The Subject
Approach to
Information

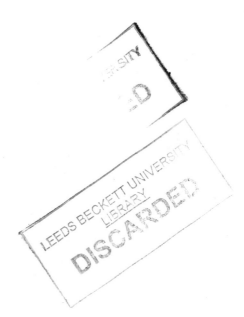

9

The Subject Approach to Information

Fifth edition

A C Foskett MA FLA AALIA
School of Communication and Information Studies,
University of South Australia

O What a tangled web we weave
When first we practise to retrieve . . .

Library Association Publishing
London

Published by
Library Association Publishing
7 Ridgmount Street
London WC1E 7AE

First published 1969
Second edition 1971
Third edition 1977
Fourth edition 1982
This fifth edition 1996

British Library Cataloguing in Publicaton Data
A catalogue record for this book is available from the British Library

ISBN 1-85604-048-8

Typeset in 10/12pt Times and Arial by Library Association Publishing
Printed and made in Great Britain by Bookcraft (Bath) Ltd, Midsomer Norton, Avon

Contents

Preface

'Another damn'd thick, square, book!', exclaimed the Duke of Gloucester, on being presented with the second volume of *The decline and fall of the Roman empire*. I do not aspire to the heights of that work, but I must admit that the description might be applied to the present volume; in order to cover my subject adequately I have had to range widely across the whole field of information retrieval. Attempts to cut down in any one area have been thwarted by the need to extend the coverage in others in order to achieve my objectives.

I produced the first edition in 1969 to meet what seemed to me to be a real need for a textbook which covered all aspects of the subject approach: not just classification or subject cataloguing (then taught as separate subjects), but also the possibilities being opened up by the computer. The Cranfield projects had shown that all information indexing languages are basically the same, and I had found that students taught these underlying principles could not only use existing classification schemes, lists of subject headings or thesauri, but could also construct their own in class assignments.

The first edition appears to have met a widespread need, and the second edition was published in 1971, incorporating revisions suggested by reviewers or arising from my own use of the book as a class text. This edition was also well received, and was translated into Portuguese for use in library schools in Brazil. In view of the continued demand, I intended to produce the third edition in 1976 as part of the centenary celebrations, but health problems made this impossible, and it appeared in 1977. The fourth edition was published in 1982, and its use became world-wide, including production as a talking book for use in Scandinavia. My original plan was to produce a new edition in 1987, but anyone who has been through the academic upheavals of the last decade will appreciate that my time was otherwise occupied!

When I did settle down to write this edition, my intention was to revise the 1982 edition, bringing descriptions of the various schemes up to date, but retaining most of the rest. It soon became apparent that the use of computers has made such major changes to the process of information retrieval that a far more radical revision was needed, and most of the book has in fact been rewritten. The basic concepts of recall and relevance remain the same, so Chapter 2 has not changed greatly; little recent work has been done on main classes in general classification schemes, so Chapter 10 has also changed little. Every other chapter has either been heavily revised or completely rewritten.

One area which has changed in every edition has been the treatment of the computer and its significance. In the first and second editions, the section on 'the future' had a chapter on the computer. By the third edition, the 'future' had become the present, and I covered the computer in Chapter 3, just before derived indexing. By 1982, it was clear that those using the text – mainly library school students – would have covered computing in sufficient detail elsewhere in their courses for me to be able to take it for granted, and refer to it as necessary. For this edition, I have in a sense gone back a step by including a chapter on information technology. My purpose is to attempt to show how developments over the past 30 years have radically changed the way we can now use computers: why, for example, it is usually easy to incorporate modern material into a computer-based system, but older materials present often costly problems. Those familiar with this background can easily GOTO Chapter 5.

Do we need to understand the theory of information retrieval any longer, now that so much material is available through the computer? I believe that the answer is a resounding YES; indeed, I believe that we must have a very clear idea of what we are doing if we are not to get lost in the mass of information at our fingertips. More serious is the risk that we run of being misled by the computer. The literature on online searching is full of examples of failures, where users have tried searching but found nothing. Even more dangerous is to find *something* and assume that what has been found is all that there is to be found. Also, recent developments have meant that we have a wider choice of search strategies; tools such as DDC, UDC and LCSH are now available online, and LCC is being processed, so that we can use a variety of approaches in online searching which were not available until quite recently – but we must know how to use them. CD-ROM, the Internet, and the World Wide Web have made vast quantities of information accessible to us – if we know where to find it, and how to evaluate it. The fact that information is available on computer does not mean that it is necessarily better than that available in print; indeed, most material in print goes through a process of evaluation which is noticeably absent from most Internet publication. I have tried to cover the methods used in online retrieval in Chapter 5, and I have returned to the question of control and evaluation in Chapter 28, for it is in this sphere that I see much of the future role of the information worker.

Previous editions have not specifically dealt with thesaurus construction, though it is implicit in the discussion of semantic relationships in Chapter 6. In view of the increased significance of thesauri I have made it explicit in this edition, showing how the analysis needed to establish relationships between terms in a subject area is in fact the basis of a thesaurus. A discussion of syntactic relationships in pre-coordinate indexing follows, leading into a chapter on alphabetical headings (including PRECIS), and five chapters on various aspects of systematic arrangement: classification. This does not mean that systematic arrangement is more important than alphabetical headings, but simply that there is more to discuss. PRECIS rated a chapter to itself in the fourth edition; as its use has been discontinued by BNB, it could perhaps have been relegated to history; however, it seemed useful to have a reasonably full description of the system as set out in the second edition of the *Manual*, which includes several features not in the earlier version.

Why do we continue to use pre-coordinate indexing despite its disadvantages?

Chapter 14 looks at manual pre-coordinate indexes, including the card and fiche catalogues which are still to be found in many libraries, while Chapter 15 is a completely new look at OPACs and the MARC records which have made them possible. Chapters 16 to 24 look at the widely used classification schemes and lists of subject headings, including a new chapter on the Broad System of Ordering. In such a review, chapters become superseded as new editions are published; in this instance, a new edition of DDC will be published very shortly after the appearance of this book. Had the book been published at any other time, some other scheme would certainly have appeared in a new edition shortly afterwards. This is a battle the author cannot win! However, I have been able to include information about DDC21, and nearly all the chapter will remain relevant in any case.

There seemed to be little point in including a chapter on manual methods of post-coordinate indexing; though these were still widely used in 1982, by 1996 they have become museum pieces. Anyone who needs a description of edge-notched, Uniterm or peek-a-boo cards can go back to an earlier edition. Similarly, the chapter on computer-based systems has been overtaken by events. There are now too many to describe in detail, while the principles on which they work are covered in Chapter 5. Videotex and teletext are not covered; they appear to have fallen by the wayside as significant providers of information.

In addition to the chapters on thesauri in science and technology, and the social sciences, I have added one on visual arts and graphics. The use of graphics on computers is now so significant that it seemed appropriate to look at two of the schemes which have been developed to control this kind of information. Both the classification scheme *Iconclass* and the *Art and Architecture Thesaurus* are of interest in themselves, as well as being the means of keeping control of the information available in this format.

The results of the Cranfield projects and those that followed have now been assimilated to such an extent into retrieval theory that there was no longer any point in having a chapter on the evaluation of IR systems; in its place I have reverted to the practice of the early editions by concluding with a chapter on 'The future'. In a field such as this, to write about the future is tempting fate, and I know that 'the digital/virtual/electronic library' already exists; however, I feel that we still have some way to go before it becomes commonplace. Many of the problems to be solved are not technological but legal and ethical: intellectual property and integrity of communication are two that present real difficulties. In addition to these aspects of the digital library, I have tried to summarize the situation in medicine as a case study of possible future developments in other subjects. The Cochrane Collaboration is an excellent example of how one kind of literature can be controlled and exploited to good advantage. It is also of course very much in line with the need for more review articles expressed at the Royal Society's Scientific Information Conference – but that was in 1948! Surely anything that old is irrelevant to the future of information retrieval?

As in previous editions, I do not present any basic philosophical arguments for my ideas. They are based on a behavioural approach: what do we have to *do* to retrieve information? If our first attempts are unsuccessful, how can we amend them, and what kinds of tool are likely to help us? It seems to me that the whole of information retrieval stems from those very simple questions, without the need to look for a philosophy. I have tried, as always, to make the presentation *readable*; I see no reason why textbooks should be boring. From time to time, I have slipped in a remark which is perhaps not to be taken too seriously. I recently had a comment from a librarian who had used the fourth edition as a student, that spotting the jokes was one of the things that made using my text popular!

To assist users, I have put words which I think are significant in italics; these are usually terms which are defined, or are important in the context. They are the sort of word which might be selected for the heading of a note by a student, or used in a handout or overhead by a lecturer. Italics are also used for titles of books and periodicals, in line with usual conventions. In describing schemes in Chapters 16 to 27, I have tried to copy the text as closely as possible for the examples I give, so that the various combinations of italic, bold, roman, sans serif, caps, small caps and lower case, and indentation are as they appear in the originals. However, I must stress that I quote *examples*, and I do so selectively to show the points I am trying to make. Students need to look at the originals at first hand to gain a full appreciation of the scheme being described. My purpose is to make such first hand study informed and thus profitable, not to replace it.

Acknowledgments

Any work such as this owes a great deal to help received from colleagues. In particular, I am indebted to Dr Ia McIlwaine of UCL for her very full and helpful comments, first on my outline and later on the first draft; without these, the book would have been a great deal less effective than I hope it now is. For information on specific chapters I have to thank the following: Chapters 4 and 5, my colleague Sue Myburgh; DDC, Joan Mitchell (Editor), Ross Trotter and Giles Martin; UDC, Ia McIlwaine (Editor, English Medium edition); BC, Jack Mills; BSO, Eric Coates; LCSH, my colleague Derek Wiblin; Sears, Joseph Miller (Editor); ROOT Thesaurus, Jean Aitchison; INSPEC Thesaurus and Classification, Jeff Pache; ERIC Thesaurus, Jim Houston (Lexicographer); the Cochrane Collaboration, Michael Brittain. For the many others who have helped form my thinking over the past years, I hope that the appearance of their names in the chapter bibliographies will prove an adequate recognition. As always, I must conclude by thanking my Wife for her continuing support over the years, without which neither this nor any of the previous editions would have appeared.

A C Foskett
February 1996

List of abbreviations

AAAS	American Association for the Advancement of Science
AACR	Anglo-American Cataloguing Rules
AAL	Association of Assistant Librarians
AARNET	Australian Academic Research NETwork
AAT	Art and Architecture Thesaurus
ABN	Australian Bibliographic Network
ABNO	All But Not Only
ACM	Association for Computing Machinery
ACS	American Chemical Society
ADDC	Abridged Dewey Decimal Classification
ADFA	Australian Defence Force Academy
AFP	Anticipated Futility Point
AID	Associative Interactive Dictionary
AIP/UDC	American Institute of Physics/Universal Decimal Classification
ALA	American Library Association
ANB	Australian National Bibliography
ANSEL	Extended Latin character set
ANSI	American National Standards Institute
APUPA	Alien-Penumbra-Umbra-Penumbra-Alien
ARPANET	Advanced Research Projects Agency NETwork
ASCA	Automatic Subject Citation Alert
ASCII	American Standard Code for Information Interchange
ASCIS	Australian Schools Cataloguing Information Service
ASSIA	Applied Social Science Index and Abstracts
ASTIA	Armed Services Technical Information Agency
BBS	Bulletin Board Service
BC	Bliss Classification/ Bibliographic Classification
BCA	Bliss Classification Association
BL	British Library
BLAISE	British Library Automated Information SErvice
BLBSD	British Library Bibliographical Services Division
BLR&DD	British Library Research & Development Department
BNB	British National Bibliography
BSI	British Standards Institution
BSO	Broad System of Ordering
BTI	British Technology Index
CATLINE	Current CATalogue onLINE (National Library of Medicine)

CATNI	Catchword And Trade Name Index
CC	Colon Classification
CC	Current Contents (ISI)
CCC	Central Classification Committee (UDC)
CCF	Common Communications Format
CCML	Comprehensive Core Medical Library
CD	Compact Disk
CD-ROM	Compact Disk-Read Only Memory
CDS	Cataloguing Distribution Service
CERN	Centre for High-Energy Physics
CIA	Central Intelligence Agency
CIJE	Current Index to Journals in Education
CIM	Cumulated Index Medicus
CITE NLM	Current Information Transfer in English, National Library of Medicine
COM	Computer Output Microform/fiche/film
COMPASS	COMPuter Aided Subject System
CORE	Chemistry Online Retrieval Experiment
COSATI	Committee on Scientific And Technical Information
CRG	Classification Research Group
CTI	Current Technology Index
DC&	Decimal Classification: Additions, Notes, Decisions
DDC	Dewey Decimal Classification
DLA	Division of Library Automation (University of California)
DoD	Department of Defense
EdNA	Australian Education Network
EE	English Electric
EJC	Engineers Joint Council
EMPST	Energy-Matter-Personality-Space-Time
ERIC	Educational Resources Information Clearinghouse
ESP	Extended Subject Program
ESS	Editorial Support System (DDC)
FID	Fédération Internationale d'Information et de Documentation
FP	Futility Point
FTP	File Transfer Protocol
GARE	Guidelines for Authorities and Reference Entries
GIF	Graphics Interchange Format
GUI	Graphical User Interface
HTML	HyperText Markup Language
HTTP	HyperText Transport Protocol
IAIMS	Integrated Academic Information Management System
IBM	International Business Machines
ICI	Imperial Chemical Industries Ltd.
ICSU	International Council of Scientific Unions
ICT	International Critical Tables

IEE	Institution of Electrical Engineers
IEEE	Institute of Electrical and Electronic Engineers
IFLA	International Federation of Library Associations and Organizations
IIB	Institut International de la Bibliographie
IID	Institut International de Documentation
IM	Index Medicus
IM	International MARC [now part of UBCIM]
INSPEC	INformation Service in Physics, Electrotechnology, Computers and control
IR	Information Retrieval
ISBD	International Standard Bibliographical Description
ISDN	Integrated Services Digital Network
ISI	Institute for Scientific Information
ISILT	Information Science Index Languages Test
ISO	International Organization for Standardization
ISONET	ISO Network
IT	Information Technology
JANET	Joint Academic NETwork
JPEG	Joint Picture Experts Group
KWIC	KeyWord In Context
KWOC	KeyWord Out of Context
LAN	Local Area Network
LASER	London And South-Eastern Library Region
LC	Library of Congress
LCC	Library of Congress Classification
LCCN	Library of Congress Control Number
LCSH	Library of Congress Subject Headings
LISA	Library and Information Science Abstracts
LP	Long Play (records)
LUCIS	London University Computer Information Service
MARC	MAchine Readable Cataloguing
MEDLARS	MEDical Literature Analysis and Retrieval System
MEDLINE	MEDLARS onLINE
MELVYL	OPAC used in the University of California libraries
MeSH	Medical Subject Headings
MIT	Massachusetts Institute of Technology
MRF	Master Reference File (UDC)
NAL	National Agricultural Library
NASA	National Aeronautics and Space Administration
NATO	North Atlantic Treaty Organization
NBS	National Bibliographic Service
NCSA	National Center for Supercomputer Applications
NEH	National Endowment for the Humanities
NEPHIS	NEsted PHrase Indexing System

NEXUS	Schools network, South Australia
NISO	National Information Standards Organization
NLM	National Library of Medicine
NREN	National Research and Education Network
NSF	National Science Foundation
NSFNET	National Science Foundation NETwork
NTIS	National Technical Information Service
OBNA	Only But Not All
OCLC	Online Computer Library Center
ODA	Office Document Architecture
ODIF	Office Document Interchange Format
OKAPI	Online Keyword Access to Public Information
OPAC	Online Public Access Catalogue
OSI	Open Systems Interconnection
OSTI	Office for Scientific and Technical Information (later BLR&DD)
PAIS	Public Affairs Information Service
PCL	Polytechnic of Central London
PMEST	Personality-Matter-Energy-Space-Time
PRECIS	PREserved Context Indexing System
RIE	Resources In Education
RIN	Reference Indicator Number
RMIT	Royal Melbourne Institute of Technology
SAERIS	South Australian Educational Resources Information Service
SAMOS	Satellite And Missile Observation System
SCI	Science Citation Index
SCIS	Schools Cataloguing Information Service
SDI	Selective Dissemination of Information
SDIF	SGML Document Interchange Format
SGML	Standardized General Markup Language
SIN	Subject Indicator Number
SMART	Experimental computer-based IR system devised by G. Salton
SPDL	Standard Page Description Language
SRC	Standard Reference Code/Standard Roof Classification
SRIS	Science Reference and Information Service
STAIRS	STorage And Information Retrieval System (IBM)
TCP/IP	Transmission Control Protocol/Internet Protocol
TEI	Text Encoding Initiative
TEST	Thesaurus of Engineering and Scientific Terms
UBC	Universal Bibliographical Control
UBCIM	Universal Bibliographical Control – International MARC
UC	University of California
UDC	Universal Decimal Classification
UDCC	Universal Decimal Classification Consortium
UKAEA	United Kingdom Atomic Energy Authority

UKOLN	United Kingdom Online Library Network
UMLS	Unified Medical Language System
UNIMARC	Universal MARC format
UNISIST	World science information system
URL	Uniform/Universal Resource Locator
USAEC	United States Atomic Energy Commission
VINITI	All-Union Institute for Scientific and Technical Information
VIP	Vocabulary Improvement Project (ERIC)
WAN	Wide Area Network
WASP	White Anglo-Saxon Protestant
WLN	Washington Library Network
WWW	World Wide Web

Part I
Theory of information retrieval systems

Chapter 1
Introduction

It is frequently said that we live in the 'Information Age', and nearly every day we learn of some new development in information technology. The human need for information is growing, as our societies grow to depend more and more on information to survive and flourish. We all need to be able to find facts, but we also need to find *information* on particular subjects – not just the bare facts, but their evaluation and assimilation into our own frame of reference. Can the computer solve all our problems, or do we still need to bring human intelligence to bear on the solutions? How do we set about finding information that we need? This book attempts to look at the kind of problems we meet in trying to find information that meets our needs, how the computer can help, and how human effort can still be valuable in easing our path to discovery.

It is helpful if we try to define some terms so that we can see their relevance to our daily lives, and to the work of the professional information worker. The following definitions are based on those in the *Concise Oxford dictionary*[1] and the *Macquarie Dictionary*.[2]

- *knowledge* is what *I* know
- *information* is what *we* know, i.e. *shared* knowledge
- *communication* is the imparting or interchange of . . . information by speech, writing or signs, i.e. the *transfer* of information
- *data* [literally things given] any fact(s) assumed to be a matter of direct observation.
- Additionally, a *document* is any physical form of recorded information.

From these definitions we can see that data consists of unprocessed facts; knowledge is what an individual possesses after assimilating facts and putting them into context; information is knowledge shared by having been communicated. *Information technology* is the equipment, hardware and software that enables us to store and communicate large amounts of data at high speed. If we record knowledge, then it may be communicated at a distance in space and time; we do not have to be face to face with the informant as we do in oral communication. This further suggests the concept of a *repository* or store of recorded information.

Before knowledge was recorded, individuals formed the repository of knowledge, the bridge between successive generations and between those who generated new information and those who required to use it. The amount of information that can be passed on in this way is limited, and society began to move forward when information of various kinds began to be recorded in relatively permanent forms which could serve as a substitute for the 'elder' in person. Knowledge only becomes generally useful when it is communicated; by recording it, we do our best to ensure that it is permanently available to anyone who may need it, instead of ephemeral and limited to one individual.

Nowadays, the amount of new information being generated is such that no individual can hope to keep pace with even a small fraction of it, and the problem that we have to face is that of ensuring that individuals who need information can obtain it with the minimum of cost (both in time and in money), and without being overwhelmed by large amounts of irrelevant matter. Sherlock Holmes[3] puts the matter well:

> ... a man should keep his little brain attic stocked with all the furniture he is likely to use, and the rest he can put away in the lumber-room of his library, where he can get it if he wants it.

Holmes himself kept not only a library of published works, but also his own personal index, to which he referred on many occasions to supplement his own knowledge. The point is that we do not have to know everything – but we must know how to find information when we need it.

So, instead of the individual store of knowledge, we now have the corporate store: libraries, information services, computers. Instead of the individual memory, we have the corporate memory: library catalogues, bibliographies, computer databases. And just as the individual whose memory fails cannot pass on wanted information, so the inadequate corporate memory will fail in its purpose. We have to ensure that the tools we prepare meet the needs of our users. It is therefore very important to try to define the needs of our users as closely as possible, particularly in view of the exponential growth of knowledge in recent years. Professional librarianship is concerned with the skills, both human and technical, needed to plan and use systems which will achieve the optimum results in meeting the needs of users. Libraries are still the main repositories of information, but computers have now become the most significant factor among the tools used.

The growth of knowledge

A valuable study[4] identified three eras of information need, to which we may add a preliminary fourth, the polymath era. There was a time when the sum total of human knowledge was sufficiently small to be comprehended by one individual. As knowledge grew, we moved into the discipline-oriented era, which lasted in effect from the invention of printing until well into the twentieth century. This was characterized by the division of knowledge into more or less water-tight compartments or *disciplines*, reflecting the way in which they were studied; new disciplines grew out of the splitting up, or 'fission' of existing disciplines as particular aspects grew in importance and developed into disciplines in their own right. Thus science developed from philosophy as a field of study; physics developed from science; electricity developed from physics; and electronics developed from electricity. In each case the new subject represented a fragmentation of the old, but remained within it. Most of the conventional retrieval tools used in libraries were developed within this frame of reference, and it is only as new eras, with changing user needs, have developed that schemes such as DDC and other library tools have begun to show serious signs of strain. We shall be examining some of these problems later.

The second era, the problem-oriented era, began to assume importance in the 1930s, and particularly in the Second World War. This was characterized by the need to solve particular problems, using whatever disciplines might be necessary, regardless of whether they 'belonged together' or not. A recent example comes from the field of micro-engineering, where parts are so small that novel methods of moving them have to be devised. Japanese scientists have 'borrowed' the methods used by cilia (the fine hairs found on mucous membranes) to move mucus, in order to be able to move the microscopic units involved. The best-known example is genetic engineering, which involves the merging, or 'fusion', of disciplines such as physics and biology which used to be thought of as fundamentally separate.

We are now in the third, or mission-oriented, era, in which demands for information may span a range of disciplines. For example, space medicine certainly requires a knowledge of medicine, but in addition involves problems related to space physics, mechanics (the phenomenon of weightlessness), diet, hygiene – the list is formidable. Clearly the old barriers between disciplines, which began to crumble in the problem-oriented era, have now effectively disappeared, presenting further difficulties in the communication of information. The more remote new information is from individuals' existing range of knowledge, the more difficult it becomes for them to comprehend and incorporate it into their own store of knowledge. The needs of today's information users place demands on information services far more acute than those experienced in past eras, and our information retrieval systems must be adequately developed to meet these demands.

It is also useful to distinguish between the retrieval of data and the retrieval of information. Retrieving information from documents is not the same as retrieving data – there are some important differences.[5] A request for data is satisfied by directly providing the desired fact(s); a request for information is satisfied by providing either references to documents or the documents themselves which will *probably* contain the desired information. Requests for data are deterministic and require no logical decisions on the part of the enquirer; the answer supplied is either right or wrong. On the other hand, requests for information are probabilistic, and may involve a series of logical decisions on the part of the enquirer. So a request for data should lead to the *right* answer, otherwise it is useless. By contrast, a request for information should lead to a *useful* answer, which does not necessarily have to be complete; its usefulness is a matter of judgement on the part of the enquirer.

Information retrieval as a form of communication

In the light of the preceding discussion, we may see that one measure of the success of an information retrieval system is its effectiveness as a means of communicating information. It is therefore helpful to look at the communication process itself, and the ways in which it is modified by the information retrieval process.

We may consider information retrieval processes as part of the overall pattern of communication. The most commonly used model of the communication process is that devised by Shannon and Weaver, shown in Figure 1.1(a). In this model, we see that a *source* has a *message* which is to be transmitted to a *receiver*; before it can be transmitted, the message must be *encoded* for transmission along the selected *channel*, to be *decoded* before it can be understood by the receiver. In information retrieval, the sources are the originators of the documents we handle; the encoding process includes the choice of the appropriate physical manifestations – words, sounds, images – and their translation into an appropriate medium; the channel is

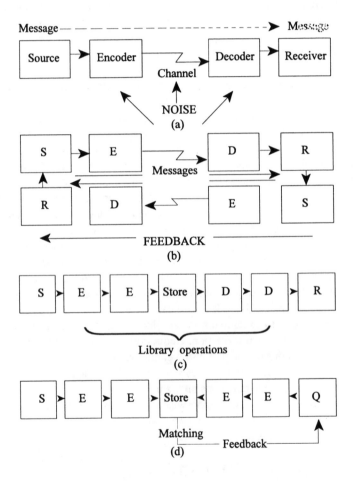

Fig. 1.1 Models of the communication process
    (a) The Shannon–Weaver model
    (b) Verbal (two-way) communication; involves feedback
    (c) The effect of library operations
    (d) The query situation: feedback through the matching process

the resulting document and its progress from source to receiver; and the decoding process involves the receiver's ability to comprehend the message in the form in which it is presented. The final element in the model is *noise*. Noise may be defined as anything which detracts from the fidelity of transmission of the message from source to receiver. Shannon and Weaver were concerned with the transmission of messages over telephone wires, but the concept of noise can be generalized to cover all kinds of interference with communication – for example, the retrieval of unwanted documents in response to a request.

If we consider normal verbal communication, we can see that the model (Figure 1.1(b)) is in fact that of Figure 1.1(a) doubled, so that the original source functions also as a receiver, and vice versa. In this situation, a further important element enters the picture: the idea of *feedback*. If the message becomes distorted on its way from source to receiver, the receiver can immediately query it (I didn't quite catch that, or, Could you explain that again, please?, or, *What?*) Feedback can thus be significant in reducing the effects of noise.

Unfortunately, when we are dealing with documents, there can be little, if any, feedback from receiver to source. The source has no control over who receives messages, and cannot therefore restrict them to a specific audience. Receivers in turn cannot be sure that they have understood a message correctly, or that they have located all – or indeed any – of the messages they were looking for. Indeed, the situation is made more difficult by the interposition of additional encoding processes, which then require further decoding processes on the part of the receiver. In libraries, we normally arrange books by putting a code on the spine: a call number; and we identify them in our catalogues by a further series of codes: catalogue entries (Figure 1.1(c)). Catalogue entries and class marks can in fact give a great deal of information, but for most library users they form an additional complication in the chain of communication, and are an inherent additional source of noise. Furthermore, we have introduced another complication: transmission of messages is delayed by their being placed in a *store* of some kind. A book may be regarded as such a store, but so may a CD-ROM encyclopedia or any other kind of document; libraries are stores, as are bibliographic databases. In this context, relatively trivial matters such as the misshelving of a book or a power supply malfunction all add their quota of noise to the communication process.

The importance of bibliographic control

Documents can take a variety of physical forms. If we consider a library as a convenient example of a store of documents, at one time we could have assumed that for many libraries the bulk of the stock of documents would have been books; in others, periodicals or technical reports might predominate. Now, libraries may contain audiovisual and computer-readable materials as well as printed, and the computer-readable materials may themselves contain the equivalent of printed and audiovisual materials in the form of multimedia presentations. We may then have the same work in several different physical forms. We may have Shakespeare's play *Hamlet* as a printed book, or as a film, or spoken word cassette. An encyclopedia may be a set of printed volumes or a single CD-ROM. The *intellectual content* remains the same, but the physical format varies.[6] It is the *work* which is important, but we can no longer rely on the physical arrangement of the documents to bring together different versions of the same work. We have to rely on a substitute – a set of surrogate *records* – of the documents we have, in order to achieve *bibliographic control*. Hagler has summarized the purposes of bibliographical control:[7]

1 identifying the existence of all possible documents produced in every physical medium;

2 Identifying the works contained in documents or as parts of them (e.g. periodical articles, conference papers, contents of anthologies etc.);

3 producing lists of these documents and works prepared according to standard rules of citation;

4 providing all useful access points (indexes) to these lists, including at least some access by name, title and subject;

5 providing some means of locating a copy of each document in a library or other accessible collection.

These records must use *words*; we can only identify and locate information if we can adequately describe it in words. (Even in a collection of art materials, where it is possible to match, say, specific examples of textures with illustrations in which they occur, it is still necessary to identify *textures* as the key word in our search.)

The situation has been further complicated by a historical division between the bibliographic control of books and that of other materials. Books have normally been treated as units, and listed – catalogued – as such, whereas since the development of the scientific periodical in the seventeenth century, and in other fields later, periodicals have been controlled through a quite separate mechanism of abstracts and indexes, normally not produced by librarians. With the development of audio-visual materials, a new apparatus of bibliographic control grew up to enable users to find what they needed. These divisions have been to some extent overcome by the development of computer databases, but there is still a major division between the bibliographic control of books and that of non-book materials. Even online library catalogues – OPACS, discussed in Chapter 15, do not normally cross this divide; for the bibliographic control of other materials we turn to other databases – though to confuse the issue still further these may be available through an OPAC.

If we only have one kind of document in our collection, for example a set of records in a computer database, we still have to have access to the records from various points of view. We might wish to identify all those on a particular subject, or by a particular author, or with a particular title, as indicated in Hagler's point 4 above. If the database contains images, we may wish to locate all the records containing a particular image or kind of image. To find specific items, bibliographic control is still needed to give us access to them through a variety of factors.

Some of these factors *identify* the item(s) they refer to. For example, if we have the number of a patent specification, there will be only one item corresponding to that description. If we have selected a particular author, then the number of works which will match our requirements is immediately limited. If we choose a particular title, we shall find only one item, or perhaps a few, which will satisfy our request (authors usually try to find unique titles for their works, but do not always display enough originality!). Furthermore, there are now standards which help us to determine the format in which we should look for the information we need; for example, the widely used Anglo-American Cataloguing Rules[8] and the MARC records (discussed in Chapter 15) now enable us to formulate a search for a factor that identifies in such a way that it becomes a search for data rather than for information.

Factors which do not identify

If we are asked for information on a particular subject, we face a rather different set of problems. To begin with, there is no set of standards to tell us precisely how to express the subject, and indeed virtually every database seems to have its own rules. Readers seek information on particular subjects, and expect our systems to be able to provide the answers. In this situation, the readers/receivers become sources, encoding messages in the form of enquiries. (Figure 1.1(d)). We now have to discover any messages in our store which appear to match these enquiries; having found some, we can pass them on to the enquirers, who can decide whether the answers match their needs. In the light of our responses, enquirers may modify their messages in an attempt to achieve a closer match with their requirements; in other words, we have a degree of feedback in the system, which may enable us eventually to satisfy a request despite initial failure. This failure may arise from a variety of causes: enquirers may not be able to express their needs clearly, or may not be very sure exactly what those needs are (if they knew the answers they would not need to ask the questions!); or our encoding processes may be inadequate; or the original sources (the authors) may not have made their messages clear, or may even have had some rather different messages in mind. For example, the answer to a question from a librarian on the optimum number of people required to staff the circulation desk may be found in a book on supermarket management. Authors write within their own particular frame of reference, which will not be the same as that of the readers. We have to try to optimize the results of any search, while accepting that we can no longer characterize the result as right or wrong.

Reference retrieval, document retrieval and information retrieval

It is also important to recognize the distinction between reference retrieval, document retrieval and information retrieval. Surrogate records used for bibliographic control, such as conventional library catalogues and bibliographies, give us *reference* retrieval; we still have to supply the actual documents. The user has then to look at the documents, and can only make a final judgment on the basis of the information in the documents. Some computer-based systems, for example those in the legal field, have included full text for some years, and thus give document retrieval at the same time as reference retrieval, but at present the majority do not, though this is rapidly changing with the development of CD-ROM and multimedia. Further, if the communication process between authors and user is to be complete, the librarian may have to act as intermediary and interpret the documents found by translating them into language which can be understood by the user. This may mean literally taking a text in, say, German and producing an English translation, or it may involve an explanation process within the one language. In either case, it is a process which is often neglected; all too often the list of references is seen as the end product, not the actual communication of information.

This book is concerned with a discussion of the problems of optimizing our responses to requests for information on subjects. This is not to suggest that identifying factors such as authors' names do not present any problems; the fact that it took some 20 years of discussions to produce a new edition of the Anglo-American Rules, which has since been revised,[8] and is still the subject of discussion, shows very plainly that they do! The problems of the subject approach to information, however, are more severe because they are more indeterminate; we never reach the stage of being able to say we have finished a search conclusively. A great deal of research has been done on these problems; much more remains to be done. This book is an attempt to show the present state of the art in a way that will be acceptable as an elementary textbook; it does not pretend to be an advanced study, of which there are many,[9] but rather to give beginners some understanding of present theories and ideas.

References

1   *The concise Oxford dictionary*, 6th edn, Oxford, Clarendon Press, 1976.
2   *The Macquarie dictionary*, St Leonards, NSW, Macquarie Library Pty Ltd, 1981.
3   Doyle, Sir A. C., 'The adventure of the five orange pips', *The adventures of Sherlock Holmes*, 1892.
4   Arthur D. Little Inc, *Into the information age: a perspective for federal action on information*, Chicago, American Library Association, 1978.
     The information society: issues and answers, edited by E. J. Losey, Phoenix, Oryx Press, 1978.
5   Blair, D. C., *Language and representation in information retrieval*, New York NY, Elsevier Science Publishers, 1990.
6   Hagler, R., *The bibliographic record and information technology*, 2nd edn, Chicago, USA, American Library Association; Ottawa, Canada, Canadian Library Association, c1991.
7   Hagler, R., ref. 6 above, 7.
8   *Anglo-American cataloguing rules*, 2nd edn, 1988 revision, London, Library Association, 1988.
9   Of the making of many books on information retrieval there appears to be no end. The following very select list is intended to act only as a guide to the student. Much of the basic work was published in the period 1960–1980 in such works as the Butterworth's series *Classification and indexing in . . .: science and technology*, by B. C. Vickery, 3rd edn, 1975; *the social sciences*, by D. J. Foskett, 2nd edn, 1975; *the humanities*, by D. Langridge, 1976. Specific refer-

ences will be made to these works in particular chapters, and a more complete list is included in the 4th edition of this work. The following list includes some of the works published since the previous edition.

Austin, D., *PRECIS: a manual of concept analysis and subject indexing*, 2nd edn, London, British Library, 1984.

Classification of library materials : current and future potential for providing access, Bengtson, B. G. and Hill, J. S. (eds.), Neal-Schuman, c1990.

Coates, E. J., *Subject catalogues: headings and structure*, reissued with new preface, London, Library Association, 1988.

Craven, T. C., *String indexing*, Orlando, Academic Press, 1986.

Hunter, E. J., *Classification made simple*, Aldershot, England; Brookfield, USA, Gower, c1988.

Lancaster, F. W. and Warner, A. J., *Information retrieval today*, Arlington, VA, Information Resources Press, 1993.

Langridge, D., *Subject analysis: principles and procedures*, London; New York, Bowker-Saur, 1989.

Milstead, J. L., *Subject access systems: alternatives in design*, Orlando, Academic Press, 1984.

Rowley, J. E., *Organising knowledge: an introduction to information retrieval*, 2nd edn, Aldershot, Ashgate, 1992.

Salton, G. and McGill, M. J., *Introduction to modern information retrieval*, New York, McGraw-Hill, c1983.

Subject access: report of a meeting sponsored by the Council on Library Resources Inc, Dublin, Ohio, 1982.

Dym, E. D. (ed.), *Subject and information analysis*, New York, M. Dekker, c1985.

Berman, S. (ed.), *Subject cataloging: critiques and innovations*, New York, Haworth Press, c1984.

Subject indexing: principles and practices in the 90's: IFLA satellite meeting August 17–18 1993, Lisbon, Munich, Saur, 1995.

Turner, C., *The basics of organizing information*, London, Bingley, 1985.

Chan, L.M., Richmond, P. A., Svenonius, E. (eds.), *Theory of subject analysis: a sourcebook*, Littleton, CO, Libraries Unlimited, 1985. A valuable collection of significant articles, referred to elsewhere as *Theory of subject analysis . . .*

Wynar, B. S. *Introduction to cataloging and classification*, 7th edn, by A. G. Taylor, Littleton, CO, Libraries Unlimited, 1985.

For developments over the past few years it is helpful to consult the chapters on classification in *British librarianship and information work*, London, Library Association, 1982–; 1976–1980, Taylor, L. J. (ed.), 1983; 1981–1985, Bromley, D. W. and Allott, A. M. (eds.), 1988; 1986–1990, Bromley, D. W. and Allott, A. M. (eds.), 1992; these also have comprehensive bibliographies. Useful series of articles include 'Subject access literature' annually in *Library resources and technical services*. Relevant chapters in the *Annual review of information science and technology* are also valuable for the student wishing to pursue the subject in depth.

Chapter 2

Features of an information retrieval system

Authors generate large quantities of information every day. Estimates made 30 or more years ago suggested that the number of useful (i.e. not merely repetitive) periodical articles published each year in science and technology alone was in excess of one million,[1] and the number has certainly increased since then. In Britain alone over 50,000 books are published each year, and the USA has now overtaken Britain as the world's most prolific book publisher. Libraries acquire a selection of this enormous output for the immediate use of their readers, and through the various schemes of interlibrary cooperation they have access to a very much wider choice. At the other end of the chain of communication we have readers, each with their own individual needs for information which has to be selected from the mass available. The readers' approach may be purposive, that is, they may be seeking the answer to specific questions, which may be more or less clearly formulated in their minds. This is the situation that we shall consider first, but we must not overlook the browsers, who are looking for something to catch their interest rather than answers to specific questions, and who form the majority of users in public libraries.

Information retrieval and document retrieval

We should distinguish between information – knowledge which is being communicated – and the physical means by which this communication takes place, as was pointed out in Chapter 1. In the past, although it has been the practice to refer to *information* retrieval, what has been described has been *document* retrieval; in other words, when asked for information, we have provided a set of documents which we believed would contain the information sought. The success of our search has been considered to be a subjective judgment, which could only be made by the individual making the request; indeed, many librarians have thought it beyond their terms of reference to make any attempt to *evaluate* the documents found unless the information sought was purely factual – and some not even then! This reticence has not been restricted to librarians; for example, the *International critical tables*, published 1927–1933, gave a selection of values for most physical data, indicating what was usually thought to be the 'best value', but giving chapter and verse for each value recorded so that users could make up their own minds if they wished. The US Academy of Sciences still maintains its Office of Critical Tables, though the sheer quantity of data now available has precluded publication of a revised edition of *ICT*.

Various attempts have been made to mechanize the document delivery part of the system, but none of these found widespread acceptance, mainly because of costs and mechanical problems. However, the development of new means of storing massive amounts of information in computers has led to a new approach to the direct retrieval of information. Factual information on a wide variety of subjects is now available in many countries through the various forms of videotext, using the TV set which is now an essential part of every civilized home (as George Orwell[2] pointed out). CD-ROM and videodisk provide access to equally large amounts of information, including sound and illustrations as well as text (multimedia), using a desktop computer. Networking allows information to be transmitted direct from computer to computer, making possible the paperless office discussed in Chapter 4 – though so far offices seem to be using even more paper than they did in the past. It has been suggested that paper consumption in the USA is likely to increase steadily until at least the year 2000!

We should not, and cannot, ignore these developments, but it remains important to recognize that they do not in fact alter the fundamentals of the communication process, though they may change some of its practical manifestations. This book is concerned with the intellectual problems associated with those aspects of information transfer most likely to be met by the librarian (using the word in its widest sense); they remain the same no matter what physical means are used.

Current scanning and retrospective searching

Our reader may be mainly interested in keeping up to date with current publications in a subject, in which case our retrieval system must also be up to date. However, because the items referred to are usually easily available, our system need only be a fairly simple guide; if an item looks interesting, the reader can obtain the original without much trouble. On the other hand, the reader may need as much information as can be found regardless of date; in this case, much of the material may be difficult and therefore expensive to obtain, and we need to be much more certain that it will be of use before we attempt to follow up a reader's request. Our information retrieval system must give us enough information about a document for us to be able to decide whether to pursue it or not. Since this second situation is the more demanding, it is the one on which we shall be concentrating in this book, but the more straightforward current scanning should not be forgotten. The contrast between the two approaches is well illustrated by such works as *Current papers in electrical and electronic engineering* and *Electrical and electronic abstracts*, both of which cover the same groups of documents but with two different purposes in mind. There are a number of similar publications covering various subject fields; within the library, current scanning needs are often met by current accessions lists, while the catalogue serves the major function of the retrospective searching tool as far as the library's own stock is concerned.

Selective dissemination of information

In addition to providing facilities for current scanning and retrospective searching, both of which imply that the user takes the initiative, for many years now libraries have themselves taken the initiative by endeavouring to see that readers are kept informed of new materials in their fields of interest. In the public library, this might be on a haphazard, 'old boy', basis, but in the special library it has always been regarded as an important part of the library's function. There are, however, certain difficulties in the way of running such a service successfully, some intellectual, some clerical. The use of a computer can solve many of these problems and enable us to give a more complete and accurate service to our readers.

A system for computer operation was developed by H. P. Luhn of IBM and is still valid today, though it has been modified in some respects. In effect, it involves readers in stating their requirements in the same method of subject description as is used in indexing the library's holdings. If the library uses a thesaurus, then terms will be chosen from this; if a classification scheme, this will be used. Natural language terms may be used, particularly in subject areas such as Science and Technology, where the terminology may be described as 'hard', i.e. well-defined and generally used; the documents may then be regarded as self-indexing, using titles, abstracts or full texts. These reader 'profiles' are fed into the computer together with the similar profiles for new accessions; when the computer finds a match between the two, it prints out a notification, or may use electronic mail facilities to give the reader a more immediate service.

Clerical problems are thus fairly easily solved. The intellectual problems are rather more intractable. A research project showed that perhaps the most pressing difficulty in setting up a viable SDI system was to obtain a valid statement of readers' needs. Users were asked to state their interest profiles, and were sent a selection of articles on the strength of this. At the end of the month they were asked to state which of the articles had been of use, and which article they had read during the month had proved most interesting to them. While the majority of the references notified by the SDI systems were of some value, the 'most interesting articles' were often found to bear little relation to the reader's profile! By asking readers to return the notification form, indicating whether the reference had been of interest or not, a degree of feedback can be obtained which can be used to modify their profiles, but there will never be any means of foretelling the 'wayout' article which may prove of interest.[3]

Despite the difficulties, the IEE developed this work into a satisfactory computer-based system, INSPEC, in which all the operations involved in the SDI service and the production of the various parts of *Science abstracts*, including *Electrical and electronics abstracts*, and *Current papers* . . . are integrated. This is only one of many such services.

While SDI systems may not be able to achieve the impossible, they can function very effectively within a particular organization, and computer processing enables us to extend the benefits to a larger audience. The success of the many services now available has shown that provided the users do their part by stating their needs precisely, a very effective service can be given on a nationwide scale.

In sum, readers will need all the information that we can collect (at least that is the hope of the authors!), but we cannot tell in advance what items of information we are likely to acquire that will be of value to any particular reader. What we have to do is organize our collection in such a way that when we search for information for a reader we do not have to scan the whole contents in order to find what he or she wants, but can go with the minimum of delay to those items which will be of use. To look at it from another angle, our organization must permit us to eliminate what is *not* wanted. This idea introduces three very important concepts: recall, relevance and precision.

Recall, relevance and precision

For any particular reader with a need for information, there will be certain items in our collection which will be relevant. Among these it will be possible to establish some sort of precedence order; some will be definitely relevant, others will be useful, but less so, while others will be only marginally relevant. To take an example, a reader might want information on Siamese cats: in our collections we may have items dealing specifically with Siamese cats, and these will probably be highly relevant. There are however factors other than the subject alone which will influence this; these items may be too detailed, or not detailed enough; they may be written at the wrong level, or in a language which the reader does not understand. The reader's background will inevitably affect any decision as to which items are most relevant. To find more information we may broaden our search: that is, present to the reader those items which, though they do not deal specifically with the subject of the enquiry, include it as part of a a broader subject. In our example, we may find items which deal with cats in general, not just with Siamese cats; or with pets in general, not just with cats. However, we must accept that the more we broaden our search – the more material we *recall* – the less likely it is that any given item will be *relevant*. There is an inverse relationship between *recall* – the number of items we find in conducting a series of searches – and *relevance* – the likelihood of their matching our reader's requirements.

Normally, readers will be satisfied with a few items, so long as these contain the sort of information wanted; that is to say, we need a system which will give us high relevance, even though recall may be low. But there will be situations when readers will require high recall – as much information as possible – even though this means that they will have to look through a lot of items which will turn out to be of little or no value. We need to be able to vary the response of our system to cater for the kind of demand. It is also clear that relevance is a subjective judgement depending on the individual; the same question posed by two different readers may well require two different answers. Indeed, we may carry the argument further. Each document revealed in our search may change a reader's view of what is relevant, so that even a single individual may make varying decisions about relevance at different times.

The problem arises from the fact that readers seek information which they can build into their own corpus of knowledge – their frame of reference – with the minimum of effort, whereas authors present information in a form dictated by *their* frame of reference; each of us has our own frame of reference, so that there will never be an exact match. We have to design our information retrieval systems to optimize the likelihood of being able to match our readers' requests, but accept the fact that they will never be perfect.

The individual view of relevance has led to the concept of *pertinence,* or *utility.* If a document is retrieved in answer to a particular request, its relevance may be assessed by a panel of those skilled in the art,[4] but its pertinence can only be assessed by the originator of the request. In other words, relevance is a consensus judgement, pertinence an individual judgement. Another way of looking at the matter is that a document retrieved in answer to a request may be *useful* to the enquirer, but its utility may change; for example, if we retrieve the same document in a second search, it will have lost its utility the second time round. Its *relevance* will not have changed, but the enquirer's view of it will.

In an experimental situation, such as a study into the effectiveness of different indexing systems, judgements on relevance may be made in advance, for example by examining all the documents in the test collection in relation to all the test questions, as in the second Cranfield project.[5] We can then arrive at an objective view of the success of a system by comparing the results achieved with that system with the predetermined answers. In this situation it is usual to refer to precision rather than relevance. The term precision is used very widely in the literature in preference to relevance, but in this text we shall be using the word relevance when a subjective judgement is involved. The various terms are discussed thoroughly by Lancaster in three articles in the *Encyclopedia of library and information science.*[6] A more recent study shows that the inverse relationship between recall and relevance, first demonstrated in the first Cranfield project,[7] can be mathematically proved. If we want to have improved recall *and* improved relevance, we have to change our search strategy.[8]

We may use Venn diagrams (see Figure 2.1) and set notation to examine these concepts further. If we take as our universe a set of documents L, then in response to any given question there should be a set A of documents which are relevant, where A is a subset of L ($A \subset L$). If we use our information retrieval system to try to find these documents, we shall actually retrieve a rather different set B ($B \subset L$), of which only the subset forming the intersection of A and B ($A \cap B$) will be relevant.

We may now define the two terms recall ratio and precision ratio.

$$\text{Recall ratio} = \frac{(A \cap B)}{A} \qquad \frac{\text{(relevant documents retrieved)}}{\text{(total of relevant documents)}}$$

$$\text{Precision ratio} = \frac{(A \cap B)}{B} \qquad \frac{\text{(relevant documents retrieved)}}{\text{(total of documents retrieved)}}$$

These are usually expressed as percentages by multiplying by 100.

Another term which is sometimes used is fall-out ratio, defined as

$$\text{Fall-out ratio} = \frac{B - A}{A'} \qquad \frac{\text{(retrieved but not relevant)}}{\text{(total not relevant)}}$$

The set $B - A$, consisting of documents retrieved but not relevant, may be regarded as noise, while the set $(A \cup B)'$, documents neither retrieved nor relevant, may be thought of as *dodged,* to use Vickery's term.

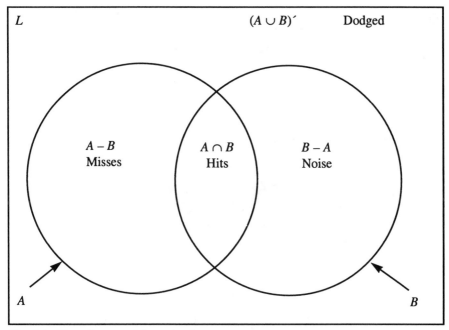

Fig. 2.1 Venn diagram of the retrieval process

Unfortunately, the set *A* is rarely clearly defined; in fact, probably only in the experimental situation can we delineate *A* precisely. In real life there is a grey area, consisting of those documents which *may* be relevant. If we draw a cross-section through *A* and plot this on a graph showing degree of relevance (see Figure 2.2), we get the result denoted APUPA by Ranganathan. U denote the *umbra*, i.e. those documents which are clearly relevant (within the *shadow* of the subject); P denotes the *penumbra* (the 'twilight zone'); and A denotes *alien*, i.e. those documents which are clearly *not* relevant. It is the penumbra which makes it impossible to define *A* clearly, and this means that we cannot use the term precision in this situation. In this text, *relevance* is used to refer to the real-life situation, *precision* to refer to the experimental situation where the set A can be predetermined.

Fuzzy sets

Ranganathan was by education a mathematician, so we should perhaps not be surprised to find that part of mathematical set theory has been used in attempts to quantify his APUPA concept. This is the idea of *fuzzy sets*. In standard set theory, given a universe *L* of which *x* is a member and *A* a subset, we can define a membership function $F_A(x)$ which will be 1 if *x* is a member of *A* and 0 if it is not; in other words, *x* either is, or is not, a member of set *A*. If *A* is a fuzzy set, then $F_A(x)$ may take any value between 0 and 1; in other words *x* is not, $(F_A(x) = 0)$; is, $(F_A(x) = 1)$; or may be, $(0 < F_A(x) < 1)$; a member of *A*. The concept has been widely adopted since its original publication by Zadeh[9] in 1965, and *Social science citation index* lists sev-

(a)

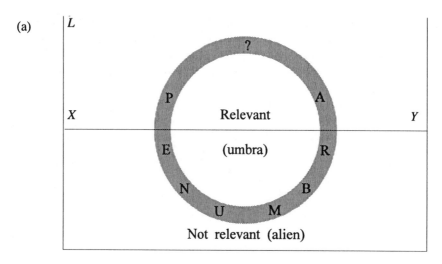

(b)

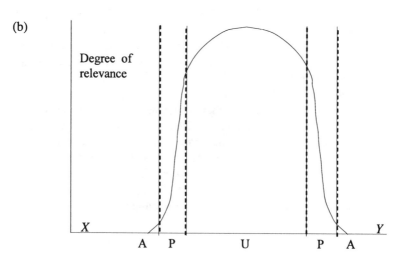

Fig. 2.2   The problem of defining the class *A* of relevant documents:
(a) the boundary between *A* and *A´* is indeterminate;
(b) Ranganathan's APUPA cross-section

eral hundred references citing this, of which only a small proportion are about information retrieval.

The object of applying fuzzy set theory to information retrieval systems is that, by
using a computer, we may be able to devise a system that will allow us to rank the
documents retrieved in probable order of relevance, instead of the 'either/or' result of
a conventional search, which sorts the relevant sheep from the irrelevant goats and

ignores the fact that there are a lot of 'maybe's' involved. Systems which rank document output do exist, using a matching function between request and document to rank the output. Other systems use probability functions for the same purpose. It remains to be seen whether fuzzy set theory can produce better results. Some mathematicians are still dubious about the value of the theory as a whole, while other writers have suggested that it is not particularly applicable to information retrieval.

The recall-precision curve

We can display the four classes of document $A \subsetneq B$, $A - B$, $B - A$ and $(A ∈ B)'$ in the form of a matrix:

	Retrieved	Not retrieved	Total
Relevant	$A \cap B$	$A - B$	A
Not relevant	$B - A$	$(A \cup B)'$	A'
	B	B'	L

From this matrix, we may see why some writers prefer to compare relevance ratio and fall-out ratio rather than relevance ratio and recall ratio. The latter two have the same numerator $(A \cap B)$, whereas fall-out ratio uses the complementary section of the matrix, giving a different numerator and denominator from either of the others $((B - A)$ and A' instead of $(A \cap B)$ and A or B).[10] However, recall and relevance are more usual. We can take the results of a number of tests and use these to plot a graph of recall ratio against precision ratio. Ideally, of course, our graph would be concentrated into the 100% recall and 100% precision corner, but in practice we obtain a curve of the kind shown in Figure 2.3.

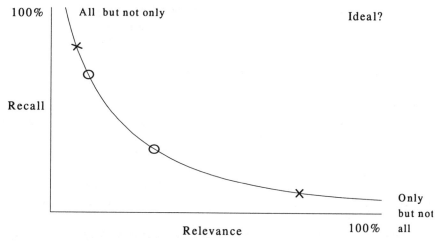

Fig. 2.3   The recall–relevance/precision curve

Flexibility of system: ability to select the appropriate operating point on the recall-relevance curve

System X–X is more flexible than system O–O (X and O mark limits of operating parameters)

The implication of this curve is that if we try to improve recall, we can only do so at the expense of precision, and conversely that if we try to improve precision, we can only do so at the expense of recall. We owe the terms recall, relevance and precision to the Cranfield Project, but the same idea was expressed some years earlier by Fairthorne in the phrases 'All but not only' (ABNO) and 'Only but not all' (OBNA).[11] One measure of the effectiveness of an information retrieval system is the freedom with which one may move from one part of the recall-precision curve to another; for example, if our first search does not reveal all the information we want, can we increase recall by moving up the curve (and thereby sacrificing a degree of precision)? If our first search reveals an overwhelming amount of information, can we increase precision and thus reformulate our search strategy to give lower recall? Ways of altering our search strategies to give such changes will be discussed in due course, when it will become apparent that not all systems have the same degree of flexibility in this respect.

We should be cautious about accepting the recall-precision curve unquestioningly. As Cleverdon himself has pointed out, it represents the average performance of any given system, and this may vary quite considerably in particular situations. For example, in the MEDLARS evaluation study Lancaster found that the system was operating on average at about 58% recall and 50% precision, retrieving an average of 175 documents per search. To achieve 85% to 95% recall would have meant retrieving an average of some 500 to 600 documents per search, with a precision ratio of about 20%. However, if we examine the results of individual searches, we find that in some cases 100% recall was achieved with 100% precision, while in others both recall and relevance were zero! Furthermore, while it may not be possible to alter the response of a system to a particular request – if we try to improve recall or precision we can only do so at the expense of the other – in practice, once we start to obtain documents from the system in response to a request, the feedback we obtain may well enable us to modify our request in such a way as to improve both recall and precision.

From the point of view of the user, it is usually relevance rather than recall which is desirable. The majority of enquiries can be satisfied by providing no more than half a dozen documents, providing they are all useful, and it is only in the minority of cases that a high recall figure is necessary. For example, the Patent Examiner needs to be sure that any relevant documents that may exist are found, since prior publication is grounds for invalidating a patent; *one* such document is enough, but the system must be such that the Examiner is certain to find that document if it exists. On the other hand, the casual enquirer would not normally need the same degree of certainty, and would rarely wish to be presented with an enormous pile of documents in response to a request.

There is also the point that many documents are repetitive: they do not add anything significant to our knowledge. R. Shaw examined a collection of documents on milkweed in detail, and came to the conclusion that all the information to be found was contained in 96 of the total of 4000![12] Of course, in order to identify the 96 he did have to examine the 4000, but this does reinforce two points. The first of these is that even literature which is claimed to be original may duplicate previous work;

the second is the importance of the intermediary whose task is to act as a filter between authors and users. There is scope for a great deal more analysis of the content of documents, as opposed to their unquestioned supply to the user who then has to sort the wheat from the chaff. It has been suggested that we are seeing a publication explosion rather than an information explosion; perhaps librarians could solve some of the problems of recall and relevance by encouraging some kind of literary contraception.

We should however not overlook the fact that there is a genuine need for a certain amount of duplication. New ideas need to be disseminated at more than one level; what would be ideal for the author's peers would probably leave the lay person no wiser, and an interpretation at a simpler level is required. With the modern trend towards increasing specialization, we may even have various levels of 'lay person', requiring a series of levels of interpretation ranging from the original article in a learned journal to the TV presentation and newspaper report. There is also the problem of publication in languages other than the original. Depending on the purpose of our information retrieval system, we may need to store information at more than one level, and ensure that we have the means of selecting the right level for any particular user.

Blair has put forward an interesting and useful concept to clarify the 'normal' attitude to recall and relevance, that of the *futility point*.[13] A relevance ratio which might be quite acceptable in a small system may be totally unacceptable in a computer-based system with access to millions of references. Two terms have been coined to characterize a user's reaction to the result of a search. To satisfy the user, a search should retrieve a small enough set of documents for the searcher to be willing to browse through them to find those which are relevant. The number of documents through which searchers are willing to browse before giving up in disgust is their futility point FP. If a searcher's FP is n, then they will be willing to look through n documents of the set B in Figure 2.1 before giving up without finding the document(s) wanted from set A. However, there is also an 'anticipated futility point' m, which is the size of the set that a searcher is willing to *begin* browsing through; for example, it is obvious that in the vast majority of cases the announcement that a search has retrieved 1,200 references will not rouse any great enthusiasm in the searcher. Based on observation, Blair suggests that in practice m is of the order of 30; with many databases now containing millions of references, we may have to rethink our ideas on acceptable relevance levels.

Confirmation of the concept of the futility point comes from a study by Lantz on the London University Computer Information Service LUCIS.[14] Users were asked to respond to questionnaires on over 2000 requests; the first asked them to estimate the number of relevant references retrieved, the second asked how many they had actually read. The responses showed that the more relevant documents were retrieved, the smaller the proportion of them that were actually read. When the number relevant was 10, the number read was about 5; when the number relevant was 100, the number read was about 28. The proportion varied according to the subject field; for engineering, the number read reached a limit at about 10, for medicine at about 60. For the social sciences, the field observed by Blair, the figure was about

30. Mathematical analysis showed that the curve of number read y against number relevant x could best fit an exponential expression:

$$y = a(1 - e^{-bx})$$

where the mean value for a is 34.1 and for b is 0.017. As $x \to \infty$, $e^{-bx} \to 0$, so that $a(1-e^{-bx}) \to a$: the mean maximum number read is then about 34. These are average figures (two readers in fact reported that they had read over 200 references) but the similarity to Blair's figure is too striking to be ignored. The University of London Library has of course very good resources for users to consult; in libraries with fewer resources, it is probable that the proportion read would be influenced by the availability factor. Users normally prefer materials that are immediately available, even if they are not the 'best possible', to those which have to be obtained from elsewhere, with an associated delay. In a library with fewer resources, it is likely that the proportion of relevant items actually read would be lower than was found in this study.

Despite the need to be aware of these findings, it is clear that recall and relevance (precision) are valuable concepts in the study of any information retrieval system. They are, however, not the only criteria by which a system may be judged. We can now consider some of the factors affecting recall and relevance, and some of the other important aspects of IR systems.

Probability of error

Indexers are human; so are users, and also the keyboard operators who produce computer-readable text. All are thus liable to make mistakes. Our system should be one which reduces the probability of error as far as possible. Research by telephone engineers some years ago[15] showed that the probability of incorrect dialling began to rise steeply as the length of the number increased to nine or more digits. (A look at trends in telephone numbers can be depressing.) If a system uses numbers for coding, for example a classification scheme, mistakes become more common if the length of the notation grows beyond the limit indicated above. Even if we use words, the likelihood of error still exists; for example, many English users of MED-LINE must have been infuriated by the inability of the system to spell even simple words such as Haemoglobin and Labour correctly. This problem is compounded in Australia, where there is an ambivalent attitude towards words ending in -our; the preferred spelling as shown in the *Macquarie dictionary* is -our, but one major political party is the Labor Party, and over a century ago one port in South Australia was named Victor Harbor!

Errors will have an effect on relevance, in that we shall get answers which are wrong; they also affect recall, in that we shall miss items that we ought to find. We should therefore try to ensure that the system we use does not have a built-in tendency to increase human error. Just as faults in a telephone line introduce audible noise and thus interfere with our reception of a message, so errors in an IR system introduce their own particular kind of noise. The fewer the errors, the less will be the noise from this source.

Ease of use

Another source of noise is the ease with which an IR system may be used. Whatever system we choose to use, there are two groups of people who must find it helpful: those responsible for the input, i.e. the *indexers*, and those trying to obtain an output, i.e. the *users*. At the input stage, how much skill do indexers need to be able to use the system? Does it help to overcome deficiencies in their understanding of the subjects dealt with? Despite their best endeavours, indexers are not omniscient! Similarly, users often find it difficult to express their needs exactly; does the system help them to formulate a satisfactory search despite this? Is the physical form of output acceptable? A system which presents the user with a set of documents, or at least abstracts, is likely to be more popular than one which gives merely a string of numbers.

Specificity and exhaustivity

There are several other factors which affect the overall performance of an information retrieval system and its potential in terms of recall and relevance. First, we may consider *specificity*: the extent to which the system permits us to be precise when specifying the subject of a document we are processing. The higher the specificity, the more likely we are to be able to achieve high relevance, and conversely, with a system that permits us only limited specificity we are likely to achieve reasonably high recall but correspondingly low relevance. In the example quoted earlier, if our system did not permit us to specify *Siamese* cats, we should have to look through all the items about cats before we could find out whether we had anything on that particular breed. Further, if the second item we found did relate to Siamese cats, there would be no guarantee that this would be the only one, or that any others would be found alongside it. If specificity is lacking, we are in fact reduced to the kind of sequential scanning that is necessary if our collections are not organized at all – though of course we have reduced the amount of material that we have to scan by partially specifying its subject content. If we are to obtain the maximum amount of control over our searching, the system must permit us to be precise in our specification of subjects; in fact, our specification should in every case be coextensive with the subject of the document. If we need to increase recall, we can always ignore part of our specification, but we cannot increase relevance by adding to it *at the search stage*. It is very important to keep clear the distinction between the *input* to our system (i.e. the specifications of the documents we are adding), and the *output* (i.e. the results of the searches we perform among these specifications). We cannot add to the input at the output stage; anything omitted at the input stage will remain outside the system, and will have to be replaced by sequential scanning of an unnecessarily large output. (We may however be able to use a systematic approach to help us formulate our search strategy, even though it is not part of the system used to specify the input, while the use of computers may enable us to get round the problem by using full texts as input and thus transfer all our 'indexing' operations to the output stage. These ideas are discussed in more detail later.)

Specificity is a function of the system, but another important factor, *exhaustivity*, is the result of a management decision. This is the extent to which we analyse any given document to establish exactly what subject content we have to specify. We may distinguish between the overall theme of a document, and the subthemes which it may contain; for example, a description of a scientific experiment may be concerned overall with the purpose and results, but it will probably also contain a description of the apparatus used. In a large general library we may content ourselves with specifying the overall themes, giving perhaps an average of one to one and a half specifications per document, whereas in a small special library, anxious to exploit the stock to the maximum advantage, we may wish to index subthemes as well, giving perhaps dozens of specifications for every document. This is known as *depth indexing*, as opposed to the *summarization* of the first method. Depth indexing might indicate that a book is about Dryden, Wycherley, Congreve, Vanbrugh and Farquhar, while summarization might say that it was about Restoration drama. It would clearly be very difficult if not impossible to index *all* the subthemes in a document in a library catalogue or a bibliography (the index to the present work contains nearly 1000 entries), so depth indexing is usually carried out in libraries where the needs of the readers can be foreseen fairly clearly; often depth indexing is applied to technical reports and similar documents which are relatively short and are therefore manageable. Some work has been done on the feasibility of using book contents pages and indexes to increase greatly the exhaustivity of indexing possible in online systems with a minimum of effort.[16] As a high proportion of the books produced today are computer-typeset, machine-readable versions are easily obtained.

Depth indexing involves the indexer in the exercise of judgement as to which themes and subthemes are worth noting. In choosing between depth indexing and summarization, the decision is ours and not a function of the system. However, there is a link between exhaustivity and specificity in that there is no point in increasing exhaustivity unless the system being used has adequate specificity.

A moment's thought should show that whereas specificity is a device to increase relevance at the cost of recall, exhaustivity works in the opposite direction, by increasing recall, but at the expense of relevance. A device which we may use to counteract this effect to some extent is *weighting*. In this, we try to show the significance of any particular specification by giving it a weight on a pre-established scale. For example, if we had a book on pets which dealt largely with dogs, we might give PETS a weight of 10/10, and DOGS, a weight of 8/10 or less. If it gave some information about dogs, but not much, we might give DOGS a low weighting of 2/10. The reader wanting high relevance now knows that this particular item can be ignored, at least for the time being, while the reader wanting high recall will have no difficulty in finding it. Search terms may be weighted in the same way, and the SMART system incorporates means for using feedback from the user's relevance judgments to amend the search strategy by altering the weighting given to the various search terms.

Time

Indexing takes time; searching takes time. By increasing our effort at the indexing stage – the input – we may well be able to reduce the amount of time we have to spend at the output stage in searching. On the other hand, in any given library situation, a proportion (which may be high) of the documents indexed will never be sought, and the effort used to index them will be wasted; if we concentrate our effort at the output stage by keeping our indexing to a minimum (for example by using abstracts or even whole texts for the input instead of subject specifications) and then perform complex searches to find relevant items, we can argue that we are eliminating a large amount of unnecessary work. As has already been mentioned, users cannot always specify exactly what it is they want, so any search will be a dialogue between the user and the system; the results of a first search will be used to modify or refine the question so that further searches can be performed until such time as a satisfactory end point is reached. By concentrating our efforts on the searching rather than the indexing, we do not hamper this dialogue in any way, but we can very easily make use of such feedback in planning future search strategies. In a system where the effort is concentrated on the input, this may not be quite so easy, as the output cannot affect the input retrospectively; to take account of experience gained in searching we may have to re-index some items – i.e. increase the input effort still further.

At present, nearly all systems involve large amounts of input effort rather than transferring this to the output stage. The complicated search strategies necessary with the latter technique, together with the very large amounts of storage necessary for the input, have only recently become available as computer technology has advanced, and there remain many situations where this approach is still either impractical or not cost-effective. Some of the SDI services referred to earlier rely on abstracts or even titles on their own, and the consequences of this in terms of search strategy and profile construction are discussed in more detail later. Searching of full texts is now becoming commonplace, but is likely to present problems of relevance, since exhaustivity is obviously 100%.

Iterative and heuristic searching

The idea of a dialogue between users and system is worthy of further examination. As has been pointed out above, users often find it difficult to express their needs precisely. In a conventional library, searches may be carried out by users, or by the librarian acting on their behalf. When they are carried out by the users themselves, searches are usually modified as they progress; each relevant document found tends to influence the user's decision as to what further information is required. In many cases the clarification that results as searches are pursued leads to a situation where users finish up with objectives rather different from those that they started out with. Such a search, where the course of events is modified continuously in the light of knowledge being gained, may be described as *heuristic*. If on the other hand the search is carried out by the librarian, this continuous modification is not possible, since modifications of the librarian's knowledge do not affect the user. For this reason it is usual for the librarian to perform a first search and present the results to the user; the search strategy may then be modified in the light of the proportion of relevant documents among those resulting from this search. A second search may then be performed, and the process repeated until the user has what is needed. This kind of search, which is modified not continuously but at intervals, may be described as *iterative*. Both heuristic and iterative searches require interaction between user and results, but heuristic searching eliminates the time delay between receiving the result of a search operation and using it to modify the search procedure.

Many information retrieval systems do not permit heuristic searching, whereas the conventional library card catalogue does. The importance of this should not be overestimated, but it is obviously a point to be considered when we are trying to estimate the relative value of different systems.[17]

Browsing

We have assumed so far that the purpose of our system is to make it possible to find information on demand – that the users will approach it with some definite objective in mind, even though they may not, to begin with, have clarified this. However, this is by no means always the case; there will be many occasions when readers will approach the collection without any particular need in mind but wishing instead to be able to select items at random. To help in this situation, our system should permit *browsing*; a reader should be able to follow a casual train of thought as well as a planned search. As was pointed out in the discussion of SDI, it is often an item which does *not* fit our existing patterns of interest which proves to be the most interesting; many of the most significant scientific discoveries have arisen as the result of *serendipity* – 'the faculty of making happy and unexpected discoveries by accident' – and a system which excludes this possibility might prove to be *too* successful in matching readers' expressed needs!

Cost

Many of the factors affecting information retrieval systems are cost factors. We have to balance the cost of so organizing our libraries that we can find information when it is required, against the cost of not finding it at all, or finding it too late for it to be of use. In libraries serving industrial firms, for example, the cost of not finding information may be high; this is why 'hard headed businessmen' add to their overheads by paying for extensive library services. (The term 'library services' is here taken to include those denoted by the more elite term 'information services'). On the other hand, public libraries have in the past tended to regard the exploitation of the information in their stocks as very much less important than its provision, because the cost to the community at large if one of its individual members fails to find information is considerably less than the cost of organizing the material adequately. However, it is now being realized that the cost to the community of wasted information is in fact very high in terms of international competition, and more effort is being devoted to providing adequate services. We still have to find out a great deal about the cost effectiveness of various methods of organizing information, though we are beginning to learn something about their comparative efficiencies as systems. Despite our relative ignorance we must not ignore cost factors altogether, but they can usually only be studied in detail in a particular set of circumstances, and will therefore only be indicated in general terms in this text.

Modern trends in the evaluation of cost significance have been towards the idea of cost effectiveness. Most of the sophisticated devices developed in recent years have been aimed at improving relevance: reducing the number of unwanted documents revealed by a search, and thus reducing also the time taken to scan through the results and select those which are of use to us. However, if it costs more to use a sophisticated system for indexing than it would cost to look through the output of an unsophisticated system, there is no point in using the more advanced system. We have also to bear in mind that a relevance level which might be tolerable in a small system might well be quite unacceptable in a large nationwide mechanized system. If a search reveals ten documents, four of which are useful, this is not too bad; but if we have the same level with a collection a hundred times as large, we might well boggle at the thought of discarding 600 documents from a total of 1000. As yet only a limited amount of research has been carried out into this aspect of information retrieval, but it is obviously a field that is likely to be explored in more depth in the future, particularly with the development of mechanized systems.

Problems of linear order

Knowledge is multi-dimensional: that is to say, subjects are related one to another in many different ways. In the example quoted earlier, it was assumed that Siamese cats were to be considered as pets, but it is obvious that they can be regarded in many other ways – as a branch of the zoological class *Felidae*, or as originating in a particular part of the world, to name but two approaches. However, when we try to arrange items in our library or catalogue, we find that we are restricted to a linear, unidimensional, sequence, just as we are if we are reading a book. We cannot *display* multiple relationships and must therefore find some other means of showing them. If we have a book with no contents list and no index, the only way we can find a given item in it is to read it through. We have only one means of access; sequential scanning. However, we can overcome this problem by providing multiple access through the contents list and index, which permit us to go direct to the information we require; but the text of the book continues to display its information unidimensionally. The sequence in the book is chosen for us by the author and we cannot alter it, though we may to a large extent minimize the effect by adequate signposting in the form of indexes and guiding.

We face exactly the same problem in organizing the information in our libraries. We can provide a sequence which we hope will be helpful to our readers, just as an author does, but we must recognize the need to cater for other modes of access. We must also realize that without these secondary modes of access we can only find information in one way, unless we are prepared to revert to sequential scanning. A simple example will demonstrate this in relation to a familiar tool, the telephone directory. These directories are arranged according to the surnames of the subscribers, set out in alphabetical order. Provided we know the subscriber's name, we can find the telephone number without much trouble, but we cannot perform the operation in reverse; we cannot find out the name of a subscriber whose number we know, unless we are prepared to look through the directory until we find it. To overcome this we can have a second sequence, arranged this time by number; but we still cannot find the number of a friend if we only know his or her forename and address.

The problem is of course largely an economic one. We do not set up multiple sequences of books and other items in our libraries because it would cost too much to try to arrange a copy of a book at every point in the library where it might be related to other items. Nor can we afford to make multiple sequences in bibliographical tools which have to be printed and distributed. We might perhaps make several sequences in our records within the library, but even this will prove very expensive if we are to be consistent and comprehensive. However, just as we can overcome the problem in a book by providing multiple access through subsidiary sequences which lead us to the required points in our main sequence, so we can do the same thing in our information retrieval system. Different systems will permit us differing degrees of multiple access; the more flexible a system is in this respect, the more likely it is to be of value. This is perhaps the major advantage of computer-based systems. Once the information is stored in the machine, it is possible for us to manipulate it in virtually as many ways as we wish; we have all the flexibility which has long been recognized as desirable but unattainable with manual systems.

Literary warrant

No matter what our system may be, the information in it must be a function of the input; that is to say, our systems must take account of the relationships between subjects shown in the items we are indexing. We may in addition built into it relationships between subjects of which we are aware *a priori*, through a study of knowledge *per se*, but if we restrict ourselves to a study of knowledge alone without taking into account knowledge as it is presented in recorded form, i.e. information, we shall find ourselves unable to specify subjects precisely. In other words, we are concerned with the organization of information rather than the organization of knowledge on its own. The term *literary warrant* is used here to denote that our system must be based on the information we put into it rather than on purely theoretical considerations. (As this term is widely used in this context, it is retained, even though computer-based systems may well hold information which is not available in any other form, and conventional systems may well hold information relating to audiovisual materials which do not fit the usual definition of 'literary'.)

There is another aspect to this particular question. It is the output of the system which is important, since this is the whole purpose of the system. But we cannot know in advance what output will be required, at least not with any degree of precision, though we may be able to form an intelligent guess on the basis of past experience. So although it would be desirable to build up our system in such a way that it matched the required output, we are unable to do this since we do not know what the required output will be. We are obliged to use the input as our basis for building up the system, adding to this whatever is suggested by studies of knowledge outside the system. If we restrict ourselves to studies of knowledge outside the system we shall, by ignoring the input, be removing our system one stage further from the required output. In any subject area there will be an accepted corpus of knowledge, but each document we index may modify this; literary warrant implies a system that is able to accept this kind of change.

There is perhaps a danger that we may take a negative attitude to literary warrant: exclude from our system the possibility of catering for subjects which have not as yet appeared in our collections. This danger is usually associated with the older kind of enumerative system described below, but there have been more recent examples to demonstrate the problems that arise if we deliberately make our system a static one. Hospitality to new concepts as they are revealed by our collections is vital if we are to maintain the desired level of specificity.

The term literary warrant was used by Wyndham Hulme to denote a rather different kind of idea, though one basically similar.[18] He considered that if we have a document entitled, say, *Heat, light and sound*, then that represents a subject for which we should make provision in our system. However, most of these are not genuine subjects but aggregates of subjects resulting from the bibliographical accident of being bound within the same pair of covers. This situation should not be confused with that of a genuine interaction between subjects, e.g. the effect of heat on sound (discussed in more detail on pp.107–110); this is a different kind of situation for which we do have to make provision. Hulme's use of the term is rarely found now, though his ideas were largely reflected in the practice of the Library of Congress, and have indeed developed into the modern theory already outlined.

Heading and description

We use the terms in our indexing system to name the subjects of the documents in our collection, but obviously a user who has found the correct subject description will require in addition some details of the documents to which that description applies. We can therefore divide an entry in the system into two parts, the heading and the description.

The *heading* is the subject description which determines whereabouts in the sequence we shall find any given entry. (The present work is restricted to considerations of the subject approach; in a full catalogue, headings will include names of authors and titles, as well as subjects.) In an alphabetical system, headings will consist of words, while in a systematic arrangement it is the notation – the *code* vocabulary – that is used for the headings. We need to distinguish between two kinds of heading. We have those which are 'preferred' terms, in the sense that we use them to lead us directly to information – a catalogue entry, or a book on the shelf. These form the *index vocabulary*. We also have those which are 'non-preferred', for examples synonyms we have decided not to use, except to lead us to terms in the index vocabulary. These non-preferred terms, together with the index vocabulary, form the 'entry vocabulary'.

The *description* is the part of an entry which gives us information about a document, and will therefore contain all those factors which serve to *identify*. There are various sets of rules for the compilation of document descriptions, e.g. those in the

Anglo-American Cataloguing Rules, or the International Standard Bibliographical Description, but for our purposes here we need only note their existence. The presence of a document description enables us to make a useful distinction: a *subject entry* consists of a heading from the index vocabulary together with a document description, while an *index entry* or *cross-reference* leads us from a heading with no document description to an entry. The heading from which we make a cross-reference may be one which appears only in the entry vocabulary, in which case the reference is one leading us from a heading not used to one which is used; or it may appear in both entry and index vocabulary, in which case the reference is one linking two headings which are both used, to show some kind of relationship.

It should be noted that in some systems the descriptions may be in the form of a number (an accessions number or document number) rather than the detailed information about author, title, imprint and so on which we find in, for example, a library catalogue. The links between related headings may form an integral part of the main sequence, as in a dictionary catalogue; part of a subsidiary sequence, as in as classified catalogue; or quite separate, as is usual in post-coordinate systems. These points will be clarified in due course; at this stage it is important to realize that these features, like the others in this chapter, are common to all information systems. Their presence or absence can make a great deal of difference to the ease with which we can retrieve information.

Term entry and item entry

The preceding section implies that we make entries for a document (which we identify by its description) under each of the appropriate headings, and file these in the correct place in our alphabetical or classified sequence. A system which works in this way is called a *term entry* system, and a card catalogue using unit cards is of this kind. It is possible to take the opposite approach, and make a single entry for each item, using a physical form which permits access to the entry from all appropriate headings. Such a system is known as *item entry*, and is used in computer-based systems. It implies a main sequence of entries supported by one or more indexes, and is discussed more fully in Chapter 5.

Separation of intellectual and clerical effort

In any system, part of the work involved will be intellectual and part will be clerical. Deciding what the access points to a particular document should be is an intellectual operation in assigned indexing systems, discussed in later chapters, but the actual mechanics of placing an entry in a file is not. Similarly, in searching we need to make an intellectual decision as to which words or headings are likely to give a satisfactory answer to an enquiry, but the task of displaying the results of the search does not involve intellectual effort.

The distinction has become important with the use of computers. Computers can perform clerical tasks very well, they are much faster and more accurate than human beings, provided they are given the right instructions. At present, we do not know enough about the way in which the human mind works to be able to give computers the right instructions to enable them to perform intellectual operations; these must still be done by human effort. However, studies such as that carried out by E. J. Coates in the computerization of the production of the then BTI showed that many of the operations which had been thought of as intellectual could be reduced to an algorithm suitable for computer operation. It is clearly advantageous to transfer as much routine work to the computer as we can, to enable us to concentrate on the intellectual tasks; by doing so we can only improve our service to users.

References

1 Vickery, B. C., *Techniques of information retrieval*, London, Butterworths, 1970. Chapters 1 and 2.

2 Orwell, G., *1984*, London, Secker & Warburg, 1949.

3 Kemp, A., *Current awareness services*, London, Bingley, 1979.

4 The phrase 'one skilled in the art' is commonly used in patent specifications to denote someone who has a sufficient working knowledge of the existing procedures to be able to utilize the invention being patented.

5 Cleverdon, C. W., Mills, J., and Keen, E. M., *Factors determining the performance of indexing systems*, Cranfield, Aslib–Cranfield Research Project, 1966, 2v in 3.

6 Lancaster, F. W., 'Evaluation and testing of information retrieval systems', in *Encyclopedia of library and information science*, **8**, 1972, 234–59.
Lancaster, F. W., 'Pertinence and relevance', in *Encyclopedia of library and information science*, **22**, 1977, 70–86.
Lancaster, F. W., 'Precision and recall', in *Encyclopedia of library and information science*, **23**, 170–80, 1978.
Swanson, D. R., 'Subjective versus objective relevance in bibliographic retrieval systems', *Library quarterly*, **56** (4), 1986, 389–98.
For a recent detailed review of the question of relevance see Schamber, L., 'Relevance and information behavior', *Annual review of information science and technology*, **29**, 1994, 3–48.

7 Cleverdon, C. W., *Aslib Cranfield Research Project: report on the testing and analysis of an investigation into the comparative efficiency of indexing systems*, Cranfield, College of Aeronautics, 1962.

8 Buckland, M. and Gey, F., 'The relationship between recall and precision', *Journal of the American society for information science*, **45**, 1994, 12–19.

9 Zadeh, L. A., 'Fuzzy sets', *Information and control*, **8**, 1965, 338–53.
Robertson, T. E., 'On the nature of fuzz: a diatribe', *Journal of the American Society for Information Science*, **29** (6), 1978, 304–7.
Cerny, B., 'A reply to Robertson's diatribe on the nature of fuzz', *Journal of the American Society for Information Science*, **30** (6), 1979, 357–8.
Bookstein, A., 'Probability and fuzzy set applications to information retrieval', *Annual review of information science and technology*, **20**, 1985, 117–51.

10 I am indebted to E. M. Keen for drawing my attention to this point in ref. 5 above.

11   Fairthorne, R., 'Automatic retrieval of recorded information', *Computer journal*, 1958, 36–41.

12   Shaw, R., *private communication*, quoted by Cleverdon in *Journal of documentation*, **30** (2), June 1974, 174.

13   Blair, D. C., 'Searching biases in large interactive document retrieval systems', *Journal of the American Society for Information Science*, **17** (3), 1980, 271–7.

14   Lantz, B. E., 'The relationship between documents read and relevant references retrieved as effectiveness measures', *Journal of documentation*, **37** (3), 1981, 134–45.

15   Conrad, R. and Hille, B. A., 'Memory for long telephone numbers', *Post Office telecommunications journal*, **10**, 1957, 37–9.

16   Atherton, P., *Books are for use: final report of the Subject Access Project to the Council on Library Resources*, Syracuse, NY, Syracuse University, 1978. Cochrane, P. A., *Redesign of catalogs and indexes for improved online subject access: selected papers of Pauline A. Cochrane*, Phoenix, AZ, Oryx Press, 1985.

17   Lancaster, F. W., 'Interaction between requesters and a large mechanized retrieval system', *Information storage and retrieval*, **4** (2), 1968, 239–52.

18   Hulme, E. Wyndham, *Principles of book classification*, London, Association of Assistant Librarians, 1950 (AAL Reprints No 1). Originally published in the *Library Association record*, 1911–1912. Included in *Theory of subject analysis . . .*

Chapter 3
Derived indexing 1: Printed indexes

As we saw in Chapter 1, we have to encode the subject of a document in order to place the document itself or our records of it in our store. This means that we must in some way be able to specify the subject. How can we establish the subject of a document so that we can specify it? We do not usually have time to read all the documents we add to stock, and in any case we might not understand them if we did. We may use short cuts: the contents page, preface or introduction, or publisher's blurb on the cover for a book; or an abstract if we are looking at a journal article or technical report; or the claims for a patent specification. All of these will give some indication of the subject and will suggest certain lines of thought if we want to pursue the matter further, for example in a dictionary or encyclopedia.

We may decide that in the interests of economy we will rely solely on information which is *manifest* in the document, without attempting to add to this from our own knowledge or other sources. This is *derived indexing*, that is, indexing derived directly from the document. We can begin by studying some of the ways in which derived indexing has been used to produce printed indexes, particularly in computer-based systems. These are now often found in online systems, but the principles remain the same.

We have seen that it is possible to distinguish between intellectual and clerical effort involved in an IR system, and computers enable us to carry out the clerical operations at high speed. Derived indexing reduces intellectual effort to a minimum, and is thus well suited to computer operations, which can enable us to get a variety of outputs from the one input. We may find that we are able to produce some forms of output that can be produced manually but are usually not attempted because of time and cost factors.[1]

Title-based indexing

There is of course one part of a document in which authors themselves usually try to define the subject: the title. In many cases this will give a clear indication of what the document is about, though we find cases where the title still leaves us in some doubt, and others where the title is obviously meant to attract attention rather than inform us about the subject. In the first category we might place *The development of national library and information services*, or *Early Victorian New Zealand*; in the second, *The design of steel structures* (Buildings? Bridges? Or all of them?), or

Steps in time (Fred Astaire's autobiography!); and in the third *Men in dark times* (a collection of biographies of men who died in the twentieth century, including Bertolt Brecht), and 'Waterfalls and tall buildings', which turns out to be a review of the *Guinness book of records*! Authors tend to generalize in the titles they select, and though they usually try to find titles which are unique to their own work, this is not always the case. There are for example several books with the rather vague title *Materials and structures*. The title *Malice in Wonderland* used by Nicholas Blake for a detective story was also used for a film starring Elizabeth Taylor. So in general we find that searching for specific titles will give low recall, though probably high relevance at the same time, but occasionally will produce false drops – titles which match the specification but are not in any way relevant.

If we consider titles given to 'serious' works, we will often find that works on the same subject have titles containing the same significant words – *keywords* – which can be used as a basis for information retrieval, e.g.:

Manual of library classification
Library classification on the march
Introduction to library classification
A modern outline of library classification
Prolegomena to library classification.

The use of keywords to give various kinds of index is well established, but has been emphasized in recent years by the use of computers to manipulate the terms.

Catchword indexing

Catchword indexing has been used for many years in bibliographical tools, particularly those produced by publishers, where it has provided a cheap and reasonably effective means of subject access to the titles listed. The titles are manipulated to bring the significant words to the front, giving perhaps two or three entries per title. The editor selects the words to be used, and the entries are generated manually. The technique was also used to produce the indexes to periodicals such as *Nature*. With the computerization of these kinds of index, catchword indexing has in effect been dropped in favour of other formats, but it will be found in many older reference tools.

Keyword in Context (KWIC) indexing

One particular form of catchword indexing was adapted for computer production by H. P. Luhn of IBM.[2] Each significant word becomes an entry point, but instead of appearing at the left-hand side of the page, the keyword appears in the middle, with the rest of the title on either side. One important point arises immediately. In catchword indexing, an editor selects the significant terms, but a computer cannot recognize the significance of a given word; instead, we have to construct a list of words which are *not* of value for indexing purposes: a *stop list*. The computer is then programmed to delete any entries which might arise under these terms. It is usual to have a fairly short list of terms which are obviously of no value as index entries –

the *articles* a, an, the; *prepositions* on, of, in; *conjunctions* and, or; *pronouns* he, she, my; and so on – and then add a rather larger list, based on experience, of words which are unlikely to be of any value. The New Grolier multimedia encyclopedia has a stop list of 132 words, including bibliography, which might not please librarians! Other terms considered to be unsought are words such as although, begun, can (which might be unhelpful to a can-maker!), different, etc. The list may be edited from time to time to take account of 'fashions' in terminology and of changes in the subject coverage of the collection. This will still leave us with words which occur too rarely for us to include them in a stop list; when they do occur, they will give rise to entries in the index, but these will be few enough not to bother the user. It is better to have a few entries that are not useful than to omit some which would be.

KWIC techniques were at one time popular as a cheap and quick means of producing indexes (KWIC is an unusually apposite homophonic acronym), but with more sophisticated methods now available, they have been largely superseded. One place where such an index is still often to be found is in a thesaurus, where the *rotated index* is used to reveal otherwise hidden words in multiword terms. An excerpt from the index to the PAIS *Subject headings list* is as follows:

	Industrial relations
Boycott	(industrial relations)
	Industrial relations consultants
Grievance procedures	(industrial relations)
	Industrial safety
Social service,	Industrial
Sociology,	Industrial
Spies,	Industrial
	Industrial surveys

Although the word 'industrial' would be at the front of many of these entries, i.e. the access point, in others it would not be found at all easily by any means other than this index. An interesting use of KWIC techniques has been introduced by DIALOG.[3] Many of the files now contain several million references, and even a well-planned search may well retrieve an unacceptably large number of references from a file this big. To facilitate looking through the results of such a search, it is possible to display titles (or in some cases text) containing the sought term in context. This should be of help in pursuing the search further to improve the relevance performance.

Keyword out of context (KWOC) indexing

Because the filing word is not in the usual place, KWIC indexing looks unfamiliar, and another method of title manipulation is to have the keyword at the beginning of the line, followed by the complete title. This has the advantage of having as familiar appearance – filing word at the left – and also of presenting the whole title as it stands, but is not as successful as KWIC in bringing together titles which contain the same pairs of words. The point is well illustrated by the British Library

Document Supply Centre's *Index of conference proceedings*; this started out in 1965 with a single-word KWOC index, but has had to develop a more sophisticated system using pairs of words as its collection has grown to some 18,000 titles each year. For example, 'A proposed new structure for food and agricultural policy' is indexed under Food policy; agricultural policy; AAAS [organizer], but not under Policy. 'Listening devices and citizens' rights: police powers and electronic surveillance' is indexed under the pairs of words Listening devices; Citizens' rights; Police powers; and Electronic surveillance. There does not appear to any way to get to this starting at the single word 'Rights'.

Using KWIC and KWOC, each title will give rise to a number of entries: as many as there are significant words in the title. For this reason, they are usually used as indexes, leading to descriptions of the documents in a separate file. Judged by the criteria for IR systems in general, they do not perform particularly well. Relevance is certainly likely to be high, in that a title found by looking for a particular word is likely to be useful, but we may have to look through a number of entries at that word before finding a title which looks like what we want. Recall, however, is likely to be low. As we have seen, authors usually look for unique titles, and we have no way of identifying related terms, such as synonyms, other than our own knowledge, which is clearly outside the system. Specificity depends on the authors' choice of words, while exhaustivity again depends on how detailed the titles are. Despite this potential disadvantage, KWOC title entries were found to be popular with users in the Bath University Comparative Cataloguing Study,[4] and must obviously be taken seriously.

Since the 1960s, authors of scientific and technical papers have been encouraged by professional societies and the US Government to give their works explicit titles. Although printed indexes based on titles are not common now, titles are an important source of terms for computer database searching in science and technology, though we should perhaps except patents from this; their titles are required to be accurate statements of the subject area of the contents, but are often made unhelpful in order to avoid helping competitors. In the social sciences and humanities there are also problems of terminology which make title-based indexing less useful.

Citation indexing

Documents of value are likely to contain bibliographies; this is the way in which authors show the foundations on which they have built. Garvey suggests that the list of references is a key part of any scientific paper, since it helps to put the research into its proper context in the development of the scientific consensus.[5] His research also suggests that the use of scientific literature occurs at two quite distinct stages of a research project. Scientists will probably begin any research work by finding some references, but their major use of the literature may not take place until their work is completed and is being prepared for publication; at this stage, they are trying to show the relevance of their work to what has gone before, and the citations may reflect this concern rather than indicate the sources actually used during the research. This would seem to lend weight to the significance of *citation indexing*.

There is a link between a document and each work cited in its bibliography; we can invert this, and say that there is a link between each item cited and the work citing it. Since documents usually cite several items, by scanning large numbers of original documents we can establish much larger numbers of such links. If we now file these according to the items cited, we shall bring together all the documents which have included a given item in their bibliographies. This is the basic principle of citation indexing.

As with title-based indexes, the use of the computer made possible the practical implementation on a large scale of an idea which had already been in use in certain subject areas, notably legal literature. The Institute for Scientific Information (ISI), established in 1961, now produces various citation indexes, notably *Science citation index* 1961–, *Social science citation index*, 1966–, and *Arts and humanities citation index*, 1977–. Between them, these indexes cover over 5,000 key periodicals; these are scanned, and all the bibliographic links found are entered into a computer. The information thus gathered is used to provide the citation indexes, source indexes and corporate indexes; it is also used for an SDI service, ASCA (Automatic Subject Citation Alert), and a 'subject index', the Permuterm index, which enters each item under pairs of significant words found in the title.[6]

To use a citation index, it is necessary to have the reference for a relevant article, but it is often the case that a search starts from such a basis. If we do not have a 'prompt' article, we can use the Permuterm index to try to find a starting point using pairs of keywords from our search formulation; this can be useful in locating information on subjects commonly described by a word pair such as 'Holy Grail', which may well be used in the title.[7] This may then give us one or more articles to use as our starting point for a citation search. From the citation index we can find brief details of other more recent articles which have cited the one we already know. We can turn to the source index for full details, and then locate the articles in the appropriate periodicals. If they are not relevant we can discard them, but if they are, we can use the articles they cite as the basis for a further search in the citation index. By this process of recycling we can compile a substantial bibliography from our single starting point. It is of course possible to do this manually, but at a very substantial cost in time and effort. A search which takes weeks to do manually may be done in minutes using a citation index.

Since every item in the periodicals scanned is entered, we can follow up amendments and corrections to previously published articles. These often contain important information – for example, the withdrawal of a claim of success! – but are usually ignored by conventional indexing and abstracting services. This advantage is of course not inherent in citation indexing, but is reflected in the cost of SCI and its fellows compared with most conventional services.

Citation links

Two articles which both cite another earlier article must have something in common; if they both cite two earlier articles, the linking is increased. This is known as *bibliographic coupling*, and if two articles have half a dozen articles in common, we should be justified in assuming that they covered very much the same subject. (An article which had all 50 citations in common with another turned out to be a translation!) This is a reflection of the fact that authors normally cite those works which constitute the basis from which they begin their own writing. Bibliographic coupling was shown to give good results in studies carried out at MIT. Another approach which has been shown to give useful results is *co-citation*, i.e. the citation together of two or more articles in more than one paper. For example, when bibliometrics began to be widely studied, it was usual to find S. C. Bradford's book *Documentation* cited, since it was in this work that he first published his ideas on 'Bradford's Law of scattering' to a wide audience. If we look carefully, we find that nearly all the works which cite *Documentation* also cite an article by B. C. Vickery in the *Journal of documentation*, **4** (3), 1948. Even if we did not have the title of this article, we could assume that it related to Bradford's Law because of the pattern of co-citation. As the study of bibliometrics developed, other works such as *Human behavior and the principle of least effort* by G. K. Zipf were also co-cited. The study of such patterns would be both difficult and tedious using manual methods, but the availability of citation indexes makes them relatively simple, and we can follow the development of an idea through various stages.[8]

Derived indexes such as SCI require no intellectual effort at the input stage, since in effect they are based on the assumption that the author has done the necessary work to establish the citation links for us. They assume that authors are familiar with the literature of their subject and will quote the appropriate sources fully and correctly; that they will not indulge in unjustified self-citation, and do not ignore documents which put forward relevant but opposing views while quoting articles of marginal relevance by their friends. All of these assumptions are by and large justified, but it would be unwise to think that authors are not as liable to sins of omission and commission as anyone else. Nevertheless, there is no doubt that these tools are an extremely important addition to the range of bibliographical services available to the information worker. They also are based on a common approach to a search for information, where users start with a document which has aroused their interest and which can be used as the start of a search in a citation index. The following example shows how a journal article is treated in a citation index.

The original appears in the **author (source) index**:

Johnson, Karl E. 'IEEE conference publications in libraries', *Library resources and technical services, 28* (4) October/December 1984, 308–314.
[IEEE = Institution of Electrical and Electronic Engineers]

It contains the following references at the end (among others):

Marjorie Peregoy, 'Only the names have been changed to perplex the innocent', *Title varies* 1:13 (April 1974).
Jim E. Cole, 'Conference publications: serials or monographs?' *Library resources & technical services* 22:172 (Spring 1978).
Michlain J. Amir, 'Open letter to IEEE', *Special libraries*, 69:6A (Nov. 1978).
Michael E. Unsworth, 'Treating IEEE conference publications as serials',

Library resources & technical services 27:221–24 (Apr./June, 1983).

The following entries would appear in the **Citation index:**

Amir, Michlain J. 'Open letter to IEEE,' *Special libraries*, 69:6A (Nov. 1978). **Johnson, Karl E. 1984.**
Cole, Jim E. 'Conference publications: serials or monographs?' *Library resources & technical services* 22:172 (Spring 1978). **Johnson, Karl E. 1984.**
Peregoy, Margaret. 'Only the names have been changed to perplex the innocent,' *Title varies* 1:13 (April 1974). **Johnson, Karl E. 1984.**
Unsworth, Michael E. 'Treating IEEE conference publications as serials,' *Library resources & technical services* 27:221–24 (Apr./June, 1983). **Johnson, Karl E. 1984.**

The following entries would appear in a **Permuterm index:**

Conference	IEEE	Johnson, Karl E. 1984.
Conference	Libraries	Johnson, Karl E. 1984.
Conference	Publications	Johnson, Karl E. 1984.
IEEE	Conference	Johnson, Karl E. 1984.
IEEE	Libraries	Johnson, Karl E. 1984.
IEEE	Publications	Johnson, Karl E. 1984.
Libraries	Conference	Johnson, Karl E. 1984.
Libraries	IEEE	Johnson, Karl E. 1984.
Libraries	Publications	Johnson, Karl E. 1984.
Publications	Conference	Johnson, Karl E. 1984.
Publications	IEEE	Johnson, Karl E. 1984.
Publications	Libraries	Johnson, Karl E. 1984.

The above examples do *not* have exactly the same layout as you will find in, say, *Science citation index*, but the principles are the same. Once the data has been entered from the original journal article, all the rest is produced by computer.

Summary

This chapter has dealt with methods of producing printed indexes by computer from information manifest in a document: the title or the bibliographical references. The citation indexes mentioned are now available online in parallel with the printed versions; the choice of which version to buy becomes an economic one depending on the amount of use made of the service. Many of the co-citation studies mentioned are really only practical with the online versions.

References

1   Craven, T. C., *String indexing*, Orlando, Academic Press, 1986. Probably the best text on KWIC/KWOC and similar indexes.
2   Luhn, H. P., *Keyword in context index for technical literature*, IBM, 1959. Included in *Theory of subject analysis . . .*

3   *Chronolog*, 15 (2), 1987, 25, 27 (announcement).
4   Bath University Comparative Catalogue Study, *Final report*, Bath University Library, 1975. 10v in 9. (BLR&DD report 5240–5248).
5   Garvey, W. D., *Communication: the essence of science*, Oxford, Pergamon, 1979.
6   Garfield, E. *Citation indexing: its theory and practice in science, technology and humanities*, New York, Wiley, 1979.
     Ellis, P., Hepburn, G. and Oppenheim C., 'Studies on patent citation networks, *Journal of documentation*, **34** (1), 1978, 1–20.
     Students should examine at least one of the citation indexes produced by ISI in depth, using it in various ways to test its effectivess; cf Brahmi, F. A., 'Reference use of *Science citation index*', *Medical reference services quarterly*, **4** (1), 1985, 31–38.
7   Mann, T. *Library research models: a guide to classification, cataloging and computers*, New York, NY, Oxford University Press, 1993.
8   Small, H., 'Co-citation in the scientific literature: a new measure of the relationship between two documents', *Journal of the American Society for Information Science*, **24** (4), 1973, 265–9; 'Co-citation context analysis and the structure of paradigms', *Journal of documentation*, 36 (3), 1980, 183–96.
     Bichteler, J. and Eaton, E. A. III, 'The combined use of bibliographic coupling and co-citation for document retrieval', *Journal of the American Society for Information Science*, **31** (3), 1980, 278–82.
     Broadus, R. N., 'Citation analysis', *Advances in librarianship*, 7, 1977, 299–335. (The application of citation analysis to library collection building.)

Chapter 4
Developments in information technology

While this book is not a text on information technology, in order to examine the use of computers for information retrieval we must look at some of the rapid developments in computer technology which have taken place during the last 35 years, and more particularly the last 15, as these have major implications, both for present practice and for the future. The techniques described in Chapter 3 were feasible with the technology available c1960, but many of the techniques to be covered later have only become possible with more recent technology. Those familiar with these developments can move direct to Chapter 5.

Computer-controlled typesetting

During the 1960s, computers were large centralized installations, with limited access. The user had little control over the end product, and almost all processing was done in batch mode, not online. Input was through the use of 80-column punched cards; printing was by high-speed (but low quality) line printers. *Computer-controlled typesetting* was developed at this time, much of the work being done for organizations such as the NLM in its MEDLARS project to computerize the production of *Index medicus*. The widespread adoption of this technology has meant that a high proportion of formally published printed material today is also available in computer-readable form; before this, anything to be processed by computer had to be specially keypunched, an expensive and time-consuming operation which in effect repeated all the work that had gone into the production of the original document. It is for this reason that bibliographic databases do not cover material published before the 1960s, and projects to make historic materials available in computer-readable form have only recently become technologically and economically feasible.

Microcomputers

Developments in semiconductor technology led to the introduction of integrated circuits and the microprocessor, which in turn led in the mid-1970s to the first microcomputers, but these were strictly for the 'amateur', that is, those who enjoyed computing and knew enough about it to be able to program the machines for themselves. It was not until about 1980 that the desktop or *personal computer* (PC) became a practical proposition for general use, and was quickly adopted by business and industry as well as in education. Since then, developments in technology and software mean that anyone can now have as much computing power on their desk as was available in mainframe computers 20 years ago.

With the increase in computing power came the need for increasing memory, both for processing and for storage. The first PCs had 64k (kilobytes: 1k = 1024 (2^{10})) bytes of *Random Access Memory* (RAM) for processing, and used floppy disks for permanent storage. (One 360k floppy disk might store the equivalent of about 100 A4 pages.) New operating system software made it possible to use 640k of RAM, then increasing amounts; the current 'minimum' is 4MB (Megabytes), and most IBM-compatible machines can have up to 32MB. Upper range desktop machines can have several hundred MB of RAM. The first *hard disks*, for large-scale permanent storage of files, held 10MB; such a disk would not now hold the operating system software needed to run the computer, and disks holding several hundred megabytes are now common.

CD-ROM

Hard disks are normally a permanent part of the machine – hence the early name fixed disk – but the development of the laser-read compact disc has given the capacity to store up to 680MB (1995 capacity) of data on a removable CD-ROM (*Compact Disc – Read Only Memory*) disc. CD is the format usually found, though it is not the only kind of laser-read disk. Another format which appeared earlier than CD-ROM was the 12 inch laser disk; this is an analog device, with data recorded in a format compatible with television standards, rather than the computer-readable digital form of CD-ROM. It has been used successfully to store illustrations, for example photographs in archive collections. As the name implies, CD-ROMs are read-only devices, but they can of course be quickly interchanged to give access to a variety of sources of information. The adoption of an international standard (ISO 9660 – also known as the High Sierra standard) led to a rapid increase in the number of databases available on CD-ROM, covering a wide range of information. Standardization meant that discs from any supplier could be read on any CD-ROM drive: the market was no longer limited to those people having the matching equipment.

One CD-ROM can store the whole text of an encyclopedia, complete with illustrations – including video clips – and sound. Perhaps more immediately significant is the possibility of storing whole bibliographic databases, including full text, so that we are no longer constrained by the need to link up to a central computer, but can carry out searches on our own PCs. For many users, this is not only more convenient but also less stressful! (It also avoids telecommunication costs.) Some of the implications of these technological advances will be discussed here, but we cannot hope to cover them in depth; further reading is essential to gain a full appreciation of the possibilities.

Networks

Unless we are able to connect our own computer to other computers, we are restrict-

ed to those databases we have on our own machine or on a portable medium such as CD-ROM. The use of external databases requires us to be able to connect computers together. In the early days of interconnection, mainframe computers were made available to multiple users through direct links to 'dumb' terminals: dumb, in that they could not operate independently of the mainframe. The development of the microcomputer meant that these could be linked to other computers, but act as intelligent terminals, in other words carry out processing on their own. It was more sensible to utilize the power of the local machine even when connected to a large central computer. In order to do this, two things were necessary: telecommunication links and suitable software.

Software

Local Area Networks (LAN) were developed using software which connected PCs to other PCs as well as to mainframes within the same organisation. At the same time, the idea of connecting computers in distant locations through Wide Area Networks (WAN) was implemented by military, academic and commercial users. In 1969, the US Department of Defense set up a network, ARPANET; its purpose was to prevent the complete dislocation of the military network in the event of a nuclear attack, by distributing the computing power to a number of widely separated sites. In the mid-1980s the National Science Foundation (NSF) saw the possibilities of using this technique to keep down the cost of research involving supercomputers; instead of every academic research centre having its own supercomputer, which would probably be underused, a limited number of centres with supercomputers linked together through NSFNET and accessible to other users would be much more cost-effective. Other academic networks have been established, for example JANET[1] in the UK, NREN in the USA, and AARNET and the Australian Education Network (EdNA) in Australia; as more and more networks were linked together, they became the basis of the *Internet*, the network of networks linking millions of users in countries all over the world. Commercial enterprises such as banks and airlines also quickly saw the value of networked computing services to link branches in the same city, same country, and internationally, and have developed highly sophisticated software to facilitate banking and travel worldwide. Unlike the Internet, such networks, and those developed for military purposes, are not for public use, though some hackers have contested this.

To facilitate the use of information on one computer by another remote computer, the concept of *client–server* software has been developed. The computer supplying the information is the server, and the software is designed to supply information in an appropriate format to other computers, possibly to more than one at once. The computer using the information is the client, which must again have the right software to utilize the information in the format supplied by the server. If we are talking about the transmission of simple text, this is not difficult, and there is little difference between client and server; the standard code for the transmission of text, ASCII, is discussed later. Files may also be transmitted in binary format; this is the format required for multimedia files, which tend to be large. To utilize these files, users must have appropriate software on their PC, in addition to the software required for the network.

Telecommunications

Developments in telecommunication links have been a major factor in the growth of distributed computing. To begin with, the existing telephone network was used; since this used electromechanical equipment, it was subject to fairly high error levels, and transmission rates were slow – originally 110 bps (bits per second), which soon rose to 300bps. (The number of bits per second transmitted is often referred to as the *baud rate*, but at the higher speeds becoming common the two are no longer exactly equivalent.) One problem is that computers produce digital signals consisting of a series of 0s and 1s; standard telephone circuits are analogue devices, which represent sound by a continuously varying electrical voltage. To transform the digital signals into a form which can be transmitted over telephone wires requires a *modem* (*mo*dulator-*dem*odulator) which converts the signals from digital to analogue at one end, and analogue to digital at the other. Not only is there the possibility of noise through the telecommunication process, there is also the possibility of error in the conversion process. In recent years, the old electromechanical devices have been replaced by electronic, and there have been improvements in both hardware and software for modems, so that the present (1995) limit is 28,800 bps, accepted as an international standard (V34) in 1994.

Compared with the speed at which computers now operate, this is still very slow, and considerable efforts are being put into increasing transmission speeds. One technique involves making more efficient use of the existing telephone network, which represents a massive investment in infrastructure. *Packet switching*, introduced in the 1970s, meant that it became possible to link networks over long distances at reasonable cost. A normal telephone call monopolizes a certain proportion of the available links between the two centres involved – the 'bandwidth' – but the amount of information transmitted only occupies a limited part of the time. In between words, for example, nothing is being sent in either direction. Computers could get through a considerable amount of processing during these dead periods, just as they can between keystrokes. Packet switching takes the input from a number of messages and divides it up into labelled compressed 'packets'; the packets are then sent in a continuous stream to the receiving station, where they are sorted out into the original messages, which are forwarded to the intended recipients. Dead time is eliminated, and much more traffic can be sent along the same transmission channel using the X.25 protocol.

In the mid-1980s the suggestion was put forward that the telephone network could be used to transmit digital signals in an *Integrated Services Digital Network* (ISDN). Such a network could not only carry telephone conversations and link computers, but would also provide the means for the delivery of video signals, at a speed of 128kbps or higher. At the moment, the change to ISDN is still slow, but it seems likely that new international standards and rapid falls in cost will soon change this. With an ISDN link, there is of course no need for a modem at either end for computers to be able to communicate, since the digital output and input can be transmitted directly without having to be converted to analogue form.

Conventional telephone lines consist of pairs of copper wires (known as 'twisted pairs'); the amount of information that they can carry is quite limited. A significant development has been the introduction of *fibre-optic cable*. Electrical signals are transformed into pulses of light and transmitted down a long, very thin glass fibre cable; at the far end they are transformed back to electrical signals. Transmission can be at very high speeds: currently, 50M bps is usual, while it seems likely that speeds of 2G (10^9) bps will be possible soon. In developed countries, inter-city telephone links are now being replaced by fibre-optic cables. The massive increase in carrying capacity means that one cable can carry the same number of signals as a very large number of twisted-pair copper wire links. Fibre-optic cables are a practical means to carry television signals as well as voice, for example. The growing network of fibre-optic cables is the main structure of the 'information superhighway' of which we hear so much. Just as a freeway can carry more traffic at higher speeds than a network of local roads, so the fibre-optic network can carry more information than the conventional telephone network.

A third type of link uses microwave transmission. This needs a dish aerial at each end of the link, but does not need other connections. This method is being used for the transmission of data in the same way as telephone lines. The limitation is that there has to be line-of-sight transmission from one point to the next, but if this can be achieved, costs are comparable with cable. The use of satellites means that microwave (e.g. TV) transmissions can also be broadcast, i.e. distributed worldwide, and dish aerial receivers for this purpose are becoming a common sight (information from the sky!). Technical problems in linking computers into networks are now largely solved, though the search for increased speeds of transmission will surely continue. We thus have at our disposal the physical means to access information held in a wide range of computers. We should now consider how this information is presented.

Graphical user interface

A significant development in the microcomputer world was the introduction of the Apple Macintosh in 1984. Prior to this, computer commands had had to be typed in, either from memory or by consulting a manual. For many users, this was a tedious and error-prone activity, which tended to restrict the use of PCs to those with the necessary skills. The Apple Macintosh was the first microcomputer to use a *graphical user interface*, GUI, in which commands were represented on the screen by icons, which were selected by a 'pointing' device such as a mouse. The mouse was used to move the cursor to the desired position on the screen; one or two clicks of the mouse button(s) then activated the required command. Alternatively, menus – lists of commands – could be selected in the same way. The typing of commands was reduced to a minimum, making the machine much simpler to use. In addition, the use of graphics within programs was made easier by the fact that the whole screen display was a graphic; inserting illustrations required less complex programming than for text-oriented screens. A GUI of equivalent quality for IBM-compatible PCs had to wait until Windows 3.1 in 1991.

Input devices

For text, the *keyboard* is still the standard means of input. Keyboards originally looked very much like a typewriter keyboard with some extra keys. Despite some changes, the standard shape is so well established that it seems likely to persist, just as the typewriter keyboard layout has persisted. (It is a sobering thought that the QWERTY layout was intended to slow typists down so that they could not type faster than the mechanics of the typewriter could operate!) A device which has proved its use in converting text to digital form is the *scanner*, which will also convert graphics, including those in colour. This has meant that whole libraries of graphics are available for incorporation into documents as needed. More recent is the use of digital video cameras, which enable us to add photographs or video clips to our documents, again in colour. Another device which will certainly grow in importance is voice input; a multimedia PC already has the facility for voice output from text, but voice input is also becoming practical, though as yet it is still basically experimental.[2]

Desktop publishing

The introduction of the laser printer in 1985 meant that computer output was no longer restricted by the limitations of less sophisticated printers. A variety of fonts could be used, with high quality graphics incorporated into the text, and software was quickly developed to take advantage of these possibilities, including printing in colour. Many people now produce their own brochures and pamphlets. Although all of these are computer-produced, by no means all go through the normal publication channels to be picked up by a bibliographic agency; those which do not become part of the rapidly increasing 'grey' literature,[3] and may only be tracked down by accident. The other side of the coin is that useful works, such as some specialized publications which only warrant a small edition, can be produced in this way and printed out on demand. Modern high speed laser printers and binding machines enable a bookshop or desktop publisher to hold the text in computer-readable form, and produce a copy 'while-you-wait'. Computer-controlled typesetting made most formally published material available in computer-readable form; desktop publishing has done the same for informal publications.[4]

Electronic publishing

One important result is the development of *electronic publishing*. Some materials, including journals, are now being published online, with distribution via the Internet.[5] Since there have been in effect no means of charging for material made available in this way, it has been suitable for publications such as academic journals, weather reports and government documents which are not intended to make a profit. With the commercialization of the Internet, charging is becoming practical, and many other journals are now becoming available in this way.

The paperless office

In many organizations now each staff member has a desktop computer forming part of the local area network (LAN). Information does not have to be distributed in the form of print on paper, but can be circulated by electronic means using suitable software.[6] Individual users can build up their own personal files of information useful to them, and information can be circulated using electronic mail to one person, to a selected group, to the organization as a whole, or to anyone who wants to read it. (Security procedures have to be in place to ensure that information only reaches those entitled to read it!) Large organizations such as ICI and the CIA were the first to adopt this method of working, but so far it has not been the panacea that was once assumed, and most offices are still paper-based. (In some cases, there are legal requirements which require documents to be on paper.) It is possible to transmit fax messages from computer to computer, but the fax machine with its paper copies is still the norm, even though most of the messages are produced by word processors and printed out for transmission.

Bulletin boards have been accessible for some years; these consist of computers accessible by modem and telephone line. Some are the work of enthusiastic amateurs, many are established by organizations of one kind or another. Messages may be put on the board by the SysOp (SYStem OPerator) who manages the BBS, or users who connect to the board from their own PC. Most are freely available, including some which are major sources of public domain or shareware programs, but others, e.g. Compuserve, charge fees but provide a wider range of information and services. The distribution of information via electronic channels is now pervasive.

HyperText

If we are reading a novel, we expect to read it straight through, in order to follow the development of the plot and the characters. If by contrast we look something up in an encyclopedia, we may well wish to follow up a reference to an article elsewhere in the work, perhaps in another volume; from there, we may well be referred on again to yet another article. Trains of thought are not linear, as was pointed out in a key article by Vannevar Bush.[7] The idea that this kind of browsing from prompt to prompt could be done by computer was first suggested by Ted Nelson,[8] but the first practical application on a wide scale came with the introduction of Hypercard on the Apple Macintosh. This enabled the user to compile a file (stack) with built-in links outside the main sequence. The name given to this form of file structure by Nelson was *hypertext*, from the idea of multi-dimensional hyperspace put forward as a mathematical concept in the 19th century. HyperText is now generally available and is widely used in databases on CD-ROM, for instance. (It is interesting that both Bush, with the Memex machine, and Nelson, with XANADU, envisaged processing by a very large central machine, not the distributed processing that has now become the norm.)

HyperText links begin with the starting point of the link, an *anchor*. It is then necessary to specify the exact location to which this is to be linked, making a hyperlink to a second *anchor*. Once this is done, the new location can in turn become a starting point anchor, with further links being generated as needed. These may be specific, taking the user to a specific location; local, taking the user to any chosen point in the current document; or generic, taking the user to any point in any document – which may reside on a totally separate computer, which may in turn lead on to a file on yet another computer. It is often easy to lose track of where one has got to!

Multimedia and hypermedia

A GUI is able to display graphics as well as text. With the growth in power of computers, sufficient memory became available to make this feasible at acceptable cost; graphics take up much more disk space than text files. Graphics also require more processing power than text. It was not until 32-bit processing rather than 8-bit or 16-bit was developed that graphics became a practical proposition, with the Apple Macintosh, followed some years later by the Intel 80386 and later processors for IBM-type PCs. Desktop computers to be used specifically as graphics workstations may use 64-bit processing. The change from 8-bit to 32-bit processing was accompanied by increases in the speed at which microprocessors could operate; where an early 8-bit processor might operate at 4MHz (1 Hertz Hz = 1 cycle per second), or 10MHz in turbo mode, 1995 models may operate at up to 130MHz. These high speeds are essential for the processing of graphics, especially video.

The digital recording of sound, first on LP records and then on CDs, meant that sound too could be incorporated into computer files. Sound files also occupy space: the chord which introduces Windows occupies about 25k for a second or so of playing time. The introduction of graphics and sound into computer files gave rise to *multimedia* presentations, which may now also include video and animations. From this, the next step was *hypermedia*: multimedia in which we can jump from one point to another via hypertext links.[9]

Interchange of data

One of the most important limitations of the text-oriented screen is the fact that it can only display a limited number of symbols: upper and lower case letters, numbers and punctuation. Various codes were developed to represent these symbols in binary code, but the one now commonly accepted is the ASCII (American Standard Code for Information Interchange) character set.[10] The sequence of codes is important, because it determines the filing order of the various symbols. The use of ASCII codes may thus dictate the filing order found in computer-based lists of subject headings.

This standard is used very widely, but it caters only for the roman alphabet, and not for any of the accents and special characters used in European languages. An extended ASCII 8-bit set exists, but this does not cover all of the requirements conveniently even for European languages. It is evident that the exchange of information is severely limited if we are restricted to the ASCII character set, yet this is still the standard code used for e-mail, simply because it is standard! There is no guarantee that the sender and receiver of an e-mail message are using the same extended symbols, but if they restrict their text to standard 7-bit ASCII it will be received as sent. Languages such as Greek which do not use the roman alphabet may be forced to adopt complex combinations of ASCII codes.

One severe limitation for anything but the most simple message is that no information can be transferred about formatting. Word processors enable us to use a variety of fonts, font sizes, emphasis (**bold**, *italic*, <u>underline</u>) and layout, to produce documents which look good and convey our meaning effectively. None of this can be transmitted using standard ASCII. Before the introduction of the GUI, this was not vital, as the effects could not be displayed anyway, except indirectly; with a GUI display, all these special effects *can* be shown on the screen – but they still cannot be transmitted to other computers using standard ASCII codes. It is possible to encode them in binary form and transmit this – most communications programs will transmit binary files – but they will make no sense at the receiving end unless exactly the same word processor is used to display them. On the other hand, the ability to display format on a GUI may lead us to neglect structure and content in favour of layout; Honan[11] argues that for large documents a text-based word processor is just as effective as one based on a GUI, since we are forced to pay attention to content rather than allowing ourselves to become unduly obsessed with presentation.

Standards

Both hardware and software are subject to change, often quite rapid. There was a need for standards to be developed which would make possible the exchange of data regardless of the software and hardware used to produce them and receive them.[12] The first step was the development of SGML: Standardized General Markup Language, in 1986.[13] This works by tagging each unit of a document, e.g. heading, title, text, so that it can be recognized as such by the receiver. Information concerning layout and type faces can also be encoded. The widely used HTML: HyperText Markup Language is a subset of SGML. It provides tags for headings, title, address and so on. Each tag must begin and end. The net result is a document which uses standard ASCII codes and can therefore be transmitted simply to another computer, where it can be decoded by suitable browser software. A simple page might look something like this:

```
<html>
<head>
   <title>Welcome</title>                        [headings]
   <h1>Welcome!</h1>
</head>
<body>
            [body tags and text]
</body>
</html>
```

Each tag begins and ends, so that the receiver can recognize the various parts of the document. The end is shown by preceding the tag with a slash /.[14] For those reluctant to undertake the coding task, there is software which will do it automatically, or (at the receiving end) strip off the codes and give plain ASCII text.

A number of other standards have been developed including Open Document Architecture (ODA) and Standard Page Description Language (SPDL). One significant venture was the Text Encoding Initiative (TEI), which was developed in the UK to permit the exchange of documents between universities.[15] To send text as an ASCII file by e-mail would have been fast, but this would have been negated by the amount of work involved in reconstituting the document complete with formatting. The TEI used a form of SGML to solve the problem. Another possible solution is to use the coding/decoding programs UUENCODE.EXE and UUDECODE.EXE; these convert computer files into ASCII strings which can be transmitted over the Internet and decoded at the receiving end.

The introduction of multimedia and hypermedia meant that further standards have had to be developed, not just to cover each format separately but also their use together, since they have to be synchronized (*in sync*). It can be disconcerting when the sound and picture are not synchronized! One of the key standards is HyTime, an SGML-based Hypermedia/Time-based Structuring language; a master encoded document serves as the hub for text files, sound files and graphics, linking them all and ensuring that data from each is used at the appropriate moment.

Another important aspect of file transmission is the amount of information to be transmitted. A computer monitor displays information as pixels, single dots of colour; a common resolution of 640 x 480 pixels contains 307,200 pixels. For 256-colour displays, each pixel requires 8 bits ($2^8 = 256$), giving a total of 2,457,600 bits of information, or 307,200 bytes. Thus a static picture in 256 colours occupies over 300kB of disk space. The Macintosh uses 16-bit colour, giving 65,536 colours, requiring twice as much space. To show moving images, it is necessary to repeat the picture 60 times a second, to take advantage of the phenomenon of persistence of vision within the parameters of the computer screen. The amount of information to be stored is obviously very large, and forms of compression have been developed to reduce this to an acceptable level. Here too standards are very important; to use a graphics file which has been compressed we must have the right software to decompress it. If we are transmitting a graphics file through a network using a modem, it is clear that even at 28.8kbps, it will take some time to transmit a file of several hundred kilobytes, possibly some minutes. The most important compression standard is the JPEG (Joint Photographic Experts Group) File Interchange Format; with this, it is possible to reduce a file of 2MB to about 100k, at the cost of some detail.[16] Fortunately the human eye is very tolerant, and the losses are not noticeable. To give some specific figures, the Kodak Photo-CD format gives about one hundred images of high quality on a CD; the Portfolio system gives up to a thousand at lower but still acceptable quality; while compression techniques can give several thousand images on one CD.

We should also not overlook industry standards. Adobe Systems Inc., which developed the Postscript printer control language, has also developed Adobe

Acrobat, software which will take a Postscript printer file and convert it into a form which can be read on any GUI screen in the original format, complete with graphics and colour.[17] Intel have developed the Indeo algorithm for the capture and compression of digital video; this is incorporated in Microsoft's Video for Windows, and Apple's QuickTime and QuickTime for Windows.[18]

The Internet

Over the years, large amounts of information have become available on the Internet,[19] and various programs have been developed to help users find their way about. It must be remembered that there is no overall control of the Internet, no central body to impose order. Any order that exists is the result of cooperation between users. To begin with, most of the traffic on the Internet was e-mail between individuals, but it soon became clear that groups were beginning to form, exchanging the same information among a number of people. This led to the establishment of *newsgroups*; mail sent to the group is automatically forwarded to all the members. There are now several thousand newsgroups around the world, each with its own listserver who manages the mechanics of the subscriber list, and usually keeps track of what goes on to remove 'unsuitable' messages. (Unsuitable may simply mean out of scope – all messages take up space on the server's hard disk –but some may offend subscribers. Walls are not the only place where one finds graffiti!)

To use the network, it is necessary to have software which conforms to the standard TCP/IP (Transmission Control Protocol/Internet Protocol). Telnet allows remote login to other sites to see material that is there. FTP (File Transfer Protocol) enables us to transfer files between our computer and others. To find one's way around we may use Gopher software. There are several hundred servers containing hierarchical menus leading to information available; many library OPACS are accessible using Telnet or Gopher, including the British Library and the Library of Congress.[20] With Gopher client software it is possible to create 'bookmarks' to identify sites that one may wish to visit again; this can save a great deal of typing! Other software such as ARCHIE and Veronica acts as means of locating servers or files.

Though TCP/IP is currently the *de facto* standard protocol for information interchange, there are problems of compatibility with ISDN, and also with the new international standard for Open Systems Interconnection (OSI). Though IBM announced in 1988 that it would begin offering OSI protocol products in 1990, OSI, the *de jure* standard, has not yet replaced the earlier standard,[21] and it may well not do so, in view of the investment in TCP/IP.

The World Wide Web

The difficulties of finding information on the Internet led to the development of a new protocol for linking to computer sites, HTTP: HyperText Transport Protocol. From an idea in 1989, this led to implementation of the World Wide Web at CERN, the European Centre for High-Energy Physics, in 1991. Full-scale operation came in 1993 with the development of the Mosaic Web Browser software by the NCSA

(National Center for Supercomputer Applications), which placed it in the public domain, so that anyone could obtain it using FTP.[22] The Web accounted for 0.1% of NSF Internet backbone traffic in March 1993, after the introduction of Mosaic; by September 1993 it accounted for 1% and by November 1994 10%; use is obviously continuing to grow very rapidly. What led to this sudden 'explosion' in the use of the Internet?

The first factor was the use of hypertext to build links between documents. The physicists at CERN were experiencing information overload, and needed a better way to keep track of the publications on the Internet that they found useful. The second factor was the use of multimedia; the Internet had been restricted to text, but the Web software made it possible to use graphics and the facilities of a GUI. Mosaic has now been replaced by Netscape, a graphics browser which enables the user to use point and click techniques to go to other sites and also to create hypertext links using bookmarks. (Other software can also be found from various suppliers.) Each site is identified by a Universal Resource Locator, URL, which may include not only the computer location but also the directory path to specific files.

Another factor in the growth of use has been the interest shown by commercial vendors. While the Internet was largely restricted to the exchange of text between academic institutions, there was little interest from those who did not already have access. With the development of the World Wide Web, demonstrating that graphics and sound could also be used, much more interest was aroused, for example from schools, and various firms have started to offer access on a fee-paying basis. (Although communication on the Internet had always been seen as free, or 'for the cost of a local call', the costs had been met by universities, governments and government funded bodies such as the NSF.) As use has increased, so have costs; the availability of graphics and sound meant that much more information is now being transferred between sites, with increased demands on telecommunication facilities. The link between Australia and North America was upgraded in 1995 to double its previous capacity; it took about a day for the additional capacity to be fully utilized!

As was mentioned earlier, there is no governing body for the Internet, nor is there for the World Wide Web. There is also very little control over the information available on it, nor on the way that the information is organized. It can take a great deal of skill to locate all the sources of information of value in a particular subject area, as shown by Westerman;[23] seven business librarians collaborated at length to identify sources of business information on the Net, to provide their users with a service which was small and focused in relation to the Net as a whole. The possibility of using the BSO (described in Chapter 20) to help organize the Net has been suggested; this classification was devised to identify institutions by their overall subject coverage, and might perhaps be used to label sources of information. Whether information providers on the Net would want to cooperate in such a way remains to be seen. Perhaps the increasing presence of commercial vendors will lead to closer control. Users paying for a service are more likely to demand ease of use than those who have access free!

References

1   McClure, C. R. *et al.*, 'Toward a virtual library: Internet and National Research and Education Network', *Bowker annual: library and booktrade annual*, 1993, 25–45.
    McClure, C. R. *et al.*, *The National Research and Education Network: research and policy perspectives*, Norwood, NJ, Ablex, 1991.
    MacColl, J. A., 'Library applications of a wide area network: promoting JANET to UK academic libraries', *Information services and use,* **10** (3), 1990, 157–68.

2   Cawkell, A. E., 'The annual 'arrival' of speech recognition', *Information services and use,* **10** (3), 1990, 133–4. (Editorial) Cawkell's scepticism is still justified, though progress is certainly being made.

3   Auger, C. P., *Information sources in grey literature*, 3rd edn, London, Bowker-Saur, 1994.

4   Yasui, H., *Desktop publishing: technology and design*, Chicago, Science Research Associates, 1989. This is one of the many books now available on DTP. Students should use a text which is conveniently available.

5   *Infotrain* is an electronic journal produced by students of librarianship, available at http://infotrain.magill.unisa.edu.au

6   Lancaster, F. W., *Toward paperless information systems*, New York, NY, Academic press, 1978.

7   Bush, V., 'As we may think', *Atlantic monthly,* **176** (1), July 1945, 101–8.

8   Nelson, T. H., *Computer lib: dream machines*, Redmond, WA, Tempus Books of Microsoft Press, 1987. This text is also available on the XANADU experimental machine.

9   'Perspectives on the human-computer interface' [special issue], *Journal of the American Society for Information Science,* **43** (2), 1992, 153–201.

10 American standard code for information exchange, American National Standards Institute X3.4: 1977.

11 Honan, J. 'Highway more than a home shopping guide', *The Australian*, June 20 1995. (Argues very strongly for the importance of text as opposed to graphics.)

12 'Workshop on hypermedia and hypertext processing', *Information services and use, 13*, 1993, 81–199. The need for standards is emphasized by G. Stephenson, 'Introduction', 85–7, and by M. Bryan, 'Standards for text and hypermedia processing', 93–102.

13 Stern, D., 'SGML documents: a better system for communicating knowledge', *Special libraries,* **86** (2), Spring 1995, 117–24.

14 Pfaffenberger, B., *World wide web bible*, New York, NY, MIS Press, 1995. Chapter 27: 'A quick introduction to HTML', 447–70.

15 Popham, M., 'Use of SGML and HyTime in UK universities', ref. 10 above, 103–9.
    Burnard, L., 'Rolling your own with TEI', ref. 10 above, 141–54.

16 Bryan, M. In ref. 12 above.

17 Fox, E. A. *et al.* 'Digital libraries', *Communications of the ACM,* **38** (4), April 1995, 23–8. (Introduction to a special issue on digital libraries, 23–109)

18 Pring, I. 'Video standards and the end user', *Information services and use,* **13**, 1993, 93–102.

19 Krol, E., *The whole Internet users' guide and catalog,* 2nd edn, Sebastopol, CA, O'Reilly and Associates, 1994. There are a number of good books on the Internet, but this is one of the best and most complete.
    Lynch, C. and Preston, C., 'Internet access to information resources' *Annual review of information science and technology,* **25**, 1990, 263–312

20 For the British Library, gopher portico.bl.uk. For the Library of Congress, tel-net marvel.loc.gov, login as marvel. (Marvel is the LoC gopher.) To use the Library of Congress catalogue, telnet locis.loc.gov and follow the menus.

21 Cawkell, A. E., 'Videoconferencing, the Information Superhighway and the second Défi', *Information services and use,* **15** (2), 1995, 73–4. (In *Le défi Americain,* J. J. Servan-Schreiber argues the decline of Europe in the face of American Cultural imperialism.)

22 Books on the World Wide Web, of which ref 14 above is one example, are forming a publication explosion of their own. Many come with floppy disks or CD-ROM, containing software to enable users to set up their own home page. Not all home pages are of value.

23 Westerman, M., 'Business sources on the Net: a virtual library product', *Special libraries,* **85** (4), Fall 1994, 264–9.

24 CRG minutes, February 24 1995.

In order to keep pace with changes it is important to scan the computer section of a quality newspaper, and also read widely in the periodical literature; the main problem is not to become bogged down in trivia!

Appendix

Some of the relevant ISO standards are as follows:

ISO 7498:1988 Open systems interconnection reference model. (OSI)
ISO 8613:1989 Information processing – text and office systems – Office Document Architecture (ODA)

Part 1 Introduction and general principles
Part 2 Document structures
Part 4 Document profile
Part 5 Office Document Interchange Format (ODIF)
Part 6 Character content architecture
Part 7 Raster graphics content architectures
Part 8 Geometric graphics content architectures
Part 9 Audio Content Architecture
Part 10 Formal specifications
ISO 8879:1986 Standard Generalized Markup Language.
ISO 8879: 1988 SGML Supplement 1.

ISO 9069: 1988 SGML support facilities: SGML document interchange format (SDIF)

ISO 9541–1: 1991 Font information exchange: Part 1: Architecture.

ISO 9541–2: 1991 Font information exchange: Part 2: Interchange format.

ISO 9660:1987 Volume and file structure of CD-ROM.

ISO 10180: 1993 Standard Page Description Language (SPDL)

ISO 10744:1992 HyTime Hypermedia/Time-based structuring language.

ISO 10918 Joint Picture Experts Group (JPEG) – compression encoding for continuous tone pictures.

ISO 11172: 1993 Moving Picture Experts Group – digital moving picture compression method.

Chapter 5
Derived indexing 2: Database access systems

Background

In Chapter 1, we noted briefly that there has been a dichotomy between biblio-graphical control systems used for books and those used for other materials. The catchword systems described in Chapter 3 were originally used for book catalogues, but the use of computers made them applicable to many other materials – for exam-ple periodical articles, technical reports and conference proceedings. Citation index-ing, as developed by Garfield, was specifically applied to periodical articles; books and other sources such as patents may appear in the citation index as items cited (the two most frequently cited authors are the Bible and Shakespeare!), but never in the source index. We do in fact find that there are now two rather different sorts of com-puter bibliographic databases, those dealing with what might be called macro-pub-lications – books – and those covering micro-publications – periodical articles and all the other similar forms of publication. A practical distinction is that books can stand on library shelves, and can therefore be arranged in some kind of helpful order which is a significant factor in subject searching. The other materials cannot be arranged in this way. It is possible to arrange periodicals as a whole on the shelves, or conference proceedings in book form, but this does not give direct access to the individual articles within them.

The real world is of course grey, not black and white, and this dichotomy is a simplification, but this practical distinction is paralleled by the way that the two streams are treated for information retrieval. Books are 'catalogued' while other items are 'indexed'. Both techniques have the same general objectives: to identify the item and provide access to it through various approaches, including the subject. However, the cataloguing of books usually involves summarization: we treat the contents as a whole, and provide subject access on a limited scale – a class number for shelf arrangement, and one or two subject headings for access through the cata-logue. The indexing of other materials tends to be more detailed: we do not have a class number for shelf arrangement, but perhaps for arrangement in a printed bibli-ography, and we tend to be rather more generous in the provision of terms for sub-ject access. To give a practical example, the 5th International Study Conference on Classification Research, which is cited in several chapters in this book,[1] can be cat-alogued as a book, shelved at 025.4, and given the subject heading Books—

Classification. In an abstracting journal such as *Library and information science abstracts*, or an indexing journal such as *Library literature*, we would expect find entries for each of the individual chapters, on DDC, UDC, LCC, thesaurus construction, reclassification and so on. While we may regret this separation, it has existed since the beginning of indexes to periodicals, and has practical consequences for information retrieval. In this section we shall be looking at databases covering micro-publications, postponing the examination of book catalogues – manual and OPACS – to later chapters.

General publications

In Chapter 4, we referred to the development of computer-controlled typesetting in the early 1960s. To begin with, this was relatively rare, but three significant groups quickly saw the advantages. Bibliographic databases such as *Index medicus* could be produced more quickly than by conventional methods, and could also be cumulated progressively into a large database which could be searched as a whole.[2] This contrasted favourably with the tedium of a search through a large number of separate printed issues. Since the first tentative experiments in the late 1960s showed that online access was practical, increasing numbers of bibliographic databases have become available online, and over 450 were accessible through the DIALOG Information Retrieval Service, the largest of the utilities of this kind, in 1994, yet this is only a small proportion of the total now available.[3]

The second group to profit from computerization were newspaper publishers. Journalists could now produce their copy on a microcomputer for direct input into the main computer, which can be used to typeset the whole newspaper without the intermediate step of having it composed on a Linotype machine. In fact, this machine, which had been the core of newspaper production for the whole of this century, disappeared from use in a surprisingly short time. In due course, newspapers became available online, and many are now accessible in this way.

The third group were governments, and Statutes and other legal documents began to be produced and made available online with increasing frequency, until this may now be said to be the norm, certainly in developed countries. Legal databases were among the earliest full-text sources to be available online.[4] Commercial publishers also use computer-controlled typesetting, but are naturally reluctant to make their publications freely available! Unlike governments, commercial publishers need to make a profit from the sale of their products. The important question of intellectual property and copyright is looked at in Chapter 28.

All in all, very large amounts of online information are now accessible through a variety of sources, some free but some on a commercial basis. When online databases first became available about 1970, users were mainly librarians and other information workers. The easy accessibility of databases today, and the (relatively) user-friendly software at hand to use them, has meant that many other people have begun to use them without the help of intermediaries. There are however certain skills which must be acquired to make the best use of the information available to us. As pointed out in Chapter 2, not all users have the same requirements for recall and relevance, and search strategies can be modified to recognize this. We must be aware of which databases are likely to prove most profitable in searching for particular kinds of information, and we may have to put some effort into presenting the information that users want in a format that will meet their needs.

DIALOG, the major online utility, was introduced in the 1960s, and was used by both intermediaries – librarians and other information workers, and by end users – users who originated the requests for information. By 1982 the numbers of intermediaries and end users searching the facility was about equal, but by 1988 end users formed about 65% of new users.[5] However, not all enquirers wish to do their own searching; one study at the University of North Carolina showed that a number of users requested help, even though various databases (ERIC, Books in print and Ulrich's Plus) were available on CD-ROM, and BRS/After Dark (specifically intended for end users) was available online. Of the reasons given for preferring an intermediary, over two thirds cited lack of search expertise and over 40% did not wish to spend their own time. Users may also use both options; many of those surveyed planned to use an intermediary again, but also to do their own searches on occasion.[6]

In a work such as this, we can only consider the basic techniques, but textbooks such as that by R. J. Hartley *et al.*[7] go into detail on searching techniques in a way not possible here, where we can only attempt to summarize the main techniques currently in use. Since databases may be online through commercial utilities such as DIALOG, BRS/Search or ESA/IRS, but may also be available on CD-ROM or through the Internet, in line with Dalrymple and Roderer[8] we have used the title database access rather than online searching.

Computer searching of text

If we knew that some information we wanted was to be found in a particular document, but there was no contents list or index, we could find what we wanted by reading through the whole of the document, looking for the words we were interested in. To use the term that we have used previously, we would be trying to *match* our requirements, as expressed in certain words, against the words to be found in the document. Now we may be prepared to do this for one document, but when we start to think in terms of a collection of documents the process clearly becomes impractical. Even to look through a lengthy list of titles can be time-consuming, as many readers have discovered from scanning booksellers' lists and similar publications.

The computer can perform this kind of matching operation at high speed; if the titles or other parts of the text are in machine-readable form, as is now usual, we can program the computer to carry out the matching process and identify the documents likely to be useful to us. All that we have to do is to feed in to the computer the words that we want it to match. With access to large quantities of text either online or on CD-ROM, finding an answer to a particular question becomes a matter of fast, painless extraction. The computer does not become tired of searching – it has no futility point! – nor does it get bored. It simply goes on searching for exactly what we have said we want until the search is completed. (We may of course discover at this stage that what we said we wanted was not really an accurate statement of our needs! Search statements often contain errors, while many are not followed through to obtain a 'best' result.)

Early information retrieval systems ran in batch mode, and used magnetic tape as the storage medium. This meant that searching was slow; even a small database of a few thousand items might take several minutes to scan, since the scanning had to be carried out sequentially. (Compare the speed of locating a particular track on an LP or CD with that of searching through a cassette tape!) The introduction of random access storage greatly improved access times, but still required considerable searching to find the items which matched a request. The solution was to create a second *inverted* file in which each term in the original (with the exception of stop words) is listed as an index entry. A search then begins with the index file, which gives the number and locations of postings of a term, and can quickly compare the postings under two terms to determine which are common to both. In some systems, one inverted file lists the terms with the number of postings, and a second lists the specific locations. Basically the same method is used with today's much larger files. The penalty for the improved access times is that additional index files are required, giving a database perhaps twice as big as the original. Services such as DIALOG require hundreds of gigabytes of storage for their holdings; a good proportion of this is taken up by the index files accompanying the databases. The majority of current databases utilize the inverted file method, but cluster analysis and similar processes are carried out on text as it stands, without the need for inverted files.

Search strategies

We can program the computer to carry out the matching program in two ways, paralleling the changes that have come about in the use of other computer programs such as word processors. The first database programs required the user to type *commands* in a more or less esoteric language, e.g. strs for stringsearch. This meant learning the commands before one could make good use of the service. Since each service used a different command language, this could lead to confusion; fortunately, since all of them perform the same tasks, once one set of commands has been learnt it is not too difficult to master others. Attempts have been made to develop a 'common command language', so that all services used the same commands, but this has not had any great success.[9] The alternative to using commands is to use *menus*; these are simpler to use, and do not have to be learnt, but they tend to be slower than using commands direct. (We are only talking of seconds, but the online user prefers to fill the unforgiving minute with sixty seconds' worth of processing done! The beginner may also wish to make use of Help screens, further slowing down the process, if the menus are not completely self-explanatory.) DIALOG and other services offer the choice for many databases; once users are familiar with the system through using the menus, they can switch to using the commands.

Online searching should then be very simple, but in practice it turns out to be rather more complex.[10] Suppose that we are interested in *classification*; we may find documents using the word *classifying* just as useful. Again, suppose that our interest is in *pollution* –a topic very much in the public mind. We could search for *pollution*, but we might then miss documents which only use the word *pollutant*, or *polluting*. The solution is simple: we can *truncate* our search term to *pollut*. We may need to show specifically that we have used truncation by adding a symbol such as the asterisk *, to show that we are interested in the stem *plus*, otherwise we may find that we get a nil response; some systems automatically take any input as the beginning of a search term, and do not require a specific indicator. We can use forward truncation, e.g. POLLUT*, or backward truncation, e.g. *CLASSIF*; the latter will now match reclassification in addition to words beginning classif . . . However, it will also match *declassification*, the process of making secret documents public. A search for information on the role of the parent could be set up as *PARENT*, to retrieve *parents, parental, parenthood, grandparent* and *grandparents*, but will also retrieve *parenthesis, parenteral*, and *transparent*! In some systems, the computer will display a list of terms which will be located by our truncations, which may lead to second thoughts! We may also be able to use a wildcard to allow for variations in spelling, e.g. WOM?N will match women and woman; F?ETUS will match fetus (US spelling) or foetus (British spelling).

It is possible to have a parsing program which will recognize suffixes, and perform the truncation process for us automatically. This is known as *stemming*, and it is important to know whether the software we are using will do this, or if we have to specify a truncation indicator like the * shown above. In the first case, POLLUT will be accepted as a search term, but in the second it will be rejected without the asterisk. Stemming can take place in two stages; the first is at a simple level, and, for example, may convert plural to singular, remove suffixes representing verbal forms (-ing, -ed) and merge variant spellings, (-isation, -ization; -our, -or). The second, more powerful, stage may remove a wide range of suffixes, e.g. -itis, -able. Stemming can be a valuable search aid, but as with manual truncation, it may also lead to disaster![11]

So far we have assumed a search for one word, but in practice we would normally be thinking of more than one word to denote the subject we are interested in. For example, we may be concerned with *water pollution* rather than pollution as a whole. In this situation we can use the ability of the computer to handle logical statements; the logic is Boolean rather than Aristotelian, and it means that we can link the words we are searching for by the operators AND, OR and NOT. Our search becomes:

WATER AND POLLUT*

However, we might remember that water includes sea(s) and river(s), and modify the search to take account of this:

POLLUT* AND (WATER OR SEA* OR RIVER*)

We might want to exclude sewage as a form of pollution:

POLLUT* AND (WATER OR SEA* OR RIVER*) NOT SEWAGE

The order of precedence among the operators is NOT, AND, OR. Thus

POLLUT* AND WATER OR SEA*

will be treated as a search for *pollut** in association with *water*, or *sea** on its own. The use of parentheses in the above example is necessary to avoid this, and is good practice in clarifying a search formulation anyway. It must also be remembered that users unfamiliar with Boolean techniques may use the wrong operator altogether; needing information on, say, 'cats and dogs', they need to specify this as 'cats OR dogs', otherwise they will retrieve only information dealing with both, rather than information dealing with either.

The example above could be set up as a series of simple searches, using the results at each stage as input into later stages, as shown here (system response underlined):

1   POLLUT*
Search 1 POSTINGS 732
2   WATER
SEARCH 2 POSTINGS 1653
3   SEA*
SEARCH 3 POSTINGS 451
4   RIVER*
SEARCH 4 POSTINGS 679
5   2 OR 3 OR 4
SEARCH 5 POSTINGS 2215
6   1 AND 5
SEARCH 5 POSTINGS 142
7   SEWAGE
SEARCH 7 POSTINGS 284
8   6 NOT 7
SEARCH 8 POSTINGS 114

The operators AND, OR and NOT apply to whole documents; in the above example, we would be looking for documents in which *pollut** was found along with *water* or *sea** or *river**, but *sewage* did not occur. We may wish to be more precise, and specify that words appear in the same paragraph, same sentence, or adjacent, and some services permit this. Note that ADJ may be qualified, e.g. ADJ(n), where n is the separation we are willing to accept. For instance, ADJ(5) means that the two sought terms must occur within five words of each other.

WATER AND POLLUT*	(same document)
WATER SAME POLLUT*	(same paragraph)
WATER WITH POLLUT*	(same sentence)
WATER ADJ POLLUT*	(adjacent)

The order of words may also be important; if we specify INFORMATION ADJ(2) RETRIEV*, we may exclude 'retrieval of information', because the words are not in the specified order, or 'information we want to retrieve', because the words are too far apart. Does the program we are using count stopwords in determining how close words are? We may need to think carefully about the order of words, and the likelihood of their being separated by unsought words, when formulating our search. A possible alternative is to enclose search phrases in quotation marks ". . ." so that they are treated as a whole. We may search for material on 'circulation' AND 'control' only to find we have retrieved *Control of the peripheral circulation in man*! Proximity searching can also be useful if we are not sure whether we are looking for one word or two, for example post-coordinate or end user.[12] For proximity searching to be possible, the inverted file has to record the location of terms very precisely, so that it becomes much larger than one which simply records that a term occurs *somewhere* in a document.

We may misspell a word used as a search term, either through ignorance or lack of typing skills, or select a word not used; the system may in this case display a list of words close to our spelling in alphabetical order, or sounding the same (assonance), enabling us to correct the error, or choose another search term. (This is very similar to the operation of a spelling check in a word processor.) A powerful method of automatic error correction uses soundex codes; this involves the removal of all other than initial vowels and reduction of the result to four characters. It involves a large dictionary and a great deal of processing, but can cope with most errors other than transposition – which for many unskilled keyboarders is a frequent error![13]

The database may include indexing by a controlled vocabulary as well as text words, that is, terms added by an indexer from a predetermined list. If this is the case, we should be able to display search terms from the vocabulary, and also any related terms, or expand our search to include them; this involves the rather alarming instruction EXPLODE in MEDLINE! In general, this technique is known as the use of *hedges*; a set of terms can be brought together 'within a hedge' to represent a broader subject for which no single term is suitable, by the use of the logical OR. For example, USA OR France OR China OR Russia OR United Kingdom could represent 'the permanent members of the UN Security Council'. Hedges represent the kind of grouping found in classification schemes or similar controlled vocabularies,[14] and are used when searching the text as it stands may produce problems. A search term may have synonyms or near-synonyms, for example drunk driving, drink driving, driving under the influence, drunken driving . . .; or be ambiguous and need context to clarify, e.g. record; or ill-defined, e.g. democracy; or it may occur too frequently to give useful search results.[15] Hedges can be created by the database producers, as in MEDLINE, or by searchers, who may also modify them on the base of experience. They may be based on semantic relationships found in a thesaurus or dictionary, or based on cooccurrence shown by computer processing.

Documents are represented in the computer by *records*; a collection of records of the same kind becomes a *database*; database records are normally organized into *fields*, so that we can restrict our search to one particular area. For example, if we know the author's name we can cut down our search time by searching only the author field, or the title field if we know all or part of the title. If the database includes descriptors from a controlled vocabulary in a descriptor field, we can make use of this in two ways. We can select descriptors from the controlled vocabulary to make our search; alternatively, once we have found a useful document, say by searching on words in the title, we can use the descriptors used to index it to revise our search strategy. Some documents may have an abstract field, or a full text field;

searching the full text of documents online may take time and add to the bill – a good argument for the use of databases on CD-ROM!

If we are carrying out a search involving several words, it is good practice to treat each one as a separate search, to obtain the postings for each, as shown earlier. We can then cut down the search time in the most effective way by beginning with the term having the fewest postings and combining it with the one with the next fewest. We may even reduce the number of hits to an acceptable number without searching on the most frequently used term, which is likely to be the least effective in rejecting unwanted references.

Problems with Boolean searching

All users of Boolean searching quickly become familiar with one of the disadvantages. For a search to be successful, the result must fall within the user's Futility Point; if the FP is m, and a search retrieves n documents, it is successful only if $n \le m$.[16] A search in a large database on one term frequently gives far too many postings, so we AND a second term; if this still gives too many we AND a third, and so on. Unfortunately, we often find that adding one more term to the search formulation reduces the number of hits from an unacceptably large number to zero.[11] Alternatively, we may begin our search by specifying a number of terms to be ANDed together, only to find that we retrieve nothing at all. How can we best reorganize our search to give an acceptable result? The obvious way in both situations is to drop one or more terms, but which? The tendency is to omit the terms which the searcher thinks are least significant, and retain those which are considered to be most significant. This has been described as the 'anchor effect', and in effect retains certain terms in every variant of the original formulation when their omission might well lead to success.

One way of manipulating the chosen terms is to search on *combinations* of them.[17] For n terms there are $2^n - 1$ combinations, so that if we start with five terms there are 31 possible combinations. Even three terms will give us seven combinations. To work all these out intellectually and try each one would be time-consuming and tedious, but the computer can do it for us, using the kind of effective search strategy mentioned above, and give us the result at each stage. We can thus stop the search while the result is still below our FP, while remaining confident that the search results will match our search closely if not exactly. Some IR systems do offer this facility, known as *quorum searching*, though it is only the more sophisticated software which is likely to have the necessary computing power.

Ranked output

Boolean searching gives us no control over the cutoff point. In other words, we cannot say how many documents we would like to retrieve, and aim for that target; we have to accept what the computer gives us. A more effective approach is to use a more sophisticated search procedure, so that the results of a search can be *ranked* in order of probable relevance. We can then select as many as we wish from the top of the list with some confidence that they will be the most useful. In contrast with

Boolean searching, where the system dictates the cutoff point, this enables *us* to set the cutoff point: we can say that we would like to see the six, or a hundred, or three, most promising documents, and ignore the rest unless we find that they are needed to broaden our search. We are no longer at the mercy of the system, but can set our own parameters for success.

One way to achieve this is to weight the terms used for indexing or searching, but how can we allocate suitable weights? We can either do it intellectually or by means of computer manipulation. In either case we can regard the document-term link as a matrix in which there are x documents indexed by y terms; w_{ij} is the extent to which term i is used to index document j.

D	o	c	u	m	e	n	t	s		
w_{11}	w_{12}	w_{13}								
w_{21}										
w_{31}										
									w_{ij}	

(vertical label: T e r m s)

In searching on unweighted terms, the value in each cell is either 1 (that term *is* used to index that document) or 0 (that term is *not* used to index that document). This is the situation found in Boolean searching.

In a search system using weights, the value of w_{ij} can range from 0 to 1, and may be regarded as the probability that a particular term will be useful in retrieving a document in response to a particular enquiry.[18] To allocate weights intellectually might be possible for a small collection, but would quickly become impractical. We therefore have to consider ways in which weights may be allocated by computer.

One approach is to use statistical methods to indicate the significance of terms. This can be done in a variety of ways. Word frequency counts on their own are somewhat simplistic, but are more powerful if we consider word frequency in relation to expected frequency, based on counts of words in a large body of literature. One method, the Associative Interactive Dictionary (AID) was developed for searching the various MEDLARS files.[19] The inverted file for the database shows us the terms used and the number of postings for each; from this can be calculated the expected frequency of occurrence in any given set of documents of a given term. Let us assume that a search recalls n documents from the total N in the collection. For any given term which occurs in these documents we can find the total number of postings for that term in the collection T. The expected frequency of occurrence E is then

$$E = T.n/N$$

If we now calculate the actual number of occurrences O, we can derive a relatedness measure (cf the statistical measure χ^2) to show the strength of association between the term being studied and the documents retrieved:

$$R = (O - E)/E$$

We can then calculate the value of R for each of the terms which occur in the set of documents, and rank them in order. A user may enter a search term, and ask to see the related terms; the results are like those found by intellectual effort, but include some unexpected results. One example started with the word 'shellfish' and located a large number of associated terms, of which the nine most highly ranked were:

Rank	XTRA-PSTGS	Term
1	390	OYSTERS
2	334	MUSSELS
3	227	CLAMS
4	185	TIDES
5	180	ESTUARIES
6	143	PARAHAEMOLYTICUS
7	138	CRASSOSTREA
8	101	SEAFOODS
9	88	VIRGINICA

While most of these might be expected, some would not appear in an intellectually derived list! However, they are certainly justified by their occurrence in the documents studied; as Svenonius points out, associations derived from full-text analysis by computer represent the logical extreme of literary warrant![20]

While it is not as powerful as *expected* word frequency, *absolute* word frequency may be of value. Words which occur very frequently in a particular document collection will obviously recall a large number of documents, many of which may be marginally relevant or not relevant at all to a particular enquiry; words which occur infrequently will give lower recall, and will thus enable us to reject unwanted documents more easily. A weighting factor could thus be based on the reciprocal of the frequency of occurrence.

The *term discrimination factor* can be calculated to determine which terms will be most useful in distinguishing one document from another. If we have two documents which are represented by sets of index terms, we can compute a measure of the similarity between them; where the sets of index terms are the same, the similarity measure would be 1, whereas if the two sets had nothing in common, it would be 0. Normally it would lie somewhere between 0 and 1. We can calculate the similarity measures for a collection of documents to arrive at an average figure. We can then recalculate the figure with each term removed in turn; the discrimination factor for each term will be shown by the difference between the similarity measure obtained with that term omitted and the average similarity measure, and terms ranked according to their discrimination factor. Terms which appear very frequently will have a low discrimination factor, and are not good indexing or search terms.

Location may be used to weight terms; words which occur in the title, for example, are likely to be highly relevant to the subject of the document, as are those found in an abstract if one is included.[12] Instead of words as they occur, we may use stemming. In the process of a search, user feedback may be used to weight more heavily those terms which retrieve relevant documents; terms from useful documents found may be added to the search formulation. A combination of search terms can now give a search formulation for each query representing the weighted combination of each of the individual terms.

Many of these methods were tried with success by Salton in the SMART experiments, and are now being incorporated into working systems.[21] Salton proposed that each term in a document should be regarded as a *vector*; the totality of n terms would then give an n-dimensional vector describing the document. A query would then be treated in the same way, and the two multidimensional vectors matched. One measure which was found useful was the cosine correlation coefficient, which is a measure of the angle between the two vectors; if they coincided perfectly, the angle between them would be $0°$; the cosine of $0°$ is 1. If the two vectors did not match at all, the angle between them would be $90°$, with cosine $90°$ being 0. In practice, a figure between 0 and 1 would be obtained for each document in relation to a query, enabling the documents to be ranked. The function is given by the equation:

$$\cos(q, d) = \frac{\sum_{i=1}^{n} d_i q_i}{\left(\sum_{i=1}^{n} (d_i)^2 \cdot \sum_{i=1}^{n} (q_i)^2\right)^{\frac{1}{2}}}$$

Alternatively, we may use the rather simpler form:

$$\text{Strength of association} = \frac{Cab}{\sqrt{(Oa^2 \times Ob^2)}}$$

where Oa is the total number of occurrences of term a, Ob is the total number of occurrences of term b, and Cab is the number of cooccurrences of terms a and b, proposed by Sparck Jones.[27]

One of the systems to use methods similar to SMART is the CITE NLM system,[22] which accepts queries in natural language and uses them as the basis of a search after deleting any stop words (about 600 are used). Using the original words, terms from MeSH, the indexing language used in the descriptor field, related terms derived from computer processing, and the use of combinations of terms as outlined above, the system can give ranked output. The user can use this to make relevance judgements, which can be used to modify the search strategy if the user is not satisfied with the first results.

Maron proposed a rather different approach to calculating the weight to be applied to each term used to index a document. Using the matrix set out above, the weight to be given to a term is the probability that a user requiring a particular document D_j would use term I_i to search for it. This probability w_{ij} can be estimated as:

$$\frac{\text{Number satisfied with } D_j \text{ and using } I_i}{\text{Number satisfied with } D_j}$$

symbolized as $P(I_i|A.D_j)$, where A represents the whole set of users. However, this weight is still based on the indexer's estimate, whereas we should be trying to rank documents according to the users' needs $P(D_j|A.I_i)$. We can convert one viewpoint to the other by mathematical manipulation:

$$P(D_j|A.I_i) = P(D_j|A).P(I_i|A.D_j).c = P(D_j|A).w_{ij}.c$$

where $P(D_j|A)$ is the probability that document D_j will meet the needs of all library users A, which is calculated by the kind of statistical techniques outlined above. On this basis it is possible to rank documents according to the probability that they will meet users' needs.[23]

The ranking process does require more computation than Boolean searching, so a possible compromise is to carry out a Boolean search to reduce the number of documents to be ranked to, say, a couple of hundred, and then rank those. The method is now a practical proposition, and is used by some databases, though the majority still use Boolean searching only. The advantages of ranking are such that we shall surely see a steady increase in its use.

Recall and relevance

Most of the work done in establishing the concepts of recall and relevance was carried out on small databases. The 1965 MEDLARS evaluation[24] was the exception, in looking at a database which already contained some 800,000 references. There are now several databases containing millions of references. It becomes apparent that a relevance ratio which might be quite acceptable in a collection of a few hundred references will probably be quite unacceptable in one containing even one million. In the MEDLARS evaluation, the average number of references retrieved for each search was 175, with an average relevance ratio of 50%; that is, of the average 175 references found, about 90 were found to be not relevant. The database is now some ten times as big; following the same search procedures, we would retrieve an average of 1750 references for each search, of which some 900 would not be relevant! The average recall ratio was about 58%, as calculated by a somewhat roundabout method; it was obviously not feasible to examine the whole database in relation to each search in order to establish the recall base. Taking the average search, and assuming that about 90 of the references found were relevant, with a recall ratio of 58% this implies that about 155 references should have been found, but 65 were missed. Again extrapolating this to the current database, we would have to assume that some hundreds of relevant documents would be missed.

We also have the consider another factor in addition to recall and relevance: *utility*, also mentioned in Chapter 2. If we carry out a search using a particular search strategy, we should recall some relevant documents, and we may assume that these will be useful to the enquirer. If we modify the search to recall more documents, we shall almost certainly retrieve some of those found already. To find them a second time is no longer useful! This point was considered in the MEDLARS study, where one of the factors measured was the 'novelty ratio': were the documents retrieved new to the enquirer, or were they already familiar? As was pointed out in Chapter 3, to use a citation index we have to have a starting point which is a document already known to be relevant. It is not a success if our searching eventually reveals the document that we began with – though it is a reassurance that our search strategy is sound. In carrying out a search by any method we will normally arrive at a point where further searching simply re-locates the documents we have already found. It is then time to stop searching, or to adopt a totally new approach!

Blair[16] argues that with the large databases we now have, past thinking on satisfactory levels of recall and relevance is no longer adequate; increases in size have led not merely to a quantitative problem, as illustrated in the previous paragraph, but also to a qualitative change in the way that we must look at retrieval. The ability to reject ('dodge') unwanted material becomes a great deal more significant; we need to achieve much higher relevance ratios, while in certain circumstances much higher recall ratios are essential. The example which Blair quotes in particular is that of a legal database, set up by two lawyers to support their arguments in a court case. Searches were formulated by the two lawyers assisted by two paralegal aides, and carried out by two information specialists. Many of the searches were carried further by manipulating the search formulations, adding terms and using the power of the database program STAIRS. Documents retrieved by the additional searches were passed to the lawyers with those found by the searches that they had formulated. In general, the lawyers felt that they were retrieving about 75% of the relevant documents by their searches, bearing in mind that they had themselves set up the database. In fact, their searches were finding about 20% of the total relevant documents revealed by the various searches. The additional relevant documents were only found by greatly expanded search strategies. In such a situation high recall and high relevance are essential if a case is to be successfully argued. With a large database it is also likely to take much longer to reach the point where we no longer retrieve useful documents. The fact that most large law firms now set up such databases to support their arguments suggests that we should not be complacent about the success at present of online text searching, since search methods are likely to be used a great deal more intensively than has been normal in the past.

Interface design

Vickery and Vickery have a lengthy and very helpful discussion of the overall design of a search interface.[25] This looks at the *functional requirements* of a system, and the *query processing techniques* that can be used to achieve them. Considering the functional requirements first, faced with the need for a search, we must establish the context. This will enable us to select suitable databases and hosts (some databases are available on more than one bibliographic utility, and may also be on CD-ROM). We then have the user's expression of the query, which we may need to clarify through the usual reference interview. We then need to merge or translate the terms used in the query into those likely to be found in the database, for example using a controlled vocabulary, to create a search statement. We can then carry out a search and obtain a set of results. After eliminating duplicate hits, we can evaluate the results, which may be ranked by the system. This procedure is of general application, and applies to manual as well as computer searching.

Among the query processing techniques, we have the need for disambiguation of search terms, possibly using thesaurus relations and classification hierarchies, and the elimination of words in stoplists. We may need to use stemming to remove suffixes. The query may then be formulated as one or more Boolean search statements, which we may need to manipulate to get the best results. Search terms which do not give the desired results may be errors which can be checked against spelling or sound, as mentioned earlier. The system may give us values for term relevance, making document weighting and ranking possible. It should be possible to modify the original query by relevance feedback based on first results.

Computer classification

Full-text databases tend to be large, which means that, as discussed above, they cause problems in use. We may be able use computer processing to help by reducing the amount of work that has to be done to carry out a given search. The similarity coefficients referred to above may be used to give *clusters* of terms or documents to assist in searching.[26] Clusters of terms may be used as hedges, while clusters of documents serve to reduce the bulk of the collection to be searched in response to a given query. To consider the two extremes, we may regard the whole collection (of documents or terms) as one cluster, or we may regard it as consisting of as many clusters as there are documents or terms; obviously neither of these is particularly helpful in processing a search, and we need to find a satisfactory intermediate value.

If we consider terms, we can compute relationships between pairs of terms from the number of times they co-occur in the same document, for example. We can then rank these and set a cut-off point, above which terms may be considered to be related; the cut-off point determines the strength of the relationship. We may exclude terms which occur in only one document, on the grounds that adding such a term can only increase retrieval by that one document; or those which occur very frequently on the grounds that their use would not be helpful. (To take the extreme again, a term which occurred in every document in a collection would have no discrimination value whatever!) Four kinds of group may be found: strings, stars, cliques and clumps. Strings occur when term A is strongly associated with term B, term B with term C, and so on. In practice, strings tend to form loops fairly quickly: term $A \rightarrow B \rightarrow C \rightarrow D \rightarrow E \rightarrow A$. Stars are found when one term is equally strongly related to two or more others. Cliques occur when a set of terms are all strongly related, each to the other. Clumps are a weaker form of clique, in which a term is related to one or more of the others in the clump, but not necessarily to all. In searching, we might begin with a given term but find the results unsatisfactory; we can then use the previously determined relationships between terms to change our search strategy, as mentioned in the earlier discussion of hedges. We normally think of the grouping of terms as a recall device, but Sparck Jones pointed out that this could be a precision device. If we begin with, say, four terms and conduct a Boolean search, we may retrieve nothing; by substituting related terms we may be able to achieve success at the level of coordination that we began with, rather than by simply dropping one or more terms to obtain results at a lower level of coordination.[27]

If we look at clustering from the point of view of documents, we can use the same kind of approach to determine which documents are likely to be related. Instead of using Salton's technique to measure the correlation between documents and queries, we can use it to measure the correlation between documents.[28] We can then form document clusters, within which all the documents will be related to each other at a level we decide. For each cluster we can determine an average 'centre of gravity' (centroid) which represents the cluster as a whole; this may either be a specific document, or a calculated quasi-document. In searching, we can now restrict our processing to the cluster of documents whose centroid most closely corresponds to the query. In practice, by using different correlation level cutoff points, we can build hierarchies of clusters; we can then begin searching at a level which seems most likely to meet our needs, depending on whether we are looking for high precision or high recall. For high precision we would use the clusters with the highest correlation values, which will of course be the smallest; for high recall we might prefer to begin with the larger clusters having lower correlation levels.

For computer-generated clusters to be useful, they must be reasonably *stable*. A method that gives clusters which change significantly each time we add a document will not be particularly helpful. Consistency is also helpful; processing should preferably give one cluster, or at most a limited number. While consistency is not absolutely necessary, in that different clusters may perform equally well in practice, stability appears to be essential. This is most likely to be achieved when the databases which are processed for clustering are large; just as a manually constructed classification scheme or thesaurus will change substantially with each new document classified or indexed while it is still small, it will eventually reach a state where the average change for each document added is relatively insignificant. So it would appear that the databases which are likely to lend themselves best to clustering techniques are those with which it is likely to prove most useful! The first attempts at developing clustering techniques were carried out on small databases; the largest database used with the original SMART experiments contained just over 1000 documents.We now have far greater computing power available to carry out the intensive processing involved in clustering techniques, and we may well see techniques once dismissed as purely experimental become not only practical but also economically viable.

Limitations on computer matching

It is important to remember that computer techniques for searching or clustering are based on matching words as collections of digits devoid of semantic content. This is most clearly seen in the Soundex techniques for word matching by truncation, described in Chapter 15, since the resulting four-character strings are clearly meaningless in themselves. Some work is in progress to develop IR systems which will take account of semantic content, and results seem promising, in that improved recall and relevance appears to be possible. Chapters 6 and 7 discuss the problems involved in doing this intellectually, but it may be that in the future computer systems may be able to simulate this approach.[29]

Expert systems

Users who come to an IR system with an enquiry lack information that they need, but may not be able to express their need clearly: if they knew the question, they would be well on the way to finding the answer. It is during the reference interview that an intermediary tries to elicit information from the enquirer which will clarify the enquiry. At the other end of the process, the information which satisfies the enquiry will probably have come from one or more experts, who are knowledgeable in the subject. We may be able to help enquirers by developing computer *expert systems*, in which we store information gathered from experts together with rules and procedures to enable the users to get to the information they need despite starting from a position of ignorance.[30] The expert system is thus intended to parallel the purpose of the reference interview, but also to eliminate the steps of reference retrieval and document retrieval by providing direct answers.

In constructing an expert system for a particular subject we face certain problems. The first of these is that of gathering available information within the carefully defined scope of the system. This may be begun by a literature search, which is likely to identify those who may be regarded as experts in the field. The next step is to consult the experts themselves, and it here that we meet the second problem. The experts should be able to confirm the accuracy and adequacy of the information we have gathered, but they may find it very much more difficult to explain how they themselves acquired the information. Over the course of years we all develop mental information gathering and processing habits which enable us, when faced with a problem, to come up with a solution heuristically; we make decisions based on past experience without identifying each step of the thought processes which lead us to the answer. For a computer program to function, each step must be clearly identified and set down, otherwise the program will not be able to perform the task for which it is intended. A third problem is that in finding answers to questions we do not rely solely on knowledge specific to the subject, but use a wide range of general knowledge to provide us with context, analogies and instances which help us to make decisions which enable us to reach our goal. It is not practical to incorporate the whole of this range of general knowledge into an expert system; in order to make the process manageable we have to limit the information we put into the system to that which is specific to the subject area covered. Enquirers, on the other hand, may well stray outside these narrow bounds, if only because they are not aware of them.

Once we have established the knowledge base for a system, and elucidated the decision-making processes used by experts, we still have to incorporate what we have learnt into a computer system, using one of the programs already written for expert system development, and design a suitable user interface, bearing in mind the target group for whom the system is intended. Once a prototype has been constructed it has to be tested and, almost certainly, modified to correct any imperfections. Ardis gives an example of a difficulty arising in the design of an expert system to help users in online patent searching; one of the problems which was not recognized at the planning stage was that many users did not appreciate the difference between a patent and a trademark. The reference librarians who normally answered these enquiries would of course have implicitly recognized the two kinds of enquiry as separate, and this had to be built into the prototype once it had been made explicit by failures with the system. The features of and requirements for an expert system are summarized as follows:

The expert system:

1   must represent the expert's domain-specific knowledge in the way that the expert uses that knowledge
2   must incorporate explanation processes and ways of handling uncertainty
3   typically pertains to problems that can be symbolically represented
4   is more tolerant of user errors than conventional programs

In order to achieve this:

1   there must be at least one acknowledged expert in the subject area
2   the sources of the expert's expertise are judgement and experience
3   the expert must be able and willing to explain his/her knowledge
4   the problem must be well-bounded
5   the problem area must have a real consensus
6   test data must be easily available.[31]

So far, only a few working systems exist in library and information science. There are systems to help map cataloguers, for reference work, and for evaluating donations, but most are very specialized. One related to another subject area is PLEXUS, which is intended for public library clients wanting gardening information.[32] We have yet to see any substantial transfer of reference work from people to computers, but this will no doubt be a future trend, now that the proponents of artificial intelligence have accepted the present limitations on their work and are concentrating on what can be achieved.

Summary

This chapter has attempted to give an overview of the use of online searching, some of the background to its present role, and an indication of the kind of techniques that can be used. The number and scope of online databases means that online searching is now the normal way of finding information for many people. By no means all databases are bibliographic; there are financial databases, for example, to enable us to gamble on the stock market, if we wish, from the comfort of our own home! Increasingly, databases are including information other than text; as mentioned earlier, technology now allows us to retrieve graphics and sound. Chemical databases have included structural diagrams for compounds for many years, but the graphics involved are very simple compared with what is now available. Statistical databases are widely used; census data is becoming available to industry and commerce, as well as to the general public, much faster now that it is computer-compiled. The first edition of the *Oxford English dictionary* took 40 years to compile, in 13 volumes, and a supplement published five years later became necessary as a result of the extended editing process; the second edition is now available on one CD-ROM, and took six years to produce. Children are becoming accustomed to using computers and CD-ROM sources at school and at home, and will expect to find the same kind of information available for work purposes later in life. Yet we have seen that controlled vocabularies compiled by intellectual effort are still frequently used to achieve satisfactory results. One small experiment showed that natural language gave higher precision but lower recall than the use of a controlled vocabulary.[33] Making both available gave the user the option of high recall or high precision. We look at some of these controlled vocabularies in the following chapters on assigned indexing.

References

1 *Classification research for knowledge representation and organization: proceedings of the 5th International study conference on classification research, Toronto, Canada, June 24–28 1991*, Williamson, N. J. and Hudon, M. (eds.), Elsevier, 1992. (FID 698)

2 Austin, C. J., *MEDLARS, 1963–1967*, Bethesda, MD, National Library of Medicine, 1968. The MEDLINE database now contains several million references.

3 *Gale directory of databases*, Detroit, Gale Research Inc, 1995. In this edition, v1 lists over 5300 online databases; v2 lists 2015 CD-ROM products and another 2200 databases available on floppy disk, magnetic tape and other media.
Tenopir, C., 'Full-text databases', *Annual review of information science and technology*, **19**, 1984, 215–46.

4 Larson, S. E. and Williams, M. E., 'Computer assisted legal research', *Annual review of information science and technology*, **15**, 1980, 251–86.

5 Summit, R. K., 'In search of the elusive end user', *Online review*, **13** (6), 1989, 485–91.

6 Cornick, D., 'Being an end user is not for everyone', *Online*, **13**, March, 1989, 49–54.
Fisher, J. and Bjorner, S., 'Enabling online end-user searching: an expanding role for librarians', *Special libraries*, **85** (4), Fall 1994, 281–91.
Harman, D., 'User-friendly systems instead of user-friendly front-ends', *Journal of the American Society for Information Science*, **43** (2), 1992, 164–74. Suggests that implementing user-friendly front-ends is an inadequate substitute for improving the power of search engines.

7 Hartley, R. J., Keen, E. M., Large, J. A. and Tedd, L.A., *Online searching: principles and practice*, London, Bowker Saur, 1990.

8 Dalrymple, P. W. and Roderer, N. K., 'Database access systems', *Annual review of information science and technology*, **29**, 1994, 137–78.

9 ANSI Z39.58:1992 *Common command language for online information retrieval*, Bethesda, MD, National Information Standards Organization, 1992.

10 Armstrong, C. J. and Large, J. A. (eds.), *Manual of online search strategies*, Boston, Mass., G. K. Hall, 1988.

11 'Public access online catalogs', Markey, K. (ed.), *Library trends*, **33** (4), 1987,

523–67. (The point is made here in relation to OPAC searching, but it is of course generally valid.)

12 Keen, E. M., 'The use of term position devices in ranked output experiments', *Journal of documentation,* **47** (1), 1991, 1–22.
Keen, E. M., 'Some aspects of proximity searching in text retrieval systems', *Journal of information science,* **18** (2), 1992, 89–98.

13 Walker, S., 'Evaluating and enhancing an experimental online catalogue', *Library trends,* **35** (4), 1987, 631–45.

14 Sievert, M. and Boyce, B. R., 'Hedge trimming and the resurrection of the controlled vocabulary in online searching', *Online review,* **7** (6), 1983, 484–94.

15 Fidel, R., 'Thesaurus requirements for an intermediary expert system', *in Classification research for knowledge representation and organization: proceedings of the 5th International study conference on classification research, Toronto, Canada, June 24–28 1991,* Williamson, N. J. and Hudon, M. (eds.), Elsevier, 1992, (FID 698), 209–13.

16 Blair, D. C., *Language and representation in information retrieval,* New York, NY, Elsevier Science Publishers, 1990.

17 Cleverdon, C. W. 'Optimizing convenient online access to bibliographic databases', *Information services and use,* **4** (1–2), 1984, 37–47.
Cleverdon, C. W. [letter to the editor] *Online review,* **14**, 1990, 35, suggests that intermediaries support Boolean searching because it needs them to make it practical!
Pape, D. L. and Jones, R. L., 'STATUS with IQ: escaping from the Boolean straitjacket', *Program,* **22** (1), 1988, 32–43.

18 Maron, M. E. And Kuhns, J. L., 'On relevance, probabilistic indexing and information retrieval', *Journal of the Association for Computing Machinery,* **7** (3), 1960, 216–44.
Maron, M. E., 'On indexing, retrieval and the meaning of about', *Journal of the American Society for Information Science,* **28** (1), 1977, 38–43.

19 Doszkocs, T. E., 'An associative interactive dictionary (AID) for online bibliographic searching', in *The information age in perspective: proceedings of the ASIS annual meeting, November 1978.* White Plains, NY, Knowledge Industry Publications, 1978, 105–9.

20 Svenonius, E., 'Classification: prospects, problems and possibilities', in *International study conference on classification research, Toronto, Canada, June 24–28 1991,* Williamson, N. J. and Hudon, M. (eds.), Elsevier, 1992. (FID 698), 5–25.

21 Salton, G. (ed.), *The SMART retrieval system: experiments in automatic document processing,* Englewood Cliffs, NJ, Prentice-Hall, 1971.
Salton, G. and McGill, M. J., *Introduction to modern information retrieval,* New York, NY, McGraw-Hill, c1983, Chapter 3.
Salton, G. and Buckley, C., 'Improving retrieval performance by relevance feedback', *Journal of the American Society for Information Science,* **41** (4), 1990, 288–97.
Kantor, P. B., 'Information retrieval techniques', *Annual review of information*

science and technology **29**, 1994, 53–90.

22 Doszkocs, T. E., and Rapp, B. A., 'Searching MEDLINE in English: a proto-type user interface with natural language query, ranked output, and relevance feedback' in *Information choices and policies, proceedings of the ASIS annual meeting, 1979*, White Plains, NY, Knowledge Industry Publications, 1980, 131–9.

23 Maron, M. E. and Kuhns, J. L., 'On relevance, probabilistic indexing and infor-mation retrieval' *Journal of the ACM*, **7** (3), 1960, 216–44.
Maron, M. E. 'On indexing, retrieval and the meaning of about', *Journal of the American Society for Information Science*, 28 (1), 1977, 38–43.

24 Lancaster, F. W., *Evaluation of the MEDLARS demand search service*, Bethesda, MD, National Library of Medicine, 1968.

25 Vickery, B. C. and Vickery, A., 'Online search interface design', *Journal of documentation*, **49** (2), 1993, 103–87.

26 Van Rijsbergen, C. J., *Information retrieval*, 2nd edn, London, Butterworths, 1979.

27 Sparck Jones, K., *Automatic keyword classification for information retrieval*, London, Butterworths, 1971.
Needham, R. M. and Sparck Jones, K., 'Keywords and clumps: recent work on information retrieval at the Cambridge Language Research Unit', *Journal of documentation*, **20** (1), 1964, 5–15. Included in *Theory of subject analysis . . .*

28 Salton, G. and McGill, M. J., *Introduction to modern information retrieval*, New York, NY, McGraw-Hill, c1983, Chapter 6, section 4.

29 Sembok, M. T. and van Rijsbergen, C. J., 'SILOL: a simple logical-linguistic document retrieval system', *Information processing & management*, **26** (1), 1990, 111–34.

30 Poulter, A., Morris, A. and Dow, J., 'LIS professionals as knowledge engi-neers', *Annual review of information science and technology*, **29**, 1994, 305–50.
Vickery, B. C., 'Knowledge representation: a brief review', *Journal of docu-mentation'*, **42** (3), September 1986, 145–59.
Alberico, R. and Micco, M., *Expert systems for reference and information retrieval*, Westport, CT, Meckler, 1990.
Artificial intelligence and expert systems: will they change the library?, Lancaster, F. W. and Smith. L. C. (eds.), Urbana-Champaign, University of Illinois Graduate School of Library and Information Management, 1992. (Clinic on library applications of data processing: 1990)

31 Ardis, S. B., 'Online patent searching: guided by an expert system', *Online*, **14** (2), March 1990, 56–62.

32 Vickery, A. *et al.*, 'A reference and referral system using expert system tech-nique', *Journal of documentation*, **43** (1), March 1987, 1–23.

33 Rowley, J. E., 'A comparison between free language and controlled language indexing and searching', *Information services and use*, **10** (3), 1990, 147–55.

Chapter 6

Assigned indexing 1: Semantics

In Chapter 3 we looked at ways in which printed indexes could be derived from information manifest in a document. In Chapter 5, we considered some of the ways in which files may be searched online, again using the information manifest in the document, e.g. titles, abstracts or full text; the discussion indicated some of the problems that are likely to arise in doing this, and we referred in passing to the use of 'controlled vocabularies' to assist in solving these problems, without at that time showing what was meant by a controlled vocabulary. We have also seen in Chapter 2 that full-text searching gives the highest possible level of exhaustivity, which tends to be associated with high recall but low relevance; we may wish to have some method of summarization to supplement the depth indexing of text searching. A discussion of these problems leads to the idea of *assigned indexing*.

Firstly, we have to choose the words which we will use in a search of the system by trying to think of all the words that the authors of the documents we have indexed might have used to describe the topic we are interested in, and, having chosen the words, we have to think of the various forms in which they might occur. Truncation serves as a means of merging different word forms, but not always; TEACH* will retrieve teaching and teacher but not taught. Secondly, we often need to search for combinations of terms; word pairs are more significant than the individual words on their own, but we often find ourselves wanting to associate more than two words. This process of *coordination* is, as we have seen, a process of class intersection. To use one of our previous examples, our collection of documents (the universe of discourse) contains a set of documents containing the word 'water', and each of these sets forms a class, and if we are searching for documents on 'water pollution' we are looking for the intersection of these two classes. Any process involving class intersection is likely to be a powerful method of reducing the total number of documents retrieved; we have also seen that a reduction in recall is often accompanied by an improvement in relevance, so we would expect *coordination* to be a useful method of obtaining improved relevance. On the other hand, class union ('A' OR 'B') increases the total number of documents retrieved, so we would expect the inclusion of alternative terms to be a device for improving recall.

We also noted that *water* on its own might not retrieve all the documents of interest, because they might use different but related terms: *sea* and *river*. We noted in Chapter 5 that computer matching does not involve semantic content, so that it can-

not lead to related terms directly; even computer classification is based on such factors as co-occurrence, not similarity of meaning. In order to carry out an adequate
search of our collection of documents, we had to think of not only the words in
which we were interested, and all the forms in which they might be used, but also
all the alternative or related forms. We then had to decide just how we were going
to coordinate these words in order to retrieve relevant documents, while at the same
time excluding words or combinations of words which would retrieve irrelevant
material. This is obviously quite a complex operation, and if we are to do it well we
need some guidance: a list of words showing their relationships and indicating ways
in which they might usefully be combined to give the class intersections we are
interested in. However, in Chapter 1 we pointed out that what we are actually trying to do is carry out a matching operation between the messages which in their
encoded form are the input to our system and the messages – also in their encoded
form – which represent the questions we put to the system. This concept of matching is of course strongly reinforced by our examination of computer-based systems,
which depend on the computer to match the words of our question against the words
in the documents.

Now if we are to use a list of words to help us in our searching, it would appear
that we would increase the chances of achieving successful matches if we used the
same list of words to encode the document at the input stage, and *assigned* the
appropriate words to the documents ourselves rather than rely on the authors'
choice. In other words, we devise an *indexing language* and use this for both encoding operations: input and question. Such systems are referred to as *assigned indexing* systems, and most of the rest of this book is devoted to the problems of
constructing and using such systems. In this chapter we examine some of the basic
theoretical problems.[1]

Choice of terms

Assigned indexing is also known as *concept indexing*, because what we are trying
to do is to identify the concepts involved in each document. (Concept: idea of a class
of objects; general notion.)[2]

One analysis suggests that there are five categories of concept: entities; activities; abstracts; properties; heterogeneous. A concept is denoted by a *term* which
may consist of more than one word. (Term: a word or expression that has a precise
meaning in some uses, or is peculiar to a science, art, profession or subject.)[3] We
may examine each of these categories in more detail. *Entities* are things which may
be given a denotative meaning,[4] i.e. we can identify them by pointing at them. They
may be physical, e.g. matter, or physical phenomena; chemical, e.g. molecular
states, minerals; biological, e.g. living being; or artefacts, i.e. manufactured items.
Activities are usually denoted by verbal nouns, e.g. building, lubricating, though in
some cases we find the passive rather than the active form, e.g. lubrication.
Abstracts usually refer to qualities or states, and are given connotative meanings,
i.e. each of us may attribute a different meaning to them depending on our particular corpus of experience. They may be physical, e.g. energy; symbolic, e.g. Justice

as a blindfolded figure; or behavioural, e.g. truth (the definition of which was questioned on at least one notable occasion). *Properties* are of two kinds, which are distinguished by their grammatical form. Adjectival forms can only be used in conjunction with a noun, which they qualify in a subjective or attributive way, once again giving a connotative meaning. They may relate to sight, e.g. dull, shiny, symmetrical; sound, e.g. loud, musical; or to the other three senses, touch, taste and smell. They may also relate to mechanical properties, e.g. loose, rigid. Noun forms describe physical properties which may be measured, e.g. rigidity, reflectivity, loudness. It will be clear at once that there will be in many cases a definite relationship between the two kinds. We may refer to the rigidity of an iron bar, for example, in which case we are thinking of the property; or we may refer to a rigid bar, in which case we are using the property to define the kind of entity that we are considering.

Heterogeneous concepts form a very mixed bag, in that they usually represent concepts which might be further analysed into two or more simpler concepts which would fit into the other categories, but are nevertheless regarded as unitary concepts and treated as such. Willetts[5] has suggested some types:

Roles of man (Entity + Activity, Entity + Property) e.g. teacher, landlord
Groups of man (Entity + Abstract) e.g. society, conference
Types of building (Entity + Activity + Property) e.g. library, theatre
Discipline (all four) e.g. Physics, Medicine
Groups of chemicals (Entity + Activity, Entity + Property) e.g. catalysts, polymers

Austin[6] would regard the Groups as Aggregates, while the rest would fit into most indexing systems quite smoothly as they stand. Are there any advantages to further analysis?

During the 1950s a team at Case Western Reserve University worked on a system of analysis known as semantic factoring.[7] The objective was to break down every concept into a set of fundamental concepts called semantic factors. Because of their fundamental nature, there would only be a limited number of these factors. A concept would be denoted by the appropriate combination of semantic factors, and the use of a complex set of roles and links enabled the indexer to write a 'telegraphic abstract' which would represent the subject of a document in a computer file.

The method is clearly a powerful one, but is open to some doubts and objections. Exactly how far does one carry such an analysis? Heat and temperature, for example, could be specified as *movement* of *molecules*. Again, it is possible to specify a concept by using only some of its attributes; or perhaps more significantly, is it ever possible to specify *all* the attributes for a given concept? For example, thermometer may be specified as instrument: measuring: temperature, and barometer may be specified as instrument: measuring: pressure. Neither reveals the fact that both may have other factors in common, for example the fact that they may be mercury-in-glass devices. Certainly for most purposes a mercury barometer has more in common with an aneroid barometer than it does with a thermometer, but this may not be the case if we are thinking of the instrument maker. If we start to think of a particular individual, we may have no difficulty in putting a name to the object of our thoughts; we may find it impossible in practical terms to think of all the possible terms that might be needed to specify an individual without naming them. Sex, age, nationality, family status, marital status, height, weight, occupation, language, religion – the list is almost endless. Furthermore, we may find ourselves in the position of not knowing all of the information we require; we have to remember that we are dealing with the information in a collection of documents, and this will usually be incomplete.

We also have a problem in analysing certain concepts which lose their significance if split up into their constituent parts. A soap opera is not a kind of opera, nor is it a form of soap;[8] 'moment of truth' cannot be analysed further; a blackbird is a specific species of bird, but there are many black birds;[9] a rubber duck is not a species of duck (despite evidence presented in some TV advertising) and nowadays it is rarely made of rubber.[10] Fortunately, though the theoretical problems involved may not all have been solved, in practice, solutions which are reasonably effective *can* be found.

Choice of form of word

During the above discussion of categories of concept it should have become apparent that – with the sole exception of adjectival properties, which cannot stand alone – all the concepts involved were denoted by nouns. Even activities are denoted by verbal nouns, active or passive, e.g. cataloguing and classification. In fact, it is the norm in indexing languages to use nouns as far as possible, and various sets of rules have been drawn up to give guidance on the use of singular and plural. Table 6.1 is based on the rules given in the EJC *Thesaurus of engineering and scientific terms*, described in Chapter 25, while the ISO,[11] BSI[12] and ANSI[13] have all published standards on thesaurus construction. A useful rule of thumb is: how much? – use the singular; how many? – use the plural.

Table 6.1 Choice of singular or plural form of noun

Type of term	Use singular	Use plural
Materials Properties	When specific, e.g. polythene density	When generic, e.g plastics chemical properties
Objects Events Objects specified by purpose		Cars Laws Wars Lubricants
Processes Proper names Disciplines Subject areas	Lubricating Earth (the planet) Law War	

Homographs

The same spelling is sometimes used for different words, which may or may not be pronounced the same, e.g. sow and sow, China and china. This may arise from a figure of speech such as metonymy or synecdoche, in which we use part of a description to mean the whole; it may be through analogy, when terms such as 'filter' from hydraulic engineering are used by electrical engineers; or it may simply be an etymological accident. Whatever the cause, there is likely to be confusion if we do nothing to distinguish such words. One way of doing this is to qualify each by another word in parentheses to show the context and thus the meaning, e.g.:

PITCH (Bitumen)
PITCH (Football)
PITCH (Music)
PITCH (Slope)

If we do not distinguish homographs we shall get reduced relevance; the seriousness of this will depend on the coverage of our system. For example, if our system only covers music there will be no problem with the word pitch, since other meanings than the musical are unlikely to arise at the input stage. However, it has been pointed out[14] that the 20 most frequently used English nouns have an average of seven meanings each, so we must obviously be aware of the problem.

Relationships

We have seen that in addition to the choice of terms and the form in which they should be used, there are two kinds of relationship between terms that we have to take into account: the recognition of terms denoting related subjects such as water, sea and river, and the association of otherwise unrelated terms to represent composite subjects. One place where we can identify the kinds of terms used by authors, and how they are associated is in the titles they give their works. If we study Table 6.2 carefully, we can see first of all that the titles, which are taken from the Library of Congress catalogue, fall into three major groups: Education, Agriculture and Cookbooks. Within each of these three subject areas we can see examples of both kinds of relationship, and it can be seen that one kind is permanent, and arises from the definitions of the subjects involved, while the second kind arises from the associations we find in documents, and represent temporary, *ad hoc*, associations. The first kind are known as semantic relationships: corn is always a kind of cereal. The second are called syntactic: Disinfestation is an activity carried out on a crop, in this instance grain, an entity; coloured immigrants are people, entities, being educated, activity, in Britain, place. This suggests that our indexing language must contain the equivalent of a dictionary, to show semantic relationships, and a grammar, to cater for syntactic relationships. In computer searching, the grammar may be the rudimentary provision of Boolean logic, but in printed indexes or shelf arrangement we may wish to show more complex relationships.

Semantic relationships

We find that these may be considered in three groups: equivalence, hierarchical and affinitive/associative. The first two groups are reasonably straightforward, but the third is much less clearly defined, and is the group which causes most problems in practice.

We can examine the various kinds of each of the three groups in more detail, with most of our examples taken from the titles in Table 6.2.

Table 6.2 Related subjects

Concept analysis

1	Education of women in India 1921–1966.
2	Acceleration and the gifted.
3	The costs of education.
4	The teaching of Physics at university level.
5	Teaching French: an introduction to applied linguistics.
6	Saga of the steam plow. [plough]
7	The main course cookbook.
8	The corn earworm in sweet corn: how to control it.
9	Wheat.
10	The potato.
11	New first year mathematics: teacher's book.
12	Radiation disinfestation of grain.
13	The education of coloured immigrants in Britain.
14	Modern corn production.
15	The elementary school: a perspective.
16	Agricultural financing in India.
17	Technology of cereals.
18	Meat, fish, poultry and cheese . . .
19	A cyclopedia of education. [i.e. encyclopedia]
20	Soups and hors d'oeuvres.
21	Curriculum theory.
22	A world of nut recipes from soups to savories.
23	Economic aspects of higher education.
24	The pecan cookbook.
25	Education improvement for the disadvantaged in an elementary setting.
26	The evolution of the comprehensive school.
27	The world book of pork dishes.
28	New media and college teaching.
29	Potatoes in popular ways.
30	Educational aids in the infant school
31	The planetarium: an elementary School teaching resource.
32	Vegetable cookbook.
33	English in the primary school.
34	Talking about puddings.

Equivalence

Synonyms and antonyms
Quasi-synonyms
  Same continuum
  Overlapping
Preferred spelling
Acronyms, abbreviations
Current and established terms
Translations

The English language is rich in synonyms and near-synonyms, because it has roots in both Teutonic and Romance languages. While it is true that Wordsworth's ode would sound less impressive as *Hints of deathlessness* than as *Intimations of immortality*, the former is as correct a statement of the subject as the latter. Many subjects have both a common name and a scientific name: potato and *Solanum tuberosum*; American usage differs from British or Australian: elementary school and primary school; authors differ in their usage: the word college is used in more than one sense. By not merging synonyms, we shall be separating literature for the lay reader from that for the expert, American from British, one author from another; this is likely to improve relevance at the expense of recall. By merging synonyms, we are likely to improve recall at the expense of relevance.

It may seem odd to include antonyms with synonyms, yet in trying to retrieve information we may often find it useful to treat them in the same way. In practice, gifted children are often disadvantaged! Quasi-synonyms often represent points on the same continuum, or the overlapping of concepts. Antonyms and quasi-synonyms may overlap; roughness and smoothness may be thought of as antonyms, but they lie on a continuum which often represents a subjective judgement. We may find difficulty in clearly distinguishing pre-school, infant school and primary school; comprehensive schools overlap secondary schools; economics, costs and financing are often not clearly distinguished; the distance between two points is a length.

The other four instances are self-explanatory: plow (US) = plough (UK), labor (US) = labour (UK); ERIC = Educational Resources Information Clearinghouse; Third World, Developing Countries, Underdeveloped Countries; Zhurnal = Journal.

The equivalence relationship implies that there will be more than one term denoting the same concept. In a controlled vocabulary it is usual to select one term as the *preferred term*, and use only that one in our indexing. We must of course make provision for those users who look for information under one of the other terms, and this is discussed below in the section on showing semantic relationships.

Hierarchical

Genus – species
Whole – part

The usual kind of hierarchical relationship is that of genus to species, which represents class inclusion (all A is B; some B is A). It is seen most clearly in the biological sciences (all mammals are vertebrates; some vertebrates are mammals), but is also found in other subject fields; indeed, much of classification is concerned with the establishment of hierarchies. Austin[15] distinguishes what he calls quasi-generic relationships from true generic, using the criterion of permanence; a potato is always a plant of the species *Solanum tuberosum*, but it may appear on our dinner plate as part of a meal, or it may be used by children to print out simple designs. A planetarium is a kind of teaching resource. Beef, veal and pork are kinds of meat.

Whole-part relationships are not generic. A wheel is not a species of bicycle, nor is a door a species of house. However, it is convenient to regard whole-part relationships as hierarchical, and it has been recommended that the two types should be distinguished as Genetic and Partitive.[12] The partitive relationship is illustrated by four particular examples:

a systems and organs of the body
b geographic locations
c disciplines or fields of discourse
d hierarchical social structures.

In each case, the name of the part should imply the name of the whole regardless of context, so that the terms can be organized as logical hierarchies.

Affinitive/Associative relationships

Coordination
Genetic
Concurrent
Cause and effect
Instruments
Materials
Similarity

Because these are the least well-defined, and often are not immediately obvious, they are the group most likely to cause problems in an indexing language. Indeed, Coates[16] criticised LCSH for including these relationships in what appears to have been a quite haphazard way. (More recently, new relationships within LCSH have been restricted to equivalence and hierarchical types.) Despite the difficulties, we should make some attempt to cater for these relationships by first of all recognizing that they exist and then trying to identify them systematically.

Some present fewer problems than others. Coordination is in effect a by-product of the generic relationship: species of the same genus are coordinate. Thus wheat and corn are both kinds of cereal crop; savo[u]ries, hors d'oeuvres, soups, entrees, main courses and puddings may be regarded as sequential courses of a meal. It is worth noting that if division of this kind is *dichotomous*, i.e. into A and A´, the result is to give two concepts which are antonyms, e.g. male and female, poetry and prose. For this reason antonyms are sometimes considered to fall into the associative rather than the equivalence group.

Genetic relationships are also straightforward, e.g. mother–son; here again we

Table 6.3 Relationships and associations

Relationships discussed	Word associations
Word forms	Word derivatives
synonyms	similar
antonyms	contrast
hierarchical	superordinate
	subordinate
coordinate	coordinate
whole-part	whole-part
cause and effect	cause and effect
instruments	verb-object
materials	material
similarity	similarity
genetic	—
—	assonance

may note that the first level of genetic division will give coordinate concepts, e.g. son–daughter. Concurrent refers to two activities taking place at the same time in association, and is thus open to much broader interpretation; an example is education–teaching. Cause and effect are rather easier to identify, though of course they have been the subject of much philosophical discourse; an optimistic example from the draft British Standard was teaching–learning. This has been replaced in the final version by the more prosaic but rather more solid diseases–pathogens. Instruments, e.g. teaching–media; and materials, e.g. plastic film–transparencies, are usually fairly obvious. The final category, similarity, is perhaps the most difficult of the affinitive relationships in that it necessarily implies a subjective judgement; how similar do two concepts have to be for us to recognize the relationship? We should not expect any great degree of consistency between different indexing languages.

It is interesting to compare the kinds of relationship discussed here with a similar categorization of relationships revealed by psychological word associations.[17] It may be that a study of such associations may throw further light on the kinds of relationship that we need to cater for in our index vocabularies (Table 6.3)

The need to recognize semantic relationships

At the beginning of this chapter we saw how the need to identify semantic relationships might arise, but in view of the fairly detailed analysis that we have just carried out, it is worth restating the problem, from two rather different points of view. We started off from the viewpoint of the searcher trying to carry out a search in a computer-based system using the texts, or parts of the texts, of the documents in our collection. Just which collection of terms do we have to use to ensure that we have covered all the possible approaches to a concept? To put it another way: if the term we first think of does not retrieve the documents we want (or perhaps does not retrieve any documents at all!) *what other terms can we substitute*? It is obviously of help in this situation if we have some kind of list of terms showing the relationships between them, to suggest substitute terms.

This list of terms – our indexing language – is equally obviously of value to the indexer who is trying to encode a document in such a way that it will be found by searchers who are likely to deem it useful. The concept the indexer is trying to encode may be unfamiliar, in which case it is useful to be able to follow a path through a network of related subjects until we find the most appropriate term. It will also indicate the terms we are likely to have used in encoding previous documents dealing with the same subject.

It is worth noting that if the concept we are dealing with has a clearly defined name used by authors and known to the searcher, the need for an indexing language with its network of relationships disappears; we will do perfectly well using a computer to match the search term with the records in a database. However, this is not always the case, and we shall often need help in conducting a search, particularly if we need high recall. We shall also find a need for indexing languages for other purposes, for example in arranging the books on the shelves of a library, or producing a printed index. We must therefore continue by looking at methods of devising indexing languages.

Showing semantic relationships

So far, we have seen that our indexing language should consist of a list of terms denoting the concepts we wish to include, together with a set of relationships linking various sets of terms. We now have to consider the question of how to arrange our terms, and how to show the relationships which exist among them.

The simplest way to arrange our terms is alphabetically, as in a dictionary. However, it is evident that alphabetical arrangement cannot show any kind of relationship except the accidental one of bringing together words which have the same stem, which at best can only cater for a very small part of the problem. The answer is to insert a series of *linkages*, usually called *cross-references*, which serve to bring semantic relationships to the attention of the user.

Equivalence relationships normally imply the selection of one form as the preferred term, as we have seen, so we make a cross-reference from the non-preferred term to USE the preferred term:

Footpaths
    USE Trails
Book-marks
    USE Bookmarks

In these examples from LCSH, the first directs us to a preferred word. The second is a preferred spelling, which may seem trivial until it is realized that in the computer filing the hyphen is treated as the equivalent of a space, and Book-marks is found between Book margins and Book numbers, some 150 headings earlier in the list! In a computer-based catalogue, it is quite simple for the user who looks up the non-preferred term to be automatically transferred to the preferred heading. In a card or printed catalogue the user must of course make the move unaided.

In the index language, we need to show the inverse of these directions to help the indexer, once again using a convention, UF, i.e. Use For:

Trails
UF Bridle paths
    Foot trails
    Footpaths
    Horse trails
        Paths

Bookmarks
UF Book-marks

In the first of these examples, we see that Bridle paths, Foot trails and Horse trails are treated as equivalent to Trails, though they might be thought of as more specific. This is a matter of practical utility; if there is not much literature on a specific heading, it can be found under the broader heading reasonably conveniently without unduly increasing the number of headings. These inverse directions do not usually appear in the catalogue, but this is a matter of historical practice rather than a theoretical consideration.

Hierarchical and affinitive/associative relationships

As we have seen, equivalence relationships are essentially one-way, taking us from non- preferred terms to preferred. By contrast, the other two categories of relationship are two-way and this implies somewhat different treatment. We shall need cross-references in both directions. To take some examples of the hierarchical relationship, if we have material in our system on the solar system, the planets, and Earth, we should draw the attention of our reader to this:

Solar system
    BT   Milky Way
    SA   names of individual planets
    NT   Asteroids
           Comets
           . . .
           Planets
           . . .
           Sun

If we turn to Planets, we find:

Planets
    BT   Solar system
    NT   Earth

where BT is Broader term, and NT is Narrower term. We can see that the relationships are reciprocal: each BT has a corresponding NT. We can also see that there are examples of both generic and partitive relationships; The Earth is a member of the class Planets, but Asteroids, Comets, Planets, Sun, are all *parts* of the Milky Way. SA [see also] is used by LCSH for references which would otherwise become overwhelming, e.g.

Flowers
    SA   names of flowers, e.g. Carnations; Roses; Violets.

Such blanket references are somewhat unsatisfactory, in that they leave us unsure of what headings we may successfully search for; on the other hand, we should not expect an indexing language to do the job of an encyclopedia. In a small collection, blanket references can be avoided altogether, since the number of headings to be referred to will be limited.

To take another example, we find:

Pressure vessels
  UF Containers, Pressurized
        Pressurized containers
  BT High pressure (Science)
        Pressure
  RT Autoclaves
        Boilers
        Caissons
        Compressed air
        Steam-boilers
        Tanks
  NT Gas cylinders
        Hyperbaric chambers
        Nuclear pressure vessels

Here, in addition to USE, BT and NT we have RT, Related Term. These too are reciprocal relationships, and each RT has a corresponding RT in the overall list.

In editions of LCSH prior to the 11th, 1988, a rather different system was used, which may still be found in some printed or card catalogues. Instead of USE we find *See*, with UF represented by *x*. BT, RT and NT were shown as *See also*, but the converse was *xx*. Thus we could have:

Forging
See also   Blacksmithing
xx   Blacksmithing
Blacksmithing
See also   Forging
xx   Forging

The older system was introduced in the 5th edition in 1948, but was confusing for users, and the current system, first fully introduced in the EJC *Thesaurus of engineering terms* in 1964 (Chapter 25), is a big improvement; its adoption by LCSH means that its use, recommended by all the various standards for thesaurus construction, is now virtually universal.

Comparison of linkages in different indexing languages

It can be both interesting and instructive to compare the networks of cross-references in two indexing languages, and Kochen and Tagliacozzo proposed two measures for this purpose.[18] The first of these is the *connectedness ratio*:

> The number of terms linked to other terms as a proportion of the total number of terms in the vocabulary.

The second is *accessibility*:

> The average number of terms leading to any given term.

Accessibility is related to the density of the cross-reference network, while the connectedness ratio is a measure of the number of *orphans*, a term coined to denote terms which have no linkages.[19] Such terms can, of course, only be found if we think of them for ourselves, since by definition no other term will lead us to them. Of the 36,000 entries in the seventh edition of LCSH, some 7,000 were found to be orphans, which seems a rather high proportion; however, Austin found a somewhat similar proportion in PRECIS, which is a much more tightly controlled system than LCSH.

Entry vocabulary and index vocabulary

From the above discussion it should be clear that terms linked by equivalence relationships are rather different from those in the other two groups, in that we select one preferred term and use only that one in our index, whereas the other two kinds of relationship occur between terms which are both used in the index. For example, if we choose **Pressure vessels** as our preferred term, rather than Pressurized containers, then all the information we have in our collection on that subject will be indexed by the term Pressure vessels and none by the term Pressurized containers; users who think of the latter term will find the instruction USE Pressure vessels. By contrast, we shall use **Autoclaves** or **Compressed air** as appropriate, since these are linked to Pressure vessels by Related term references. In our indexing language we will therefore have both preferred terms, which are used for indexing, and non-preferred terms, which are not. The preferred terms on their own form the *index vocabulary*, while the preferred terms and non-preferred terms together form the *entry vocabulary*. The entry vocabulary is very important; there will be many occasions when we decide for one reason or another not to use a particular term, but to use one already in the index vocabulary instead. It is essential that both indexers and searchers should have thorough access to the index vocabulary without having to know the preferred terms in advance. The MEDLARS evaluation project[20] showed very clearly that an inadequate entry vocabulary leads to failures in both recall and relevance, and Lancaster[21] emphasizes the point that terms in the entry vocabulary should reflect not only literary warrant but also enquiry warrant: in other words, not only those terms found in the literature, but also those used by readers looking for information. We must be aware of the terms used by the users of our information retrieval system as well as those used by the authors whose works we are indexing.

The lack of an adequate entry vocabulary is well illustrated by the frustration of trying to find information in a book with a poor index or no index at all. At least the reason for our failures in recall is very obvious in this situation!

Thesaurus construction

The simplest kind of indexing language consists of a list of terms denoting single concepts, showing the semantic relationships between them. Such a list is usually referred to as a *thesaurus*,[22] though in examining some typical examples we shall see that they do not always adhere strictly to the idea of single concepts. This may have practical value. For example, in the ERIC *Thesaurus* we find 'Electronic classrooms' as a pre-coordinated heading; this avoids the false drop of 'electronic equipment in mobile classrooms'. In this chapter, we have discussed the essential points to be noted in constructing such a list, and can now see how they might be put into effect, employing the same techniques of analysis used earlier. Let us consider the titles enumerated in Table 6.4. It quickly appears that they fall into two main groups, literature and metallurgy, and that these groups are homogeneous and distinct; such distinct, homogeneous subjects are called *basic classes*. The next step is to consider each basic class separately to see what principles we can use to analyse them further.

If we look at the titles carefully, we find that in literature, such terms as German, French, English, Spanish and Latin occur, and form a group of *languages*; drama, poetry, novels suggest a group characterized by *literary form*; while seventeenth century, 1901–1915 and 1800– are clearly periods of *time*. If we now go through the whole of the group, we find that all the important concepts fall into one or other of these groups. In metallurgy, we find a number of terms denoting *metals*, either individual or families (e.g. non-ferrous), and others which indicate that some kind of operation is carried out, e.g. heat treatment. These groups, resulting from bringing together concepts which relate to the basic class in the same way, are referred to as *facets* of the subject, and individual concepts within them are known as *foci* (plural of *focus*).

Once we have analysed subjects into basic classes and the appropriate facets, we can identify the relationships within the facets. Each facet will probably contain examples of equivalence relationships: two or more words which represent the same concept. It is the act of defining what they represent that identifies synonyms and near-synonyms, and enables us to decide what action we should take – choose one as preferred term and use the others only in the entry vocabulary, or try to define them in such a way that their use signifies slightly different concepts. For example, in the titles in Table 6.4 we find 'fiction' and 'novel'; 'drama' and 'playwriting'; 'verse' and 'poetry', 'thermal treatment' and 'heat treatment'. We can also identify hierarchical relationships: 'non-ferrous metals' and 'aluminium', 'copper', 'beryllium'; 'iron and steel', which may be identified as 'ferrous metals'; 'rare metals' which is a third group; 'heat treatment' is a method of 'manufacture'. We have already seen that 'German', 'French', 'English', 'Spanish' and 'Latin' fall within the general heading 'Languages'. From the hierarchical relationships we can identify some of the associative relationships; for example, each of the non-ferrous metals has a coordinate relationship with the others.

Table 6.4 Analysis into basic classes and facets

1　The study of literature
2　Select methods of metallurgical analysis
3　The growth of the English novel
4　Elements of heat treatment of metals
5　Modern drama 1800–
6　A textbook of metallurgy
7　Playwriting
8　Methods for the analysis of aluminium
9　The poet's task
10　Iron and steel
11　The French drama of today
12　The metallurgy of beryllium
13　The literature of the Spanish people
14　The manufacture of iron and steel
15　A history of English drama 1600–1900
16　Equipment for the thermal treatment of non-ferrous metals
17　English literature of the twentieth century
18　Rare metals handbook
19　The background of modern English poetry, 1901–1915
20　Methods for the analysis of raw copper
21　Latin literature
22　Heat treatment of aluminium
23　English literature and its readers
24　Heat treatment of steel
25　Some principles of fiction
26　Copper: the science and technology of the metal
27　A short history of German literature
28　Methods for the analysis of iron and steel
29　The temper of the seventeenth century in German literature
30　Twentieth century German verse
31　A few facts about aluminium
32　The decline of the Spanish novel, 1516–1600

We thus have enough information to begin constructing a *thesaurus* covering the subject area of a basic class. Obviously we have a lot more work to do before the thesaurus could be said to be complete or even useable, but once we have recognized the basic structure of facets and hierarchies within them, it will not be too difficult to incorporate new terms as they arise. We must build up our network of linkages, based on the hierarchies and preferably avoiding associative or affinitive links which do not stay within this framework.

From the equivalence relationships that we identify we can decide on which USE and UF links to make. For example, we might decide to prefer Heat treatment:

Heat treatment
   UF   Thermal treatment
Thermal treatment
   USE   Heat treatment

Hierarchical links should modulate, that is, link one step at a time. For example, we have identified three major groups within the metals facet, ferrous metals, non-ferrous metals and rare metals. We will therefore have:

Metals
   NT   Ferrous metals
             Non-ferrous metals
             Rare metals

Within Ferrous metals we have iron and steel, within non-ferrous metals we have aluminium, copper, beryllium. We do not yet have any specific example of rare metals. So we should find the following links:

Ferrous metals
   NT   Iron
             Steel
Non-ferrous metals
   NT   Aluminium
             Beryllium
             Copper

What we must avoid is such links as:

Metals
   NT   Aluminium

This omits a step of division, and opens the way to a situation where every term is related to every other – in which case, of course, we would be equally well off with no links at all. (If the logic of this is not immediately obvious, it is worth giving some thought to the matter; it will be considered again later in relation to some of the thesauri described.)

We can recognize coordinate links as related terms:

Aluminium
   RT   Beryllium
             Copper   [and the same treatment for Beryllium and Copper]
Ferrous metals
   RT   Non-ferrous metals
             Rare metals

We would however *not* have:

Aluminium
   RT   Iron

because Iron is in a different hierarchy.

It has also been recommended that we use caution in making RT links between coordinate headings. Consider the following example:

Vehicles
   NT   Boats
           Ships

In common usage there is overlap between the two headings 'ships' and 'boats', and we should therefore remind users who find one that they should also consider the other. On the other hand, 'oaks' and 'elms' are both NT to 'trees', but there is no overlap in meaning, and therefore no necessity to remind users who find one, of the existence of the other. This is quite true, yet it means that we may have to make a judgement about including an RT link between terms for every term in our hierarchies. The method suggested above is a mechanical means of generating RT links and does not require the exercise of judgement; it does however enable us to maintain control over our network of linkages, and ensure that it is complete, yet without unnecessary cross-references.

To complete the thesaurus, we must arrange our terms in alphabetical order. We may also add some auxiliary sequences, but the basic work of thesaurus construction will have been done. The auxiliary sequences may include a rotated index, to reveal words hidden in multi-word terms, and a hierarchical display, to show the classificatory relationships. While these are not an essential part of a thesaurus, in most cases they are very useful adjuncts, as will be seen from the practical examples discussed in Chapters 25 and 26. It must of course be remembered that the above discussion is an illustration only; there are more than three facets in literature, and more than two in metallurgy, as further examination of the literature would show. However, the process remains the same, and provides us with a sound and reasonably simple method for developing an indexing language. There are now various computer programs to assist in the development and maintenance of thesauri, which vary from the basic to the highly sophisticated needed to maintain a complex thesaurus; the requirements for such programs are discussed in detail by Milstead.[23]

Social science literature may present particular problems if we try to carry out this kind of analysis. Words are often taken over from other subject fields and used with particular meanings – jargon – so that their use in that way is specific to perhaps one branch of the social sciences. 'Political correctness' dictates that certain words should not be used; for example, *illiteracy* may be thought to imply a slur, so it is replaced by *non-readers*, which means that a term with a clear meaning for most people is replaced by one which is vague, and can refer to more than one condition. It may be necessary to include definition notes DF as well as scope notes SN, so that the thesaurus then becomes prescriptive rather than descriptive. Much of the literature in the social sciences falls into the category of 'grey literature', and is not covered by standard bibliographical sources; if the thesaurus is used by field workers who do not have the skills necessary to index the material, the results can be less than satisfactory.[24]

The above technique begins with a study of the words used in a particular subject area, but moves towards the idea of *concept indexing* by eliminating synonyms and recognizing relationships. If we follow this through, we can identify the same basic concept wherever it occurs, even though there may not be any common factor in the words used for it. We might connect stream, current, flux, flow and evolution as being manifestations of motion; expurgation, disinfection, refining, Bowdlerization and whitewashing as being manifestations of cleaning. Such a list is the meaning intended by Roget for the word 'thesaurus' in his *Thesaurus of English words and phrases*, from which the two examples quoted are taken; there are other examples.[25]

Systematic arrangement

The above discussion on showing semantic relationships is related to one method of arrangement, the alphabetical. We can also show relationships by *juxtaposition*, that is, grouping related concepts together in a systematic arrangement to form a *classification scheme*. Such an arrangement will show hierarchical relationships as well as coordinate relationships, and may well also show others such as instruments and materials. In this way, a substantial part of the cross-reference structure required by an alphabetical arrangement is eliminated, because the relationships are shown by the way that the concepts are grouped. We normally arrange books on the shelves of a library in this way in order to help the users, who will, we hope, find all the books they are interested in shelved in the same area.

There is however a price to be paid for this advantage. If we group our preferred terms systematically, then the order in which they occur is no longer self-evident, and we are forced to introduce a *notation* or *code vocabulary* to show the order and enable us to find particular concepts among the systematic arrangement. The entry vocabulary now becomes doubly important, because not only does it contain all the non-preferred terms as well as the preferred terms, but – being arranged alphabetically – it also forms our only means of access to the systematic arrangement, via the code vocabulary. We need to look up the terms in which we are interested in the entry vocabulary, which will tell us what codes have been used to denote them:

Electronics	621.381	(DDC)
Cyclotrons	621.384.61	(UDC)
Preaching	PXP	(BC1)
Disease (Medicine)	L:491	(CC6)
Amplifiers	TK6565.A55	(LCC)

Equivalence relationships are catered for by simply showing the same code for each; in fact, all the entries in the entry vocabulary may be regarded as equivalence relationships, in that they show the heading used for arrangement (in this case a piece of notation) for both preferred and non-preferred terms. In the *schedules* of the scheme, i.e. the list of index vocabulary terms in systematic order, we shall find only the preferred terms.

A further problem arises because, as we have seen already, a concept may appear in more than one hierarchy, where we find both generic, permanent, relationships, and quasi-generic relationships representing applications. So the same basic concept may be represented by more than one code, depending on the context within which it appears:

Tobacco
botany	583.79
hygiene	613.8
social customs	394.1

Systematic arrangement can show many of the categories of relationship we have identified, either by juxtaposition in the schedules or by the complementary juxtaposition of entries in the alphabetical sequence of the entry vocabulary. However, this does not cover all the affinitive/associative group, some of which may actually be hidden by the arrangement. The only way in which these may be drawn to the attention of the indexer or searcher is through cross-references in the schedules or in the entry vocabulary. Unfortunately, such cross-references are the exception rather than the rule in most classification schemes; this may well be a reflection of the fact that only in recent years have we begun to clarify the nature of the relationships which may occur between concepts.

The function of semantic relationships

As we have seen, the inclusion of a network of semantic relationships in our indexing system enables us to improve our indexing or searching formulations by suggesting substitute or additional terms that we may use. At the indexing stage, we are trying to foresee ways in which users will later wish to find a document; at the searching stage, we are trying to achieve a better match between our formulation of a query and the terms used by indexers or authors.

Semantic relationships have therefore the improvement of recall as their primary function, but this may be at the expense of relevance. If we have to substitute another term for the one we first thought of, it *may* be an inferior substitute, though not necessarily; the term we first thought of may itself have been wide of the mark. It is often difficult to find exactly the right term to represent a concept, especially when it is remembered that the searcher is starting from a position of relative ignorance. If however we *are* certain of the right term, then even a synonym may be less acceptable; it may be argued that in the case of terms having connotative meanings there can be no exact synonyms. The merging of synonyms and other equivalence relationships, the groupings achieved by hierarchical and affinitive/associative relationships, are both primarily means of ensuring that more documents are retrieved in response to a query, i.e. they are devices to improve recall. On the other hand, they may be used as devices to improve relevance by enabling indexers or searchers to arrive at the optimum selection of terms to use in a given situation.

References

1 Cleverdon, C. W., Mills, J. and Keen, E. M., *Factors determining the performance of indexing systems*. Cranfield, Aslib-Cranfield Research Project, 1966. 2v in 3.

2 *The concise Oxford dictionary*, Oxford University Press, 6th edn, 1976.

3 *Webster's seventh new collegiate dictionary*, Springfield, Mass, Merriam, 1971.

4 Berlo, D., *The process of communication*, New York, Holt, Rinehart and Winston, 1960. 191–6.

5 Willetts, M., 'An investigation of the nature of the relation between terms in thesauri', *Journal of documentation,* **31** (3), 1975, 158–84.

6 Austin, D., *PRECIS: a manual of concept analysis and subject indexing,* 2nd edn, London, The British Library, 1984, 86–7.

7 Perry, J. W. and Kent, A., *Tools for machine literature searching: semantic code dictionary: equipment: procedures*, New York, Interscience Publishers Inc, 1958.

8 Lancaster, F. W., Elliken, C. and Connell, T. H., 'Subject analysis', *Annual review of information science and technology,* **24**, 1989, 35–84.

9 Jones, K. P., 'Compound words in thesauri', *Journal of documentation,* **37** (2), 1981, 53–68.

10 Ref, 6 above, 62.

11 International Organization for Standardization, *Guidelines for the establishment and development of monolingual thesauri,* Geneva, ISO, 2nd edn, ISO 2788:1986.

12 British Standards Institution, *Guide to establishment and development of monolingual thesauri,* Milton Keynes, BSI, 1987. BS 5723:1987.

13 National Information Standards Organization, *American standard guidelines for the construction, format and management of monolingual thesauri,* Bethesda, MD, NISO, ANSI/NISO Z39.19: 1993.

14 Vickery, B. C. and Vickery, A., 'Online search interface design', *Journal of documentation,* **49** (2), 1993, 103–87.

15 Ref. 6 above, p80.

16 Coates, E. J., *Subject catalogues: headings and structure*, London, Library Association, 1960. (This has been reissued with a new preface, 1988.)

17 Miller, G. A., *Language and communication*, New York, McGraw Hill, 1951. Ch9.

18 Kochen, M. and Tagliacozzo, R., 'A study of cross-referencing', *Journal of documentation,* **24** (3), 1968, 173–91.

19 Sinkankas, G. M., *Study in the syndetic structure of the Library of Congress list of subject headings*, Pittsburgh University, Graduate School of Library and Information Science, 1972. (Pittsburgh studies in library and information sciences 2).

20 Lancaster, F. W., *Evaluation of the MEDLARS Demand Search Service*, Bethesda, MD, National Library of Medicine, 1968.

21 Lancaster, F. W., *Vocabulary control for information retrieval*, 2nd edn, Arlington, VA, Information Resources Press, 1986.
22 Aitchison, J. and Gilchrist, A., *Thesaurus construction: a practical manual*, 2nd edn, London, Aslib, 1987.
    Foskett, D. J., 'Thesaurus', in *Encyclopedia of library and information science*, New York, NY., Dekker, v30, 1980, 416–63.
    Townley, H. M. and Gee, R. D., *Thesaurus making: grow your own word stock*, London, Deutsch, 1980.
23 Milstead, J. L., 'Thesaurus management software', *Encyclopedia of library and information science,* **51**, 1993, 389–407.
24 Hudon, Michèle, 'Term definitions in subject thesauri: the Canadian Literacy Thesaurus experience', in *Classification research for knowledge representation and organization: proceedings of the 5th International study conference on classification research, Toronto, Canada, June 24–28 1991*, Williamson, N. J. and Hudon, M. (eds.), Elsevier, 1992. (FID 698), 255–62.
25 Neaman, J. and Silver, C., *In other words: a thesaurus of euphemisms*, London, Angus & Robertson, 1991, is an entertaining example.

Chapter 7
Assigned indexing 2: Syntax

In the opening sections of the previous chapter we saw that two kinds of relationship were involved in searching: semantic, arising from the need to be able to search for additional or substitute terms; and syntactic, arising out of the need to be able to search for the intersection of two or more classes defined by terms denoting distinct concepts. In this chapter we shall mainly be concerned with the ways in which we can carry out this process of class intersection or *coordination*.

We can approach the problem in two quite different ways. If we use terms from an indexing language to denote the individual concepts present, we are able to coordinate terms at the time of searching by using a computer, as we have seen in Chapter 5. This method is known as *post-coordinate indexing*, and had its origins in physical forms such as Uniterm or optical coincidence cards which have now been superseded by the computer. We may however decide that we want to represent subjects consisting of more than one concept as units, by coordinating the appropriate terms at the time of indexing; this method is known as *pre-coordinate indexing*, and is still very widely used for printed indexes, for subject headings such as LCSH, and for shelf arrangement. In both cases we have to decide whether we are to show syntactic relationships, and if so, how we are to show them. Pre-coordinate indexing involves more problems than post-coordinate; if we can see how to tackle those for pre-coordinate indexing, then post-coordinate indexing becomes relatively simple.

We should clarify one problem of terminology before going further. What is now referred to as post-coordinate indexing was first known as *coordinate indexing*. It was only after the theoretical background had been developed that it was seen that all kinds of indexing involve coordination of concepts, either at the time of indexing or at the time of searching. The terms *pre-coordinate*, to denote indexing in which concepts were coordinated at the time of indexing, and *post-coordinate*, to denote indexing in which concepts were coordinated at the time of searching, were established to clarify the difference while confirming the essential similarity.

We can begin by considering some quite general questions concerning relationships between concepts. In Figure 4.1, we see that all relationships between concepts may be regarded as basically dyadic: that is to say that even if we have several concepts involved in a *composite subject* such as 'the manufacture of multiwall kraft paper sacks for the packaging of cement', we may regard it as a series of *pairs* of concepts linked together. There are three ways in which we can express such a relationship. The first is simply to say that a relationship exists, without specifying what kind of relationship is involved; this is the kind of coordination we get from a

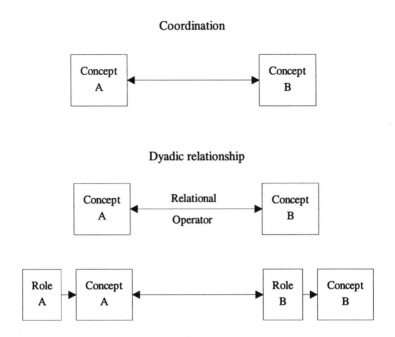

Fig. 7.1 Coordination – methods of showing dyadic relationships

simple computer search for the cooccurrence of two terms. If we use a simple AND link, then we know that the two words occur in the same document—possibly a very tenuous relationship indeed. The second method is to define the kind of relationship that exists between two concepts by using a *relational operator* to link them. Two systems using relational operators have been devised, by J E L Farradane[1] and J C Gardin respectively,[2] but neither has made any significant impact on the general direction of information retrieval systems, though some of their ideas have influenced other workers.

Farradane based his system on the learning process and the way it develops. The system consisted of nine operators, which were used to link terms to construct *analets*. One interesting feature was that an analet did not have to be a linear string of terms; two-dimensional structures were possible, an idea later adopted in PRECIS. Farradane himself claimed that analets were easy to construct, taking about two minutes; experience in the ISILT project[3] was that half an hour was a more realistic figure!

Gardin's scheme arose out of the need for a common method of indexing to be used within the EURATOM group. Only four kinds of relationship were recognized, and these were necessarily very general. The most useful contribution was perhaps Gardin's identification of *a priori* and *a posteriori* relationships: those arising from the structure of knowledge, and those arising from the temporary association of terms in a document. We have used the terms 'semantic' and 'syntactic' to describe these relationships; Gardin went further to suggest that the same relationship may fall into either class depending on the document in which it was found. Semantic relationships are normally permanent, but quasi-generic relationships might be thought to fall within Gardin's claim.

Role indicators

Relational operators are necessarily associated with pre-coordinate indexing, since they permanently link the concepts involved. Role indicators are linked to the concepts to which they refer, and can thus be used in both pre-coordinate and post-coordinate indexing. They are, however, most commonly found in pre-coordinate indexing, where they may be explicit, as in MeSH, or implicit, as in DDC. But before launching into a discussion of how they may be used, we must first define what we mean by the word *role*.

In the previous chapter, we saw that it was possible to identify five broad categories of concept, and this analysis was of value in demonstrating that, apart from adjectival properties, all the concepts were denoted by nouns. However, for most practical purposes analysis into these five categories is only helpful up to a point, and we need to identify more specific categories. We can do this at the general level, to give categories of wide application, e.g. raw material, product; or we can devise categories which fall into one of these general groups but can be given specific names because they relate to specific subject fields, e.g. crops (the *product* in the specific field Agriculture). By placing a concept in one of these categories, we are in effect defining its *role* in relation to concepts in other categories.

We can illustrate the point by considering some examples. 'Heat treatment of metals' involves an *operation* heat treatment on a *patient* metals by an *agent* heat; 'Ultra-high temperature pasteurization of milk' gives us exactly the same categories. 'Aluminium windows' involves a *product* windows made from a *raw material* aluminium: 'plastic bags' gives the same categories. 'Heat treatment of non-ferrous metals', 'welding of plastic bags', 'polyethylene films', may all be analysed in the same way to fit into categories which define their role in relation to the other concepts involved. A particular concept may not always fit into the same category, depending on its role in the subject we wish to represent; for example, in the subject 'extraction of aluminium from bauxite', aluminium is the *end product* and bauxite the *raw material*, with extraction as the *operation*.

Various systems of categories have been devised by different indexers, and these will be discussed in detail as each system is described. The point at issue here is that all these categories represent roles, and are shown as such either explicitly, by the use of some kind of symbol, or implicitly, by their relative position. In pre-coordinate systems we may find either method used; for example, in the heading from BTI 'BOTTLES; polyethylene, blow moulded' the semicolon before polyethylene indicated that it is a *material*, while the comma before blow moulded indicated that this is a *kind* of polyethylene, whereas in the Dewey Decimal Classification notation 823 we know from a study of the structure of this section of the scheme that 2 indicates a *language* (English) and 3 a *literary form* within the class of Literature denoted by 8. In the first example the role indicators are explicit: they appear in the form of additional symbols. In the second case, the role indicators are implicit in the form of the notation. In post-coordinate systems, if role indicators are used at all, they must be explicit; for example, we may find 'Paint (B)' in an index using the American Petroleum Institute list of terms, where (B) indicates *product*, or 'Penicillins-therapeutic use' and 'Penicillins-analysis' in *Index Medicus,* where the roles are spelt out in the form of subheadings.

Combination order

Although we can, obviously, use role indicators with single concepts, we are normally concerned with composite subjects, i.e. those involving two or more concepts. In pre-coordinate systems we assemble these into a *string* of terms corresponding to phrases or sentences in natural language. The question must therefore arise: why do we not use phrases from natural language as they stand? Why go to all the trouble of constructing an artificial syntax as well as an artificial vocabulary? (Artificial in the sense that we control the form of the words, using only nouns or adjectives, and select preferred terms where natural language gives us a free choice.) The reason lies in the flexibility of natural language; just as we may have more than one word denoting the same concept, so we may have more that one grammatical construction to express the same subject. For example, we may say 'manufacture of paper sacks' or 'paper sack manufacture'; 'the process of communication' or 'the communication process'. Clearly we may have a form of equivalence relationship arising not from the semantic association between words but from their syntactic association. Just as we find it advantageous to control semantic equivalents, so we shall achieve consistency only if we control syntactic equivalents in the same way. What this means is that we must decide on the order in which we assemble the terms in a particular string, so that we retain the correct sense but eliminate alternative possibilities.

In all pre-coordinate systems, combination order is a major feature, though not always under that name. In classification schemes it is usually known as *citation order*, while Coates used *significance order* to stress the principle on which he constructed his string of terms. Whatever the name, the principle remains the same: to ensure that the same composite subject is always treated in the same way, no matter how it may be expressed in natural language.

This element of consistency is extremely important, not only from the point of view of the indexer seeking guidance on how to treat a particular subject, but also from the point of view of the user. For the indexer, it is obviously important not to index a document one way if a colleague has already indexed a similar document in another way; research has shown that inter-indexer and even intra-indexer consistency are very hard to achieve,[4] but the problem is surely lessened if there are clear rules to follow.

For the users, the effect is twofold. In the first place, it means that once they have found out how a subject has been indexed, they will find all similar documents, which will presumably have some degree of relevance, indexed in the same way. In the second place, it means *predictability*: the ability to foresee how documents involving other concepts, but in a similar pattern, will be indexed. Some examples will make this clear.

One of the rules used by Coates is that when we have a *Thing* defined by the *Material* of which it is made, the thing precedes the material. The user finding the heading 'Tanks, Aluminium', and learning its meaning, will know on another occasion that the heading wanted is 'Bridges, Concrete'. No such rules are apparent in LCSH; what is the geographer to make of the sequence under the word Geographic. . .? (Preferred terms are in bold type.)

Geographic information systems
Geographic models
    USE Geography, economic—Mathematical models
Geographical distribution of animals and plants
    USE Biogeography
Geographical distribution of man
    USE Human geography
Geographical distribution of plants
    USE Phytogeography
Geographical location codes
Geographical models
    USE Geography—Mathematical models
Geographical museums
Geographical myths
Geographical names
    USE Names, geographical
Geographical photography
    USE Photography in geography
Geography—models
    USE Relief models

Where are we to look for information on the use of **models** in geography? Where might we find information on Geographical features? Such examples are to be found time and time again in LCSH, and their psychological effect on the user must be devastating. If there is a cross-reference to the preferred heading, this can only lessen, not eliminate, the frustration at not being able to guess right the first time, and on the all too frequent occasions when there is no cross-reference, what are we to do? Consistency is a key feature of a sound indexing language.

Some recommended combination orders

The first writer to discuss the order in which terms should appear in a heading for a composite subject was Cutter, who recommended the use of natural language order 'unless some word other than the first is decidedly more significant'. To Cutter, the word 'significant' had a perfectly clear meaning in this context, but this was lost sight of over the years, with consequences discussed in Chapter 8.

Kaiser (Chapter 8) proposed the simple formula Concrete-Process, which is basically sound, and is still used by most modern systems, but does not go far enough. Ranganathan postulated five fundamental categories: Personality; Matter; Energy; Space; Time (cf the five basic categories discussed in the last chapter) and laid down the most famous (or notorious, depending upon one's point of view) combination order PMEST for systematic arrangement, or EMPST for alphabetical headings. Coates (Chapter 8) developed Kaiser's order further to give Thing-Part-Material-Action-Agent, while Vickery (Chapter 9) has proposed Substance (Product)-Organ-Constituent-Structure-Shape-Property-Patient (Raw material)-Action-Operation-Process-Agent-Space-Time.

Fortunately, we do not have to remember all these different answers – and the above is not a complete list – to the same problem. In analysing a particular subject field, a combination order can often be found in the structure of the subject itself, but these generalized proposals serve to remind us of the kind of categories to look for, and ways in which they may usefully be combined. We should also point out that a fixed combination order can present problems, especially in systematic arrangement, where the groupings resulting from the combination order may not suit all our users. These problems are discussed further in Chapter 9. In post-coordinate indexing, where terms are combined at the moment of searching, there are no problems of combination order, but on the other hand we lose the element of meaning provided by the syntax of the string of pre-coordinated terms.

Problems of pre-coordination

What are the problems referred to in the previous paragraphs, and what criteria can we establish for solutions to them? As with the problems discussed so far, we can then measure the particular solutions found in various indexing languages against these criteria.

There are two fundamental problems. The first is that our choice of combination order may not suit all our readers, who may find that we have scattered on the shelves or in the catalogue the concepts that are of primary interest to them. The second is that, as we saw in Chapter 2, any linear representation of multi-dimensional knowledge can only give us direct access to *one* term, the one that comes first in our combination order and thus forms the filing element. In effect, both of these are different aspects of the same problem: the fact that any term after the first is hidden, and cannot be found directly. It should be noted that the problems are the same whether our chosen indexing language gives us alphabetical arrangement or systematic; however, they are probably more acute with systematic arrangement, since the major objective of this is to show relationships by grouping together related subjects in a helpful way. If our groupings do not show the relationships which are of interest to our users, they will prove more of a hindrance than a help. Unfortunately, we have to accept the fact that we can rarely find a combination order that will give grouping of related subjects which will satisfy all our readers, and we must normally aim to please *most* of the people *most* of the time.

There are three different approaches to these problems. The first is to make one *main entry* (ie heading plus document details) and then give access to this from other search points through cross-references. The second is to make *unit* entries: to file copies of the main entry under as many different access points (headings) as are thought necessary. The first method is economical, in that one cross-reference from a non-preferred to a preferred heading will serve no matter how many entries are involved at the preferred heading. However, the second is more satisfactory from the readers' point of view, since it means that they are not referred from the heading they first thought of to one filed somewhere else.

It is important to distinguish between an entry and a cross-reference, since in manual or printed systems the difference can be quite significant economically. Suppose that we have one document, and we are faced with the choice of making one main entry and four cross-references, or five unit entries; either way will give us the same number of entries all told, though the five unit entries will take up more space in a printed index. If we add to the catalogue another nine documents on the same subject, the first method will give us ten main entries and the same four cross-references, while the second would give 50 unit entries. If we now think in terms of 20 similar subjects, the first method would give 200 main entries and 80 cross-references, but the second would give us 1000 unit entries. The distinction is that a main entry contains information about a document, and can therefore relate only to that specific document, whereas a cross-reference links related access points and thus holds good for everything for which those access points are relevant. Both are however entry points into the sequence, and we have to provide an access point under each term that a reader is likely to use in a search, insofar as we can establish this in advance.

Over the years, the economics of the situation have changed. In the days of printed catalogues (and the early days of computer-produced printed catalogues) the cost of added entries was high, and cross-references were used, or possibly abbreviated entries. As card catalogues became the norm, unit entries became more common, particularly with the introduction of printed cards such as those from the Library of Congress; however, there was still the high cost of filing and storing the cards.

The third approach has come with the introduction of MARC records and computer-based catalogues. With a computer-held database, there is only one record with multiple access points, and the distinction ceases to exist. O'Brien[5] suggests that 'Keyword access is a liberating by-product of computerized retrieval, while controlled systems are a legacy of manual catalogs which are two-dimensional browsing systems'. However, there are still many printed bibliographies, for which production costs are high, and we still find the use of cross-references leading to a single main entry.

A distinction should also be made between terms which are in the index vocabulary and those which are in the entry vocabulary. It is usual to make USE cross-references from the latter to the preferred terms; non-preferred terms are not access points. Here again, a sophisticated computer system can automatically take us from a non-preferred term to the preferred access point.

Cross-references

In Table 6.4 we mentioned the subject 'Heat treatment of aluminium'; in most indexing languages this would be entered as:

Aluminium - Heat treatment

using the generally accepted principle that Thing (Concrete) is more significant than Action (Process), and should therefore precede it in the combination order which determines the form of the string of terms we construct. For this particular heading, one method of constructing a cross-reference suggests itself:

Heat treatment - Aluminium USE Aluminium - Heat Treatment

By inverting the terms, we can make an equivalence cross-reference. Alternatively, we may make a hierarchical cross-reference:

Heat treatment NT Aluminium - Heat treatment

But how can we use this straightforward approach if we are indexing an article on 'Ethnic minority adolescents' identity in the new Europe: a trans-cultural approach [using psychotherapy]'? The heading for this in ASSIA is:

Ethnic groups - Young people - Ethnic identity - Psychotherapy - Cultural aspects

Such a heading tries to represent the subject fully, giving a specific single entry , but it raises in an acute form the problems we are considering. In the first place, although we hope that the significance order will enable users to find this straight away, there is no guarantee that this will be successful every time, and we must cater for the user who looks under one of the hidden terms. In the second place, users who are interested in 'Young people' may well wish to know of this article on ethnic minority adolescents.

Chain procedure

Ranganathan specified a method, chain procedure, whereby we can make the minimum number of cross-references, yet still be sure that readers will find an entry point under every significant term in such a composite heading. It was in fact the method used by Dewey to construct the 'Relative index' to his classification, but Ranganathan first identified the theoretical principle. We begin by writing down the 'chain' of terms:

Ethnic groups - Young people - Ethnic identity - Psychotherapy - Cultural aspects

To construct the cross-references, we write down the last term in the chain, following it by each of the preceding terms in turn; this forms the entry under that term, and leads us to the preferred heading in full:

Cultural aspects - Psychotherapy - Ethnic identity - Young people - Ethnic groups
   See
Ethnic groups - Young people - Ethnic identity - Psychotherapy - Cultural aspects

We can now move on to the next to last term, and follow the same procedure:

Psychotherapy - Ethnic identity - Young people - Ethnic groups
   See
Ethnic groups - Young people - Ethnic identity - Psychotherapy

By making similar entries for each significant term we can ensure that we have access to at least part of the heading, beginning with the lead term, no matter which term we think of. If there are n significant terms, then we need $(n-1)$ additional access points.

Computer production means that each entry in ASSIA can be numbered. The entries are filed by the full heading, while the subject index is constructed by chain procedure to lead to the appropriate abstract number(s) rather than the heading. For this example, we find the index entries:

Cultural aspects - Psychotherapy - Ethnic identity - Young people - Ethnic groups   4333
Psychotherapy - Ethnic identity - Young people - Ethnic groups   4333
Ethnic identity - Young people - Ethnic groups   4333
Young people - Ethnic groups   4333
Ethnic groups   4325 – 4333

We also have the related term cross-reference:

Adolescents
   see also
      Young people

This gives us a system of 'main entry', consisting of the full heading, bibliographical reference and abstract, backed up by a subject index giving access at every significant term in the heading, and an author index. The use of abstract numbers rather than headings avoids one of the problems with chain procedure: it may lead us to non-existent headings, or to broader headings than we want. For example, Ethnic groups leads us to several abstracts, because it is a much broader heading than the one used for this particular abstract. We will not find the heading Young people – Ethnic groups except in the reverse order **Ethnic groups – Young people** as *part* of the more specific heading for this abstract. Similarly, a user who looks in the index to DDC under Engineering when what is wanted is Transportation engineering will need to work through the schedules and summaries to get from 620 to 629.04.

Chain procedure is simple and can be easily computerized. It should also logically give the minimum number of additional entries leading to the required heading. However, in experimental situations, for example the EPSILON project,[6] chain procedure does not appear to give the expected economy of entries. The reason for this is not clear, but it is evidently a point to bear in mind. It is to some extent borne out by the findings of *BNB*; the introduction of PRECIS indexing to replace the chain index used from 1950 to 1971 was expected to lead to an increase in the size of the index, but this did not occur. It would be interesting to investigate the reasons why chain indexing does not live up to expectations.

Rotation and permutation

As we saw in Chapter 3, it is possible to construct a KWIC index by keeping the filing position of the key term constant, but moving the full title across the page so that each word appears in the filing position in turn. For example, we might take the ASSIA heading shown above and construct a KWIC-type index:

Ethnic identity - Psychotherapy -   **Cultural aspects/** Ethnic groups - Young people   4333
Psychotherapy-Cultural aspects/   **Ethnic groups-**Young people-Ethnic identity   4333
Ethnic groups-Young people-   **Ethnic identity-**Psychotherapy-Cultural aspects/   4333
Young people-Ethnic identity-   **Psychotherapy-**Cultural aspects/ Ethnic groups   4333
Cultural aspects/ Ethnic groups   **Young people-**Ethnic identity-Psychotherapy   4333

This kind of index is a *rotated index*,[7] and, as mentioned in Chapter 3, it is most often found as a supplement to thesauri, to reveal hidden words in multi-word headings.

Permutation is a mathematical term referring to the construction of all possible arrangements of a given set of elements; if we have the three elements A, B, C then there are six possible arrangements or permutations:

ABC;   ACB;   BCA;   BAC;   CAB;   CBA

The number of permutations of n things is $n!$ (n factorial = $n \times n-1 \times n-2 \ldots 3 \times 2 \times 1$), so that for the heading looked at above we would have 5! or 120 possible entries, rather than the five that we constructed using rotation. For reasons which are not clear, rotated indexes in thesauri are often referred to as *permuted* indexes, but this name is unsound and should be avoided.

Multiple entry

So far we have considered the situation where we make one main entry supported by indexes of various kinds. The alternative is to make unit entries, where an entry having the full details is filed at each appropriate heading. The example of chain procedure given earlier came from the British publication ASSIA; unit entry is more common in American indexes such as *PAIS International*. For example, the following entry is found under three headings:

Seeger, N. Liechtenstein: the differential tax treatment of offshore and domestic enterprises, *Bul Internat Fiscal Docum, 48* 579–81 N 1994 [four-line abstract]

The headings and subheadings used are:

International business enterprises – location
Liechtenstein – Tax policy
Taxation – Liechtenstein

There is also a cross-reference:

Business enterprises
　See also
International business enterprises

A similar comparison can be made between *Library and information science abstracts* (British) and *Library literature* (American). The following article is covered by both:

Klein, S. S. 'Your right to privacy and the AIDS virus: a selective bibliography', *Legal reference services quarterly, 13* (3) 1994, 115–127.

In LISA there is one entry 94–2955, with abstract, under the heading **Collection development.** In the subject index, we find:

Privacy – Patients – Acquired Immune Deficiency Syndrome – Bibliographies – Selection aids – Acquisitions   2955
Patients – Acquired Immune Deficiency Syndrome – Bibliographies – Selection aids – Acquisitions   2955
Acquired Immune Deficiency Syndrome – Bibliographies – Selection aids – Acquisitions   2955
Bibliographies – Selection aids – Acquisitions   . . . 2955 . . .
Selection aids – Acquisitions   . . . 2955 . . .
Acquisitions   . . . 2955 . . .[twelve blocks of entries, one for each month]

and an entry for Klein, S. S. in the separate author index.

In *Library literature* we find three entries and a cross-reference in the single dictionary sequence:

Right of privacy – Bibliography
Legal literature – Bibliography
Klein, Sandra S.
Bibliography
　　See also subhead Bibliography under specific subjects and under specific types of literature.

Phase relationships

So far, we have made the assumption that it is possible to construct a string of terms, using syntactic relationships either implicitly, or explicitly in the form of role indicators, to produce a consistent representation of any given simple or composite subject (i.e. involving only one concept or several), and then manipulate this string according to various straightforward methods to enable users to find them not merely through the term denoting what we consider to be the most important concept, but through any of the other terms as well. We may not explicitly indicate the role or category into which a particular term falls, but we make the assumption that this will be evident from the context. The examples we have looked at so far do in fact justify these assumptions.

If we consider Table 7.1, however, we can see that we have not yet made provision for the kinds of relationship demonstrated. The term used to denote such relationships is that coined by Ranganathan, *phase relationships*, and we can identify four particular kinds.[8] In the first group we find subjects treated with a particular audience in mind; the subject itself remains the same, but the examples used to illustrate it will come from the subject interest of the intended audience. An introductory book on statistics written for librarians may well be of use to a business student, but it is unlikely to be of much use to a student wanting a book on, say, reference work. In these examples of *bias phase*, the subject treated is the subject of the book, not the intended audience.

In the second group, we see one subject influence by another; in these examples of *influence phase*, it is the subject influenced which is the core. In the third, *exposition phase*, it is the subject expounded, not the 'tool' subject, which is the significant one. In the fourth group, showing *comparison* or *interaction*, we find that both subjects are of equal importance.

Table 7.1 Phase relationships

1	Middle management for nurses
2	Fluid mechanics for civil engineers
3	Basic statistics for librarians
4	Methylmercury in fish: effects on human health
5	The literary impact of *The golden bough*
6	The effect of PAS on the resistance to streptomycin of tubercle bacilli
7	Typewriter behaviour: psychology applied to teaching and learning typewriting
8	Literature through art: a new approach to French literature
9	Hamlet: an analytic and psychologic study
10	Science and politics
11	Church and state
12	Religion and science

When we come to try and write strings to represent phase relationships fully, we find that we are obliged to make them explicit by using terms to denote the kind of relationship involved. For example, the heading:

Aluminium – heat treatment

does not use prepositions, yet few users could misunderstand it. Even the much more complex subject quoted earlier:

Ethnic groups – Young people – Ethnic identity – Psychotherapy – Cultural aspects

takes very little effort to comprehend. By contrast, if we omit the subsidiary words, the headings:

Middle management – nurses
English literature – *The golden bough* (instead of *The golden bough* – influence on English literature)
French literature: art (instead of French literature – exposition through art)
Science: politics

are either ambiguous or misleading. Phase relationships can be recognized by this characteristic: the need to make the kind of relationship explicit – in an alphabetical system by the use of words denoting such as ideas as *influence, effect, audience, interaction, comparison,* in a classified system by the use of notation such as –024 . . . in DDC. There is a further point about phase relationships which it is essential to grasp. They are necessarily *ad hoc* relationships; though we know in advance that books will be written in which one subject is treated in comparison with another, or to show how it has been influenced by another, or with a particular audience in mind, we cannot know which subjects will be so treated. Phase relationships cannot be predicted in the same way that we can predict that, for example, metals will be subjected to various forms of treatment, or that crops will be affected by pests. All that we can do is to make adequate provision for them by recognizing the possibility of their occurrence.

In the first three kinds shown in Table 7.1, we can identify one of the two concepts as the key concept. In bias phase, where a subject is treated for a particular audience, it is the subject treated which is the primary phase; in influence phase, it is the subject influenced; in exposition phase, it is the subject expounded. In these three cases it is possible to construct a string of terms which will represent the subject unambiguously, and we can construct cross-references by changing the connecting words or the order. Thus we may have:

Statistics *for* librarians
Librarians – statistics *for*
The golden bough – *influence on* English literature
English literature – *influence of The golden bough*
French literature – *expounded through* Art
Art – *expounding* French literature

However, the only way we can deal with the interaction relationship, which could be regarded as a two-way influence, is by treating both concepts involved as being of equal importance.

Science *in relation to* Politics
Politics *in relation to* Science

We might use the word *and*, as in Science *and* Politics, but this may be misleading. If we have a typical physics textbook entitled *Mechanics, heat, and sound*, we can be confident that this is a physical association of three separate works within one pair of covers as an economy measure, rather than showing some kind of interaction. If we have a work on *The mining of silver and lead*, we have in fact two separate subjects: the mining of silver, and the mining of lead. When Quintin Hogg wrote *Science and politics*, he was writing about their interaction: the effect that political decisions may have on science, for example by deciding which projects receive funding, and conversely, the effect that science may have on politics, for example by enabling politicians to reach a world-wide television audience. We might, however, have a work which dealt with 'the science of politics', discussing the methods by which decisions are made and implemented. This would be a permanent relationship, not the kind of interaction that we have been discussing.

In concluding this discussion of syntactic relationships, perhaps it is worth offering a word of warning. As Gardin pointed out, syntax and semantics go together, and should be regarded as two aspects of the process of formulating clear and unambiguous statements of a subject and its relationships. A sentence may fulfil every requirement of syntax yet be meaningless: Austin[9] quotes Chomsky's well-known example 'Colourless green ideas sleep furiously'. Equally, the same words with different syntax may have totally different meanings: to quote one of Austin's own examples, 'pollution of oil by water' is by no means the same as 'pollution of water by oil', though the words used are identical.

The purpose of syntactic relationships

We saw that the purpose of semantic relationships was to enable us to improve the recall performance of our system. By contrast, the purpose of syntactic relationships is to enable us to improve the relevance performance, by allowing us to specify subjects more precisely. We can do this through semantic relationships to some extent, by realizing that there is a more specific term than the one we first thought of, but the most powerful method of increasing specificity is by coordination. The specificity of an indexing language has to be measured not only in terms of its vocabulary, but also by the amount of coordination that it permits. We saw in Chapter 5 that coordination through the uncontrolled use of the Boolean AND could lead to failure, but in an assigned indexing system, terms are coordinated when and only when that is appropriate. To use one of the examples already cited, if we find Young people – Ethnic groups among the indexing terms, we *know* that there is information to be found by combining those terms.

Closed and open systems

If we are to be consistent in the use of an indexing language, we must record somewhere any decisions that we take, for example on the choice of preferred synonyms or significance order. The record thus compiled becomes our *authority file*, and it may be entirely our own or it may be based to a greater or lesser degree on a published list. In the interests of standardization, it is usual for libraries to make use of published lists, and indeed Parts III and IV of this work are given over to descriptions of such schemes. However, they may present a problem summed up in Ranganathan's phrase: *autonomy for the classifier.*

Knowledge, as we have stressed, is not static, and an indexing language needs continuous revision if it is to remain current. Furthermore, since general schemes may relate to the literary warrant of a particular collection, or to that of a hypothetical collection, they may exclude some subjects which we find represented in our collections. What are we to do if we find that this is the case? Can we insert a new heading in the authority file ourselves, or must we wait until the compilers have produced a new edition or an amendment sheet? If the first of these is the case, the system is said to be *open*, while the second situation is a *closed* system. Dewey saw the problem at an early stage, and suggested that if a particular topic was not represented in his scheme, we should classify the document at the nearest inclusive heading, on the theory that new subjects usually arise from the splitting up, or 'fission' of already existing subjects. The compilers would then make a place for the new topic in subsequent editions, an optimistic hope which has not always been borne out by practice. As we saw in Chapter 1, the growth of new subjects by fission was normal in the discipline-oriented era, and Dewey's solution was therefore quite reasonable at the time – though it is fair to point out that it made no provision for phase relationships, particularly those in which it is not possible to identify the key subject. The 'nearest inclusive heading' solution presents the indexer with an impossible choice in trying to find a place for a new subject which has developed through the fusion of previously separate disciplines, while the multi-disciplinary approach of the mission-oriented era is obviously precluded by an approach dependent on the unambiguous separation of established disciplines.

Since alphabetical order is self-evident, it is rather easier to insert a new heading into an alphabetical list than into one which is systematically arranged; all that we need to know is the form of a heading, e.g. whether we should use the singular or plural form of a noun. Alphabetical lists such as LCSH and Sears have rules for the insertion of headings for named individuals of a species, e.g. persons, flowers, places, animals. There are also 'pattern headings' showing the model on which we should construct headings dealing with works about, say, specific authors and their oeuvres.

It is rather more difficult to establish in advance the correct notation for a new topic in a classification scheme, since we are dealing with a wholly artificial language, and no satisfactory solution has been proposed. Ranganathan's *seminal mnemonics*, discussed in Chapter 21, offer a temporary solution, but one in which the arrangement is dictated by the notation rather than by the needs of the subject. It is for this reason that the method of revision adopted by a classification scheme is so important, and this point is discussed in relation to each of the schemes studied in Part III.

Enumeration and synthesis

In a pre-coordinate indexing language we have to provide for both single concepts and composite subjects, and the problems of a closed system become that much more acute. Older systems set out to list, or *enumerate*, all the subjects which seemed appropriate, both single concepts and composite, leaving the individual classifier no autonomy to insert new subjects which might arise in a particular collection.

More recent schemes tend to use *synthesis* to cater for composite subjects. Such schemes list only single concepts, but give the classifier rules for the construction of headings for composite subjects. The method is obviously a great deal more powerful than the purely enumerative, but does depend on the individual concepts being listed, or there being rules for the construction of headings for them. A synthetic language is thus a great deal more open that an enumerative one, but may still not give the indexer complete autonomy. It is for this reason that many special libraries which deal with new subjects arising from research have avoided being tied to a possibly out-of-date published list by constructing their own indexing languages, systematic or alphabetic.

As we have emphasized, phase relationships are essentially *ad hoc*: it is therefore very difficult to deal with them in an enumerative scheme. Only those relationships which have already arisen can be enumerated; thus in DDC we find 'Religion and science' because that was the subject of a number of books by the time that Dewey constructed his classification in 1876, arising out of the publication, among other significant works, of Darwin's *Origin of species* in 1859 – but we shall look in vain for 'Science and politics'. A synthetic scheme can make provision for phase relationships much more easily.

There is of course no hard and fast line between the two types of system; we may expect to find a complete range between the closed enumerative scheme where the indexer has no freedom at all, and the open synthetic scheme which permits the indexer to specify any subject which arises. Most systems fall somewhere between the two extremes, and it should perhaps be mentioned that although one of the advantages claimed for post-coordinate schemes is that they are much freer than pre-coordinate schemes, this is not necessarily the case. A language such as that used in ASSIA can be almost unrestricted, while some thesauri offer a strictly limited vocabulary.

Critical classification

Indexers are intermediaries between authors and users: to what extent are they justified in imposing their own ideas and prejudices? The immediate answer is, not at all, but in practice this is very difficult to achieve. An indexing language inevitably reflects the social and cultural background of its compiler, and while it serves users of a similar persuasion this is not necessarily a bad thing; it is when we try to impose one culture on users of another that problems are likely to arise. Examples of chauvinism used to be common, though fortunately most of those in LCSH and Sears have gone:

World War II: Germany's Conquest of Europe, Rescue by the United States (BC1)

or we may find genuine differences of approach:

compare the schedules for *government* in, say LCC and CC
or *education* in UDC (European view) and LCC (US)

or invidious distinctions:

Disabled USE Handicapped   (LCSH)
Disabled students USE Handicapped students
Disabled veterans USE Veterans, Disabled

or intellectual arrogance:

821.9 Minor poets [e.g. John Donne!] (early editions of DDC)

or euphemism ('political correctness'):

Falkland Islands
   SN As a geographic subdivision this heading is used directly (LCSH)

This neatly avoids the question of whether the standard *indirect* entry should include Argentina or Great Britain!

Whatever the reason, *critical classification* – the imposition of the indexer's viewpoint on the user – is found rather more widely than we would wish to admit.[10] Even such schemes as UDC, which has a definite international policy, are not entirely free from bias.

Prior to the 10th edition, 1986, LCSH had no heading for Muhammad; at the entry for **Islam,** there was a scope note: Here are entered works on the religion of which Muhammad is the prophet. In the 10th edition, LCSH introduced the heading **Muhammad d.632**, thus offending a large proportion of the Islamic world by ignoring his status as Prophet.[11] In the 11th edition of LCSH the heading was changed to **Muhammad, Prophet, d.632** The indexer should be careful not to introduce bias unwittingly, and the user has to be aware of its possible existence, if our systems are to achieve the objective of making information freely available to all who ask.

Indexing languages

A system for naming subjects in the way that we have described is called an *indexing language,* and, like any other language, it will consist of two parts: *vocabulary* and *syntax*. If we use terms as they appear in documents without modification, we are using *natural language*. However, as we have seen, this can lead to problems. Where vocabulary is concerned, different authors may use different terms to express the same idea – synonyms – leading to a decrease in recall. Where syntax is concerned, the same idea may be expressed in more than one way: child psychology or psychology of children; adult education or education of adults. For these reasons, assigned indexing systems introduce a measure of control over the terms used: we use a *controlled vocabulary*. We also formalize the flexible syntax of natural language by permitting only certain constructions: instead of heat treatment of aluminium, we use aluminium – heat treatment; instead of using libraries for children, or children's libraries, we use libraries, children's. We are then using a *structured language*. A controlled vocabulary and formalized structure are features of an *artificial indexing language*. The extreme example of an artificial language is the notation of a classification scheme; instead of the natural language terms, heat treatment of aluminium, or the more formalized aluminium – heat treatment, we use 669.71.04.

The use of an artificial language enables us to use *concept indexing* rather than *term indexing*. In term indexing we rely on the words used by each author to give us the subject descriptions we require, and hope that when we are trying to find information we can match the different words used by different authors; this is the word matching that we use in carrying out a keyword search by computer. In concept indexing, we try to establish a standard description for each concept and use that description each time it is appropriate, whether it has been used by the author or not. When we are searching our files, we again use the standardized description, and should be able to match these more consistently and reliably. Natural language is very flexible, particularly in a highly developed language such as English; this is a tremendous advantage for authors, who can vary their terminology to maintain the reader's interest, but it is a handicap for the indexer, who is more concerned with the ideas conveyed than with the niceties of a graceful literary style.

If we use words for our subject descriptions, then the only way in which we can arrange them is alphabetically; if we try to arrange them any other way we shall not be able to find them when we want them. But there are many occasions when alphabetical arrangement may not be particularly helpful; for example, if we want to follow the progress of a railway train, an alphabetical list of stops will be of much less use than a chronological sequence. An artificial language such as the notation of a classification scheme enables us to arrange concepts in any order we wish, and improve our chances of finding information when we look for it, organized in the way that we want it. An assigned indexing language involves work on the part of the indexer and of the searcher; in return, it should help us to improve both recall and relevance as needed.

Relevance and 'aboutness'

So far, we have assumed that we can decide what documents are about, and what kind of information is sought by readers, so that we can make judgements on which documents are relevant to a particular request. In discussing retrieval in computer-based systems, we assumed that by matching the words of a reader's enquiry with those used in the document, perhaps using various devices to modify the original request, we could locate documents which would meet the reader's needs. In manual systems, we have indicated ways in which we could construct and manipulate headings which should enable us to match readers' needs. How can we allocate such headings appropriately? How do readers decide whether a particular document is relevant or not? What are the criteria for judging the performance of the indexer/searcher or computer? As we have seen, relevance is a subjective judgement, so we should not expect any easy answer to this question, but we can look at some of the ideas which have been proposed.

At the beginning of Chapter 3 we looked at some of the ways in which we might establish the subject of a document; from this we can agree with Hutchins[12] when he quotes the PRECIS manual[13] to the effect that 'the indexer, having examined the document, has established in his mind some meaningful sequence of words which summarizes its subject matter'. This is a reasonable description of a practical technique, but it does not really take us much further. Hutchins suggests one way in which we might decide what a document is about, based on linguistic structures. In any piece of text, there will be certain information which the author states as 'given', i.e. he/she assumes that it will already be known to the reader. There will be other information which is assumed to be 'new', i.e. not already known to the reader. So in reviewing a document for indexing purposes, we can identify the given information and the new information as two separate packages. Readers can also be divided into two groups: the novice, who knows little about the subject but wishes to learn something of it, and the expert, who knows a great deal about the subject but wishes to extend his or her knowledge if possible. (As mentioned earlier the real world is grey, not black and white, but the generalization does reflect to a large extent the provision of library services: the public library caters largely for the generalist, and the special library largely for the specialist.) Ideally, the 'given' information in a document should match the reader's knowledge at the time, while the 'new' information should match the current need. Since the communication process is not as precise as this, we shall not be able to match this model exactly, but it is a goal at which we can aim. We need therefore to be clear as to which type of reader we are trying to serve.

A computer cannot distinguish between 'given' and 'new' information. The 'given' information is unlikely to exceed the expert's knowledge, while any 'new' information is welcome, and the expert is thus likely to be satisfied with the results of a computer search. On the other hand, as Hutchins argues, for beginners it is better to use only the 'given' information as a basis for indexing, since this will lead to the kind of documents which will best meet the need for them to enlarge their existing knowledge.

In practice, we find that indexers in general libraries do indeed rely largely on those parts of the document where the author sets out the assumed knowledge which forms the basis of a work: preface, introduction, contents list and so on. By contrast, indexers in special libraries do tend to use depth indexing of as many themes in the document as possible. Hutchins points out that abstracting services provide a ready-made summarization of the document, including both given and new information, and thus meet the needs of the expert for whom they are usually intended. This is in line with the results of evaluation experiments such as Cranfield 2,[14] which showed that systems based on abstracts appear to give optimum results. Lancaster has argued strongly that abstracting and indexing are two sides of the same coin.[15]

At the same colloquium, Swift[16] argued that the criteria for aboutness which are useful in science and technology may not be so helpful in the social sciences. This point has been taken up again more recently by Ellis[17] and Pickens.[18] Ellis suggests that social scientists follow rather different information gathering patterns from scientists and technologists, while Pickens proposes that database structure should be geared more closely to the needs of the users. For example, Education has four major fields: subjects; content; zone; and form. Subjects (educands) may be characterized by age or by institution; content (subject matter) may be characterized by descriptors, which may be major or minor; zone (place) may be place of origin or place written about; and form (document type) is important is matching the kind of document to the reader. In the ERIC database, all of these are catered for, but in the same descriptor field, with the exception of place, which is treated as an identifier. It would be more helpful for the typical user if they were treated separately. Pickens suggests that database design is still being constrained by past limitations (of information technology) which are no longer important.

Lancaster[19] identifies the same factors in a slightly different way. 'Aboutness' may be regarded as *intrinsic* – the subject of the document – or *extrinsic* – external considerations such as the purpose for which a document is required, or by whom. Document descriptions, queries and matching algorithms are all interdependent and should not be considered in isolation. We should also distinguish between index language devices such as roles, and indexing/searching devices such as weighting. Roles are essentially part of the input process, in which the indexer seeks to add to the specificity of the indexing; they are thus tied to the indexer's view of relevance. Weighting is normally part of the search process, and reflects the user's assessment of relevance. As discussed in Chapter 5, Maron suggests that by calculating the weighting of each cell w_{ij} in the document-term matrix, we can arrive at a measure of the 'aboutness' of a document as the weighted column vector for that document.[20]

We must also consider the different ways in which progress is made in different subject areas. Science progresses essentially by consensus,[21] whereas progress in the social sciences and humanities is normally based on a process of dialectic, and consensus is not the primary objective. As we have seen, relevance is a consensus judgement, which may thus not be appropriate beyond the fields of science and technology.

Consistency

We have seen that consistency is a very important factor in successful information retrieval. We need consistency in our choice of terms to represent particular concepts, and also in the way that we represent composite subjects, but there are a number of factors which militate against this. Some of these relate to the indexers; since we are all individuals, we all have our own particular frame of reference, our own educational background, our own experience of life, it may be difficult for us to be consistent one with another in the way that we interpret what we are trying to index. Our own views change with time; as Heraclitus pointed out, it is not possible to step twice into the same river. There is an inherent tendency towards inconsistency. How can we counteract this?

In this and the previous chapter we have looked at various ways in which we can try to achieve consistency. If we have clear rules on the selection of terms, set out in a controlled vocabulary, we are more likely to be consistent than if we rely solely on the words used by authors. If we have clear rules on how to treat composite subjects, again we are more likely to be consistent than if we have none. The amount of time spent on indexing a document will affect the way we index it. Too little, and we can only skim the surface, without fully grasping the full import of a document; too much, and we may begin to dream up unlikely aspects which will not be helpful to those who eventually retrieve the document. Experience of both indexing and retrieval is important; the days when cataloguers could sit in the back room without ever having to meet the people they were supposed to be helping are fortunately dead, at least in most situations. However, it is likely that we will have to accept that inconsistency is a hazard that we must live with, and be prepared to cope with it, while trying to keep it to a minimum.[22] Unfortunately, it seems that hypertext links are just as liable to inconsistency as any other kind of indexing,[23] and the ease with which bookmarks can be created in the World Wide Web suggests that they too can present a fruitful source of problems!

Summary

We have seen that a substantial proportion of information retrieval is now carried out by computer, relying on the natural language of the documents in the database. We have also seen that for certain purposes – shelf arrangement, printed indexes – this is not useful, and that we need to assign index terms to documents to replace the text; this indexing may also be of value in computer searching to supplement the text in certain cases. A set of terms, together with relationships between them, can form an indexing language, with a vocabulary and possibly also syntax. The needs of users may differ from discipline to discipline, making it difficult to establish a generally acceptable measure of 'aboutness'. Inconsistency, both intra-indexer and inter-indexer, is a permanent feature of all information retrieval systems. However, the purpose of those systems remains that of matching the needs of readers to the output of authors as effectively and efficiently as possible.

References

1 Farradane, J. E. L. *et al.*, *Report on research into information retrieval by relational indexing: part 1: methodology.* London, City University, 1966.
2 Gardin, J. C., *Syntol*, Rutgers, The State University School of Library Science, 1965. (Rutgers series on systems for the intellectual organization of information.)
3 Keen, E. M. and Digger, J., *Report of an information science index languages test.* Aberystwyth, College of Librarianship Wales, 1972. 2v.
4 Chan, L. M., 'Interindexer consistency in subject cataloging', *Information technology and libraries,* **8**, 1989, 349–58.
5 O'Brien, A., 'Online catalogs: enhancements and developments', *Annual review of information science and technology,* **29**, 1994, 219–42.

6   Keen, E. M., 'On the generation and searching of entries in printed subject indexes', *Journal of documentation,* **33** (1), 1977, 15–45.
Keen, E. M., 'On the processing of printed subject index entries during searching', *Journal of documentation,* **33** (4), 1977, 266–76.
Keen, E. M., *On the performance of nine printed index types: a selective report of EPSILON,* Aberystwyth, College of Librarianship Wales, 1978.
7   Foskett, D. J., 'Two notes on indexing techniques', *Journal of documentation,* **18** (4), 1962, 188–92.
8   The phase relationships demonstrated here are those identified by *BNB.*
9   Chomsky, N., quoted by Austin in the PRECIS *Manual,* 1st edn, Chapter 16.
10   Berman, S. *Prejudices and antipathies,* Metuchen, NJ, Scarecrow Press, 1971.
Berman, S., *Worth noting: editorials, letters, essays, an interview and bibliography, with a foreword by Bill Katz,* Jefferson, NC, McFarlane, c1988.
Much of Berman's writing is concerned with this aspect of indexing languages.
Fina, M., 'The role of subject headings in access to information: the experience of one Spanish-speaking patron', *Cataloging and classification quarterly,* **17** (1/2), 1993, 267–74. (The WASP bias causes problems for minority groups.)
Foskett, A. C., 'Misogynists all: a study in critical classification', *Library resources and technical services,* **15** (4), Spring 1971, 117–21.
Foskett, A. C., 'Better dead than read: further studies in critical classification', *Library resources and technical services,* **28** (4), Oct/Dec. 1984, 346–59.
Rogers, M. N., 'Are we on equal terms yet? Subject headings concerning women in LCSH 1975–1991' *Library resources and technical services,* **37** (2), 1993, 181–96.
Wilson, A. 'The hierarchy of belief: ideological tendentiousness in universal classification', in *Classification research for knowledge representation and organization: proceedings of the 5th International study conference on classification research, Toronto, Canada, June 24–28 1991,* Williamson, N. J. and Hudon, M. (eds.), Elsevier, 1992. (FID 698), 389–97.
11   Sheriff, S., 'Library of Congress insults Islam', *Library Association record,* **88** (8), August 1986, 371.
12   Hutchins, W. J., 'The concept of 'aboutness' in subject indexing', *Aslib proceedings,* **30** (5), 1978, 172–81. Coordinate Indexing Group Colloquium on aboutness, April 1977.
13   Austin, D., *PRECIS: a manual of concept analysis and subject indexing,* London, British National Bibliography, 1974, 4.
14   Cleverdon, C. W., Keen, E. M. and Mills, J., *Factors determining the performance of indexing systems.* Cranfield, Aslib–Cranfield Research Project, 1966. 2v. in 3.
15   Lancaster, F. W., *Indexing and abstracting in theory and practice,* London, Library Association, 1991.
16   Swift, D. F., Winn, V. and Bramer, D., '"Aboutness" as a strategy for retrieval in the social sciences', *Aslib proceedings,* **30** (5), 1978, 182–7. Coordinate Indexing Group Colloquium on aboutness, April 1977.
17   Ellis, D., 'A behavioural approach to information retrieval system design',

Journal of documentation, **45** (3), 1989, 171–212.

18 Pickens, K., 'The relationship of bibliographic database design to the structure of information: a case study in education', *Journal of documentation,* **50** (1), March 1994, 36–44.

19 Lancaster, F. W., Elliken, C. and Connell, T. H., 'Subject analysis', *Annual review of information science and technology,* **24**, 1989, 35–84.

20 Maron, M. E., 'On indexing, retrieval and the meaning of about', *Journal of the American Society for Information Science,* **28** (1), 1977, 38–43.
Stone, A. J., 'That elusive quality of "aboutness": the year's work in subject analysis, 1992', *Library resources and technical services,* **37** (3), 1993, 277–98.

21 Ziman, J., *Public knowledge: the social dimension of science,* Cambridge, Cambridge University Press, 1969.

22 Leonard, L. E., *Inter-indexer consistency studies 1954–1975: a review of the literature and a summary of study results,* Urbana, IL, University of Illinois Graduate School of Library Science, Occasional papers No 131.

23 Ellis, D., Turner-Hines, J. and Willett, P., 'On the creation of hypertext links in full-text documents: measurements of interlinker consistency', *Journal of documentation,* **50** (2), 1994, 67–98.
Langford, D. and Brown, P., 'Creating hypertext comments: is it worth the effort?', *Aslib proceedings,* **45** (4), 1993, 91–5. Suggests the use of commentary (hidden text) to explain reasons for links.

Part II
Pre-coordinate indexing systems

Chapter 8

Alphabetical subject headings: Cutter to Austin

Cutter

The first attempt to establish a generalized set of rules for alphabetical subject headings was Charles Ammi Cutter's *Rules for a dictionary catalogue,* published in 1876[1] (the year which also saw the first edition of Dewey's *Decimal classification*: truly an *annus mirabilis*!). Cutter had been brought up within a particular educational frame of reference, which coloured his whole approach to the question of what was, or was not, an acceptable heading in an alphabetical subject catalogue. He viewed knowledge within a classificatory framework where every *subject* had its predetermined place based on the way in which it had developed. New ideas which had not yet found their permanent place within the framework were not *subjects* but *topics*. Subjects had names, which were known to everybody – or at least that majority of the educated population who had had the same kind of education as Cutter. Once a topic had become established within its proper place, and given a name, it became a subject. When a subject name consisted of more than one word, the classificatory structure from which it was derived indicated which word was the most significant. Cutter used 'natural language' for his headings, but it was natural language constrained by carefully defined rules.[2] We shall see this approach repeated in the 'scientific and educational consensus' which formed the basis of the work of H. E. Bliss.

Without a knowledge of the basis for Cutter's thinking, we may well find problems with some of his examples. A subject name was one that was 'generally accepted', but it is often difficult for us to see why one term was to be treated as 'generally accepted' while another very similar term was not. For example, the heading:

Circulation of the blood

is acceptable, but the very similar

Movement of fluids in plants

is not. Some odd phrases *may* be used 'if the name is accepted by usage or likely to be accepted by usage', e.g.

Capture of property at sea

but the more probable

    Gothic architecture in Spain

is not. The cataloguer was of course expected to be familiar with the consensus, and therefore able to use judgement as to what constituted accepted usage.

The classificatory background to Cutter's thinking is also shown by another very important rule that he introduced. This was the idea of *specific entry*: a subject was to be entered under its name, not that of an inclusive class. If we consider this carefully, we realize that what Cutter was referring to was *direct entry*, rather than specific. 'Cats' is the heading to be used, not 'Domestic animals – cats' or some similar *indirect* entry, i.e. entry under one or a series of containing classes.

We have used the term specific in this text in the sense of making a heading coextensive with the subject it is intended to represent; Cutter, with his reliance on accepted names, recommends that when there is no name for the subject being dealt with, two or more entries should be made which together cover the subject. Thus 'Gothic architecture in Spain' must be entered under 'Gothic architecture' and 'Spain: *architecture*'. In effect, to find the documents having the specific subject we need, we have to find the intersection of two or more classes; now we have seen that the act of coordinating at the time of searching is a characteristic of post-coordinate systems, which use physical forms which permit this. Cutter was thinking of the printed book catalogue or the card catalogue, which do *not* lend themselves to this approach. Yet Cutter's idea of double entry, or if necessary multiple entry, is still very widely accepted in order to retain as far as possible 'names in common usage' as headings, and avoid the use of complex but specific headings of the kind advocated in this book. For example, we are told that 'a phrase Mathematics in secondary schools . . . would need to be reduced . . . to the two code terms Mathematics and Secondary schools, *both of which are specific*'.[3] [Italics added] If we accept the meaning of *specific* used in this book, it is the coordination of the two terms which gives the specific subject in this instance; neither term is specific on its own *in relation to this particular document*.

The question of where we draw the line also arises: 'Secondary schools' is acceptable, although it is actually a composite subject involving *institution* and *level*, so why not 'Secondary school mathematics' a composite subject involving *institution*, *level* and *curriculum subject*? It could be argued that this is a name in common usage to at least the same extent as some of the headings in LCSH.

Cutter went on using his system of subject headings, but the rest of his life was devoted to the development of his classification scheme, and he appears to have devoted no more effort to refining his *Rules*. By the time the Library of Congress opened its new building in 1897, and with it its new dictionary catalogue, the essential philosophical structure of Cutter's thinking had been lost. As discussed in Chapter 23, the two people most involved, J. C. M. Hanson and C. Martel, adopted a pragmatic approach where Cutter had been systematic; Cutter advocated a *syndetic* approach, that is, one in which subjects are linked together in an underlying classificatory structure, but this does not appear to have been fully appreciated even by his contemporaries.

It is hardly surprising that those who came later, and had not gone through the same kind of educational experience as Cutter, should not grasp the structure of his reasoning. The consequence was that Cutter's *Rules*, based on one particular approach to knowledge, were later adapted for LCSH along rather different lines, with results that are often less than satisfactory.[4]

Cutter's acceptance of natural language names as the only source of headings brought him face to face with another problem which we examined in Chapter 7: the order of terms in a heading involving more than one word. Cutter saw that a strict adherence to natural language order would often lead to headings in which the first word was not the most significant. His solution to the problem of significance was based on his acceptance of a structure of knowledge which clearly indicated which was the most significant word and should therefore come first. This led to the practice of inverted headings, which are certainly not natural language, but do fit into Cutter's structure. Without the structure, which is the most significant word becomes almost a matter of guesswork, with consequences which we have already seen in the example from LCSH under the term 'Geographical . . .'.

In some cases Cutter does give definite rulings, as for example when there is a clash between subject and place. Here we are instructed to enter under subject, qualified by place, in scientific and similar areas, but under place, qualified by subject, in areas such as history, government and commerce where the country might reasonably be expected to be taken to be the main focus of interest. For the humanities – literature, art – we are recommended to use the adjectival form of the country or language as the entry word: English drama, French painting.

As mentioned above, Cutter recommended that related subjects should be linked by a network of references to give a *syndetic* catalogue. We can only compile such a catalogue if we adopt a classificatory approach; a purely alphabetical approach will not show hierarchical relationships, though we can see syntactic links when two unrelated terms are used together in a heading. For example, the heading English drama itself shows the need for a link with the broader term Drama, (in this case the 'hidden' term), but does not show the relationship with the broader subject Literature; to reveal this, we need to carry out the kind of systematic subject analysis outlined in Chapter 6. We can then make the complete network of references needed. However, on economic grounds Cutter restricted the links shown in practice to downward references, i.e. from broader to narrower terms, and recommended that we ignore both upward links (Narrower term to Broader term) and collateral (Related term) links between subjects of equal rank. Thus Cutter would have cross-references such as

> Literature *see also* Drama

but *not*

> Drama *see also* Literature

nor

> Drama *see also* Poetry

Now it is certainly true that many users begin a search by specifying a much broader subject than they in fact want: needing information on the 'Dark tower' theme in literature, they ask for the Literature collection.[5] We certainly need links to take us from broad subjects to narrower, to help clarify the specific subject of a request. But we do also need to be able to go to broader and related subjects if we do not find what we want, and we can only do this systematically if there are the NT-BT and RT-RT links normal in thesauri, not just BT-NT links. Despite its disadvantages, Cutter's advice was followed as standard practice, and it is only in recent years, with the adoption of thesaurus conventions by LCSH and Sears, that this limitation on search strategy in alphabetical subject catalogues has been removed.

The dictionary catalogue, first rationalized by Cutter, has been the basis of subject cataloguing practice in the USA this century.[6] LC began to distribute its printed cards at the beginning of the century, complete with subject headings; cards are still (1995) available, though they have been largely replaced by MARC records. Smaller libraries which found LC practice too detailed for their needs have been served by Sears *List of subject headings*, compiled on the same lines as LCSH. This influence has not been restricted to the US; the vast majority of Australian libraries, for example, follow the same practice, despite the efforts of such writers as Metcalfe to bring some degree of rationalization to Australian subject heading practice. In the UK, the classified catalogue was somewhat more popular, but with the introduction of MARC records in 1971, BNB began to give LCSH in its entries for international consistency, and also for the relatively small number of British libraries using LCSH. Lack of funds caused the British Library to cut down on its cataloguing activities, as announced in *Currency with coverage*[7] in 1987; though LCSH formed part of the subject 'packages' developed for use with PRECIS, and 75% of entries were found to be covered by existing subject packages,[8] LCSH headings were dropped. However, by this time many libraries had adopted LCSH and dictionary catalogues, and the steadily rising tide of complaints led to the official reintroduction of LCSH on January 1 1995, though some entries were made beginning in October 1994.

It is unfortunate that many of the features for which Cutter is now remembered – multiple entry, inverted headings, downward references only, for example – have tended to outweigh his real achievement: the introduction of direct entry in natural language backed by a syndetic network of cross-references. His *Rules* can still be read with profit (and, more unusually, pleasure) today.

Metcalfe

One of the strongest supporters of the Cutter type of catalogue was J. W. Metcalfe, who wrote three major works[9] on the subject approach, yet received little attention outside his adopted country – a case of a prophet without honour save in his own country. His case for the alphabetico-specific catalogue is worth careful consideration.

He first defines the alphabetico-specific catalogue as consisting of known names in a known order: i.e., terms in natural language arranged in self-evident alphabetical order. He lays stress on the importance of this to the reader, who should be able to use the catalogue with the minimum of difficulty, though as we have seen in Chapters 6 and 7 (and as Metcalfe admitted) this may not always be as simple as it appears. Entry should be direct, according to Cutter's rule; any departure from direct entry leads to alphabetico-classed arrangement, which is contrary to the specific approach. To clarify this point, Metcalfe introduced the important differentiation between *specification* and *qualification*; specification refers to division into species by adding a term, while qualification refers to division by aspect, process or form. Thus 'prestressed concrete' is a species of concrete, and it would be wrong to enter it as 'concrete – prestressed', because this would be class entry; but 'concrete – pouring' is correct, because pouring is a process applied to concrete, not a species of concrete.

The next question for discussion is what is meant by 'specific' entry. Metcalfe argued that the purpose of subject cataloguing is to indicate the subject classes into which a document falls, *not* necessarily to indicate precisely the precise subject of the item itself. This view is of course directly contrary to the view advocated in this book, which is that the subject specification should be coextensive with the subject of the document. Metcalfe recognized that many subjects that appear in documents involve the coordination of subject classes, and that the card and book catalogue do not lend themselves to this approach, but he suggested that in many cases a reader faced with a non-specific heading would only have to look through a limited number of entries to find items on the specific subject he requires, and that this would be simpler than looking through the network of cross-references involved in single entry, coextensive headings. An analogy might be drawn here with *Index medicus* and MEDLINE; many users find the arrangement in IM, with multiple entry under non-specific headings, quite satisfactory for current scanning, but find that they need MEDLINE, with its potential for post-coordination, for retrospective searching.

In an attempt to take the ideas of Cutter and Kaiser and bring them up to date, Metcalfe published a *Tentative code for alphabetico-specific entry* in 1959. In this he suggested in Rule 2.41 that the extent of subject qualification by subheadings is entirely a matter of judgement according to the number of entries and the specialization of literature under particular headings. This either implies a static collection, or a potential need to recatalogue documents on subjects that grow too unwieldy as more literature in the subject field is published. Some of the rules appear to contradict Metcalfe's own ideas on direct, specific entry; nevertheless, they did represent an attempt to provide a *modus operandi* for the multiple entry under known names approach. Unfortunately, much of Metcalfe's writing is difficult to follow, and is marred by what appears to be a deep-rooted prejudice against the classified approach. A more moderate approach is found in a short pamphlet by R. K. Olding,[10] which is a clear exposition of the method, though this too seems to stop at a point where something like the theories of Coates would have to take over.

Specificity, coordination, recall and relevance

It is worth recapitulating briefly some of the points made in earlier chapters in order to put the multiple entry/single entry controversy into perspective. We have seen that coordination is a device to improve relevance, whereas class entry is a means of improving recall. Single entry systems attempt to provide specificity by means of pre-coordination; multiple entry systems attempt to provide the same degree of specificity without using coordination, since the kinds of bibliographic tool they are used in, e.g. the printed or (more rarely now) card catalogue, do not permit coordination of entries under two or more headings. Do readers prefer to go to a specific heading, perhaps via one or more cross-references, in a form that is clearly not 'natural language', or do they prefer to scan a number of entries under a less specific heading which is closer to natural language – though it must be stressed again that any controlled vocabulary cannot claim to be 'natural' language. If the latter, how many entries would they be willing to scan? To use the term introduced in Chapter 2, what is their anticipated futility point? The answer to this question depends on the reader and the type of search being undertaken, but, as we have seen, in most cases it is likely to be about 30. The results of evaluation tests seem to indicate that post-coordination is the most powerful device for achieving specificity, and one may suspect that the enthusiasm with which post-coordinate indexing was welcomed in the USA may have been the result of disillusionment with the multiple entry method divorced from the possibility of coordination by the physical form of the card catalogue. Perhaps the computer will resolve the debate by giving us the possibility of enjoying the best of both worlds, as discussed in Chapter 15.

Kaiser

In England the practice of subject indexing tended to take a rather different path, towards greater specificity in headings. One of the first significant workers was J. Kaiser, who in 1911 published a work called *Systematic indexing*,[11] which took the practice of alphabetical subject indexing an important step forward. His ideas formalized the practices he had developed in trying to index information relating to business and industry, and they represent the first attempt to find a sound and consistent answer to the problem of significance order, and are still valid and useful in many cases. Kaiser pointed out that many composite subjects can be analysed into a combination of a *concrete* and a *process*, and stated that in such a combination the concrete should be cited first; for example, 'Heat treatment of aluminium' is entered:

> Aluminium – Heat treatment

If *place* is involved, Kaiser makes double entry, once under concrete and once under place; entry for localities is indirect, i.e. under country subdivided by more specific locality. Thus 'Steel production in Sheffield' would be entered:

> Steel – Great Britain, Sheffield – production
> Great Britain, Sheffield – Steel – Production

Concretes are linked by a complete network of cross-references, to superordinate and coordinate as well as subordinate headings. For concretes involving more than one word, e.g. 'Aluminium windows', natural language order is used, though this would tend to break down with some of the complex subjects met with today, e.g. 'Gas-cooled natural uranium fuelled nuclear power reactors', where natural language permits more than one arrangement.

Kaiser also illustrated in his example the effect of using systematic arrangement of subheadings as opposed to straightforward alphabetical filing. For example, if we have a concrete subdivided by place and also by process, we can file the subheadings alphabetically or we can group places and processes. We could have, for example:

Steel – Great Britain, Sheffield – Production
Steel – Smelting
Steel – United States of America, Pittsburgh – Smelting
Steel – Welding

or

Steel – Smelting
Steel – Welding
Steel – Great Britain, Sheffield – Production
Steel – United States of America, Pittsburgh – Smelting

A further sequence may arise if we include bibliographical forms as subdivisions, e.g. Periodicals, Dictionaries, Indexes, etc, as once again it may be helpful to avoid interfiling these with other kinds of subheading. The principle followed by Kaiser has been more fully investigated in the field of classification and is considered under the heading *Principle of inversion* in Chapter 9. However, the ideas of grouping subheadings is followed by most alphabetical subject catalogues, as is shown by the following headings from LCSH, in which the computer filing gives the arrangement:

Sales	(single word)
Sales—taxation	(subheading)
USE Sales tax	
Sales—Rome	(geographical)
USE Sales (Roman law)	
Sales, conditional	(qualifier)
Sales (Roman law)	(context)
Sales accounting	(two or more words)

The problem with introducing systematic arrangement into an alphabetical sequence is that the order is no longer self-evident, and in consequence users may not be able to find their way around as easily as they should.

Kaiser identified many of the problems which arise frequently in the indexing of periodical literature, technical reports and so on, but are less commonly met with in cataloguing books, which tend to deal with broader subjects. His methods were not widely adopted, but his ideas did have an important influence on the thought of later workers such as Coates and Austin.

Coates

Undoubtedly the most important contribution to the theory of alphabetical subject headings for many years was the work of E. J. Coates. In his book *Subject catalogues*[12] Coates summarized succinctly the previous approaches, both theory and practice, and put forward his own theories as to the correct formulation of specific subject headings. He also had the challenge of putting his ideas into practice on a large scale in *British technology index*, of which he was editor from its inception in 1963 until his retirement in 1976 – an opportunity of a kind which rarely presents itself to the theorist.

Coates began his study of order in composite headings by trying to establish the reason for Kaiser's selection of concrete rather than process as the entry point, and suggested that there is a sound psychological reason for this. If we try to visualize an *action* out of context, it is very difficult; we normally have to think of some *thing* which is involved in the action. For example, we can visualize a piece of steel or aluminium undergoing heat treatment, possibly glowing, changing shape and so on, but it is much more difficult to visualize *heat treatment* on its own.[13] We can therefore establish an order of significance reflecting this, and in this simple case it is the same as Kaiser's Concrete-Process, which Coates named Thing-Action. Similarly, if we think of a thing and the material of which it is made, it is once again the thing which conjures up the more definite mental image. So we can develop our significance order one stage further, to give Thing-Material-Action; from here we can again move forward to incorporate *parts*, which must depend on the things to which they belong, thus giving us Thing-Part-Material-Action. Further variants can be built up using the same basic principles.

In addition to the problems of combination order, Coates took Cutter's ideas on place *versus* subject further, and proposed the following ranking of subjects:

1 Geographical and biological phenomena (flora and fauna)
2 History and social phenomena
3 Language and literature
4 Fine arts
5 Philosophy and religion
6 Technology
7 Phenomena of the physical sciences.

Groups 1, 2 and 3 are entered under place, with a few specific exceptions, and the rest under subject. This is very much in line with Cutter's view, but gives rather more detailed guidance.

Cross-reference structure

An index constructed on these principles shows the problems of related subjects in an acute form. We have to establish a network of semantic relationships, but we must also cater for those who look for a word other than the first in what can be a very complex heading. Coates used a number of classification schemes to establish semantic relationships, and a sophisticated form of chain procedure to give all the necessary cross-references. In 1968, the production of BTI was computerized, to speed up the production schedule. To begin with, Coates was sceptical whether the cross-reference structure could be computerized, because of the complexity of the string manipulation, but it was found that the only purely intellectual task was the writing of the original string. Punctuation was used to show the relationships between terms, and this was all that was needed to operate the algorithms to produce all the cross-references. Obviously detailed thought must go into the preparation of the algorithms, and it requires a thorough understanding of what they are to achieve, but the manipulation can be reduced to a clerical task that can be done by a computer. It is important to identify the separation of intellectual and clerical tasks, and to avoid attaching an intellectual mystique to indexing operations which turn out to be amenable to computer manipulation; apart from anything else, it tends to imply that computers *are* capable of intellectual operations.[14]

There is no doubt that the system devised by Coates was a very good solution to the problem of generating specific subject headings for the complex subjects written about in periodical articles in the field of technology. However, there were also disadvantages in its practical application. The headings were too complex for some users; more importantly, the network of cross-references became very large, forming a substantial proportion of each issue of BTI. Although the economy of chain procedure kept the number of cross-references to a minimum, the fact that the procedure was so thorough meant that it gave rise to a much larger number of cross-references than users were accustomed to. Also, as we have seen in Chapter 7, chain procedure gives cross-references which are specific in only one instance; thus a user looking for information on 'the determination of neutron flux in boiling water reactors' might well look under the word reactors, only to find a cross-reference

Reactors, nuclear
   see
NUCLEAR REACTORS

In the annual volume of BTI there might well have been a large number of entries at this heading, and the user might have had to look through a good proportion of them before finding what was wanted, in effect giving the same result as entry under non-specific headings.

When Coates retired, the opportunity was taken to review the overall policy of BTI, including the indexing techniques used. In 1981, the name was changed to *Current technology index* and the coverage was increased. The thesaurus of terms was revised, and the layout was changed to give a more pleasant print effect. The number of cross-references was reduced, and an author index was added. (Coates had left this out in order to keep costs down. Two commercial ventures of a very similar kind had failed previously, and economy was essential.) There is also a quarterly supplement, *Catchword and trade name index* (CATNI) giving full details with each entry. The indexing method is still basically that devised by Coates, but the improved layout, additional indexes and wider coverage have led to greater acceptance by users.

The entries are grouped into 25 numbered categories, corresponding largely to those in the *ROOT thesaurus*, discussed in Chapter 25. To take an example, an article on *Personal-computer-based control and evaluation of Langmuir probe characteristics* (CTI95-6948) is included in category 10 Electronic engineering under the broad heading Electrical discharges, and has the detailed heading:

**Low temperature plasmas – Measurements – Langmuir probes –
Microcomputers – Programs**

In the subject index, we find the following entries generated using chain procedure:

Low temperature plasmas 6947–6948
Langmuir probes
  Measurements – Low temperature plasmas 6948
Programs
  Microcomputers – Langmuir probes – Measurement – Low temperature
  plasmas 6498
Microcomputers
  Langmuir probes – Measurements – Low temperature plasmas 6948
together with the NT cross-references:
Computers
  narrower term
  Microcomputers
Plasmas
  narrower term
  Low temperature plasmas
Probes
  narrower term
  Langmuir probes

The only term from which it is *not* possible to reach this entry is Measurement, which is a weak indexing term, likely to be unsought. CTI is now available from 1981 as CTI Plus on CD-ROM, with over 270,000 entries (1995) and quarterly updates.

PRECIS

During the 1960s, the Classification Research Group was involved in work sponsored by NATO intended to lead to a new general classification scheme.[15] This was prompted by the problems encountered by the BNB in using DDC to arrange the national bibliography as a classified catalogue, and by the need to develop a scheme which could be used in computer production. By the late 1960s, enough work had been done to show that analysis into facets and identification of the relationships between the foci found was progressing well, but that problems with the notation were causing delays. However, the strings of terms representing composite subjects could be manipulated by computer quite satisfactorily.

At the same time, the MARC project (Chapter 15) had led the BNB to accept that in the interests of international cooperation they should use DDC in its standard form, rather than the version which had been developed by them over the years, and for which they had also built up a detailed chain index. DDC18, the edition adopted for the BNB switch to MARC format in 1971, still contained enough anomalies for it to be unsuitable for chain indexing, and there was an urgent need for a suitable method of indexing the classified arrangement used in the bibliography. Further pressure arose from two other factors: the MARC format allowed for classification schemes other than DDC, whereas a chain index is geared specifically to one arrangement; and users had expressed dissatisfaction with the chain index, mainly because of its failure to provide specific leads at every entry point.

The work done on the CRG classification had reached a stage where it could be used to devise an indexing system which would meet the four requirements specified for the new alphabetical access scheme to replace the chain index:

1 headings should be coextensive with the subject at all access points
2 the scheme should not be geared to any particular classification scheme
3 each entry should be meaningful to the user without explanation
4 all manipulation of entries was to be done by computer.

The system devised mainly by Austin was called PRECIS: PREserved Context Indexing System. Use in BNB for the 1971–73 cumulation showed the need for some refinements in the preliminary version, and a slightly amended version was introduced in 1974. Further refinements were introduced later to take account of work done on the use of PRECIS with languages other than English, and the final version was fully described in the revised edition of the manual published in 1984.[16] The following account is necessarily brief, but gives the main features of the system. PRECIS was devised as an indexing system for BNB, but could very well have been used to generate subject headings for an alphabetical catalogue; it was proposed as a possible alternative to LCSH when the Library of Congress closed its card catalogue in 1981.

The first step in creating a set of PRECIS entries is to write down the subject as a string of terms forming a title-like statement. This is formulated in a suitable way, and each term is then allocated a role operator. There may be additional secondary operators within a multiword term. Terms which are to be used as access points, i.e. appear as the first in an index entry, are marked ✓, and other codes may be added, for example (LO) to show that a term is only to be used when it appears in the lead position. It is usual to write down the string complete with role operators as a series of lines, one mainline operator to a line. Semantic relationships are added for each term in the string as necessary, to generate any *see also* references needed; computer manipulation codes are added, and the computer then generates an entry for each term marked as an access point.

The output is in shunted form, with the *lead* term in bold, followed by the *qualifier* in roman (with rare exceptions) and the *display* on the next line in roman or italic depending on the role operator. The lead terms are the most important, as these are the access points. Terms are always in natural language order; inverted headings are never used. Each term marked as a lead term gives rise to an entry with that term in the lead position; the remainder of the terms in the string are shunted into the qualifier or the display depending on which operator introduces them. In each case the layout, punctuation and typography of the entry are automatically provided by the computer program, using the manipulation codes linked to the operators and other instructions. The intellectual input lies in writing the original string.

Over the years the BNB built up a thesaurus of preferred terms, and the indexer checked this to see if a term had been used before; if it had, it would be identified in the computer-held thesaurus by a random number, the RIN (Reference Indicator Number), which locates a package consisting of the term together with any semantic links. (The use of random numbers avoids any suggestion that a term is restricted to one particular hierarchy.) Including the RIN in the string will cause the computer to print out all these cross-references as well as the appropriate entries. A complete string may have been used before, in which case it is part of a package identified by a SIN (Subject Indicator Number), which includes not only the PRECIS string but also any DDC, LCC or LCSH subject designations associated with it. By 1987 some 75% of the items handled by BNB dealt with subjects for which a SIN already existed, significantly reducing the amount of time taken to index them.

The operators fall into various groups which serve different purposes. The following is a very abbreviated discussion; for full details it is necessary to consult the *Manual*.

Primary mainline operators

The first group consists of the operators (0), (1), (2) and (3). (0) is used to show the *environment* of the *core concepts* introduced by (1), (2) and (3). A string must begin with one of the operators (0), (1) or (2), and all strings must contain a concept introduced by either (1) or (2). (1) introduces the *key system*; this will be an entity (which may include abstract or heterogeneous concepts), and the normal rules for singular and plural are followed – these are in effect identical with the EJC rules set out in Chapter 6. (2) introduces *actions* and *phenomena*; the passive form of nouns signifying actions is preferred, e.g. classification rather than classifying. There may be more than one concept introduced by (1) and (2). The operator (3) denotes an *agent*, which may be an entity or an action causing the action introduced by (2) affecting the entity introduced by (1). An example will show the method of writing strings and the kind of results that can be obtained.

String:

(1)   organic compounds✓
(2)   synthesis✓ $wof
(2)   catalysis✓ $wof
(3)   noble metals✓

Entries:

Organic compounds.
        Synthesis. Catalysis. Noble metals
Synthesis. Organic compounds
        Catalysis. Noble metals

Catalysis. Synthesis of organic compounds
    Noble metals
Noble metals
    Catalysis of synthesis of organic compounds

The first group of operators are thus the key to the whole system; all strings must contain at least one of them, and they may be repeated if necessary. The terms introduced by them are always printed in roman, no matter in which of the three positions they appear, the only difference being that, in common with all others, they are printed in bold in the lead position.

Extra-core mainline operators

The second group consists of operators (4), (5) and (6), introducing *extra-core concepts*, which differ in three important respects from the previous group. The first is that once the string has incorporated one of this group of operators, it is not possible to go back to the first group; the second is that they are printed in italic in the display, preceded by a dash, and also in the qualifier if the occasion arises; the third is that they give rise to an inverted form of entry. Although they are regarded as mainline operators, they represent less significant concepts than the first group.

Terms introduced by (4), viewpoints and perspectives, are not usually of a kind that warrants lead status. Every book is written from some point of view; (4) should only be used when the author's viewpoint has some significant effect on the presentation. Common examples are sociological, political or religious (for example, '*in vitro* fertilization from the Roman Catholic point of view'). (6) is used to introduce both target (bias phase) and bibliographical form. It may thus be used twice and the order can affect the meaning, as this example shows:
String:

    (2) multivariate analysis✓
    (6) librarianship✓ $hfor
    (6) bibliographies
    (2) Multivariate analysis✓
    (6) bibliographies
    (6) librarianship✓ $hfor

Entries:

Multivariate analysis
    – For librarianship – Bibliographies
Librarianship
    Multivariate analysis *–For librarianship – Bibliographies*
Multivariate analysis
    – Bibliographies – For librarianship
Librarianship
    Multivariate analysis *– Bibliographies – For librarianship*

The difference between these two sets of entries should be clear.

Place

Place may be treated in several ways, depending on the sense. If Place is the only focus, or the principal focus, (1) is used; this operator is also used where a natural feature is defined by its location, or if an action implies a whole community. In such cases, the name would be a lead term. If on the other hand Place is simply the environment, or the location of a man-made feature, (0) is used, and Place does not normally appear as a lead term. If Place is used in the sense of a 'selected instance' from which the author draws general conclusions, it is treated as a *study region*, introduced by (5) from the extra-core group of mainline operators. Occasionally Place may be regarded as an agent, e.g. 'the role of Australia in the East Timor dispute', in which case (3) would be used, but this is rare. (0) is probably the most used operator for Place. An example of the use of 'Study regions' is as follows:
String:

- (1) man
- (p) spina bifida✓
- (4) social aspects
- (5) study regions
- (q) Scotland✓ (LO)
- (p) South-east Scotland✓

Entries:

Spina bifida. Man
    – Social aspects – Study regions: South-east Scotland
Scotland. *Study regions*
    Man. Spina bifida *– Social aspects – Study regions: South-East Scotland*
South-east Scotland. *Study regions*
    Man. Spina bifida *– Social aspects – Study regions: South-East Scotland*

In this example, Scotland only appears in the lead position. When the sequence introduced by (5) moves into the lead position, Place becomes the lead term; *Study regions* never becomes the lead term, but moves into the qualifier, remaining in italic, while the rest of the entry moves into the display in an 'inverted' format. Note also that while terms introduced by (5) are still in the display, the term *Study regions* is followed by a colon which introduces the place.

Secondary operators

We now come to the next group of operators, the *secondary operators*. These cannot be used on their own; they must be used with one of the primary operators. The first three indicate elements which depend in some way on the operator to which they are subsumed: (p) indicates parts or properties, (q) is used to denote quasi-generic relationships. An example illustrates some of the features:

String:

- (0) Great Britain
- (1) higher education institutions✓
- (p) curriculum subjects
- (q) mechanical engineering✓
- (3) degree courses✓

Entries:

Higher education institutions. Great Britain
    Curriculum subjects: Mechanical engineering. Degree courses
Mechanical engineering. Curriculum subjects. Higher education institutions.
      Great Britain
    Degree courses
Degree courses. Mechanical engineering. Curriculum subjects. Higher
      education institutions. Great Britain

Two points should be noted about this example. The first is that (q) automatically causes the colon to be printed in the display after the containing term, in this case curriculum subjects; the second is that if the qualifier overflows on to the next line, it is indented eight spaces, to distinguish it from the display, which is indented two spaces, with four spaces indent for any overrun.

Operator (r) is used to show assemblies. The first kind of assembly is the aggregate; the second kind covers associates, e.g. the wives of Henry VIII. Neither is likely to occur often, but this operator can be used to solve certain otherwise intractable indexing problems.

Operators (s), (t) and (u) are denoted *concept interlinks*. (s) is used when an unusual role is involved, or an indirect agent, or an indirect action; the last of these is more familiar as *influence phase*; (t) denotes author-attributed associations, specifically the phase relations *exposition* and *relation to*; (u) is used for the phase relationship *comparison*.

String:

                        (1) states✓
                        (p) size✓
(sub 2↑)   (1) size of state
                        (s) effects $von $wof
                        (3) democracy✓

Entries:

States
    Size. Effects on democracy
Size. States
    Effects on democracy
Democracy
    Effects of size of state

This example also shows the use of substitute phrases to give entries that are more easily read.

The final operators in this group are (f) and (g), denoting coordinate concepts, e.g. silver and lead in 'The mining of silver and lead', e.g.:
String:

    (1) silver✓ $v&
    (g) lead✓
    (2) mining✓

Entries:

Silver
    Mining
Lead
    Mining
Mining. Silver & lead

Codes within PRECIS strings

Operators beginning lines in a PRECIS string are shown in parentheses. Codes falling within a line are shown by a conventional sign – in the case of BNB, the $ sign was used. The major *secondary codes* are those used as *differences*. Instead of Coates' Thing, Kind, and Kind of kind, PRECIS treats the results of such qualifications as a single concept consisting of a *focus* and one or more *differences*. The differences may be direct (Kind of Thing) or indirect (Kind of kind); lead or non-lead; close-up or not.

    $0   non-lead, space-generating
    $1   non-lead, close-up
    $2   lead, space-generating
    $3   lead, close-up
    $01   non-lead, space-generating, direct (i.e. level 1)
    $32   lead, close-up, indirect (here level 2)

Differences and focus are written down in the reverse of natural language order, but are printed in the correct order by the appropriate algorithm.
Examples:
String:

    (1) compounds $21 inorganic $21non-metallic   [kind of thing, kind of thing]

Entries:

Non-metallic compounds
    Non-metallic inorganic compounds
Inorganic compounds
    Non-metallic inorganic compounds

String:

   (1) peas $21dried $32 freeze-   [kind of thing, kind of kind]

Entries:

Peas
   Freeze-dried peas
Dried peas
   Freeze-dried peas
Freeze-dried peas

In an Appendix to the *Manual* Austin discusses the order of adjectives which should be followed when we have more than one difference acting on the same focus. Date is treated as a difference, introduced by $d, and is printed in italics. The connectives $v (downward) and $w (upward) are used to link terms within strings, for example to restore prepositions which clarify the relationship between terms, as seen in some of the above examples.

The syntactic structure of PRECIS is obviously complex, and the preceding notes do not cover all the features by any means. The advantage of PRECIS is that it gives a complete subject statement at each entry point, which chain procedure does not. Critics have claimed that it is unduly complex and time-consuming, and does not in practice give better results than would a simple KWOC index, though other tests have shown that it does perform better. Despite its complexity, in some ways it appears to be imprecise in some aspects; for example, in many instances it does not appear to make any difference whether a concept is coded (1) or (2), which suggests that the operators would not be of much help in searching a computer file, where they might be included (the operators were only used to control the computer manipulation for the printed index).

To set against these criticisms, we have the fact that PRECIS has been shown to work in a number of languages other than English. It appears to reflect the principles of transformational grammar as elaborated by Chomsky and other modern linguistic analysts. The differencing operators can be made to cater for inflexions in languages such as German, and the set needed for English become in effect a subset of the whole, and the *Manual* becomes specifically a manual of English-language practice. The complete set of operators can deal with compound words such as armchair, (where 'chair' is effectively lost), 'portmanteau' words, for example in German, inflexions, and various syntactical constructions in languages which have these. PRECIS appears to be the only indexing system with real possibilities for multi-lingual application, and the number of languages in which it has proved successful is impressive. It has been used in Canada to produce a bi-lingual bibliography, and seems to be well suited to the indexing of audiovisual materials, where most existing systems are not detailed enough.[17] It has also been used in experimental systems in China.[18]

COMPASS (COMPuter Aided Subject System)

During the late 1980s, the growing popularity of online searching, together with the need for financial stringency, led to a review of the work of BLBSD. The position paper *Currency with coverage*[7] proposed a number of changes, including the separation of BLBSD into three separate organizations, one (NBS) responsible for the National Bibliographic Service, one for Telecommunications and Computing, and the third for Acquisitions, Processing and Cataloguing. The NBS is responsible for, among other things, UKMARC and BLAISE.

PRECIS was intended to be a complete subject statement in a form that was suitable for a printed bibliography, and this was not necessarily the best format for online searching. For example, its complex system of role operators served to produce the output strings for printing, but were not otherwise utilized – though there is no reason why they should not have been. PRECIS includes Place in several ways as part of the subject string, introduced by operators (0), (1), (5) and occasionally (3). Persons as subjects, for example of biographies, also form part of the PRECIS subject string, so entries for an individual may be found in both the Author/Title file and the subject file. Common practice for many years has been for libraries to file such entries in the Author/Title file, making this a *name* file. If a record is being searched online, it is to some extent immaterial whereabouts in the record a piece of information occurs, so long as it is there to be found.

It was decided to revise UKMARC and introduce a simplified system of subject indexing, COMPASS,[19] using much the same kind of basic principles as PRECIS. These include an open-ended vocabulary; the arrangement of terms in subject strings organized by PRECIS principles of context dependence and role operators; and the re-use of previously existing subject strings. (As mentioned above, some 75% of the items handled by BNB had an entry in the SIN file already.) In effect, PRECIS mainline operators (1), (2) and (3) have been retained, together with the subsidiary operators p, q and r. Operators (0), (4), (5) and (6) are not used. Some of the content of PRECIS strings has been transferred to other tags. Tags 650, topical subject headings, 651, geographic names as subjects, and 690, 691 and 692, associated with PRECIS, were discontinued, and in their place 660 is used for Subject topical descriptors and 661 for Subject geographical descriptors. The PRECIS network of related terms (the RIN file) was retained, and a new authority file is being developed using WLN software; this will incorporate entries from the old file as appropriate. Proper names as subjects are located in the MARC tag for personal names as subjects, and are found in the Author/Title index, marked † to distinguish them from the same name as author or title.

Historical periods may be listed; in Literature, for example, the period subdivisions used in DDC are used, so that the subject string and class number coincide. Connectives are also used to show phase relationships and to disambiguate strings, for example those involving agents, e.g. Children. Abuse. By adults.

The PRECIS strings were used to generate the DDC class numbers and also feature headings for the BNB classified sequence, so that users could find their way through the file without being unduly reliant on the class numbers; both these links were incorporated in the SIN file. COMPASS was not used for this purpose at all. The DDC class numbers are now linked direct to the bibliographic records rather than through the subject string. There are guide headings in bold throughout the sequence, usually for the three-digit numbers, e.g. 296 **Judaism**, but sometimes for four-digit numbers, e.g. 332.7 **CREDIT**, or even five-digit numbers such as 629.23 MOTOR VEHICLES. CONSTRUCTION, but there are no feature headings for more detailed subdivisions. The COMPASS string is given after the main body of the entry, in italic. Thus from the subject index one may be referred to a class number:

Judaism
    Christianity *related to* Judaism   200

Turning to class 200 in the classified sequence, we find a number of items, and have to scan the entries carefully to select the one which has at the *end* the subject heading 'Christianity *related to* Judaism'; the title, *Children of one God*, is not immediately obvious. The subject index entry also leads us to four other class numbers, and with the subdivision *History* to two others.

The printed subject index to BNB was certainly much shorter, though the PRECIS index itself was nothing like as large as was originally predicted. However, the decrease in size was at the expense of the user, who had to work a great deal harder to find what was wanted, frequently by searching in a number of different places in the classified sequence. For example, in the 1990 PRECIS index at the word **Antiquities** there are first ten *see also* references, then 54 entries, each modified by terms either in the qualifier or the display to give a specific subject statement, leading to 54 different class numbers. In the 1991 COMPASS index we find the heading **Antiquities**, with the subheading Antiquities [!] 28 times, each leading to a different class number, but with no clue at all to distinguish one from another. **Antiquities** is fairly obviously a heading where place will be important, but the printed subject index ignores it. The heading **Cognitive psychology** has the subheading Cognitive psychology four times, with different class numbers for each but no other help for the enquirer. The end result is to increase recall, but at the very obvious expense of relevance. It was assumed that relevance could be improved by searching for other factors in the online file; the printed version was certainly an incentive to do so.

Some 25% of libraries surveyed in 1993 reported using LCSH, including several large research libraries. The increase in demand for LCSH led the NBS to conclude that it had taken the wrong direction with COMPASS, and in January 1995 LCSH headings were reintroduced, though COMPASS will continue in use until at least the end of 1966. The NBS has in fact proudly announced its first British contribution to LCSH, **Ring Ouzel**; this bird is not found in North America, so that no cause to include the heading had previously arisen.[20] We can see that the British influence may soon lead to major changes in LCSH.

NEPHIS

The NEsted PHrase Indexing System was devised by Craven[21] as a simple way of generating strings from which index entries could be generated by computer. Four symbols are used: < > to generate a nested phrase, ? to introduce a connective, and @ to mark a term not to be used as an access point. As a simple example we may take the following string:

Higher education institutions. Degree courses. Mechanical engineering.

We can rewrite this as a NEPHIS string of nested phrases:

<Degree Courses ?in <Mechanical <Engineering>>> ?in <Higher Education Institutions>

This would give us the entries:

Engineering. Mechanical. Degree Courses in Higher Education Institutions
Mechanical Engineering. Degree Courses in Higher Education Institutions
Degree Courses in Mechanical Engineering in Higher Education Institutions
Higher Education Institutions. Degree Courses in Mechanical Engineering

NEPHIS is a relatively simple method to use, and has been shown to give rather better results than PRECIS in Chinese, though PRECIS has been used successfully.[22]

Filing order

If our subject headings are more than one word long, we may find that they present filing problems, particularly if they introduce symbols other than letters, such as the comma, parentheses or the dash. As headings in an alphabetical catalogue become more complex, it becomes necessary to introduce filing rules to govern the overall arrangement, which may themselves influence the form of the headings. This has proved particularly true as computer filing becomes common; for example, in both LCSH and Sears *List* we find that dates are now specified numerically, so that eighteenth century 1700–1799 files *after* seventeenth 1600–1699. Are we to file *letter by letter* (all through), ignoring spaces, or *word by word*? The index to this book is word by word: thus 'index vocabulary is found *before* 'indexing'. In a letter by letter arrangement the converse would be true. There are arguments on both sides, and the case for each was argued out in the *Indexer*,[23] though Wellisch[24] argues forcibly in his practical guide that word by word is the only acceptable method. Are hyphens to be taken as splitting words or joining them? For example, in the index to this work they are taken as joining words into one whole, so that 'Cross-references' follows 'Crossley', whereas 'Cross references' without the hyphen would precede 'Crossley'. The reverse convention is used by LCSH, where we find the sequence:

Pitch pine
Pitch-pipe
   USE Pitchpipe
Pitching (Aerodynamics)
Pitching (Baseball)
Pitchpipe

in which the hyphen is in effect treated as a space.

The second decision is the one already mentioned in our consideration of Kaiser's rules: the problems of grouping. Again we have two possibilities: either we can use a strict alphabetical order, or we can group certain subheadings to give what may be a more helpful arrangement. The punctuation in headings consisting of more than one word has an effect; if it is ignored, we get one order, if, as is more usual, it is given a filing value, a considerable amount of grouping can take place at some headings, e.g. in LCSH:

Shakespeare, William, 1564–1616
Shakespeare, William, 1564–1616. Hamlet
   —Bibliography   [etc – model for other works]
Shakespeare, William, 1564 – 1616
   —Characters
   —Characters—Falstaff [Margaret of Anjou, etc]
   —Chronology
   —. . .
   —Poetic works
   —Poetry
Shakespeare, William, 1564–1616, in fiction, drama, poetry etc.

Women
Women—Portraits
Women—Vocational education
Women—Great Britain
Women, Black
Women (International law)
Women air pilots
Women and religion
Women in motion pictures
Women motion picture producers and directors
Women's colleges

Pipe
Pipe—Welding
Pipe, Aluminum
Pipe, Wooden
Pipe (Musical instrument)
Pipe bending
Pipe-fitting
Pipe music
Piperonal
Pipes, Deposits in

(In the above examples, a selection of headings is given to illustrate the filing order; there will be other headings in the list at the points shown.)

It is evident that the use of groupings such as those shown is a step away from the direct alphabetical approach; in an attempt to provide helpful groupings, direct access becomes more difficult. Without a knowledge of LCSH, how would we find 'Falstaff' in the above arrangement? (At least it is an improvement on the 8th edition, in which the subheading 'Characters', with sub-subheadings for 'Falstaff' *et alia*, came *after* class headings such as 'Welshmen' and 'Women'! Though such anomalies have disappeared from present practice, they may still be found in older printed or card catalogues.) The 'Pipe' example shows how the use of both singular and plural forms can lead to a considerable separation between closely related headings; similar separations are found at such headings as 'Plastic' and 'Plastics'. PRECIS has a mechanism to allow a backward reference, e.g. from 'Ceramics' to terms beginning 'Ceramic'; a forward reference is not found necessary, as we normally read forwards anyway. Computer filing has imposed consistency,[25] but the results are not always what one would expect, as is shown by the sequence under 'Women'.

This chapter has been devoted to methods for the construction of alphabetical subject headings, and to the various systems that have been devised. We have to have rules for filing, otherwise we may not be able to find the headings we construct, but their implementations seem to suggest that even those who favour the alphabetical approach may see some value in systematic arrangement!

References

1   Cutter, C. A., *Rules for a dictionary catalogue*, Washington DC, Government Printing Office, 4th edn, 1904 (reprinted by The Library Association) Part III, Subjects included in *Theory of subject analysis* . . .

2   Miksa, F. L., *The subject in the dictionary catalogue, from Cutter to the present*, Chicago, American Library Association, 1983.

3   Balnaves, F. J., *A workbook in information retrieval*, Canberra, Canberra College of Advanced Education, 2nd edn, 1975.

4   Milstead, J. L., 'Natural versus inverted word order in subject headings', *Library resources and technical services*, **24**, Spring 1980, 174–8.
    Chan, L. M., '"American poetry" but "Satire, American"; the direct and inverted forms of subject headings containing national adjectives', *Library resources and technical services*, **17**, Summer 1973, 330–9.
    Chan, L. M., *Library of Congress subject headings: principles and application*, Littleton, CO, Libraries Unlimited, 1978.

5   Mann, T. *Library research models: a guide to classification, cataloging and computers*, New York, NY, Oxford University Press, 1993.

6   Haykin, D. J., *Subject headings: a practical guide*, Washington, DC, Library of Congress, 1951.

7   *Currency with coverage*, London, British Library, 1987.

8   'Currency with coverage subject indexing proposals', *British Library Bibliographic Services newsletter*, (45) February 1988, 1–3.

9   Metcalfe, J., *Subject classifying and indexing of libraries and literature*, Melbourne, Angus and Robertson, 1959.

Metcalfe, J., *Information indexing and subject cataloguing*, Metuchen, NJ, Scarecrow Press, 1957.

Metcalfe, J., *Alphabetical subject indication of information*, Rutgers State University, Graduate School of Library Science, 1965.

10 Olding, R. K., *Wyndham Hulme's literary warrant and information indication*, University of California, Los Angeles, Graduate School of Library Service, 1965.

11 Kaiser, J., *Systematic indexing*, London, Pitman, 1911. Included in *Theory of subject analysis* . . .

12 Coates, E. J., *Subject catalogues: headings and structure*. London, Library Association, 1960, reprinted with a new preface 1988.

13 Foskett, A. C., 'E. J. Coates, The British Technology Index and the theory of subject headings: the man who loved cat springing' in *The variety of librarianship: essays in honour of John Wallace Metcalfe*, Sydney, Library Association of Australia, 1976.

14 Coates, E. J. and Nicholson, I., '*British Technology Index* – a study of the application of computer type-setting to index production', in Cox, N. S. M. and Grose, M. W., *Organization and handling of bibliographic records by computer*, Newcastle, Oriel Press, 1967, 167–78.

See also Svenonius, E., Songqiao, Liu and Subrahmanyan, B., 'Automation of chain indexing', *in Classification research for knowledge representation and organization: proceedings of the 5th International study conference on classification research, Toronto, Canada, June 24–28 1991*, Williamson, N. J. and Hudon, M. (eds.), Elsevier, 1992, (FID 698) 351–64.

15 Austin, D., 'Prospects for a new general classification', *Journal of librarianship*, 1 (3), 1969, 149–69.

16 Austin, D., with M. Dykstra, *PRECIS: a manual of concept analysis and subject indexing*, London, British Library, 1984.

17 Dykstra, M., *PRECIS: recent applications*, Halifax, Nova Scotia, Dalhousie University, School of Library Services, 1986.

Jacobs, C. and Arsenault, C. 'Words can't describe it: streamlining PRECIS just for laughs', *Indexer*, 19 (2), October 1994, 88–92. (Indexing film and video extracts in the Musée de rire, Montreal.)

18 Hseuh, L-k, 'The application of PRECIS in indexing Chinese documents: an experimental study', *Library and information science (USA/Taiwan)*, 19 (1), April 1993, 40–75. [In Chinese; abstract in LISA 94–01908]

19 'The new British Library subject system'. *Select: National Bibliographic Service newsletter*, (1), June/July 1990, 3.

'COMPASS: a rose by any other name'. *Select*, (2), Winter 1990, 3.

Wilson, N., 'COMPASS: news from the front', Select, (4) Summer 1991.

McIlwaine, I. C., 'Subject control: the British viewpoint', *Subject indexing: principles and practices in the 90's*, R. P. Holley (ed.), *et al.*, Munich, K. G. Saur, 1995, 166–80. (UBCIM Publications – New series Vol 15.)

20 *Select: National Bibliographic Service newsletter*, (14), Winter 1994/5, 7.

21 Craven, T. C., *String indexing*, Orlando, Academic Press, 1986.

22 Hong Yi, 'Indexing languages: new progress in China', *Knowledge organiza-tion,* **22** (1), 1995, 30–2.
23 *The indexer,* **3**, 1962–3, 15, 21, 93–5, 158.
24 Wellisch, H. H., *Indexing from A to Z,* New York, NY, H. W. Wilson, 1991. *See also* British Standards Institution, *recommendations for alphabetical arrangement and the filing order of numerals and symbols.* Milton Keynes, British Standards Institution, 1985, BS 1749:1985.
25 Harris, J. L., *Subject analysis: computer implications of rigorous definition,* Metuchen, NJ, Scarecrow Press, 1970.

Chapter 9
Systematic arrangement

In Chapter 6, we saw that one way of showing semantic relationships is by juxtaposition: by arranging related subjects together systematically. By grouping subjects in this way, we hope to present the user with a helpful order: one in which the subjects sought together are in fact grouped. In Chapter 8 we saw that a systematic (syndetic) approach can also be helpful in constructing the network of cross-references needed in an alphabetical system. The most common use for systematic, or classified, arrangement is for the arrangement of books on open access shelves, but we will also find classified bibliographies and catalogues.

Classified arrangement is not self-evident; as we saw in Chapter 6, a concept may be found in a variety of contexts. If we use this kind of arrangement, we must have some authority to turn to tell us what relationships we have decided to show: we do not want to have to keep making the same decisions over and over again, quite apart from the hazard of making different decisions! Such an authority is a *classification scheme*, and consists of four parts: the *schedules*, which are the index vocabulary in which subjects are listed systematically, showing their relationships; the *notation*, which is the code vocabulary, having a self-evident order and thus enabling us to find our way around the arrangement; the *alphabetical index*, which is the entry vocabulary, linked to the index vocabulary by means of the notation; and an *organization* to maintain and revise it. In the next few chapters we shall be considering each of these in turn, but it is essential to remember that the key part of a classification scheme is the schedules – the index vocabulary. In particular, the notation is *not* the classification scheme, though to many people it appears to be.

Schedules

Before we can arrange subjects systematically we have to establish what exactly are the subjects we wish to arrange. Using the titles in Table 6.4 in Chapter 6, we were able to identify various terms and arrange them in such a way as to show relationships between them. To construct a thesaurus, we had then to arrange the terms alphabetically. We also saw in Chapter 6 that an alternative way of showing the relationships was by juxtaposition: arranging related terms together, to form the index vocabulary – the schedules – of a classification scheme. We saw that the titles fell into two *basic classes*, literature and metallurgy. If we want to arrange the concepts represented systematically, then the first stage must evidently be to consider each basic class separately, to see what principles we can use to arrive at a helpful order within them.

We therefore need to consider the titles carefully to see whether any further groups suggest themselves. We find that in literature, such terms as German, French, English Spanish and Latin occur and form a group of *languages*; drama, poetry, novels suggest a group characterized by *literary form*; while seventeenth century, 1901–1915, and 1800– are clearly periods of *time*. If we now go through the whole of the group, we will find that all the important concepts fall into one or other of these groups; no matter how many more titles we take, they will still fall into the same pattern. We find a separate minor facet including *techniques*, and other minor facets may well be found, but the major facets remain constant. In metallurgy, we find a number of terms denoting *metals*, either individual or families (e.g. non-ferrous), and others which indicate that some kind of *operation* is carried out, e.g. heat treatment.

In Chapters 6 and 7 we saw that we might analyse concepts in such a way as to fit them into five fundamental categories, but that in practice it is more useful to identify specific categories within a particular subject. In classification theory it is usual to call these specific categories *facets*. If we consider a topic such as copper, we can place it in a number of different contexts; for example, there will be a metals facet in metallurgy, as we have already seen, but there will also be a materials facet in engineering, a substances facet in chemistry, and so on. Copper taken out of context is an *isolate*, but if we place it in context in a facet within a particular basic class we can refer to it as a *focus* (plural *foci*) in that facet. We can tell if we have carried out our analysis adequately by the fact that the foci within a particular facet should be *mutually exclusive*; that is, we cannot envisage a composite subject which consists of two foci from the same facet. We cannot have the 17th-century 1800s, or German English, or copper aluminium, but we *can* have composite subjects consisting of combinations of foci from different facets: English novels, 17th-century German literature, analysis of copper, heat treatment of aluminium.

Once we have organized the concepts into basic classes, and then into facets, there are two important decisions to be made before we can incorporate terms into an arrangement which will be helpful to our users. We have to decide on the order of terms within each facet, but we also have to decide on the order in which we cite the terms in a composite subject – the combination order, usually referred to as the *citation order* in a classification scheme.

Order within facets

Whereabouts in the sequence does any given subject appear? We are trying to arrange subjects systematically, but it is important to remember *why* we are doing this; it is because we believe that by arranging related subjects together we will be helping our readers. Our efforts to find a sound systematic arrangement must therefore be directed to finding a *helpful order*. There are a number of general principles which may be appropriate, particularly in the neutral situation where we cannot foresee the needs of the users.

Chronological: this is obvious where arrangement in periods may be envisaged, such as in Literature, but it is also applicable where operations may be considered sequentially, e.g. Natural gas technology, where we find

> processing
> storage
> transportation
> distribution
> use

Evolutionary: this is frequently similar or identical to, the previous arrangement. It suggests itself for the biological sciences, but may also be used elsewhere, and is also related to the next principle.

Increasing complexity: in many subjects we find a steady development from basic ideas to their most complex application, a good example being mathematics:

> arithmetic
> geometry
>> Euclidean
>> non-Euclidean
>> trigonometry
>> descriptive
>> coordinate
> calculus
>> differential
>> integral

Size: many subjects lend themselves to a quasi-arithmetical arrangement, e.g. music:

> solos
> duets
> trios etc

and government:

> central/federal
> regional/state/provincial
> metropolitan/city
> urban/town
> rural/village

Spatial: this is the obvious choice for place, where we would try to arrange together countries which are contiguous, but it may also be used elsewhere, e.g. transport:

> ground
>> railway
>> car *etc*
> water
>> inland

```
        rivers
        canals
      marine
  air
      balloons
      aircraft
  space
      rockets
```

Preferred category: we often find that our users are likely to be interested in one or a few of the foci within a facet far more than in the rest. The normal approach is to begin at the beginning of a sequence, and work through it from left to right (on the shelves) or forward (in a catalogue or bibliography). It will therefore be helpful if we arrange our sequence so that the most wanted items are at the beginning rather than in the middle or at the end. We may remove the *preferred category* from its normal place in the sequence and bring it to the beginning; for example, in Linguistics or Literature we may begin with English (or the mother tongue), even if this means that it will not fall into its logically correct place according to whatever principle we are using. It must be remembered that we are aiming at a *helpful* order, not necessarily a logical one (though in general of course a clear principle of arrangement logically followed *will* be helpful). An example of spatial arrangement with an exception made for preferred category may be found in astronomy:

```
Planets
    Earth (preferred)
    Mercury
    Venus
    Mars
    Jupiter etc
```

Canonical: in some subjects we find a traditional order, named by Ranganathan *canonical order*; this will often in such cases form a useful basis for our arrangement, particularly as it will almost certainly be reflected in literary warrant. For example, in Physics we often find in textbooks the sequence Heat, Light, Sound, and unless we wish to use a different principle we can usefully follow this order in our arrangement. The archetypal canon is of course that of the books of the Bible, which are gathered together in a fixed and unchanging order. However, we must be prepared for the fact that where subjects are concerned, few groupings are likely to show this kind of permanence; new approaches call for different groupings from the traditional, and other arrangements are likely to prove more helpful.

Alphabetical: if we are arranging individual topics each of which has a distinct name which is likely to be used to identify it, there is a strong argument for using these names and arranging them in alphabetical order. The obvious examples are found in Biography, where the individual topics are people, and Literature, where we reach a point where we need to arrange by author's name but still need to arrange each author's works systematically. Individual makes of car form another group where alphabetical arrangement may be helpful.

There will be occasions when it is difficult to see any helpful principle; for example, in what order should we arrange grain crops, root crops, legumes etc. in the crops facet in Agriculture? If after careful study we are unable to establish any principle to guide us in our choice of a helpful order, then it is equally unlikely that our users will expect any particular order; we should choose one of the general principles listed above and use that. In other cases, there will be an order which is unique to a particular subject, and is suggested by the structure of the subject itself. The careful study of the literature which is necessary before we start our analysis will reveal this.

Citation order

We have already seen that it is very important when using alphabetical headings to choose the most significant term in a composite heading as the entry word. We have exactly the same choice to make with systematic arrangement, but this time the effects are if anything even more important. The links in the chain forming a composite heading must come from different facets (foci from the same facet cannot be combined), so we are faced with the problem of deciding which facet is the most important, which is next most important, and so on down to the least important. This order of precedence – the order in which we cite the facets – is called the *citation order*. The effect of the citation order is to group material on topics which fall into the *primary facet*, but to scatter information on topics which fall into any of the other facets. Table 7.1 shows the effect of changing the citation order in Literature, using the titles from the list we have already studied in Table 6.4.

The first section shows the groupings which result from citing Language first, then Literary Form, then Period, while the second shows the effect of citing Literary Form first, then Language, then Period. In the first case, users interested in English literature, French literature, or the literature of any language group, will find all this material together; but the student of Poetry will have to look in several different places. In the second case, the user interested in a particularly Literary Form, e.g. Poetry, will find all such material together, but the student of English Literature will have to look in several different places. Whichever citation order we choose, we have to accept the fact that we cannot please all of the people all of the time. Systematic arrangement brings related subjects together only if they fall into the primary facet. We accept the fact that secondary topics will be scattered because we consider that the groupings brought about by systematic arrangement will be helpful to an extent which will outweigh the disadvantages.

There is another point to having a definite citation order; this is, to provide one, and only one, unambiguous place for any given composite subject. Suppose that we have a document dealing with the Heat treatment of aluminium, and we do not have a fixed citation order; we do not know whether this item ought to go with others in Heat treatment, or with those on Aluminium. Suppose again that we decide that this particular document ought to go with others on Heat treatment; next week, we may have another document on the same subject, but because of its different treatment

Table 7.1 Effect of citation order on grouping

Literature grouped by Language, then by literary form:

    Playwriting
    Modern drama, 1800–
    The poet's task   (no language specified)
    Some principles of fiction

    English literature and its readers
    English literature of the twentieth century
    The growth of the English novel
    A history of English drama, 1660–1900
    English poetry, 1901–1915

    German literature, a short history
    The temper of the seventeenth century in German literature
    Twentieth century German verse

    The French drama of today

    The literature of the Spanish people
    The decline of the Spanish novel, 1516–1600

Literature grouped by literary form, then by language:

    English literature and its readers
    English literature of the twentieth century
    German literature, a short history   (no form specified)
    The temper of the seventeenth century in German literature
    The literature of the Spanish people

    Some principles of fiction
    The growth of the English novel
    The decline of the Spanish novel, 1516–1600

    Playwriting
    Modern drama 1800–
    A history of English drama 1660–1900
    The French drama of today

    The poet's task
    The background of modern English poetry, 1901–1915
    Twentieth century German verse

---

of the subject we may decide to place it with other items of Aluminium. We now have two items on the same subject in two different places; the user trying to find information will find one, and assume that he or she has now found all that we have. The system has an inbuilt tendency to error which will cause us to miss items which we should find; the potential for recall will be greatly lowered. Placing the same composite subject in more than one group is known as *cross-classification*, and it cannot happen if we have a clearly defined citation order to which we adhere. If we are using an enumerative classification, we may have to make up our own rules if it does not cater for the composite subjects we have to deal with.

This is obviously another manifestation of the important factor of consistency and its corollary predictability which we referred to when discussing alphabetical systems. Not only can the classifier avoid cross-classification, by having one and only one possible place for any given composite subject, but the users can begin to recognize the pattern for themselves. This can help in two ways; it can make using the arrangement easier, but it can also help in those situations where the users are not sure exactly what it is they want. In such cases the existence of a predictable pattern is an aid in the formulation of a satisfactory search strategy.

As with order within facets, there are some general principles which will help when we are trying to establish the correct citation order.

Subject before bibliographical form: in general, the subject of a book is more significant than the bibliographic form in which the information is presented, i.e. an encyclopedia of chemistry should be grouped with other works on chemistry, not with other encyclopedias; *New society* should be grouped with other works on the social sciences, not with other periodicals. However, there will be occasions when we will disregard this principle in favour of grouping by bibliographic form. We may have a periodicals room where we keep all periodicals, or perhaps only current issues; we may have an abstracts and indexes room where we keep all our tools for bibliographic searching, rather than scatter them by subject; if we have an active translations section associated with the library, as is the case in many special libraries, we may decide to keep all our technical dictionaries together; or we may decide to keep all 'quick reference' works together so that people using them do not disturb other users of the collections. All these decisions relate to the locating of physical items within the library, but will be reflected in the catalogue; we can however make additional entries in the catalogue using the preferred citation order.

Purpose/product: many basic classes represent subjects in which the objective is to construct some particular product, or achieve some particular purpose. In such cases, the primary facet will normally be the end product or purpose. For example, the purpose of agriculture is to produce crops; the crops facet will therefore be the primary one in the basic class Agriculture. This principle may be used throughout most of Technology.

Dependence: it is difficult to imagine such operations as Heat treatment without the materials they are applied to, as we have seen earlier when discussing Coates' ideas on significance order. These operations are in fact *dependent* upon the existence of the material; without the materials, there would be no operations. In such cases, the dependent facet should follow the one on which it depends.

Whole–Part: an extension of the idea of dependence is that of Parts being subsidiary to the Wholes to which they belong. Thus in the various branches of Engineering, Machines are more important than Parts, so the Machines facet should precede Parts facets in the citation order. In general, *kinds* of things are more important than *parts*. For example, in Packaging, kinds of container (cans, composites, paper boxes) is the primary facet, with parts (bodies, ends, lids) subsidiary to it.

Decreasing concreteness: Ranganathan has suggested that one, and only one, correct citation order can be established, reflecting an order of decreasing concreteness. This order is usually known as PMEST, from the initial letters of Ranganathan's *fundamental categories*, Personality, Matter, Energy, Space, Time. These are studied in more detail in Chapter 21 on Colon classification; for the present, we should note that their generality frequently leads to doubts as to their precise mode of application, particularly in the case of Personality. In addition, a facet which is Matter in one basic class, e.g. Materials in Library science, may become Personality in another basic class, in this case Bibliography; other similar changes are possible.

The above lines may be followed to give a generalized facet order: Things – Kinds – Parts – Materials – Properties – Processes – Operations – Agents. However, it is by no means obvious how we can apply this to Literature, or some of the social sciences. We are faced with the same problem as in alphabetical order: what exactly is the most significant part of a subject? Once again we have to restate the purpose of systematic arrangement: to provide an order which will be helpful to the user. We must try to group those foci which a user is likely to want to find grouped; if we can discover this, we have established at least the primary facet. As with significance order in alphabetical headings, it is when we have difficulty in establishing users' needs that we are obliged to rely on general principles, in the hope that these will prove valid for a good proportion of our users.

The idea of one place and one place only for any composite subject is central to the idea of shelf arrangement, or the ordering of items in a bibliography. However, the essential corollary of the one place requirement, a fixed citation order, can lead to problems, and has been the source of most of the criticism of systematic arrangement and pre-coordinate systems. It assumes that we can satisfy our readers by one fixed grouping, but as has been pointed out, we cannot please all the people all of the time. Two examples may help to demonstrate this, one from Literature, the other from Engineering.

In a general library, the user's approach to Literature will usually be primarily through language, secondly through literary form. Our readers often take it for granted that all the English literature is together, and ask for novels, or plays, or whatever form is of interest to them. Period is usually less important, but has a role in that most readers are interested in *modern* literature. The situation in an academic library is rather different; here students will usually be interested primarily in a particular language, as before, but within that language are likely to be studying a particular period rather than a particular form. Indeed, it can be argued that division by literary form is a hindrance to them, because it separates the works of an author who has written in more than one form. We have here two situations which differ in that the needs of the users in one is for a different set of groupings from that required by users in the other. One citation order cannot cater for both, and it is interesting to note that the Dewey decimal classification (DDC), which is directed mainly towards the general, public, library situation, has the language, form, period, citation order first outlined, whereas the Library of Congress classification (LCC), intended to arrange a library for scholars, to a very large extent ignores form in its Literature schedules.

A fixed citation order implies that there is a 'standard' approach to a subject; but what of the situation in a library serving a research establishment? The essential characteristic of research is that it is intended to upset the accepted order of things, and we must therefore expect research workers to find an arrangement based on the old order something less than helpful. Such a situation arose in the central library of the English Electric Company, where a classified catalogue was in use arranged by the library's own classification for engineering; this had the citation order

Machines: Parts: Materials: Problems

A topic such as metal fatigue, which assumed a new importance in the 1950s as the unexpected cause of at least two major air disasters, is a Problem, and thus fell into the least important facet. For most of the users of the library, this was acceptable; the company produced machines, and most of its research was concerned with these – motors, generators, nuclear reactors, aircraft. However, this citation order did mean that fatigue was scattered at a very large number of places in the classified (helpful!) sequence, simply because it fell into the last facet and was thus not used for grouping; in fact, it was to be found in more than 300 places. It is not surprising that this did not appeal to the groups of engineers who were working on this very problem; they could not be expected to regard as helpful an arrangement which scattered their interests to over 300 places (even though it could truthfully be said that every one of the 300+ could be identified through the alphabetical index to the classified sequence). A similar difficult was met in the library of the Atomic Energy Research Establishment, Harwell, where it proved impossible to find a satisfactory citation order in some subject areas covered by the catalogues. Some methods of solving the problem by making multiple entry under various forms of the same heading have been described in Chapter 7; D. J. Foskett suggested rotation in conjunction with the *London education classification*, while cycling is widely used in catalogues based on UDC. These solutions are mainly found in special libraries, and of course they can only apply to the catalogue, not to the arrangement of books on the shelves; we may assume for the time being that, for the general library at least, it *is* possible to find a citation order which will result in groupings helpful to the great majority of users, while remaining aware of the fact that in certain situations this is less likely to be the case.

Filing order

We have now established the need for a careful study of the literature of a subject to determine the concepts likely to arise, and the facets into which we can group these concepts; the need for order within the facets; and the need for a citation order which will determine the order of precedence of facets in composite subjects. We now have to study the way in which we must write out the schedule which will show clearly whereabouts in the sequence any given subject – simple or composite – will be found.

It is a commonly accepted principle of systematic arrangement that general should precede special. This can apply both to subjects related as genus to species and to those in which the relationship is syntactic. For example, Metals should precede Non-ferrous metals, which in its turn should precede Aluminium (though this does not indicate whether Aluminium should precede or follow Ferrous metals – aluminium does not lie in the same chain of division). At the same time, Aluminium should precede Heat treatment of aluminium, as should Heat treatment, since both are more general than the composite subject of which they form part. But should Aluminium precede Heat treatment, or *vice versa*? We cannot say that Aluminium is more general than Heat treatment since we have no basis of comparison; we cannot determine a special/general relationship between foci from different facets, only between those in the same facet. We have determined the order of facets when more than one is represented in a composite subject, but we still have to determine the order in which the facets themselves should be written down so that we can arrange simple subjects in which only one facet is represented. The citation order, together with the general principle enunciated above, that general should precede special, will enable us to do this.

Principle of inversion

Consider the following seven titles, falling within the basic class Literature:

The English novel
Trends in twentieth century literature
The novel as a literary form
Twentieth century English literature
English literature
The English novel in this century
The modern novel, 1900–

Using the citation order Language – Literary form – Period, we can re-state these subjects in the formal manner:

English: novel	(1)
Twentieth century	(2)
Novel	(3)
English: twentieth century	(4)
English	(5)
English: novel: twentieth century	(6)
Novel: twentieth century	(7)

Having done this, we can group them according to the citation order into those in which a language is specified; those in which no language is specified but we have a literary form; and those in which neither language nor literary form is specified but we have a period.

Group A	English: novel	(1)
	English: twentieth century	(4)

	English	(5)
	English: novel: twentieth century	(6)
Group B	Novel:	(3)
	Novel: twentieth century	(7)
Group C	Twentieth century	(2)

Now, however we arrange them, we must keep the groups intact, because that is the purpose of having a citation order. Consider the three subjects (6), (7) and (2); if we are to arrange these so that general precedes special, it must be in the order (2), (7), (6).

Twentieth century	(2)	(Group C)
Novel: twentieth century	(7)	(Group B)
English: novel: twentieth century	(6)	(Group A)

If we are to keep the groups intact, then equally *Group* C must precede *Group* B, which in turn must precede *Group* A. Within *Group* B, clearly (3) must precede (7). Within *Group* A, (5) must come first, since it is more general than any of the others, and (6) must come last, as being more special than any. This leaves us with (1) and (4) to sort out, but (1) must be grouped with (6), since within the general group English literature, they both deal with the novel, which is in the next facet to be considered. So we end up with the arrangement:

Group C	Twentieth century	(2)
Group B	Novel	(3)
	Novel: twentieth century	(7)
Group C	English	(5)
	English: twentieth century	(4)
	English: novel	(1)
	English: novel: twentieth century	(6)

We have now followed the two guidelines we established to begin with, the citation order Language – Literary form – Period, and the general-before-special principle. If we now study the result, we find that (perhaps contrary to expectation) it is the least important facet Period which comes first, with the most important, Language, coming last; that is to say, the filing order is the reverse of the citation order. This effect, which arose because we wish to preserve the idea of general before special for both semantic and syntactic relationships, is known as the *Principle of inversion*. If we do not follow this principle, then we shall find that general precedes special for semantic relationships, i.e. relationships between foci within the same facet, but that for some syntactic relationships general will follow special.

The principle of inversion is in conflict with the suggestion put forward under the heading *Preferred category* (page 150) that users like to find the material of most interest to them at the beginning of the sequence. In the example worked out above for Literature, before we come to any particular language (English will probably be the first), we shall have to scan through entries relating to the whole of Literature limited only by Period, and entries relating to particular literary forms – yet we have said that Language is the most important element. For this reason, some classification schemes have ignored the principle of inversion, for example the English Electric Company's scheme for *Engineering* previously mentioned, and the scheme for *Occupational health and safety* devised by D. J. Foskett. However, the introductions to editions of the English Electric scheme after the first pointed out that in practice this did not work satisfactorily. The problems with the citation order led to the abandonment of the classified catalogue in favour of post-coordinate indexing, with the classification used only for shelf arrangement. In the complete revision published in 1970 as *Thesaurofacet* (Chapter 25) the editors did follow the principle of inversion in the classification, and linked it to a thesaurus for their post-coordinate index.

The principle of inversion is one that often causes students an unnecessary amount of difficulty. The easiest way to understand it is to arrange a set of examples using first a scheme following the principle, then a scheme ignoring it. The difference in the overall arrangement will then become clear. In the example used above to demonstrate the principle, we used the citation order Language: Literary form: Period. This gave us the groups A, B and C, since this is the function of the citation order; we chose that citation order because it would give us those groups, which represent the kind of grouping that we think our readers will find useful. If we ignore the principle of inversion, we will make our filing order also A B C, so let us consider the effect this will have on the overall filing order. In Group B, if general is to precede special, Novel must precede Novel: twentieth century. For the same reason, in the Group A (ignoring title 4 for the moment) we shall have the sequence:

English
English: novel
English: novel: twentieth century

and since Period now follows literary form we can add title 4 at the end of this sequence. The overall order will thus be:

English
English: novel
English: novel: twentieth century
English: twentieth century
Novel
Novel: twentieth century
Twentieth century

It will be seen that the result here is not the orderly progression from general to special that we had before, but a progression which moves from general (English) to less general (English: novel) to least general (English: novel: twentieth century), then back to more general (English: twentieth century) to more general (Novel) to less general (Novel: twentieth century) to more general (twentieth century). The same kind of result will occur whenever the principle is not followed. Later in this chapter a schedule is worked out for Library science, using a particular citation order; the way in which the principle of inversion works can be seen very clearly if the titles on pages 164–5 are arranged first using the schedule with the citation order suggested, then using it with a different citation order but keeping the same filing order. (The exercise is easier if the schedule is given a notation, but can be carried out without this. The method is outlined within the next section, schedule construction). The principle will be ignored if we keep the same citation order and alter the filing order, as we did just above, or keep the same filing order but alter the citation order, as is suggested for the exercise. In both cases the result is the same; instead of an orderly progression in which a general heading always precedes headings more specific, we shall find an order in which it is difficult to predict exactly whereabouts a particular degree of generality is to be found. We shall still be able to find subjects, and the order will still give us the groupings which we have decided are likely to be the most helpful, but if we do not find what we want straight away, altering our search strategy is likely to be confusing.

Schedule construction

We have now established all the information that we need to enable us to construct a schedule, or table, in a given subject area. We have decided on the order of importance of the facets of the subject – the citation order; the order of foci within each facet; and, using the principle of inversion, we know that the order in which the facets should appear in the schedule is the reverse of the citation order. We now have to make a decision as to whether our schedules should be enumerative or synthetic; since the latter are very much easier to construct and use, let us consider them first.

In a synthetic schedule we need only list simple subjects; we do not try to list any composite subjects. All we need to include in the schedule will be the foci within the various facets; the citation order tells us how to combine these whenever this is necessary. To write down the schedule, all that has to be done is to write down the facets, beginning with the least important and ending with the most important. Within each facet, the foci will of course be arranged according to whatever principle we have adopted. In this instance, we will use the order found in DDC: chronological for periods; Poetry, Drama, Novel for literary forms; and English, German, French, Spanish, for languages. There does not appear to be any significant reason for departing from this, and many people will already be familiar with it. (Equally, a different order could be justified for both the languages and the literary form facet; there does not appear to be any overriding principle at stake, so let us follow precedent!)

To arrange composite subjects using such a schedule, we must first analyse them into individual foci, and rearrange these according to the citation order, so that the most important focus in each case is the first in the formal statement. Taking some of the titles from Table 6.4 and using the citation order Language, Literary form, Period, we arrive at the following formal statements:

3	English: novel
5	Drama: 1800–
7	Drama: techniques
9	Poetry: criticism
11	French: drama: twentieth century

15	English: drama: 1600–1900
17	English: twentieth century
19	English: poetry: 1901–1915
20	Novel
29	German: seventeenth century
30	German: poetry: twentieth century
32	Spanish: novel: 1516–1600

(Note that in addition to putting these into our preferred citation order we have eliminated various synonyms, e.g. fiction, verse, plays). Using the schedule we have constructed, we can put the primary foci into order:

Poetry	9
Drama	5, 7
Novel	25
English	3, 15, 17, 19
German	29, 30
Spanish	32

We have thus settled the order for some but not all of our examples. We still have to sort out those which have the same primary focus, once again using the schedule, but this time applying it *within* each group of items:

Drama:	techniques
	1800–

(because techniques comes from a facet less important than period and thus precedes it), and:

English:	twentieth century	17
	poetry	19
	drama	15
	novel	3
German:	seventeenth century	29
	poetry	30

We have now arrived at the correct placings for each of the subjects in our list:

9	Poetry: criticism
7	Drama: techniques
5	Drama: 1800–
25	Novel
17	English: twentieth century
19	English: poetry
15	English: drama: 1600–1900
3	English: novel
29	German: seventeenth century
30	German: poetry: twentieth century
11	French: drama: twentieth century
32	Spanish: novel: 1516–1600

In this particular case we did not have to go beyond the second concept in any of the statements, but if we had been obliged to the procedure would have been exactly the same. Suppose for example that we had reached a stage where we had:

English: drama: Restoration (1660–1700)
English: drama: Jacobean (1603–1625)
English: drama: techniques
English: drama: 1800–
English: drama
English: drama: 1840–1890

We should now have to arrange these according to the third concept in the formal statement, to give us:

English: drama
English: drama: techniques
English: drama: Jacobean (1603–1625)
English drama: Restoration (1660–1700)
English: drama: 1800–
English: drama: 1840–1890

and so on, until we had arrived at the most complete systematic arrangement possible. In a normal library situation, there will of course be more than one item at most points in our systematic arrangement, and these can then be arranged according to author's name, in chronological sequence, or by some similar characteristic additional to the subject specification. This may well be signified by a Cutter number, to give a shelf mark.

The schedule is thus very simple, yet from it we are able to find an unambiguous place for any given composite subject (provided of course that the concepts involved in it are listed in our schedule). Because we list only single concepts, with none of their possible combinations, the schedule can be very brief, yet be as powerful in arranging our schedules as a much longer enumerative schedule.

If, however, we decide to compile an enumerative schedule, we have to follow a similar procedure, but this time for any and every composite subject. For each focus in the primary facet we have to envisage which foci from the second facet will be likely to co-occur in a composite subject, and list these; in addition, for each of these we have to consider which foci from the third facet are likely to co-occur, and then list the composite subjects formed in this way. Then, when we come to classify by the scheme, we do not have to build up the composite subject represented in the item we are dealing with, but will instead find it, ready made, in the scheme.

An example will help to make the distinction clearer. If we are using the Universal Decimal Classification (UDC), we find that in the basic class Literature we have a completely synthetic schedule, which occupies about a page of the schedules; to classify a composite topic such as *The English novel of the 1840s* we have to find English, novel and 1840s, and combine these elements. If we are using an enumerative classification such as the Bibliographic Classification (BC1), we turn to Literature, then find English literature, then find Nineteenth century English literature, and finally the period 1837–1870, which is the closest we find to the precise one we require; then we find listed under that period : novelists (as well as the other literary forms). Problems of synthesis are mainly notational: can we combine the notation for the various elements to give us the correct composite notation? These are discussed in a later section. The problems of enumeration, on the other hand, are mainly those of quantity: can we enumerate all the composite subjects we are likely to need, or do we make a selection? LCC is an enumerative scheme, and its schedules for language and literature occupy over 2,000 pages of print, as opposed to UDC's one; but even this is only a selection of the possible combinations, because LCC only includes subjects if there is literary warrant for them in the Library of Congress *and* it is thought that they need to be specified for the shelf arrangement. What usually happens in enumerative schemes is that a rather limited selection of composite subjects is listed and that others which are not listed have to be accommodated with their most important focus but without specifying other foci. In addition, enumerative schemes do not usually have a clear facet structure, so that one is often left in doubt as to which is the most important focus.

Consider the subject 'The lighting of museum display cases'. The idea of dependence suggests that 'lighting' depends on having 'display cases' to light; we would not have the display cases if there were nothing to display, and that this in turn depends on the existence of 'museums'. We can therefore turn to the schedules in the confidence that the primary focus is museums, and in DDC20 this takes us to 060, where we find:

	060	General organizations and museology
	069	Museology (Museum science)
	069.2	Management & use of physical plant
	069.29	Utilities and related facilities *inc* lighting
or	069.3	Equipment, furniture, furnishings
	069.31	Exhibit cases, screens, pedestals
or	069.5	Collections and exhibits of museum objects
	069.53	Maintenance. . . display . . .

Which is the correct citation order? The Principle of Inversion says 069.53 'Display of museum objects' is correct, but we could argue a case for 069.31 'Exhibit cases', or a much weaker case for 069.29 'Lighting'. To take another example, 'A collection of Anglican wedding sermons'; looking through the schedules for Christian church we find:

	250	Christian orders & local church
	252	Texts of sermons
	252.03	Anglican
or	252.1	For baptisms, confirmations, weddings, funerals

Here again the Principle of Inversion tells us that 252.1 is better than 252.03, though we cannot really use the principle of dependence here. In neither of these cases is there any specific instruction on citation order in the schedules; however, there is guidance in the Editor's Introduction, (Section 5.13), which lays down some principles to follow in such circumstances. Each new edition of DDC covers more eventualities as the need for rules in specific instances is noted, either in rules for citation order or in Tables of precedence, discussed in Chapter 17, but there are still places where we have neither and must rely on general principles such as the Principle of inversion.

Another problem that is found in practice in enumerative schemes, despite the fact that theoretically it cannot occur, is that concepts of different kinds are found to be mixed up, so that cross-classification becomes not so much a danger, more a way of life. Consider the following excerpt from the abridged UDC schedules:

628	PUBLIC HEALTH ENGINEERING
628.3	Sewage, rain-, foul-water. Purification etc.
628.33	Physical and mechanical treatment
.334	Screening. Grit and grease removal
335	Flocculation: tanks etc.
.336	Sludge: handling, disposal
.337	Electrical treatment of sewage
.34	Chemical treatment processes etc.

It will be seen that in the middle of a series of methods of treatment (Actions, Operations, Processes) we find a material 'sludge' which is the result of a process of settling, not mentioned in the schedule. In another example we find:

361	SOCIAL RELIEF IN GENERAL
.9	Relief or aid in emergencies, disasters
.91	Earthquakes, storms, hurricanes
.92	Floods
.93	War, civil war
.94	Epidemics
.95	Famine
.96	Fires, conflagrations
.98	Technical (volunteer) relief services

Either technical (volunteer) relief services are to be regarded as disasters in themselves, or we are faced with considerable problems in finding the correct place for technical (volunteer) services for earthquake relief. We shall be in the same position as we found in the last paragraph, uncertain of the correct place to choose for a composite subject not specifically listed in the schedules.

As has already been indicated in Chapter 7, all systems enumerate to some extent; a synthetic classification has to list the foci in each facet, and if it fails to list the particular focus we are searching for on some occasion we shall again be faced with the problem of lack of specificity. For example, the subject *Design and construction of transistor superhets* implies a specification:

Communication engineering – radio – apparatus – receivers – superheterodyne – using transistors

If we are using the Colon Classification (CC6), which is as completely synthetic a scheme as possible, we find that this can only be classified with radio engineering; the scheme simply does not enumerate anything more detailed in this subject area. Even with UDC we find (using the abridged edition) that we can only specify receivers, not superhets, and are thus unable to be specific.

It should be remembered that we have been thinking so far of the classifier trying to find a place in the overall arrangement for each new subject as it arises. From the point of view of the user, who only sees the results of the classifier's work, there is no difference between a synthetic scheme and an enumerative, except in those instances where the enumerative scheme has failed to foresee a composite subject. If we were to write out all the possible combinations of concepts arising from the use of a synthetic scheme, we should have an enumerative scheme. The real problem for the classificationist, i.e. the compiler of a classification scheme, is that the number of possible combinations is enormous. Mathematically speaking, if we have a schedule containing four facets, with four foci in each facet, the number of possible subjects we can specify is 624! And this from a ridiculously simple schedule containing only 16 concepts! It is small wonder that an enumerative scheme usually only lists a selection – but provided that it lists the *right* selection, it will prove just as effective as a synthetic scheme, and the user will have no means of telling the difference. The real problem is that enumerative schemes are usually *closed*; if we do have to deal with a subject not enumerated, we have to wait for the compiler to tell us where we can put it in our schedule, rather than insert it ourselves as we can with a synthetic scheme.

Construction of a classification scheme

It may be helpful to demonstrate how we may set about constructing a classification schedule in a limited subject area, in this case Library science. By studying the following list of titles carefully, we can establish certain facets; we can then decide on a citation order and helpful order within each facet. Finally we can write down the schedule and use it to arrange the items (titles taken from *Library science abstracts*).

1 Progress of the Universal Decimal Classification in the USSR
2 Baltimore County Public Library initiates book catalog
3 An art reference library for children
4 Automation in the Detroit Public Library
5 Cooperation in government libraries
6 Non-standard material at the National Lending Library for Science and Technology
7 The National Library of Canada
8 Libraries and librarianship in Saskatchewan
9 Book selection tools for agricultural documents
10 An information retrieval system for maps
11 Aspects of recent research in classification
12 La Roche College classification scheme for phonograph records
13 The economics of book catalog production
14 Classification of law books in the University of South Africa Library

15 Book selection and acquisition processes in university libraries
16 Administrative problems of university libraries
17 Revision of classification schemes for Nigerian needs
18 Acquisitions
19 School libraries
20 Federal assistance to special libraries
21 The hospital library service in Lincoln
22 A mechanized circulation system
23 Automation in university libraries
24 Newspapers in technical college libraries
25 Library services to the blind in New Zealand
26 Public libraries in the New York Metropolitan area
27 Metropolitan areas growing and under stress: the situation of Detroit
   Public Library

If we try to group the concepts arising from the titles, we find that a first approximation gives us four groups:

Libraries	*Materials*	*Operations*	*Common facets*
special	non-standard	cooperation	
government	newspapers	administration	automation
university	books	selection	research
technical college	phonorecords	acquisition	revision
public	(i.e. records)	cataloguing	economics
municipal	maps	catalogues	various places
county	agriculture	bookform	
national	law	classification	
hospitals		schemes	
blind		UDC	
children		circulation	
reference		finance	
art		Federal aid	
science			

It is clear that there is a group of 'Libraries' but that these fall into more than one subfacet:

kind	*people served*	*mode of use*	*subject coverage*
special	hospitals	reference	art
government	blind		science and
academic	children		technology
university			
technical college			
school			
public			
municipal			
county			
national			

We can of course extend the above lists even without literary warrant, by the addition of, for example, lending, or industrial, under kind, once we have identified the facets.

We can also subdivide the Materials facet into two groups:

subject
agriculture   law
form
books   maps   newspapers   non-standard   records

Within the Operations facet we find some concepts which depend on others, e.g.

classification–schemes
cataloguing–catalogues

In each case, further subdivision by kind can be made. It would be possible to separate these into another facet, but for the time being we may keep them with the operations to which they belong.

We find a group of topics which may appear in any basic class, called common foci; as we shall see in the next chapter, there are usually four of these groups, but in the present example only two are represented, place and common subjects.

Having identified the facets, we need to decide on a citation order. For the neutral situation, this might well be Libraries – Materials – Operations, though in the context of a library school a citation order which brings Operations to the most significant place might well be more useful. Within Libraries, we may decide that kind is most important, then population served, then mode of use and finally subject; Materials may be arranged primarily by subject, then by physical form. Of the two common facets, place is more important than common subjects. This gives us an overall order:

Libraries – kind – population served – mode of use – subject – Materials – subject – form – Operations – Place – Common subjects.

If we decide to follow the principle of inversion, we shall arrive at a schedule outline as follows:

Common subjects
Place
Operations
Materials
  by form
  by subject
Libraries
  by subject
  by mode of use
  by population served
  by kind

Within each facet we need to arrive at a helpful order. In the Common subjects none suggests itself; for Place, we may use the schedule from an existing scheme; those Operations which form a logical sequence in time may be arranged chronologically, with circulation perhaps moved to a place under administration rather than its chronological place following technical services; in kind of library, a progression by size of population served is a possibility. We can thus build up a schedule as shown in Figure 9.1.

There are several points to note from this schedule. The first is that it is very incomplete in its listing of foci, but that despite this it probably identifies most of the major facets of library science. The more literature we study, the more foci we can insert, but additional facets are likely to be few. Secondly, this analysis is identical to the kind of analysis we looked at Chapter 6 in trying to identify semantic relationships; we can in fact use the layout to show the hierarchical relationships in constructing a classification schedule, or use BT-NT-RT links to show the relationships if we are constructing a thesaurus. The subject analysis process for both is the same. Thirdly, we need to carry our analysis further than we have done so far; for example, we could have blind children as the population served – but we have said that it is not possible to combine foci from the same facet! We can introduce *subfacets* within the persons facet, to distinguish people by age, sex, and other relevant characteristics; it is possible to identify as many as 15 subfacets in this particular facet. Experience may also suggest modifications to the citation order. A scheme of the kind adumbrated here was devised by the CRG,[2] and was used in the Library Association library, and also to arrange *LISA* in 1969 and 1970. This had the schedule order:

Ab/D	Common subdivisions
E/F	Equipment
G/K	Processes – Technical and administrative
L/M	Library materials
N/Z	Library services and use,

the citation order being the inverse of this. As a result of user reactions, the citation order was changed from the original Libraries – Materials – Operations to Operations – Materials – Libraries at the beginning of 1971, with the revised schedule order:

Ab/D	Common subdivisions
E/H	Types of libraries and users
J/M	Materials and use
N/R	Operations and agents
S/Z	Processes – Technical

The LA library continued to use the original scheme, until the classification was replaced by DDC. The use of the notation was discontinued in *LISA* in 1993, and it is now arranged under a much simpler notation reflected by broad subject headings, though in effect the arrangement still uses the detailed revised classification, with a full subject index derived by chain procedure For example, we have:

Common subject subvisions
  revision
  research
  automation
  economics
Common place subdivisions
  (no schedule needed)
Operations
  Administration
    selection
    acquisition
    circulation
  Technical services
    cataloguing
      catalogues
        book form
    classification
      schemes
        UDC
  Cooperation
  Finance
    government aid
Materials
  Books
  Serials
    periodicals
    newspapers
  non-standard (i.e. non-printed word)
    maps
    records
  by subject
    (no schedule needed)
Libraries
  by subject
    (no schedule needed)
  by mode of use
    reference
  by population served
    children
    hospitals
    handicapped
      blind
  by kind
    special
      government
      industry
    academic
      school
      technical college
      university
    public
      municipal
      county
      national

Fig. 9.1 Tentative schedule for library science

4   USERS AND USER SERVICES
4.1   LIBRARIES AND SERVICES BY TYPE OF USER
4.11   CHILDREN AND YOUNG PEOPLE

An article under this heading, *The need for cultural diversity in preschool services* (LISA 93-4179) has index entries based on the full string:

Public libraries – Children's libraries – Role in – Multicultural education – Preschool children – Users – Libraries

corresponding to the detailed classification.

A computer-based approach

A new approach has been advocated by Losee, who begins by posing a series of questions.[3] Many of these relate to order, but the main focus is on the use of a different kind of notation, Gray codes, which were used in the 1950s in the design of telephone switching circuits.[4] If we look at the sequence in which a series of switching relays operate, we find that they change position in such a way that only one changes at a time. This can be represented by a series of binary codes in which each code differs from those on either side of it in one digit only. If we compare the series of three-digit codes with the usual binary notation the difference becomes apparent:

Binary codes 000 001 010 011 100 101 110 111
Gray codes   000 001 011 010 110 100 101 111

The usual binary codes change 1 digit at a time (000 to 001), 2 (101 to 110) or 3 (011 to 100), whereas the Gray codes always change only one digit at a time. Two-digit codes can be visualized as the four corners of a square coded 00, 01, 10 and 11; longer codes can be imagined as the vertices of an n-dimensional cube. Losee suggests that computer processing of documents could show similarities and differences in such a way that they could be given Gray codes to arrange them in a sequence in which the most similar documents are close together, whereas the least similar would be furthest apart.[5] While this is one of the desired objectives of classification, it is not clear just how the scheme would be implemented. The sequence would be dependent on the items in a given collection, their number and the aim of the collection, which presumably means that we would find the same works differently arranged in different libraries. This is not necessarily a bad thing, but it would prevent any kind of centralized processing such as we have at present. Users might also find it disconcerting! Binary codes of any kind are longer than the corresponding decimal codes as found in DDC; there would be practical problems in labelling books for shelf arrangement. The idea is still to be fully worked out, but may find a place in the digital library of the future.

Summary

In this chapter we have looked at the analysis that must form the starting point of any controlled vocabulary, alphabetical or systematic. If we are to have an orderly approach to vocabulary construction, it must be based on a methodical study of the terms found in the literature and the relationships between them. We must then organize them in such a way as to show the terms and their relationships in a way which will be helpful to the user and facilitate the retrieval of information, whether this be by shelf arrangement, printed indexes or computer searching of databases. We do have a method of constructing a controlled vocabulary, even though it still needs refining.[6] One thing we must always bear in mind is the needs of the user for whom we are constructing the vocabulary. We should also remember that in a computer-based system, a controlled vocabulary can be used in conjunction with natural language searching to give results which are better than either could give on its own.

References

1   There are many works on analytico-synthetic classification, of which the following list is a brief selection. Most of the basic theoretical work was completed in the 1950s or earlier, and older texts are still valid in many cases.
Brown, A. with Langridge, D. W. and Mills, J., *An introduction to subject indexing*, London, Bingley, 2nd edn, 1982 (programmed text)
Foskett, D. J., *Classification and indexing in the social sciences*, London, Butterworths, 2nd edn, 1975.
Foskett, D. J., 'Concerning general and special classifications (with examples from the 1990 revision of Bliss Class J, Education), *International classification*, **18** (2), 1991, 87–91.
Hunter, E. J. *Classification made simple*, Aldershot, Gower, 1987.
Langridge, D. W., *Classification and indexing in the humanities*, London, Butterworths, 1976.
Langridge, D., *Subject analysis: principles and procedures*, London ; New York, Bowker-Saur, 1989.
Vickery, B. C., *Classification and indexing in science and technology*, London, Butterworths, 3rd edn, 1975.
Knowledge organization has regular bibliographies of current literature in classification.
2   Daniel, R. and Mills, J., *A classification of library science*, London, Library Association, 1974.
3   Losee, R. M., 'Seven fundamental questions for the science of library classification', *Knowledge organization*, **20** (2), 1993, 65–70.
4   Gilbert, E. N., 'Gray codes and paths on the n-cube', *Bell system technical journal*, **37**, May 1958, 815–26.
5   Losee, R. M., 'A Gray code based ordering for documents on shelves: classification for browsing and retrieval', *Journal of the American Society for Information Science*, **43**, 1992, 312–22.
6   Svenonius, E., 'Unanswered questions in the design of controlled vocabularies', *Journal of the American Society for Information Science*, **37**, 1986, 331–40.

The best way to learn the significance of facet analysis, citation order, the Principle of inversion, and other matters discussed in this chapter is to work through them for oneself. Take a collection of, say, 50 titles within a particular subject field (an abstracting or indexing journal could be a good source), identify the significant terms listed, write each term on a separate card, sort them into heaps (facets), and select a suitable order within the various facets and a citation order. Construct a schedule using the Principle of inversion and arrange the titles; then construct a schedule disregarding the Principle, and compare the resulting arrangement with the first. It is not necessary to allocate any notation to a schedule of this size in order to carry out the exercise.

Chapter 10

General classification schemes

So far we have been considering the problems that arise within a particular basic class. If we wish to include more than this, we have to face additional problems, in particular the one of overall order; in what sequence do we arrange a collection of basic classes? In the early years of library classification in the modern sense (i.e. from Dewey's introduction of his decimal classification in 1876) it was assumed that the order of main classes was the one important feature of a scheme, and such classification theorists as H. E. Bliss devoted much time and thought to this. When Ranganathan introduced the idea of consistent facet analysis applied to all basic classes in the first edition of Colon Classification (CC), published in 1933, interest began to concentrate on the development of 'special' classifications, i.e. those applied to a particular, limited, subject field, usually a single basic class, and during the 1950s the Classification Research Group in Britain devoted most of its thought to this problem. Techniques of analysis and synthesis, and the notational devices required to permit them, were developed, and several notable schemes were produced. In the 1960s, there was a swing back towards the general scheme and its problems, with the objective of developing a new classification of the whole of recorded knowledge, and some practical work was done with the aid of a grant from NATO. We have therefore to consider now the problems of arranging basic classes in a helpful order, and the additional features which we must provide in a general scheme if it is to function properly.

Common facets

If the titles listed in Table 10.1 are studied carefully, it will appear that there are certain kind of concept which keep recurring, and which may be found in any basic class. We find for example dictionary, periodical, illustration, encyclopaedia: all kinds of bibliographical form. Statistics, law, societies, research: all kinds of subject which exist in their own right, yet may be found as features within other subjects as well. We also find that all subjects may be considered from the historical and geographical points of view, or to use the more common terms, time and place. There are in effect four groups of subjects which may occur within any basic class: four *common facets*. In providing a schedule for a basic class, we may decide that it is not appropriate to include these common subdivisions, but obviously in a general scheme they must appear.[1]

Table 10.1 Identify the common factors

1	*Metal industry* handbook and directory
2	Glossary of terms relating to iron and steel
3	English poetry and prose: an anthology
4	Metallurgical dictionary
5	British miniature electronic components data annual 1967–68
6	Colliers encyclopaedia
7	The Oxford English dictionary
8	*Life* magazine
9	XIX century fiction: a bibliographical record
10	Cassell's encyclopaedia of literature
11	*Washington Post*
12	Bibliography on steel converter practice
13	Instrumentation in the metallurgical industry
14	The *Voice of youth*: the Poetry Society's junior quarterly
15	Aluminium Development Association: Directory of members
16	Winston Churchill: the early years
17	The Highlands of Scotland in pictures
18	The rules of the game of netball
19	Statistical assessment of the life characteristics: a bibliography
20	A year with horses: John Beard's sketch book
21	American scientists of the 19th century
22	Handbook of chemistry and physics
23	Education in Scotland
24	Scientific and learned societies of Great Britain
25	Annual abstract of statistics
26	International who's who

The titles in Table 10.1 indicate that in some cases the bibliographical forms and the common subjects may be applied to the whole of knowledge as a unit, not just to a limited area such as a single basic class. A general encyclopaedia presents information on the whole of knowledge in a particular form; a general periodical may treat any or every subject. In a general scheme we shall therefore find it necessary to make provision for this, in what is known as a generalia class. Some general schemes also include in this class topics which may be regarded as pervasive or tool subjects: DDC includes Library science and Documentation, for example.

Main class order

In a general scheme, we have to continue our process of grouping by arranging related basic classes together in sequence, and imposing some sort of overall plan. To start in this way with the elements and build them up into larger groups is the inductive approach; in the past, the deductive method of taking the whole of knowledge and dividing it up into smaller areas has been the one more often used. The results are similar, but we find that in many cases the number of areas discovered by the deductive approach bears a close relationship to the number of notational symbols available, the most striking example being DDC, where Dewey freely admitted that 'Theoretically division of every subject into just nine parts is absurd', but nevertheless went ahead to do exactly that. By using induction we are more likely to avoid this kind of trap.

A major problem has always been to define the term main class, which is commonly used for these large areas or groups. We can see that heat, light, sound, electricity and magnetism can be grouped with various other basic classes to form a group of subjects which we call physics; but physics can itself be grouped with such subjects as chemistry and astronomy to form the group of physical sciences, while these can further be grouped with the biological sciences to form the natural sciences group. Finally, we can group this with a similar large assembly to form science and technology. We can carry out a similar series of groupings in other disciplines, ending up with three assemblies: science and technology, social sciences, and humanities. At what point do we stop? Or do we conclude that there are only three main classes? The question is evidently one of terminology, and in practice we find no agreement between the compilers of general classification schemes as to what constitutes a main class. Ranganathan defines main class: 'any class enumerated in the first order array of a scheme of classification of the universe of knowledge. This definition is valid only for the scheme concerned' (Tables 10.2a, b and c).[2] Elsewhere he suggests that main classes are conventional, fairly homogenous and mutually exclusive groups of basic classes, and also introduces the idea of 'partially comprehensive' main classes as a means of differentiating the 'supergroups' such as physical sciences. The idea that main classes are merely conventional groups may serve to free us from having to find any theoretical justification for our selection and ordering, and it emphasizes the fact that there is unlikely to be long-term stability in any particular selection we may make. However, it is important to study the arguments which have been advanced to justify one order or another of main classes, and to see what effect this factor has on the overall arrangement given by a scheme. It is certainly the case that the major classification schemes are discipline-oriented (discipline: branch of instruction or learning), and Brown's *Subject Classification* was one of very few attempts to construct a scheme in which the primary division was not by discipline. The introduction to *Sears list of subject headings* (Chapter 24) states:

> Books are classified by discipline, not by subject. A single subject may be dealt with in many disciplines . . . The cataloger must examine the book in hand and determine the discipline in which the author is writing. On the basis of that decision the cataloger classifies the book, not the subject of the book.

This obviously takes a different view of the subject of a document from the one used in this book, but the emphasis on classification by discipline is correct.

Dewey

Dewey credits his arrangement of main classes to 'the inverted Baconian arrangement of the St Louis library . . .', but also points out that 'In all the work, philosophical theory and accuracy have been made to yield to practical usefulness'. Palmer[3] suggests that if literary warrant be taken as the criterion, BNB identified no fewer than 54 main classes in DDC, rather than Dewey's ten. In many ways, the order in DDC is poor, separating Language (400) from Literature (800), and History (900) from the other Social sciences (300). It also reflects the state of knowledge of the latter half of the nineteenth century, with, for example, psychology shown as a division of philosophy. It illustrates the point that an order of main classes which may be justified at one point in time may well cease to be acceptable as time passes; despite its groundings in Baconian theory, nobody would now claim that Dewey's main class order is particularly helpful or theoretically valid.

Bliss

Bliss devoted a great deal of time to establishing the correct order of main classes, and the introductions to the two volumes of his scheme contain much that is of value in this discussion, as does his other work.[4] He introduced several ideas which are still of value. Perhaps the most basic of these is the idea of the 'educational and scientific consensus'. Bliss thought it vital that a classification scheme for recorded knowledge should reflect the structure of knowledge as recognized and taught by scientists, philosophers and educators, and that the more knowledge we acquire, the more clearly we shall see this desired structure. Unfortunately, this is not the case: knowledge changes, the structure of knowledge changes, and any widely accepted pattern is likely to be out of date, for the purpose of research is indeed to change the structure of knowledge as well as to expand it. Bliss himself recognized that 'the old order changeth', and that any classification scheme will inevitably become gradually more and more divorced from helpful order; what he does not seem to have recognized is the speed with which this process can take place.

To establish the order of subjects within the educational and scientific consensus, Bliss used three main principles. The first of these is *collocation of related subjects*. For example, Bliss considers that Psychology is related to both Medicine and Education, so that the relevant part of his outline is as follows:

Anthropological sciences
  Medicine
  Psychology
  Education
  Social science

Here it will be seen that psychology is linked to both of these other topics. However, it may also be seen that Bliss did not follow his own second principle, *subordination of specific to general*, for in order to collocate it with psychology, education has to precede the more general heading social science. However, in general these two principles are sound and can give a helpful arrangement.

The third principle Bliss called *gradation in speciality*, and it relates to what is in effect a kind of progression of dependence. If we compare mathematics and physics, we can see that though we use the ideas of mathematics in physics, the converse is not true; we do not use the ideas of physics in mathematics, and to this extent therefore physics depends on and should follow mathematics. If we now compare physics and chemistry we find that on similar grounds chemistry should follow physics. We can arrive at an order within the sciences which can be justified in this way:

logic
mathematics
physics
chemistry
astronomy
geology
geography

It becomes rather more difficult to apply this idea to the biological sciences and social sciences, but within its limitations it is a valuable principle.

Apart from Bliss we find few efforts to produce a philosophically justifiable order of main classes. Ranganathan has argued the case for his own order in CC, but without conveying any great conviction; he clearly recognizes the fluid nature of such groupings, and is in any case more concerned with order within classes. LCC does not claim any sort of theoretical basis – it reflects the holdings and use of that library and is thus justified for its own purposes. UDC is based on DDC, but is trying to arrive at a more satisfactory order by a slow process of change; so far there has been one major relocation, placing language together with literature, and others are foreshadowed.

Phase relations

Assuming that we use the synthetic principle and thus restrict our needs to those of listing simple subjects in our schedules, we can compile a classification scheme that will now serve most purposes. We can analyse basic classes into facets, list the foci in each facet and state the citation order; the basic classes themselves can be grouped into a helpful order, with a generalia class and common facets added. We have accounted for semantic relationships by showing related subjects together in the sequence, and we have allowed for syntactic relationships within the basic classes, by permitting the combination of foci from different facets.

There is, however, one further kind of subject that we have to make provision for: concepts linked by one of the *phase relationships* discussed in Chapter 7 and illustrated in Table 7.1. As we saw there, these relationships are necessarily *ad hoc*, since though we can tell that they are likely to occur, we cannot foresee in advance which concepts may be linked in this way. It is in fact here that we see the final distinction between the enumerative and the synthetic approach. In an enumerative scheme, all that we find will be provision for phase relations that existed before the scheme was compiled; e.g. in DDC we find *science and religion* listed (the Darwinian controversy) but not *science and politics*. Phase relations can only be accommodated as they arise in a synthetic scheme; even here there is a need to recognize the different kinds, e.g. in UDC the colon, :, is used to link the notation for the two phases in this kind of relation, but it is used for all four kinds and is thus not very precise. CC is the only scheme to set out detailed provisions for phase relationships, though the four given in Chapter 7 are in fact taken from BNB rather than CC.

The examples given of phase relationships in Table 7.1 all illustrate the linking of concepts from essentially different basic classes, but this is not necessarily the case. Phase relationships can occur between foci in the same facet, e.g.

The influence of Goethe on Sir Walter Scott

We have pointed out that foci from the same facet cannot normally be combined; indeed, this is the criterion by which we judge whether we have carried our analysis to the point where foci in one facet are mutually exclusive. Phase relationships are obviously one kind of relationship in which foci cannot be mutually exclusive. This also illustrates the point that phase relationships do not in general present serious problems in alphabetical systems, except that it may be necessary to use a phrase to specify them; it is in systematic arrangement that we have to make special provision for them.

We saw in Chapter 7 that in the case of bias, influence and exposition phase relationships, there is a primary phase and a secondary phase, the primary phase being the key subject. Thus in the subject 'anatomy for nurses' it is anatomy which is the primary phase, and we shall therefore classify such a work with others on anatomy, *not* with those on nursing. Similarly, 'a psychological study of *Hamlet*' goes with other works on *Hamlet*, not with other works on psychology. But what of the comparison or interaction phase?

We saw that in this case both phases are equal: there is no primary phase. This presents a problem if we are thinking in terms of shelf classification, where we have to find one place at which to locate a given book. Most general classification schemes have a simple rule that in this situation, the primary phase is to be the one appearing first in the schedules. This is an arbitrary rule intended to save the trouble of making a decision on merit each time the occasion arises; it means that using DDC, 'Science and politics' will be classified with politics, whereas using CC, it would belong with science. In each case it would be necessary to make provision for the secondary phase, for example by making an added entry in the catalogue.

Having seen the need to include them, we now have to decide whereabouts in the overall order we want to file them. CC files all phase relationships immediately after the subject treated generally. The *BNB Supplementary schedules*, used in BNB between 1960 and 1971, made provision for bias phase to be filed there, but the others to be filed after the common facets but before the first facet of the basic class. DDC now makes provision for bias phase by the standard subdivision –024, but this places such items in the middle of 'miscellany' with 'the subject as a profession' on one side, and 'directories' on the other. Other kinds of phase are occasionally enumerated in DDC, but there is no consistent synthetic provision for them.

Recent trends

Traditional classification schemes rely on main classes which reflect the traditional disciplines. Modern developments in all areas of knowledge tend to cross the boundaries between disciplines; new subjects develop not only by fission, but also by fusion – the merging of previously distinct disciplines. It is very difficult to accommodate interdisciplinary or multidisciplinary subjects within a traditional framework, and existing schemes are subjected to increasing criticism for their failure to keep pace with changes in knowledge. The pace of change is itself increasing, yet we are still constrained by yesterday's thought patterns.[5]

One way to cater for the multidisciplinary approach is through the recognition of Phenomena and entities; one scheme which specifically allows this is the BSO (Chapter 20), in which we find:

088   PHENOMENA & ENTITIES
          This class is for phenomena or entities treated from a multidisci-
          plinary or non-disciplinary point of view. It is to be used only
          when emphasis on one discipline is lacking. The content of this
          class will be mainly materials and organisms

which *precedes* the main sequence in disciplinary order. Similar provision is made in the Generalia class of BC2 (Chapter 19), again preceding the main sequence of disciplines.

It can be seen that the problem of finding a satisfactory overall order that will last for anything more than a few years is one of the most difficult problems facing systematic arrangement. Traditional approaches do not serve as a helpful basis for placing new interdisciplinary subjects in relation to the disciplines from which they arise; novel methods may fail to accommodate the mass of published information that still falls into the conventional framework. As Mr Bennet observed, 'it seems an hopeless business'.[6] The solution may lie in the recognition of the fact that any user of a scheme can only be aware of a relatively small part of it at any time, even in a small library; the overall order will in practice not be visible. It seems likely that information will continue to be presented in conventional ways, even though the conventions may change from decade to decade; the problem lies perhaps more in the area of keeping up to date than in that of theoretical study.

Table 10.2(a) Comparative classification: social sciences
NB A line between two subjects indicates that another subject intervenes. Two lines indicate a considerable gap.

DDC and UDC	LCC	BC	CC
Psychology	Psychology	Geography	Humanities and social sciences
Ethics	Ethics	Anthropology	----------
----------	History	Psychology	Psychology
Social sciences	Geography	Education	Social sciences
Sociology	Anthropology	Social sciences	Education
Statistics	Folklore and customs	Sociology	Geography
Politics	Social sciences	History	History
Economics	Statistics	Social welfare	Politics
Law	Economics	Ethics	Economics
Government	Transport	Politics	Transport
Military science	Commerce	Law	Commerce
Social welfare	Sociology	Economics	Sociology
Education	Social groups	Business methods	Anthropology
Commerce	Welfare		Social work
Transport	Political science		Law
Folklore and customs	Law		
========	Education		
Business methods	========		
========	Military science		
Geography			
History			

Table 10.2(b) Comparative classification: humanities

NB Opinions differ as to whether a subject such as 'recreation' is in the humanities or the social sciences; it is included here if that appears to be the intention of the scheme. LC treats 'language' and 'literature' separately for the major Western languages; UDC permits either approach.

DDC	UDC	LCC	BC	CC
Philosophy	Philosophy	Philosophy	Philosophy	Humanities and Social sciences
-------	History of Philosophy	Logic	Logic	Spiritual experience and Mysticism
Philosophy – topics	Philosophy – topics	-------	-------	Humanities
Logic	-------	Religion	Religion	Fine arts
History of Philosophy	Logic	-------	-------	Literature and Language
Religion	Religion	Recreation	-------	Literature
-------	-------	-------	Fine arts	Language
-------	-------	Music	Literature and Language (together)	Religion
Language	Fine arts	Fine arts		Philosophy
-------	Photography	Literature and Language		Logic
-------	Music	(sometimes together, sometimes not)		
Fine arts	Recreation			
Photography	Literature and Language			
Music	Language			
Recreation	Literature			
Literature	(or together)			

Table 10.2(c) Comparative classification: science and technology

NB Two approaches are shown: 'science' as a whole followed by 'technology' as a whole, or each individual science followed by its related technology. DC in 'medicine' and BC in 'physics' depart from their normal practice of separating the two.

DDC and UDC	LCC	BC	CC
Science	Science	Science	Science
Mathematics	Mathematics	Mathematics	Mathematics
Astronomy	Astronomy	Physics (including	Astronomy
Physics	Physics	some applications)	Physics
Chemistry	Chemistry	Chemistry	Engineering
Crystallography	Geology	Chemical technology	Chemistry
Mineralogy	Natural history	Astronomy	[Chemical] Technology
Geology	Botany	Geology	Biology
Biology	Zoology	Geography	Geology
Botany	Anatomy	Biology	Mining
Zoology	Physiology	Botany	Botany
Technology	Medicine	Zoology	Agriculture
Medicine (including	Agriculture	Anthropology	Zoology
scientific aspects)	Technology	Medicine	Animal husbandry
Engineering	Engineering	————	Medicine
Agriculture	Building	————	Useful arts
Domestic economy	Mechanical engineering	Useful arts	
Business methods	Electrical engineering	Agriculture	
Chemical technology	Chemical engineering	Engineering	
Manufactures	Manufactures	Manufactures	
Building	Domestic economy	Domestic arts	
		Building	

References

1   Grolier, E. de, *A study of general categories applicable to classification and coding in documentation*, Paris, Unesco, 1962.
2   In the rules for main classes in CC6.
3   Palmer, B. I., *Itself an education*, London, Library Association, 1971. Chapters 2 and 3.
4   See Chapter 19 for details of the writings of H. E. Bliss.
5   Toffler, A., *Future shock*, London, Bodley Head, 1970.
6   Austen, J., *Pride and prejudice*, 1813. Chapter 20.

Library resources and technical services has a literature review each year with the subtitle 'the year's work in subject analysis'. Other periodicals to watch include *Knowledge organization* 1993– (previously *International classification*, 1974–1992), and *Cataloguing and classification quarterly*. The appropriate chapters in *British librarianship and information work* are valuable summaries.

Chapter 11
Notation

Unlike alphabetical arrangement, systematic order is not self-evident, and we may find that there are differing views as to the best (i.e. most helpful) arrangement at any point. It would be most unhelpful if we had to work our way through the schedules every time we wished to find a particular subject on the shelves or in the catalogue, even if the guiding was of a much higher standard than is usually found. To make systematic arrangement a practical proposition we must add to the schedules a set of symbols – a notation – which *does* have a self-evident order; we can then use the notation to find the subjects we want on the shelves or in the catalogue in a clearly organized order.[1]

There are two important points here. The first is that the notation is something *added* to the schedules, and only when we have decided on the arrangement can we begin to think about the notation. It is an unfortunate fact that notation is often taken to *be* the systematic arrangement, and classification schemes have been criticized for poor arrangement when it has been the notation which has failed, not the schedules. The notation cannot turn a bad schedule into a good one, but it can so hamper the use of a good arrangement that it becomes unacceptable to its users. To quote H. E. Bliss, 'notation . . . does not make the classification, tho it may mar it'.[2]

The second point is that the notation has to show the order: that is its function. The notation itself must therefore have a self-evident order, otherwise it will not serve its purpose. The order must be self-evident not only to the professional information handler, but also to the general user, who cannot be expected to appreciate results which are not immediately obvious, no matter how intellectually satisfying they may be to the compiler.

There are two sets of symbols which have a widely recognized order: Arabic numerals, used world-wide, and the roman alphabet, understood wherever a Western European language is used. Using letters, we have the choice of upper and lower case (capitals and small letters) which means in effect that we have three sets of symbols we can use rather than just two. A notation which uses only one set of symbols is called a *pure* notation, while one that uses more than one kind is known as a *mixed* notation. It is clear that only a pure notation will give us the completely self-evident order we have stated to be necessary, but other factors enter into the picture which may make mixed notation superior to the extent that it may be worth while accepting the loss of consistency.

Memorability

Notation is the means by which we get from a subject expressed in words in an alphabetical listing of some kind to that same subject in context in the systematic arrangement. It has to appear in catalogue entries, on the backs of books, in stock records, shelf guides – anywhere that we need to find our way around the systematic arrangement. We must therefore be able to carry it mentally with ease, write or key it without error, inscribe it on book spines which may be relatively narrow. It must also lend itself to the maintenance of the desired systematic arrangement, for example in the shelving of books by non-professional staff in a busy library. The notation must be easily used for all of these purposes; to do so it must possess certain qualities which between them add up to what is called *memorability*, but might also be denoted by the 'in' term *user-friendliness*.

The first quality is *simplicity*, by which we mean that it must be easy to grasp mentally. Consider the following ten digit number:

6183022262

This looks long and clumsy, and most people would find it difficult to grasp as a whole, but if we split is up into three shorter section:

618 302 2262

it at once becomes much simpler, because we can recognize the structure of a telephone number. By splitting the number up, we have increased its length by two digits (counting each space as a digit), but this actually makes it easier to grasp despite the increased length.

This leads us to a consideration of the ease of use of different kinds of notation. The following pieces of notation are all of much the same length, but clearly some of them are easier to grasp than others:

1	7382159142	
2	738 215 9142	[telephone number]
3	JVG XBF 8EAD	[BC2]
4	Z695.1.E5E5	[LCC]
5	921,52,15,76	[BSO]
6	621.312 424	[DDC]
7	621.315.5:669.14	[UDC]
8	Si(61)NoHm+Hf	[CRG classification of library science]
9	ntx.city.unisa.edu.au	[Internet node]
10	O,111,2J64,HE+8	[CC7]

We find that on the whole devices which normally act as separators – punctuation marks, spaces – are psychologically acceptable for this purpose in notation, though because separators are *empty digits* which convey structure but not meaning they lengthen the notation. Mixed notation *may* be easier to grasp than pure notation – but only if we can grasp the pattern to the mixing; and numbers are for most people more acceptable as a notation than letters. In practice, we also find that familiarity is a great help; if we regularly use the notation of a scheme, we quickly recognize the patterns even if they are not immediately obvious.

The second quality which is important is *brevity*. Other things being equal, a short piece of notation is more easily grasped than a long one; as we have seen, other things are not always equal, but there is no doubt that brevity is important. For example, it is difficult to put a long piece of notation of the spine of a book for shelf arrangement, unless we can split it up into shorter units, and the longer the notation the less likely it is to be memorable. Brevity depends on two factors: the *base* of the notation, and the *allocation*. The base is simply the number of symbols available in the system: for numbers this is ten (0/9) or nine if we ignore the zero; for letters it is 26. If we mix the notation by using both numbers and letters we may have 35 (there are dangers in using both O [capital letter o] and 0 [zero], as can be seen in CC), while if we use both upper and lower case letters and numbers we will have about 60. (There is the possibility of confusion between 1 (one) and l (lower case l), between i and l, and hand-written b and 6, as well as O and 0.) If we use numbers, we shall have longer symbols than if we use letters. For example, if we have about 2,000 items in our schedule and need to show their order, we have to use up to four figures but only three letters. The longer the base, the larger the number of items that can be arranged by a given length of symbol; mathematically, if the base contains x symbols, then by using up to n digits we can construct

$$x^n + x^{n-1} + x^{n-2} + x^{n-3} + \ldots + x^3 + x^2 + x$$

different notational symbols. The general preference for numbers has to be set against the fact that letters will in general give shorter symbols.

Another factor affecting brevity is the way that the notation is allocated. Some subjects are static: they have not developed much in recent years. Others are dynamic, and develop steadily, or sometimes rapidly, over the years. When we allocate the notation for a classification scheme we should try to make sure that we give a large share to dynamic subjects, even if this means relatively long notation for static subjects to begin with. After a few years, the notation for static subjects will not be any longer, while that for dynamic subjects will inevitably have grown. Of course, we cannot tell in advance which particular subjects are most likely to grow in years to come, but can at least make some sort of intelligent guess, bearing in mind that if we could indeed foretell the future the construction of classification schemes would probably not be our chosen profession.

In his first edition, Dewey gave the same spread of notation to Logic as he did to Engineering: ten three-figure numbers. (It must be remembered that this was the age in which a US Senator could recommend the closure of the Patent Office on the grounds that everything of use had already been invented!) As a consequence, in DDC21 we still find three-figure numbers in Logic (which has been static now for the best part of 2,000 years) but in Engineering, particularly those branches which have had to be inserted since the scheme was first drawn up, we find that six digits are common, and ten digit numbers are by no means uncommon. What makes the situation worse is that most libraries have a lot of material on Engineering but relatively small collections on Logic – so the short notation is rarely used.

It must be remembered that, although we can make some provision for the growth of dynamic subjects, it is not possible to make sure that they will retain a brief notation indefinitely; as we have seen, any systematic arrangement will need revision over the years to keep pace with the growth of knowledge, and we are unlikely to be able to keep pace with this growth and still retain a convenient notation indefinitely.

A further factor affecting brevity is *synthesis* of notation. We have seen the contrast between enumerative and synthetic classification schemes; in the latter, only simple subjects are listed, and the classifier has to select the appropriate ones for any subject in hand and combine them according to the specified citation order. In practical terms, the notation for the individual elements is combined to reflect the composite subject, and this will usually lead to longer notation than if the symbols had been evenly distributed over all the required subjects enumerated, simple or composite. For example LCC uses two capital letters and four figures for most subjects in its schedules – though it is fair to point out that many composite subjects are not listed and must be classified with one of their elements.

UDC has often been criticized for the length of its notation. Because it was based on DDC5, and has been developed in areas of technology where Dewey's allocation of notation was inadequate to begin with, it frequently has long notation for single concepts; with synthesis built on to this base, the results can often be clumsy, repeating certain sections of the notation. For example, at one time the notation for the subject 'Power supplies for the electromagnet of a proton synchrotron' was:

621.384.61:539.185:621.318.3:621.311.6

Nobody can claim that this is brief or user-friendly, and it repeats 621.3 (Electrical engineering) three times. It was however specific, and UDC was the only classification scheme detailed enough to specify this subject and others like it. If we want specificity, that is, high relevance, we have to accept that the consequence will often be long notation. If the allocation of notation was poor to begin with, the situation is likely to be compounded. Eventually we reach a stage where the only solution is to revise the scheme, and this is discussed in Chapter 13.

It is often suggested that *mnemonics* in notation are an aid to memorability – as indeed they should be! *Systematic mnemonics* are found where the same concept is always denoted by the same piece of notation: for example the use of (410) for Great Britain in UDC, which has many mnemonics of this kind. In DDC we find mnemonics which fall into this category, but only in a limited way; for example, in Literature, Drama is always denoted by 2:

English literature	820	English drama	822
German literature	830	German drama	832
French literature	840	French drama	842

However, 2 does not always mean Drama, even within Literature. England is often denoted by 0942, but it may be shown by 942, 42, 042 or even 2, and while 0942 does nearly always mean England, the other symbols do not. We do not have the consistency needed for a piece of notation to be truly mnemonic.

Literal mnemonics are associated with the use of letters for notation; the theory is that by using the initial letter of a subject for its notation we shall find it easier to remember. Thus in BC1 C is Chemistry (but Physics is B); in LCC Music is M (but Fine Arts is N). This kind of mnemonic is so haphazard that it is of little value, and it certainly should not be used to affect the systematic order, as appears to be the case in the Generalia class in LCC.

In general, mnemonics are of minor importance. The general reader will not normally be aware of them, while the classifier will have little difficulty in remembering large amounts of the notation of a scheme regularly used, mnemonic or not. However, the use of systematic mnemonics takes on a new importance in searching computer-held files, since they can then be used to carry out searches which would be impractical with manual files. The MARC format for classification (Chapter 15) will make computer searching for notational elements much simpler, though we shall still have to be wary of unexpected pitfalls with schemes such as DDC.

Memorability is important, and the factors contributing to it must be carefully weighed when selecting a notation for a classification scheme. There is no doubt that much of the success of DDC is owed to its simple, easily understood and widely known notation, rather than to any theoretical excellence in its schedules. Despite this, it is important to reaffirm that notation is subsidiary to the needs of the schedules, and that it is possible to worry too much about the difficulties caused by long or complex symbols. Far more important is the need for the notation to possess other qualities, of which the most important is hospitality.

Hospitality

Notation shows the order of the schedules, but the schedules are merely a helpful way of listing subjects; since knowledge is not static, our schedules cannot be static; we must be prepared to add new subjects as they arise, in the correct place (as far as we can see it) in the overall order. The notation must therefore also be able to accommodate insertions, at any point where we may find it necessary to make them. We will most often need to insert a new focus in a facet, but we may occasionally have to accommodate a new facet, or even new basic classes. The notation must allow us to insert a new subject in the correct place: it must be *hospitable*.

If we are using Arabic numerals, we may use them as integers (whole numbers) or as decimals. Integers give a clear order which is known to everybody: 12 comes later than 2 but earlier than 115, for example. But suppose we have a series of foci in a facet, and we giver them the numbers 1 to 7; if we now need to insert a new focus between the third and fourth, we cannot do so, for there is no whole number between 3 and 4. One solution is to leave gaps when we are allocating the notation originally, as is done in LCC, but of course this is merely postponing the time when we run out of places; there is also the temptation to insert new subjects in the schedule at points where we have left gaps in the notation, rather than in their correct, systematic places in the schedules. And since it is very difficult to foresee where new subjects will arise, we shall often leave gaps in the wrong places, but none where they are needed.

If, however, we use numbers as decimals, we can insert new symbols at any point in the sequence. Between 3 and 4 we can insert 31, 32, 33 . . . 39; between 33 and 34 we can insert 331, 332, 333 and so on. Now there is no longer any need to worry about leaving gaps in the right places, or to waste notation by leaving gaps in the wrong places The facility of decimal numbers to incorporate new symbols at any point was seen by Dewey, and proved to be one of the most vital parts of his scheme – indeed, it gave the scheme its name.

The term decimal applies to Arabic numbers and relates to division by ten. The idea can of course be applied equally well to letters, where it will mean division by 26, so the term decimal is strictly speaking not correct, and instead we should speak of 'radix fraction'. As the word decimal is widely understood, it is used in this text to apply to letters as well as numbers. In a letter notation, between B and C we can insert BA, BB, BC . . . BZ; between BB and BC we can insert BBA, BBB, BBC and so on. If we wish to have complete hospitality at all points, we must never finish a piece of notation with the first symbol of the base: 0, A or a; unless we follow this simple rule we shall find that we cannot insert new subjects at the beginning of a schedule. For example, if we use all ten digits 0 to 9, between 3 and 4 we can insert the ten numbers 30 to 39, but we then cannot insert anything between 3 and 30. If we do not use the first number 0, then we have nine left, so we can insert 31 to 39 between 3 and 4; if we want to insert a new focus between 3 and 31, we can use 301 to 309 and still retain complete decimal hospitality. We reduce the base by 1: 1 to 9, B to Z, b to z; in return, we gain hospitality at all points. Lack of hospitality is likely to lead to distortion of the schedules – notation dictating order – which we must avoid.

Expressiveness

Another quality which notation is often expected to have is *expressiveness*. This means that the notation reflects the structure of the schedules, and such a notation may be *structured* or *hierarchical*. A hierarchical notation reflects the genus-species structure of each hierarchy in our schedule of single foci; narrower terms have a longer notation than broader, while coordinate related terms have the same length of notation. A structured notation reflects the syntactic relationships in composite subjects, which may well involve the addition of *facet indicators* to our notation, as will be demonstrated shortly.

A hierarchical notation has the advantage of showing the structure of the classification. It is important to remember that the arrangement of books on the shelves, or items in a printed catalogue or bibliography, is a linear order which cannot show any structure other than the one-dimensional. We should use guiding to help users find their way around the arrangement, but a hierarchical notation can help. It also has the advantage that computer searching is made more obvious: to get greater recall, we shorten the notation we are using for our search, while to increase relevance we lengthen the notation. For example, we might begin a search in an OPAC by looking for English drama in 822; if we do not find what we want, we might broaden the search to 82, which will enable us to scroll through the whole of English literature, substantially increasing recall, though at the cost of relevance. Alternatively, we might decide that we want Elizabethan drama, and lengthen our search notation to 822.3, decreasing recall and hopefully increasing relevance. An expressive notation facilitates this kind of search strategy, but it is not necessarily excluded by a non-expressive notation. For example, we may do a search for material on Swedish language at 439.7; if we decide that this does not find enough material, it is not too difficult to move up the hierarchy, but we have to know that Scandinavian languages are at 439.5, *not* 439. Again, the MARC format for classification will make searching easier by showing the steps of a hierarchy, whether these are reflected in the notation or not.

Unfortunately, we find that hospitality and expressiveness are mutually exclusive; sooner or later one or the other breaks down. The reason for this becomes clear if we consider a practical example such as the schedule for Engineering in DDC. In the first edition, Electrical engineering was not included, but it found a place in the second edition as a subdivision of Mechanical engineering. This might perhaps have been considered an acceptable subordination at the time, but it would certainly not be so now. We have also seen various other branches of engineering develop, all of which might lay a claim to be of equal status: nuclear engineering, aviation engineering, control engineering, car engineering, for example. Dewey realized that new branches of engineering might develop, and allocated 9 for 'Other . . .':

600	Technology
620	Engineering
621	Mechanical
621.3	Electrical
622	Mining
623	Naval
624	Civil
. . .	
628	Sanitary
629	Other

Clearly, car engineering and aviation engineering are similar to mechanical engineering rather than civil or sanitary, while control engineering, as one of the more theoretical studies applicable throughout engineering, surely belongs at the beginning of the schedule with the other theory subjects rather than with the more practical branches of engineering listed later. However, there is no notation left to show the status of these subjects, nor can they be slotted into the right place in the schedules; control engineering, car engineering and aviation engineering are found in 629, as 'other branches of engineering', while nuclear engineering is found in 621.48, which may be approximately the right place in the schedules, but hardly reflects the relative significance of this new basic class.

The fact is that immediately we start to require our notation to be expressive, we limit ourselves to an integral use of the final digit; in the above example, Dewey only had the numbers 1 to 9 to list all the branches of engineering and at the same time show their equal status. As we have already seen, an integral notation cannot be hospitable; for the same reason, an expressive notation cannot be hospitable. Hospitality is more important than expressiveness, because it is the quality which allows us to govern the notation according to the needs of the schedules, instead of having notation dictate the order in the schedules. Ranganathan sought to overcome the problem by making the final digit of the base, 9 or Z, an *empty* digit; it could be used to extend the base by making 91, 92 . . . 991, 992 and so coordinate with 1, 2, 3 etc. This is of course a rationalization of Dewey's use of 9 for 'Other'. In CC7 it does enable us to insert new notation wherever we wish, but at the cost of losing any semblance of expressiveness; it is difficult to recognize that 2, 4, 91 and 991 are all coordinate pieces of notation.

We must also ask whether we *ought* to seek expressiveness in the notation. The purpose of the notation is to show the order of the sequence, of books on the shelves, or items in a bibliography, say; should we in addition expect it to show the structure which the sequence cannot show? Furthermore, we may find that the structure itself may cause difficulties by concealing the fact that certain foci are coordinate; consider the following schedule:

MUSIC
    Individual instruments and instrumental groups arranged according to their basic mode of performance
        Keyboard instruments
          Piano
          Organ
        String instruments
          Bowed
            Violin
            Viola
          Plucked

If we apply an expressive notation to this schedule, Violin and Viola will have the same length of notation, which will be three digits longer than the general heading; Piano, Organ, Bowed and Plucked string instruments will all have a notation two digits longer than the general heading; while Keyboard and String instruments will have notation one digit longer. We can see that because of the number of steps in the hierarchy taken to define them, individual instruments – which presumably ought to be coordinate – will have differing length of notation. The problem is inherent in hierarchical classification, and we can find other examples in DDC; for example, in Metal manufactures 673, Tin 673.6, Mercury 673.71, and Magnesium 673.723 are all individual metals and are thus coordinate, but are reached through different steps of division.

We saw earlier that expressive notation can be useful in searching a computer database, since it enables us to move up and down the hierarchy, to broaden or narrow our search. However, because of the problem of accommodating more subjects than is allowed by the notational base, and also the different hierarchies which take us to subjects we expect to be coordinate, we find that problems may also arise with synthesized notation. For example, we saw that in DDC, 'drama' is represented by

2 in Literature: English literature is 820, English drama is 822. If we try to search for drama in whatever language by using an internal wildcard 8?2, this will be successful for the major languages as identified by Dewey: American, English, German, French, Italian, Spanish, Latin and Greek. It will not work for the rest, which DDC includes in 890; 892 takes us to Afro-Asiatic literatures. Looking at the schedules, we find that Russian literature is in 891.7, Russian drama in 891.72, so that our wildcard search has to be 8???2 or 8?2 OR 89??2. 89?2 will take us to Sanskrit, 891.2, and Vietnamese, 895.2, literatures; Japanese drama, including Noh theatre, is at 895.62. The problem can be avoided in a scheme which uses facet indicators, such as UDC, where drama is -2; to search for all drama we can search for 8 AND -2 if our OPAC allows this.

Although the lack of expressiveness may make the overall arrangement that much harder to follow, we can help to overcome the problem by adequate guiding. It is also doubtful whether users are actually aware of the role of the notation in showing the structure; they are much more concerned with following the sequence of books on the shelves or entries in the catalogue.

Synthesis

We have briefly mentioned synthesis as one of the factors affecting brevity of notation, and it is worth re-examining this point in the light of the discussion on synthesis in Chapter 7. We saw there that coordination of single concepts was an extremely important device for improving retrieval performance from the point of view of relevance, and analytico-synthetic classification schemes are one important method of achieving coordination in an ordered fashion, according to a predetermined combination or citation order. By listing single concepts in the index vocabulary, and providing rules for their combination, we can give the classifier a much more powerful tool than the enumerative scheme, which attempts to provide in advance for composite subjects, but inevitably cannot foresee all that are likely to arise. In particular, we have seen that phase relationships are a form of coordination which cannot be predetermined, and *must* therefore be provided for by synthesis at the time of classification. The implication of this is that each single concept must have its own piece of notation, and that it must be possible to combine these pieces of notation – the *code vocabulary* – to specify any composite subject, including those involving phase relationships. We must therefore now consider in some detail the problems that arise if we try to synthesize notational symbols.

If we take the outline schedule for Library science that we constructed in Chapter 9, we can allocate an expressive notation, giving the kind of result that we have in Figure 11.1 column 1. Here we see that *History* (the generalized Time facet) is 3, and *Academic libraries* is 75; so the notation for *History of academic libraries* ought to be 753. But we can see at once that this will not do: 753 is the notation for *Technical college libraries*. We are of course trying to divide the heading *Academic libraries* in two different ways using the same notation: synthetic, *Academic libraries* AND *History*; and hierarchical, *Academic libraries* NT *Technical college libraries*. The same piece of notation could mean more than one subject. We have to label not only the foci within facets, but also the facets themselves; if we do this, we can combine elements from different facets to denote composite subjects without causing confusion with hierarchical subdivision within the same facet. We shall have *hospitality in chain and in array*.

The problem is one that arises regularly in DDC, which has no specific facet indicators. Where we have a general heading with hierarchical subdivisions, it is not possible to use synthesis at that heading; by contrast, where we have specific subdivisions which are not divided hierarchically, synthesis is possible. In DDC17 the convention of using an asterisk to denote those places where synthesis is possible was introduced; an example will help to make this clear. In Agriculture we have the general headings:

633   Field crops
633.4   Root crops

Both of these are extended hierarchically, 633 obviously to include root crops and other kinds of crops at 633.1, 633.2, 633.4 and so on, and 633.4 to specify particular root crops, e.g. 633.49 Tubers, which is itself extended to specify Potatoes at 633.491*. To synthesize the notation for 'injuries to crops' we are told to add 9 to the notation for the crop, then add the appropriate number from 632 Plant injuries, diseases, pests and their control (the 'Problem' facet). Injuries to crops in general is 632.1, so to specify Injuries to root crops we would take the base number 633.4, add 9, then add 1 (from 632.1) to give us 633.491 – which is the notation for Potatoes! Because the notation is extended hierarchically (*in array*), we cannot extend it syntactically (*in chain*). However, when we get to the end of the hierarchical subdivisions, in this case at 633.491 Potatoes, we *can* synthesize a number for Injuries to potatoes because there will be no notational conflict. To 633.491 we add 9, then 1, to give 633.49191 Injuries to potatoes. The asterisk is used to show that synthesis is possible, and we are instructed not to use synthesis unless the base number has an asterisk. The only kind of synthesis permitted at all points is the use of the common subdivisions from Table 1, introduced by the zero 0.

How can we label facets so that we can synthesize notation unambiguously? We may find different kinds of notation used for different facets; for example, BC1 used lower case letters only for Place, while CC6 used them only for the common facets of bibliographical form and subject. In both cases it is possible to add these symbols directly to another piece of notation without confusion:

BC	Cricket (sports)	HKL
	Australia	ua
	Cricket in Australia	HKLua
CC	Physics	C
	Encyclopedia	k
	Encyclopedia of Physics	Ck

This method is clearly limited by the fact that there are only three kinds of notation we can use. Another method is shown in column 3 of Table 11.1 (*see* pp.194–5); this uses capital letters to denote the facets, with lower case letters for foci within the facets. We can now combine the notation for the foci in a composite subject without any possibility of confusion. This was the kind of notation used by the CRG *Classification of library and information science*, and seen for many years in LISA. Arbitrary symbols may be used as facet indicators, for example in UDC, where we find (1/9) for Place, (01/09) for bibliographic forms, ". . ." for Time, and the colon : as a general indicator of relationship. In CC we find the comma , used to label Personality, semi-colon ; for Materials, colon : for Energy, dot . for Place and ' for Time. Synthesis is possible in both schemes, but clearly we have to lay down a filing order for these arbitrary symbols, both in relation to each other and in relation to the main notation.

Retroactive notation

The use of mixed notation or arbitrary symbols loses the great advantage of pure notation: its completely self-evident order. It also tends to make the notation more complex. Is it possible to have a pure notation which will nevertheless permit synthesis? We have had a hint of the answer when looking at the example from DDC earlier, when we saw that the subdivisions from Table 1 may be used anywhere, *because they are introduced by the zero* 0. The 0 is in effect reserved to act as a facet indicator, giving us the possibility of synthesis while retaining a pure notation.

If we have a subject with, say, three facets, we may use 1 to introduce the least important, which should file first. We can now use 2 to introduce the second facet, and combine notation from the two facets according to the citation order, *provided that we never use the figure 1 in the notation for the second facet*. Similarly, we can use 3/9 to introduce the third facet, the primary facet in this simple case, and still achieve complete synthesis, but we cannot use 1 or 2 in the notation for this facet. The penalty that we have to pay for the ability to synthesize within a pure notation is the progressive diminution of the base available. In the second facet above, the base is no longer 1 to 9 but 2 to 9; in the third it is 3 to 9, and so on. If we have nine facets, we might finish up with 9 as the whole of the base, giving 9, 99, 999, 9999 etc as the only pieces of notation possible in the primary facet! This is clearly unacceptable; we must begin by allocating an adequate amount of notation to the primary facet and work back from there. Further, because letters have a larger base than numbers, the method is likely to be more successful with notation using letters, and this is the kind of notation used in BC2. Because the elements must be combined in order working backwards (i.e. following the Principle of inversion) it is known as *retroactive* notation. Column 4 in Table 11.1 illustrates how the method may be used, and further examples will be found in Chapter 19. We may also find examples in DDC, where more than one zero is used to permit synthesis while retaining the pure notation. However, because of the length of the potential notation resulting from the use of this device, we are warned in the Introduction not to use more than one level of synthesis in such situations. An example from DDC20 is 350 Public administration, where 354 is for central governments other than the United States; we find that the facets are as follows:

0001 – 0009	Standard subdivisions
001 – 009	Administrative activities
01 – 09	The executive
.3 – .9	Specific countries from Area Table 2

The primary facet needs no facet indicator, and the three less important facets are introduced by one, two and three zeroes respectively. Theoretically, we could synthesize notation for a bibliography of legislation introduced by the Attorney-General of Australia – but with some 16 or more digits it would hardly be practical!

Table 11.1 Possible notational systems for the library science schedule
The four columns show how various kinds of notation might be allocated to the schedule for Library science. Since the schedule itself is tentative, so are the attempts at the allocation of notation. Column 1 is a simple expressive notation (cf DDC). The facets need indicators to permit synthesis. Column 2 is a non-expressive notation which tends to assume that the schedule is now fixed; it is usually shorter than 1, but less accommodating (cf LCC). Column 3 uses capitals for facets, lower case for foci, and is non-expressive (cf CRG). Column 4 is a non-expressive retroactive notation using letters; it does not need facet indicators (cf BC2).

Schedule	*1*	*2*	*3*	*4*
Bibliographic forms	1	10	A	B
Common subjects	2	20	B	C
revision	21	21	Bb	CC
research	22	22	Bf	CF
standards	23	23	Bj	CJ
automation	24	24	Bm	CM
economics	25	25	Br	CP
Time	3	30	C	D
Place	4	40	D	E
Operations	5	51	E	EZZ
administration	51	52	Eb	F
selection	511	53	Ec	FG
acquisition	512	54	Ed	FK
circulation	513	55	Ee	FM
technical services	52	56	Eh	FZ
cataloguing	521	57	Ei	G
catalogues	5211	58	Ej	GG
by physical form	52111	59	Ejz	GL
book form	521113	60	El	GP
classification	522	61	En	H
schemes	5221	62	Eo	HJ
UDC	52215	63	Er	HP
cooperation	53	64	Ew	J

finance	54	65	Ex	K
funding	541	66	Ey	KL
federal	5413	67	Ez	KM
Materials	6	69	F	LZZ
books	61	70	Fb	M
serials	62	71	Ff	N
periodicals	621	72	Fj	NN
newspapers	622	73	Fm	NP
non-standard	63	74	Fpz	NZZ
maps	631	75	Fr	O
records	632	76	Fw	P
Libraries	7	78	H	QZ
by subject	71	79	J	R
by mode of use	72	80	L	RZ
reference	721	81	Lb	SS
by population served	73	83	N	SZ
children	731	84	Nb	T
hospital	732	85	Nc	TT
handicapped	733	86	Nd	TU
blind	7331	87	Ne	TV
by kind	74	88	Q	TZZ
special	741	89	Qb	U
government	7411	90	Qc	UU
industry	7412	91	Qe	V
academic	75	92	Qh	W
school	751	93	Qi	WR
technical college	753	94	Qm	WV
university	757	95	Qr	X
public	76	96	Qu	Y
municipal	761	97	Qv	YR
county	762	98	Q	YS
national	77	99	Qx	Z

The schedule for particle accelerators introduced into UDC in 1961[3] used retroactive notation, though this was not made plain at the time in deference to the large number of users who preferred to use UDC in the conventional way. Those who wished could use the schedule in the usual way, with the colon to link the notation for foci from the various facets, while those who wanted shorter notation could use it retroactively. This tentative experiment did work, but made no impression on UDC practice in general.

Though there is normally no need for a facet indicator for the primary facet, this may alter if we need to denote combinations of foci from subfacets; for example, a Children's reference library on art might have the notation 731,721,71(Art), where the comma enables us to combine the three foci satisfactorily.

We can see how the four systems compare by classifying two of the titles from the list, using the facet indicators from CC where necessary:

2   Baltimore County Public Library initiates book catalog
12   LaRoche College classification system for phonograph records

Notation	Title 2	Title 12
Column 1	762:521113;4(Baltimore)	757;632:522.4(LaR)
Column 2	98,60,40(Baltimore)	95;76:61.40(LaR)
Column 3	QwElD(Baltimore)	QrFwEnD(LaR)
Column 4	YSGPE(Baltimore)	XPHE(LaR)

These examples show that allocation has an important effect on length of notation, and that length itself is not the only factor involved in ease of use. In a fully developed scheme we would have a schedule for place, or perhaps 'borrow' one from a general classification. We may also use *identifiers* such as (LaR) if this is helpful.

Flexibility

If we use arbitrary symbols as facet indicators, we have to lay down a filing order for them, since there is no established sequence. This obviously has disadvantages, since the general user will no longer be able to follow the sequence unaided. On the other hand, it can have the advantage of allowing us to alter the citation order. As mentioned in Chapter 9, it is not always possible to find a citation order which will suit everybody, as shown by the two approaches to Literature exemplified by DDC (Language – Literary form – Period – Author) and LCC (Language – Period – Author – Literary form). If we use arbitrary symbols, as in UDC, we can use whichever of these citation orders we please, and we can even alter the schedule order to preserve the Principle of inversion, since we shall be determining the filing order of the symbols introducing the facets. This ability to change the arrangement by altering the citation order is one aspect of a feature of notation known as *flexibility*. Many schemes provide alternatives in specific schedules; for example, DDC permits us to shelve bibliographies with the subject, or all together, and to decide which arrangement we prefer for our Law books. In each case, there is an editor's preference, and it is this which determines which notation appears in the MARC records, but we may use the alternative if we wish. BC1 had a number of alternative schedules to give classifiers the flexibility to decide which they preferred. However, we should not forget that flexibility is a transient phenomenon; once we have decided which arrangement we prefer, all others must be excluded. We cannot vary our practice from week to week, and a change of citation and schedule order must be a rare event. Flexibility is not a primary consideration in notation; hospitality is far more important.

A classification of notations

We may work out a small matrix to clarify the various kinds of notation, ending up with a tabulation as follows:

Hierarchical but not structured

shows genus-species division but does not allow synthesis (e.g. DDC in parts)

Non-hierarchical and structured

permits genus-species division and synthesis, but does not display hierarchy (e.g. BC2)

Hierarchical and structured

permits genus-species division and synthesis and displays both (e.g. CC)

Non-hierarchical and non-structured

permits genus-species division but not systematic synthesis, and shows neither (e.g. LCC)

(A scheme like LCC does permit composite subjects to be included, and some are enumerated on nearly every page, but they must be fitted into the existing sequence, not denoted by notational synthesis. Hierarchies are shown by layout but not by the notation, except where it has been necessary to introduce decimal subdivision to accommodate new subjects.)

Because a synthetic scheme lists only single concepts, and has to provide means for notational synthesis to represent composite subjects, it makes the distinction between hierarchical and structured notation in the above table very obvious. We have discussed semantic relationships in Chapter 6 and syntactic in Chapter 7; we expect the notation of a classification scheme to accommodate both, but it is not possible for it to display both indefinitely. As we have seen, hospitality and expressiveness are mutually exclusive in the long run, and although CC claims both, it is at the expense of a number of devices which make the notation of the scheme much less practical than we would wish.

A cautionary tale

It is a fact of life that most people are not mathematically minded to any great extent. We have been discussing notation as a device to reflect the order of the schedules in a classification scheme, but for most library users it is solely a locating device. A piece of notation is found in the schedules or the catalogue, and the user can then go to the place in the classified sequence and find what is wanted by browsing the shelves, using authors and titles rather than notation. The kinds of notation which are accepted by people in general are telephone numbers and car registration numbers; in neither case are we concerned with order, but with *identification*. The only sequences which are readily accepted are alphabetical, as in a dictionary or telephone directory, and integral, as in house numbers. It is easy to look at the desirable properties of a notation from a theoretical point of view, but much harder to get users to make practical use of the result.

When *Library and information science abstracts* (LISA) began in 1969, the abstracts were arranged by the CRG classification of library and information science, as discussed in Chapter 9. In 1971 the citation order was changed, but the notation still consisted of upper case letters for facets and lower case for foci. Many users found it unhelpful, and the indexing was amended to give only a short notation sufficient to take the user to the general area, while the annual indexes, which were not under quite so much pressure of time, indexed direct to abstract numbers. In 1976, computerization made it possible to index direct to abstract numbers in the bi-monthly issues, and in 1993 the notation was dropped completely. The abstract numbers are of course in a simple integral sequence beginning at 1 each year, which is familiar to everyone. We would expect the users of LISA to come very largely from the ranks of qualified librarians, who might be expected to cope with any kind of notation with equal ease, but this appears to be over-optimistic! If librarians find themselves ill at ease with a mixed alphabetical notation, we cannot reasonably expect the general public to find it acceptable.

A similar situation was found with the classification devised by E. J. Coates for the *British catalogue of music*.[4] This was used from the beginning of the service in 1957 until 1982, when it was replaced by the 'Proposed revision of 780 Music' published as a draft phoenix schedule for DDC and formally adopted in DDC20. The new schedule was firmly based on the BCM *Classification*, adapted to fit into the general structure of DDC, using the more familiar decimal notation rather than the non-expressive alphabetical notation of Coates' scheme. Its adoption by BCM was part of the internationalization of BL services, but also a recognition of the fact that other kinds of notation are not welcomed by the users at large.

Summary

Notation is a device to mechanize the use of classified arrangement: to serve as a set of convenient ordering symbols, and to enable users to get easily from a subject expressed in words to the same subject slotted into its place in what is intended to be a helpful sequence. To get a notation which will give us hospitality in both hierarchical (semantic) expansion and in structured (syntactic) synthesis, we find it necessary to introduce some modifications to the kind of simple notation that is most easily accepted by users, but this conflicts with the need to provide users with the most simple access to information possible. With abstracting and indexing services, the computer can make the notation transparent to the user, giving a detailed classified arrangement with access through a separate easily grasped sequence of integers. We still have the problem of shelf arrangement, where simplicity is still essential if shelving is to be carried out quickly and accurately by clerical staff, who cannot be required to understand the niceties of a complex notation. It seems that we must accept a loss in specificity and thus a poorer relevance performance in order to have a practical shelf arrangement notation. However, the user does not find it too difficult to scan a shelf full of books, so perhaps concerns on this score are not acute. It is clear from experience that the majority of attempts to provide greater specificity by using an unfamiliar notation have been at the least unwelcome to the majority of users, to whom, in a reversal of the old proverb, unfamiliarity breeds contempt. With the development of the digital library, the computer may solve the problem by taking over the role of shelf arrangement as well as that of detailed subject access.

References

1   Most of the work on notation was done in the 1950s, and recent discussions have related to the use of class numbers in online retrieval, discussed in the chapter on OPACS. The following references cover all the essentials:

Coates, E. J., 'Notation in classification' in *Proceeedings of the International Study Conference on Classification Research*, Dorking, 1957.

Foskett, D. J., *Classification and indexing in the social sciences*, London, Butterworths, 2nd edn, 1974, Chapter 4.

Vickery, B. C., *Classification and indexing in science and technology*, London, Butterworths, 3rd edn, 1975, Chapter 9.

2   Bliss, H. E., *The organization of knowledge in libraries*, New York, H. W. Wilson, 2nd edn, 1939, Chapter 3.

3   Coblans, H., Sabel, C. S. and Foskett, A. C., 'Proposed schedule for Particle accelerators 621.384.6', adopted by UDC 1961.

4   Coates, E. J., *The British catalogue of music classification*, London, Library Association, 1960.

Chapter 12
Alphabetical index

Systematic order is not self-evident; we need notation to show whereabouts in the sequence we shall find a particular subject. However, we also need some way to find the notation, and this must be through an alphabetical sequence, for we inevitably use words in our first approaches to the system. A classification scheme must therefore have an alphabetical index to serve as its entry vocabulary, leading us to the schedules which form the index vocabulary by means of the notation which forms the code vocabulary.[1] The importance of the entry vocabulary has already been demonstrated in Chapter 6, and in this chapter we consider some of the practical implications. To begin with, how do we construct the entry vocabulary to a classified arrangement?

The obvious place to find the required words is in the schedules, where we have listed all the terms we wish to arrange. As a first approximation, we can indeed take the words in the schedule, together with their appropriate notation, and re-arrange them in alphabetical order. This is however something of a simplification, since there are several problems to be solved before we can claim to have produced a good index. The first of these is *synonyms*. In the schedules we shall normally only use one, preferred, term for a particular focus, but there may well be others; both the preferred term and its synonyms must form part of the entry vocabulary. For example, in the index to DDC20 we find:

Hats	391.43
Headgear	391.43

The second problem is that of *homographs*. We must distinguish the same word used with different meanings in a classification scheme, just as we must with alphabetical headings. Again from DDC20, we find

Models (Fashion)	746.92092
Models (For molding)	
Sculpture	731.43
Models (Representations)	688.1
	T1 —022.8
Models (Simulations)	003
	T1 —011

The same term may appear in a number of different places in the schedules, denoting the same concept but in different contexts. As we saw in Chapter 6, these occurrences represent generic and quasi-generic relationships. In the index to DDC20 we find:

Tobacco	583.79
agriculture	633.71
customs	394.14
ethics	178.7
see also Ethical problems	
manufacturing technology	679.7
toxicology	615.952 379
Tobacco abuse	362.296
Medicine	616.865
personal health	613.85
social welfare	362.296
see also Substance abuse	
Tobacco industry	338.173 71
agricultural economics	338.171 71
law	343.076 371
manufacturing	338.476 797
Tobacco industry workers	679.7092
occupational groups	T7 —6797

This is an example of a word that occurs several times in the schedules of a general classification scheme, scattered within a variety of disciplines; it is represented by several pieces of notation, but each of these represents it in only one particular context. In indexing such a word, it would be less than helpful to give merely the word and several pieces of notation – though this would certainly lead us to all the places in the schedules where the word may be found. As mentioned in Chapter 8, COMPASS, the indexing method used by BNB from 1990 to 1994, leads us in the 1991 index to 28 places in the classified sequence at the entry **Antiquities**; a user would need to be more than usually enthusiastic to follow up all these leads – though they certainly do all lead to entries in the classified sequence. To help the user, we give the context in which a particular piece of notation represents a given term; this is the *relative index* first devised by Dewey.

In effect, every entry in the index to a classified arrangement is a USE or *see* reference, taking us from the concept in words to the notation which is the heading used for arrangement. It is therefore not usual to make *see* references within the index, though this has been done, for example in DDC19, where we find:

Endometritis	
see Uterine infections	
Uterine infections	
gynecology	618.142
. . .	

These *see* references were all removed from DDC20, where we find:

Endometritis
gynecology   618.142
Uterine infections
gynecology   618.142

A similar situation arises with terms which are synonyms or near-synonyms but are found in a number of places in the schedules. In such a case we may find a single entry under one with a reference to the other, where a variety of entries are made:

Hats   391.43
   see also Headgear
Headgear   391.43
   commercial technology   687.4
   customs   391.43
   home economics   646.3
   home sewing   646.5
   see also Clothing

Systematic arrangement is intended to arrange related subjects together, but the linear sequence can only show one kind of relationship. The alphabetical index can help by bringing scattered aspects together, as we have seen, but we can also make links within the schedules to complement the arrangement still further. In DDC20 we find both *see* and *see also* cross-references in the schedules:

001   Knowledge
  .4   Research
  .42   Research methods
  .422   Statistical methods
         See also 310 for collections of general statistical data, notation 021 from Table 1 for statistics on a specific discipline or subject

641   Food and drink
  .5   Cooking
         For cooking specific materials, see 641.6; specific cooking processes and techniques, 641.7; cooking of composite dishes, 641.8

The combination of classified arrangement and relative index with cross-references in both the schedules and the index gives us a thorough guide to locating concepts.

Composite subjects

If we are using a synthetic scheme, it will list only single foci, which are relatively simple to index, though we saw in Chapter 6 that some concepts may be denoted by terms involving more than one word. An enumerative scheme will however contain a good proportion of composite subjects, and we have to ensure that all the terms in a composite heading are present in the entry vocabulary as access points. The most convenient way of doing this is by using chain procedure , as described in Chapter 7. We make an entry for each term in the chain, qualifying it by as many of the previous terms as necessary to show the context. The notation may help here if it is expressive, but we can use the procedure whether it is or not; the important thing is that the chain of division is correctly stated in the first place.

Even if we use a synthetic scheme, we shall of course have composite subjects in the classified sequence, for example the main section of BNB, which we shall have to index. We must draw a distinction between the index to a classification schedule and the index to a catalogue compiled by using it. The difference is most clearly seen with a synthetic scheme, where the catalogue will obviously include subjects not enumerated in the scheme. A good example is the index to LISA from 1969 to 1992, where the subject indexes led to both single concepts, which were listed in the CRG *Classification of library science*[2] used for the arrangement, and composite subjects, which were not. By contrast, the index to the scheme listed only single concepts.

Unsought links

We may find that chain procedure is not an entirely automatic procedure because of the nature of hierarchical structures. We may need to insert steps of division that are necessary to show the structure but are not in themselves useful access points. To refer back to an example in Chapter 11, we have:

MUSIC
    Individual instruments and instrumental groups arranged according to their
    basic mode of performance
      Keyboard instruments
        Piano
        Organ
      String instruments
        Bowed
          Violin
          Viola
        Plucked

It is most unlikely that anyone would look under the word 'individual', or indeed for the general heading as a whole; this is an essential step to show the rationale of division, but is not in itself likely to be looked for: it is an unsought link. We may find such facet indicators in both classification schemes and thesauri, since both display hierarchies of terms; the American standard[3] specifies that they may be included in square brackets, and not used for indexing.

It is normal practice to omit also such weak access points as periods of time, common terms of wide application but low significance such as Methods, Equipment, Production, Calculations, Research and so on. To index bibliographical forms could lead to a large increase in the number of index entries with limited value; we would normally expect users to turn to the subject of, say, a dictionary rather than look under the word Dictionary itself.

A related problem is that of *false links*, which may arise if we place too much reliance on the notation to indicate the chain that we have to index. There may be errors on the part of the compiler of the scheme, or changes in the structure of knowledge, so that subjects appear to be subdivisions of other subjects when in fact they are not. For example, early editions of DDC showed Electrical engineering as a subdivision of Mechanical engineering, and the notation continued to show this until the terminology was changed from Mechanical engineering to Applied Physics:

620	Engineering
621	Mechanical
621.3	Electrical

In such instances, if we rely on the notation we may go wrong and create false links in the index, but this cannot happen if we rely on the systematic chain of division. In recent editions of DDC, careful attention to terminology as well as the layout of the schedules has made such errors unlikely. The converse effect may also be seen if we rely on the notation and it is not expressive:

400	Language
430	Germanic (Teutonic) languages German
439	Other (Teutonic) Germanic languages
439.5	Scandinavian (North Germanic) languages
439.7–439.8	East Scandinavian languages
439.7	Swedish

Here Swedish appears from the notation to be on the same hierarchical level as Scandinavian languages, which is clearly incorrect. This example from DDC20 is untypical, as the notation is as far as possible expressive, but it is the norm with a scheme such as LCC in which a largely integral notation is used. Once again, provided that we follow the chain of division carefully through the schedules, we can apply chain procedure, as the following examples show:

ND	Painting
ND1700–2399	Water-color painting
ND2290	Still life
ND2300	Flowers
ND2305	Reproductions. Facsimiles

which would give index entries:

Facsimiles. Reproductions. Flowers. Still life. Water-color painting ND2305
Reproductions. Flowers. Still life. Water-color painting ND2305
Flowers. Still life. Water-color painting ND 2300
Still life. Water-color painting ND2290
Water-color painting ND1700-2399
Painting ND

Another example, again from LCC:

NB	Sculpture
NB60–198	History
NB69–169	Ancient
NB135–159	Special materials
NB145	Terra-cottas
NB150	Figurines
NB155	Greek
NB157	Tanagra

which would give index entries

> Tanagra Greek figurines. Terra-cottas. Ancient history. Sculpture NB157
> Greek figurines. Terra-cottas. Ancient history. Sculpture NB155
> Figurines. Terra-cottas. Ancient history. Sculpture NB150
> Terra-cottas. Ancient history. Sculpture NB145
> [Special materials – unsought]
> Ancient history. Sculpture NB69–169   [probably unsought]
> History. Sculpture NB60–198
> [or History of a subject *see* the subject]
> Sculpture NB

The problem in applying chain procedure to a scheme with a non-hierarchical notation is that it is sometimes difficult to follow all the steps of division through the schedules, particularly if they are not clearly set out, as was the case with, for example, BC1. It is also sometimes necessary to modify the method in order to take account of unsought links and redundant qualifiers; for example, we do not need to qualify Water-color painting by the superior term Painting.

Distributed relatives

We have already seen in Chapter 9, particularly in Table 9.1, that systematic arrangement only brings together the topics which we have decided shall form our primary facet; all the rest are systematically scattered. It is therefore useful to make explicit a point which is implicit in much of this chapter, that is, that foci which are scattered by the systematic arrangement are brought together by the alphabetical index. These *distributed relatives* (concepts which are related but scattered) are shown clearly in the index, as is demonstrated clearly in the 'tobacco' example from DDC. The index to a classification scheme or classified arrangement thus has a dual role; not only does it enable us to find the notation for a particular topic, and thus its place in the overall arrangement, it also shows all the several places where a concept is to be found even though they are scattered throughout the arrangement.

The index is thus much more than a convenience, it is an essential, integral, part of a classified arrangement. As is emphasized in Chapter 17, Dewey realized the importance of the index to his classification scheme from the very beginning, but all too often the compilers of classified catalogues appear to regard the index as an expensive luxury. The BNB had a chain index from its beginning in 1950 until 1971, when PRECIS was introduced to index the standard use of DDC18 in the

MARC records. Both systems supplemented the classified arrangement in the appropriate way. With the introduction of COMPASS in 1990, BNB ceased to have a relative index, and with the substitution of LCSH for COMPASS in 1995 the classified arrangement has no index at all; instead, it has a parallel but not complementary alphabetical sequence – as is also the case with the ANB. Systematic searching in a classified sequence, whether in a printed bibliography or online in an OPAC, is not possible without an adequate alphabetical index related specifically to the classification scheme used.

References

1   As with notation, most of the work on indexing classified arrangements was done some time ago. It is worth studying the index to DDC20 to see how an index to a classification scheme can be constructed; the index to UDC Medium edition BS 1000M 1988, which was produced by computer, can be usefully contrasted with that to BS 1000M:1994, which was compiled by skilled indexers. Volumes of BNB up to 1971 show the chain index used, 1971–1990 the use of PRECIS, 1991–1994 the use of COMPASS. The following references are useful:

Austin, D. with Dykstra, M., *PRECIS: a manual of concept analysis and subject indexing*, 2nd edn, London, British Library, 1984.

Coates, E.J., *Subject catalogues: headings and structure*, reissued with new preface, London, Library Association, 1988, Chapters 8 and 9.

Foskett, D. J., *Classification and indexing in the social sciences*, 2nd edn, London, Butterworths, 1974, Chapter 10.

Mills, J., 'Chain indexing and the classsified catalogue', *Library Association record*, **57** (4), 1955, 141–8.

'The new British Library subject system'. *Select: National Bibliographic Service newsletter*, (1), June/July 1990, 3 [COMPASS].

Wilson, T. D., *An introduction to chain indexing*, London, Bingley, 1971.

2   Daniel, R. And Mills, J., *A classification of library science*, London, Library Association, 1974.

3   National Information Standards Organization, *American standard guidelines for the construction, format and management of monolingual thesauri*, Bethesda, MD, NISO, ANSI/NISO Z39.19: 1993.

Chapter 13
Organization

Knowledge does not stand still, and a classification scheme left unrevised will, sooner rather than later, become unusable. There are several implications here, beginning with those for the compiler. In the first place, continuing revision implies some sort of organization, rather than an individual, to carry it through. Individuals are mortal, but an organization can continue indefinitely. We find that those schemes which have relied on the genius of their compilers, without the backing of an adequate organization, have gradually fallen into obsolescence, whereas those schemes which have adequate backing continue to progress. Examples of the first kind are the *Subject Classification* of J. D. Brown[1] and Rider's *International* classification,[2] both of which are now of historic interest only. While valiant efforts are being made to complete the second edition of BC, it remains to be seen whether this attempt will be successful; it is still very much in the hands of a few individuals. Even the latest general classification scheme, the BSO sponsored by UNISIST, faces severe management problems.

In the second category we find DDC, LCC and UDC. LCC has the backing of the Library of Congress, and since LCC class numbers appear on virtually all MARC records, it is widely used by other libraries as well, particularly American academic libraries. DDC has its editorial office in the Library of Congress, and DDC class numbers appear on a substantial proportion of MARC records; in addition it now has the financial backing of OCLC, the largest utility of its kind. Despite the fact that both schemes show serious theoretical deficiencies, and compare unfavourably with those parts of BC2 which have appeared, they are likely to remain the dominant schemes in the future, because of their organizational strength.

UDC is a mixture of success and failure. For many years it has been the classification of choice for large numbers of special libraries, and it was adopted in the USSR as the official classification for science and technology. It had the backing of the Fédération Internationale d'Information et de Documentation (FID), but despite all this it went through a period of steep decline, caused by lack of money and a poor management structure, and also by lack of any ties to a large library. As described in Chapter 18, it is now showing signs of a strong revival, thanks to substantial changes in management policy and practice, which will, it is hoped, make the scheme financially viable.

If a scheme as widely used and well established as UDC can have problems in surviving, it is hardly surprising that other less widely used schemes face difficulties. Many special classification schemes are developed for specific purposes, but often when the person who devised the scheme moves on, the scheme itself is abandoned or substantially altered, no matter how good it may be

Methods of revision and publication

There are various ways of keeping a scheme up to date. The most obvious is to publish a new edition from time to time, but this may not necessarily be the best way. In a large and detailed scheme, some sections may need revising frequently, e.g. science and technology (and even within these areas particular topics may present peculiar problems), whereas other sections will need little or no revision. (The schedule for logic in DDC20 closely resembles that in DDC2!) It may therefore be more effective to publish the scheme in parts, and revise each part on an *ad hoc* basis, in this way keeping the whole scheme current with the minimum of publishing effort. DDC is an example of a scheme which appears in a new edition at regular intervals (the editorial policy has been to publish a new edition every seven years), while LCC exemplifies the policy of piecemeal publication. UDC is interesting in that it has used both methods; for the full editions, publication has been in fascicules, while the abridged editions were published as a whole. The new English medium edition is likely to follow the same pattern as the abridged in being published as a whole; the French edition is published in three parts over a period of time. The adoption of computer technology means that it will be very much simpler to keep the master copy up-to-date and thus produce new editions as necessary. There is some doubt as to whether the full edition will continue to be maintained.

Whichever of these methods is adopted, with a well-organized scheme revision will be continuous, and it is therefore usual to have some means of publishing current revisions at regular intervals, so that users do not have to wait until the new schedules are published formally. DDC is kept up to date through *Decimal classification: additions, notes, decisions* (DC&); LCC through *LC classification – additions and changes*, and UDC through *Extensions and corrections to the UDC*. One point that is perhaps rather surprising is that it seems to have taken a long time for the use of computers to play a significant role in the revision of classification schemes. It was not until the 19th edition that DDC was successfully produced by computer, after an abortive attempt with the 18th. Since the publication of the 19th edition, new schedules have been published as separates for both Computer science and Computer technology, reflecting perhaps an increased awareness of the potential of modern computer technology. Certainly the present situation is that DDC is at the forefront of computer production, and DDC21 will probably be the first complete scheme to be produced using the new USMARC format for classification. (LC has already (1995) produced new schedules for H Social sciences in MARC format.) The AIP project mentioned in Chapter 18 demonstrated in the 1960s that UDC schedules could be successfully produced by computer, but progress since then has been painfully slow. It was not until the Medium edition of 1985 that part of the schedules were computerized, but the Machine Readable File was completed by 1993; the 1994 medium edition quickly followed, and future amendment will be very much simpler. The MARC format for UDC has been devised, which will help in standardization. Work is currently in progress on fitting the rest of LCC into the MARC format for classification, and this scheme too will be completely computer-produced in the future.[3]

Alphabetical systems are now regularly produced by computer; the thesaurus used by CTI is computer maintained, though it has never been published, while that for PRECIS was produced by the British Library on microfiche. LCSH is now regularly produced from computer-held records, and policy is to produce a new edition annually in print form, as well as in the microforms which have been available quarterly since the eighth edition, though these have tended to lag behind the scheduled publication dates. LCSH is now also available on CD-ROM as well as online through the Library of Congress Internet node. The ERIC thesaurus is computer-produced, and is available through the ERIC Online CD-ROM version produced by DIALOG, as well as in the printed form.

Problems with revision

Revision must obviously be carefully planned, with the needs of users in mind. Editions of DDC up to DDC14 showed very clearly the problems of haphazard revision; Medicine occupied some 80 pages of the schedules, while the equally important topic Chemical Technology (including for example fuel, food, industrial oils and metallurgy) had two pages. Later editions have shown the editors' concern that revision should be appropriate to the needs of the literature. In the past, the revision of UDC was left very much to the initiative of users, who were encouraged to develop new schedules they themselves found necessary. While this certainly related the development of new schedules to expressed user needs, it also meant that much of the work was done on a voluntary basis, and led to the same sort of uneven development that characterized early editions of DDC. One of the most detailed schedules was that for nuclear science and engineering, produced by a team from the UK Atomic Energy Authority working with similar organizations overseas. Other schedules which needed revision did not have the same resources to call on.

From the point of view of the individual trying to use a scheme to arrange a library or a catalogue, revision presents other problems, many of them economic. Once a particular scheme or list of subject headings has been adopted, the library begins to build up a vested interest in the scheme as it stands; there will be increasing numbers of books and other records with pieces of notation on them. If the scheme is changed, the librarian has to consider whether changing all the notation and re-arranging the books is worthwhile *and* economically feasible. Now that most catalogues are computer-held, changing records is simple, but shelf arrangement is a different matter. Dewey recognized this very early, and DDC2 introduced his policy of 'integrity of numbers': a piece of notation would not be reused with a different meaning, and topics would not be relocated to new notation, though there might well be expansion at a particular heading. This policy certainly contributed to the success of the scheme, since librarians welcomed this concession to administrative convenience. On the other hand, it also meant that the scheme became further and further removed from the changing structure of knowledge. Every edition since

DDC15 has introduced major changes in the form of phoenix schedules, intended to replace the previous schedule. (The graphic term 'phoenix' has now been replaced by 'completely revised'). While there is no doubt that these changes have been jus-tified, there is equally no doubt that they have met with strong criticisms from some users.[4] One Canadian study showed that librarians reluctantly accepted the need for change, but few reclassified their existing collections.[5]

The problem of keeping pace with knowledge is not restricted to classified arrangement, of course. Terminology changes, new terms have to be introduced, new relationships arise, and all these changes will affect any system, systematic or alphabetical. Some 60 years ago the suggestion was put forward that libraries should in effect start again every ten years![6] While this seems unrealistic when applied to libraries, it is in fact exactly what is found in many bibliographical tools. Each BNB cumulation has differed from its predecessors, but as far as possible changes are not made *within* cumulations. Indexes and abstracts have, in their print-ed versions, usually worked on a year-by-year basis, with only a few, e.g. *Chemical abstracts*, cumulating indexes into longer periods. Even the computer databases of the larger services tend to split their records into manageable spans of a few years. As with so many problems, the root of the matter is economic: can libraries afford the effort of keeping pace with changes, either continuous or at periodic intervals? Perhaps we should instead ask the question, can the library afford *not* to keep pace with changes? Our readers expect the arrangement on the shelves to be helpful, and if it is obviously not helpful they may decide to take their custom elsewhere. For example, DDC17 introduced a phoenix schedule for Psychology, reusing many class numbers with new meanings, and moving topics to new places in the sched-ule. To interfile books classified by the new schedule with those filed by the old results in an arrangement which certainly does not meet the essential criterion of 'helpful to the user', and the same is of course true of any major change. The increasing availability of computer-based services means that libraries now have strong competition to contend with in the provision of information, and it would be short-sighted to ignore this.

Choice of classification

From time to time, new libraries are established, often in small organizations but occasionally in a larger context. What classification should be adopted for shelf arrangement? The question is again largely one of economics. Most cataloguing is done now from MARC records, so the fact that these nearly all contain an LCC call number, and a DDC number for most books in English, puts considerable pressure on the librarian of a new library to adopt one or other of these schemes. One impor-tant factor will be a form of peer pressure: what are comparable libraries using? For example, in the USA LCC is the choice preferred by most academic libraries, whereas in Australia DDC is almost universal. Similarly, a new public library in most English-speaking countries would probably adopt DDC, which is rather more suited to the needs of the ordinary user (the reader on the Clapham omnibus?) than is LCC. In the UK, a number of education libraries have stayed loyal to the

Bibliographic classification, despite its publication problems, and the lack of BC class numbers in MARC records, because they feel that it is better suited to their needs.

Many special libraries find themselves in the position of finding very little of their intake covered by MARC records; there is in this situation not the same pressure to adopt one of the two major classifications. UDC may well be the preferred choice, because its synthetic nature makes it well suited to the kinds of specialized materials likely to be added. Now that the medium edition is available and likely to be kept up to date more effectively, it may well be the best choice, particularly for libraries dealing with science and technology – though it is only fair to point out that one major revision recently has been 'language and literature'![7]

For the small special library, the possibility arises of devising a special classification to match the needs of the organization and its members as closely as possible. Existing schemes do not usually provide the right emphasis, in terms of citation order or even order within facets, for this kind of library. The principles of constructing a special classification have been outlined in this book, and in more detail in other texts, and for a small collection it is quite feasible. However, the question of organisation is just as important in this situation as it is for larger schemes. It is essential to prepare not only the schedules and index but also a manual on how the scheme is to be used *and maintained*, if the scheme is to continue in use beyond the enthusiasm of its originator.

Summary

It may seem out of place to devote a chapter on administrative problems in a book mainly dealing with basic principles, but the principles can only flourish in a favourable economic climate! Experience shows that the schemes which are successful are those which have a good solid organization behind them, whether they are sound in principle or not; the administrative tail wags the theoretical dog. The essential point is to try to choose a scheme which will meet the needs of the users while remaining within the economic framework of the organization using it.

References

1   Brown, J. D., *Subject classification*, 3rd rev edn, J. D. Stewart, 1939. Though the scheme was originally welcomed by British librarians, it gradually became so out of date that it was abandoned by the 1960s.

2   Rider, F., *International classification for the arrangement of books on the shelves of general libraries*, 1961. (Published by the author.)
Poole, H., 'Fremont Rider and his *International classification*: an interesting tale of American library history', *Library resources and technical services*, **24**, Spring 1980, 106–13.

3   Williamson, N. J., Suliang Feng and T. Tennant, *The Library of Congress Classification: a content analysis of the schedules in preparation for their conversion into machine-readable form*, Washington, DC, Library of Congress Cataloging Distribution Service, 1995.

4   Arawaka, E. and Knecht, F. W., 'Don't buy DDC 19', *Library journal*, August
    1980, 1555–6. [Letter to the editor]
    Berman, S., 'DDC 20: the scam continues', *Library journal*, **114**, Sep. 15 1989,
    45–8.
5   Howarth, Lynne C, 'Factors influencing policies for the adoption and integra-
    tion of revisions to classification schedules', in *Classification research for
    knowledge representation and organization: proceedings of the 5th
    International study conference on classification research, Toronto, Canada,
    June 24–28 1991*, Williamson, N. J. and Hudon, M. (eds.), Elsevier, 1992, (FID
    698), 247–54.
6   Lund, J. J. and Taube, M., 'A nonexpansive classification system: an introduc-
    tion to period classification', *Library quarterly*, **7** (3), 1937, 373–94.
7   Amies, P., 'The new Linguistics classification', *Extensions and corrections to
    the UDC*, **17**, 1995.

Chapter 14
Uses of pre-coordinate indexing

Having considered the basic essentials of alphabetical and classified pre-coordinate systems, we can now consider the ways in which they may be used, looking at the advantages and disadvantages of different methods. The three areas to be covered are:

1 Shelf arrangement of books
2 Library catalogues and bibliographies
3 Book indexes.

All these depend on the fact that pre-coordinate indexes are 'one-place' indexes, in that they give a place which we consider to be the primary statement of the subject, though they may need supporting secondary listings in a different order to give full access. In this chapter we will consider manual methods, with MARC records and OPACS to be dealt with in Chapter 15.

Shelf arrangement

It is generally accepted that libraries should have a good proportion, if not all, of their stock on open access; wares which are not on view are harder to market! (One hundred years ago, the eminent British librarian James Duff Brown was thought to be mad when he put open access into practice in the London borough of Islington!) We have to arrange the books on open access in some helpful way, and the consensus seems to be that systematic arrangement by subject is the most useful of the choice of author, title or alphabetical subject. The major classification schemes have in general been compiled with this purpose in mind: DDC (though Dewey did envisage its use in a classified catalogue); LCC, specifically to arrange the books in the Library of Congress; BC1 and BC2 are for shelf classification, as is CC. UDC is the only major scheme to have been compiled primarily to arrange a catalogue, but this is used for shelf arrangement in many special libraries.[1]

Why is classified shelf arrangement helpful? There are two important reasons. The first is to satisfy the browsing function; readers like to wander round the shelves and find books which attract them. Although this may seem to be a form of random selection, it is rarely completely without purpose; readers usually browse in a *subject* area which interests them, and classified arrangement facilitates this. The second is in many situations more important: what do we do if the specific book we are looking for is not there? Other readers do selfishly borrow books which we would like to obtain, particularly in academic libraries. In this situation, *can we find a substitute*? Is there another book which will serve our purpose as well as the original? Classified arrangement optimizes our chances of finding a satisfactory substitute.

These two purposes only hold good if we have an open access collection; if books are in a closed stack (i.e. closed to the readers), then the question of browsing does not arise, nor does the idea of finding a substitute. The only person who can select a satisfactory substitute is the reader, since we are very much concerned here with pertinence, i.e. relevance to a particular individual. If they do not have access to a collection, readers cannot browse, nor can they pick a suitable substitute off the shelf. Shelf classification only makes sense in an open access collection.

We have seen in previous chapters some of the practical problems that arise in shelf classification. If the notation is long, it is difficult to put it on the back of a book, or – worse still – a pamphlet, yet this is necessary for the practical work of shelving. Rider devised a classification scheme expressly for this purpose, with the aim of providing a notation no longer than three digits, yet able to arrange quite a substantial library. Unfortunately, he did not appear to realise the problems inherent in composite subjects, and his allocation of notation can only be described as eccentric in places. His scheme was well-intentioned, but was regarded by most as irrelevant, despite his attempt to meet their wishes for a short shelf notation.[2]

Immediately we put a piece of notation on a book, we have a vested interest in obsolescence; we do not want the structure of knowledge to change, because that will mean altering our past practice. Further, unless we guide our shelves thoroughly, readers will find it difficult to follow the arrangement, particularly if the notation is mixed. In a lending library, many of the books will be on loan at any given time, with the books not in place varying from day to day. This makes it that much more difficult to maintain the sequence in good order, and the actual position of the books will also vary; readers who find 'their' books moved from their regular place see this as a cause for dissatisfaction!

Despite all the problems, libraries in general do provide classified arrangement on their shelves, though many librarians, particularly in the United States, tend to regard it as merely a means to 'mark and park', ignoring the purpose of systematic arrangement. If shelf classification is indeed simply a location device, there are other much cheaper ways of achieving the purpose.

Any classified arrangement will only please some – we hope a majority – of our readers. We must therefore use other arrangements to complement it, for example through displays bringing together topics scattered by the classification. The 'new books shelf' reflects the fact that a great many readers are interested in the latest publications, sometimes almost regardless of subject matter. After the novelty has worn off, the books are returned to the main sequence.

We also need some kind of alphabetical access to the arrangement. This should properly be an index compiled for the purpose, but sometimes as an economy measure the index to the scheme is used. As we have seen, there will be subjects in our sequence which do not appear in the scheme because we have synthesized the notation; equally there will be subjects in the scheme not represented on our shelves, for which the index entries will simply mislead users. Another method, used in OPACS and also in dictionary catalogues, is to give access through a set of subject headings, which may bear little or no relation to the structure of the classification scheme; the class mark is then a separate part of the catalogue entry. In the USA and some other countries such as Australia, the class mark is part of the *shelf mark*, which includes a Cutter number to represent the author's name and possibly the copy or edition number. This tends to emphasize the function of the classification as a finding device rather than an arranging device.

Another problem mentioned in Chapter 13 was that of keeping pace with knowledge. Any scheme will need to change over the years, as new subjects develop and relationships change. Any changes will mean disruption to our established order, but the problem is rather deeper than this. Classification schemes change in order to reflect changes in the organization of knowledge: the way that books are written and the subjects that they cover. If new subjects fit uneasily into an old classification, is it not true that old subjects, as represented in books written at the time, will fit uneasily into a new classification? Perhaps a solution would be to keep only the modern books on open access, and relegate the older books to the stacks – which can be arranged by a more space-efficient mode of fixed location, since the arrangement does not need to be helpful to the readers.

Another solution which has been used is to abandon formal classification altogether for shelf arrangement and use 'categorization' instead, i.e. broad subject groups incorporating fiction as well as non-fiction.[3] Those systems which have been described have been limited to libraries holding fewer than about 30,000 volumes on open access, and close examination shows that 'categorization' is simply classification by another name. The groupings used are not those of any of the major schemes, and usually have a different citation order from the discipline-based organization of most schemes, but are not fundamentally distinct. They certainly do not throw classification out with the Dewey bathwater, as is sometimes suggested, and the catalogue, perhaps classified by DDC in the UK, remains as a tool for the serious reader. The answer we choose depends on how seriously we consider the classified shelf arrangement as an aid to readers, and perhaps even on the needs of our readers, who should not be entirely overlooked in the discussion.

Library catalogues and bibliographies

A library catalogue is intended to record the stock of that library; a bibliography, on the other hand, is not limited to the stock of any one library, but usually has some other kind of limitation, e.g. national, language or subject. As far as the subject approach is concerned, both are very similar and can be considered together. For example, the theory of subject headings developed by Coates was applied in BTI, a bibliography, but could also have been applied in a library catalogue. Many special libraries use UDC for their catalogue, and for their shelf arrangement (possibly in an abbreviated form), but UDC is also used by some bibliographies for their primary arrangement. LCSH is intended for use in library catalogues, but is the basis of headings used in several indexing services.

Bearing this point in mind, we can evaluate the different kinds of manual subject catalogue still to be found, and point out the relative advantages and disadvantages. It must be stressed that if we start with systems having the same degree of specificity, and adopt the same policy with regard to exhaustivity, and build in the same network of relationships, there will be no difference in the information that can be found through the systems; what will differ is the way the systems will give answers to particular types of enquiry. All systems are equal, but in any given situation, some are more equal than others.[4]

Alphabetical subject catalogue

The alphabetical catalogue contains subject entries and cross-references arranged alphabetically in one sequence. The form most commonly found is the *dictionary catalogue*, in which subject entries are interfiled with author and title entries, to give a single complete sequence; an alternative is the subject list accompanied by a *name catalogue*, which lists names as authors and as subjects. There are three situations in which the dictionary form is found: the first is periodical indexes, of which those compiled by the H. W. Wilson Company are probably the most widely used; the second is library catalogues published in book form in the past, for example those produced by the New York Public Library;[5] and the third is card catalogues which have not yet been retrospectively converted to OPAC form. A study by UKOLN[6] identified some 28,000,000 card catalogue records still to be converted in UK libraries; there is no reason to suppose that figures for the USA and Australia would not be comparable. There is therefore a need to be aware of the format despite the change to OPACS for many library catalogues.

As we have seen in Chapter 2, subject entries consist of a heading, from the index vocabulary, and a description which identifies the document. There may also be cross-references in the sequence, of two kinds: USE or *See* references, which lead from headings which appear only in the entry vocabulary to headings in the index vocabulary; and RT, BT and NT, or more usually in this situation *See also*, references, which serve to link headings in the index vocabulary, either to show semantic relationships or to reveal 'hidden' terms in composite headings, as discussed in the section on chain procedure in Chapter 7.

Headings for the index vocabulary are usually maintained separately. In general, library catalogues have relied on published lists such as LCSH or *Sears list of subject headings*, but we do need to keep in addition some kind of *authority file* to show what our usage has been. We shall need to show which headings we have used in a published list, to help in maintaining consistency in practice, and also headings we have used which are not in the list. Both LCSH and Sears give the local user scope to introduce additional headings: as specific examples of general 'blanket' headings, or as headings generated by analogy with a 'pattern' heading, or by the addition of subheadings of general application. The lists used for some indexes, e.g. *PAIS International*, are published; the PAIS list is discussed in Chapter 26.

We may summarize the advantages and disadvantages of the alphabetical approach as follows:

Advantages:
- self-evident order (though we must be aware of the filing order of subheadings).
- hospitality: we can insert new topics at any time simply by filing the new headings in the correct place in the alphabetical sequence, provided that the index vocabulary that we are using permits us to add terms.
- flexibility: we can show more than one genus-species relationship by making cross-references; this freedom can be important when we are dealing with interdisciplinary subjects, though we must maintain careful control of the syndetic structure.

Disadvantages: To set against these, we have to consider some of the problems.
- alphabetical scatter: if we look under Zoology, we may be referred to Animals; having made our way to the other end of the sequence, we may find that we should really have been looking for Zebras. In other words, related subjects are scattered according to the accident of their names.
- conflict with natural language: if we are to be consistent in our selection of headings, we shall be forced to abandon natural language in favour of an artificial index vocabulary: artificial in the sense that the choice of terms will be strictly controlled, and headings will not necessarily conform to normal usage. We try to eliminate synonyms, so a proportion of users will look for a term that we have not used, and are directed from their choice to ours. We may have inverted headings such as Art, American; though LCSH practice is now to avoid these, older catalogues will still have many examples. We may also have a similar problem with headings and subheadings, e.g. Corn – Harvesting. The end product of a list of subject headings is not in natural language. However, users are accustomed to artificial conventions in looking for information: how many authors put their surname before their forenames on the title-page of their books? So perhaps we should not exaggerate the importance of this factor.
- generic searching is tedious: to start with a particular term and then follow through all of the related terms which may lead us to useful information is not easy. Alphabetical arrangement works well in a situation where terminology is clearly defined, and where users are mainly concerned with requests for information on specific topics with generally accepted names.

Classified catalogue

Systematic arrangement brings related subjects together by using notation as its code vocabulary; there is therefore no question of combining the subject and author/title sequences in one. Entries consist of a heading, which is a notational symbol, and a document description. We need a separate file to enable us to identify the notation we should be looking for; as discussed in Chapter 12, this is an integral part of the catalogue, but is often neglected.

Genus-species relationships and syntactic relationships are both shown by a combination of juxtaposition in the classified sequence and juxtaposition in the alphabetical index, but whereas in an alphabetical arrangement it is difficult to show *kinds* of relationship (the syntax of the index language), in a classified arrangement these are shown by the notation if it is expressive, as well as by the arrangement.

Feature headings

In a systematic arrangement, it is the notation which forms the headings by which the entries are arranged, but notation is merely a means to an end, that of arranging entries according to the schedules. It does not help users who find a piece of notation if they do not know what it stands for. Suppose that a user thinks of too broad a subject, and finds the notation for this through the alphabetical index; the next step is to locate this notation in the classified sequence, where the content of the entries will show that the heading is too general. The classified sequence is intended to help users find their way from broad headings to more specific, but how do they know when they have got to the right place? We cannot expect the users to be able to translate the notation into words. The solution was proposed by Dewey: we should ourselves translate the notation into words, through the use of *feature headings*. These give the users the same facility that they have with the alphabetical catalogue of finding subject headings which they can understand for each entry. A very good example of the use of feature headings was BNB, where in the classified section we found a liberal use of words to clarify the systematic arrangement. Feature headings were also used by BNB as a source of terms for its index to the classified arrangement.

If the classification scheme we are using is not specific enough for our needs, we may use feature headings which go beyond the notation to state the subject precisely; the words which are not represented by notation are *verbal extensions*. They can be used for indexing, but may present a problem in the arrangement; do we arrange the items at a particular piece of notation extended in this way alphabetically by the verbal extensions, or in some classified arrangement which goes beyond that provided by the classification scheme? The resulting arrangement may not be at all obvious to the user. The best example of the use of verbal extensions is the early volumes of BNB; using DDC14 to classify a large collection of literature in detail quickly revealed deficiencies which were overcome by the use of this device, which was signalled by ending the class number with [1]. However, in places it led to quite lengthy sections in which the entries were systematically arranged by a system which was unknown and invisible to the user, except through the feature headings and verbal extensions. Particularly in the five-year cumulations, this could become very confusing. The advantages were those of [presumably] helpful order and specificity; the searcher would find related topics together, and if there were two books on the same specific topic they would be found together. Without the use of verbal extensions these two advantages would have been lost; users would still have had to look through as many entries, with no guarantee that if they found one document on a subject they had found them all.

With the introduction of MARC records in 1971, BNB adopted the current edition of DDC, DDC18, and stopped using the [1]. PRECIS was used as the indexing system from 1971 to 1990; it also served to produce feature headings, but this was dropped with the introduction of COMPASS. Up to three levels of heading from DDC were given, and the COMPASS string appeared at the end of the entry, but this was certainly not as effective as the feature headings which used to be given. With the abandonment of COMPASS in 1995, BNB no longer shows any direct translation of the notation.

Feature headings and verbal extensions, as well as being a major source of terms for the alphabetical index, will indicate the terms which should be used for guiding for the shelf arrangement. In general, libraries provide quite inadequate guides to their systematic arrangement, assuming that readers can find their way around the shelves with a minimum of effort – an optimistic view which does not appear to be justified by experience.

We may summarize the advantages and disadvantages of the classified catalogue as follows:

Advantages:
- helpful order – the arrangement is intended to bring related subjects together in a way which is helpful to users. Search strategy within the main hierarchy is simple – to broaden a search we need only look at the entries at broader class numbers, which is very simple if the notation is hierarchical but not particularly difficult if it is not, since we need only move backwards through the sequence. More specific subjects can be found in the same area by moving forwards, rather than backwards, through the order. The index to the classified catalogue will also provide an index to the shelf arrangement, enabling the reader to go straight to the shelves.

Disadvantages:
- indirect access – we have to have a secondary index file in alphabetical order to find the appropriate notation to get to the desired place in the systematic arrangement. Any search, no matter how simple, thus requires two stages, whereas with an alphabetical catalogue we may need only one.
- systematic scattering – only the foci in the primary facet will be brought together, those in other facets will be scattered. Also, a subject which can appear in more than one discipline will be scattered by the usual discipline-based classification.

The classified catalogue is best suited to broad searching, where a reader starts at one particular point and then follows up the ramifications of the subject, which can become tedious in an alphabetical sequence. For readers who know the right terminology the alphabetical subject catalogue will give more direct entry, but the larger the catalogue, the more likely it is that the terminology used will depart further and further from expectation. Fortunately, many of the difficulties in both types of arrangement are solved by computer-based catalogues, but there are still many printed catalogues and bibliographies in use, and an understanding of the principles on which they are based will make their use much easier and more productive.

Physical forms of catalogue

In theory, the effectiveness of a catalogue should not be affected by its physical form, but in practice this is not the case. The physical form can affect both the input, from the point of view of the librarian keeping the catalogue up to date, and the output, from the point of view of the readers trying to find information.

In any system that is open-ended, we need to be able to insert new items as necessary, and also to withdraw items. If we have a fixed location serial file, that is, one in which we give each item a permanent place, there is only one place where we can add items: at the end. If we need to withdraw items, this is feasible, but it means leaving gaps in the sequence which it is impractical to fill. We cannot add in the middle, because that will disrupt the existing order. The only kind of order that can be displayed is a chronological one, with the new items added at the end. Such a file is the accessions file which used to be an essential feature of library stock control, or a file of data on magnetic tape, and to find a particular entry means scanning the whole file sequentially until we come to it; we do not have *random access*, i.e. the ability to go direct to any specific point in the file that we may wish. (Most of us are familiar with the difficulty of finding a specific item on a cassette tape compared with locating a track on a record; even a CD is less flexible than an LP in this respect.) The various physical forms must be considered from this point of view as well as the intellectual content.

The card catalogue

The most commonly found form of manual catalogue is the card catalogue. Though increasingly many libraries now offer online catalogues, there are still many card files in use. These may be in small libraries and other organizations where the benefits of computerization do not as yet outweigh its costs, or in very large libraries which have not yet converted all of their past catalogue entries to online form, again because of cost.

The cards in a card catalogue are usually of standard 12.5 × 7.5 cm size. For any particular item to be catalogued, there will be a set of cards, each usually containing the same information; this is known as *unit entry*. For each desired access point the appropriate heading from the indexing system is added to a card, and the set of cards are then arranged according to these headings. New cards can be inserted at any point, and we can go direct to any access point we want, provided that it is used as a heading. The more entries we make, the larger and more costly the catalogue becomes, with the required infrastructure of drawers and cabinets. Using a large catalogue also becomes quite difficult, whichever arrangement we choose. It has therefore been the practice for the number of entries to be limited, so that the average number of subject entries made by the Library of Congress has been put at about 1.7 per document. It is important to realize that this is an economic consideration, because it has been carried over into online catalogues, where the same economic arguments have no validity, and we suffer an unnecessary restriction on subject access.

There are various other points which might be considered, but to sum up, the card catalogue is very flexible: it permits us to arrange any number of entries in any way we wish, and to add or withdraw entries as necessary. To set against this, it is relatively expensive, both in capital costs and in upkeep, it is not convenient to scan, and it is essentially a single copy device; it costs twice as much to maintain two copies as to maintain one. Many readers are reluctant to use a card catalogue, and regard it as a barrier to their use of a library – if indeed they regard it as a tool for their use at all; many assume that it is for the use of the staff only. Perhaps it is unduly cynical to regard it as an effective barrier to library use, but the card catalogue was always seen as a benefit by librarians rather than readers. Yet for small files it is still a simple and useful form of index, and should not be entirely overlooked. The National Information Standards Organization is in fact preparing a new standard Z39.65-199x for permanent and durable catalogue cards, and LC is still supplying sets of catalogue cards to libraries using the form.

Book form

At one time, the printed catalogue in book form was the standard method used by public libraries, particularly those with closed access. The book form has several advantages: it is portable, it can be produced in multiple copies very easily, and it is convenient to use – the eye can scan a column of entries very easily instead of having to look at one at a time. It suffers however from one major disadvantage: it is completely inflexible. The time taken to print it can mean that it is out of date as soon as it is available, and though withdrawals can be shown by crossing out (though this is hardly practical in multiple copies!), additions cannot be shown at all. The printed catalogue is thus suited to the situation where withdrawals are few, and additions are also a small proportion of the total stock. We find this situation in such large national libraries as the British Library, though even here it is probable that the last complete printed catalogue has been produced, the *General catalogue of printed books – 1975*, or in a library concentrating on a particular subject. A good example of the latter is the *Catalogue of manuscripts of Australia and the South Pacific in the Mitchell Library, Sydney*, which is the major historical collection of its kind in Australia. In both cases, the catalogue is of use to a much wider audience than can actually visit the library, and the production of multiple copies is more important than absolute currency.

During the 1960s a number of libraries began to use computers to produce their printed catalogues. In some cases this was part of the overall computerization of the library, but in others it was a solution to problems posed by the card catalogue. The local government reorganization in London in 1965 meant that a number of library services were merged, facing the librarians with the task of rationalizing perhaps three different catalogues. A simple short-title form of catalogue produced by computer was a quick way of achieving this objective. Computer-produced book form catalogues became quite widely used, and were reasonably acceptable to the readers, despite the poor print quality and inconvenient paper size which were all that were available at that time.[7] The MARC project, discussed in the next chapter, combined with Computer Output Microform to produce a new physical form to replace the computer printout.

COM

The computer could be used to produce output in the form of microfilm or micro-fiche, though for catalogue purposes the latter proved to be the popular form. The photocomposing machines used had a wide range of fonts and special characters suitable for cataloguing, and could produce output which was very much more pleasant to use than the line printer output direct from the computer. Fiche was also cheap enough to make the production of multiple copies economically feasible; as an example, the British Library Document Supply Division found that it was cheaper to give a copy of a report on microfiche to a borrower than to set up a loan record. This meant that libraries could produce multiple copies of their catalogues, with new cumulations at regular intervals. During the 1970s and much of the 1980s, the COM catalogue was the preferred form in many libraries,[8] and was also used for bibliographical tools, for example regular quarterly cumulations of LCSH; the Library of Congress now supplies the *National Union Catalog* on fiche. BNB is available on fiche, as is *Books in English*; a cumulation containing 1.25 million records covering 1981–1992 was published in 1992. However, for many libraries COM was seen as an interim stage towards the online computer-based catalogue which has now taken its place. COM is still used for other purposes; for example ERIC documents are supplied to deposit centres round the world in COM fiche form, as are other similar reports.

Bibliographies

Unlike library catalogues, bibliographies are normally printed and intended for wide distribution. Multiple entry is therefore almost unknown, because of its cost; instead, we have a single main entry, which may range in detail from author, title and date to a full informative abstract, with various secondary indexes to give access through factors thought likely to be useful. We have exactly the same problems of access as in library catalogues, but some other considerations arise from the nature of bibliographies.

Bibliographies may be either current or retrospective. In the latter case, we select the entries to be included, and the list is then closed; we are thus in a position to choose whatever method of primary arrangement we wish, and can opt for one which will reflect, as far as we can tell in advance, the needs of likely users. Current bibliographies, on the other hand, are normally produced under pressure of time, and it may prove necessary to abandon any pretence to helpful order in the main sequence, and instead use chronological order of receipt. For example, in *Resources in education* we find that the main sequence is arranged by report number, i.e. order of receipt. (It is important here not to overlook the fact that for report literature, the report number is a significant identification factor.) If the main order is arbitrary, the need for indexes to provide access becomes acute if we are to be able to conduct a search for a particular item or on a subject. A major advantage of computer-based services is that they use a single-entry sequence supported by indexes which give us easy access through a variety of approaches.

This need relates to the use likely to be made of a current bibliography. We have already seen in Chapter 2 that there is a difference between bibliographies intended for current notification and those intended for retrospective searching; those that are intended for the latter purpose will normally have more, and more detailed, secondary sequences than those meant for temporary use only. The cost of producing an abstracting journal intended to be of permanent value is now high: much higher than that of producing, say, a guide to current contents. The librarian also has to weigh the cost of having the printed version against that of conducting the same searches online, through one of the utilities providing the machine-readable version. It must be remembered that the printed version involves acquisition, processing and storage costs as well as the actual subscription. If only a limited number of searches are carried out in a particular printed bibliography each year, it may well be considerably cheaper to cancel the subscription and rely on online searching. Careful and realistic costing is needed to arrive at the correct break-even point, including of course staff time taken in searching the printed version as opposed to online searching.

Many of the techniques described in earlier chapters were developed for use in printed abstracting and indexing services rather than for library catalogues. However, it must be realized that the arrangement of, and access to, bibliographical tools are in essence no different from the comparable features in library catalogues, and both should be evaluated in the same way.

Book indexes

The indexing of individual books is usually also regarded as something quite separate from other kinds of indexing, but this is not the case.[9] We can employ the same kinds of approach as we would with any other classified sequence, since a book itself presents information in a systematic way; in particular, it is possible to use chain procedure to give a full and detailed index which is nevertheless within economic bounds, as may be shown by examples taken from the index to the fourth edition of this work:

Notation *def* 150, ch 10 188+
    DC: on Library of Congress cards 339
    DC19 335   [the abbreviation DC was used in that edition]

These three entries tell us that notation is defined on page 150; Chapter 10, beginning on page 188, deals with notation in general; and there are two other pages we should turn to for further information. If we now turn to the name Dewey we find:

Dewey, M
    integrity of numbers 316
    see also DC

If we follow the instruction *see also* and turn to DC, we find:

DC ch 17 313+
    notation
    lack of facet indicators 307

not always expressive 200
not hospitable 195
segmented 209
used in *Sears list* 430

By following up the various references we have found we can discover everything in the book relating to Dewey's use of notation, but some of the searching may be indirect. Under Notation, we are referred to Chapter 10, but are not told exactly where in that chapter we should find information on Dewey, while if we follow up the references under Dewey and DC we may find ourselves reading through the whole chapter, or at least looking for section headings. The only entries under Notation which are specific are those leading to places not in the general chapter; similarly, the entries under DC which are specific are those not leading to Chapter 17. This is not entirely satisfactory, but the alternative soon begins to look impractical if we consider that under Notation we should have to list all the significant contents of the whole chapter on notation, and under DC the whole contents of that chapter, in addition to all the entries which are there already. In order to gain an economic advantage we sacrifice a degree of specificity, giving us a result which is consistent (even in its imperfection!) and is of reasonable size in relation to the book.

As in the classified catalogue, chain procedure forces us to rely to a considerable extent on the use of headings within chapters, and on the systematic presentation generally. (Despite impressions to the contrary, authors do in general try to present their work systematically!) Since the index leads us to pages, or possibly even to paragraphs, the scanning which may be necessary is not intolerable, and may even be useful in drawing our attention to, for example, other features of notation mentioned in Chapter 10 but not necessarily associated with Dewey. The systematic collocation of distributed relatives which is one result of applying chain procedure does at least make sure that we can find everything on notation indexed under that heading, and on Dewey indexed under his name, even though the information we want may be scattered through the book.

In compiling indexes to individual books, we do not need to rely on an external source of subject headings or terms; we can use the terminology in the book. Since we are trying to pinpoint ideas *within* the text, we have to formulate quite specific subject terms; we are looking at a combination of high exhaustivity with specificity if the index is to be useful. Since we are indexing a systematic presentation – the text of the book – we will gain little from a systematic index, which would also itself need a further alphabetic index. We do however sometimes find examples of indirect alphabetic entry, which is open to exactly the same kind of objection. Index entries should be direct as well as specific.

It is desirable to avoid *see* references within the index, for the same reason that we discussed in Chapter 12: they take us from one place in the index to another place *still in the index*, so that we have yet to find our way into the text of the book. In the index to the fourth edition of the present work, the presence of long lists of entries under synonyms – the reason why we might use *see* references – has been avoided to some extent by indexing only the preferred synonym in full, but giving entries under non-preferred synonyms which lead to the preferred term, but also to the main section in the text. For example:

References (cross-references) *def* 33

leads us to the place where reference is defined, but also indicates that the user will find more entries by turning to the preferred synonym cross-references, where indeed there are 26 entries:

Cross-references *def* 33, 77, 96+
    alphabetical subject catalogues 281
    alphabetico-classed arrangement 144
    book indexes 301
    . . .
    Thesauri 441
        TEST 484
        WRU education thesaurus 511

Once again we have an economy measure intended to keep down costs while nevertheless providing users with complete access at the cost of a little more effort on their part. Since publishers are invariably anxious to keep costs as low as possible, authors are obliged to use economical methods; like hanging, indexing a book concentrates the mind wonderfully.

Search strategy

So far we have looked at the theory and practice of the construction of manual pre-coordinate indexes, but we should also give consideration to their use.[10] How do we set about getting the best results from such a index? What procedure should we follow in conducting a search? We are faced with a question posed by a user, possibly not very well phrased, perhaps asking for something other than what is really wanted, but normally triggered off by some particular event or events. This question has to be resolved into an answer which in a manual system usually consists of a set of document descriptions identifying items which we think will provide the information wanted. (Computerized systems do not necessarily provide anything further.) The index or catalogue is the tool we use to perform this transformation, and, as in pantomime transformation scenes, the effectiveness with which it will do so depends on how well the machinery works and how carefully we have maintained it. (For some of our readers, no matter how we wave the magic wand of persuasion, the library catalogue remains obdurately a pumpkin – computerized, perhaps, but still a pumpkin.)

The first piece of advice may seem something of a counsel of despair: it is that if we have some identifying factor, such as an author's name, it is easier to follow this up than to try to formulate a subject search. The success of tools such as the ISI citation indexes is linked to their avoidance of subject specification and their reliance on manifest information such as bibliographical references. Similarly, if during the course of a subject search it appears that a few authors are major figures in the subject field concerned, it is worth following their names up in a large-scale abstracting or indexing service such as *Chemical abstracts*, or the appropriate citation index. We may use a biographical reference work, since this will frequently reveal items which it would have been difficult or even impossible to find through the subject approach.

If we do not have any identifying factors to go on, we have to pursue our search through the subject. The first point is to establish as closely as possible the exact nature of the subject we are interested in, and this can be quite difficult. Users often find it difficult to express themselves; they may well not be quite sure what it is they are looking for. They may not realize the range of tools at their disposal; few patrons have any idea of the variety of approaches that are available to carry out a search.[11] However, enquiries are usually prompted by some kind of springboard or trigger, and if we can establish this through the *reference interview* we can work forwards from a satisfactory starting point. Lancaster's classic research on the MEDLARS system[12] showed that such an interview is best carried out without reference to any indexing language; enquirers should be encouraged to express themselves freely and if necessary at length, so that we have as complete statements as they can give of what is wanted, in their own words. Once we have these statements, we can think about translating them into the various languages used in the tools we decide to search.

If the search is for a single concept, it will be relatively simple. We have to determine which terms have been used to denote that particular concept in our indexing language; in an alphabetical system this should be straightforward, provided that the term is listed in the entry vocabulary, but in a classified arrangement we have to determine the appropriate notation depending on the context in which the concept is sought. Having established our first point of entry, we can turn to the subject sequence and find what is filed under the appropriate heading. If we find nothing, we have to consider what other headings to consult; in an alphabetical sequence, we should look for *see also* references, in a classified sequence try searching round about the place we have found. In both cases we are looking for related headings, but whereas in an alphabetical sequence these will be scattered, in a classified sequence many of them should be juxtaposed. By moving back through the classified sequence, i.e. in the direction of earlier class numbers, we can normally come to a broader heading; by moving forward, in the direction of later class numbers, we may come to useful material at more specific headings. For example, if we are looking for information on 'potato blight' in a catalogue classified by UDC, the class number representing the subject will be 633.491–24. If we find nothing at this point, we can move forwards to the more specific subject 'treatment of potato blight' at 633.491–24–293.4; alternatively, we may move back to the more general heading 'potatoes' at 633.491. If neither of these moves gives any useful information, we can move further back to even more general headings: 'control of plant diseases' 632.93, 'fungus diseases of plants' 632.4, 'diseases of plants' 632.

As we have seen already, it is not usual to make upward references in an alphabetical catalogue. If we find nothing at Potato blight, or Potatoes – blight, we can obviously look under Potatoes or Blight, but there will be no guidance to headings broader than these. We have to turn back to the authority list, e.g. LCSH, to find what more general headings might be worth trying, e.g. Plant diseases. If we are using a tool for which the authority list is not published, we may have some difficulty in deciding on a suitable broader heading, and it could be useful to consult a classification scheme!

At all times the needs of the users have to be borne in mind. If they are satisfied with one document, then we can stop our search directly we have found one relevant answer; we do not need to worry about whether there are other answers, or even whether one of them might not be better. If the enquirers are satisfied, we have achieved our objective. This is not to say that we should not advise them if we think we might find something better by expending more effort (and perhaps more money!); they may still be quite happy for us to stop searching. There will be other occasions when we shall need to find as much information as we can, by making our search as complete as possible. This will normally require some knowledge of at least the terminology of the subject area, as well as skill in the use of catalogues and bibliographies, as is shown by some of the examples quoted by Vickery.[13]

Catalogue use studies in the past have generally been carried out by questionnaire rather than direct observation. The general conclusion that has been drawn has always been that users preferred to carry out author/title rather than subject searches, but one study carried out at City University has called this into question.[14] The main catalogue was on COM, and consisted of classified and author/title sequences. The main subject access was through a printed PRECIS index to the classified sequence (which was also the shelf arrangement). Nearly three-quarters of all searches were subject searches, though some appeared to begin as title searches. Many users reformulated their searches while scanning the PRECIS index, and of those who began looking for titles, many were actually making subject searches on the title words. Many users also continued their searching at the shelves once they had found a suitable class number. The study has implications not only for manual catalogues but also OPACS, discussed in Chapter 15.

Summary

Pre-coordinate systems are basically one-place systems, but problems arise from the necessity for a fixed combination or citation order. Post-coordinate systems avoid the need for combination order. Why then should we bother with pre-coordinate systems at all?[15]

There are situations where a one-place system is a practical necessity. We do not scatter multiple copies of books round the library to ensure that one is found at every possible access point, and the single sequence of entries in a current bibliography, dictated by economic considerations, can be helpfully arranged by a precoordinated system. In a particular library, it is often the case that we can find an order which will satisfy the vast majority of users; it is then economic sense to keep costs down by using this, and spending more money finding information in those few cases where the order is not helpful. Pre-coordinate systems also lend themselves to changes of search strategy; having started a search at one particular point, we can follow up a narrower, broader or related subject search without having to start again from scratch. The matter may be resolved by the computer, which can search a pre-coordinate file as if it were a post-coordinate file of single terms. We may find that this is one situation where we can have our cake and eat it: use pre-coordinate arrangement for the shelves or bibliography, but carry out post-coordinate searches on the bibliographical records.

References

1   Foskett, A. C., 'Shelf classification – *or else*', *Library journal*, **95** (15), 1970, 2771–3.
    Hyman, R. J., *Access to library collections*, Metuchen, NJ, Scarecrow Press, 1972.
    Hyman, R. J., *Shelf classification research: past, present – future?*, University of Illinois, Graduate School of Library Science, 1980 (Occasional papers 146.)
    Hyman, R. J., *Shelf access in libraries*, Chicago, American Library Association, 1982
    Hyman, R. J., *Information access: capabilities and limitations of printed and computerized sources,* Chicago, American Library Association, 1989.
    Hyman is not convinced of the value of shelf classification, but Mann (ref. 11 below) believes browsing the shelves to be far superior to browsing catalogue records.
2   Rider, F., *International classification,* 1961.
3   'Categorization' has been discussed during the 1980s in a number of short articles and letters to the editor in the *Library Association record* from time to time, e.g.:
    Tyerman, K., 'Alternative arrangements: children's non-fiction categorisation in Waltham Forest', *Library Association record,* **91** (7), 1989, 393–4.
    Pejtersen, A. M., 'The role of domain, task and users in providing subject access to information', *Cataloguing Australia,* **19** (3/4), 1993, 85–124.
    Alternative arrangement: new approaches to public library stock, Ainley, P. and Totterdell, B. (eds.), London, AAL, 1982. Includes several case studies.
4   Bath University Comparative catalogue study, *Final report*, Bath University Library, 1975. 10v in 9.
    Bryant, P. 'The catalogue', *Journal of documentation,* **36** (2), 1980, 133–63.
5   New York Public Library. Reference Division, *Dictionary catalog of the music collection*, Boston, Mass, G. K. Hall, 1964. 33v.
    New York Public Library. The Research Libraries, *Cumulative supplement 1964–1971,* Boston, Mass, G. K. Hall, 1973. 10v. Photographed from cards.
    New York Public Library. The Research Libraries, *Dictionary catalog of the research libraries.* 1972– . Photocomposed automated book catalogue.
6   'FIGIT retrospective catalogue conversion study', *UKOLN newsletter* (4), October 1995, [3].
7   Dolby, J. L., *Computerized library catalogs: their growth, cost and utility*, New

York, NY, Stechert-Hafner, 1969.

8 Stecher, E., *Catalogue provision in Colleges of Advanced Education*, Melbourne, RMIT, 1975.–
The Bath University Comparative catalogue study showed a very definite preference for fiche among users. P. Bryant (ref 5 above) mentions several other studies which reached similar conclusions. The 'Automation in libraries' survey carried out by the NBS found that of 3007 responses, 318 libraries had COM catalogues. (Reported in *Select,* (14) Winter 1994/5.)

9 *American national standard for library and information services and related publishing practices – basic criteria for indexes*, New York, NY, American National Standards Institute, 1984, Z39.4: 1984
Anderson, M. D., *Book indexing*, Cambridge University Press, 1971.
Guidelines for the content, organization and presentation of indexes, Geneva, ISO, 1994. ISO 999: 1994.
Knight, G.N., *Indexing, the art of: a guide to the indexing of books and periodicals*, London, Allen and Unwin, 1979.
Langridge, D., 'The use of classification in book indexing', *The indexer*, 2 (3), 1961, 95–8.
Recommendations for examining documents, determining their subjects and selecting index terms, Milton Keynes, British Standards Institution, 1991, BS 6529:1991.
Recommendations for preparing indexes for books, periodicals and other documents, Milton Keynes, British Standards Institution, 1988. BS 3700:1988.
Wellisch, H. H., *Indexing from A to Z*, New York, NY, H. W. Wilson Co., 1991.

10 Bates, M., 'Search strategy', *Annual review of information science and technology*, **16**, 1981, 139–69.

11 Mann, T. *Library research models: a guide to classification, cataloging and computers*, New York, NY, Oxford University Press, 1993.

12 Lancaster, F.W., 'Evaluating the performance of a large computerized information service', *Journal of the American Medical Association*, **207** (1), 1969, 114–20. (Included in *Theory of subject analysis. . .*)

13 Vickery, B. C., *Techniques of information retrieval*, London, Butterworths, 1970, 140–5.

14 Hancock, M. 'Subject search behaviour at the library catalogue and at the shelves: implications for online catalogues', *Journal of documentation*, **43** (4). 1987, 303–21.

15 Svenonius, E. 'Pre-coordinate or post-coordinate?', *Subject indexing: principles and practices in the 90's*, Holley. R.P. (ed.), *et al.*, Munich, K. G. Saur, 1995, (UBCIM Publications – New series Vol. 15).

Chapter 15

Online public access catalogues

Standardization to improve accessibility to information

If we are to have the international exchange of bibliographical information, then it is necessary for international standards to exist, so that records produced by different sources are compatible.[1] Attempts to devise a common cataloguing code for the UK and US began early this century, and resulted in the Anglo-American Cataloguing Rules of 1908. Work on the revision of this code began in the 1930s, but the UK members of the committee had to withdraw on the outbreak of war in 1939. The American Library Association (ALA) continued the work, producing a draft code in 1941, and a new code, the ALA Rules, was published in 1949. This continued the AA-1908 practice of working from cases, without trying to identify the underlying principles; dissatisfaction with this approach led to the International Conference on Cataloguing Principles held in Paris in 1961. This Conference asserted the importance of drawing up a code of rules based on sound theoretical principles rather than on *ad hoc* solutions to practical problems, and led to the production of the Anglo-American Cataloguing Rules in 1967. Though this was generally agreed, the Library of Congress (LC) decided to continue past practices in some areas, and there were in consequence two versions of the code, one for the UK adopting the new principles in full, the other for the US adopting most but not all.

One of the areas which needed further work if it was to be internationally accepted was the area of description, and in 1969 the International Federation of Library Associations (IFLA) sponsored an International Meeting of Cataloguing Experts which led in 1971 to the publication of the first edition of the International Standard Bibliographical Description (ISBD). This was developed further for various non-book materials, leading to the publication in 1977 of a generalized version ISBD(G); a revised version for monographs ISBD(M) was published in 1978.[2] ISBD laid down rules on a range of matters, including the preferred sources of information (e.g. title-page rather than cover); punctuation to be used to introduce and identify specific parts of the entry regardless of language; and three levels of cataloguing, from 1, minimum to 3, full. Much of this was incorporated into the second edition of AACR, published in 1978; the value of international standardization led to the acceptance of a single set of rules, with LC agreeing to change its practices to conform with the new standards, finally adopting the rules in full in 1982. A major revision was published in 1988, (AACR2R) and further minor amendments in 1993.[3] This has meant that there is now a very large measure of international agreement on the content of catalogue entries. This has been paralleled by the adoption of computer-based methods for the physical manipulation of catalogue records.

MARC

In the early 1960s, a study was carried out of the potential for using computers to store and maintain the whole of the bibliographical records of the Library of Congress (LC), and possibly also some of the documents themselves. At the then state of the art, some of the proposals were seen as unrealistic, but the King report,[4] as the final report on *Automation and the Library of Congress* came to be known, had a profound effect on thinking in libraries. One of the results of this study was the setting up of the MAchine Readable Cataloging (MARC) project, which began in 1966 as a cooperative venture involving 16 libraries other than LC. Each library was sent computer tapes from which it could produce catalogue records in a variety of formats, each entry containing information similar to that contained on LC cards.[5]

The experiment, which lasted a year, was successful, though it revealed certain problems, of which the most serious was fixed field working. Computer programs had largely been developed for business, where the length in letters or figures of information to be put in each field, for example the date, or the number of sales, could be predetermined. Information which could not fit into the field allocated, for example a lengthy address, was simply cut short, in line with the well-established Procrustean model. (Most people will recognize that this practice still continues.) For library cataloguing, this was clearly unsatisfactory if not useless. To accommodate long titles, a long field had to be allocated, which would waste storage for the vast majority of titles; a field which would accommodate personal authors would be totally inadequate for most government bodies. The project therefore lent weight to the development of variable field programming, which was at that time regarded as an expensive luxury. Another interesting outcome of the MARC I project was that libraries found that they could use the information for purposes other than cataloguing; it was used for acquisitions checking, SDI, and selection and ordering of materials. One library incorporated some of its own data in the same format. The results led to a much more ambitious project, MARC II, with international implications.

The MARC II project was seen as the basis of an international exchange of bibliographic data; any country that wished to cooperate could produce a full entry in the accepted format for all the documents catalogued by its national bibliographic service, and the information could be made available on magnetic tape to any other country requesting it. The project implied a much more detailed description of the document than was usual; each item of information had to be identified and tagged, for two reasons. The first was the use of variable fields; the computer had to be given instructions on the beginning and end of each field, and its contents, as well as each record. The second was that the information would be available to the whole range of libraries; some might want very detailed cataloguing, while others might well be satisfied with something rather briefer. Further, it was envisaged that a whole range of subject descriptions might be given: not merely DDC and LCC class numbers but also possibly UDC and NLM, or any other scheme; not just LCSH, but also PRECIS, or any other alphabetical system. Even those libraries using very full cataloguing would not necessarily want all this information.

LC started its MARC distribution service in 1969, and BNB also started experimenting with the production of MARC format records at the same time, adopting MARC as the basis for all its operations at the beginning of 1971, to coincide with the start of a new cumulation. The MARC project has been very successful, and bibliographic records are now freely exchanged among the English-speaking countries UK, USA, Canada and Australia.

Universal Bibliographic Control

The success of the MARC project among English-speaking countries led IFLA to develop a programme for Universal Bibliographic Control (UBC) beginning in 1974.[6] The purpose of this was to extend the idea initiated by Unesco after the Second World War to further the production of national bibliographies; if all countries produced a national bibliography, then a high proportion of the world's book production would be listed. The UBC programme is intended to achieve this goal by standardizing the format of records produced in different countries. A parallel programme was begun to develop a Common Communications Format (CCF), the International MARC (IM) programme. This merged with the UBC programme in 1987 to become the UBCIM.[7] There are now over 20 national MARC formats; unfortunately, slight differences in approach have led to slight differences in the 'standard' format, and UBCIM is leading continuing efforts to produce a generally accepted standard, UNIMARC.[8] The position is complicated further by the fact that MARC formats have been developed for various non-book materials, and these have yet to be generally agreed. One study which was begun in 1977 led to the publication in 1984 of the Guidelines for Authorities and Reference Entries (GARE), which sets out the format in which authority files should be compiled. This led logically to a similar set of guidelines for subject authority files, published in 1993.[9]

Integrated library operations

When computers first began to be used for library purposes, this was done on a piecemeal basis. Because of its nature, the circulation was one of the first areas to attract attention, while it quickly became clear that the processes used by libraries to order, acquire and process materials differed little from those used by other organizations for this purpose. The information required for circulation control is much less that that required for acquisition, which in turn needs less than does cataloguing. However, computers are most efficient when the same information is used for a variety of different purposes. The MARC I project had shown that the records could be used for other purposes than cataloguing, and libraries gradually adopted the idea of integrated computer systems, where one record could serve to represent a document from the time that it was ordered to its appearance in the catalogue and on the shelves. All that was necessary was to add any necessary local information to the MARC record.

The complete MARC record database now contains several million records; by 1994, LC records alone occupied some four gigabytes of storage space. The majority of libraries do not need all this information for their own collections; a practical solution was that records needed should be obtained wherever possible from a central agency. Processing centres have been established in several countries, on which libraries can draw for their own needs. The largest of these is OCLC,[10] which provides a variety of services to over 17,000 customers in 51 countries as well as in the USA. Its computing facilities can handle 4,000 simultaneous users at a rate of 100 transactions/second! In the UK, the British Library (BL) provides the BLAISE service, and in Australia the Australian Bibliographic Network (ABN) database produced by the National Library of Australia provides not only cataloguing copy but also locations, making it an effective union catalogue for interlibrary loan and collection building purposes, similar to the LASER project in the UK.[11] Not everyone views these developments with equal enthusiasm; it has been suggested that access to MARC records has been taken over by middlemen, and that to obtain MARC records now costs as much as buying the original document, though this seems to be a somewhat extreme view.[12]

By the late 1970s, the idea of making the catalogue available to the public online had begun to be accepted, and has been implemented throughout the period since. The advantages of using computer processing for all library systems have meant that most libraries now have their catalogues available as Online Public Access Catalogues: OPACS.[13] Not only can users find the documents they want through the catalogue, they can also find out their availability – on the shelf, on loan, missing, – and place holds on those they need that are not immediately available. (This facility has become particularly important for academic libraries with the growth of multi-campus universities.) Overdue penalties can be avoided by keeping track of what one has on loan!

MARC and the subject approach[14]

Not all the information in the MARC record is relevant to the subject of a document, but certain fields are likely to be more productive than others. Some fields relate specifically to classification notation:

050	LCC call number
060	NLM
080	UDC
082	DDC
083	Verbal features
086	government document classification

Others relate to subject headings:

600	Personal name as subject

610	Corporate name as subject
611	Conference name as subject
640	Uniform title as subject
645	Title subject heading
650	Topical subject headings
651	Geographical subject headings
653	Uncontrolled subject headings
655	Genre
69X	Locally assigned subject headings, e.g.
690	PRECIS descriptor string
691	SIN
692	RIN

Other relevant fields are those containing title information:

214	Augmented title
240	Uniform and collective titles
245	Title

Subfields and indicators are used to show, for example, the kind of subject heading used and the source.

Unfortunately, we do not always find the degree of consistency that we might hope for between the various MARC services. For example, LC has never used PRECIS; following the publication of the policy statement *Currency with coverage* in 1987, BNB stopped including LCSH headings until protests from users finally led to their reinstatement in 1995. (It must be noted that use of the PRECIS SIN file went on until PRECIS was dropped; this covered some 75% of the throughput in BNB, so for those items LCSH headings would still have been included.) PRECIS was replaced by COMPASS, which is used by nobody else, in 1990. Even when the two services were running more or less in parallel, they were not always in step. One study looked at 82 titles in library science which appeared in BNB in 1987 and were also catalogued by LC; both gave headings from LCSH, but these coincided for only 11% of the sample; if partial matches were included, the figure went up to 36%. This is still a rather disconcertingly low figure when one considers that the two groups involved are assumed to be 'the experts'! Even in the USA, which has a tradition of using LCSH, a study by Chan reported by Svenonius found discrepancies between LCSH headings given by LC and those chosen by other libraries.[15] In the interests of cost-sharing, the BNB now accepts records from the other five copyright libraries, which may lead to further inconsistencies.[16]

Subject searching in OPACs

OPACs normally work through a main menu, which enables users to select the kind of search they wish to make. The design of this interface is an excellent example of the truth of the Latin tag *quot homines, tot sententiae*; however many libraries we have, there will be that many menus. An academic library may in fact have more than one menu, depending on whether the user is on campus or external.

Standardization seems unlikely while vendors are eager to demonstrate the superiority of their own product.

One advantage of a computerized system is that a transaction log can be compiled; each search can be recorded and studied to follow through the path(s) followed by each user. (One difficulty is that users do not have to log into most OPACs, so it can be hard to see where one search ends and another begins.) Research into catalogue use can thus be based on observation of actual user behaviour. One rather surprising discovery was that a much higher proportion of searches were subject searches than had been thought previously. Earlier catalogue use studies, which mainly used survey techniques such as questionnaires rather than direct observation,[17] had indicated that relatively few users carried out subject searches, but this was shown to be untrue, at least as far as OPACs are concerned. In addition, many searches which started out as known item searches turned into subject searches; once the user had found the right place to search on the shelves, or the correct subject heading to search the catalogue, the nature of the search changed. It became apparent that the subject access facilities available in conventional catalogues – LCSH, DDC, LCC – were not adequate, and that user dissatisfaction had been mitigated by the fact that libraries had most of their stock on open access. Transaction logs were able to reveal what the card catalogue had concealed: that many users experienced frustration and failure in their attempts to find the material they wanted through the catalogue. Of course, it must be realized that OPACs in their turn introduced searching hazards which did not exist in manually produced catalogues; one study[18] showed that typographical errors, spelling mistakes and failure to clear the line before starting again accounted for a quarter of the search failures. However, it has become painfully clear that subject access to OPACs is inadequate for any but the simplest searches; Lancaster[19] asserts that the OPAC presents 'the most primitive of subject access' (a description which must presumably apply even more strongly to the card catalogue), and various ways of improving the situation have been suggested.

Augmented subject access

During the mid-1970s, Atherton carried out the Subject Access Project[20] to see whether including contents pages and indexes for books would improve subject access to them through an online catalogue. Some 2,000 books had their subject description augmented with about 300 words taken from the contents lists and indexes; a comparison of searches carried out in this database with one having only the MARC records showed improved recall and relevance, with reduced searching costs. Although the idea has not been generally accepted, it has been successfully implemented in one Australian library.[21] In the Extended Subject Program (ESP) at the Australian Defence Force Academy (ADFA) library, over a period of five years some 40,000 books had an average 75 words or 20 phrases added to the MARC record in field 653; the additions were selected from the contents pages or indexes, with the criterion that they must relate to at least five pages of the text. The improved access given has justified the continuation of the programme.

Classification in OPACs

Svenonius[22] suggested in 1983 that classification could be of value in online catalogs. Recall could be improved by using a classification to suggest related headings,
while the schedules would give context to homographs and thus improve relevance.
DDC class numbers are included in nearly all MARC records, and OCLC sponsored
a detailed study from 1983 to 1986 to discover whether having the schedules of
DDC online would enable users to get improved access to materials through
OPACs. The transition from manual to online catalogues was investigated before
the DDC project began; this work has been summarized by Markey,[23] who was also
responsible for the DDC project.[24] Although DDC19 was not computer-produced,
the schedules were available in machine-readable form, and were used in a detailed
study to find out the value of using both the schedules and the relative index to
enhance subject searching. Although the terminology in some of the schedules
needed improving, DDC proved to be as good as, or better than, LCSH in the choice
of words for subject retrieval. Not only did the DDC schedules and index add to the
vocabulary of entry terms available, they also provided the possibility of browsing
through the shelf arrangement at the catalogue. The importance of an enhanced
entry vocabulary was emphasized by Bates,[25] who found, for example, that PRE-
CIS and LCSH gave similar results, but that the performance of both was greatly
improved when they were used in conjunction with title words. Bates suggests the
need for a 'superthesaurus' to give access to both controlled vocabularies and title
words through a very large entry vocabulary. (The importance of the entry vocabulary had been stressed by Lancaster in his study of MEDLARS.)

Some work was also done on the use of LCC,[26] but this confirmed one important
problem that had arisen in the DDC project. Many composite subjects are represented in DDC by synthesized notation, either using the Tables or by adding fragments of
schedules from a different place in the schedules from the primary facet. It is very difficult to locate such fragments and identify them correctly when searching by computer. Suppose that we have to classify a document on 'biological control of the cotton boll weevil'. We can establish that this is *Anthomus grandis*, a member of the cur-
culionidae subclass, classified at 585.768, which *includes* weevils, i.e. is not specific.
We then turn to the schedules to find cotton, which is a crop in Agriculture:

630	Agriculture
633	Field & plantation crops
633.5	Fiber crops
633.51	Cotton
633.51l9	Injuries, diseases, pests *from* notes at 633–635
633.519l7	Insect pests *from* 632.l7
633.5197l68	Boll weevil *from* 595.7l68 *inc* weevils

(The l is used solely to illustrate the steps of division; it is of course not part of the
notation.) It is clear that we can only construct the number by a detailed study of the
schedules, and that the various digits borrowed from elsewhere – 9, 7, 68 – would
be impossible to track down without in effect reclassifying the document. Although

LCC does not synthesize notation in the same way as DDC, it does have its own way of shortening the schedules through the use of tables, e.g. for subdivision of authors; these are inserted into gaps left in the notation at the main number for a given author. (See Chapter 22). There are several such tables; the correct one to use depends on the importance (in terms of literary warrant) of the author. Here too it would be very difficult to follow the construction of the class number in an online catalogue. Additionally, the notation in DDC is largely hierarchical, whereas that in LCC is not, making it more difficult to follow through the various steps of division. The centred headings in DDC represent steps of division which were not originally shown, but have been inserted using notation which is not itself used in classifying.

Another problem arises from changes in the classification. Each edition of DDC lists changes made from the previous edition, but not those which took place earlier; so DDC20 lists changes from DDC19 to DDC20, but not those from DDC18 to DDC19. Libraries with material classified by different editions (that is, not reclassified when new editions appear) will have class numbers in their catalogues which will not tally with the current edition, and could not be traced through an online version.

US MARC format for classification data

The difficulties which arose in the DDC project, together with the need to keep both DDC and LCC up to date in computer-produced form, led to the development of an expansion of fields not previously used in the MARC record to provide a format for classification data.[27] This would enable hierarchical steps to be followed through even when not shown by the notation; the origins of fragments used in synthesis; and notation used in earlier editions for a given concept. It would also facilitate the production of schedules by computer typesetting, which had necessitated the development of special software for DDC20,[28] and was not possible at all in any systematic fashion for LCC. Some of the important fields in the new format are as follows:

084	Classification scheme and edition
153	classification number, includes caption and superordinate hierarchy
154	General explanatory index term
253	complex see references – lead away from 153
353	complex see also references – lead away from 153
453	invalid number tracing – wrong number, leads back to number in 153
553	valid number tracing, leads back to 153
680	scope note
681	classification example tracing note
683	application instruction note
684	auxiliary instruction note – primarily for DDC manual
685	history note (past changes)
700–754	index terms, e.g. LCSH, MeSH
761	add or divide like
763	internal subarrangement or add table entry
765	synthesized number components
768	citation and precedence order instructions

The first LCC schedule to be prepared and published using the new format is class H, Social sciences, available in 1995. DDC21, to be published 1996, will also use the format, but will have an additional advantage from being published by OCLC; each class number can be linked to records in the OCLC database showing how it has been used by other classifiers.[29] This could be potentially confusing if used in conjunction with an OPAC; users might assume that their library held the books given as examples when it did not.

Alphabetical headings

A majority of MARC records contain LCSH headings, and these are obviously a source for subject searches. Some of the problems with LCSH have been indicated in Chapter 8, and further discussion will be found in Chapter 23. Markey has investigated the use of LCSH in an experimental online catalogue[30] with interesting results. LCSH in book form was made available beside the online catalogue, but was never used. The machine-readable form of LCSH for the catalogue was constructed from the 6XX fields in the MARC records, and had advantages over the printed form. It contained headings with subdivisions, and headings subdivided according to 'pattern' headings, neither of which is in the printed version. However, it still caused users not familiar with its methods some problems. It was difficult for them to identify characteristic forms of heading: for example, that New York City should be New York (City). Many of them assumed that topics listed together in the alphabetical sequence were related, and there was clearly a need for users to be able to browse backward as well as forward from a selected heading in order to find additional headings. (This point has been discussed in Chapter 8 in relation to such headings as Ceramics and Ceramic . . .) Automatic spelling correction could avoid some problems, and an algorithm to ignore punctuation would also help with problems such as that illustrated above with New York. There is also a need for some kind of access to hidden terms in headings, i.e. any term other than the first; either a rotated index of the kind found in most thesauri or keyword access online. This reinforces once more the need for an adequate entry vocabulary. There is also a need for the display of related terms, which is of course found in the printed version; many users began their search with a broad term, often only representing one facet of the subject they were interested in, and could have been guided to a more suitable heading by the display of narrower or related terms. Now that LCSH is available online, and also on CD-ROM, it is important to make users aware of the problems revealed by this project and others.[31]

Computer processing of queries

If the catalogue is online, then it should be possible to apply the kinds of technique mentioned in Chapter 5 to the processing of enquiries. One experimental system which has tried several of these techniques is OKAPI,[32] which began at the Polytechnic of Central London (now the University of Westminster), and transferred in 1989 to the City University. One point became clear quite quickly. The PCL library had some 90,000 volumes, and many searches were for items not listed because they were not in stock. It is important to let users know as soon as possible that this is the case, otherwise they can waste time conducting increasingly complex searches which are doomed to failure. Experiments in the USA have either been on catalogues of large libraries, where chances of failure were much less, or on experimental collections where the users were aware of the limitations.

The first experiments took the words of a subject search and compared them with an index to words from titles and subject headings, and from corporate name headings. If an implicit AND search failed, words were weighted on an inverse frequency basis of their occurrence in the index, and searches conducted using subsets of the whole search word set. The use of weights in this way enabled the output to be ranked. Experience has shown that Boolean AND searches on three or more words fail most of the time, so the fallback mechanism could often produce results where a straightforward Boolean search would fail.

In the second set of experiments, automatic stemming was introduced at both the weak and strong levels, as described in Chapter 5. Matches found by strong stemming were less heavily weighted than those found by weak stemming. Use of both levels at once, rather than sequentially after feedback from the user, was chosen because it simplified the process, though it did involve more processing. The method of weighting gave results which were likely to meet the users' needs without confusing them with additional search formulations. Spelling errors which led to no matches were referred back to the user with suggested alternatives, as in a word processor; these were right most of the time, or could prompt the user to try again. (Spelling checkers can use various techniques, including assonance, which can sometimes lead the user astray; a simple typo giving accewss instead of access leads to the suggested replacements accuses, accuse and access, in that order!) A third aid was the use of a synonym dictionary to link words which would not be merged by stemming. These include irregular plurals (mouse, mice); abbreviations (BBC = British Broadcasting Corporation, – but ITA can have more than one meaning); alternative spellings (labour, labor); and words which are used casually as synonyms though they may differ in their precise meanings (Great Britain, United Kingdom, Britain, British Isles). In addition to the usual stoplist, there was a 'go-list' for phrases which cannot be broken down; these were treated as single words.

Weak stemming was found to be effective almost all the time; there are some plural words which cannot correctly be reduced to the singular or have 'ing' removed, and these must be identified and given special treatment. Some words are not suitable for strong stemming (e.g. viable); these again have to be identified. Experience is likely to reveal any of these which have been missed on a preliminary scan. Words linked by cross-references in the synonym dictionary can be dealt with by weighting; a second hit on the same document by adding a related term should not increase the weight, while additional documents found by using related terms rather than the original can be weighted more lightly.

The second round of experiments had shown that a high proportion – some 80% – of searches were short and successful; the users were apparently satisfied with a couple of references selected from those retrieved in their first search. (This may of course simply be a reflection of their level of expectation, as with most facets of librarianship. If users' expectations are not high, they will be satisfied with very little; if their expectations *are* high, based perhaps on a high level of service in a previously used library, they are likely to be far more demanding.) Some sessions were short, with the users quickly giving up after failing to find anything. There remained a proportion of users who persisted for long periods, looking through perhaps hundreds of records in search of an answer. The OKAPI system philosophy was that the system should adapt to the user rather than the user to the system, and this involved an interactive system which could adapt as far as possible to the users' needs and level of expertise. The next stage was thus to introduce the use of relevance feedback through automatic query expansion; additional search terms could be found in references already retrieved and judged by the user to be relevant. However, this introduced a psychological problem; users seemed to be very reluctant to modify their search strategies, even when this meant merely browsing through a classified sequence based on a successful hit – which would in effect be the equivalent of browsing at the shelves, which most users seem willing to do. The system needed to be able to model the users' experience, skills and persistence level in order to be able to present suggestions which would both improve the likelihood of success *and* involve the user in a minimum of effort – hence the need for *automatic* query expansion.[33]

MELVYL

The OKAPI experiments were carried out in a relatively small library with the objective of improving user access through a variety of methods of computer processing. MELVYL was planned on the very different basis of providing access to a number of collections together forming a major information resource. It is therefore instructive to see the similarities between the two approaches as well as the differences. The University of California has nine campuses and some 100 libraries. In 1977 a ten-year plan was drawn up for the development of the university library services as a whole; one of the most significant items was the introduction of an online union catalogue of the whole of the collections, which together constitute a major bibliographic resource of several million volumes. The system was implemented by the Division of Library Automation (DLA) at the beginning of 1982; progress has been reported regularly in the *DLA bulletin*, and its tenth birthday was celebrated in three issues of *Information technology and libraries*.[34] The scheme has many features of interest, though of course only a proportion of these relate to the subject approach. (The name was coined from MEL[ville Dewey] and WYL[BUR], a utility program developed at Stanford University that was used in the early stages.)

MELVYL started life as a first generation OPAC: a straightforward conversion to computer format of existing catalogues. It quickly moved to a second generation model, with keyword searching and Boolean operators, but still with some limitations. The BROWSE facility, enabling users to scan the list of subject headings, for example, was not introduced until 1985, and still did not permit users to scan subheadings within a particular heading. External databases have been added, enlarging the scope of the system considerably beyond its first goals. Now, the system is moving to replace the character-based screens which have been used since the beginning with a Windows-type environment with bitmapped displays; however, the character base will continue until the end of the decade, since it is much more practical for external users with slow phone lines.

The service is on a large scale; by 1991 it contained over six million records, and queries exceed half a million a week during busy periods. It was originally intended for use within the various libraries, but it soon became evident that general on-campus access would be greatly appreciated by users. The idea of networking to give off-campus access and eventually general access and electronic delivery was one that was pursued by the DLA without undue publicity, as it was felt to be rather more ambitious than would be acceptable to the administration![35] Despite this caution, MELVYL was one of the first OPACS to be available through the Internet, in the mid-1980s.

Good response time has always been seen as an essential, and this has affected some of the services offered. For example, some searches involve lengthy processing because of the number of hits; these have been identified, and users are warned not to use them during the busy afternoon period. One of the reasons for slow processing is that each search has to be carried out separately; it is not possible to search on an already established set. For example, Alcohol is a widely used term, and is counted as a long search. A user seeking information on the effects of alcohol on sex behaviour keys in:

FIND SU SEX BEHAVIOR AND SU ALCOHOL

The system searches for the first subject term, SEX BEHAVIOR, then for the second, ALCOHOL, and only then matches the two sets; if it were possible to restrict the search to the already established – and much smaller –first set, much less processing would be required. This problem is of course not peculiar to MELVYL; it is the normal way of processing Boolean searches. However, within the limitations of a specific system as opposed to a major utility such as DIALOG, the additional processing does cause problems by noticeably slowing the response time.[36]

MELVYL is the union catalog of the UC libraries; it is not an *integrated* catalogue in that it does not contain information about the availability of particular items found in a search. For this purpose, the various campuses have their own OPACS, which can have unexpected consequences.[37] As mentioned, a major step forward for MELVYL was the introduction of external databases; MEDLINE was the first, with *Current Contents* (CC) from ISI added more recently. Recent additions include Eureka™ and FirstSearch™.[38] The use made of CC at the Davis campus, which is relatively small, is three times that at the UCLA campus, one of the largest. UCLA has had its own integrated OPAC (ORION) since the mid-1980s, which is evidently in competition with MELVYL; as a large campus, with its own library of several million items, UCLA is probably less in need of a union catalogue than the smaller sites, so users appear to be less aware of the additional facilities offered by MELVYL.

The use of external databases presents some interesting features. Because the availability of these services is covered by a site licence, they are not available to external users, and have to be kept separate from the general catalogue. Access to this is anonymous, so that there is no opportunity to build up the knowledge of users which would enable more sophisticated search procedures to be developed to match the users' level of expertise. Despite this limitation, MEDLINE is one of the most popular segments of MELVYL, accounting for about one tenth of the enquiries. The use of the system illustrates the Futility point concept very well: although the average search reveals about 100 records, it is unusual for users to display more than about 15 of these. Since most displays begin at the beginning of the alphabet, authors whose names fall into that section tend to be favoured![39] There is also the general problem of Boolean searching, that it tends to retrieve either too little or too much.[40]

Another problem which is not apparent to many users is that of making two different kinds of database available through the same OPAC. The library catalogues which form the basis of MELVYL are essentially the original catalogues; the subject access points are LCSH and LCC or DDC, to which the OPAC adds the facility for keyword searching on titles and other parts of the record. The additional databases which are available through the same OPAC use quite different methods for subject access; for example, MEDLINE uses MeSH, which includes its own hierarchical tree structure, so that the search techniques needed to obtain satisfactory results differ significantly from those used with the catalogue records. The ISI databases are constructed on yet another set of principles. How is the lay user to realize that new search techniques must be used? The switch from one kind of database to another is made transparent, but perhaps we should take heed of the experience of architects. Floor to ceiling glass panels were introduced as a means of expanding the views available from within a building – but they now have markings to warn the unwary not to walk through them.

One area of development for the future is that of a transparent entry vocabulary which will translate users' enquiry words into the appropriate terms used by the system. Once a heading from LCSH has been found, it may well appear plausible, but all too often it is not something that occurs to the user without prompting. Using Boolean logic, the complexity of a search can often exceed the expertise of the searcher. OPAC designers must develop ways of simplifying searching to match the abilities of the general user.[41] To facilitate the use of additional databases, the NISO Z39.50 standard interface is being implemented in a client-server environment, which will also benefit external users.[42]

Other considerations

Most if not all computer retrieval systems use stopwords, as was pointed out in Chapters 4 and 5. In an OPAC, which is specifically directed at use by the public as opposed to skilled intermediaries, it is necessary to keep the list of stopwords under review. There will usually be two lists: hard stopwords, which are built into the software and consist of articles, prepositions, adverbs and similar parts of speech; and soft stopwords, which will depend on the environment. Experience shows that the choice of these to begin with is not necessarily a good guide. A check can be kept on the number of uses made of soft stopwords, and the number of postings for each.

If their use is compared with that of other search terms, it may well show that some stopwords are either used very rarely or they retrieve very few documents. Such words can be removed from the stoplist with little effect. On the other hand, other words may show up as being used frequently and retrieving large number of documents; their discrimination power is low, and they are obvious candidates for a revised stoplist.[43]

Another, perhaps more serious problem, is the question of misspellings. We have already seen the possibilities of correcting spelling errors made by searchers, with the aim of telling the user of failure and suggesting alternatives. Far more intractable is the occurrence of spelling errors in the databases themselves. These can be found in data downloaded from a utility, in online searching, and in databases on CD-ROM. The consequence of a spelling error in a database is that the word becomes an orphan; it will not be found when searching for the correct form, and will usually only be found by accident. The information in databases is not normally in a format which lends itself to word processing, with relatively straightforward spellchecks. In addition, much of the information, such as authors' names, cannot be checked in this way in any case. There are other hazards; Shakespeare's name is spelt in more than one way, and correct transcription from a title page may give a form that is not accepted by a spelling check. A database which includes foreign-language (i.e. not English) material may cause further confusion; 'language' in English becomes 'langage' in French, but this would be identified as a spelling error. One method that has been used is to construct a keyword inventory and scan this for potential errors; though this requires human effort, it can be very successful in cleaning up a database; it can also identify possible additional terms – such as variant forms of Shakespere's name – for an automatic entry vocabulary program.[44] It is encouraging to know that OCLC undertook a record cleaning programme to try to eliminate at least a good proportion of errors in its very substantial database.

National collections

Both the British Library and the Library of Congress have completed retrospective conversion projects. Both libraries have recent acquisitions in full MARC format, the BL since 1950, LC since 1968. (BNB, which began in 1950, carried out its own retrospective conversion programme for entries from 1950 to 1970.) The entries for LC were completed by Carollton Press, Inc, those for the BL by SAZTEC in 1992. In both cases, the conversion was based on existing catalogue data, for example the British Museum Library *General catalogue of printed books*; though the data is in MARC format, the entries are not the full MARC entries that we now expect. Nevertheless, both catalogues are now available online through the Internet,[45] as are the OPACS of many other libraries. The BL and LC catalogues are also available on CD-ROM, BL (i.e. BNB) on three disks, LC on 7–8. It should be noted that the BL now has three databases: in addition to the conversion of the *General catalogue*, which covers the period up to 1975, there is the Humanities and Social Sciences catalogue since 1975, and a third database for the Science Reference and Information Service, which originated in the old Patent Office Library.

Using OPACs from other libraries

There are two important points to note when using OPACs from other libraries. The first is that there are a number of suppliers of software, so that the screens will differ from library to library; however, most of them work through menus, so that they are reasonably simple to follow. One option to establish as soon as possible is how to exit gracefully! The second point is that they will not necessarily be using the ASCII character set. The BL warns that a GUI will be needed to make use of the non-roman characters in the entries for many foreign language books. LC uses 8-bit ASCII (the extended ASCII character set, ANSI X3.4) and ANSEL: extended Latin alphabet coded character set for bibliographic use (ANSI Z39.47: 1993). There is also a USMARC character set for Chinese, Japanese, Korean, produced in 1987. Users should be aware of these potential hazards. It is also necessary to know whether a command has to be followed by <Enter> or is accepted as it is typed. For example, for an author search we may have to type 2<Enter> using one OPAC, or A using another; in the second case, the use of <Enter> would in effect give a null author search and return us to the main menu. There appears to be little likelihood of a 'standard' user interface for some time to come.

Limitations on subject access

The amount of subject information included in standard MARC records is, as we have seen, limited. There will be a DDC classmark in most, an LCC classmark in most, LCSH headings in current records, PRECIS for BNB entries 1971–1989 and COM-PASS entries since. We may also make use of words found in the title fields or geographic name fields. The author information may be of value, if an individual or a corporate body is closely associated with a particular subject. However, the sum total of all this is very small compared with what is available for, say, periodical articles. A four-page article may be accompanied by an abstract of about 100 words, of which about 25 could be considered significant; while the estimates given by various authors of the average number of LCSH headings allotted to a book differ, the figure appears to be no more than 1.5. The fourth edition of the present work was unusual in being given five: subject cataloging; indexing; abstracting and indexing; book classification; subject headings. However, the seven significant words (subject, cataloging, indexing, abstracting, book, classification, headings) represent over 500 pages and some 150,000 words of text. The density of subject access is obviously not comparable with that given to periodical articles. No matter how sophisticated our systems, if there is not much input there will not be much output. We return to this point when considering the digital library of the future in Chapter 27, but it may be that we shall need to rethink the subject access provided through OPACs if they are not to fail to live up to their promise. On the credit side, we must recognize the unifying power of the OPAC, the precursor of the digital library. Before OPACs, users would have a workplace; they would go to the library and look in a second place to consult the catalogue; and then look in a third place to find the documents they needed. The OPAC gives us the power to bring the catalogue, and also the documents, to the user's workplace. This is a major step forward for the dissemination of information.

References

1 *Standards for the international exchange of bibliographic information*, McIlwaine, I.C. (ed.), London, Library Association, 1991. Covers standards in other fields as well as ISBD and MARC.
2 IFLA ISBD(M). *International Standard Bibliographical Description for monographic publications*, 1st rev edn, IFLA International Office for Universal Bibliographic Control, 1978.
   Curwen, A. G., 'International Standard Bibliographical Description', *Standards for the international exchange of bibliographic information*, London, Library Association, 1991, 73–81.
3 *Anglo-American Cataloguing Rules, 2nd edition, 1988 revision*, London, Library Association; Washington, DC, American Library Association; Ottawa, Canadian Library Association, 1988. Now incorporates the 1993 revisions.
4 Council on Library Resources, *Automation and the Library of Congress*, by D. W. King *et al.*, Washington, DC, USGPO, 1963.
5 Gredley, E. and Hopkinson, A., *Exchanging bibliographic data: MARC and other international formats*, London, Library Association; Washington, DC, American Library Association; Ottawa, Canadian Library Association, 1989.
6 Anderson, D., *Universal Bibliographic Control: a long term policy, a plan for action*, Munich, Verlag Dokumentation, 1974.
7 The *IFLA newsletter* changed its name to *International cataloging and bibliographic control* in 1971; this is now the main source of information on the IFLA UBCIM programme.
8 UNIMARC: universal MARC format recommended by the IFLA Working Group on Content Designators set up by the IFLA Section on Cataloguing and the IFLA Section on Mechanization. 2nd rev edn, London, IFLA International Office for UBC, 1980.
   Holt, B. P. *et al., UNIMARC manual*, Frankfurt, IFLA UBCIM program, 1994.
   Hopkinson, A., 'Information transfer and exchange formats', *Standards for the international exchange of bibliographic information*, London, Library Association, 1991, 169–76.
   'Permanent UNIMARC Committee: terms of reference and procedures', *International cataloging and bibliographic control*, **21**, 1992, 51–2.
   Bourne, R., 'The IFLA UBCIM programme: standards in the changing world', *Standards for the international exchange of bibliographic information*, London, Library Association, 1991, 18–22.
   Roberts, W. D., The Universal Bibliographic Control and International MARC Program (UBCIM)', *IFLA journal*, **16** (23), 1990, 231–8.
   Long, A., 'UK MARC and US MARC: a brief history and comparison', *Journal of documentation*, **40** (1) 1984, 1–12.
   Truitt, M., 'USMARC to UNIMARC/Authorities: a qualitative evaluation of USMARC data elements', *Library resources and technical services*, **36** (1), 1992, 37–58.
9 *Guidelines for authority and reference entries (GARE)*, London, IFLA

International Programme for UBC, 1984.

IFLA section on Classification and Indexing, *Guidelines for subject authority and reference entries*, Munich, K. G. Saur, 1993.

10 Olvey, L. D. 'Library networks and electronic publishing', *Information services and use*, **15** (1), 1995, 39–47.

11 Plaister, Jean M., *Computing in LASER: regional library cooperation: London and South Eastern Library Region*, London, Library Association, 1982.

12 Culkin, P. B., 'The MARC format: private road or public highway', *Advances in librarianship*, *16*, 1992, 83–91.

13 Hildreth, C. R., *Online public access catalogs: the user interface*, Dublin, OH, OCLC, 1982.
Matthews, J. R., *Public access to online catalogs*, 2nd edn, Weston, CT, Online Inc., 1985.
'Public access online catalogs', Markey, K. (ed.), *Library trends,* **35** (4), 1987, 523–667.
The online catalogue: developments and directions, Hildreth, C. R. (ed.), London, Library Association, 1989.
O'Brien, A. 'Online catalogs: enhancements and developments', *Annual review of information science and technology*, **29**, 1994, 219–42.

14 Aluri, R., Kemp, D. A. and Boll, J. J., *Subject analysis in online catalogs*, Englewood, CO, Libraries Unlimited Inc, 1991.
Subject control in online catalogs, Holley, R. P. (ed.), New York, NY, Haworth Press, 1989.

15 Tonta, Y., 'A study of indexing consistency between Library of Congress and British Library catalogers', *Library resources and technical services,* **35** (2), 1991, 177–85.
Svenonius, E. and McGarry, D., 'Objectivity in evaluating subject heading assignment', *Cataloging and classification quarterly,* **16** (2), 1993, 5–40.

16 McIlwaine, I. C. 'Subject control: the British viewpoint', *Subject indexing: principles and practices in the* 90's, Holley, R. P. (ed.), *et al.*, Munich, K. G. Saur, 1995, 166–80. (UBCIM Publications – new series vol 15.)

17 Hancock-Beaulieu, M., 'Online catalogues: a case for the user', in *The online catalogue: developments and directions*, 25–46.
Zumer, M. and Zeng, L., 'Comparison and evaluation of enduser interfaces', *Cataloging and classification quarterly,* **19** (2), 1994, 67–98.

18 Peters, T. A., 'When smart people fail: an analysis of the transaction log of an online public access catalog', *Journal of academic librarianship,* **15** (5), 1989, 267–73.

19 Lancaster, F. W. *et al.*, 'Identifying barriers to effective subject access in library catalogs', *Library resources and technical services,* **35**, 1991, 377–91.

20 Subject Access Project, *Books are for use: final report of the Subject Access Project to the Council on Library Resources*, Syracuse, NY, Syracuse University, School of Information Studies, 1978, Pauline Atherton, Director.
Cochrane, P. A., *Redesign of catalogs and indexes for improved online subject access: selected papers of Pauline A. Cochrane*, Phoenix, AZ, Oryx Press, 1985.

21 Beatty, S., 'ESP at ADFA after five years', in *Cataloguing for online access: proceedings of the 9th annual cataloguing conference, 1991, Cataloguing Australia,* **17** (3/4), 1991, 3–155, 65–79.
See also Piascik,J. M., 'Enhanced subject access in OHIO public libraries', *Cataloging and classification quarterly,* **16** (4), 1993, 77–87. This survey found enhanced access was of more use to the public than to library staff . . .

22 Svenonius, E., 'Use of classification in online retrieval', *Library resources and technical services,* **27** (1) 1983, 76–80.
Svenonius, E., 'Classification: prospects, problems and possibilities', *in International study conference on classification research, Toronto, Canada, June 24–28 1991,* Williamson, N. J. and Hudon, M. (eds.), Elsevier, 1992, (FID 698), p5–25.

23 Markey, K., *Subject searching in library catalogs: before and after the introduction of online catalogs,* Dublin, OH, OCLC, 1984.

24 Markey, K. and Demeyer, A. H., *Dewey Decimal Classification online project: evaluation of a library schedule and index integrated into the subject searching capabilities of an online catalog,* Dublin, OH, OCLC, 1986.
Markey, K. and Demeyer, A. H., 'Findings of the Dewey Decimal Classification online project', *International cataloging,* **15** (2), 1986, 15–19.
Markey, K., 'Subject searching strategies for online catalogs through the Dewey Decimal Classification' in *The online catalogue: developments and directions,* 1989, 61–83. A useful short account.
Drabenstott, K. Markey, *et al.,* 'Analysis of a bibliographic database vocabulary enhanced with a library classification', *Library resources and technical services,* **34** (2), 1990, 179–98.
See also Taylor, A. C., 'Enhancing subject access in online systems: the year's work in subject analysis', *Library resources and technical services,* **36** (3), July 1992, 316–32.
Kinsella, J., 'Classification and the OPAC', *Catalogue and index,* (105–106), 1992, 1, 3–10.

25 Bates, M., 'Rethinking subject cataloging in the online environment', *Library resources and technical services,* **33** (4), 1989, 400–12.

26 Chan, L. M., 'Library of Congress classification as an online retrieval tool: potential and limitations', *Information technology and libraries,* **5**, 1986, 181–92.
Williamson, N. J., 'The Library of Congress classification: problems and prospects in online retrieval', *International cataloguing,* **15**, 1986, 45–8.

27 Library of Congress, Network Development and MARC Standards Office. *USMARC format for classification data, including guidelines for content designation.* Washington, DC, Library of Congress, 1990–. For the latest news search the LC online services: gopher marvel.loc.gov
Guenther, R. S., 'The USMARC format for classification data; development and implementation', in *Classification research for knowledge representation and organization: proceedings of the 5th International study conference on classification research, Toronto, Canada, June 24–28 1991,* Williamson, N. J.

and Hudon, M. (eds.), Elsevier, 1992, (FID 698), 235–45.

28 Beall, Julianne, 'Editing the Dewey Decimal Classification online', in *International study conference on classification research, Toronto, Canada, June 24–28 1991*, Williamson, N. J. and Hudon, M. (eds.), Elsevier, 1992, (FID 698), 29–37.

29 Vizine-Goetz, Diana, 'The Dewey Decimal Classification as an online tool' in *International study conference on classification research, Toronto, Canada, June 24–28 1991*, Williamson, N. J. and Hudon, M. (eds.), Elsevier, 1992, (FID 698), 373–80.

30 Markey, K., 'Alphabetical searching in an online catalogue', *Journal of academic librarianship,* **14** (6), June 1989, 353–60.

31 Cochrane, P. A., *Improving LCSH for use in online catalogs: exercises for self-help with a selection of background reading,* Littleton, CO, Libraries Unlimited, 1986.

32 OKAPI appears to be a name that became an acronym, Online Keyword Access to Public Information. The okapi is an African mammal related to the giraffe, shy and elusive and with a long gestation period; it is presumably this latter quality which prompted the name!

33 Walker, S., 'The Okapi online catalogue research projects' in *The online catalogue . . .* 84–106.
Hancock-Beaulieu, M. and Walker, S., 'An evaluation of automatic query expansion in an online library catalogue', *Journal of documentation,* **48** (4), 1992, 406–21.
Hancock-Beaulieu, M., 'User friendliness and human-computer interaction in online library catalogues', *Program,* **26** (1), 1992, 29–37.

34 'Happy [tenth] birthday to MELVYL', *Information technology and libraries,* **11** (2), 1992, 146–81; (3) 1992, 271–304; (4) 1992, 405–19.

35 Lynch, C. A., 'The next generation of public access information systems for research libraries: lessons from ten years of the MELVYL system', ref 27, 405–15.

36 Farley, L., 'Dissecting slow searches', *DLA Bulletin,* **9** (1), 1989, 1, 3–6.

37 Ritch, A., 'Ten years of monitoring MELVYL: a librarian's view', ref 27, 172–9. This article contains a useful chronology.

38 Kanter, E., 'Eureka™ and FirstSearch™: two world class database services join the MELVYL system', *DLA bulletin,* **14** (1), 1994, 1, 3–6.

39 Berger, M. G., 'The MELVYL system: the next five years and beyond', ref 27, 146–57.

40 Larson, R. R., 'Between Scylla and Charybdis: subject searching in the online catalogue', *Advances in librarianship,* 15, 1991, 175–236.
Larson, R. R., 'Evaluation of advanced retrieval techniques in an experimental online catalog', *Journal of the American Society for Information Science,* **43** (1), 1992, 34–53.

41 Buckland, M. K., 'Agenda for online catalog designers', *Information technology and libraries,* **11** (2), 1992, 157–63.

42 Needleman, M. H., 'Z39.50: new doors opening', *DLA bulletin,* **12** (2), 1992, 14, 24.
Tibbetts, M., 'The prototype Z39.50 client', *DLA bulletin,* **14** (1), 1994, 14–15.
National Information Standards Organization, *Information retrieval service definition and protocol specification for library applications,* ANSI Z39.50: 1992.

43 Johnson, B. and Peterson, E., 'Reviewing initial stopword selection', *Information technology and libraries,* **11** (2), 1992, 136–9.

44 Ballard, T. and Lifshin, A., 'Prediction of OPAC spelling errors through a keyword inventory', *Information technology and libraries,* **11** (2), 1992, 139–45.

45 Pountain, D., 'The British Library's catalog is online', *Byte,* May 1995, 62–70. For free access to the LC catalogue, within specified time limits, telnet locis.loc.gov.

Part III
Pre-coordinate indexing languages

Chapter 16
Introduction

So far we have studied the theoretical considerations which affect every system. In this section we shall be studying indexing languages that are widely used, to see how they measure up to the criteria we have established in Parts I and II. The schemes are discussed in the following order.

1 The Decimal Classification of Melvil Dewey (DDC). This was the first library classification in the modern sense, and in it we see foreshadowed many of the ideas we have been discussing. It is the first scheme to have been computer-produced, maintaining its status as a pioneer.

2 The Universal Decimal Classification (UDC). Originally based on the fifth edition of DDC, UDC is basically enumerative, but has many synthetic devices grafted on to its main core, which give it a great deal of flexibility. The full schedules of UDC are probably the most detailed of any classification scheme, but at present it is not intended to include them in the computer database which forms the master file; this is now the basis of the medium edition, which seems likely to become the standard.

3 The Bibliographic Classification of H. E. Bliss (BC). This was perhaps the last of the great enumerative schemes, and though Bliss did include many synthetic tables he does not seem to have appreciated the importance of the principles of analysis and synthesis he himself used. The main class order of BC is probably the most satisfactory of the major schemes. Until recently, it has lacked a satisfactory financial structure, though the efforts of a committee of devotees have helped to keep the scheme alive. It seems possible that a solution to this problem has been found, and the second edition is now in course of publication. This will mark a great advance on the first; in addition to the satisfactory main class order there is now consistent use of facet analysis within main classes, and possibilities for synthesis will be found throughout the schedules. Despite this, one may still doubt whether libraries will feel sufficiently attracted to the scheme to wish to change to it from one of the longer established schemes such as DDC, though these may in theory be inferior. The fact that BC class numbers are unlikely to be included in the MARC records will also militate against its general adoption, but it does have firm adherents.

4 The Broad system of ordering is the latest general scheme to be developed. Originally planned as a means of updating the main class outline of UDC, it was adopted by UNISIST as a switching language to facilitate the handling of foreign language documents. It is held as a computer file, but does not appear to have fired

the imagination of those who might use it.

5   The Colon Classification of S. R. Ranganathan (CC). This is the only completely synthetic general scheme and has many interesting and significant features, though from time to time one feels that the scheme is more a testing ground for Ranganathan's theories than a practical means of arranging documents and catalogues. The schedules of the seventh edition are now available, but not the index.

6   The Library of Congress Classification (LCC). This scheme is unique in that it is intended for use in one library only, yet because of the significance of that library it is used in many others. Here we have a scheme in which the compiler and classifier are one and the same; the published version is almost completely enumerative, and the external classifier has to accept the scheme as it is or not at all. Another aspect is that it was intended for the shelf arrangement in the Library of Congress, to be complemented by an alphabetical subject catalogue, in LC practice a dictionary catalogue arranged according to LCSH, now superseded by an OPAC. The scheme is now being put into computer-based form using the MARC format for classification.

7   Library of Congress Subject Headings. (LCSH). This is the most important general list of subject headings, and it is valuable to see how it fits in with LC classification. and also how it measures up to our criteria.

8   Sears list of subject headings is a much smaller work intended for the medium sized library. It has been widely used in Britain in the past in libraries using dictionary catalogues, whereas in the USA LCSH is far more popular. In Australia, LCSH is universally used by public and academic libraries, and Sears list was widely used by school libraries; its place has now been taken by the SCIS list.

In each case the object of the discussion will be to highlight what appear to be the significant aspects, particularly those concerning the background which affect the nature of the scheme. Little attempt will be made to go into the fine details of each scheme; it must be stressed that familiarity with these can come as the result of first hand study. Similarly, facility in use will only come as the result of practice. However, it is hoped that the student who works through the following chapters will then be in a position to make good use of such first hand examination, and will be able to estimate the overall importance of the individual schemes, both in isolation and in relation to each other. All the schemes are here subjected to criticism (though perhaps less than that levelled by Bliss at all schemes other than his own!), but we have as yet nothing better to replace them; they are used in libraries all over the world, and librarians have to learn to live with them. We shall, however, be in a much better position to overcome their defects if we are aware of them and know what countermeasures to take.

It may be argued that it is not fair to judge the older schemes by criteria which did not exist when they were compiled. This is a plausible point of view, but it will not stand up to close examination. Classification schemes, like circulation control systems, are tools, devised to carry out particular tasks in the overall organisation of libraries; we have to judge them in the light of how well they perform their set task today, not yesterday, and we must also bear in mind how well they are likely to stand up to tomorrow's demands.

Some features of the schemes, for example main class order, have been discussed in some detail already, and as far as possible this will not be repeated. Occasionally, it may be necessary to reiterate a point already made in order to put it in a different context, but the discussion of the practical schemes should not be divorced from the discussion of the theoretical framework into which they fit.

It should perhaps be stressed that the length of each chapter should not be treated as being a reflection of the relative importance of the scheme discussed. DDC, as to be expected of a pioneer, introduced many new ideas, which are described in that chapter, though they now apply to most schemes; UDC, with its synthetic devices, requires more explanation and examples than does LCC, which has, in effect, none. The main feature of CC, analysis into facets and notational synthesis, has become so much a part of modern theory that it is covered in detail in Part II, and does not therefore appear in the discussion of CC except insofar as that scheme has certain unique methods of applying it.

The lists of subject headings do not involve problems of order (except in a very minor fashion); they have no notation, or index. There is therefore much less to describe when writing about them than there is in a classification scheme, but in practical terms the two Library of Congress publications, LCSH and LCC, are of equal importance; indeed in both the USA and Australia LCSH is used almost universally, but LCC less so.

Bibliography

Readings for the individual schemes are given at the end of each chapter. The following general works contain good accounts of the schemes as well as more general considerations.

Chan, L. M., *Cataloging and classification: an introduction*, 2nd edn, New York, NY, McGraw Hill, 1994, Part IV: Classification.

Mann, T. *Library research models: a guide to cataloging, classification and computers*, New York, NY, Oxford University Press, 1994.

Marcella, R. and Newton, R., *A new manual of classification*, Aldershot, Gower, 1994. This is the latest edition of the *Manual of library classification* originally written by W. C. Berwick Sayers; the 4th and 5th editions were prepared by A. Maltby. This edition has been completely revised, with a lengthy section on 'Information technology and classification'.

Rowley, J., *Organising knowledge*, 2nd edn, Aldershot, Ashgate, 1992. This has a rather wider sweep than classification, which is covered in Part III Subjects.

For comments on the present state of the art in several of the schemes, see 'Classification: options and opportunities', *Cataloging & classification quarterly*, **19** (3/4), 1995.

Chapter 17

The Dewey Decimal Classification

Melvil Dewey was born in 1851, and at the age of five, we are told, he rearranged his mother's larder in a more systematic fashion; an early beginning for a career which was to transform librarianship! In 1872, at Amherst College, he obtained a post as a student library assistant, and in the following year put forward a plan for rearranging the library in a more systematic fashion. He was promoted in 1874 to Assistant College Librarian, and in 1876 published anonymously a work which was to have far reaching effects: *A classification and subject index for cataloguing and arranging the books and pamphlets of a library*. When we consider that Dewey also became the first editor of the *Library journal* in 1876, was a founder member of the American Library Association in 1876 and became its first secretary, founded the first library school in the United States (Columbia University) in 1887, promoted the standard (12.5cm x 7.5cm) catalogue card, and in the course of a long life (he died in 1931) took an active interest, not only in all aspects of librarianship, but also in related topics such as spelling reform, we may realize the full stature of the man and respect him, even though the classification scheme which bears his name and the best known of his contributions to librarianship may in some ways look inadequate for today's needs.

Dewey's first edition consisted of 12 pages of introduction, 12 of tables and 18 of index, and its novelty lay in three main areas: the first of these was the assignment of decimal numbers to books rather than shelves; the second was the specification of relatively detailed subjects; the third, the provision of a relative index. It is possible to argue that these three principles were in fact a greater contribution to the progress of library classification than the scheme itself, despite its wide acceptance throughout the world. Their significance may be judged by the fact that they are taken for granted in Part II of this work, and are described here to illustrate the historical development of Dewey's ideas.

Relative location

Dewey did not introduce subject arrangement into libraries; many libraries had previously been arranged by subject. What he *did* do was to introduce the idea of relative as opposed to fixed location. It was the practice to allocate certain areas of the library to various subjects, arranging the books within each area by accession number and giving them a *shelf mark* which identified their exact position: room, bay, tier, shelf, place on shelf. Once allocated, the shelf mark indicated the permanent home of a book in that library. New additions within any given subject area were invariably at the end of the sequence. Dewey introduced the idea of using notation for the subjects in his scheme, and *applying the notation to the books*, not to the shelves. A new book on a given subject could be inserted into the middle of an existing sequence, in a position indicated by the notation; no longer was the end of the sequence the only place where new additions could be accommodated. The tool that enable Dewey to do this was his decimal notation: the use of Arabic numerals, arranged as decimals. As we have seen, there are certain problems arising out of the use of a pure notation, and Dewey did not foresee these; in places this inhibits synthesis in the scheme today, when subjects are far more complicated than Dewey could have envisaged a century ago. There is, however, no doubt that the simplicity of the notation has been an important factor in the widespread adoption of the scheme throughout the world.

Detailed specification

Before Dewey introduced his idea of relative location, the number of subject groups into which the books in a library could be arranged was strictly limited. It is not practical to leave large numbers of shelves empty so that books can be added at the end of a multiplicity of sequences. Once the idea of moving books at any particular point to accommodate additions is accepted, then it becomes far more feasible to specify more detailed subjects. Dewey listed nearly a thousand, and was criticized for giving unnecessary detail; the seventeenth edition, listing over 20,000 topics, was criticized for its lack of detail. Much of this change in attitude is due to Dewey himself, who made it practical for librarians to arrange their collections in a detailed fashion instead of broad groups. The history of DDC has, in general, been one of the provision of ever increasing amounts of detail to match the needs of documents which themselves treat of increasingly narrow areas of knowledge. By the adoption of the principle of detailed subject arrangement, Dewey made this progress possible.

Relative index

One of the objections raised to detailed subject specification was that it would be impossible to find any given subject in the complex systematic arrangement. Dewey overcame this problem by the provision of a relative index, showing exactly whereabouts in the scheme any given topic was to be found, and listing synonyms also in some instances. Indeed it seems that Dewey was if anything inclined to favour the index over the classification; in the second edition we find the statement 'an essential part of the Subject Index is the table of classification', and Dewey also wrote 'A clerk, if he only knows the subject of his book, by the use of the index can class just as the chief of the catalog department would class . . .'. While Dewey's enthusiasm for the index seems over-optimistic, there is no doubt that the detailed index was an important factor in the success of the scheme as a whole. It must, however, also be considered as a major source of the 'subject index illusion' so trenchantly condemned by Bliss, as mentioned below.

The three 'innovations' described here are now taken for granted in library classification, and it is important to remember that it was not always so. In his scheme Dewey foreshadowed many of today's developments, even if he did not always recognize them explicitly.

Decimal notation

Dewey's plan was to divide the whole of knowledge into ten main classes, then to divide each of these into ten divisions, then each of these divisions into ten sections. In the first edition he suggested that in a catalogue it would be possible to continue the division to a fourth or fifth place, though he did not recommend this for shelf arrangement; for example, *geology of Mexico* might be given the number 5578. The point was used to introduce the book number: 513.1 was the first book on geometry 513. Another method of division after the point was by size; 421.3.7 was the seventh book on the *philology of the English language* 421 filed in the third (i.e. oversize) sequence. Dewey recognized that decimal division might lead to some anomalies, but claimed that it worked in practice; his devotion to practice as opposed to theory led him in fact to distort the hierarchical structure of the notation in places, as is shown by the second edition of 1885, in which a number of changes led to the scheme which is very largely the basis of the latest editions.[1]

Dewey claimed: 'we have not sacrificed utility in order to force subjects on the decimal Procrustean bed.' However, in the second edition, when there are fewer than nine subdivisions of a subject, the 'spare' notation is used for further subdivision, while if there are more than nine, some – the 'minor' subdivisions – are all accommodated at one number. In this edition we find the three figure minimum notation, with a point following the third figure if further notation is used; we also find many of the synthetic devices which characterize the scheme. For example, whereas in the first edition the form divisions (common facets) were enumerated at the main class headings and could only be used there, in the second we find a table of form divisions which may be used anywhere. There are instructions to 'divide like' various numbers; e.g. 016 Bibliographies of subjects, divide like the classification. Division by period under a country is possible, using a zero to introduce the notation. What is even more interesting is that we find in some places, notably Class 400 Philology, a very clear facet structure. Dewey does not appear to have seen the significance of this, and it was left to Ranganathan some 50 years later to make explicit and generalize the principle which is implicit and restricted in this example; nevertheless, in this as in so many other points, Dewey showed the way ahead at a very early stage.

Integrity of numbers

Just as the notational pattern was set in the second edition for all succeeding editions, so also was the systematic arrangement crystallized. Dewey realized that a scheme which changed substantially from edition to edition would not succeed, because librarians would not accept it; change means reclassification, altering notation on catalogue entries and books, reshelving, refiling – a great deal of work. In the second edition Dewey announced that the structure of the scheme would thence-forth not be changed; expansions would be introduced as necessary, but the basic outline would remain constant. This has certainly been an important factor in the success of the scheme, but has led to severe problems in keeping pace with the growth and development of knowledge. Dewey wrote: 'Even if the decisions reached were not the wisest possible, all practical purposes are served.' H. E. Bliss named this attitude the *subject index illusion* – the idea that the overall order is rel-atively unimportant, provided that each subject has its own little pigeonhole where it can be found.[2]

It is in this edition that we also first find Dewey's simplified spelling. Dewey, who was keenly interested in reforming the spelling of the English language, lost no oppor-tunity of pursuing this particular hobby; christened Melville, he soon dropped the final le, and even went to the extreme of spelling his final name Dui for a time. The classi-fication scheme reflects this interest from the second edition to the 14th, so that we find headings such as filosofy and jeolojy used throughout the text. Unfortunately, Dewey's simplified spelling did not take account of all the problems of expressing 42 sounds using only 26 letters, and in consequence some of his 'improved' spellings were ambiguous. They also caused problems for users whose first language was not English. This feature was dropped after the 14th edition, except for a reprint of Dewey's own introduction to the 12th edition which appeared in editions up to the 18th. With the death in 1977 of Dewey's son Godfrey, this was also dropped in the 19th edition, which used standard English spelling throughout with the exception of such words as 'thru' which are now common American practice.

The 15th (standard) edition

Up to DDC14 progress was mainly in the form of increased detail, but on a very *ad hoc* basis. The 1951 15th edition was intended to bring the scheme up to date, bas-ing the amount of detail in each section more firmly on relative literary warrant. The method chosen was to cut all the schedules down to size, rather than cut some but expand others. From 31,000 headings in DDC14, we find a slashing reduction to 4700 in DDC15. In History, 942 stood for England, Thames river; apart from the period divisions the schedule was completed by the inclusion of 942.1 London; 942.34 Channel Islands; and 942.89 Isle of Man. The criterion used was that sub-jects not represented on the shelves of the Library of Congress were omitted, but the reduction clearly went much further than this. There were also many relocations; of the 4700 topics, about 1000 were in different relative positions. The index was also greatly shortened, to such a extent that a new index was published a year later to meet the criticisms.

DDC15 was very badly received, with many libraries (and BNB) deciding to ignore it. However, there were some good features. The typography and layout were greatly improved, with the schedule structure shown by indentation and typestyle. Terminology was brought up to date, and scope notes were added to many headings. Following editions saw a reversion to the kind of detail previously found in the schedules, but the good features of DDC15 were retained.

A seven-year publication cycle was adopted, and DDC16 appeared in 1958. Some headings were relocated back to their places in DDC14, but the improvements in presentation of DDC15 were retained, and changes from DDC14 and DDC15 were carefully tabulated to help those making the changeover. DDC16 also introduced the first of the 'phoenix' schedules: schedules which completely replaced the existing outdated schedules. These major changes have become a feature of each new edition, and have also appeared between editions. DDC16 had new schedules for 546 and 547, Inorganic and Organic Chemistry; DDC17 (1965) for 150 and 130 General and Special Psychology; DDC18 (1971) for 340 Law and 510 Mathematics; and DDC19 (1979) for 324 and 329 in a new schedule for the political process, and a complete new schedule for Sociology, expanding 301.1 to cover 301 to 307. However, many found this new schedule to be in effect an outline, and a fuller schedule was published as a separate in 1982, for immediate adoption as part of a new policy of continuous revision. In 1985 another complete new schedule was published as a separate, for 004–006 Data Processing. DDC20 had only one major phoenix schedule, for 780 Music; this was published as a separate in 1980 to gauge reaction to the totally faceted schedule, and was adopted as part of the scheme after a few minor amendments. The name 'phoenix' has now been changed to 'complete revision'.

The 20th edition[3]

With the publication of the 19th edition, the question of a seven-year publication schedule was reviewed, and it was ten years before the new edition appeared in 1989. As has been mentioned, during that time the expansion of 302–307 Sociology, and also the new schedule for 004–006 Data processing and computers, had been published as separates. Both of these were adopted as 'official' without delay, but the phoenix schedule for 780 Music, which had been the centre of a certain amount of controversy, was left to lie on the table until finally being incorporated into the new edition.[4] On the retirement of Ben Custer in 1980, John Comaromi was appointed editor, and remained in that position until his unexpected death in 1991.

An important tool which followed publication of the nineteenth edition was the *Manual on the use of the Dewey Decimal Classification: Edition 19*.[5] This appeared in 1982, and was a serious attempt to answer as many of the likely questions on usage as possible, with guidance on problems likely to face the practising classifier. It was incorporated into DDC20 in a modified form, and now forms an integral part of the scheme. Many notes have been included in the schedules, and the summaries within classes are more frequent and more detailed; *see-also* notes have been added in places. There have been numerous minor revisions, such as those for Japan and Germany in the Area Table 2.

Changes are listed in a section on 'New features in Edition 20'. Among these is a note on the index, which has been reduced in size: entries unlikely to be used have been dropped, and *see* references have been eliminated by giving the class number instead. Names which might appear as entries are now indexed in accordance with AACR2 as well as under any other commonly used forms. All in all, considerable effort has obviously been devoted to making the scheme more 'user-friendly' as it has moved into the computer age.

The scheme

The 20th edition is in four volumes: Introduction and Tables; Schedules 000–599; Schedules 600–999; Relative index and Manual. Volume 1 begins with the Publisher's Foreword, in which two significant events are listed, both taking place on the same day: July 29, 1988. The first was the delivery of a computer tape containing the text of the new edition produced on a microcomputer by the editorial staff using a sophisticated editorial support system. The second was even more important: Forest Press and the Dewey Decimal Classification became part of OCLC, probably the most significant non-government organization of its kind. With the continuing support of the Decimal Classification Division of the Library of Congress, the future of DDC now seems assured.

The preface by the Editorial Policy Committee lists the major changes which have been made in this edition, and is followed by Acknowledgments. Next is a new section, New Features in Edition 20, which lists changes which have been made in some detail, beginning with a statement of the aim of 'user convenience'. There are more and clearer instructions in the schedules, and increased use is made of summaries. This is an influential improvement, in that it makes *classification*, as opposed to 'looking it up in the index', much easier. Other changes listed are mentioned later.

The *Introduction to the Dewey Decimal Classification* is intended for the beginner, but as usual contains much advice which is of value as a reminder to the experienced classifier. Section 5, *Determining the subject of a work*, includes guidance on selecting the right discipline for a work, and on citation order, concluding with a *Table of last resort*, which is a general citation order (Kinds of thing, Parts, Materials, Properties, Processes, Operations, Instrumentalities) which may be used in the absence of any other rule. Citation order is also covered in Section 9, *Number building*. Section 7, *Key features of the schedules and tables*, includes a clear explanation of the various kinds of notes to be found throughout the schedules. The introduction is followed by a glossary, and an index to the introduction and glossary.

This section is followed by the seven auxiliary *Tables of common facets*. These begin with a brief note explaining their use, which emphasizes that they are not to be used on their own, and that the notation begins with a dash in the tables to show this; in use, the dash is omitted. Table 1 is the standard subdivisions, and starts with a page of notes on their use, including a lengthy precedence table; for example, a work on a subject written as a programmed text (—077) for a specific group of users (—024) has the ss —024, *not* —077, which comes lower in the table of precedence. The summary of the table gives the nine divisions, as follows:

—01 Philosophy and theory
—02 Miscellany
—03 Dictionaries, encyclopedias, concordances

—04 **Special topics**
—05 **Serial publications**
—06 **Organizations and management**
—07 **Education, research, related topics**
—08 **History and description with respect to kinds of persons**
—09 **Historical, geographical, persons treatment**

Further summaries are given at —02, —07, —08 and –09, e.g.:

—070 1–070 9	**Geographical treatment**
—071	**Schools and courses**
—072	**Research**
—074	**Museums, collections, exhibits**
—075	**Museum activities and services Collecting**
—076	**Review and exercise**
—077	**Programmed texts**
—078	**Use of apparatus and equipment in study and teaching**
—079	**Competitions, awards, financial support**

We still find the intermingling of bibliographical forms —02, —03 and —05, and common subjects —01, —06, —07, and —08, with Place and Time covered in —09, and —04 as pig in the middle. Since there is really no practical way in which this can now be avoided, it remains as an unfortunate feature which we must be aware of.

There are notes of one kind or another at nearly every heading. These are a prominent feature of DDC20, and are a major development of the network of notes found in previous editions. Those found in Table 1 include:

Definitions, e.g.
    —083 5   Young adults
                            Aged twelve to twenty
'Class here', including comprehensive works, e.g.
    —071 55   In-service training and residency
                            Class here on-the-job education
'Class elsewhere' directions, e.g.
    —07   Education, research, related topics
                            Do not use for textbooks; class textbooks in 001–999
                            without adding notation from Table 1
See references, e.g.
    –068 8   Management of distribution
                            For physical distribution, see —0687
Relocation, e.g.
    —074 1–074 9   Geographical treatment [*formerly —07401–07409*]
    —[074 01–074 09] Geographical treatment
                            Relocated to —074 1–074 9

'Standing room' notes refer to topics which are narrower than the heading to which they are attached, but do not at present justify their own class number. A document on such a topic should be classed at the heading *with no synthesis*; to subdivide further would be to ignore a step of division, e.g.

—07   **Education, research, related topics**
                 Including training teachers, practice teaching
—068 7   Management of materials
                 Examples: physical distribution . . .
Synthesis, e.g.
—070 1–070 9   Geographical treatment
                              Add to base number —070 notation 1 or 3–9 from Table
                              2, e.g. education in France—07044

The standard subdivisions are followed by the Area table 2. The notation from this may be added directly at places specified in the schedules; where it is not specified it may be added if appropriate by interpolating —09 from T1, e.g.

338.93–99   **Economic development and growth in specific continents,**
                              countries, localities
                              Add to base number 338.9 notation 3–9 from Table 2,
                              e.g. economic policies of United Kingdom 338.941
526.99   **Hydrographic surveying** [no notes]
526.990 916 576   in the Great Australian Bight

Table 3 provides subdivisions for individual literatures and literary forms. This was introduced in DDC18 to try to make the instructions for synthesis simpler. In DDC19 it was divided into Table 3 and Table 3A. In DDC20 we find Tables 3–A, for works by or about individual authors; 3–B, for the works by or about two or more authors, and for rhetoric in specific literary forms (808.1–.3); and 3–C, used mainly with Table 3–B. The instructions need to be followed very carefully if the correct result is to be obtained. For the period subdivisions for a particular literature, we have to go back to the main schedules. For example, to find the class number for critical appraisal of 20th century English poetic drama we have to find the base number 82 from the main schedules at 820; then to Table 3–B to find the table of precedence, which tells us that poetic drama goes with drama in —2, not poetry in —1; then to the schedule in Table 3–B, which tells us that we go to 820 to find the period number 91 to add to the base number 822, then back to Table 3–B to find that critical appraisal is 09, giving us 822.9109. If we have a large collection of the works of a specific author, we can subdivide it using the detailed table found at 822.33 Shakespeare.

Table 4 is for the subdivision of those individual languages marked * in 420–490. Table 5 is for racial, ethnic and national groups, Table 6 for languages, and Table 7 for Groups of persons. These Tables may only be used where specified.

Following the Tables are three lists to help those making the change from DDC19. The first is of relocations, in DDC19 order, with the DDC20 equivalent in a second column. The second is of reductions, where for one reason or another a subject has been reclassified to its inclusive heading, or from one of the Tables to the main sequence. The third covers the new schedules for Music and British Columbia: each has three sequences, the first alphabetical, the second giving DDC19 to DDC20 class number conversions, the third giving a similar DDC20 to DDC19 conversion.

The second volume begins with the Summaries. The first summary lists the ten main classes:

000   Generalities
100   Philosophy & psychology
200   Religion
300   Social sciences
400   Language
500   Natural sciences & mathematics
600   Technology (Applied sciences)
700   The arts
800   Literature & rhetoric
900   Geography & history

The second lists the hundred divisions, e.g.

600   Technology (Applied sciences)
610   Medical sciences   Medicine
620   Engineering & allied operations
630   Agriculture
640   Home economics & family living
650   Management & auxiliary services
660   Chemical engineering
670   Manufacturing
680   Manufacture for specific uses
690   Buildings

The third summary lists the 1000 sections, e.g.

620   Engineering & allied operations
621   Applied physics
622   Mining & related operations
623   Military & nautical engineering
624   Civil engineering
625   Engineering of railroads, roads
626
627   Hydraulic engineering
628   Sanitary & municipal engineering
629   Other branches of engineering

The schedules are carefully set out to show the various hierarchies and to define headings or illustrate their use. Examples are always given to demonstrate notational synthesis. Instructions given at a broad heading normally apply to the more specific headings within that hierarchy, and it is therefore necessary to study the schedules carefully to establish exactly how to deal with composite subjects. At times, the classifier is referred to another heading to find out how to synthesize a particular piece of notation. For reasons which have been discussed in Chapter 11, it is sometimes the case that synthesis is only possible at some headings within a particular class; in such cases the asterisk * or obelisk † or both are used to indicate headings where synthesis is possible, with a note at the bottom of the page explaining their purpose.

In general, the classification is prescriptive; however, there are places where there are genuine differences of opinion among users as to which is the preferred citation order. In such cases the various options are set out, with the Editor's preference being the way that class numbers will be generated for MARC records. (For Law, opinion is so divided that *three* options are provided; in addition to the Editor's preference, class numbers in accordance with Option B are provided in MARC records by agreement between the British Library and the Decimal Classification Division.) Options are shown in parentheses. Another use for options is for international users who may wish to emphasize, say, their own religion rather than Christianity. At 292–299 **Religions other than Christianity** there are in fact five options. The Editor's preference for bibliographies is to collect these together at 016, but for those who prefer to shelve them with the subject, the option is provided. Options are shown in parentheses in the main schedules:

016 **Bibliographies and catalogs of works on specific subjects or in specific disciplines**
      (Option: class with the specific discipline or subject , using notation 016 from Table 1 . . .)

In Table 1:
      (—016) Bibliographies, catalogs, indexes
      (Optional number, prefer 016)

The following excerpts are intended to show some of the more important features of the schedules. Each is selected to illustrate a particular point, and does not necessarily represent the full schedule at that point. The numbers at the left-hand edge are *not* part of the schedules, but refer to the notes following these excerpts.

1)   **000**   **Generalities**
2)   *See Manual at 000*
3)   **SUMMARY**
            001   **Knowledge**
            002   **The book**
            003   **Systems**
            004   **Data processing**   **Computer science**
            005   **Computer programming, programs, data**
            006   **Special computer methods**
  001   **Knowledge**
4)   General aspects: history, description, critical appraisal of intellectual activity in general; increase, modification, dissemination of information and understanding
5)   Class here discussion of ideas from many fields
6)   Class epistemology in 121

		.1	**Intellectual life**
7)			Nature and value
8)			*For scholarship and learning, see 001.2*
	[.14]		Intellectual cooperation
9)			Number discontinued; class in 001.1
10)	**.3**		**Humanities**

Including relative values of science versus the humanities

.4   Research

| .42 | Research methods |

11)   Class here research methods not otherwise provided for *[formerly 001.43]*, scientific method

.422   Statistical methods

12)   *See also 310 for collections of general statistical data, notation 021 from Table 1 for statistics on a specific discipline or subject*

.422 6   Presentation of data

13)   Examples: charts, graphs, nomograms

14)   [.424]   Operations research

Relocated to 003

15)   .43   Historical, descriptive, experimental methods

Research methods not otherwise provided for relocated to 001.42

.432   Historical method

      example: case studies

.433   Descriptive method

      Including collecting, field work, questionnaires, surveys

.434   Experimental method

16) **350   Public administration and military science**

SUMMARY

17)   350.000 1–.9   **Standard subdivisions; specific aspects of public administration**

18)   Add to base number 350 the numbers following 351 in 351.0001–351.9, e.g. Personnel management 350.1

19)> **351–354 Administration of central and local governments**

Class comprehensive works in 350

351   Administration of central governments

20)   **.000 1–.000 9   Standard subdivisions** (enumerated)

.000 5   Serial publications

21)   Class serial administrative reports in 351.0006

22)   .000 6   Administrative reports

23)   **.001.–.009   [Bureaucracy, chief executives, cabinets**

and councils of state, fundamentals of
administration, special agencies] (enumerated)

24)   .01–.09   [Specific departments and ministries of
cabinet rank, intergovernmental administration (enumerated)

25)   .1   Personnel management

26)   ... [summaries not listed]

641   Food and drink

.5   Cooking

27)
Preparation of food with and without use of heat
Unless other instructions are given, observe the following
table of precedence, e.g., outdoor cooking for children
641.5622 (*not* 641.578)

For special situations, reasons, ages	641.56
Quantity, institutional, travel, outdoor	641.57
Money-saving and timesaving cooking	641.55
With specific appliances, utensils, fuel	641.58
For specific meals	641.52–.54
By specific types of person	641.51
Characteristic of specific geographical environments, ethnic cooking	641.59

Class menus and meal planning in 642
*For cooking specific materials, see 641.6; specific
cooking processes and techniques, 641.7; cooking
of composite dishes, 641.8*

663   Beverage technology

.9   Nonalcoholic brewed beverages

28)
Add to notation for each term identified by * as follows:
028 Auxiliary techniques and procedures; apparatus, equipment
     Class materials in 1

1   Materials
2   Preliminary preparations
3   Fermentation and oxidation
4   Firing, roasting, curing
5   Blending
7   Specific varieties
8   Concentrates
9   Packaging

.92   *Cocoa and *chocolate

.93   *Coffee

.94   *Tea

.96   Herb teas
>   Examples: catnip, maté, sassafras, other aromatic and
medicinal teas
.97   Coffee substitutes
>   Examples: acorns, cereal preparations, chicory

929   Biography, genealogy, insignia
>
920.1–928.9 Biography of specific classes of persons

29)   (Option A: Use subdivisions identified by *
(Option B: Class individual biography in 92 or B, collected
biography in 92 or 920 undivided
(Option C: Class individual biography of men in 920.71, of
women in 920.72
(Prefer specific discipline or subject, using notation 092 from
Table 1, e.g., Collected biography of scientists 509.22)

30)   Add to notation for each term identified by † notation 3–9
from Table 2, e.g., Baptists from Louisiana 922.6763

1)   Major headings in bold type
2)   The *Manual* has a discussion of this class
3)   Summaries are given to help the *classifier* as opposed to the index-searcher
4)   *General aspects* notes indicate coverage not specified in the standard subdivisions
5)   Class here topics which might fall into a range of headings
6)   A related subject which is classed elsewhere
7)   Scope note
8)   See reference to clarify structure within the class
9)   Subdivision from an earlier edition no longer used
10)   A topic in 'standing room' included at this entry
11)   Topic reclassified from a previous edition [*formerly* . . .], plus a topic which approximates the whole of the heading
12)   A reminder that the word 'statistics' has more than one usage
13)   Concrete examples to clarify an abstract heading
14)   Topic moved to a more helpful position
15)   Heading showing a step in division, but unlikely to be used in practice.
16)   350 actually includes two separate classes: Public administration in 350 to 354, and Military science in 355 to 359. There is a 10-page discussion of classification problems in this division in the *Manual*
17)   350 is for public administration in general, when works relate to both central and local administration. The subdivisions to be used are those enumerated at 351. Standard subdivisions have in effect four zeros, e.g. 350.0003 Encyclopedia of public administration, from 351.0003
18)   Notational synthesis is shown by the instruction Add to base number . . . the numbers following . . . An example is always given to make the synthesis clear

19) The notation 351–354 for the centred heading shown by > is not used, and there is therefore a need for an instruction on where to place comprehensive works

20) Standard subdivisions have three zeros, which is the practice to be followed in 351 to 354. Placing the subdivisions at 350 could cause confusion over the need for a fourth zero

21) Citation order specified

22) The ss is used with a meaning other than the usual, which would be tautologous in this context

23) The most general facet specific to public administration. The bracketed headings are in fact the individual subdivisions

24) Next more specific facet

25) Most specific facet

26) Summaries are given of all nine subdivisions of 350, 351–359 (not shown here)

27) The Table of precedence and *see* references set out the citation order clearly in what would otherwise be a difficult situation for the classifier. In DDC, the term Precedence order is used when facets cannot be combined because of notational problems, Citation order when they can

28) An asterisk is used widely to distinguish numbers which may be further subdivided from those which may not. In this case, .96 and .97 cover a range of headings which may at some time be given notation as a specific subdivision; they therefore cannot be divided by the common subdivisions, as this could lead to a future notational clash. The obelisk † is also used for this purpose

29) In some subjects, notably 340 Law and 920 Biography, different approaches have to be recognized. One is chosen as the Editor's preference; this is the way in which notation for MARC records is generated. Other options may be adopted in individual libraries; for example, it is common practice in many libraries to arrange biography alphabetically by biographee at 92 or B, and this option is allowed for in the schedules

30) In some cases, both * and † may be used to denote various alternatives.

Because of Dewey's original allocation of the notation, this varies in length quite considerably. There is a three-figure minimum, so that for the main classes and the 100 divisions the final 0s are retained, e.g. 600, 510. In a few places this is not exceeded, e.g. 160 Logic, where the schedule bears a close resemblance to the original of 1876; in others, e.g. 621 Applied physics, six figure numbers are almost the norm, and many 10-figure numbers can be found. Applied physics includes Mechanical, electrical, electronic, electromagnetic, heat, light, nuclear engineering – all subjects which have grown since 1876, particularly in recent years. On the other hand, 626 does not even appear in the outline, though a note in the schedules points out that it has not been used since DDC14. The subject to which it was allocated by Dewey, Canal engineering, has so decreased in importance that it no longer justifies a separate section, and has in fact been subsumed under 627.13 Canals as a subdivision of 627 Hydraulic engineering, and 386.4 Canal transportation, as a subdivision of Inland waterway and ferry transportation in 380 Commerce, communications, transportation. The use of 9 to accommodate the unforeseen 'other' is well illustrated by:

629   Other branches of engineering
             SUMMARY
629.04   Transportation engineering
   .1   Aerospace engineering
   .2   Motor land vehicles, and cycles
   .3   Air-cushion vehicles (Ground-effect machines, Hovercraft)
   .4   Astronautics
   .8   Automatic control engineering

While it has proved possible to accommodate all these subjects in 629, it cannot be argued that they are in the most helpful or logical place in the schedules; they are obviously more closely related to Applied physics in 621 than to 628 Sanitary and municipal engineering with which they are collocated.

To make the notation easier to use as it gets longer, it is divided up into units of three digits, first by the point after the third digit, then by a space after each third digit in both schedules and index. The space is not an essential part of the notation, and is often ignored in practice, but has been included in the examples given above, which reflect as closely as possible the typography and layout of the original.

The index

The fourth volume begins with the Relative index, which occupies 730 pages of the 961 total. The index is an integral part of the scheme, and in the second edition Dewey stressed its importance, as we have seen. With the exception of those to DDC15 and DDC17, the indexes have always been well received. The index to DDC20 is no exception, and contains several features intended to make it more helpful to the classifier.

In any classified arrangement, the index is an essential complement to the schedules. The classified order is intended to be helpful, but it can only show one set of relationships; others – the distributed relatives – must be brought together in the index. Dewey recognized this point, and the name Relative index which he coined illustrates this. To take an example, Marriage is found in a number of contexts in the schedules, which are collocated in the index:

Marriage	306.81
citizenship issues	323.636
customs	392.5
ethics	173
religion	291.563
Buddhism	294.356 3
Christianity	241.63

Hinduism	294.548 63
Islam	297.5
Judaism	296.385 63
folklore	398.27
sociology	398.354
law	346.016
literature	808.803 54
history and criticism	809.933 54
specific literatures	T3B—080 354
history and criticism	T3B—093 54
music	781.587

. . .

Synonyms always present a minor problem. If there are a number of subdivisions at an index entry, as for Marriage above, how does one deal with synonyms or near-synonyms? In DDC16 through to DDC19 the index contained both *see also* and *see* references, but all the entries in an index to a classified arrangement are in effect *see* references, since they refer the user to a place in the schedules by means of the notation. The index to DDC20 contains some *see also* references, but *see* references have been replaced by making a direct index entry. However, this does emphasize the importance of referring to the schedules, which is of course correct practice, but sometimes skipped. For example, to take a near-synonym for marriage, weddings:

Wedding clothes	392.54
commercial technology	687.16
customs	392.54
home sewing	646.47
see also Clothing	
Wedding music	781.587
Weddings	
customs	392.5
dress	392.54
etiquette	395.22
flower arrangements	745.926
handicrafts	745.594 1
interior decoration	747.93

There seems to be some redundancy:

Wedding clothes	392.54
customs	392.54
Weddings	
customs	392.5
dress	392.54

And why not:

Weddings
music   781.587

when we have a parallel entry:

Marriage
music   781.587

The entry in the schedules within 780 Music is:

781.587   *Weddings and marriage

whereas the entry in the schedules within 390 is:

392.5   Wedding and marriage

It is obviously important to take the Editor's advice and refer back to the schedules each time we use the index. If we turn to Clothing, for example, to which we are led by the *see also* reference to the broader concept, it is difficult to see any index entries which might be specifically relevant to wedding clothes. However, if we turn to the schedules, we find that 392.54 is the interdisciplinary number for Wedding clothes.

Proper names are entered according to AACR2, so we have:
Shakespeare, William   822.33
Smith, Adam
economic school   330.153

However, we find that John Maynard Keynes as an individual misses out; the entry is:

Keynesian economic school   330.156

as the subject is identified by the adjectival form rather than the originator's name.

It would not be difficult to find other minor anomalies of this kind, but the index as a whole is a very good piece of work, which serves its purpose well. Nevertheless, it must always be remembered that the index is *not* the schedules; the Editor's advice to go back to the schedules each time we use the index to find a piece of notation is not just sound, it is essential.

The manual

The second part of the fourth volume is the Manual, which is intended to help practising classifiers by describing the practice of the Decimal Classification Division of the Library of Congress. It begins with notes on the use of the Tables of common facets. For example, in discussing the standard subdivisions, there is a very useful discussion of the six kinds of subdivision found in the Table, followed by a warning on the danger of using unwanted subdivisions: unwanted, that is, by the users. If we have a work which deals with the current status of a subject, we do not need to add a period subdivision, e.g. 09049, since this will simply separate the book from those in the main sequence. Notation from the Tables should also not be added when the subject forms only a part of the heading; for example, we find

398	**Folklore**	
398.2	**Folk literature**	
398.24		Tales and lore of plants and animals
398.245		Animals
398.245 4		Legendary

Examples: dragons, phoenixes, unicorns, werewolves

Drawings (—0222) of unicorns should be classified at 398.245 4, *not* 398.245 402 22, since that would mean skipping a step of subdivision; at some time in the future, there may be enough literature on unicorns to justify listing in the schedules with its own notation, but this is not the case at present.

There are 20 pages of notes on the use of the standard subdivisions, an indication of their significance and widespread use. The remaining Tables are only to be used where specified in the schedules, with Table 2, *Geographic areas, Historical periods, Persons*, the next most commonly used. The six pages of text are accompanied by eight pages of maps, a very useful addition to the *Manual*, since they indicate the areas to which particular pieces of notation belong. The instability of political entities is exemplified by the inclusion of —47 Soviet Union, which has had to be amended in DC&, v5, no.4.

Table 3, *Subdivisions of individual literatures*, for specific literary forms, has 12 pages of text and three detailed flowcharts. Like the detailed explanations for Table 1, these are a reflection of the problems involved in classifying a class which often accounts for a substantial part of a library's holdings. Table 4, *Subdivisions of individual languages*, has a page of notes; Table 5, *Racial Ethnic, National groups*, has three; Table 6, *Languages*, has a paragraph on Bantu languages; while Table 7, *Groups of persons*, has no comments at all, as the schedule and notes leave little room for ambiguity.

In the notes on the main schedules, the lengthy explanations are to be found in those areas which experience has shown to cause classifiers problems, and for the new schedules included in DDC20. There are nine pages on the new schedules for Computers and data processing in 004–006; seven pages on the Social sciences and the new schedules for 301–307; eight pages on 340 Law; eight pages on 350–354 Public administration; and 12 pages on the new schedule for 780, including a flowchart. The flowchart has been revised in DC& v5, no.4, in response to a problem raised in a letter to the Decimal Classification Division. There are also flowcharts for 910 Geography and travel, and 930–990 History.

An Appendix lists Policies and procedures of the Decimal Classification Division, as shown by the following examples. For *segmentation*, in a long piece of notation, a segmentation mark ´ indicates the end of the notation to be found in the Abridged edition, or the beginning of a standard subdivision from the Tables. For example:

323´.025´73	Directory of civil rights leaders and organizations in the United States
323	Civil and political rights, as in the Abridged edition

.025   Directories (ss from Abridged edition Table 1)
73   United States (notation from T2 added to –025 from the
                Unabridged T1)

Occasionally, two DDC numbers are allocated to one work. This happens regularly in 340 Law, where two options are widely used; the notation for the non-preferred option is shown in brackets, e.g. [347.3058]. Biographies are given the 'official' notation, but also the notation [B] for those libraries who prefer this method. Volumes which form part of a series are given a class number for the series, but also a class number for the subject of that volume. The third and fourth sections relate to the treatment of juvenile literature.

Abridged editions

The aim of the full edition of DDC has always been to provide as much detail as is likely to be necessary in the largest library, but for many years there has been a parallel series of abridged editions intended for smaller libraries with collections of 20,000 or fewer, such as school libraries. The first abridged edition was published in 1894, and the latest, ADDC12,[6] in 1990, shortly after DDC20 on which it is based. The tenth edition was a departure from the norm in that it was an adaptation rather than an abridgement; in some subject areas long notation was shortened by adapting shorter notation which would otherwise have been unused. This clashed with the segmentation used in the MARC records, and subsequent editions have been true abridgements. This has meant that the first segment of DDC20 notation found in the MARC records now parallels the shorter notation in ADDC12. In addition to the 'official' edition, there is also *Dewey decimal classification for school libraries: British and International* edition;[7] published in 1986, this is a revised and expanded version of the *Introduction to the Dewey Decimal Classification for British schools,* of which the third edition was published in 1977.

Organization

Dewey was nothing if not practical, and he devoted some of his tremendous energy to setting up the Lake Placid Club, a 'self-help' real estate development which turned out to be highly successful. Profits from this went to the Lake Placid Club Education Foundation, which then provided funds through the Forest Press for the continuation of the scheme, which has itself been highly successful. Over 50,000 copies were printed of both DDC18 and DDC19, which makes the scheme a bestseller. DDC19 was adopted by the Library of Congress in 1980, prior to publication, and by BNB in 1981, to coincide with the start of a new cumulation. DDC20 was adopted by both libraries on publication.

The Library of Congress started supplying catalogue cards to other libraries in 1901, and in the late 1920s discussions took place on the feasibility of including a DDC number on these cards for the benefit of those libraries which bought the cards but used DDC rather than LCC. In 1923, the Editorial Office was moved to the Library of Congress to form the Decimal Classification Office. In 1930 the Library set up the Decimal Classification Section to start supplying DDC numbers for LC cards. In 1953 the Decimal Classification Office was awarded the contract for the preparation of DDC16. In 1957 the editorial office and the Decimal Classification Office were merged, with the Editor given overall responsibility for both; the merged Office later became the Decimal Classification Division of LC. In 1987 the position of Editor and Chief of the Division was split into two positions, but the editorial office remained a part of the Division.

With the publication of DDC20, Forest Press became part of OCLC Online Computer Library Center. The Decimal Classification Division continues to function as before, but the actual publication in printed and electronic form is now carried out by OCLC Forest Press. The link with OCLC's computer database should provide the scheme with a secure future, without in any way detracting from its links with the users. There is a ten-member international Editorial Policy Committee consisting of representatives of the users; this now includes a representative of the [British] Library Association, an indication of the close working relationship which has developed following a period during which the BNB and the DCD were at loggerheads over BNB's notational adaptations. There are also representatives from Canada and Australia. With its full-scale introduction of the MARC records in 1971, BNB dropped its modifications and adopted standard DDC18 in the interests of international standardization. The phoenix schedule for music was first prepared in the UK, and has its roots in the classification developed by E. J. Coates for the *British Catalogue of Music*. Other countries have also contributed, particularly to Table 2; BNB devised the schedule for the United Kingdom which was necessitated by local government reorganization in 1974, while Australia and New Zealand have both drawn up expansions for their own areas, the latter being included in DC& v5 no.4; regrettably there is still no place for Australasia as a whole, though Australasia is indexed to T2—9. The new schedule for UDC (94) may prompt a revision of DDC. Canada supplied the new schedule for British Columbia.

Over 100 000 titles are now classified by the DCD each year (115,000 in FY 1995); adding those prepared in the UK, Australia, New Zealand, Canada and elsewhere, the total number of MARC records must now contain a substantial proportion with DDC numbers. The scheme is certainly being used very widely – more than 135 countries worldwide,[8] in 35 languages – and its link to national bibliographies means constant contact with literary warrant, without which a scheme becomes steadily more and more out of touch. It has been adopted by the British Library[9] for some of its reading rooms, for example the collection on librarianship which used to form the Library Association library and is now known (optimistically!) as BLISS.

Aids for the user

The fact that DDC is so widely used has led to the production of several tools[10] for the student, as well as the *Manual* for the user. In addition to an 'official' workbook, there are at least two others, and also a programmed text. The production of the schedules in computer-based format has made it possible to produce an electronic version, which can be used by the practising classifier, but also by the student.

Electronic Dewey

DDC in computer-based form is now conveniently available in the *Electronic Dewey*[11] published by OCLC Forest Press in January 1993 and revised in March 1994. This consists of a CD-ROM disk containing the bulk of the text of DDC20: schedules, tables, index, manual; additions and corrections from *DC&*; LCSH associated with DDC20 class numbers, taken from LC records contributed to the OCLC bibliographic database; a sample bibliographic record for each class number, again from the OCLC database; schedule and table summaries and hierarchies for all schedule and table records in the DDC database. In addition, segmentation marks are included for schedule numbers. Excluded from the CD-ROM are: the glossary, maps (Table 2) and flow charts, which are included as Appendices to the *User guide;* the Introduction, which is included as a separate booklet; and the minor tables showing changes between 19th and 20th editions.

The database is organized into records, which correspond to entries in the schedules, tables or manual in the printed volumes, plus synthesized numbers from the index. Each record may contain fields for DDC class numbers from schedules and tables; index terms from the DDC relative index; related DDC index terms; captions from the schedules; notes; relevant LCSH headings. Each field may have indexes for DDC class numbers, keywords, or phrases. The file can thus be searched by DDC class number or by terms. The two kinds of alphabetic index give access to single keywords or to whole phrases; both can be browsed, obviously an important point in using a phrase index where the whole phrase must be matched.

There are a few important points to note when using the indexes. As usual, the keyword indexes do not include stop words; however, these do occur in phrases, which must therefore be enclosed in quotes, e.g. 'strength of materials', where *of* would normally prevent a match. For ease of use in printed form, long class numbers are segmented by gaps after each third digit following the point; these must be ignored in searching the computer file, as must the segmentation marks. Hyphens are significant for indexing, but other punctuation is not, except for the point in DDC numbers. Because the Relative index includes some synthesized numbers, there are 'built number' records for these, tagged to show that they will not be found in the schedules as they stand.

Boolean searches can be carried out using the normal operators AND, OR, and NOT. Parentheses are used to clarify Boolean expressions. WITH can be used to specify that two words must occur in the same field, while ADJ[N] limits separation to *n* words. Truncation (* and ?) can be used, with the normal caution, and character masking (?). Queries can be saved and used again if necessary. The schedule summaries can be viewed, and both schedules and tables can be browsed. The facility to view bibliographic records showing how class numbers have been used in practice should prove very useful in confirming a choice of class number.

The whole package is well planned, and easily understood, unlike many computer manuals. A version is now available for Windows. It will be interesting to see how many users switch to using the electronic version rather than the printed version as they become accustomed to the idea.

Computer production[12]

The program for the production of the DDC20 database was the Editorial Support System ESS, developed before the USMARC format for classification data was available. For DDC21, changes are being made to facilitate the production of a database in either format. Three particular lines are being followed to make this possible. The first is changes to the ESS database to make conversion to USMARC format simple; this involves revising the codes for various kinds of notes, and making changes to the way that some information is preserved. For example, the USMARC field 685 contains information about the history of changes; at present, information regarding, say, relocations is published in the edition to which it relates, but is then dropped. Changes made from DDC18 to DDC19 were detailed in DDC19 but did not appear in DDC20. In future, information relating to changes will be preserved in field 685, though it is not economically practical to undertake any kind of retrospective exercise.

The second area is the identification of the various parts of synthesized numbers. In many places in the schedules we find instructions to 'add to base number . . .'; this often means dropping part of the 'borrowed' notation, losing the link to the original schedule from which it was borrowed. For example, as shown in Chapter 15, in the notation 633.519768 representing the cotton boll weevil, the fact that the 68 comes from 595.768, the 7 from 632.7, and the 9 from the instructions at 633–635, is lost, and can only be revealed by going back to the schedules and following through the instructions. In DDC21 add notes will be formulated in such a way that they can be incorporated in the appropriate USMARC format fields, e.g. 761 (add or divide like instructions) or 765 (synthesized number components). This will make it possible to search on the various parts of a synthesized number online.

The third area is that of showing hierarchical relationships. Much of the notation of DDC is already hierarchical; we can broaden a search by dropping the final digit of a class number, or narrow it by adding a digit. However, this is not always true, and presents particular problems with centred notations. These were introduced to fill in steps in the hierarchy which Dewey had omitted, or which represent changes in the way we look at subjects now. (Dewey's omission of a place for Christianity is an example of a different way of looking at the world. For him, Religion *meant* Christianity.) There are also many places where Dewey departed from strict hierarchical notation in order to save a digit in the class number. In future, steps in the hierarchy which are not reflected in the notation will be noted in such a way that they can easily be converted to USMARC field 553 (valid number tracing), so that hierarchical searches will be possible online. The whole exercise will involve a lot of work on the part of the editorial staff, and particular attention to accuracy and completeness; once done, it should bring DDC as a classification truly into the online age.

In another approach to the same end, OCLC have been working on ways of improving the ESS database to produce Electronic Dewey. As mentioned earlier, the database used for editing purposes has been enhanced in three major ways. The addition of information about DDC hierarchies means that these can be displayed; this particular exercise will presumably become redundant when the ESS database contains all the information necessary for the USMARC classification format. The availability of the OCLC bibliographic database has meant that each class number can be linked to bibliographic records in which it is used. In addition, LCSH headings from these records give enhanced access through the terms used, so that the classifier is no longer wholly dependent on the index and schedules of DDC itself. The combination of the increased information provided in the USMARC format and the user interface developed by OCLC will provide a powerful tool for both classifier and online searcher.

Revision

The main method of revision is by the publication of new editions at regular intervals. With the publication of DDC19, suggestions were made[13] that a more practical method would be to publish new schedules as separates, and additions and corrections in DC& as they arose, for immediate adoption; new editions of the whole scheme would be published at infrequent intervals. There was in fact a ten-year interval between DDC19 and DDC20, but it is intended to revert to the seven-year cycle, with the publication of DDC21 planned for mid-1996. In between editions, users are kept informed of new developments through *DC&: Decimal classification: additions, notes, decisions*, now in its fifth volume. This originated in three series of *Notes and decisions on the application of the decimal classification* published by the Decimal Classification Office 1934–1955; the title was changed after the publication of the 16th edition, and the second volume began with the publication of the first issue in Spring 1967, after publication of the 17th edition. Although the intention was to publish DC& on a regular basis twice a year, in the event publication has been irregular until volume 5, which has been published regularly once a year. DC& provides a vehicle for communication with users and the publication of corrections and short revisions. For DDC19, new schedules were proposed for 301–307 Sociology, 780 Music, and 560–590 Life sciences. In the event, the Sociology schedule appeared in outline in DDC19, to be filled in by publication as a separate in 1982. Music was left on the table for further discussion, because of its radical nature, and finally appeared in DDC20.

The twenty-first edition

Planning has been under way for this edition for several years, and it is to be published in mid-1996. Though it will follow the overall plan of DDC20, there will be some significant complete revisions ('phoenixes') and partial revisions. Life sciences were put in the too-hard basket for DDC20, and a new schedule has been produced for DDC21. In this, Process will be preferred over Organism, so that Physiology of the cat will be classified with Physiology rather than with Cat as at present. Extensive revisions of 350–354 Government administration have been made; it should be noted that this will invalidate examples 16–26 from the section of examples given earlier in this chapter, which apply only to DDC20. 370 Education has been extensively revised, including the vacating of 376 Education of women and 377 Religious education, both of which had become anachronistic in today's culture.296 Judaism and 297 Islam have been revised as part of a large-scale revision of Religion generally to remove some of the inherent bias towards Christianity. 200 is now Religion, and the standard subdivisions 201–209 have been vacated as part of a two-stage operation to be completed in DDC22. The content of the standard subdivisions has been moved to various places in Christianity, reflecting the fact that in the past there has in effect been no proper place for Religion as a whole. The standard subdivisions of Comparative religion 291 have been relocated to 200.1–200.9; in DDC22, Comparative religion, now in 291.1–291.9, will be relocated to 201–209, and 290 will become solely Religions other than Christianity. Christianity, now at the class heading 200, is transferred to a centred heading 230–280 Christianity, with comprehensive works in 230. This move eliminates the anomalous position of the Bible, to part of which at least Judaism can lay claim, as solely part of Christianity. The overall result is a schedule which gives a much more rational approach to Religion and removes the now somewhat embarrassing emphasis on Christianity which was part of Dewey's view of the world.

The future

Despite the many criticisms which have been made of the scheme, it is obviously very successful. It has been criticized for not being sufficiently up-to-date, and for introducing new schedules; for not reflecting the current state of knowledge[14] and for introducing too many revisions.[15] Despite all these unfavourable (and contradictory!) comments, it has continued to flourish, and seems likely to become even more entrenched with the introduction of the electronic version. With versions in over thirty languages, used in 135 countries in some 200,000 libraries, and its place in the MARC records, it seems that DDC will continue to be the major library classification scheme.

References

1 Facsimile editions of the first two editions were produced; that of Edition 1 was produced by Forest Press as part of the centenary celebrations, while DDC2 was made available from University Microfilms. It is instructive to go back to these and see how the scheme as we know it today had its beginnings.

2 Bliss, H. E., *The organization of knowledge in libraries and the subject approach to books*, New York, NY, H. W. Wilson, 1933.
   For a discussion of the need for a proper classificatory approach to a subject, see Soudek, M., 'On the classification of Psychology in general library classification schemes', *Library resources and technical services*, **24**, Spring 1980, 114–28.

3 *Dewey decimal classification and relative index: devised by Melvil Dewey; edition 20*, edited by John Comaromi [*et al.*], Albany, NY, OCLC Forest Press, 1989. 4v.
   Comaromi, J. P. and Satija, M. P., *Dewey decimal classification: history and*

current status, New Delhi, Sterling Publishers, c1989.

Intner, S. S., 'Dewey decimal classification: a review article', *Library resources and technical services*, 33 (2), April 1989, 186–91.

4   *In celebration of revised 780: music in the Dewey decimal classification, edition 20*, compiled by Richard B. Wursten, Canton, MA, Music Library Association, 1990.

5   *Manual on the use of the Dewey Decimal Classification: Edition 19*, prepared by J. P. Comaromi [*et al.*], Albany, NY, Forest Press, 1982.

6   *Abridged Dewey decimal classification and relative index: devised by Melvil Dewey; edition 12*, edited by John Comaromi [*et al.*], Albany, NY, OCLC Forest Press, 1990.

7   *Dewey decimal classification for school libraries: British and International edition*, Albany, NY, Forest Press, 1986.

8   *Dewey: an international perspective: papers from a workshop on the Dewey Decimal Classification and DDC20*, ed. R. P. Holley, New York, NY, K. G. Saur, 1991. Includes: Sweeney, R., 'An overview of the international use of the DDC', 11–31.

9   Byford, J., 'The British Library, DDC and the new building', *Catalogue & index* (103–104) Spring/Summer 1992, 1, 3–5.

10 Batty, C. D., *An introduction to the twentieth edition of the Dewey decimal classification*, London, Bingley, 1992. [Programmed text]

Chan, L. M., *Cataloging and classification: an introduction*, 2nd edn, New York, NY, McGraw Hill, 1994, Chapter 12.

Chan, L. M. *et al.*, *Dewey Decimal Classification: a practical guide*, Albany, NY, Forest Press, 1994.

Comaromi, J. P., *Exercises in the 20th edition of the Dewey Decimal Classification*, with M. P. Satija, New Delhi, Sterling Publishers, 1990.

Davis, S. W., *DDC20 workbook: a practical introduction to the Dewey Decimal Classification*, Albany, NY, OCLC Forest Press, 1992.

Dewey decimal classification, 20th edition: a study manual; revised and edited by J. P. Comaromi, Englewood, CO, Libraries Unlimited, 1991.

Downing, M. H. and Downing, D. H., *Introduction to cataloging and classification*, 6th edn, Jefferson, NC, McFarland, 1992.

Sifton, P., *Workbook for DDC20: Dewey Decimal Classification, edition 20*, Ottawa, Canadian Library Association, 1989.

11 *Electronic Dewey*, Dublin, OH, OCLC, 1992, updated 1994. CD-ROM.

12 Beall, Julianne, 'Editing the Dewey Decimal Classification online', in *International study conference on classification research, Toronto, Canada, June 24–28 1991*, Williamson, N. J. and Hudon, M. (eds.), Elsevier, 1992, (FID 698), 29–37.

13 Jelinek, M., 'Twentieth Dewey: an exercise in prophecy', *Catalogue and index* (**58**), 1980, 1–2.

14 Bull, G. and Roberts, N., 'Dewey decimal classification and relative index, 19th ed.' *Journal of librarianship,* **12** (2), 1980, 139–42.

15 Berman, S., 'DDC20: the scam continues', *Library journal,* **114**, Sep 15 1989, 45–8.

Chapter 18
The Universal Decimal Classification

In 1984 two Belgians, Paul Otlet and Henri LaFontaine, conceived the idea of a 'universal index to recorded knowledge', to which people all over the world would contribute, and which would in its turn be available to all.[1] An alphabetical arrangement was out of the question in so aggressively international an enterprise, and they turned their minds to systematic arrangement. The decimal classification of Melvil Dewey was then in its fifth edition, and used arabic numerals as its only notation – a system used world-wide. Otlet and LaFontaine secured Dewey's agreement to allow them to extend the detail in his scheme to make it suitable for their purposes, and managed to classify several thousand documents in time for the First International Conference on Bibliography in 1895. The conference welcomed the idea of an international index, the *Répertoire universel bibliographique,* and established the Institut International de la Bibliographie (IIB) to act as the organization responsible. The development of the scheme went ahead, and it was published in 1905 as *Manuel du Répertoire universel bibliographique,* stressing its primary purpose. It was already more detailed than DDC, its parent, and it was adopted in many libraries and other organizations in Europe; it is still the most widely used classification in Europe, and particularly in the French-speaking world.

The index barely survived World War I, and fell into disuse in the 1920s. However, by this time the classification scheme had achieved recognition in its own right, and a second edition was published over the years 1927–1933, under the name *Classification décimale universelle,* with Otlet and LaFontaine responsible for the Humanities and Social Sciences, and Frits Donker Duyvis, employed by the Dutch Patent Office, to supervise Science and Technology. (Donker Duyvis remained as the mainstay of the scheme until ill-health obliged him to retire in 1959.) To emphasize the international nature of the scheme, the third edition was the German *Dezimal Klassifikation*; this edition, begun in 1934, was interrupted by World War II, and was not completed until 1953. The IIB changed its name in 1931 to Institut International de Documentation (IID), and again in 1937 to Fédération Internationale de Documentation (FID). In 1986 the name was changed again, to Fédération International d'Information et de Documentation, retaining the acronym FID.

Publication in English

In Britain the scheme was enthusiastically adopted by Dr S. C. Bradford, Librarian of the Science Museum Library; most of his book *Documentation*[2] is about UDC, and he produced the first English version, the abridged schedules used in the Science Museum Library: *Classification for works on pure and applied science in the Science Museum Library*, publishing the third edition in 1936. In due course, the British Standards Institution became the official British editorial body, and publication of the full English-language edition, the fourth overall, began in 1943; unfortunately, like FID itself, BSI always suffered from a lack of funds to prosecute this work. The situation changed radically in 1967, when OSTI made a grant to BSI to enable them to increase the scope and quantity of their documentation activities, including UDC; as a result of this, by 1980 the first full English edition was virtually completed, though some parts – for example the biological sciences 57/59 – were still some 40 years old. (By contrast, the schedule for Electrical engineering 621.3 was already in its third edition!) Work began on the second full edition, with particular reference to those parts of the schedules which most needed revision.

Other editions

Other full editions then in preparation included revisions of the German and French editions, and new ventures in Spanish and Japanese. Though the full schedules were available at the FID headquarters, publication meant translation into the desired language, and since most work was done voluntarily in the national committees there was little access to the master copy. The master copy itself consisted of the French edition of 1927–33, with additions since then (in French, English or German, the three official languages of UDC) taken from the *Extensions & corrections* without any overall editorial control. To provide a practical alternative to the incomplete full editions as published, abridged editions were prepared in over 20 languages. The first English language edition was published in 1948, and was based on the Science Museum Library schedules. The second, published in 1957, was more detailed as well as being more up to date, and had a far better index, with 20,000 entries as opposed to 2,000 in the 1948 edition. The third abridged English edition BS 1000A was published in 1961, and served for many years as the basic edition, supplemented in many special libraries by the full schedules (where available) for subjects of specific interest. Work on a revised abridged edition was set aside in favour of completing the full edition and, later, the medium edition.

In 1958 FID published a trilingual abridged edition, BS 1000B. The text of this was in the three official languages of UDC, English, French and German, and four columns held the notation and the appropriate text in each language. A supplement was published in 1968, which could be used to update the English abridgement of 1961.

In 1967 the first medium edition was published in German, and work began on a 'Basic medium edition' to form the basis of medium editions in other languages. The revised German schedules appeared in 1980, but the English edition, originally intended to be published in 1976 as part of the DDC centenary celebrations, did not in the event appear until 1985. It contained about 40,000 entries, twice as many as the abridged edition, and proved to be very successful, superseding the abridged edition, which was by then some 24 years old. The second English medium edition was published in 1994, and marks a very significant development.

Computer production

In March 1993, a machine readable version of UDC, the Master Reference File (MRF), based on the 1985 English medium edition supplemented by changes made since then, was completed. In future, this will replace the old master copy as the basis for the revision of all editions of UDC, and will be available in various formats to others wishing to make use of it. The English second medium edition contains some 60,000 headings, about 50% more than the first, and has a detailed index compiled by subject experts who are also professional indexers. Because the MRF is now computer-maintained, subscribers can receive regular updates. The only problem appears to be that as the full edition will no longer be maintained as part of the computer-held master copy, any English parts of the full edition to appear in future will have to be the responsibility of BSI, who will also have to bear the costs. The same is of course true of any other organization wishing to publish more detail than is in the MRF, or – at least for the time being – in any language other than English. It is intended to cover other languages in the MRF, with German as the first candidate.

BSI intends to continue publication of the full English edition, though progress is likely to be slow. Class 8 has been published, but is in fact identical with the MRF; 54 Chemistry has also been prepared in conjunction with the revision of the MRF schedules. A new schedule for 611 is planned, though a full-scale revision of Medicine is in progress for the MRF. VINITI is undertaking the preparation of the third Russian edition for possible publication in 1995, though suffering seriously from shortages of staff and money.

The lack of progress on the full edition led to the production of several special subject editions; these were usually based on the practice of a large library, e.g. the UKAEA for nuclear science and engineering, or the Iron and Steel Institute for mining and metallurgy, and gave the full schedules for the core subjects, together with scope notes, cross-references and instructions, and abridged schedules for related subject areas. Because they were based on the practical application of the scheme, they could give the user more help than the abridged edition while presenting the full edition detail in their special subject field. With the publication of the medium edition, the need for such schemes has been greatly reduced, but a new edition of that for polar research was published in 1991 by the Scott Polar Research Institute, and another for astronomy is in preparation.

Organization

The IIB was set up to run the Répertoire universel and to develop the UDC as its means of arrangement. With the change of name to IID, then FID, came a broadening of the organization's sphere of interest and influence, and UDC became only one of many functions. Responsibility was therefore delegated to national committees and subject committees, with the FID/UDC Assembly as the governing body and the Central Classification Committee (CCC), consisting of the editors of the major full editions, having the overall editorial responsibility. The day-to-day work was done by the Classification Secretariat, (for many years quite literally a 'one-man-band'!) who maintained the central records by coordinating all the submissions from the various national committees. The national committees themselves consisted of librarians and others who used UDC, and who were usually those responsible for devising new schedules, mainly to help them in their daily work. In Britain, a small secretariat was provided by BSI; the grant from OSTI already mentioned enabled BSI to triple the size of this, from one to three. (The staffing has now reverted to the norm, one.) National and international subject committees were also involved in the editing of such proposals, while preliminary publication laid any new schedule on the table for four months for anyone to comment and suggest amendments.

It is hardly surprising that the adoption of new schedules was slow; a proposed new schedule for Aerospace took ten years to gain acceptance, by which time it was somewhat out of date and had undergone a number of changes. Even a proposal which met no opposition could take two years to become part of official UDC. Criticism of the management structure grew steadily, and in 1986 both the FID/UDC Assembly and the CCC were replaced by the UDC Management Board. In 1989 a small Task Force was set up to consider the future of the scheme. In 1991 their report to the Management Board made some major recommendations; the most important of these was the creation of the MRF, but of almost equal significance was the abolition of the existing committee structure, which had been described by G. A. Lloyd, for many years FID Classification Secretary, as 'hyperdemocratic'. Instead, a small advisory group was set up to oversee the revision process. At the beginning of 1992 FID transferred the responsibility for UDC to the UDC Consortium (UDCC)[3], a non-profit making foundation, and in 1993 the UDCC set up an Editorial Board, with an honorary Editor-in-Chief (I. McIlwaine). The six founder members of the UDCC were the FID itself and the publishers of UDC, usually standards organizations, in Spain, The Netherlands, UK, Belgium and Japan. It is hoped to extend the membership to include, for example, Germany, where DIN has discontinued its association with the German edition; despite this, plans for a German edition of the MRF are going ahead, as mentioned earlier. The return of stability to Eastern Europe should lead to the restoration of contributions from VINITI. For many years VINITI was a regular contributor, but after helping with the planning of MRF ceased to play any active role in 1992. Following a meeting with the Editor in May 1995, VINITI has agreed to cooperate in revision work, and to contribute a revised schedule for Eastern Europe to the *Extensions and corrections* for 1995. It is perhaps somewhat ironic that the FID, the body which was originally set up as the IIB to maintain the UDC, has now been obliged to transfer this work to a separate organization.

Revision

The change in management structure has led to important changes in revision procedures. Originally, after the need for a new schedule had been identified, someone (usually the original proposer) would be invited to prepare a proposal. After acceptance by the national subject committee and national committee, this would be forwarded to the CCC, there to be examined by the international subject committee as well as the CCC itself. Any major revisions at this stage would be referred back to the national committee. Eventually an agreed proposal would be published as a *P-Note*, to lie on the table for four months for comment by any user, informed or not. Having undergone this further scrutiny, if there were no objections the schedule would be added to the master copy, and published in *Extensions and corrections to the UDC*. This was cumulated into three-year series. The first five series of *Extensions* were cumulated into five volumes; a further six-volume cumulation covered most of the next four three-year series. Because of the long delays in the publication of the full editions, users had to look in several different places to make sure that they had the latest schedule for any given subject.

With the changes in management structure, *P-Notes* have now become unnecessary. The *E&C* will continue publication yearly, with annual volume 17 being published in 1995; from Volume 16 onwards they now include information about revisions in progress, proposed revisions for comment (replacing P-Notes), an annual update of the Area table for nation states, news about the scheme, and an annual bibliography of writings on UDC. Approved revisions will be incorporated into the MRF, and an annual update of this will be circulated to all subscribers. The UDCC also intends to play a much more proactive role in schedule revision. A revision programme for the rest of the decade has been drawn up, with new schedules being commissioned on a more commercial basis than in the past, when changes were introduced by users on an 'amateur' basis. Had it not been for the indirect support of such organizations as the UKAEA through its library services, and VINITI in the USSR, the revision process would have been even less effective than it was. Provided that enough revenue can be generated from the sale of schedules and fees for the use of the computer-based MRF, the future should see revision proceeding in a smoother fashion – and at a faster pace – than in the past.

Major changes

UDC was originally based on the fifth edition of DDC, but the two schemes tended to drift apart, though attempts were made to retain the same outline at the three-figure level. In 1961, two studies of the UDC commissioned by Unesco[4] were published, both of them highly critical. Much of the criticism arose from the outdated overall outline, and the CCC took the decision to try to carry out a large-scale revision. The first move was to transfer Language from its place between the Social and Natural Sciences to a more helpful place with Literature. The notation 4 could then be reused, after the 'starvation policy' period of ten years, for a subject such as Communication, which might be seen as bridging the gap between the Social and Natural Sciences. (Notation which had remained unused for ten years could be reused with new meanings; in the special libraries which are the major users of UDC, most material would probably have been discarded after ten years.) Such a major change would involve concomitant costs; in view of the continued financial struggles of the FID it is perhaps not surprising that the notation 4 still remains unused, some 30 years after the removal of its contents. The starvation policy has now been rescinded, and changes take place in previously unused notation. Communication is now likely to be redeveloped in Class 0, which is relatively empty and is a reasonable place for a subject which can be regarded as pervasive. The decision to concentrate on the more manageable medium edition should make the overall management of the scheme more effective and less costly.

The scheme

The major edition of the UDC in English is now the medium edition BS 1000M,[5] and it is that which will be considered here. The scheme is in two volumes: 1 contains the systematic tables, 2 the alphabetical index. The Introduction to Vol. 1 begins with a brief history of UDC, then continues with a discussion of the nature of classification, with particular reference to UDC. The main classes are listed, still looking very similar to the first outline of DDC, without the three-figure minimum:

    0   Generalities
    1   Philosophy. Psychology
    2   Religion. Theology
    3   Social sciences
    5   Mathematics and Natural sciences
    6   Applied sciences
    7   Fine arts. Applied arts. Entertainment. Games. Sport
    8   Language. Linguistics. Philology. Literature
    9   Archaeology. Geography. Biography. History

This is followed by a discussion of the main schedules and the notation, which is generally hierarchical. Because in some places the notation can be very long, it is broken up by a dot after every third digit unless some other indicator is applicable. These other symbols are the facet indicators for the *Auxiliary tables*, which are a key part of the scheme, since they permit almost any kind of synthesis. They are divided into two groups: the common auxiliaries and the special auxiliaries. The common auxiliaries may be used anywhere with the same meaning, whereas the special auxiliaries may only be used as specifically instructed.

The common auxiliaries fall into two groups: independent and dependent. The independent auxiliaries, such as those for Place, may be used on their own, or attached to a main number; they also are more flexible in that they may precede or follow the main notation, or even be inserted in the middle if that is appropriate. The dependent auxiliaries, such as those for Points of view, must be added to a UDC number from the main schedules.

As mentioned above, there is no three-figure minimum for the notation; in consequence, the 0 can be used as a significant digit, e.g.:

9	Geography. Biography. History
93/94	History
930	Science of history

Many of the schedules are short, because they rely on synthesis to denote specific subjects. For example, the Literature schedule occupies about a page; supplemented by the Language and other common auxiliaries, it can accommodate as much detail as the more than 2000 pages in LCC's Literature schedules. There are some cross-references, indicated by an arrow, e.g.:

621.384.6	Particle accelerators
	→ 539.1.076; 621.039.5; 621.386.2

drawing our attention to nuclear physics, nuclear engineering and X-ray tubes. Subdivisions in one area which parallel those in another are indicated by the symbol ≅. For example, the schedule for 616.1/.9 Special pathology includes:

616.11	Pericardium
616.12	Heart
616.13	Arteries
616.14	Veins

At 611.1 Angiology. Cardiovascular system. Blood vessels, we find the instruction:

611.11/.14 ≅ 616.11/.14, e.g.	
611.11	Pericardium
611.12	Heart
611.13	Arteries
611.14	Veins

This is a useful space-saving device, which also emphasizes the parallel nature of subdivision in related subjects. However, the simpler method of identifying the common foci as a facet which may be used as needed will be adopted in the future. Medicine is currently being revised, but the device is used elsewhere, and will be found for some time in other schedules. A similar purpose is served by the use of . .. preceding a final digit to show a subsidiary facet; this means that the final digit(s) may be applied to any of the subdivisions of that number:

539.12	Elementary and simple particles
539.12 ... 1	Characteristics, properties, behaviour
539.12 ... 13	Decay
539.122	Photons
539.122.13	Decay of photons
539.128.4	Alpha particles
539.128.413	Decay of alpha particles

Terminology is good, and shows the care that went into the production of the edition. There are some choices of word given, e.g. Dosemeters (Dosimeters). Words and spelling chosen reflect English usage rather than American, e.g. Archaeology.

However, if we judge UDC purely on its main schedules it gives little idea of the power of synthesis afforded by the auxiliaries. These are, in fact, a set of common facets and facet indicators which enable the classifier to find or construct a suitable notation for almost any subject. They appear in the scheme in the following order:

a)   Coordination. Extension +, /. The plus sign + may be used to give a single piece of notation for two subjects which are commonly associated but are separated in the main schedules. Because the second number is effectively hidden, this symbol must be used with care. The combined number files before the first number on its own.

Example: 539.1+621.039 Nuclear science and technology

The stroke (slash) / is used to join consecutive UDC numbers to denote a broader heading for which no notation exists. (This is the same principle as the centred headings in DDC.) These numbers also file before the first number on its own.

Example: 23/28 The Christian religion

b)   Relation. Subgrouping. Order-fixing :, [ ] :: . The colon sign : is the most widely used of the synthetic devices. It can be used to join two pieces of notation to indicate a relationship of some kind, including a phase relationship.

Examples   821.111:22 English literature – influence of the Bible
              621.384.634:621.318.3 Synchrotrons – electromagnets
              635.965:632.38 Indoor plants – virus diseases

The colon is certainly a powerful tool, but because of its range of uses it is also rather imprecise; it shows that there is a relationship, but tells us nothing about the kind of relationship, or the correct citation order.

Square brackets are used to remove ambiguity in some colon combinations.

Example   23/28:294.3(540) Christian religion in relation to «Buddhism in India»
             [23/28:294.3](540) «Christian religion in relation to Buddhism» in India

The colon implies that the subjects related are of equal importance; either could come first, and in many card catalogues classified by UDC a second entry would have been made by reversing the colon combination: 632.38:635.965 as well as 635.965:632.38. (This is unnecessary in an OPAC.) We may not always wish to do this; there are situations where the second concept is clearly subsidiary. In this case we can use the double colon ::

Example   621.311.6::621.318.3 Power supplies for electromagnets, when we do not want an entry under electromagnets.

c)   Common auxiliaries of language = (equals sign). The notation for this common facet can be used as specified in the Languages schedule in class 811, Literatures of individual languages 821 and the common auxiliaries of ethnic grouping (f) below). The use of =03 for translations can be very useful.

Examples   53=112.2 Physics text in German
53=03.112.2=111 German physics text translated into English
53(038) =111=112.2 German-English dictionary of physics
811.111'36 English grammar (note that = is replaced by .)
821.111 English literature

It should be noted that the schedule for class 81 and for this auxiliary from all editions prior to 1992, including the 1985 English medium edition, have been completely revised. The example above will not be found in any edition of UDC prior to 1994.[5]

    d)   Common auxiliaries of form (0...). These schedules are worked out in great detail. Normally the bibliographical form is subordinate to the subject, and the notation is added to the subject notation. It is possible to reverse this if there is reason to group all instances of a particular bibliographical form together.

Examples   53(038) Dictionary of physics (filed with books on physics)
(038)53 Dictionary of physics (filed with other dictionaries)

    e)   Common auxiliaries of place (1/9). This schedule is well worked out, containing not only the geopolitical divisions but also several other subfacets of place, such as (1-08) unexplored regions. The notation may also be used to specify place in class 9 for geography and history, replacing the subdivisions spelled out prior to 1994.

Examples   26/28(94) Christian church in general in Australia
(1-15)   The West
23/28(1-15) Christian church in general in the western world
91(94)   Geography of Australia (previously 919.4)
94(94)   History of Australia (previously 994)
329(410)LAB The British Labour Party [grouping British political parties at 329(410)]

Auxiliaries which have notation that opens and closes may be interpolated, as in the above example. This applies to bibliographical forms, place, ethnic groups and time. In some cases, geopolitical divisions have changed over time. For the United Kingdom, the traditional divisions are listed at (411/429); modern divisions (following local government reorganization) are listed at (410).

    f)   Common auxiliaries of ethnic grouping and nationality (=...). This notation is largely derived from the table for languages. Political nationality may also be denoted, using the place auxiliary notation, but this will only be needed rarely, if at all. However, the place auxiliary can also be used to denote people living in particular physiographic regions.

Examples   (=111)   English-speaking peoples
398(=411.16)   Jewish folklore
(=1.253) Forest dwellers
78(=214.58) Gipsy music

g)   Common auxiliaries of time ". . . ''. Dates and times may be expressed exactly; spread of time is shown by using the /; forms of time other than dates may be expressed by "3/9" – though this does preclude the expression of dates after 2999 A D.

Examples   "19" twentieth century (Arabic numerals must be used)
"1994.08.22" August 22 1994
"1994.08.22.17.58" August 22 1994, 2 minutes to 6pm
"321" Spring
"1914/1918"   period of World War 1
53"1945/. . ." post-war physics
050"53" weekly periodicals

One possible problem is the separation of the history of a subject in general from the history of a particular period:

050(091) History of periodicals
050"19" [a history of] periodicals in the twentieth century

If this is likely to cause difficulties, (091) could be interpolated before the time subdivisions to give a focal point.

h)   Notation from non-UDC sources. This may be used in two different ways: notation from another source is preceded by an asterisk *, while alphabetical specification may be used directly wherever useful, e.g. in Literature.

Examples   Postcodes might be used to denote place:
(94*5000) → Adelaide, South Australia (5000 is the postcode)
(73*90210) → Beverly Hills
Names may be used for specific authors in literature, either in full or in standard abbreviated form, and may be interpolated:
821.111-2"15"Shakespeare7Hamlet → Literature – English –
                drama – 16th century – Shakespeare – individual
                works – Hamlet
821.133.1Molière → Literature – French – Molière

i)   Common auxiliaries of point of view .00 These must be added to a main number at the end, and are intended to specify the various points of view from which a subject may be considered.

Example   631.52.003.3 Agriculture – applied genetics – accountancy point
          of view

They may also be used to act as a kind of facet indicator, to give a more helpful order to colon combinations:

621.384.634   Particle accelerators – Synchrotrons
621.384.634.003.3   Synchrotrons from the accountancy point of view
621.384.634.004.62   Synchrotrons from the point of view of deterioration

Additional notation for various costs etc can be colonned at .003.3, while various causes of deterioration can be gathered at .004.62, avoiding a mishmash of colon combinations at the main number. The resulting notation is of course complex, and these auxiliaries should only be used where their addition is likely to result in a more helpful order for the user. A further use is that of .000.0/.9 to express the author's point of view:

Example   23/28.000.335.5 Christianity from the Marxist point of view

k)   Common auxiliaries of materials -03, of persons -05. -03 and its subdivisions may be used throughout the schedules as appropriate, wherever the material is a subordinate concept. Materials as primary concept are most commonly found in 66/67.

Example   699.844 Soundproofing materials
               699.844-037.52   made of fibreglass
               677.52   Fibreglass as a manufacturing product

-05 is similarly used to denote persons throughout the schedules where they are the subordinate concept.

Examples   02-055.1   Male librarians
               02-052   Library users

In addition to the common auxiliaries there are three other facet indicators used for the special auxiliary subdivisions. These are the hyphen -1/-9, the .0... and the apostrophe ', which have different meanings according to their context. These are used to introduce facets special to the containing heading:

Examples   62-31   Engineering – reciprocating valve gear parts
               821.111-31   Literature – English – novels
               621.3.066   Electrical switch mechanisms
               66.066   Clarification as a chemical engineering process
               669.22'24   Nickel-silver, from 669.22 silver, 669.24 nickel

Notational problems

It will have become clear from the above examples that the notation of UDC tends to be clumsy. This is due to two major causes. The first is that the schedules are frequently very detailed, far more so than other classifications. The second follows from the fact that most of the expansion has taken place in Science and Technology, to which Dewey allocated an inadequate notational base. For example, in the German full edition completed in 1952, Technology already accounted for 53% of the schedules, but only had one tenth of the notational base, Class 6. Since 1950, there have of course been further major developments in Technology. The base notation in this class thus tends to be long; when we add any of the auxiliaries, the notation of course gets longer still. Colon combinations can be lengthened by the need to repeat base numbers, e.g.

621.384.6:621.318.3:621.311.6 Power supplies for the electromagnets of
                               particle accelerators

in which 621.3 is repeated twice. This example, based on the full edition current in 1960, has fortunately been superseded! The medium edition has in general shorter notation, but this is often at the expense of detail; however, facilities for synthesis will always lengthen notation in any scheme. If we need to specify detailed subjects, then the resulting notation will be long; this is no different from the use of a long string of words to express the same subject.

UDC notation does have some advantages for computer searching. The same concept is normally represented by the same notation whenever it occurs, and the notation is largely hierarchical. However, neither of these is yet completely consistent, though UDC is rather better than DDC, where, as has been shown, the same concept may be represented by rather different notation in different situations.

The index

The index to BS 1000M 1985, published in 1988, was computer-generated, and the introduction was somewhat apologetic for the disadvantages of the method while pointing out that it does have the advantage that every term is indexed. The index to the second medium edition BS 1000M 1994 is produced by subject experts who are also skilled indexers, and thus avoids the kind of pitfall that befalls unedited computer production. Because of the amount of detail in the schedules, it is, as with any classification scheme, essential to refer back to the schedules from the index each time the correct piece of notation for a concept is sought, though the revised index is very much more helpful. The index also cannot help in leading to notation which is synthesised according to the rules of the scheme. For this reason, users must compile an *authority file* of the notation as it is used in their catalogue or arrangement. The authority file lists all of the results of synthesis, which are not shown in either the schedules or in the index, and must also show the citation order adopted; without such a control, the possibility of inconsistency becomes a certainty, particularly with colon combinations representing facet synthesis within a basic class.

Aids for the user

In 1963 BSI published a very useful *Guide to the use of the Universal Decimal Classification*, by J. Mills. This not only gave detailed explanations of how to use the schedules as they then existed, but also contained a very valuable introduction to the ideas of faceted classification, which at that time were still unknown to many people. A new *Guide to the use of UDC*[6] has now been prepared by I. McIlwaine, who heads the UDCC editorial panel. This omits the discussion of faceted classification which was an important part of Mills' work, on the grounds that students now learn this as a matter of course. The *Guide* gives a general introduction to the scheme, its history and background and current status, then discusses the auxiliaries. There is a detailed discussion of each class, with a wide range of examples to show how the schedules, and particularly synthesis, are used. A final chapter on the uses to which UDC may be put is followed by an additional chapter on the use of UDC in online systems by A. Buxton. From this latter chapter, it can be seen that some of the problems first identified by Freeman and Atherton in the AIP/UDC Project[7] still remain to be solved. The availability of the MRF may well lead to the solution of most if not all of these problems, which arise from the use of various punctuation marks as facet indicators in synthesis. The rationalization of the use of such auxiliaries as Place (. . .) and date in the History and Geography schedules, and the use of explicit facet analysis in schedule revision, will gradually eliminate many of the anomalies. The scheme has also been fitted into the MARC format, which may well solve many of the manipulation problems. A rather different approach to the same problem was proposed by Perrault,[8] who devised a very detailed set of relators to replace the colon using letter notation. Originally published in 1965, the schema has recently been revised and republished.

The future

UDC is widely used, particularly in special libraries, in the UK, throughout Europe, and in Australia, South America and North Africa. It was also the official classification for science and technology in the USSR, strongly supported by VINITI. Use has declined in recent years, for a variety of reasons. The main one was the inadequate revision and publication structure; several studies, including one by the present author,[9] set out ways in which the management might be improved. The publication of the English medium edition in 1985 was a major step forward; at last users had a reasonably up-to-date, full schedule to work with, in a manageable format – a notable improvement over the many fascicules of the full edition. The production of the MRF must be another major consolidation, giving as it does the possibility of regular updating (a subscription to the MRF includes any updates for three years), with the easy incorporation of extensions and corrections as they are completed, and annual publication of *E & C*.

Will all these changes be enough to enable the scheme to survive the financial stringencies of the future? Will the absence of UDC numbers from MARC records be a millstone round its neck? It does look as though the new structure is likely to be more financially successful than the old. Also, much of the material which is important in the special libraries which use UDC does not get into the MARC records in the first place, so that particular factor is not likely to be as important as it might be in, say, a public library. The move towards a totally faceted structure will make the use of the scheme easier for the classifier, and there is the planned collaboration with the BCA, to consider the use of some of the schedules, e.g. that for Medicine, compiled for the second edition of BC.[10] After a lengthy period of torpor, it seems as though once again UDC is alive and well, throwing off the lethargy of the past. With satisfactory computer retrieval of UDC notation a very real possibility, the scheme may see a bright future.

References

1   Rayward, W. B., *The universe of information: the work of Paul Otlet for documentation and international organization*, Moscow, VINITI for FID, 1975. (FID 520)

2   Bradford, S. C., *Documentation*, 2nd edn, Shera, J. H. (ed.), London, Crosby Lockwood, 1953.

3   Gilchrist, Alan, 'UDC: the 1990s and beyond' in *International study conference on classification research, Toronto, Canada, June 24–28 1991*, Williamson, N. J. and Hudon, M. (eds.), Elsevier, 1992, (FID 698), 69–77.
    Strachan, P. and Gilchrist, A., *The UDCC: essays for a new decade*, London, Aslib, 1990.
    'Report of the UDC Editor in Chief (I. C. McIlwaine)', *Extensions & corrections to the UDC*, **16**, 1994, 9–18.

4   Kyle, B., 'The Universal Decimal Classification: a study of the present position and future developments with particular reference to those schedules which deal with the humanities, arts and social sciences', *Unesco bulletin for libraries*, **15** (2), 1961, 53–69.
    Vickery, B. C., 'The UDC and technical information indexing', *Unesco bulletin for libraries*, **15** (3), 1961, 126–38, 147.

5   *The Universal decimal classification; International medium edition: English text*, The Hague, Universal Decimal Classification Consortium, 1994. 2v.

6   McIlwaine, I. C., *Guide to the use of UDC: an introductory guide to the use and application of the Universal Decimal Classification*, 2nd edn, The Hague, FID, 1995, (FID 703).

7   Freeman, R. R., 'The management of a classification scheme: modern approaches exemplified by the UDC project of the American Institute of Physics', *Journal of documentation*, **20** (3), 1964, 137–45.
    For a more recent study see Buxton, A. B., 'Computer searching of UDC numbers', *Journal of documentation*, **46** (3), 1990, 193–217.
    Buxton, A., 'Computer searching of UDC numbers', *Encyclopedia of library and information science*, **51**, 1993, 132–51.

8   Perreault, J. 'Categories and relators: a new schema', *Knowledge organization*, **21** (4), 1994, 189–98.

9   Foskett, A. C., *The Universal Decimal Classification*, London, Bingley, 1973.

10 Williamson, Nancy, 'Restructuring UDC: problems and possibilities' in *International study conference on classification research, Toronto, Canada, June 24–28 1991*, Williamson, N. J. and Hudon, M. (eds.), New York, Elsevier, 1992. (FID 698) p381–387.
    McIlwaine, I. C., 'UDC: the present state and future developments', *International cataloguing and bibliographic control*, **23** (2), 1994, 29–33.
    McIlwaine, I. C. and Williamson, N. J., 'Future revision of the UDC', *Extension & corrections to the UDC*, (**15**), 1993, 11–17.
    Williamson, N. J., 'Future revision of the UDC', *Extensions & corrections to the UDC*, **16**, 1994, 19–27.
    Strachan, P. D. and Oomes, F. M. H., 'Universal Decimal Classification update', *Classification and cataloging quarterly*, **19** (3/4), 1995, 119–32.

Chapter 19
The Bibliographic Classification

Henry Evelyn Bliss devoted his life's work to the study of classification, and BC1, the first edition of the Bibliographic Classification, was the result of his efforts, tested over a number of years in the library of the College of the City of New York, where he was librarian. In addition, he wrote two major works on classification: *The organization of knowledge and the system of the sciences*, 1929, and *The organization of knowledge in libraries*, 2nd ed. 1939. Yet despite his great erudition and powerful writings, his scheme had little practical success, and was virtually ignored in the USA, finding favour mainly among librarians in colleges of education in the UK. Also, Bliss does not always seem to have appreciated fully the ramifications of some of his ideas, particularly his tentative attempts at facet analysis. The scheme was published postwar, but many of the schedules show little effect from the changes in knowledge arising from the war. Volume I, containing the common facets and classes A to G, was first published in 1940, volume II, classes H to K, in 1946; these two volumes were revised and published as one in 1951. Volume III, classes L to Z, appeared in 1953, as did the index, Volume IV. Bliss died shortly afterwards. Volume I opened with a lengthy (188p) introduction in two parts, covering problems of classification in general, and of the Natural sciences in particular. Like most of Bliss's writings, this is a valuable contribution to classificatory thinking, though his comments on schemes other than his own tend to be as scathing as those of Metcalfe on analytico-synthetic classification!

Bliss considered the order of main classes to be the most important feature of the scheme, and devoted most of his efforts to finding one that should be widely acceptable. The principles on which he based his order of main classes have been discussed in Chapter 9: collocation of related subjects, gradation by speciality and subordination of special to general, together forming the scientific and educational consensus. While on the whole these ideas are sound, they did lead to some odd results, such as the separation of science from technology by the whole of the social sciences. However, it is worth pointing out that the main class order of the BSO, which was arrived at by a quite different approach, does bear a strong resemblance to that of Bliss. One result of Bliss's concentration on the overall order was that he had less time to devote to detail; the modern approach would be to build up from the detail, arriving at the overall order by a process of induction.

In looking at detail, Bliss saw the need for some synthesis – *composite specifi-*

cation – and provided a set of common facets, to be used anywhere in the scheme, as well as some facets for specific subjects. He did not accept the need for the completely analytico-synthetic approach taken by Ranganathan, so his approach was somewhat erratic; though he provided for a good measure of synthesis, he also enumerated many subjects which could well have been synthesized, in some cases giving them notation which did not conform to the synthesized notation.

The notation of the scheme generally was also variable in quality. Bliss held strongly that notation should be short and simple, and used capital letters to give a longer base than numerals. The notation was not expressive, so little-used headings could be given long notation while their more widely used subdivisions had shorter, e.g.:

AK	Science in general
AZ	Physical science in general
AZD	Physics and chemistry
B	Physics
C	Chemistry

Unfortunately, from time to time Bliss allowed his zeal for short notation to distort the order, so that Shakespeare in YF comes not only after YEN Shakespeare's contemporaries, which is legitimate but not in accordance with favoured category, but also *after* YEW Caroline period, which is blatantly incorrect. (Shakespeare died some ten years before Charles I came to the throne!). Bliss also used mixed notation, with numerals for the common facets and lower case letters for place; the results of synthesis could not be said to be either short or simple. Bliss himself gives as examples TSQ,BbSVU and JTNbd,06,L, neither of which seems to meet his own criteria of brevity and simplicity. When one adds in the other devices used by BC1, such as the apostrophe and the hyphen, and tries to sort out the filing order,[1] the notation looks highly impractical. Bliss also made the same mistake as Dewey in allocating his notation; an undue proportion went to History, L to O, and far too little to Technology, subsumed in U Arts in general, and useful and industrial arts.

The index also appears to be very detailed, but on inspection turns out not to be constructed as a relative index; in other words, many of the entries simply repeat the schedules, while many entries which would have been useful are not there. A revised edition would no doubt have corrected most of these errors and omissions. The overall production of the scheme left much to be desired; Bliss typed out the whole of the schedules himself, using a very limited range of type sizes, with italic and reverse italic for scope notes and cross-references. The scheme was also unpaginated, which makes using it much more difficult, since the auxiliary schedules used for synthesis within subjects are rarely where one would expect them to be. (It is perhaps only fair to point out that the first edition of DDC to be paginated was DDC15!).

The second edition

The scheme was published by the H. W. Wilson Company, but at the end of 1966 they decided to hand over the rights to the British Bliss Classification Association (BCA). Money was raised to employ a research assistant under the direction of J. Mills, and work began on a complete revision of the scheme. Plans were made to publish the second edition in two volumes in 1973, but this proved impossible, and work is still in progress over 20 years later, though many of the schedules have now been published, and others are to appear shortly. Education is in fact now in its second edition, reflecting the fact that many of the users are in the field of education; Social Welfare is now also in its second edition, and is the most widely used class.

The main class order is very much as planned by Bliss except that Bibliology, Bibliography, Documentation and Libraries, previously in Z, have been moved to the beginning of the scheme in the Generalia class, and some other minor changes have been made. Each class is worked out on strict analytico-synthetic principles, and a computer program has been written to produce the schedules and the index for each class; this will also facilitate the compilation of an overall index when the schedules are complete. There will normally be no composite subjects in the scheme, so an authority file of usage will be an essential tool for the classifier using the scheme. The scheme remains discipline-oriented, but provision has been made in the Generalia class to accommodate works about Entities, Processes or Attributes from all aspects – the situations where DDC has an instruction Class comprehensive works here; alternatively such works may be accommodated in the main schedules at their place of 'unique definition' – in other words, within their permanent generic hierarchy rather than any of the quasi-generic locations where they may also be found.

Analysis into facets is accompanied by a strict citation order, usually following the idea of dependence. The schedule order is the reverse of the citation order, in accordance with the principle of inversion. The notation has been greatly simplified, and now uses only upper-case letters and numerals; the latter are used to introduce the common facets, and to act as phase indicators where necessary. The notation is retroactive, which allows synthesis without the need for facet indicators in most situations; it does however oblige the classifier to use the specified citation order, which may not always be the best in a particular environment. In this case, it is possible to use the hyphen as a facet indicator to give a different citation order; however, as we have seen in Chapter 9, this will mean that general will not always precede special.

Bliss provided a number of alternative treatments for certain classes, and the new edition also allows for some preliminary choices; once the choice has been made, other alternatives must of course be deleted. Geography in BC1 was scattered in a number of places in addition to its main location collocated with History; BC2 gives the possibility of locating all aspects of Geography in Earth sciences. Religion, normally found between History and Social Welfare, may be transferred to the end of the main class sequence following Language and literature. At the subclass level, International law may be placed in Law rather than in Political science; Social psychology may be included in Sociology rather than in Psychology.

The Generalia class represents a new approach. It begins with a classification of documents by physical form, e.g. Motion pictures, Sound recordings, followed by

Forms of presentation and arrangement, e.g. Periodicals and Encyclopedias, for documents *about* these forms, not documents *in* these forms (which are represented by the bibliographical form facet). Next is the section on Entities, Processes and Attributes mentioned earlier. Finally comes the Universe of knowledge, and Communication and information, which includes Computer science and Documentation.

The Main classes are preceded by volume 1, which contains the Introduction and Common facets. The Introduction is a lengthy (over 100 pages) explanation of the basic principles of analytico-synthetic classification and their application in BC2. Chapters 4 and 5 can be read with profit by anyone interested in the theory of classification. The Auxiliary schedules (common facets) are comprehensive, and include the following:

1	Common forms
	Common subjects, including Persons (Schedule 1A)
	Phase relations
	Time (Schedule 4)
	Place (Schedule 2)
1A	Persons
2	Place
3	Language (for use where specified in the schedules)
3A	Ethnic groups
4	Time (History), with three alternatives

Full instructions are given with each; the use of an Auxiliary schedule is normally indicated by a number taken from Auxiliary schedule 1 to serve as a facet indicator, e.g. 7 Time, 8 Place. Volume 1 concludes with three summaries of progressively great detail, corresponding to the three summaries in DDC; these are a major aid to the classifier, particularly as the scheme will have no general index until all the parts have been completed.

Notation

The notation uses only upper case letters and numerals; the hyphen may also be used by the classifier wishing to depart from the specified citation order. The filing order is 1/9–A/Z, so that the Generalia class and the auxiliary schedules file before the main classes and their subdivisions. Within classes, the notation is retroactive; this allows synthesis of notation for composite subjects while preserving the general to special order. Retroactive notation has some disadvantages, one of which is that the room for subdivision becomes restricted as one moves through the notation. To resolve this, a letter may be used as a facet indicator, though this is not always as simple as might be expected; though full instructions are always given, the classifier must have a sound grasp of notational synthesis if these are to be followed properly. As mentioned earlier, an authority file is an essential complement to the schedules. Some examples from the Education schedules will illustrate the method:

J	Education	[not repeated in synthesizing notation]
JI	Teaching methods and aids	
JIB	Teaching aids	
JIE	Audiovisual materials	
JIP	Television	
JL	Educands and Educational institutions	
JLD	Schools by various characteristics	
JLD E	Urban schools	
JLD EIP	Television in urban schools	
JV	Special categories of educand	
JVE	Socially disadvantaged	
JVE M	Immigrants	
JVG	Language and ethnic groups	
JVG X	*By cultural or ethnic group*	
JVG XBF	Coloured persons	(From Table 3A)
JVG XBF EM	Coloured immigrants	
JVG XBF EM 8EA	Great Britain	(8 facet indicator; Table 2)

= The education of coloured immigrants in Britain

5V	Bibliographies	(From Table 1, common sub-

division)

JIB	Teaching aids, educational materials *etc*	
JK	Curriculum	
JKA IB	Curriculum materials	(A = facet indicator)
JU	Adult education	
JUK AIB	Curriculum materials for adult education	
JUK AIB 5V	Bibliographies of curriculum materials for adult education	

For convenience, the notation is split up into groups of three digits, as is DDC. It is not expressive, so that in Q Social welfare we find QR Offenders as a subdivision of QO Criminals; as shown above, in J Education, Television JIP is a subdivision of Audiovisual materials JIE, which is a subdivision of Teaching aids JIB. The purely ordinal value is helpful for shelving and locating, but does not display the hierarchy; this would making searching by computer more difficult, but could be accommodated by the USMARC format: classification.

Indexes

Each part has its own index as it is published, produced by the computer program which produces the printed schedules. The indexes are produced on strict chain principles, and the final index will be produced once the schedules are all completed. However, it is important to remember that, as the scheme is completely analytico-synthetic, no composite subjects are listed in the schedules, and therefore none will be indexed. The classifier will not only need an authority file in classified order, but also an index to it. The lack of a complete index to LCC and the Full edition of UDC has always been seen as a disadvantage, and the nature of the BC2 schedules makes it just as important, but still not a final answer to practical everyday use.

Production of schedules

Early volumes in the series were produced from typescript reduced in size; with the introduction of computer production, the standard has greatly improved, and the schedules are now clear and readable (they were always *legible*, but this is not the same thing!). Following is an up-to-date list of schedules published or soon to be published.[2]

	Introduction and common facets (Auxiliary schedules) (1977)
2/9	Generalia, Phenomena, Information and communication (?; to be done)
A/AL	Philosophy, Logic (1991)
AM/AX	Mathematics, Statistics (1993)
AY/B	General Science and technology; Physics (1996?)
C	Chemistry (1996?)
D/DG	Astronomy (?; to be done)
DH/DY	Earth sciences (?; to be done)
E/G	Biological sciences (drafts prepared)
GR/GY	Applied Biology (1997?)
H	Anthropology, Health sciences, Medicine (1981)
I	Psychology and Psychiatry (1978)
J	Education (2nd ed 1990)
K	Social sciences (1984)
L/O	History, Geography, Biography
P	Religion, The occult (1977)
Q	Social welfare (1977) (2nd revised and enlarged ed 1994)
R	Politics (1995?)
S	Law (1995?)
T	Economics, Management of economic enterprises (1987)
U/V	Technology (?; well advanced)
W	Art and Design (1996?)
WV	Music (?)
X/Y	Language and Literature (?)

Several volumes have now been published, while dates with a ? are proposed on the basis of current progress. Many are already in draft form, and some have already been used by bodies such as the National Library of Agriculture (NAL) as the basis for their new thesauri.[3] If publication continues at the present rate, the full scheme could be completed by about 1998. As mentioned, the computer program used to produce the schedules also produces the indexes, which speeds up the publication process. Many of the schedules not yet published are available in draft form, some needing only final checking and the addition of notation to complete them. The scheme is being used by a number of significant libraries in Britain, and the revision seems to have gathered enough momentum to carry it through to completion. There is also a suggestion that the schedules might form a basis for the revision of UDC.[4]

The future

Despite these efforts, it would be optimistic to assume that the scheme has an assured future. It is still very much in the hands of the Editor, J. Mills, who has now 'retired', though others are becoming involved in the revision of some classes, and the BCA is certainly very active. Economics preclude the inclusion of BC class numbers in BL MARC records, while other major libraries contributing to the MARC database, such as LC and NLA, are most unlikely to take part in this kind of exercise. While PRECIS was used as the indexing system for the *BNB*, it could also have been used to generate BC2 class numbers from the revised scheme, but this is no longer relevant. It is a pity that this modern scheme, with its superior main class order and detailed analytico-synthetic schedules, seems likely to remain on the sidelines except in a limited number of libraries in the UK, though its potential use in UDC could change the picture radically. There is no doubt that it will continue to be a rich source for thesaurus construction, as well as those who wish to use their own special classification. Mills believes that the scheme will be self-supporting, with the money being gained from sales for thesaurus construction, as well as sales of the schedules. Certainly library schools wishing to demonstrate analytico-synthetic classification would find this by far the best model.

References

1   Mills, J., 'Number building and filing order in BC', *Bliss classification bulletin*, **II** (1), 1957.
2   Maltby, A. and Gill, L., *The case for Bliss: modern classification practice and principles in the context of the Bibliographic Classification*, London, Bingley, 1979.
    Thomas, A. R., 'Bliss regained: the second edition of the Bliss Bibliographic Classification', *Wilson library bulletin*, **67**, March 1993 56–7; June 93, 10.
    Thomas, A. R. 'Bliss Bibliographic Classification 2nd edition: principal features and applications', *Cataloging & classification quarterly*, **16** (4), 1993, 138.
    [Report on progress by the CRG and BCA] *International classification*, **18** (3), 1991, 159.
    Thomas, A. R., 'Bliss classification update', *Cataloging and classification quarterly*, **19** (3/4), 1995, 105–18.
3   Aitchison, J., 'A classification as a source for a thesaurus: The Bibliographic Classification of H. E. Bliss as a source of thesaurus terms and structure', *Journal of documentation*, **42** (3), 1986, 160–81. (Education courses and occupations thesaurus; Department of Health and Social Security thesaurus)
4   Williamson, N. J., 'Restructuring UDC: problems and possibilities', *Classification research for knowledge representation and organization: proceedings of the 5th International study conference on classification research, Toronto, Canada, June 24–28 1991*, Williamson, N. J. and Hudon, M. (eds.), Elsevier, 1992, (FID 698), 381–7. (Using BC2 as a mapping device.)
    McIlwaine, I. C. and Williamson, N. J., 'Future revision of the UDC',

Extension & corrections to the UDC, **(15)**, 1993, 11–17.

Williamson, N. J., 'Future revision of the UDC', *Extensions & corrections to the UDC*, **(16)**, 1994, 19–27.

Chapter 20

The Broad System of Ordering

The Royal Society's scientific information conference[1] in 1948 demonstrated the concern of the scientific community that existing methods of publishing and disseminating information were proving inadequate to cope with the ever-increasing flood of scientific and technical publication – the information explosion. Several possible lines of action were pursued. The Royal Society published two bibliographies, one a guide to scientific journals reporting original work, the other a list of journals containing abstracts; both of these were indeed useful when they were published, but the Society appears to have assumed that they would remain valid indefinitely, an assumption unfortunately ill-founded. Professor J. D. Bernal suggested the replacement of the scientific journal by the publication of abstracts only instead of complete papers, which would be available as separates on demand, a suggestion which has been revived by Garfield,[2] while more recent advocates of paperless publishing see electronic journals as the means of publication of the future – in effect, the disappearance of the journal in its present physical format altogether; however, as with Mark Twain, the death of the journal seems to have been greatly exaggerated. All in all, there was agreement that serious problems existed, but few practical solutions could be found.

In 1958, the Scientific Information Conference in Washington[3] was dominated by the computer, with its glittering prospects of good things to come. Many of the predictions proved to be overoptimistic, and though one could not envisage information retrieval now without the computer, developments have tended to be linked to the improvement of existing services and their exploitation rather than in any startling new directions. Even *Science Citation Index*, possibly the only completely novel publication to have appeared in this field since 1958, is based on a principle which had been recognized many years earlier. Recent developments in information technology have enabled us to exchange large quantities of information, including graphics, through our computers, but for the vast majority of people methods of publication and dissemination of information remain basically unchanged.

UNISIST and the BSO

During the 1960s, a new force began to make itself felt. Those countries which were already to the fore in science and technology certainly faced problems in the handling of information, but were on the whole managing to keep these problems under control; the situation for Developing Countries was very different. They felt that they were increasingly at a disadvantage in not having the same access to the free flow of scientific and technical information as the industrialized world. In 1967, a joint central committee was set up by Unesco and ICSU to carry out a feasibility study of a world science information system, to be given the name UNISIST. The committee produced a detailed report[4] after some four years of deliberation, and this was largely approved at an international conference in October 1971, at which 111 countries and 62 international organizations were represented. one of the recommendations of the report was that:

> The attention of scientists, learned societies, and information associations should be drawn to the need for joint efforts in developing better tools for the control and conversion of natural and indexing languages in science and technology.

In particular, a need was seen for a universally acceptable 'switching language' which could be applied to all publications to indicate the subject field they covered.

The concept of a switching language needs some examination here. The generally accepted meaning has been an indexing language into which one could translate any existing index language as an intermediate stage in converting it into any other indexing language; for example, one might use UDC in this way, in those areas where the schedules are up to date. A German librarian faced with the term 'optical character recognition devices' could look this up in the Full English edition of UDC and find the notation 681.327.5'12; the German edition would then show the equivalent in German of this piece of notation. Coates[5] has pointed out that in order to make this possible, the switching language must be at least as detailed as the most detailed language it is expected to switch, otherwise the specificity of the original subject will be degraded. However, this was not the kind of switching language that UNISIST had in mind; what was envisaged was a much broader classification, to be applied to whole blocks of information, e.g. a journal, rather than to individual documents. It could also be used to denote the subject coverage of an institution; for example, the International Atomic Energy Agency would be given the appropriate notation for nuclear science and technology. Such coding would be of considerable help to librarians faced with publications in an unfamiliar language (such as Japanese, for the vast majority of English speakers), and would facilitate the flow of information.

Aslib was commissioned as part of the study to examine existing classification schemes to see whether any of them would fill the bill satisfactorily, and came to the conclusion that UDC was probably the best of those available, but that none of them was particularly good. UDC might have shown up better if the schedules had been available in full, but as is shown in Chapter 18, this was not the case; at the time of the comparison a substantial part of the English full edition was either not available at all, or was so out of date as to be in effect unavailable. UNISIST therefore came to the decision that a completely new scheme should be developed, to be known as the Standard Reference Code. An alternative name was also suggested, the Standard Roof Classification; this also abbreviates to SRC and was intended to emphasize the purpose of the scheme in providing a 'roof' which would serve to cover the whole of scientific and technical information at the broad level required.

A sub-committee of FID was set up to develop the proposed new scheme, including G. A. Lloyd, then Head of the Classification Secretariat of FID and thus the man directly responsible for the day to day running of UDC. In 1974 the FID/SRC Working Group was succeeded by a three-man panel consisting of Lloyd, E. J. Coates and D. Simandl, and in 1975 a provisional draft, without notation, was circulated to some 400 experts for comment. In 1976 a first draft of the scheme, complete with notation, was produced, taking the comments received on the provisional schedule into account. This was followed in 1977 by a second draft, with alphabetical index, incorporating the results of further study by the Panel; this draft was tested by 26 institutions in 1976, and the final draft, once again revised in the light of this test, was published in 1978.[6] The scheme then underwent further testing, and was extensively reviewed in an issue of *International forum for information and documentation* containing an introduction by Coates and five comments, ranging from favourable to hostile.[7] A *Manual*[8] was published including detailed notes on how to use the schedules and notation; since the scheme used non-hierarchical synthetic notation, these instructions were essential, especially for the inexperienced.

More significantly, a change was made which distinguished the scheme radically from other schemes discussed in this book. Rather than literary warrant, institutional warrant was used to justify inclusion or exclusion of a subject. It was intended to provide a level of detail adequate to specify information-generating institutions and their publications as wholes, but not for specific items such as periodical articles. Further testing took place between 1981 and 1983, which confirmed both the overall validity of the scheme and the need for more detail. Work continued under the auspices of FID until 1990, when responsibility was passed to the newly-formed BSO Panel Ltd. The revised scheme has now been published in computer-readable (ASCII) files, which is seen as a more practical method of publishing a small edition than print.

Looking at the overall order, one is immediately struck by the similarity between this and the main class order of BC, even extending to the separation of science from technology by the social sciences. However, the panel did work from first principles, and point out in the introduction that while it is relatively straightforward to separate the physical sciences from their technologies (a point which one may doubt in these days of solid-state devices), it is more difficult to separate the biological sciences from their application, and – as Dewey found – almost impossible in medicine.

The amount of detail in the scheme has increased from some 3,500 headings in the first edition to about 12,000 in the revision, and the index has also been greatly expanded, to about 12,300 entries, though this still represents a much lower intensity of indexing than is found in, for example, DDC. The notation is synthetic; each of the 'main classes' is described as a *combination area*, and detailed instructions are given on how the notation for composite subjects is to be constructed.

Although the setting up of the BSO Panel Ltd, together with the use of computer files for editing, has made the existence of the scheme more secure, it still needs to sell a reasonable number of copies each year to cover the costs of updating and revision. Publication in machine-readable format will certainly keep the production costs to a minimum, though whether users will find this method convenient remains to be seen. The same thing applies of course to DDC, which is however available in print form as well as machine-readable, and has a very much larger customer base already well established. The BSO editorial panel are, with one exception, near or beyond retiring age, which must also raise doubts about the long-term prospects. The scheme faces a Catch-22 situation; with more users the scheme can keep going, but it will be difficult to get more users unless the scheme can keep going. The next few years should show whether the scheme is to continue, or fall by the wayside like so many others.

The scheme

The layout of Figure 20.1 is intended to show that we can think of the sequence of subjects as an endless chain; the list ends with Esoteric practices and movements, which could well be said to lead into Philosophy. A linear sequence of classes is obtained by cutting into this cyclic structure at a chosen point. The classes separated at the point of division are the first and last classes of the linear sequence. The editors suggest that the circle could be cut at almost any point to give a starting point and end, but that the one they have chosen is a convenient one. A more conventional layout is used in Figure 20.2, which shows the 'main classes' set out in the more usual linear order. At this level, the notation is always three digits, and is not hierarchical; for example:

200	Science and technology
203	Natural sciences
300	Life sciences
359	Applications of the life sciences
370	Forestry

The schedules

In addition to the 'endless belt' presentation, the schedules are given at three levels. The first outline, giving the 60 'main classes', shows the general structure of the scheme, though somewhat unevenly; **Applications of the life sciences** are given in some detail, with six subdivisions listed, but **Technology** has no sub-divisions. In the second outline, **Applications of the life sciences** lists 27 headings, while **Technology** has 98. These outlines serve the same purpose as the **Summaries** in DDC, and provide a convenient guide to the overall structure. The full schedules are given in a lengthy file; because of the synthetic nature of the scheme, the possibilities for specification are much greater than the headings actually listed. Instructions, indicated by an asterisk *, are given wherever necessary, but may not always strike the generalist as helpful, since they may assume a level of knowledge which is not shared by all classifiers.

480 Sports/games	Humanities/social studies	500
470 Human needs	History/related sciences	510
460 Education	Area studies	520
450 Psychology	Society	527
445 Behavioural sciences	Social sciences	530
420 Medicine	Sociology	535
410 Biomedical sciences	Demography	537
390 Environment	Politics	540
380 Wildlife exploitation	Public administration	550
370 Forestry	Law	560
366 Animal husbandry	Social welfare	570
360 Agriculture	Economics	580
359 Applications of life sciences	Enterprise management	588
340 Zoology	Technology	600
330 Botany	Production technology	620
320 Microbiology	Materials handling	625
310 Biological sciences	Packaging/storage	627
310 Life sciences	Energy technology	631
290 Geography	Materials technology	635
270 Geology	Nuclear technology	640
260 Earth sciences	Electrotechnology	650
250 Space & earth sciences	Thermal engineering	670
230 Chemistry	Mechanical engineering	680
228 Crystallography	Construction technology	710
210 Physics	Environmental technology	730
205 Physical sciences	Transport technology	740
203 Natural sciences	Military science/technology	760
200 Science & technology	Mining	780
188 Metrology	Process industries	800
186 Testing & trials	Metal technology	860
182 Research	Wood/pulp/paper technology	871,95
166 Standardisation	Textiles technology	877
165 Management	Particular products manf.	890
160 Systemology/cybernetics	Language/literature	910
150 Communication sciences	Arts	940
140 Information sciences	Religion/atheism	970
120 Mathematics	Esoteric practices	992
118 Logic		
112 Philosophy		

Fig. 20.1 Endless chain presentation of BSO order

088 Phenomena & entities from multi- or non-disciplinary point of view
SUBJECT FIELDS

100	Knowledge Generally	460	Education
112	Philosophy	470	Human Needs
116	Science Of Science	480	Sports & Games
118	Logic	500	Humanities & Social Studies
120	Mathematics	510	History & Related Sciences
125	Statistics & Probability	520	Area Studies
128	Computer Science	527	Society
140	Information Sciences	528	Social Groups & Communities
150	Communication Sciences	530	Social Sciences
160	Systemology & Cybernetics	533	Cultural Anthropology
165	Management	535	Sociology
182	Research	537	Demography
186	Testing & Trials	540	Political Science & Politics
188	Metrology	550	Public Administration
200	Science & Technology (Together)	560	Law
203	Natural Sciences	570	Social Welfare
205	Physical Sciences	580	Economics
210	Physics	588	Management of Enterprises
230	Chemistry	600	Technology
250	Space & Earth Sciences	700	Technology
300	Life Sciences	800	Technology
359	Applications of Life Sciences	910	Language & Literature
360	Agriculture	940	Arts
368	Veterinary Science	943	Plastic Arts
370	Forestry	945	Graphic Fine Arts
380	Wildlife Exploitation	947	Photography as Art
390	Environment	949	Decorative Arts & Handicrafts
410	Biomedical Sciences	950	Music & Performance Arts
445	Behavioural Sciences	970	Religion & Atheism
450	Psychology	992	Esoteric Practices & Movements

Fig. 20.2 Main class order in BSO: first summary

The main schedules are preceded by three tables. The first of these is a table of types of information source, permitting the classifier to specify organizations and secondary sources of information, e.g. abstracts and indexes; these can be further divided if necessary by place of origin or language. Second comes the Time facet, which has six broad periods, e.g. Mediaeval times (c500–c1500 AD), followed by an alternative which allows one to specify specific dates, though only to the year.

The third is the Place facet, which is somewhat unusual for a classification scheme. It begins with Physical zones or areas e.g. Tropical zones, Water areas, then the two Hemispheres, East and West. Next comes areas defined by ethnic, linguistic or religious features, then politically defined areas, which parallels the Physical areas.

Finally comes a list of specific countries, designated by the two-letter codes from ISO 3166; this is not of course a systematic arrangement, for which one would presumably have to turn to the physical areas section. Like all other schemes, the list has been overtaken by events in Eastern Europe; the USSR is there, with notation SU, but the individual states, e.g. Russia, are not mentioned. Revisions to ISO 3166 will be made in due course, and will then presumably lead to changes in the BSO listing.

The schedules proper begin with a place for entities and phenomena from a multi- or non-disciplinary point of view. This was found necessary because of the disciplinary approach taken in the scheme, but this location is only to be used when a subject cannot be accommodated in the normal arrangement. Detail in the schedules is uneven, being based on the needs found in the various tests which have been carried out. There is of course no reason why additional detail should not be included as it arises, but this does imply the need for an active editorial panel in contact with new situations as they occur. However, the editors do point out that the structure of the scheme is intended to make future additions straightforward, while also making the point that the facilities for synthesis will often remove the need for special provision for new subjects.

Notation

The basic notation for all the major divisions consists of three digits; further subdivision is shown by commas followed by two digits, to whatever detail is found necessary. This combination of millesimal and centesimal notation is intended to give plenty of notational space. As the notation is not intended to be expressive, it should be possible to insert a new concept at any point in the schedules, though this may eventually mean losing the 3,2,2,. . . pattern. Basic classes within which synthesis may take place along normal faceted lines are listed in a table of 'Combination areas'. Synthesis within a specific combination area is referred to as 'internal', while synthesis involving subjects from another combination area is 'external' Synthesis takes place within Combination areas according to reasonably straightforward rules, using the zero 0 and the hyphen. The schedules are constructed on faceted lines, following the Principle of inversion, so that combination of various elements within a Combination area is always in reverse schedule order. 'External' relationships use the hyphen, relying on general principles to indicate which is the primary phase; in cases of, e.g., comparison, double entry is made, using the specific notation -08. To link foci from within the same Combination area, write down the two pieces of notation in reverse schedule order, with space for two digits between them. Delete the first digit of the second item, then insert ,0, to link the two remaining pieces of notation. For example:

370   Forestry
370,40   Forest management
370,60   Special forests and forestry
370,63   Coniferous forests
Management of coniferous forests 370,63,0,70,40

Within Technology 600/890, the method differs slightly; instead of deleting the first digit of the second item, insert a comma after it, and ,0 between the two pieces of notation. For example:

811   Chemical engineering
811,65   Distillation technology
825   Petroleum technology
825,40   Petroleum products
825,47   Petrochemicals
Distillation of petrochemicals 825,47,08,11,65

In many cases, provision for synthesis already exists. For example,

910   LANGUAGE & LITERATURE = Philology
915   LITERATURE = Belles lettres = Literary art
915,30   Literary genres
                *   Expand 915,30 to 915,48 with meanings as
                      at 940,30 to 940,48, [Art history] using -01...
                      (see File BSO16) to specify time & date as needed
915,52   Folk literature
915,54   Popular & light literature
915,56   "Serious" & intellectual literature
915,64   Biography & memoirs
          * For biography in history, see 510,24
915,66   Travel literature
915,67   Adventure literature
915,68   Mystery & detection literature
915,70   Literary forms
915,72   Poetry & verse
915,74   Prose
              * Including literary essays
915,76   Novel & short story = Fiction
915,76,30   Genres of the novel
                     *   Expand 915,76,52 to 915,76,68 with
                           meanings as at 915,52 to 915,68
915,76,70   Science fiction
915,78   Drama = Plays
              *   For performance & production aspects of
                    drama, see 955
920   SPECIAL PHILOLOGICAL STUDIES
          *   Language & literature taken together
          *   The following numbers may be added to any BSO
                code 921 to 928 for a particular language or
                language group
          . . .
          ,15 Literature (not language & linguistics)

      *   Expand ,15,10 to ,15,78 with
            meanings as at 915,10 to 915,78

       . . .

921	Indo-European languages & literatures
921,50	Germanic languages & literatures
921,50,15	Germanic literature
921,52	English
921,52,15	English literature

So *English detective novels* has the notation   921,52,15,76,68

The schedule begins with Class 088, Phenomena and entities from a multi- or non-disciplinary point of view. This is only to be used for very general works which cannot be fitted into the disciplinary structure of the main schedules. It uses notation from the main schedules as necessary; an example shows both the power and the problems of the method:

088   PHENOMENA & ENTITIES
          This class is for phenomena or entities treated from a multidisciplinary or non-disciplinary point of view. It is to be used only when emphasis on one discipline is lacking. The content of this class will be mainly materials and organisms

088,225,80   Liquids
          *   In all their aspects
          *   Liquids are uniquely defined by properties covered by the discipline of Physics, within which Physics of Liquids is coded 225,80

088,235,50,1-2,8   Water
          *   In all its aspects
          *   Water is uniquely defined by its formula representing properties belonging to the discipline of Chemistry, within which Chemistry of Water is coded 235,50,1-2,8

Turning to Physics, we find:

200   SCIENCE & TECHNOLOGY
          *   Science & technology treated together
          *   For natural science, see 203
          *   For individual sciences, see 210 to 345
  210   Physics
  222   Bulk matter physics = Macrophysics
          *   The properties of bulk matter whether in fluid or solid
state
  224,83   Fluid physics
          *   Gases & liquids taken together
  225   Condensed matter physics
          *   Liquids & solids together

225,80   Physics of liquids
    *   Expand 225,80,18 to 225,80,79 with
         meanings as at 225,18 to 225,79.
         Some examples follow, together with addition-
         al notations & captions for concepts special to
         this area which are not found explicitly within
         225,18 to 225,79

So the notation for liquids as a multi-disciplinary concept is constructed by adding
the notation for liquids from Physics to 088. For water, which is an inorganic chemical compound, we have to turn to Chemistry:

230   Chemistry
    *   For chemical technology, see 812
235   Inorganic chemistry
235,50   (Specific inorganic compounds)
         *   Specify as for radicals at 234,28 by adding atomic num-
              bers of constituent elements, separated by a comma, with
              number of atoms (when more than 1) denoted by -2, -3
              etc.,
         e.g.. 235,50,1-2,16,8-4 Sulphuric acid H_2SO_4
              235,50,(7,1-4),-2,16,8-4 Ammonium sulphate
              $(NH_4)_2SO_4$.
              235,50,13-2,8-3 Alumina Al_2O_3.
              235,50,20,6,8-3 Calcium carbonate $CaCO_3$
              235,50,80-2,17-2 Mercurous chloride
              Hg_2Cl_2

While this certainly allows you to specify any chemical compound, and file the
results in a reasonable order, it does require a knowledge of chemical formulae and
the Periodic Table which may mean much thumbing of reference tools. Of course,
once the notation for a particular compound has been entered in the authority file, it
does not have to be reconstructed each time, but can be found through the alphabetical index constructed by the classifier.

    To link subjects which are from different combination areas ('external' combi-
nations), the hyphen is used. The order in which the combination is made depends
on the sense, and follows the kinds of rules we have suggested for phase relationships; thus:

125   Statistics and probability
125,20   Descriptive statistics
143   Libraries and library science
143,68   Public libraries
    Statistics for public librarians 125-143,68
    Public library statistics 143,68-125,20

Publication

The scheme is available on three 720k floppy disks, which contain various ASCII files which can be read by any word processor or editor. The first file of significance contains the introduction to the third revision of 1978 (BSO12) and the introduction to the 4th revision (BSO13). BSO14 gives instructions on notational synthesis and filing order, while BSO 15, 16 and 17 contain the optional form facet, the time facet and place facet. BSO18 contains the first and second outlines, while the full schedules occupy the whole of the second disk (BSO20). The index is on the third disk in file BSO21. The layout of the schedules is straightforward, so that they can be easily read on the screen, though one does not have the full two-page spread of a printed version. For those who prefer print, the instructions can be printed out – as indeed could the schedules, though the result would have only very simple formatting because of the limitations of the ASCII character set.

The future

Will the new revision be successful? Or will it become one of the interesting sidelines in the history of classification, like Brown's *Subject classification* or Rider's *International classification*? Interest has been shown in Europe, and it might well be used in developing countries which do not have the same vested interest in DDC as the USA, UK and Australia. Will the scheme have the active support of Unesco, who commissioned it in the first place as part of UNISIST? Could it find a place in helping to organize the Internet? It has been thoroughly tested as a classification, and has all the facilities for growth and synthesis that one could wish, but the organization remains weak compared with the massive backing for DDC and LCC. It will be interesting to see whether the computer-readable format gains acceptance.

References

1   Royal Society, Scientific information conference, *Proceedings*, London, Royal Society, 1948.
2   Garfield, E., 'Is there a future for the scientific journal?', *SciTech news*, **29** (2), 1975, 42–4.
3   International conference on scientific information, Washington DC, 1958, *Proceedings*. Washington, DC, National Academy of Sciences, 1959, 2v.
4   *UNISIST: Study report on the feasibility of a world scientific information system*, Paris, Unesco, 1971.
5   Coates, E. J., 'Switching languages for indexing', *Journal of documentation*, **26** (2), 1970, 102–10.
6   *BSO: Broad System of Ordering schedules and index*, 3rd edn, proposed by the FID/BSO Panel: Eric Coates, Geoffrey Lloyd, Dusan Simandl. Paris, Unesco, 1978, (FID 564).
7   'The Broad System of Ordering', *International forum on information and documentation*, **4** (3), 1979, 3–27.

Madeley, H., 'The Broad system of Ordering', *Australian academic and research libraries*, **14** (4), 1983, 235–46.

Dahlberg, I., 'The Broad System of Ordering (BSO) as a basis for an integrated social sciences thesaurus?', *International classification*, **7** (2), 1980, 66–72. Also editorial 'Classification and the social sciences' and review by I. L Travis in the same issue, and reply by E. J. Coates, **8** (1), 1981, 46.

8   *The BSO manual: the development, rationale and use of the Broad System of Ordering*, by E. J. Coates, G. A. Lloyd, D. Simandl. The Hague, FID, 1979, (FID 580).

Chapter 21
The Colon Classification

Shiyali Ramamrita Ranganathan, the 'onlie begetter' of the Colon Classification (CC) began his career as a mathematician, until in 1924 he was appointed Librarian of the University of Madras. One of the conditions of his appointment was that he should spend some time in England studying library science, and it was while attending a series of lectures by W. C. Berwick Sayers[1] on classification at the University College London School of Librarianship that he began to formulate his own ideas on the subject, spurred by his dissatisfaction with DDC and UDC.

Undeterred by the warnings of Sayers as to the task he was setting himself, Ranganathan determined to compile his own classification scheme; the basic essentials were in fact worked out during his passage home to India. (He remarked that as the only Indian on board he was able to get on with his work undisturbed by the other passengers.) The first draft was used to classify the books in the University of Madras library, and the experience gained led to the publication of the first edition of CC in 1933. This was largely based on trial and error, and Ranganathan felt the need to develop the basic theory to further the scheme. In 1937 he published the first edition of his *Prolegomena to library classification*,[2] and put the theory into practice in the second edition of CC in 1939. The War held up further work until 1947, and the third edition appeared in 1950. The important theory of Fundamental categories led to major changes in the fourth edition, 1952. The fifth edition was published in 1957, which also saw the second edition of the *Prolegomena*. The sixth edition, 1960, included a few Greek letters in the notation to accommodate some new subjects; a revised version was published in 1963 in which Roman letters replaced the Greek, and a few other matters were tidied up. The third edition of the *Prolegomena* was published in 1967. Ranganathan died in 1972, but the work on developing CC into a freely faceted classification continued at the Documentation Research and Training Centre under the direction of M. A. Gopinath, with the 7th edition volume 1: schedules, published in 1987. This is a rate of publication which has only been equalled by DDC, but, unlike Dewey, Ranganathan never accepted the idea of integrity of numbers, and from time to time introduced major changes. Few Western libraries have adopted the scheme (a not unexpected result of its Eastern orientation and continual state of flux), yet it has been one of the most influential classifications ever published, and the ideas incorporated in it have affected the whole of classification theory.

As we have seen, Dewey incorporated some synthetic elements in his scheme as early as the second edition, but only in a very limited fashion; Ranganathan developed the theory of facet analysis, demonstrating that analysis and synthesis apply throughout a classification, and could be systematized. He also developed his own terminology in a correct scientific fashion; much of this is now widely used, for example throughout the present work, though some of it has excited the contempt of unsympathetic critics unwilling to accept the sometimes flowery metaphors he used. However, differences in terminology do not necessarily mean a change in the underlying concept. In Chapter 9 we referred to the idea of 'dependence' as a means of deciding citation order; Ranganathan called this the 'Wall-Picture principle', but the meaning is the same.

As stated above, there have from time to time been major changes in the scheme. One such change was the decision after the fifth edition to develop two parallel editions, the basic classification (Stage 1) and the depth classification of microthought (Stage 2); in effect, an abridged and a full edition comparable with UDC. A further similarity to UDC lies in the fact that the abridged edition is published as a whole, whereas the full schedules are published in an *ad hoc* fashion in parts; some have appeared in *Annals of library science, Revue internationale de la documentation,* and *Library science with a slant to documentation,* while another important source has been the *Proceedings of the DRTC annual seminars.* A further unfortunate parallel with UDC lies in the fact that the publication schedule has been very erratic; the seventh edition was originally promised for 1972, but did not in fact appear until 1987, and then only the schedules volume, not the index or the promised volume of examples. Because of these changes, the following comments are linked as far as possible to the edition in which the features described appear.

In the first edition, we find each basic class analysed into facets, but only one notational device for synthesis, the colon; the use of this symbol was so much a part of the scheme that it gave it its name, just as Dewey's notation did to his scheme. However, we have seen in Chapter 11 and elsewhere the problems that can arise in notational synthesis if the devices used are inadequate, and his struggle with these problems led Ranganathan to develop one of his most important theories: the citation order of decreasing concreteness, PMEST. This idea was first introduced in the fourth edition, and led to a complete reconstruction of the scheme.

PMEST

In the first three editions Ranganathan had used the kind of *ad hoc* analysis described in the earlier chapters of this work, but in this, as in all aspects of library science, he was continually seeking the underlying principles which had led him to select one method rather than another. By studying carefully the kind of facet to be found in different basic classes, he was able to establish that despite their apparent surface differences they could be accommodated in five large groups, which he denoted *Fundamental categories.* He was always at some pains to point out that these were *postulates*: ideas put forward as a convenient framework for analysis, and thus liable to change in the light of experience. We have seen that Time and Place are common facets, but can also be significant in such subjects as History; Ranganathan denoted them Time [T] and Space [S] in his fundamental categories.

In the fourth edition, he isolated the concept of Energy [E] as being the common factor in such subjects as 'Exports' in Economics, 'Curriculum' in Education and 'Grammar' in Linguistics. The fourth Category Matter [M] was seen as straightforward, including 'Ivory' in Painting, 'Instruments' in Music and 'Periodicals' in Library Science. The fifth category, Personality [P], is hard to define, but easier to understand; it is what we have referred to as the primary facet, and usually contains Things or Kinds of Thing. It includes such examples as 'Persons' in Sociology and Psychology, and 'Christianity' in Religion. The same isolate did not always fall into the same fundamental category; Periodicals were [M] in Library Science, but [P] in Bibliography; in Fine Arts, the primary facet 'style' [P] was a combination of [S] and [T]. Each category is introduced by its own particular facet indicator, discussed later.

In the seventh edition, further analysis has led to the identification of three aspects of Matter: Matter [M], Matter-Property [MP] and Matter-Method [MM]. Many of the isolates which were found as [E] in the sixth edition are now seen as [MP] or [P]. Thus in Book Science (previously Bibliography) 'Periodicals' are now seen as [P]; in Linguistics, 'Grammar' is now [MP]; in Education, 'Curriculum' is now [P]. Though this has of course altered the notation, changing the facet indicators has not necessarily altered the citation order; the overall arrangement may well not change significantly. As we have seen, the existence of five fundamental categories was seen as a postulate, and changes in the light of experience were to be expected.

The same fundamental category can appear more than once in the same basic class; if this were not the case we would have the very restrictive facet order [P] [M] [E] in all cases. To accommodate this, we find the idea of *Rounds*, denoted by a figure before the fundamental category, e.g. [2P], [1MM]. Each round may consist of [P], [M] and [E]; after the [E] category, a new round begins. Within a given category, in any particular round we may have more than one *Level*, shown by a figure after the fundamental category. For example, in Literature **O**, we find that there are four levels of [P]: language [1P1]; literary form [1P2]; author [1P3]; work [1P4]. (Authors are arranged chronologically; the final result is an arrangement very similar to that found in DDC.)

Each class has its own facet formula which is stated at the beginning. In Class **J** Agriculture we have J,[1P1],[1P2];[1MP1];[1MP2],[2P1];[2MM1]; however, in Table 2, which lists the changes in facet formula from the sixth to the seventh edition, we find it given as J,[P],[P2];[MP]:[E][2P]. In the schedules, we find schedules for (1P1); (1P2);(1MP1);(1MM);(1MP2);(1E);(2P1);(2M1), though it would appear that the last should indeed be (2MM1). Unfortunately, the production of the schedules is marred by a number of misprints, of which these are typical, and which are likely to cause particular difficulties for the inexperienced user.

The idea of fundamental categories has given rise to a great deal of criticism, not all of it well-informed. Ranganathan stressed the ideas of PMEST as a postulate which could be helpful in facet analysis, but which was always subject to review. The seventh edition shows that there have been quite significant developments in the 24 years since the revised sixth edition, but that the basic concept is still used.

It can be useful to bear these categories in mind even when analysing a subject into facets along the *ad hoc* lines indicated in this book. We find another example of rounds in the re-use of operators (2) and (3) in PRECIS. The idea of levels is a useful one when analysing a complex facet such as Persons, though in this work we have preferred the term subfacets. The terminology may differ, but the concepts remain the same.

Self-perpetuating classification

One of the other basic ideas behind CC is that of 'autonomy for the classifier'. We have seen that in an enumerative classification we have to wait for the decision of the compiler before we know where to classify a composite subject not already listed, and in an analytico-synthetic scheme we may find ourselves in the same position if the foci we need are not listed – though we can cater for composite subjects if the individual foci are listed. Ranganathan has tried to go one stage further: to give the individual classifier the means to construct class numbers for new foci which will be in accordance with those that the central organization will adopt, by means of a set of rules and devices of universal applicability. In this way, the need for a strong central organization is reduced, though it still exists. In CC there are a number of such devices, which may apply to the formation of new basic classes or to the enumeration of new foci.

Devices for the incorporation of new foci

Within a basic class we may from time to time have to make provision for new foci, and CC has five main ways in which this may be done. The first of these is the Chronological Device (CD): a new focus is specified by means of its date of origin. This is used in Literature to denote a particular author, where the date of birth is to be used (though Ranganathan had a rather tetchy note about the difficulty of establishing this in some cases, which has been dropped from CC7). The second is the Geographical Device (GD), which simply means the use of the Place facet other than in its usual way; for example, as mentioned earlier, a combination of (CD) and (GD) is used to represent Style in Fine arts. The third device is the Subject Device (SD), where notation from another class is used, very much like DDC's Add . . . , except that the added notation is in parentheses. For example, 2 is Library Science, T is Education, TL Curriculum; Library science as a curriculum subject is TL (2). The fourth is Alphabetical Device (AD), which is to be used when no other method of arrangement suggests itself as more helpful. The fifth device is Enumeration Device (ED), about which CC7 is somewhat ambivalent. New foci are to be enumerated in a sequence preferred on the basis of the Canon of Seminal Mnemonics, or similar principle, for which we are referred to section AH7. Unfortunately, the volume does not contain such a section; Part A ends at AF. Whether this was intentional, or whether it was merely another example of the errors of which CC7 is regrettably full, is not clear. The idea of seminal mnemonics is that the same notation represents the same fundamental concept throughout the scheme: for example, 1 is used for unity, one-dimensional, solid state, first, etc; 2 is used for two-dimensional, second, constitution, etc. Though we may wonder about 'constitution', the rest do not look too unreasonable. However, when we find that 5 stands for 'instability', as represented by energy, water, motion, controlled plan, women, sex, crime ... we may begin to doubt. The real objection to seminal mnemonics is not that they are not well worked out, but that they are an example of notation dictating order, which is unacceptable. Ranganathan himself warned that the use of seminal mnemonics required an uncommon degree of 'spiritual insight', which is not a good basis on which to construct a sound classification scheme. Differences in spiritual insight are a notorious source of inconsistencies.

There is also provision for other groupings of subjects. A System is a particular way of looking at a whole subject field – a school of thought – and is denoted by (CD); thus Socialism has the notation X-M2; X for Economics, M for 19th century, 2 for second decade. Which date one chooses may well depend on the reference books to hand at the time! The notation which would normally be added to X is added to X-M2. Some more examples are given in Medicine L: LA is systems by (CD), e.g. LB Ayurveda, LL Homeopathy. Specials are specializations within a particular subject: again taking Medicine as an example, we find L9A Specials, including L9C Child [pediatrics], L9F Female [gynaecology] and L9X Industrial.

The scheme

CC6 consisted of a single volume in three parts. Part 1 contained the rules; Part 2 the schedules; and Part 3 schedules of classics and sacred books with special names. (In earlier editions, there were some 4,000 examples of CC class numbers, but this list was dropped, presumably on the grounds that there were enough textbooks to make it unnecessary.) Work began on CC7 soon after the publication of CC6, but Ranganathan's contribution was ended with his death in 1972, the intended publication date. Ranganathan donated all the profits from his books to set up the Sarada Ranganathan Endowment for Library Science, which has provided much of the finance – an interesting parallel with Dewey and the Lake Placid Club Education Foundation.

CC7 introduces many new ideas, some of which have already been mentioned, e.g. the more complex facet formulas now found. It is claimed to be a 'free faceted classification', though precisely what this means is not clear, since there is still a facet formula for each class, and detailed rules for most classes. The single volume so far published consists of five parts. Part A is the introduction, giving a history of the development of the scheme and its underlying theory. Part B is a short section of 'Guidance to the beginner'; Part BB deals with 'how to classify a simple subject', using the example *Eradication of virus in rice plants in Japan (1971)*, while BC explains 'how to classify a complicated subject'. (A simple subject is one which can be classified using only the standard facet formula for the class; a complicated subject is one involving other devices such as phase relations.) Part C is a lengthy section on general rules, which explains the principles on which the scheme is constructed. Part D covers General divisions and common isolates, including a list of traditional main classes similar to DDC's first summary, and a much more detailed

Schedule of Basic subjects. Even a brief examination of this calls into question the allocation of notation: Medical jurisprudence LYX and Operations research BTT have three digits, but so do Stamp collecting MMD and Shorthand MXP. The common facets listed are those for Language; Time; Place; Common Energy isolates, e.g. diagnosis; Common Matter – Property isolates, e.g. physical properties (mass, weight), optical properties (refractive index, colour) and nutritive properties (growth promotion, toxicity); common forms and subjects; and phase relations. The section concludes with a list of the facet indicators used, and a table showing the changes in facet structure from CC6 to CC7. A paragraph at the end tell us that Part F will contain the index; Part G the schedule of classics; and Part H the index to Part G. Part E contains the schedules, with the rules for each class immediately following the class – a much more helpful arrangement than their separation in CC6.

Notation

Ranganathan was a mathematician, and does not seem to have been worried by mixed notation; most of those using the scheme will not be in that fortunate situation, and will find the notation of CC7 disconcerting. It uses a wide variety of symbols, including upper and lower case letters, Arabic numerals, and 14 indicator digits. The latter include the original facet indicators: , [Personality] ; [Matter] : [Energy] . [Place] ' [Time]. To these have been added various other symbols. & is used for phase relations, e.g. &b for bias phase. The hyphen - and equals sign = are used for subdivisions other than the normal facet structure, e.g. 2W56-4411=0M British Council library in Madras City, where 2 is Library science, W is contact library, 56 is UK, 4411 is Tamil Nadu and =0M is Madras. Unfortunately, 4411 is misprinted 4111, which puts Tamil Nadu in China, and 0 is printed O, though from the rules it is not clear which it is meant to be, as they are used indifferently. (. . .) is used for Subject device, e.g. 2B(A), where B is national library system and A is Science (main class). Where Alphabetical Device is used, and the name consists of more than one word, + is used between the initial letters, e.g. O,111,2J64,L+L+L, where O is Literature (misprinted 0 in the rules), 111 is English, from the Language facet, 2 is drama, J64 is 1564 (date of Shakespeare's birth) and L+L+L is Love's Labour's Lost. Bibliographical forms are introduced by ", while * is used to show a spread of notation, e.g. S*Z Behavioural sciences, where S is Psychology, T is Education, etc. This files *before* S, in the same way as the stroke in UDC, where 5/6 files before 5. Bibliographical forms also file before the unqualified subject, so that we would find the sequence:

T*Z"k	Encyclopedia of the social sciences
T*Z	The social sciences
T"k	Encyclopedia of education
T	Education

Forward and backward ranges are shown by → and ←, e.g. M94←92 in the time facet is 1892 to 1894. (The order in which the dates are cited affects the filing order.)

The notation is claimed to be infinitely hospitable. The main notation consists of lower case letters a to z, except for i, l, and o, which can cause confusion in writing or typing; Arabic numerals 0 to 9; upper case letters A to Z, except that I, O and Z are only used to denote the main classes Botany, Literature and Law respectively; and the Greek letter Δ (delta) which is used to denote Mysticism, filing between M and N. Notation is used decimally, so that additional concepts can be inserted in the schedules in their correct places, and various digits may be used as 'empty' digits; for example, the sequences 1 to 8, 91 to 98, 991 to 998. . . are to be taken as being on the same level hierarchically. A table sets out the complete range of possible notational sequences, showing 66 sectors with a total capacity of 1,166 digits. New classes may be interpolated using T, V or X; for example we find in the Place facet 434 Philippines, 434T Marshall Islands, 434V1 Gilbert Islands, 434X1 New Caledonia 435 New Guinea, all of which are to be treated as coordinate.[3] This discussion has not exhausted the possibilities, but should illustrate the point that the notation is hardly helpful, and is likely to cause clerical staff involved in shelving a great deal of confusion. Hospitality is achieved, but at a high price, and one that is hardly in accordance with Ranganathan's fourth Law of Library Science: save the time of the reader.

The schedules

The main classes in CC7 are as follows; there is a list of the traditional main subjects and a separate, much larger, list which includes a number of others which are obtained by one or other of the devices. The traditional main subjects are:

B	Mathematics	
C	Physics	
D	Engineering	
E	Chemistry	
F	Technology	(much of this is similar to DDC class 660 Chemical engineering)
G	Biology	
H	Geology	(appears to be out of place)
I	Botany	
J	Agriculture	
K	Zoology	
L	Medicine	
M	Useful arts	(includes printing, reprography, smithy [hardware], clothing etc)
Δ	Mysticism and spiritual experience	
N	Fine Arts	
O	Literature	
P	Linguistics	
Q	Religion	
R	Philosophy	
S	Psychology	

T   Education
U   Geography
V   History
W   Political science
X   Economics
Y   Sociology
Z   Law

In general, science and technology are kept together, though Geology seems out of place between Biology and Botany.

When we come to look at the very much longer schedule of basic subjects, we find a large number of additional classes, some of which could have been included in the list of traditional main classes. For example:

01   Generalia
0X   Entity-Phenomena study   (as found in the BSO)
1   Communication science
2   Library science
3   Book science
4   Mass communication
5   Exhibition technique
6   Museology
7   Systems research
8   Management
A   Natural sciences (there are no schedules for this)

and a number of partially comprehensive main classes (agglomerates), for example:

B*Z   Mathematical and physical sciences
B*ZZ   Mathematical sciences
C*Z   Physical sciences
C6*Z   Electricity and magnetism
C9B*Z   Microphysics
etc.

The degree of detail in the schedules, which are printed in two columns, varies considerably from class to class. Physics begins with six columns of rules, followed by 36 columns of schedules. Engineering has eight columns of schedules, Medicine twelve columns, but there are no rules for either. Mysticism has two columns of schedules and nearly three of rules. Literature has half a column of schedules, but nine columns of rules; however, we must remember that the languages facet, which fills three columns of schedule and three of rules, is found in the common facets. It is difficult to escape the parallel with DDC14, which suffered from much the same imbalance of schedule development.

We may in fact draw several parallels between Ranganathan and Dewey. Both devised a classification scheme which took its name from the notation used; both first tried out their scheme on their university library, Madras and Amherst College;

both affected a wide range of library activities in addition to classification; both set up endowments to enable their work to continue; CC7, the first edition produced after Ranganathan's death, has resemblances to DDC14, the first produced after Dewey's death. Sadly, one cannot see the same future for CC as we have seen for DDC. In fact, it would perhaps be fair to claim that the best continuation of Ranganathan's work is not seen in CC7, but in BC2 and other work by the CRG.

Summary

CC7 represents a further stage in the development of Colon Classification; unfortunately, it contains many errors and misprints which make its use problematic, even by those familiar with the scheme. The development of the schedules is uneven, ranging from some which are still in need of basic expansion to those which are almost at depth classification level. The notation has become more complicated with each edition since the fourth, and is now so complex, even for some straight-forward subjects, as to cause serious problems for those using it. The index volume is still not available eight years after the publication of the schedules. Reviewers, even those inclined to support the scheme, have found it difficult to do so whole-heartedly.[4] The scheme is used by some libraries in India, but it is difficult to see it being adopted elsewhere. CC7 should not be taken as a true reflection of Ranganathan's contribution to librarianship.

References

1   Ranganathan, S. R., 'Library classification on the march', in *The Sayers memorial volume: essays in librarianship in memory of William Charles Berwick Sayers*, Foskett, D. J. and Palmer, B. I. (eds.), London, Classification Research Group, 1961.

2   Ranganathan, S. R., *Prolegomena to library classification*, London, Asia Publishing House, 1st edn, 1937; 2nd edn, 1957; 3rd edn, 1967.

3   Husain, S. 'A theoretical basis for the accommodation of new subjects in Colon Classification Edition 7', *International classification, 16* (2) 1989, 82–8.

4   Dhyani, P., 'Colon Classification Edition 7: an appraisal', *International classification, 15* (1) 1988, 13–16.
    Satija, M. P., 'A critical introduction to the 7th edition (1987) of the Colon Classification', *Cataloging and classification quarterly, 12* (2), 1990, 125–38. This review contains a bibliography of 32 articles about CC7.

Chapter 22
The Library of Congress Classification

In 1814, the Capitol of the United States, together with its collection of 3,000 books, was burnt to the ground by British soldiers. Thomas Jefferson, third president of the US, offered his own library to Congress to replace the books lost, and with this library of 6,000 books came a classification scheme, devised by Jefferson himself, which was to be the basis of the Library's arrangement until the end of the century. The range of Jefferson's collection was also wider than that of the previous library of Congress, and formed the basis of an increasing breadth of coverage, which was greatly accelerated when Ainsworth Spofford become Librarian in 1864. Spofford set out to make the library, in fact if not in name, the national library of the United States, and to this end increased the rate and scope of accessions to such an extent that towards the end of his 33 years as Librarian a new building had to be provided. When the move took place in 1897, shortly after Spofford's retirement, it was found that some three-quarters of a million books needed reclassification or recataloguing, and that there was a backlog of some 30 years of uncatalogued and unbound material.[1]

Jefferson's classification, though it had been modified and extended, was no longer adequate for a library of the size to which this had grown, and the decision was made to reclassify the whole collection – but by what scheme? Three possibilities were considered carefully: Dewey's *Decimal classification*, the *Expansive classification* of C. A. Cutter,[2] and the Halle *Schema*, used in the library of the German University of Halle. None of these commended itself for the particular situation of the library, and in 1900 Herbert Putnam, Librarian from 1899 to 1939, decided that the staff should proceed to devise a new scheme, intended to fit the Library's collections and services as precisely as possible, without reference to outside needs or influences. The classification which resulted, LCC, reflects this situation very clearly, and some of its special features can only be understood in this context.

The first part of the new scheme to be developed took shape before the decision to had been made to develop a new scheme at all. The urgent need to be able to make use of the uncatalogued material led logically to the recognition of the bibliographical collections as the key to this, and the first outline of class Z Bibliography was compiled in 1898, drawing on Cutter's unpublished seventh expansion. Since then, the various classes have been drawn up over the years and published separately, with no apparent overall plan. American history was the first of the schedules to be published, in 1901, and Law of Asia and Eurasia, Africa, Pacific Area and Antarctica the latest, in 1993, but many of the schedules have been revised several times, for example Science, now in its seventh edition. For many years, a strange omission was Law; this was used as a subdivision under many topics, but there were no schedules for Law as such. In 1949, the decision was made to end this anomaly in the library of the law-making body of the United States, and all works on Law were transferred to a new Law library – a move involving the reshelving of over a million volumes! Since then, the schedules for Law have been appearing at intervals, with American law KF the first, published in 1969, and Law of Asia . . . KL-KWX the latest.

The scheme

The outline of the classification most closely resembles that of Cutter's *Expansive classification*, but is dictated by the organization of the library rather than by theoretical considerations. Because the scheme is primarily an internal one, in which the schedules are matched exactly to the needs of the collections – that is, compiler and classifier are one and the same – there is no need for synthetic devices, and the scheme is very largely enumerative. In some classes there are tables, e.g. for subdivision of the works of particular authors in Literature, but these are not synthetic in the sense used in this book, and there are no common facets such as we have found in other schemes. In consequence, the schedules are very bulky: in all, the 21 classes occupy some 10,000 pages in 48 volumes, with Literature and Language accounting for about a third of this.

The notation is mixed, but the different symbols fall into a clear pattern, so that no problems arise. Main classes are denoted by a capital letter, and in most of them a second capital is used to denote the major sections, e.g. Q Science, QD Chemistry. Arabic numerals are then used to denote the divisions; they are used integrally, from 1 to 9999 if necessary, with gaps left liberally to accommodate new topics as they arise. However, there is no question of notation dictating order; if a new topic has to be inserted where no gap exists, a decimal point is used for further subdivision. Further arrangement is often alphabetical rather than systematic, using Cutter numbers after a point; these consist of a capital followed by one or two figures, to give a shorter arranging symbol than the name of the topic. Alphabetical arrangement is in fact used very frequently, even in places where its use would seem to be unhelpful, e.g. in Science. In some places, no facet analysis has been carried out, which gives the possibility of cross-classification; for example, at TK6565, Other radio apparatus, we find arranged alphabetically:

.A55   Amplifiers (circuit)
.C65   Condensers (part) [NB outdated terminology]
.R4   Recording apparatus.

Capacitors (Condensers) may be used in amplifiers, and amplifiers are used in recording apparatus, but we are given no guidance as to which of these is the primary facet. In other cases, straightforward alphabetical arrangement scatters topics within the same facet which would be more helpfully brought together; e.g., in Psychology we find

BF575		Special forms of emotion
e.g.	.A5	Anger
	.A9	Awe
	.B3	Bashfulness
	.F2	Fear
	.H3	Hate
	.L8	Love
	.S4	Self-consciousness

(among others) where some grouping would have been more useful. At some points an indication of facet order is given; for example, at the above number BF575 there is an instruction: Prefer BF723 for emotions of children. Such instructions are the exception, and the external user finds little help in the scheme from this point of view; within the Library, of course, procedures are well established, and the answers to questions of facet order are found by reference to past practice.

Gaps are left in the notation to accommodate the tables referred to above, which are inserted rather than added; for example, in Literature we find within English literature, 19th century, individual authors:

PR5400–5448   Shelley, Percy Bysshe (II)

This shows that the numbers allocated to this author are to be defined by using Table II from the set at the end of the schedules; turning to this we find that 3 or 53 is the number for Selections, 24 or 74 the number for Parodies. Inserting these numbers in the gap, we have:

PR5403   Selections from Shelley
PR5424   Parodies of Shelley

Had we instead been looking at Wordsworth, PR5850–5898, we should have used the second set, thus:

PR5853   Selections from Wordsworth
PR5874   Parodies of Wordsworth

There are thirteen such tables in Literature; the one to use depends on the importance of the writer, and is shown in the schedules. (Note the citation order Language–Period–Author–Literary forms, as opposed to Dewey's Language–Literary forms–Period–Author.) Class H Social sciences also includes a number of tables, particularly for division by place.

Organization

The way in which the schedules are compiled is again unique to LCC among the general schemes. Literary warrant is very important; there are no provisions for subjects not represented in the library. The original technique for compilation was to arrange the books in what seemed to be a helpful order; this order was written down and studied carefully to remove anomalies, and the arrangement of the books was revised to take account of any changes. There was thus a constant interaction between the collections and the scheme, with the latter matched as closely as possible to the needs of the former. In the case of Law, this technique has had to be somewhat modified – it is not practical to experiment with the arrangement of over a million volumes – but there is still the very close interaction.

An example will illustrate the pragmatic approach to revision. The increasing number of books on Buddhism prompted its removal from BL, Religions in general, to a new subclass BQ Buddhism, the schedule being first published in 1972 in *LC Classification—Additions and Changes*. The revised schedule for BL, BM, BP, BQ, Religion: Religions. Hinduism, Judaism, Islam, Buddhism, was published in 1984 as the third edition of that section.

B	Philosophy. Psychology. Religion
B–BJ	Philosophy
BF	Psychology
BL–BX	Religion
BL	Religions in general
BM	Judaism
BP	Islam. Baha'ism. Theosophy etc
BQ	Buddhism
BR–BX	Christianity
BS	Bible

The sections on Christianity have been published separately as BR-BV, Religion: Christianity. Bible, and BX, Religion: Christian denominations.

Although each class is developed as an independent unit, there are some general guidelines covering division within classes, so that there is a similar pattern:

General form divisions: periodicals, societies, collections, dictionaries, etc
Theory. Philosophy
History
Treatises. General works
Study and teaching
Special subjects and subdivisions of subjects progressing from the more general to the specific and as far as possible in logical order.[3]

In the past, each class has been revised on its own, without reference to the revision schedule for any other class. The process is continuous; as books on new subjects are received, new places are made in the schedules to accommodate them; the changes are published quarterly in *LC Classification—Additions and Changes*. As the number of changes in a year can be several thousand, keeping track of them is not always an easy matter. When it has seemed appropriate, a new edition of the class has been published, though this has often been in the form of the old edition with a supplementary table and index listing additions and changes. This has meant looking in two places to make sure that one had the latest schedule for a particular topic. New editions of classes are listed in the weekly Library of Congress *Information bulletin,* and the complete classification is listed in the CDS (Cataloging Distribution Service) *Catalog,* published annually with a six-monthly supplement. A complete edition in 44 volumes has also been published by Gale Research, together with a cumulation of additions and changes in 43 volumes.[4]

With the development of the USMARC format: Classification, referred to in Chapter 15, the situation has changed radically.[5] The whole scheme is to be incorporated into the MARC format, and this will make possible the publication of the full schedules on CD-ROM, beginning in 1995, as well as in a standard printed format. This has not been without its difficulties. As mentioned earlier, it has often proved necessary to insert additional notation by using a point followed by a Cutter number; however, Cutter numbers are also used for geographic place names and names as subjects, as well as the normal means to represent an author's name. No control has ever been maintained over the spread of books at each class number; in consequence, many headings represent only a very few books, while others represent so many that they really need subdivision. The notation is non-hierarchical, which may cause additional problems in computerization; this is also further complicated by the use of Cutter numbers for subject subdivisions. A possibility which could be exploited when both the classification and LCSH are in database form is that of extending the role of LCSH as a complement to the schedules rather than a totally separate tool. In future, the MARC format will make revision of the scheme much simpler, and publication of separate classes will be possible on a much more up-to-date basis than at present. The first to be produced using the new format is Class H, Social sciences, published in 1994.

LC has never produced a complete index to the scheme. Class numbers given in LCSH serve as a kind of index (but only a third of the headings have a class number), and the Outline to the scheme is recommended by CDS as a guide to the overall arrangement, with the sixth edition published in 1990. Indexes to each class have been the rule (with a few exceptions) in the past, though two attempts have been made to produce a general index.[6] The first of these was sponsored by the Canadian Library Association, and was compiled by a cut-and-paste method, using the indexes to the individual schedules, supplemented by typed indexes specially compiled to the then unindexed European literature schedules. No attempt was made to produce a chain index, as this would have greatly added to the cost. The single (large) volume was stated to be a preliminary edition, but it has not been updated. A much more ambitious index in 15 volumes was sponsored by the United States Historical Documents Institute. This was computer-produced, all in upper-case – a reflection of the technology available at the time. Entries marked [*] were based on the schedules, while those marked [B] were based on the LC shelflist. There are five sets of entries; the first, in two volumes, (A–K, L–Z), is an 'Author number index to the Library of Congress classification schedules', with entries as follows:

PR4350   BYRON, GEORGE GORDON, LORD   (TABLE 2)   [*]

Set 2 is a 'Biographical subject index . . .' in three volumes (A–F, G–N, Q–Z) covering philosophers, musicians, historical figures, educators, scientists etc., e.g.:

QC16.E5   EINSTEIN, ALBERT, 1879–1955

Set 3 complements the first two by giving a 'Classified index to persons . . .', again in three volumes: B128 – PQ4886; PQ6271 – PT3919; PT4846–Z8999. Set 4 is the 'Geographical names index . . .', which specifies which volume and edition the entry leads to, e.g.:

LINCOLN COUNTY, OKLAHOMA
  F702.L5   [E–F (3RD ED)]
LINCOLN COUNTY, OKLAHOMA (MAPS)
  G4023.L5 [G (3RD ED)]

Set 5, in six volumes, is a 'Subject keyword index . . .', which shows most clearly the lack of chain procedure; one needs a good knowledge of the scheme to see the context of some of the entries. The following are taken from the 51 entries at the word AVIATION:

AVIATION
        HE9911–25 [H (3RD ED)]
NAVAL AVIATION
        VG90–95   [V (2ND ED)]
        Z6834.A4   [SUPPLEMENTS]
AVIATION, TAXATION
        KF6614.A9 [SUPPLEMENTS]

As with the other index, this has not been updated.

The lack of an overall index is a reflection of the structure of the Library, which in effect consists of a collection of special libraries working in isolation. In this context, indexes to the individual volumes are clearly necessary, but a general index less so; those working with books in, say, Naval science V will not be classifying books on Aviation taxation, or Bibliographies. However, this situation is not true of other libraries using the scheme, who would surely welcome the help given by a good up-to-date general index; certainly one could not envisage using DDC without the index volume – nor would Dewey have wished us to!

Outline of the scheme

Outline	6th ed 1990. Gives an overview of the whole scheme.
A	General Works. 1911. 4th ed 1973. Some literal mnemonics e.g. AE Encyclopedias. AZ is now used for History of the Sciences in general, scholarship, Learning.
B–BJ	Philosophy. 1910. 4th ed 1989. Includes Psychology, Ethics, Etiquette.
BL–BX	Religion. 1927. Now split into three parts:
BL–BQ	Religion: Religions, Hinduism, Judaism, Islam, Buddhism. 3rd ed 1984.

BR–BV	Religion: Christianity. Bible. 1987.
BX	Religion: Christian denominations. 1985.
C	Auxiliary Sciences of History. 1915 (Except Epigraphy, 1942). 4th ed 1993. Includes Archeology and Numismatics. Collective Biography is classed here, but biography is normally classed with the subject.
D–DJ	History (General); History of Europe, Part 1. 1916. 3rd ed 1990. DA is Great Britain (favoured category); other European countries in approximately alphabetical order, with Greco-Roman world between France and Germany.
DJK–DK	History of Eastern Europe: General, Soviet Union, Poland. 1987.
DL–DR	History of Europe Part 2. 3rd ed. 1990
DS	History of Asia 1987
DT–DX	History of Africa, Australia, New Zealand, etc 1988. Gipsies included at DX (an afterthought?)
E–F	History: America. 1901. 4th ed 1995 The first of the main schedules to be published, this does not use a second letter in its notation. There are special tables for Jefferson and Washington.
G	Geography. Maps. Anthropology. Recreation. 1910. 4th ed 1976. Includes Folklore.
GE	Environmental Sciences. 1990 (Available only in *LC Classification: Additions and Changes, list 247, July–September 1990*)
H	New combined 5th edition of Social Sciences 1994 is the first to be published in USMARC format. Social Sciences was originally published in 1910 (except Social Groups 1915), and was divided into two parts in 1981.
H–HJ	Social Sciences. Economics. Includes Statistics HA.
HM–HX	Social Sciences: Sociology. HV Social Pathology includes Social and public welfare followed by Criminology. HX Socialism, Communism, Anarchism.
J	Political Science. 1910. 2nd ed 1924 (1966s. Unindexed revision through 1991. New edition in preparation). Place is the primary facet in many of the basic classes in this group, e.g. Local government JS, where the schedule under United States consists largely of a long list of individual towns etc arranged alphabetically. JX International law.
K	Law: General. 1977. There was no published schedule for Law prior to 1969, though the decision to reclassify all law books in one class was taken 20 years earlier.
KD	Law of the United Kingdom and Ireland. 1973.
KG–KH	Law of the Americas, Latin America and the West Indies. 1984.
KE	Law of Canada, 1976.
KF	Law of the United States. Preliminary ed 1969.
KJ–KKZ	Law of Europe. 1989.
KJV–KJW	Law of France. 1985.
KK–KKC	Law of Germany. 1982.

KL–KWX Law of Asia and Eurasia, Africa, Pacific Area and Antarctica. 2v. 1993.

L Education. 1911. 5th ed 1996. Curriculum is subordinate to grade of school, but study and teaching of particular subjects goes with the subject. Much of the schedule is simply a listing of educational establishments under country.

M Music. 1904. 3rd ed 1978. M is used for scores, ML History and criticism, MT Instruction. Ballet music M1520 appears to be a subdivision of Vocal music.

N Fine Arts. 4th ed 1970. This edition was completely revised and was available printed on one side only of the paper to facilitate updating.

P Language and Literature. 1909–1948. This class, which forms something like one third of the schedules, has been published in 12 parts, each of which is revised as a unit, e.g. PQ, Part 1 French literature. 2nd ed. 1992. For 'Minor' languages, language and literature are treated together; for major languages, the two are treated separately. The very detailed enumeration includes provision for particular editions of the more important works, but 20th century literature is poorly treated in comparison with earlier periods. Literary form is usually ignored as a major facet, except for the Elizabethan period of English Literature, where Drama is an important feature. Fiction and Juvenile Literature were classified in PZ, but this caused some problems of cross-classification with the other schedules, and the use of PZ1–4 was discontinued in 1980.

Q Science. 1905. 7th ed 1989. There is no synthesis in this class at all, and though science might be expected to lend itself to systematic arrangement, especially in the 'classificatory sciences', the schedules are notable for their use of alphabetical order.

R Medicine. 1910. 5th ed 1995. Primary division is by medical discipline, e.g. RD Surgery.

S Agriculture. 1911. 4th ed 1982. Crop subordinate to Pest at SB608. SB975 ends with SB987 General works. There is no provision for the treatment of a particular pest by a particular method.

T Technology. 1910. 5th ed 1971. [New edition in preparation] This edition incorporated all the amendments found necessary since the 4th ed 1948, but retains the same structure, which is little changed from that of the 3rd ed 1937. Most of the recent expansions have used alphabetical arrangement by Cutter number.

U Military Science. 1910. 5th ed 1992.

V Naval Science. 1910. 4th ed 1993.

Z Bibliography and Library Science. 1902 (but the first schedule actually prepared). 6th ed 1995. Includes Book industry. Subject bibliographies are arranged alphabetically by subject; at the time that the schedule was prepared it was obviously not possible to parallel the schedules.

Aids for the user

In 1992 LC published its *Subject cataloguing manual: Classification*, the manual used by LC classifiers to facilitate consistent use of the schedules. This is illustrated by examples from LC MARC records. It is complemented by *Subject cataloguing manual: Shelflisting*, Second edition, 1995, which provides guidelines for the assignment of Cutter numbers to give a unique call number for every book, and parallels the *Subject cataloging manual: Subject headings*. The nature of the classification makes such assistance very useful for the classifier dealing with material not covered by MARC records.

The future

LCC is obviously well established, and has been for many years. Many academic libraries in the USA adopted it with the provision of LCC class numbers on Library of Congress catalog cards, and during the 1960s many which had been using DDC switched to LCC; all LC cards contained an LCC class number, but only a selection contained a DDC number, and to adopt LCC was seen as a move to reduce cataloguing costs. However, it has never been as popular outside the USA; it is virtually non-existent in Australia, and though it is used in some British academic libraries, the proportion is not as great as in the USA. LCC class numbers appear in the MARC records which have replaced the LC card service, and the MARC format: classification will make the production of the schedules very much simpler.

There was some discussion at one time in the Library of Congress on whether the stacks, which are not open to the public, should be arranged by some more cost-effective method. This would have removed a substantial part of the justification for the scheme, but the open access reading room collections would remain, and would need to be in some kind of helpful arrangement; also, a high proportion of the other libraries using the scheme do not have closed stacks, and therefore need the full classification. In the event, the Library agreed to maintain the scheme regardless of its own needs, and this particular suggestion seems to have evaporated. The scheme appears set to remain as the classic example of an enumerative scheme, which is successful despite its peculiarities because of its position as the scheme used by the most influential library in the Western World, if not in the world generally.

The SRIS classification scheme

It is perhaps appropriate to mention here the classification scheme devised for the British Library Science Reference and Information Service, which has much in common with LCC. The British Museum Library had never collected material in science and technology to the same extent as in the humanities and social sciences, and when the British Library was first proposed the government of the day established in 1966 a National Reference Library for Science and Invention as part of the British Museum, by merging the science collections already held by the Museum with those of the Patent Office, the most significant library in engineering and technology in the country. The collections were not physically merged with the main collection in the BM, as there was no room; the physical sciences and engineering were held at the site of the Patent Office library, with the life sciences in another separate site some distance away.

The Patent Office library was originally classified by Wyndham Hulme at the beginning of the century, and by the time of the merger the scheme he devised was beginning to show signs of strain. The staff were faced with the decision as to whether to revise the existing scheme, adopt another scheme (UDC was the obvious possibility) or devise a new scheme. The decision was to revise the existing scheme,[7] probably because of the fact that by 1966, UDC was in a management black hole, with the full English edition still well away from completion; there seems to have been little enthusiasm for a completely new scheme. From 1966 to 1978, the schedules were revised, and the concomitant reorganization of the shelves took place. Perhaps if the same amount of effort had been directed towards revising UDC and bringing it up to date, a great many other people might have benefited as well. The life sciences were not well represented in the Patent Office library, so LCC schedules formed a basis for the construction of new schedules; with their emphasis in the classificatory sciences on 'systematic subdivisions alphabetically arranged', this choice seems odd.

After this major revision, nothing was done for nine years, by which time the schedules were once again showing signs of being out of touch with the needs of the Library, which had become the British Library Science Reference and Information Service. Resources were insufficient to carry out a full-scale revision, and, after confirming that the scheme should be maintained and not replaced, the staff set in motion a system of continuous revision. Schedules which urgently needed upgrading were dealt with one by one in such areas as Computing, Robotics and Pathology. This pattern is very similar to that used by the Library of Congress.

The scheme itself is intended for the shelf arrangement of the books in the collection, and uses a simple non-expressive notation consisting of two letters and two figures, e.g. JM02 Antimony. New classes can be accommodated by decimal subdivisions, so that a sequence might run JH20, JH201, JH202, JH21 etc. Without any kind of decimal point the notation looks as though it consists of integers, which could mislead users into searching for JH201 after JH200, and being puzzled by not finding it. The scheme is totally enumerative, with no facilities for synthesis at all; composite subjects are classified with the primary facet if the complete subject is not enumerated.

Arrangement is by discipline, with one major difference from the other schemes we have looked at. The science and technology of a particular discipline are collocated, on the grounds that modern technology is closely linked to its basic science. There are cross-references leading the user to other hierarchies where a topic might appear, and detailed scope notes are given at many headings – a practice which could well be adopted more widely by other schemes. Because of the nature of the collection, Humanities and Social sciences are treated as fringe subjects.

The schedules have now been computerized, so that the production of up to date schedules is facilitated. The scheme is available in three volumes: Rules for classing; Schedules; Index. Because the scheme is enumerative, the index to the scheme is also the index to the shelf arrangement and classified catalogue; there is no need for the separate authority file which is needed with synthetic schemes. On the other hand, an outside user needing to classify a subject which is not already in the scheme must wait for the Library to catch up and publish the new schedules. Unlike LCC class numbers, these will not be disseminated through the MARC records – though there is no theoretical reason to exclude them, any cost-benefit study would surely find them an expensive luxury. We are left wondering why all the effort needed to produce this scheme was not directed towards an existing scheme, particularly UDC, which has always been strong in science and technology. We might have had a greatly improved scheme which would be of use to a large number of information agencies rather than just one.

References

1   LaMontagne, L. E., *American library classification, with special reference to the Library of Congress,* Hamden, Conn, Shoe String Press, 1961. The scope of this work is broader than the title suggests.
     Miksa, F. L., *The development of classification at the Library of Congress,* Urbana-Champaign, IL, University of Illinois Graduate School of Library and Information Science, 1984.
2   Cutter, C. A., *Expansive classification.* The idea of this scheme was to permit librarians to select a scheme detailed enough for their needs, but not too detailed. The first expansion has seven classes, the seventh was intended to be detailed enough for the largest collection. The seventh expansion was never completed, but the first six were published together by Cutter in 1891–1893.
3   Chan, L. M., *Immroth's guide to the Library of Congress classification,* 4th ed., Englewood, CO, Libraries Unlimited, 1990.
     Chan, L. M., *Cataloging and classification: an introduction,* 2nd edn, New York, NY, McGraw Hill, 1994, Chapter 13.
     Downing, M. H. and Downing, D. H., *Introduction to cataloging and classification,* 6th edn, Jefferson, NC, McFarland, 1992.
4   *Library of Congress classification schedules: a cumulation of additions and changes through 1992,* Gale Research, 1993, 44v.
5   Williamson, N. J., 'The Library of Congress classification: problems and prospects in online retrieval', *International cataloguing,* **15**, October 1986, 45–8.
     Williamson, N. J., *The Library of Congress classification: a content analysis of the schedules in preparation for their conversion into machine-readable form.* Washington, DC, Library of Congress, 1995.
     Micco, M., 'Suggestions for automating the Library of Congress classification', in *International study conference on classification research, Toronto, Canada, June 24–28 1991,* Williamson, N. J. and Hudon, M. (eds.), Elsevier, 1992, (FID 698), 285–94.
     Guenther, R. S., 'The Library of Congress classification in the USMARC format', *Knowledge organization,* **21** (4) 1994, 199–202.

Larson, R. R., 'Experiments in automatic Library of Congress classification', *Journal of the American Society for Information Science*, **43** (2), 1992, 130–48. (An attempt to generate LC class numbers automatically from LCSH headings according to the guidelines in the *Subject cataloging manual*.)

6 Elrod, J. M. *et al., Index to the Library of Congress classification . . . preliminary edition*, Canadian Library Association, 1974.

Olson, N. B., *Combined indexes to the Library of Congress classification schedules*, Washington, DC, United States Historical Documents Institute, 1975. 15v.

7 Grimshaw, J. 'The SRIS classification scheme', *Catalogue and index*, (**112**), 1994, 7–9.

Chapter 23

Library of Congress subject headings

History

When the Library of Congress moved to its new building in 1897, two problems had to be faced: the selection and development of a more satisfactory classification scheme, discussed in Chapter 22; and the choice of the kind of catalogue to be compiled. In the 19th century several classified catalogues of the Library's holdings were published, but the practice was discontinued by Spofford, who was not in favour of the classified catalogue. It was decided to conform to the majority practice in US libraries at the time and compile a dictionary catalogue as the main information retrieval tool. Although Dewey had advocated the use of his scheme for library catalogues as well as shelf arrangement, Cutter's *Rules for a dictionary catalogue*[1] had been more influential in deciding cataloguing practice.

Work began on the compilation of a list of subject headings in 1897, based on the ALA *List of subject headings for use in dictionary catalogs* published in 1895, and the first edition was published in two volumes, 1909–1914, as the *List of subject headings used in the dictionary catalogues of the Library of Congress*. Supplements were issued at intervals until the publication of the second edition in 1919. Since then, the list has grown steadily, and the latest editions contain over 200,000 headings in four large volumes: the 'red books' which are a familiar sight in American and Australian libraries, and in recent years in the UK.

The basis for the LC list was devised largely by J. C. M. Hanson, Chief of the Catalog Department from 1897 to 1910. In 1901, the distribution of LC catalogue cards was begun; although at first subject headings appeared on a limited proportion of the cards, by 1910 about 50% included them, and they became a major source of subject cataloguing copy for American libraries. A second edition of the ALA *List* had been published in 1898, but the third edition, published in 1911, borrowed much of its content from LC practice, though covering the whole of knowledge rather than that part which had by then been catalogued by LC, and no further editions of the ALA *List* were published. The development of the LC *List* has been thoroughly described by Miksa.[2]

Hanson was faced with the task of cataloguing more than a million books and providing subject access to them through subject headings. Though he had used Cutter's *Rules* before joining the LC, he did not have the same philosophical approach as Cutter, with its grounding in a classificatory view of knowledge.

Instead, he adopted a pragmatic approach, which led to decisions which were not always consistent, and which have in their turn led to problems which have only recently been addressed. He did not feel restricted in the choice of headings by the need to find an established subject name, but introduced new headings as he saw the need arise; on the other hand, he did not have the structure which Cutter relied on for the form of headings and the choice of cross-references. Where Cutter had only used phrase headings when they were generally accepted as subject names, Hanson used them when they conformed to usage as found in the books being catalogued. Subheadings were introduced by a dash, e.g. Heart—Diseases, and inversion was used where it might help by bringing together specific subjects related to a general topic, e.g. Heart, Fatty. It will be seen that this corresponds largely to what Metcalfe denoted as *qualification* and *specification*, as discussed in Chapter 8. However, Hanson carried the idea of grouping through inversion to a degree which led to a change in the nature of the catalogue away from Metcalfe's 'known names in a known order' to a form unique to the LCSH list – but, through the wide use of LC cards, a form widely used in other libraries. Because of the possibility of creating new headings as required by a book to be catalogued, individual cataloguers could generate headings without necessarily following the same principles as other colleagues. The overall result grew over the years into a list for which several writers tried to find a theoretical justification; attempts were made by Mann, Pettee, Haykin, Metcalfe and Chan,[3] though Chan came to the conclusion that there was none to be found.

The 5th edition, 1948, introduced the *xx* and *x* notation for 'refer from' cross-references briefly described in Chapter 8. They had been printed separately to accompany the fourth edition in 1943, but now for the first time the full cross-reference structure could be easily seen within the *List*. Though these conventions are no longer used, they may well be found in older card catalogues, as many libraries have not converted their card catalogues prior to their adoption of MARC records.

With the eighth edition in 1975, the name was changed to the more familiar *Library of Congress Subject Headings* (LCSH). Various other significant changes are also linked to this edition. Perhaps the most significant was the introduction of 'free-floating subdivisions'. Until this edition, subdivisions (corresponding largely to the common facets in classification schemes: bibliographical form; subject; place; time) had been included in the list by enumeration, except for bibliographical forms, which were found in a separate list to be used as needed; the eighth edition brought all subdivisions together in a separate list with annotations for each on its use. Some of the annotations were lengthy, for example that for Dictionaries, which occupied a column. The introduction of free-floating subdivisions was not greeted with unmixed enthusiasm. Previously, most subdivisions had been enumerated in the list as they were used with each heading affected. By detaching the subdivisions, users could no longer see from LCSH where they had been used, and had to decide for themselves whether to use them or not for each heading they selected. In addition, there was the very real possibility of confusion in places where a phrase heading already existed which made the subdivision unnecessary – but would cataloguers realize that the phrase heading existed? For example, one had to know that the correct heading was not:

Health—Study and teaching

using the subdivision, but the established phrase heading

Health education

Arguments on both sides were thoroughly discussed at a conference in 1991,[4] which finally established the preferred form Topic—Place—Chronology—Form. Since then, headings in LCSH have been reviewed with a view to establishing also the order Topic—Topic—Place rather than the previously possible Topic—Place—Topic. The list of *Free-floating subdivisions* is now published separately, the seventh edition in 1995.

A minor inclusion was the *Subject headings for children's literature*, which had previously been published separately following the introduction of the Annotated Card Program for children's materials in 1965; this list contains a few hundred headings which have been modified for use with children's books, and is still included in the printed volumes.

Division by place

One major change was announced shortly after the publication of the eighth edition. Division by place is used throughout the list; to begin with, this was indirect, i.e. the name of the country was interposed between the heading and the specific place, e.g. Construction industry—France—Paris, in line with the grouping sought by Hanson. Later the policy changed, and direct subdivision was used except where indirect had already been used. Headings were shown as (*Direct*) or (*Indirect*), depending on LC practice. Despite some preference being shown by users for direct subdivision, LCSH decided to standardize on indirect subdivision, and the only place headings now divided directly are those relating to the USA, Great Britain, Canada, Australia and the (now dismembered) USSR. Headings may be shown as (*May Subd Geog*) or (*Not Subd Geog*); the latter are usually headings such as names for which geographical subdivision is inappropriate. Headings with no qualification are those for which no decision has been made to subdivide by place; again, in most cases this is because the question does not arise.

There is no rule to show whether a topic is divided by place, or place by topic, so we find, for example:

Labor supply—France
Massachusetts—History

These two headings are in line with the guidelines set out by Coates and discussed in Chapter 8. The headings **France**, **Great Britain** and **United States** show some of the topic subdivisions that may be used with other place headings. Date subdivisions are specific to each place, and are enumerated; those listed under the subheading —History may also be used under the subheadings —Foreign relations and —Politics and government.[5] However, to be certain that correct practice is being followed it is necessary to consult the *Manual*.[6]

The *List* becomes computer-based

With the computerization of the Library's bibliographic operations on January 1, 1981, the card files were closed, and new computer files were opened. Users were canvassed beforehand as to what action they would prefer on various aspects of cataloguing, including subject headings: one suggestion was that a new list should be started once rules had been laid down on the formation of headings; another was that LC should adopt PRECIS. In the event, the opportunity for a completely new start was not taken, but since then, there have been several quite major changes in LCSH. The fact that subject headings are found only in catalogues, and are not linked to physical objects such as books, means that changes can be made relatively easily in the list itself and in catalogues using the MARC records, though it has to be remembered that MARC records generated before a given change will still have the old headings, unless a library goes to the expense of changing them.

In 1986 the present computer-produced format was introduced in the 10th edition, and with the 11th edition in 1988 *See* and *See also* references and the complementary *xx* and *x* were replaced by the thesaurus conventions BT, NT, RT, UF, USE and SA.

The introduction of thesaurus conventions was roundly condemned by Dykstra,[7] who argues that the rules for thesaurus construction, as set out in the various national and international standards (see Chapter 6), relate to terms representing single concepts. Because of its frequent use of phrase headings, LCSH cannot be described as using single concept terms, and many of the cross-references in it do not conform to the hierarchical structure for which BT–NT and RT links are appropriate. Dykstra suggests building a new thesaurus based on LCSH, but with headings for single concepts only, as laid down in the standards; thesaurus conventions could be used in this without any problems, but would not be used in LCSH. Eventually, the precedent-based LCSH would be subsumed into the rule-based thesaurus.

Though this radical proposal was not adopted, with the introduction of thesaurus conventions came the decision that in future cross-references would be built up on a strictly hierarchical basis. However, the conversion of the old structure to the new was done by computer, and in consequence some relationships are still left which would not now be made. These are being tidied up as they are noted, and it is still the case that phrase headings cause problems in making cross-references strictly according to the rules. Also, as Coates pointed out,[8] many of the cross-references in LCSH in the past seem to have been made without any kind of plan in mind, prompted perhaps by a particular book, and would be hard to justify on a basis of strict rules. Such links are also being removed, but all changes which have to be made on an individual basis will necessarily take a long time to complete in a list of this size.

Inverted headings, introduced by Hanson to give an element of grouping, are now used only for specific purposes. Here too we find that past practice is still represented, though it is being eliminated slowly. For example, we find:

Bridges, Iron and steel

and similar headings for some kinds of bridges, but not all. However, the anomaly under Libraries, where we found, for example, the contradictory:

Libraries, Catholic
Libraries, Jewish
　　See Jewish libraries

has been resolved, and all headings are now direct.

The scheme

At the time of writing, the latest printed edition available is LCSH18 (1995). Despite the removal of compound heading—subheading entries, the list has grown from 145,000 headings (LCSH10, 1986) to 163,000 (LCSH11, 1988) to 186,000 (LCSH14, 1991) to 192,000 (LCSH16, 1993) to 206,300 headings (LCSH17, 1994). Of these, 160,000 are topical (subject) headings, 30,000 are geographical, and 13,000 are names, including 11,000 family names. There are 189,000 USE references from non-preferred headings and 191,922 cross-references. From the (bulky!) single volume of LCSH8 the list has now grown to four large volumes with 213,800 headings.

The list contains the complete entry vocabulary of the LC catalogues, with certain exceptions mentioned below; terms in the index vocabulary, i.e. headings which are used, are in bold type, while those in the entry vocabulary only, e.g. synonyms, are in light type. LC class numbers are given for about 36% of the headings (LCSH17). Related headings are shown by the use of BT, NT and RT linkages. There are 389 general USE references, and 3097 general SA (*see also*) references, which are of two kinds. The first is from nouns to adjectives, e.g.

Sun
　　SA　　headings beginning with the word Solar

The second kind relates main headings to subdivisions, e.g.

Ability—Testing
　　SA　　subdivision Ability testing under topical headings . . .
　　UF　　Ability testing

with the complementary

Ability testing
　　USE　　*subdivision* Ability testing *under subjects*
　　　　　　Ability—Testing
Chemistry　　　　　[May Subd Geog]
　　[QD]
　　SA　　headings beginning with the word Chemical
　　BT　　Physical sciences
　　NT　　Acids
　　　　　Agricultural chemistry
　　　　　etc . . .
Flowers　　　　　　[May Subd Geog]
　　[QK (Botany)]
　　[SB403–SB450 (Culture)]

SA   names of flowers, e.g. Carnations; Roses; Violets
UF   Flowering plants
BT   Inflorescence
       Plants

There are 40 pattern headings, which are listed in the introduction; for example **Heart** and **Foot** for Organs and regions of the body. None of the subdivisions listed at these pattern headings is repeated under the related headings to which they might apply, for example **Chest**.

Scope notes are given for some headings, though not as many as one might wish; these are usually instructional, though some are definitions. For example, we find:

Ceramics

Here are entered general works on the technology of fired earth products, or clay products intended for industrial and technical use. Works on earthenware, chinaware, and art objects are entered under Pottery or Pottery craft. Particular objects and types are entered under their specific names, e. g. Bricks; Pipe, Clay; Refractory materials; Tiles; Vases.

UF   Ceramic technology
       Industrial ceramics
       Keramics
BT   Building materials
       Chemistry, Technical
       Clay
       Mineral industries
NT   Abrasives
       Ceramic capacitors
       etc . . .

Some scope notes might be more helpful, for example that found at the heading

Alcoholism and crime

Here are entered works on the relation between alcoholism and criminal behavior or the incidence of crime. Works on alcoholic intoxication as a criminal offense or as a factor of criminal liability are entered under the heading Drunkenness (Criminal law).

The cataloguer must consider soberly whether a book to be catalogued is about Alcoholism *as a crime*, or *in relation to* a crime? Or about Drunkenness? Authors unaware of the problems they might be causing may even write about both.

Where headings have been changed, this is now shown explicitly:

Online catalogs

UF   Catalogs, online [former heading]

Drawing

UF   Drawings [Former heading]
SA   *subdivision* Drawings under technical topics for collections of drawings, plans etc. . . . e.g. Automobiles—Drawings; Automotive drafting

Some headings are qualified to avoid ambiguity with homographs:

Annuals (Plants)
Bases (Chemistry)

Some headings may be subdivided by place, shown in the above examples as [May Subd Geog]; this has been discussed earlier.

Where a heading might have had a USE reference from the inverted form, this is not now done if the entry term would then be a broader term, for example:

Exterior lighting
  BT   Lighting

rather than the inverted

  UF   Lighting, Exterior

Similarly, inverted forms still used have a BT reference to the containing heading in strict accordance with the hierarchical principle, though this was not previously thought necessary, since the BT is the first word of the inverted term, e.g.:

Bridges, Iron and steel
  BT   Bridges

It is clear that the list has been greatly improved over the period since 1986, but equally many oddities still remain. One writer complained of the need for further standardization, quoting the example of FORTRAN and BASIC, two programming languages which were differently treated,[9] in LCSH17 they appear to be treated in exactly the same way, but reveal a rather different anomaly. We find the entries

FORTRAN (Computer program language)
BASIC (Computer program language)

each with the appropriate links. However, often qualifiers are *not* preferred terms:

Computer program languages
  USE   Programming languages (Electronic computers)
Electronic computers
  USE   Computers

We also find headings which can make us wonder about their value:

Alleyn, Roderick (Fictitious character) (Not Subd Geog)
  UF   Chief Inspector Alleyn (Fictitious character)
          Chief Inspector Roderick Alleyn (Fictitious character)
          Chief Superintendent Alleyn (Fictitious character)
          Chief Superintendent Roderick Alleyn (Fictitious character)
          Superintendent Alleyn (Fictitious character)
          Superintendent Roderick Alleyn (Fictitious character)

While yielding to no-one in our admiration for this fictitious character, we may ask whether there are enough books *about* him to warrant a heading to himself, and whether all of the cross-references are really necessary? Is a reader wanting information tion likely to look under the word 'Chief' rather than a name? The heading is in fact applied to the detective fiction written by Ngaio Marsh. Since LCSH is now a very large list, this kind of entry might be said to bulk it out needlessly, since the information tion it provides is easily available from reference works such as *Fiction index.*

Filing order

The filing order is very much as set out in Chapter 8. Numbers and symbols precede letters, giving:

C-coefficient
C. F. & I. Clause
C.O.D. Shipments
Ca Gaba Indians
Cazcan Indians
CCPM test
Crystals
CTC system (Railroads)

However, we also find the unfortunate anomaly that two versions of BASIC are quite widely separated because of their distinguishing tags:

BASIC–80 (Computer program language)
Basic Bantu language
Basic Christian communities
Basic . . .
BASIC–PLUS (Computer program language)

CDMARC Subjects

Since LC computerized its bibliographical operations in 1981, it has been working to exploit the advantages to be gained from this. One benefit from the availability of LCSH in machine-readable form is LCSH on CD-ROM, the CDMARC Subjects file. This represents all headings from the subject heading authority file since 1898, with certain exceptions. For the period up to 1976 the list contains topical headings only; since then, various categories of names used as headings have been included, for example names of sacred books, gods, legendary characters, geographic regions and features and streets. Some of these were affected by the adoption in 1981 of AACR2, and the list does not contain those names which were printed between 1976 and 1981 but did not conform with AACR2.

Because LC collects material from all over the world, some of the subject headings, as well as matter in the body of the entries in its catalogue, are in languages other than English. This means that symbols other than those found in the standard ASCII set may be used. The software may be set up for standard ASCII, extended ASCII, or the ALA character set; only the latter can cater for all the possible diacritical marks, and the display and printer must also be able to handle them if they are to be used. The appropriate selections must be made when installing the software and hardware.

Since subdivisions may be widely used to construct a complex heading, only a small proportion of possible heading-subdivision combinations are included. As in the printed version, certain headings may be used as patterns, and the Reference manual which accompanies the CD-ROM software contains as an Appendix an edited version of the Introduction from the printed list, including the table of pattern headings.

There are three types of display. A search leads to a simple list of headings, from which the user may select term(s) to follow up. Non-preferred terms are preceded in this list by an asterisk. Those selected may be shown in a thesaurus display, which reflects the entry as it appears in the printed list, or in a tagged record display, showing all the associated MARC tags and their codes.

A subject heading may, as has been described, contain various elements. Not all of these can be searched through the software, and the manual lists each part and states whether it can be searched or not. Headings may be sought, as may the LCC class number in those headings for which it is given. USE references fall into two categories: for specific references, the complete USE reference is shown in a window; for general USE references, e.g. for subdivisions which may be used under appropriate subjects, an example is given. Broader and Narrower terms, and Related terms, may be sought, but only as headings; in the Thesaurus display, they will of course show up in the normal way. Broader and Related terms are shown in the Tagged record display, but not Narrower terms. Finally, the LC control number (LCCN), consisting of the two-digit year plus a sequential number allocated to the heading on first use, can be sought, but is only displayed in the tagged MARC display format.

Other parts of the entry cannot be searched for. These include geographic subdivisions, scope notes, and general *SA* references. Kinds of subdivision other than geographic are also excluded except when they form part of an established heading.

The software operates through windows, which may be used for searching or browsing. There are two kinds of menu, the bar menu, which appears at the top of the base window, and option menus. Once a function is selected from the bar menu, the options menu for that function appears. The six functions are Search, Browse, Format, Action, Database and Quit. Each function has a chapter in the manual, and another chapter is devoted to the Mnemonics which can be used to speed up the search process. For all except the Search function, the options menu has a default value.

To begin a search, the Search option is selected from the bar menu. Two windows appear: the smaller left-hand window contains the search mnemonics, while the right-hand window is for the search statement. Searches can be entered in upper or lower case, and diacritics are ignored; these will be displayed if the right hardware is available, but not otherwise. Wildcards may be used: ? represents a single character, as usual, but instead of the * the dollar sign $ may be used for truncation, though the search does automatically right truncate sought terms word by word. Boolean operators AND, OR, and ANDNOT can be used in formulating the search string. Parentheses can be used in constructing a complex search, while headings which contain one of the operators (usually 'and') must be enclosed in quotes to avoid misinterpretation. A further important point is that two of the search mnemonics, sc (Subject – Complete term) and su (Subject Undivided) imply a search for terms at the beginning of a heading; two cannot be ANDed, as this will necessarily lead to a nil result.

Search statements are numbered, and the list grows until the user clears it. For each search the number of headings containing the sought term(s) is shown, and searches can be combined to reduce the number to an acceptable level for further action. The results can be browsed, and those which look suitable can be viewed in either the thesaurus or the tagged display format. (One of these is chosen as the default, but the other can be selected at any time as needed.) The thesaurus display shows related terms and their relationships, and can thus help in refining a search, whereas the tagged display only shows some of the related terms and does not demonstrate the kind of relationship.

The Browse function allows the user to look through five lists: subject terms; keyword – complete term; keyword – unsubdivided term; LC class number; LCCN. On selecting the subject terms list, the user is presented with a window showing the beginning of the list, and can type a starting point in a further small window. With the other lists, the user scans through using the cursor keys; when a term is selected, the number of postings for that term, i.e. the number of headings in which it occurs, is shown, and the user can then browse through these. Results can be saved in a file on disk, or printed.

The future

Computer production enables LC to print a new edition each year, incorporating all the previous year's changes. LCSH is now available in printed form; on microfiche, revised quarterly; on CD-ROM, revised quarterly; and online through the LC Internet node locis.loc.gov. Weekly lists of additions are available through the LC gopher marvel.loc.gov, replacing the monthly printed version, which was discontinued at the end of 1994. We now have a list in which future additions will be made according to rule, and past anomalies will be gradually eliminated. However, critics such as Studwell[10] make the point that there is still much to be done before LCSH can truly be said to be completely rule-based. Others like Berman[11] have not failed to point out the examples of bias implicit in many LCSH headings. There is still a lot of work to be done before we can totally dismiss Dykstra's opinion of LCSH as 'a professional disgrace'. We may of course adopt the pragmatic approach of Downing and Downing:[12]

> All terms appearing in boldface type in LCSH are valid headings. Since all invalid terms include references to usable ones, there is little need to learn the rationale behind LC's choice of valid headings. Furthermore, you will find numerous exceptions to any rules we might provide.

They do add the proviso:

> However, the ability to deduce the correct heading in at least some cases can save both time and frustration.

We should remember that this point applies to the user as well as the cataloguer, as we saw in Chapter 7.

Use online enables us to find words other than the first in a heading, overcoming a major difficulty with the use of phrase headings. Yet we may wonder whether it will serve us well in the online age. In the research on the use of LCSH in OPACS, discussed in Chapter 15, the point was made that very often the headings, when found, looked very plausible, but were not in a form which users would think of in searching. There are problems even with natural language searching, as Bates[13] points out:

> The average likelihood that any two people will use the same term for a concept or a book, or that a searcher and an information system will use the same term for a concept is in the range 10–20%.

Librarians and other intermediaries realize that LCSH is an artificial indexing language, and use it as such, but users probably do not, thus placing yet another barrier between them and the information they are seeking.

It must also be remembered that LCSH lists only a proportion of the headings to be found in the LC catalogue; free-floating subdivisions and pattern headings mean that the potential number of headings is not of the order of 200,000, but many millions. Yet the depth of indexing is in fact quite shallow: about 1.5 subject entries per book. Does the online age mean that we shall have to rethink our ideas on the subject coverage of books and the use of LCSH? We certainly cannot afford to be complacent.

References

1   Cutter, C. A., *Rules for a dictionary catalogue*, 4th edn, Washington, DC, Government Printing Office, 1904. Part 3, Subjects, included in *Theory of subject analysis. . .*

2   Miksa, F. *The subject in the dictionary catalog from Cutter to the present*, Chicago, ALA, 1983.
     See also the brief section on History in the Introduction to the current edition of LCSH.

3   Mann, M., *Introduction to cataloging and classification of books*, 2nd edn, Chicago, ALA, 1943.
     Pettee, J. *Subject headings: the history and theory of the alphabetical subject approach to books*, New York, NY, H. W. Wilson Co., 1946.
     Haykin, D. J., *Subject headings: a practical guide*, Washington, DC, USGPO, 1951.
     Metcalfe, J. W., *Information indexing and subject cataloguing*, New York, NY, Scarecrow Press, 1957.
     Chan, L. M. *Library of Congress subject headings: principles and application*, 2nd edn, Littleton, CO, Libraries Unlimited, 1986.
     Chan, L. M. *Library of Congress subject headings: principles of structure and policies for application*, Washington, DC, Library of Congress, 1990.

Chan, L. M. 'Subject access systems in the USA', *Subject indexing: principles and practice in the 90's*, Holley, R. P. (ed.), *et al.*, Munich, K. G. Saur, 1995, 181–212. (UBCIM Publication – New Series Vol 15.)

4   *The future of subdivisions in the Library of Congress subject headings system: report from the Subject Subdivisions Conference Sponsored by the Library of Congress, May 9–12, 1991*, edited by M. O. Conway.

5   Wiblin, D., *A guide to Library of Congress subject headings*, Adelaide, University of South Australia, 1994.

6   Library of Congress., *Subject cataloguing manual: subject headings*, 4th edn, Washington, DC, Library of Congress, 1991.
    See also Burgett, T. H. and Roberts, C. W., *Library of Congress Subject Headings: significant changes 1974–1988*, Lake Crystal, MN, Soldier Creek Press, 1988.

7   Dykstra, M.., 'LC subject headings disguised as a thesaurus', *Library journal*, **113** (4), 1988, 42–6.
    Rolland-Thomas, P., 'Thesaurus codes: an appraisal of their use in the Library of Congress Subject Headings', *Cataloging and classification quarterly*, **16** (2), 1993, 71–91.
    Dykstra, M., 'Can subject headings be saved?', *Library journal*, **113**, Sep 15 1988, 55–8.

8   Coates, E. J., *Subject catalogues: headings and structure*, London, Library Association, 1960, reissued with a new introduction 1988.

9   Bloomfield, M., 'A look at subject headings: a plea for standardization', *Cataloging & classification quarterly*, **16** (1), 1993, 119–24.

10 Studwell, W. E., *Library of Congress Subject Headings: philosophy, practice and prospects*, New York, NY, Haworth Press, 1990. Studwell has also written numerous articles in *Technicalities*.

11 Berman, S., *Prejudices and antipathies*, Metuchen, NJ, Scarecrow Press, 1971.
    Berman, S., *Subject cataloging: critiques and innovations*, New York, NY, Haworth Press, 1984.
    See also references quoted on critical classification in Chapter 7.

12 Downing, M. H. and Downing, D. H., *Introduction to cataloging and classification*, 6th edn, Jefferson, NC, McFarland, 1992.

13 Bates, M. 'Rethinking subject cataloging in the online environment' *Library resources and technical services*, **33** (4), 1989, 401–12.
    LC publishes two search guides for those wishing to use its catalogues through the Internet: *LOCIS reference manual*, 1994, and *LOCIS quick search guide*, 1994.

Chapter 24
Shorter lists of subject headings

LCSH has always been very detailed – the current edition contains over 200,000 headings – and early in the century a demand arose for a list which should be less comprehensive and more suited for the needs of small libraries. Minnie Earl Sears prepared a *List of subject headings for small libraries*. This was based on the practice found in 'nine small libraries known to be well cataloged'. The headings adopted were edited to conform with LCSH practice, so that libraries using LC cards or wishing to add headings from the larger list would be able to do so. This edition, published in 1923, contained *see* references and their corresponding refer froms, but not *see also* references. At the suggestion of teachers of cataloguing using the list as a textbook, Sears added these in the very much enlarged second edition published in 1926. To help further, she added a section on 'Practical suggestions for the beginner in subject heading work' in the third edition, 1933, which in various forms has been an important part of the work ever since.

The fourth (1939) and fifth (1944) editions were edited by Isabel Stevenson Monro. Some important changes were made, notably the addition of DDC numbers to headings; these were based on usage in the H W Wilson *Standard catalog for public libraries*, which was also the source of new headings for the list. The subtitle referring to the previous source, *Compiled from lists used in nine representative small libraries*, was dropped. Subdivisions of general application, e.g. *Bibliography*, were printed in italic.

In the sixth (1950), seventh (1954) and eighth (1959) editions, edited by Bertha M. Frick, further changes were made. As a tribute to the initiator, the name was changed to *Sears list of subject headings* in the sixth edition, and the reference to small libraries was dropped in recognition of the fact that the list was used by many larger libraries than Sears originally had in mind. 'Refer from' was replaced by x (*see* ref.) and xx (*see also* ref.), in line with the change in practice introduced in the 5th edition of LCSH (1948).

Barbara M. Westby took over as editor for the ninth edition (1965), which introduced one major change, in that the DDC numbers were omitted by the publisher; some users felt that their inclusion led to confusion between the purpose of subject headings and that of classification. The tenth edition (1972) also left them out, but they were restored in the eleventh edition (1977) as a worthwhile aid to those librarians who had been left with little help in the classification of their collections. The

'Practical suggestions' were revised, and in the eleventh edition (1977) were renamed 'Principles of the Sears List of subject headings', to emphasize the theoretical approach, and a section on non-book materials was added. Sexist, racist and pejorative terms were eliminated, with the exception of **Man**, which was retained for use in the anthropological and generic sense. (The English language lacks a neutral term corresponding to *On* in French or *Man* in German.) The term **Blacks** and its related headings, which had been included as an appendix in the tenth edition, were incorporated into the eleventh, replacing Negroes which had previously been used. (The 15th edition introduces an NT **African Americans** to improve precision.) The 12th edition (1982) continued the main tradition, but introduced two modifications. Filing order was to be as laid down in the ALA *Filing rules* with the exception of punctuation; terms with modifiers – e.g. **Crack (Drug)** – and phrase headings, e.g. **Buildings—Earthquake effects,** were to be filed after the term on its own. Two lists of common subdivisions were included; the first was words which were of quite general application, while the second included terms such as Chemotherapy which could be used to subdivide a number of terms but by no means all.

The 13th edition (1986), edited by Carmen Rovira and Caroline Reves, continued in the same mould, with some significant changes, many the result of producing the list from an online database for the first time. Filing was according to the ALA *Filing rules* without the previous exception, so that all entries were interfiled regardless of subdivisions (**Moon—Surface**), inversion (**Architecture, Domestic**), phrases (**Fathers and daughters**) or parenthetical modifiers (**Dating (Social customs)**). This is one result of automation; where catalogue entries are to be filed by computer, exceptions to rules must be avoided wherever possible. Direct entry is preferred to inverted, e.g. **Natural childbirth** rather than Childbirth, Natural; however, revision of older headings is done as needed, so we still find **Concrete, Reinforced** rather than Reinforced concrete. The class numbers given are from ADDC11, with the exception of Computer science and Computer engineering, where the schedules from the then forthcoming ADDC12 were made available. Many terms were updated in line with LCSH, others in accordance with appropriate usage, e.g. **Expo '89 (Paris, France)** replaced the previous **EXPO '70 (Osaka, Japan)**. Headings from *Subject headings for children's literature* from LC were incorporated except where they conflicted with existing headings or pattern headings. The two lists of subdivisions from the 12th edition were merged into one.

The 14th edition, edited by Martha T. Mooney, was published in 1991, and did not introduce any major changes. It continued the programme of revision along the lines of the previous edition, and reflected the increasing pace of change brought about by the use of computers for the production of such lists, and also the widespread use of OPACs in public libraries. **Concrete, Reinforced** became **Reinforced concrete. Motion pictures, Silent,** was replaced by **Silent films.** Some headings from LCSH were merged or simplified, e.g. **Generic drugs,** where LCSH has **Generic drugs** *and* **Drugs—Generic substitution**; LCSH9 split **Acrobats and Acrobatism** into **Acrobats** and **Acrobatics,** but Sears preferred the combined heading **Acrobats and Acrobatics.**

The scheme

The 15th edition (SEARS15)[1] begins with a Preface which outlines the development of the scheme, including any changes from previous editions. This is followed by the *Principles of the Sears list of subject headings*, the very practical introduction to subject heading use which has again been substantially revised for this edition. It is well worth study by anyone involved in alphabetical subject cataloguing, not just those wishing to use this particular list. It gives a concise description of the process of subject cataloguing using specific entry, drawing attention to problems that may arise. For example, common usage as the source of headings is stressed, making the point that this may well differ from the USA to the UK. Plural nouns are generally preferred, but the singular form is used for abstract concepts. One example of this which seems unusual is the substitution of the singular **Tariff** for the previously used plural Tariffs. The distinction is drawn between Arab, relating to the people; Arabian, referring to the geographical area; and Arabic, for the language, script and literature, with the recommendation that this pattern should be used for similar headings. Qualifiers may be used to distinguish homographs, but in practice, careful choice of terminology means that there are in effect no homographs left, e.g.

Transmutation (Chemistry)
> Use for materials on the transmutation of metals in nuclear physics. Materials on medieval attempts to change base metals into gold are entered under
> **Alchemy**

Ensembles (Mathematics)
> USE   **Set theory**

Ensembles (Music)   782; 784
> Use for materials on small instrumental or vocal groups and for the music written for such groups
> SA   Kinds of vocal or instrumental ensembles, e.g. **Jazz ensembles**; to be added as needed
> NT   **Jazz ensembles**

Compound headings may be used, e.g. **Free trade and protection**, but a word of caution suggests that in computer-based retrieval systems they have limited value except when indicating a phase relationship, e.g. **Art and religion**. Direct entry is now preferred to inverted for all headings except battles and massacres and the one heading **State, The**. Phrase headings may be necessary for subjects which cannot be reduced to a single word without losing their meaning, e.g. **Crimes without victims**. A work which covers several topics within a broader heading is given up to three headings, otherwise the broader heading is used – a solution very much on line with that recommended in DDC.

There are various forms of subdivision, mostly included in the List of commonly used subdivisions, which may be used to extend the list of headings, beginning with subject subdivisions. These may be of wide application, e.g. **Analysis**; or more limited, e.g. **Religion**, used as a subdivision for ethnic groups or countries, e.g.

Italy—Religion. Bibliographical forms, e.g. **Periodicals**, or common subjects, e.g. **Statistics**, are also in the main list, with instructions on their use. Period subdivisions are used where appropriate, as an extension of the subdivision History, e.g. **Japan—History—1945–1952, Allied occupation**. Specific dates have been used since the 12th edition in order to facilitate computer filing; the name of a specific period may be added after the dates. Place subdivisions may be used where a note is found in the list, e.g. **Libraries** (may subdiv. geog.). Art and music take the adjectival form, e.g. **Asian Art**.

There are lengthy discussions of the forms of heading appropriate for Biography and Literature, both subjects which are widely found in public libraries. (120 new headings have been added to give improved access to imaginative literature[2] through subject and genre, e.g. **Horror films**). These are followed by brief notes on Nonbook materials, in which it is pointed out that these may need additions to the list, since they often deal with very specific topics; and Terminology, which looks at the problems involved in establishing the intension and extension of headings, especially new terms. The List has a good supply of scope notes, e.g.

Boring 622
Use for materials on the operation of cutting holes in earth or rock. Materials dealing with workshop operations in metal, wood, etc., are entered under **Drilling and boring**

though a few of these are less useful:

Hieroglyphics
Use for materials on that form of writing distinguished by stylized pictures . . .

where the scope note adds little to a dictionary definition.

Sears now uses thesaurus type cross-references BT, NT, RT, SA, USE and UF. There is a detailed explanation of how these relate to the previously used *see* and *see also* references, which are still recommended for cross-references in public; this is illustrated by diagrams of catalogue cards showing how they may be set out. These examples also show how a scope note from the List may be modified for use by the public. References from RT to RT are made both ways only if both headings are in use in the catalogue, and upward references from NT to BT are not made.

A bibliography of useful works is included so that those who wish to follow the theory of subject headings in more detail may do so. A list of headings to be added by the cataloguer is given, e.g. names of places, names of government bodies (Proper names); and birds, vegetables, diseases, chemicals (Common names). Altogether, there are over 500 places where headings may be added by the cataloguer, either through inclusion in this list or by notes or examples in the List itself. Seven headings, e.g. **Presidents—United States**, **English language**, are used as key headings to illustrate how similar headings may be subdivided. There is throughout an emphasis on the fact that each library should expand the list to meet the needs of its own collections, following the principles and examples set out. The preliminaries conclude with a list of headings which have been changed, showing the replacement headings. In the List, headings which have been replaced are shown as *[Former heading]*, e.g.

Bicycles and bicycling
    USE   Bicycles
            Cycling
Bicycles
    UF   Bicycles and bicycling *[Former heading]*
    NT   **Mountain bikes**
    RT   **Cycling**

SA (*see also*) references are used to draw attention to the existence of a potentially large set of related terms, e.g.:

Education [may subdiv. geog] **370**
    SA   types of education to be added as needed, e.g. **Vocational education**; classes of person . . . e.g. **Deaf—Education**; and subjects with the subdivision Study and teaching, e.g. **Science—Study and teaching**; to be added as needed

The List is well set out in two columns, though the right-hand column is no longer left blank for any additions or alterations the cataloguer needs to make, as it was in previous editions. To do so would have greatly increased the size (and cost) of the List, which is already 758 pages long. Preferred headings are always in bold type, even in cross-references; this makes it very simple to identify those headings which are to be used and those which are not. American usage is preferred, but often with cross-references which make amendment for an English library simple, e.g. Trams. *See* **Street railroads**. A considerable effort has obviously been made to 'tidy up' the list by removing unwanted headings, e.g. Stokers, Mechanical; and including new headings such as **Pacific Rim, Multiculturalism**. Every heading has been examined to try to ensure its currency and usefulness; for example, Philology, Comparative has been replaced by **Linguistics**. We do still find the occasional anomaly, e.g. **Ping-Pong**; surely this has by now enough international status to be known by its proper name Table tennis.

The political turmoil in Eastern Europe has led to a similar upheaval in the relevant headings:

Soviet Union 947.084; 947.085
    Use for materials on the Union of Soviet Socialist Republics between 1917 and 1991. Material on Russia or the Russian Empire before 1917 are entered under **Russia**. Materials on the independent republic of Russia since its establishment in December 1991 are entered under **Russia (Republic)** . . .

The class numbers given are from ADDC12, with a normal limit of four digits, though standard subdivisions may be added. Usually one class number is given, but if a subject covers two important areas two class marks may be given, as in the Ensembles and Soviet Union examples above.

There are some interesting differences from LCSH. Sears has **Geographic names**; LCSH Geographical names USE Names, Geographical. Sears has **Free universities**, which does not appear in LCSH at all. As a musical instrument, oboe is one of the headings which the cataloguer will add as necessary in Sears; in LCSH, **Oboe** and its accompanying headings run to five columns, reflecting the strength of the music collection in LC. **Oak** appears in Sears, with BT references to **Trees** and **Wood**; in LCSH, **Oak** has 22 Narrower Terms. Sears has the compound heading **Free trade and protection,** UF Protection; LCSH has **Free trade**, UF Free trade and protection, with BT International Trade and NT Free ports and zones. Sears has **Geographical myths**, UF Cities, imaginary; Fictitious places; Imaginary places; Islands, imaginary; Places, imaginary. LCSH again has far more detail: **Geographical myths** UF Cities, imaginary; Fictitious places; Imaginary cities; Imaginary islands; Imaginary places; Islands, imaginary; Mythical places; Places, imaginary. However, it also has some 36 NT, including OZ, Thrush Green (Imaginary place), and Vulcan (Imaginary planet).

For the small to medium sized library for which LCSH is too detailed, Sears List is a practical tool which can be very helpful. Because it is based on LCSH practice, it can be used with MARC records to produce suitable headings, and can also be adapted for British practice without too much difficulty. As a companion to ADDC, it is a practical and manageable tool.[3]

SCIS Subject headings list

During the 1970s, education authorities in several Australian states started to offer centralized cataloguing services. In South Australia, for example, the South Australian Educational Resources Information Service SAERIS was established, using a central computer to produce cataloguing copy for distribution to schools. At that time schools did not have their own computing facilities, and used card catalogues; the idea of a computer-based union catalogue was therefore seen as impractical, and SAERIS produced a catalogue on COM fiche for all the books added to school libraries, which were bought through the central purchasing agency. In each school library an aide could copy cataloguing information from the fiches, which were updated regularly, for the books added to that library.

At that time, *Sears List* was widely used in Australian school libraries, but the introduction of the new computer-based systems was seen as an opportunity to produce headings which would use Australian terminology. Various lists of subject headings were devised for SAERIS and the parallel services. In the early 1980s a Federal government project to establish a centralized service for the whole of Australia was successful, and led to a need for a suitable national subject headings list. The headings obviously needed to be suitable for school students, and a target of reading age 10 years was set, with the recognition that for senior secondary school materials, more complex headings would be needed. Emphasis was also placed on subjects covered by school curricula.

A further important consideration was that it should use Australian English. In general, libraries in Australia use LCSH and DDC. LCSH in particular causes problems, as it ignores many terms used throughout Australia in favour of the American equivalents. While this can be remedied for adults through cross-references or general knowledge, it was felt that for schools a list reflecting Australian usage was necessary. (It is worth mentioning that an attempt was made to produce a list of Australian subject headings; a preliminary list LASH was produced in 1978,[4] and a final list FLASH[5] in 1981; the National Library of Australia adopted some of the changes for its cataloguing practice. The object of that list was not to produce a complete self-contained list, but one which would supplement, and be used in conjunction with, LCSH, then in its eighth edition.) For the Australian Schools Catalogue Information Service ASCIS, the Macquarie Dictionary was adopted as the authority for terms and spelling, supplemented by the Concise Oxford Dictionary of current English, and the first edition was published in 1985 as the ASCIS *Subject headings list*. Unlike LASH, the list was always intended to be self-contained, and to replace *Sears List* rather than complement it.

A second edition was produced in 1989, containing an additional 700 headings. For the third edition, published in 1993, the decision was made to broaden the scope to include New Zealand, and the title was changed from ASCIS to *SCIS Subject Headings List*.[6] The List now contains some 6,000 preferred terms, with a rather larger number of non-preferred. Preferred terms are listed in bold upper case wherever found, with non-preferred terms in lower case. There is a list of over 100 standard subdivisions which may be used generally. Headings are restricted to one subheading; to express more complex subjects, multiple headings should be used. Some headings have subheadings enumerated, and others have instructions to subdivide geographically. **AUSTRALIA** and **NEW ZEALAND** are to be used as models for the subdivisions applicable to countries, **VICTORIA** for states, and **MELBOURNE (VIC.)** for cities. There are other model headings, e.g. **ANIMALS, BIBLE, ENGLISH LANGUAGE** and **MOTOR VEHICLES**, listed in Section VI of the Introduction. The List thus has the potential to generate far more than the basic 6,000 terms listed. Cross-references are shown by *see* and *see also*, with the complementary x (*see* from) and xx (*see also* from).

Each preferred heading may have various notes. In the order in which they appear, these include instructions to divide geographically; scope notes; instructions on subdivisions; related or narrower terms (see also); blanket references; non-preferred terms for which the term is used (x); other preferred terms which are linked to the term (xx). Not all of these will be found at all headings, of course, but the appropriate ones are given in each case. Certain categories of heading are not included, but may be added by the cataloguer as the need arises; these include proper names, e.g. ethnic groups, languages, places; corporate names, e.g. ships, government bodies, religious sects; and common names, e.g. diseases, minerals, organs and regions of the body. In addition, wherever a blanket reference is made the cataloguer may add appropriate headings. In most cases an example is given, which the cataloguer can follow.

As with *Sears List*, the printed list itself is to be used as the authority file, by marking those headings which have been used, and writing in any headings added. The list is printed in one column, but does not specifically leave a second column blank. However, there is enough space left for additional headings to be written in at the correct place, or close to it. Careful instructions are given in Section III of the introduction; it is recommended that if the list is used in microfiche form, the authority file should be on cards, while the online version may require an authority file on cards, or may be annotated itself, depending on the software in use.

Some examples will illustrate the way that the above points work in practice.

MERCHANT NAVY
    (may subdiv. geog.)
    see also **CARGO SHIPS; SHIPPING**
    x   Mercantile marine; Merchant marine
    xx   **MARITIME LAW; SAILORS; SHIPPING; SHIPS; TRANSPORT**

TELEVISION
    (May subdiv.geog.)
    Use for general works on television as well as works
    limited to the technical processes. For works limited to the media aspects of
    television see **TELEVISION BROADCASTING**

FRUIT
    see also **APPLES; BERRIES; CITRUS FRUIT; DATES (FRUIT); DRIED FRUIT; FRUIT JUICES; JAM AND JAM MAKING; STONE FRUIT; TROPICAL FRUIT**
    see also names of fruit, e.g. **APPLES**; etc.
    xx   **FARM PRODUCE; FOOD**

If we turn to CITRUS FRUIT, we find:

CITRUS FRUIT
    xx   **FRUIT**

Although there is no explicit instruction at **CITRUS FRUIT**, we can use terms such as **LEMONS** as headings, following the blanket reference at the broader term **FRUIT**.

BIBLE
    The subdivisions under this heading may also be used for
        any part of the Bible under the same form of entry as
        for the texts of such parts, e.g.. **BIBLE. N.T. GOSPELS – USE**; etc.
    These subdivisions may also be used under the names of
        other religious scriptures if appropriate, e.g. **KORAN – COMMENTARIES**; etc.
    see also **COMMANDMENTS; KORAN – COMMENTARIES; TEN COMMANDMENTS; WOMEN IN THE BIBLE**
    x   Holy Bible; Scriptures, Holy
    xx   **HISTORY, ANCIENT; SACRED BOOKS**

BIBLE. N.T.
>Use the same subject subdivisions as those given under
>>**BIBLE**
>See also **SERMON ON THE MOUNT**
>See also names of special events, e.g.. **SERMON ON THE MOUNT**
>x   Bible. New Testament; New Testament

All in all, there are about four pages of headings for the Bible, perhaps the contribution of the Religious education subject headings contributed by the Catholic Education Office of Victoria.

Because this is an Australasian list, Aborigines and Maoris are treated differently from other ethnic groups. For example, we find **ABORIGINES – ART**, not Art, Aboriginal, whereas at **ART** we find:

ART
>(May subdiv. geog. adjectival form or by ethnic group)

with no link to **ABORIGINES – ART** at all. Similarly, we find **MAORI – LAND RIGHTS**, while at **LAND RIGHTS** we find:

LAND RIGHTS
>(May subdiv.geog.)
>See also   **ABORIGINES – LAND RIGHTS; MAORI – LAND RIGHTS**

where there is a cross-reference to the two special cases. We also find Australian terms preferred to American, e.g.:

Railroads
>See **RAILWAYS**
Ranch life
>See **FARM LIFE**
Civil service
>See **PUBLIC SERVICE**

In general, natural language form is used, but some headings are inverted, though it is difficult to determine the principles on which a decision is made. Thus we find:

BRITAIN, BATTLE OF, 1940
COOKERY, FOOD PROCESSOR
BLIND, BOOKS FOR THE
HISTORY, ANCIENT   [but **MIDDLE AGES – HISTORY**]
GOVERNMENT, RESISTANCE TO

Where necessary, homographs are distinguished by parenthetical qualifiers, e.g.

SEALING (HUNTING)
SEALS AND SEALING (TECHNOLOGY)
SEALS (ANIMALS)
SEALS (NUMISMATICS)

It is perhaps an interesting comment on technological development to see that Apple and Amiga win out over IBM in the microcomputer field:

MICROCOMPUTERS
  See also **APPLE II (COMPUTER); COMPUTERS IN EDUCATION MICROPROCESSORS; MINICOMPUTERS**
  See also names of specific microcomputers, e.g.. **APPLE II (COMPUTER)**
  x   Home computers; Personal computers
COMPUTERS
  See also **AMIGA (COMPUTER)** . . .

though of course one can always add a specific make. There are over five pages of entries under the word Computer, which indicates the significance of computing in education today.

Care has been taken to avoid terms which imply discrimination of one kind or another. In consequence, some headings are a little clumsy, until such time as a generally agreed term can be adopted. There are also some where terminology lags behind current thought.

DISCRIMINATION IN EMPLOYMENT
  x   Equal opportunity in employment

though the arm of government concerned with this is the Equal Opportunity Office.

DISABLED
  See also **DISABLED CHILDREN** . . .
DISABLED CHILDREN
  See also **BRAIN–DAMAGED CHILDREN** . . .

Government policy in Australia is to mainstream children with disabilities so that they are educated in normal schools with other children; these headings are not in tune with modern usage.

Despite some minor criticisms, the List is a useful one which serves its purpose well. Like *Sears List*, it was developed for small libraries where the detail of LCSH would be inappropriate. It also represents a major effort to produce a list of headings in the language used in Australian schools, rather than continue the adherence to American practice as exemplified in *Sears List*. Further editions will no doubt appear as necessary now that the List is widely accepted throughout Australasia.

References

1   *Sears List of subject headings*, 15th edition, edited by Joseph Miller. New York, NY, H. W. Wilson, 1994.
2   Hennepin County Library (Minn.), *Unreal! Hennepin County Library Subject Headings for fictional characters and places*, 2nd edn, Jefferson, NC, McFarland & Co., 1992, was one of the sources used in this exercise.
3   The references given for LCSH also apply in large measure to *Sears List*, but

the best introduction is the *Principles of the Sears List* found in the book itself.

4   McKinlay, J., A list of Australian subject headings, preliminary edition. Bundoora, Library Association of Australia, Cataloguers' Section, 1978.

5   A list of Australian subject headings, compiled by John McKinlay for the Cataloguers' Section of the Library Association of Australia. 1st edn. (Flash). Sydney, LAA, 1981.

6   SCIS subject headings list, 3rd edn. [Schools Catalogue Information Service (SCIS)]. Melbourne, D W Thorpe in association with Curriculum Corporation, 1994.

Part IV
Post-coordinate indexing languages

Chapter 25
Science and technology

A large number of indexing languages have been devised for post-coordinate index-ing; these are usually called thesauri, though it is often difficult to distinguish many of them from what are normally referred to as lists of subject headings. The major distinction appears to lie in their use in computer systems (and their manual precur-sors) in post-coordinate fashion, rather than in library catalogues. There is however no equivalent of the large general classification scheme such as DDC or LCC, or list of subject headings such as LCSH, nor is any scheme generally accepted. Many abstracting and indexing services have their own thesauri, as have many small spe-cial libraries and information centres. However, some of the lists are significant either as models of thesaurus construction or in being used in major databases. This chapter and the next will cover a small selection of the total available; the explana-tions given will often apply to other lists not specifically covered.

EJC thesaurus

The Defense Documentation Center was at one time called the Armed Services Technical Information Agency ASTIA. To give access to its collections ASTIA compiled a list of subject headings, the fourth edition being published in 1959 as the *ASTIA subject headings list*. This list was the basis of one of the earliest attempts to evaluate different indexing languages in the early 1950s, when a test was run to compare its effectiveness with that of the Uniterm system proposed by Taube. The test was inconclusive because it proved impossible to arrive at agreement on whether documents retrieved by the two systems were relevant. It was this test which prompted the first Cranfield Project, in which comparisons were made under controlled laboratory-type conditions for the first time. The ASTIA tests were inconclusive, but the agency was also investigating the possibility of computerizing its retrieval systems, and decided to adopt post-coordinate indexing. For this pur-pose the first *Thesaurus of ASTIA descriptors* was compiled, the first edition being published in 1960, and the second in 1962. At the same time the other three major US government agencies which provided abstracting and indexing services were also looking at the possibilities of developing their own lists, and a joint project to develop a common indexing vocabulary was carried out, Project LEX. (The other three agencies were the USAEC, now the Energy Commission; NASA; and the Office of Technical Services, now NTIS.)

At the same time, the scientific and engineering societies were also becoming concerned with the problems of the dissemination of information. Much of the major scientific and engineering literature in English is produced by these societies, and it was increasingly evident that much of it was not being used as well as it should have been. They began a programme to improve standards of writing and presentation, including the use of clear and specific titles (which could be used in KWIC indexing), the submission of abstracts with papers, and the use of suitable terms for indexing. To further this latter end the Engineers Joint Council produced the EJC *Thesaurus of engineering terms*, published in 1964. This contained some 8,000 preferred terms and over 2,000 non-preferred entry terms. It was however much more significant for some of its features. Relationships were shown by the BT, NT, RT, USE and UF codes now standard; however, there was no apparent classificatory base, and it was difficult to see the justification for some of the relationships, which seemed to have been made in a haphazard manner. Scope notes were used to clarify some headings, though not a high proportion; however, they did include both instructions for use and definitions, e.g.:

ELECTRIC POWER
(USE MORE SPECIFIC TERM IF POSSIBLE)
BURSTS (MINES)
(EXCLUDES EXPLOSIONS)

The list also contained a set of roles for general use; their use raised a number of problems, and they were not widely adopted.[1]

The list was the subject of several critical reviews, and in 1965 a large-scale revision was begun, with the intention of enlarging the vocabulary, rationalizing the network of cross-references, and merging the list with that being produced as a result of Project LEX. The result was the publication in 1967 of the *Thesaurus of engineering and scientific terms*, usually known as TEST. One of the first steps was to formulate rules and conventions governing the selection of terms and the construction of cross-references; these rules are printed as Appendix I and include, among other things, one of the few clear tabulations giving guidance on the use of singular or plural forms of nouns. Most of the rules set out were restatements or refinements of rules which had been used in subject headings since Cutter's *Rules*, but it was certainly valuable to have them gathered together in this concise form.

The list contained 17,810 preferred terms and 5,554 USE references from entry terms. The relationships between terms were much more clearly based on the kind of analysis now considered to be essential. Some terms were qualified by context in parentheses, and some scope notes are given, e.g.:

Microorganism control (sewage)
Microorganism control (water)
Control of organisms such as bacteria, viruses, plankton, algae and protozoa

Some composite terms were to be replaced by two single terms, e.g.:

Membrane filters
USE   Filters
and   Membranes

Three other features of TEST have become standard parts of thesaurus construction, though not usually in the exact form used. The first is the 'permuted index', though why this mistaken term was adopted is not clear. It consists of a list of single words showing all the headings in which that word appears in the main sequence, e.g.:

Membrane
>Hyaline membrane disease
>Ion exchange membrane electrolytes
>Membrane filters

Membranes
>Webs (Membranes)

Membranes is a preferred term, and is shown in bold *italic*, an unfortunate reversal of the convention used in the main sequence; Membrane is not, and is shown in bold roman.

The second feature is the Subject category Index, which is in effect a very broad classification into 22 major subject fields, each of them divided into groups, of varying sizes. Computers is Group 02 of Category 09; in the main sequence we find:

Computers   0902

The classification is a modified form of one devised by COSATI, but we may wonder why an existing scheme such as UDC was not chosen.

The third feature is the Hierarchical index. Any term in the main sequence with no BT links, but at least two levels of NT links, is tabulated, showing all the terms which are linked to it through NT references, thus:

Addition resins
>.Vinyl resins
>..Vinyl copolymers
>...Styrene copolymers
>....Styrene butadiene resins

These hierarchies only appear for top terms, i.e. those with no broader terms; it is not possible to look for Styrene copolymers, for example, and find its place in the overall structure.

All three of these features are commonly found in current thesauri in this or similar form, and the main importance of TEST lies in its introduction of these important conventions. One vital aspect seems to have been overlooked: the scheme has never been revised, and is in consequence no longer a practical indexing tool. Its place has been taken by various other thesauri, but its importance as a model has been great.

Thesaurus of scientific, technical and engineering terms[2]

From the name, we might expect that this would be a successor to TEST, but the link appears to be indirect. This thesaurus is based on the NASA *Thesaurus* and the DoD *Thesaurus of scientific and engineering terms*. It is therefore not surprising that term selection was based on a term's significance and use in aerospace literature. The list is nominally divided into two volumes, though both are presented in one physical volume.

The first is the hierarchical listing, the second the access vocabulary, though the actual arrangement in each volume is not quite what one would expect.

In the hierarchical listing, BT-NT relationships are not used; instead, the term is shown within its generic structure (GS) in a somewhat similar fashion to the hierarchical index in TEST, but more fully. Preferred terms are entered in bold upper case, with non-preferred terms in lower case. Homographs are distinguished in two ways; in general, a *gloss* is added as a parenthetical qualifier, which forms part of the term, but in a few cases there is a parenthetical scope note, which does *not* form part of the term. It is difficult to identify these SN from the conventional kind, which are also found. Yet another kind of SN is used to expand headings which are longer than 42 characters, which, for reasons which are not explained, are truncated; there are again very few such truncations – 42 characters is a much longer heading than is normally found in a thesaurus! Terms are entered directly; inverted terms are found through the Access vocabulary. Some headings are considered to be necessary as part of the structure, but have the SN (*Use of a more specific term is recommended – consult the terms below*); these are known as *array headings*, and are identified by an ∞ (infinity symbol). The terms to be consulted are all listed as RT, which leads to some hierarchical confusion. Identifiers, for example specific models of aircraft or computers, are included as descriptors without distinction. Abbreviations are usually spelled out, but some abbreviations in common use in technical or aerospace literature are found. The filing order is dictated by the computer coding, so that (precedes A, with figures filing after letters. Some illustrations will show these features:

CRACKING (CHEMICAL ENGINEERING)
CRACKING (FRACTURING)
SPECTROSCOPIC ANALYSIS
  SN   (FOR SPECTROSCOPIC TOOLS IN CHEMICAL ANALYSIS)
  GS   CHEMICAL TESTS
         .CHEMICAL ANALYSIS
         ..SPECTROSCOPIC ANALYSIS
         SPECTROSCOPY
         .SPECTROSCOPIC ANALYSIS
         ..FLAME SPECTROSCOPY
DAWN CHORUS
  UF   CHORUS (DAWN PHENOMENON)
         CHORUS PHENOMENON
  GS   ATMOSPHERIC RADIATION
         .DAWN CHORUS
         ELECTROMAGNETIC INTERFERENCE
         .RADIOFREQUENCY INTERFERENCE
         ..BLACKOUT (PROPAGATION
         ...ELECTROMAGNETIC NOISE

....ATMOSPHERICS
.....IONOSPHERICS
......**DAWN CHORUS**
RT   AURORAS
           MAGNETIC STORMS
           WHISTLERS

(Ornithologists may consider this use of the term to be a cuckoo in the nest!)

SL 1
   USE   SKYLAB 1
SLV
   USE   STANDARD LAUNCH VEHICLES

but

Handley Page HP 115 Aircraft
   USE   HP 115 AIRCRAFT
Metal-semiconductor-metal semiconductors
   USE   MSM (SEMICONDUCTORS)
Controlled avalanche transit time devices   [40 characters]
   USE   CATT DEVICES
Trapped plasma avalanche triggered transit   [42 characters]
   USE   TRAPATT DEVICES

The word devices appears to have been omitted to shorten the heading.

MARS (PLANET)
MARS ATMOSPHERE

The very brief introduction mentions that there is no limit on the number of NT that may be shown in a Generic Structure, and points out that MEASURING INSTRUMENTS has over 300. As would be expected in a thesaurus based on NASA terminology, SATELLITES has well over 500 – six columns of 95 lines – plus 36 RT links. Of the narrower terms forming the GS under Satellites, only five are first level: Active satellites; Artificial satellites; Natural satellites; SAMOS; and TDR satellites. (The SN excludes Planets.) Apart from the fact that it is quite difficult to follow through the hierarchies, it is difficult to see why SAMOS [Satellite And Missile Observation System] and TDR satellites (which have no NT) are not listed as subordinate to Artificial satellites. The use of Array terms also makes it difficult to follow the hierarchical structure, since all the terms one is recommended to consult are listed as RT, when they are clearly not all at the same level.

∞   **CHEMICAL COMPOUNDS**
      SN   *(Use of a more specific term is recommended – consult the terms below)*
      RT   ...
      ∞   METAL COMPOUNDS
      ∞   ORGANOMETALLIC COMPOUNDS

∞   ALKALI METAL COMPOUNDS
CALCIUM COMPOUNDS

    · · ·

RT   ∞ ALKALINE EARTH COMPOUNDS
        ∞ CHEMICAL COMPOUNDS
        ∞ METAL COMPOUNDS
SODIUM COMPOUNDS

    · · ·

RT   ∞ ALKALI METAL COMPOUNDS
        ∞ CHEMICAL COMPOUNDS
        ∞ METAL COMPOUNDS

Metal compounds are surely a BT to Alkali metal compounds but NT to Chemical compounds, with a parallel hierarchy for alkaline earths.

Following the hierarchical listing there is a two and a half page Supplement of terms which presumably were added after the compilation of the main sequence. The place of these terms in the sequence is shown by †, e.g.:

WEAR INHIBITORS
    GS   INHIBITORS
               .WEAR INHIBITORS
    RT   RETARDANTS
†
WEAR TESTS

The † indicates that an additional term will be found in the Supplement, in this case WEAR RESISTANCE.

The second 'volume' contains the Access vocabulary, which is in effect a kind of KWOC index to the main sequence, allowing the user to find words other than the first. The list is referred to as one of 'pseudo-terms', but the reason for this name is not explained; comparable indexes are found in every thesaurus of any importance. It is mainly computer-produced, but contains some very useful entries which had to be intellectually compiled. These give access to parts of compound words which would not normally generate entries by straightforward computer manipulation, for example parts of names of chemical compounds. Some other entries are those for chemical elements, and states of the USA, which are spelled out in full in the main sequence.

Mn
    USE   MANGANESE
MN
    USE   MINNESOTA
(Computers), Memory
    USE   MEMORY (COMPUTERS)
Computers, Micro
    USE   MICROCOMPUTERS
Fluorides, Oxy

USE OXYFLUORIDES
ACCLIMATIZATION
Acclimatization, Altitude
    USE ALTITUDE ACCLIMATIZATION
Formula, Moliere
    USE   SPATIAL DISTRIBUTION
              SECONDARY COSMIC RAYS
              COSMIC RAY SHOWERS

Summary

The scheme has very little explanation or history, and it is not clear whether its purpose is general use or specifically for NASA. There are no guidelines on use, and the introduction sets out the ground rules very sparsely. It obviously represents a fairly large effort, and it is surprising not to have the necessary background information to make its use straightforward. Despite this, there are some features worth studying; the generic structure approach in effect merges two sections of the TEST model, the alphabetical list and the hierarchical index. The segmentation of terms to give access through prefixes is obviously relevant to many subject fields. Perhaps in any future edition the compilers (who are not identified) could expand the preliminary pages to be rather more helpful.

Thesaurofacet

The English Electric Company, now lost to view in a large conglomerate, had a very active library service, and the librarian and other members of the CRG devised the EE *Classification of engineering*, which reached its third edition in 1961. As the library began to use computer techniques and post-coordinate indexing, it was decided that a new version should combine a classification and a thesaurus. The result, with the rather ugly name *Thesaurofacet*, was published in 1970,[3] and consisted of a classification and a complementary alphabetical sequence. As has been pointed out in earlier chapters, a classification scheme can only display one set of genus-species relationships at a time, though a particular term may appear in more than one hierarchy, of course. The alphabetical sequence was used as the index to the scheme; on looking up a term, the user would find a class number, but possibly also some related terms. If we are asked for information on Thinners, we turn to the thesaurus and find:

    Thinners *use*
    Solvents

At Solvents we find:

    Solvents   **HXG**
        UF   Thinners
        RT   Dispersants
             . . .

　　　　　　　　Solvent extraction
　　NT(A)　　　Paint thinners
　　　　　　　　Turpentine

At HXG in the classification schedules we find:

HX	**Materials by purpose**
HX2	Additives
HXG	Solvents

Looking at the display in the thesaurus may however have clarified that we are actually interested in Paint thinners; we find that the class number for this is VGD in the hierarchy:

VF	**Paint technology**
VG	Paint constituents
VGD	Paint thinners

By using the combination of thesaurus and classification, we can find related terms as well as the terms we first think of, but with the classification schedule to help us by displaying the relationships in the broader context.

The importance of *Thesaurofacet* lay in the combination of two tools, but it was also welcomed in the UK as having a British bias rather than the American bias of the EJC thesaurus and TEST. Like TEST, it has not been kept up to date, but it served an important function in emphasizing the interrelationship of thesaurus and classification. By looking at these early thesauri we can see the features which appear in one way or another in thesauri in current use.

BSI ROOT thesaurus

Thesaurofacet had no direct successor, but it formed the starting point for a similar project. In 1966, the British Standards Institution began a service to exporters which drew on its large collection of overseas standards; in order to do so, BSI devised a thesaurus based on *Thesaurofacet*. In 1977 the need for an expanded and revised tool was seen, not merely in connection with BSI's own collections but also to provide a standard vocabulary for ISONET, the international network of standards organizations. In 1981, after considerable work to develop its existing thesaurus, BSI published the first edition of its *ROOT thesaurus*, which was adopted by ISONET; the second edition was published in 1985, and the third in 1988.

Like *Thesaurofacet*, the scheme has as its main basis a classification scheme, with a complementary alphabetical sequence, computer-produced from the main schedules. The notation reflecting the structure is of course independent of language, and in consequence the scheme lends itself to the production of editions in languages other than English; the first edition was made available in French as a computer printout, and translations have also been made into German, Japanese and Portuguese. Other standards organizations are using it to provide access to their collections, so its future seems assured.

The scheme comes in two substantial volumes. The first of these is the subject display, which lists over 12,000 preferred terms and some 5,500 non-preferred entry terms in a classified arrangement. Facet analysis has been generally used to show the structure of each subject; in some cases this is self-evident, but where it is not the facet structure is specified by notes *(By . . .)*. At each heading in the display, the hierarchies are demonstrated by type size, emphasis and indentation, while related terms from other hierarchies are shown by means of codes, which are also used in the alphabetical sequence. Because the scheme is intended to be used internationally, the usual BT–NT–RT codes have been replaced by symbols which are language independent and reasonably self-explanatory. The full list is given in the helpful Introduction:

Symbol	Meaning
<	BT
>	NT
–	RT This code is for use in the alphabetical sequence, and is not used in the Display, where RT in the same hierarchy are collocated, while those from other hierarchies have an asterisk to distinguish them.
*<	BT from another hierarchy
*>	NT from another hierarchy
*–	RT from another hierarchy
=	UF
→	USE
+	used between two terms needed to synthesize a concept
**	synthesized term (two terms replacing a non-preferred term)
=**	precedes a non-preferred term represented by synthesis
[. . .]	SN
(By . . .)	facet indicator (not used for indexing)

The notation used consists of capital letters in blocks of up to three separated by a period. A spread of notation is indicated by the solidus (slash) / as in UDC, e.g. IA/IV Food technology. The notation is not intended to be rigidly hierarchical, so that additions can be made in the right place as necessary; as the notation is not intended for shelf arrangement or subject searching, it does not have to be expressive. The display begins with the Subject display contents list. This is an overall outline of the scheme, and a look at coverage in terms of pages per 'main class' quickly confirms the fact that this is a tool for organizing collections of standards, rather than a general classification. Those areas such as Mechanical engineering which are widely standardized have a good spread, while the whole of Social sciences and Humanities is covered by ten pages, with Literature having five lines, consisting of a heading and four UF references! The classes are divided in the Introduction into two sections: the core, which is the main purpose of the list, and ancillary subjects – such as Social sciences and Humanities – which can be expanded in the future as the need arises. Ancillary subjects are marked + in the following list (*not* in the thesaurus):

		pages
+A	General section	20
B	Measurement, testing and instruments	36
+C/E	Science	127
F	Medical sciences	19
G	Environmental and safety engineering	19
+H	Agriculture	8
+I	Food technology and tobacco	10
J	Energy technology	7
K	Electrotechnology	41
L	Communication	31
M	Control and computer technology	18
N	Mechanical engineering	44
+O	Military technology	1
P	Production engineering	16
Q	Transport engineering	29
R	Construction	58
S	Mineral extraction technology	2
+T	Materials	6
U	Metallurgy	8
V	Chemical technology	22
W	Wood, paper and textiles	14
X	Consumer goods and services	20
+Y	Administrative science	11
+Z	Social sciences and humanities	10

Some examples extracted from the schedules will show some of the features mentioned:

A	GENERAL SECTION	Major heading
AP/AW	Common terms	Next step of division
	[Prohibited term. Use a more specific term]	Instruction (prohibition)
AQ/AR	Time	Next step of division
	*>Exposure time LPU	NT in another hierarchy
	*>Operating time MBC.DP	NT in another hierarchy
	*–Time measurement BI	RT in another hierarchy
AQC	Dates (Calendar)	Indented subdivision
AQE	Seasons Indented subdivision	
	=Autumn	UF
	=Spring(season)	UF homograph qualified
	=Summer	Alphabetical order, not
	=Winter chronological	
AT	Properties	
	[[Use a more specific term if possible]	Instruction (recommendation)

KB/KO	Electrical engineering	BT in hierarchy
KD	Electric power systems	NT in same hierarchy
KDV	Electrical installations	NT in same hierarchy

	(By voltage) Facet indicator	
KDV.C	High-voltage installations	NT in same hierarchy
	(Use this term with care as voltage values vary for each country]	Instruction (caution)
	=Very-high-voltage installations	UF
	*–high voltage CLP.H	RT in another hierarchy
KE/KJ	**Electrical equipment**	**BT in hierarchy**
KGP/KGR	**Transformers**	NT in same hierarchy
KGP.J	Power transformers	NT in same hierarchy
	*<Power inductors KHC.PH	BT in another hierarchy
	*>Autotransformers KGP.Q	NT in another hierarchy
	*–Transformer substations KDS.SD	RT in another hierarchy
KGP.JD	Small-power transformers	NT in same hierarchy

The second volume contains the alphabetical sequence, emphasizing the resemblance to the original Roget's *Thesaurus*, in which the alphabetical sequence is an index to the main classified sequence. Using the same examples as those above, we can see how the two sequences complement each other. Preferred terms are in bold, non-preferred in regular type.

Transformers KGP/KGR		
<	Electrical equipment	BT in same hierarchy
. . .		
>	Power transformers	NT in same hierarchy
Power transformers KGP.J		Notation in display
<	Transformers BT in same hierarchy	
>	Small-power transformers	NT in same hierarchy
*<	Power inductors KHC.PH	BT in another hierarchy
*>	Autotransformers KGP.Q	NT in another hierarchy
*–	Transformer substations KDS.SD	RT in another hierarchy
Autumn	non-preferred term	
→	Seasons AQE	preferred term, notation
Common terms AP/AW		
[Prohibited term. Use a more specific term]		
> ...		24 NT listed
Copper alloys UQE		
Copper alloys UQE		
+	Lead-containing alloys UGA	synthesized term
=**	Copper lead alloys UQE.Q	non-preferred term
Metal spraying PLH.C		Preferred term, notation
<	Metallizing	BT in the same hierarchy
>	Arc spraying	NT in the same hierarchy
*<	Spraying (coating) PLP	BT in another hierarchy

The word Tubes has six different meanings:

Tubes, (electronic) non-preferred		
→	Electron tubes KW	USE ...
Tubes (glass) non-preferred		
→	Glass tubes BPJ.T	USE ...

Tubes (packages)   QQQ.GT   SN (explanation)
    [For pastes, etc; contents ejected by squeezing]
    =   Collapsible tubes   UF
    <   Deformable packages   BT in the same hierarchy
Tubes (pipes)   non-preferred
    →   Pipes   NJV/NJX   USE . . .
Tubes (spinning and doubling)   WPX.PJ
    –   Spindles (textile machinery)   RT in same hierarchy
Tubes (winding yarn)   WPN.CC
    –   Winding heads   RT in same hierarchy

The main alphabetical sequence is followed by a short Chemical formula index, where the formula leads to the spelled out form. The list only covers inorganic compounds.

P_2O_5 formula
    →   Phosphorous pentoxide   DJW.F   alphabetical term, notation
**SrCrO4
            synthesized term
    →   Strontium inorganic compounds   DLJ.J   USE this term . . .
       + Chromates   DMF.G   AND this
    =** Strontium chromate   DLJ.JL   non-preferred; use
                         synthesis

The list obviously represents a considerable effort to match a particular objective, that of providing a standard thesaurus for organizations concerned with standards. It has been used by other bodies as a source to enable them to compile their own more specialized thesauri, and is regularly updated by BSI. It is a good example of the way that a thesaurus based on systematic arrangement can be the basis of multilingual use.

MeSH (Medical subject headings)

The National Library of Medicine (NLM) is the centre of medical information services in the USA, having developed from the Surgeon-General's Library set up in 1879. The library has been involved in the bibliographical control of medical literature through its *Current catalog of books*, and through *Index medicus* (IM), which has been its major index to journal literature (under a variety of names) from its inception. By the late 1950s it became apparent that the increasing quantity of literature to index was causing increasingly unacceptable delays. A preliminary project carried out in 1958-1960 explored the possibility of using a computer to speed up production of IM. This was successful in its limited objectives, though the computer-printed product was not particularly pleasant aesthetically. The decision was taken to embark on a much more ambitious project, which would not only produce a printed version of IM of high standard but would also yield a computer-readable database which could be used later for subject searching. This project, begun in 1960, was known as MEDLARS (MEDical Literature Analysis and Retrieval System), and led to the online services MEDLINE (IM) and CATLINE (*Current catalog*), available since 1970, as well as greatly improving the then rudimentary state of the art of computer-controlled typesetting. With the introduction of MED-

LARS, the NLM also took over responsibility for the publication of IM from the American Medical Association. *Cumulated Index Medicus*, a cumulation of a year's IM, began publication in 1960; from 1960 to 1963 this was published by the AMA, but since 1964 has also been published by the NLM.

A new set of subject headings, MeSH, was developed to provide suitable headings for both the *Current catalog* and IM; as a result of the study by Lancaster in 1965, the whole system was reviewed, and MeSH was substantially revised. The present online file dates from 1966, when the new headings came into effect, but the headings were used in the printed IM from 1960 onwards. MeSH now appears in two formats: the first is the annual publication representing usage in IM, distributed with the January issue of IM and in Book 1 of CIM, while the second is the MeSH *Annotated alphabetic list* intended for online users. It is the latter which will be considered here. Each is accompanied by a complementary tree structure (classification), and the Annotated list by the *Permuted medical subject headings list*.

The list is preceded by a lengthy introduction describing the features to be found. All headings listed are in bold capitals, but those used are in large caps while those not used (non-preferred) are in small caps. Following the 1965 review, descriptors were divided into major and minor; major descriptors were used as headings in IM, while minor descriptors were used only in the computer file; with the growth of the literature and the complexity of the subject matter covered, this distinction became unhelpful, and in 1991 it was removed. From 1963–1990, minor descriptors were listed in small caps in MeSH with the instruction *see under* [a major descriptor]. All preferred descriptors are now in large caps; indexers usually allocate 10 - 12 to each article, but those thought to be most significant are preceded by an asterisk in the computer file, and only these are used as headings in IM, in order to keep down the cost of additional printed entries. The distinction is now the importance of a particular descriptor in relation to a given article, rather than the significance of the descriptor in itself. No distinction is made in searching the computer file. Each descriptor has a substantial amount of information intended to help the indexer and searcher. This may include cross-references of various kinds, one or more tree structure codes, indexing or cataloguing annotations, instructions for online searching, and backward cross-references, which are discussed below. Included in the main sequence are subheadings, printed in lower-case type, and some types of descriptor which do not appear in IM and are never given an asterisk; they can however be important in searching the computer files. These include publication types, check tags, geographics and Non-MeSH terms.

Subheadings

There are four types of subheading: topical; form; language; and geographic. Topical subheadings are for use by cataloguers, indexers and searchers, while the other three are used only by cataloguers for the *Current catalog*. There are separate lists of the four types of subheading. There are over 80 topical subheadings, a few of which, e.g. 'in adolescence', are only used in cataloguing. Each one has the tree structure codes denoting the subject areas where it may be used, and a brief note on its purpose, e.g.

> **mortality** (C, E4, F3)
>> Used with human and veterinary diseases for mortality statistics, and with procedures for deaths resulting from the procedure. (1967)
>
> [C = Diseases; E4 = Surgery, Operative; F3 = Behavioral and mental disorders]

In addition to the topical subheadings, for cataloguing there are 17 pages of form subheadings, e.g., abstracts, CD-ROMs, nomenclature; each has an annotation showing the date adopted and the way it is to be used. There is a list of about 350 geographic subheadings (the cataloguer's version of the tree structure category Z (discussed below)), and another of over 100 languages.

Publication types

These were introduced in 1991 to specify the nature of the information or the way in which it is published, to expand on the previous Citation types; they do not relate to the subject of the document, but the way in which it is presented or published. Thus **BIBLIOGRAPHY** is a subject heading in the main list, for works on the subject of bibliography, but it also appears in the list of publication types, for use in indexing a work which is a bibliography. For this reason, publication type terms are always in the singular. Thus there is a heading in the main list **CLINICAL TRIALS**, but there is also a publication type **Clinical trial**. There are some 50 publication types in the list, with detailed scope notes and the date of first use.

Check tags

There are ten 'check tags' which were introduced after the 1965 review to specify the kind of study indexed, where this would be helpful. For example, it is often important to know whether a trial of a new drug is on animals or people, in the field or in the laboratory, so we find check tags ANIMAL, HUMAN, MALE, FEMALE, IN VITRO. Three relate to the source of support for a piece of research: SUPPORT, NON-U.S. GOVT; SUPPORT, U.S.GOVT, NON-P.H.S; SUPPORT, U.S.GOVT, P.H.S. The other two are CASE REPORT and COMPARATIVE STUDY. These are not used in IM.

Geographics

For indexing, as opposed to cataloguing, geographic headings are taken from Category Z of the tree structures, though it is not clear why there has to be different treatment. In the classified arrangement, ILLINOIS appears three times. Under UNITED STATES BY INDIVIDUAL STATE we find ILLINOIS, with CHICAGO as a subdivision; other cities listed are Los Angeles, San Francisco, Baltimore, Boston, New York City and Philadelphia. In the list of UNITED STATES BY REGION, ILLINOIS is listed under GREAT LAKES REGION and MIDWESTERN UNITED STATES. Apart from this kind of duplication arising from the classified arrangement, the places listed appear to be the same.

Non-MeSH headings and 'explosions'

Some headings appear in the tree structures as necessary steps of division but are not helpful indexing or searching terms. For example, UNITED STATES BY INDIVIDUAL STATE is an essential part of the tree structure, but is hardly likely to be used as an indexing term, or sought by a user. These terms are referred to as Non-MeSH terms, and can serve a very useful purpose in searching. Terms which have subdivisions in the tree structure have this shown by a + after the tree structure code in the entry, e.g.

GASTRITIS
C6.405.748.369+

If a searcher wants to retrieve documents indexed by a particular term and all its subdivisions, he can instruct the computer to 'explode' the search on that term. The search is then expanded to take in not only that heading but all the tree of which it forms the head. In the list we find

UNITED STATES BY INDIVIDUAL STATE (NON MeSH)
Z1.107.567.875.100+

This means that we can 'explode' on this heading and find all the information indexed by its subdivisions, even though nothing is indexed by the heading itself.
Some headings are frequently used in this way, and contain a number of subdivisions; in such cases, the heading is 'pre-exploded', to reduce the amount of computer time that would be taken by rerunning the instruction each time it occurred. There are about 75 pre-exploded headings, and 11 subheadings. These headings are preceded in the list by a large dot, while the subheadings are shown by an inverted triangle, e.g.

●CELLS
▼/physiology

MeSH for IM lists the major descriptors, tree codes and history notes, but does not include geographics, non-MeSH terms or check tags. The tree structures are included in the same volume, instead of being separate, as they are from the annotated alphabetic list.

Cross-references

MeSH does not use the now conventional BT, NT, RT etc codes for linkages; instead, it has a very explicit set developed particularly for MEDLARS. Since 1991, 'consider also' links have been introduced; these draw the user's attention to terms which may be linguistically related (e.g. drawn from Latin or Greek roots rather than Teutonic), and usually apply to anatomical terms, e.g.

KIDNEY
consider also terms at GLOMERUL-, NEPHR-, PYEL-, and RENAL

See links are references from non-preferred (entry vocabulary) to preferred terms;

these are now rather wider than the synonyms originally found, e.g.

EEG see ELECTROENCEPHALOGRAPHY
 E1.236.257.401+   E1.399.277+
MOOD DISORDERS, NON-PSYCHOTIC see AFFECTIVE DISORDERS
 F3.709.438.100+   [tree structure code]
MOOD DISORDERS, PSYCHOTIC see AFFECTIVE DISORDERS,
 PSYCHOTIC
 F3.709.680.80+   [+ indicates subdivisions in the tree structure]
EMERGENCY MEDICAL SERVICE COMMUNICATION SYSTEMS
 DF EMSCS   [data form – speeds indexing and searching]
DOWN SYNDROME   [no 'S]
 was DOWN'S SYNDROME 1975–92 & 1963–64; was MONGOLISM
 1965–74
 use DOWN SYNDROME to search DOWN'S SYNDROME 1975–92
 and MONGOLISM 1966–74
    [NB the period before 1966 is not covered by the online service]
SELF ASSESSMENT (PSYCHOLOGY)
 DF SELF ASSESSMENT [Omits parenthetical qualifier]

Some headings might appear in a variety of forms depending on word order or spelling; one form of these is listed; and variant forms are automatically generated in the computer file, but do not appear in the printed list. This example is thus necessarily taken from the introduction:

HOSPITALS, PSYCHIATRIC [preferred form]
HOSPITAL, PSYCHIATRIC [none of these three terms appears
PSYCHIATRIC HOSPITALS [in the printed list, but would be
PSYCHIATRIC HOSPITAL [found in searching the computer file]

As mentioned, there are various subheadings which may be used. In some cases, it was decided in 1992 that it would be better to use a precoordinated heading, e.g.

BRAIN/injuries see BRAIN INJURIES
BRAIN/analysis see BRAIN CHEMISTRY

Perhaps the most important group of linkages are the 'see related' cross-references. These link terms related in a variety of ways likely to be of help to the indexer or searcher. Originally mainly BT-NT links, they now cover a wide range of RT links as well.

BT-NT
 PREGNANCY
  see related
   PRENATAL CARE
Organ – procedure
 ARTERIES
  see related

ANGIOGRAPHY
Organ – physiological process
BLOOD
see related
HEMATOPOIESIS
Physiological process and corresponding disease
RESPIRATION
see related
DYSPNOEA
Organ and drug acting on it
VASOMOTOR SYSTEM
see related
VASODILATOR AGENTS
Physiological process and drug acting on it
DIURESIS
see related
DIURETICS
Disease and drug treating it
TUBERCULOSIS
see related
ANTITUBERCULAR AGENTS
Organism and drug acting on it
MYCOBACTERIUM LEPRAE
see related
LEPROSTATIC AGENTS
Drug and clinical deficiency or excess
POTASSIUM
see related
HYPOKALEMIA
Drug and receptor
DOPAMINE
see related
RECEPTORS, DOPAMINE

It is clear that many of these types of relationship are unlikely to be paralleled in other subjects, but they do illustrate the effort put into helpful indexing and consequent help in searching. *See* references have the complementary code X in the entry under the preferred term, while see related have the complementary code XR, e.g.

DISEASE OUTBREAKS
X   EPIDEMICS
XR   SPACE-TIME CLUSTERING

Notes

The notes which are found under a high proportion of headings are equally helpful.

These too are of various kinds:

right word?
ESOTROPIA
do not confuse with EXOTROPIA
definition
CORD FACTORS
toxic glycolipids from Mycobact tuberc   ['official' abbreviations]
use notes for searching
DIAGNOSTIC TESTS, ROUTINE
use DIAGNOSTIC TESTS, ROUTINE, to search PHYSICAL
EXAMINATION, PREADMISSION Aug 77–81
permitted subheadings
CORONARY ANGIOGRAPHY
/drug eff /rad eff permitted; do not use /util except by MeSH definition
history (indexing dates first used and usage changes)
CORD FACTORS
91(80); was see under GLYCOLIPIDS 1980–90; was CORD FACTOR
see under GLYCOLIPIDS 1975–79
use CORD FACTORS to search CORD FACTOR back thru 1975
annotations
LABORATORY PERSONNEL
coord IM with type of lab or occup (IM), as hosp lab personnel =
LABORATORY PERSONNEL (IM) + LABORATORIES, HOSPITAL
(IM) or hematol ab personnel = LABORATORY PERSONNEL (IM) +
HEMATOLOGY (IM)

Revision

The list is updated annually, with particular attention paid to areas which appear to need revision, as well as to the addition of new terms. In 1993, for example, 421 new terms were added, 94 were revised and 54 deleted; an additional 824 *see* references (entry terms) were also added. The list contains a complete list of new headings with complete scope notes. These headings are also listed in the categories in which they are found in the tree structures, and further lists show new headings with the headings they replace, e.g.

ANGIOSCOPY   ENDOSCOPY (77–92)

and replaced headings with the new headings which replace them, e.g.

ARTHUS PHENOMENON   ARTHUS REACTION

Permuted medical subject headings

This volume forms a companion to the annotated alphabetic list. Though it is difficult to see why it should be referred to as 'permuted', it is in fact a detailed index to all the significant words used in the alphabetic list, with the exception of subheadings. It also includes some links which supplement the list. For example, we find:

CELLULOSE
    ABSORBABLE CELLULOSE see **CELLULOSE, OXIDIZED**
    CARBOXYMETHYL CELLULOSE see
        CARBOXYMETHYLCELLULOSE
    CELLULOSE
    CHROMATOGRAPHY, DEAE-CELLULOSE
    DEAE-CELLULOSE
    DEAE-CELLULOSE CHROMATOGRAPHY see
        CHROMATOGRAPHY, DEAE-CELLULOSE
    ELECTROPHORESIS, CELLULOSE ACETATE

Not all of these links could have been found by scanning the annotated alphabetic list. Under Child we find (among many other entries):

CHILD
    FATHER-CHILD RELATIONS
    MOTHER-CHILD RELATIONS
    PARENT-CHILD RELATIONS

These particular links also cannot be found from the alphabetic list, and only with great difficulty through the tree structures. The Permuted list is thus a valuable addition to the tools available to the indexer, and more particularly the searcher. It does however raise the question of why it is not simply incorporated into the annotated alphabetic list? Several of the entries under cellulose, for example, could have been found from the alphabetic list starting at Cellulose, but not all. Only those links which are not already in the alphabetic list would have to be added, and the resulting tool would be easier to use than the two separate volumes. However, computer production may mean that it is simpler to produce the two lists.

Tree structures

The alphabetical lists are complemented by the categorized list containing the tree structures. These form a detailed classification of all the concepts in MeSH, including the Non-MeSH headings; as mentioned, these form part of the tree structure but are not useful indexing or searching terms. There are 15 major categories (main classes), denoted by the letters A to N and Z, the geographic listing. Each main class has one or more subclasses; D: Chemicals and Drugs, the largest class, has 26, while H: Physical Sciences, has one. Other main classes with only one subdivision at present are K: Humanities; L: Information science; M: Named groups; and surprisingly J: Technology, Industry and Agriculture. Subclasses are denoted by the main class letter plus a one- or two-digit number. Further subdivision is by blocks of up to three-digit numbers used as integers, not decimals, and separated by full stops. The notation is not intended to be mnemonic, but serves solely as an ordering device; the same concept may be represented by quite different notation in different trees. Each step of division is reflected by a further block of notation, with large gaps left to accommodate new concepts if necessary. As a result, the notation can be quite lengthy, but since it is intended to be used in a computer- based system, this is not a problem. For users, access will normally be through a MeSH descriptor, either to search for related terms to help in a search or in indexing, or to 'explode' on a term, which is done by the computer using the notation. To take an example, in the alphabetical list we find:

THEOPHYLLINE

D3.132.956.826+   D3.438.759.758.824.751+

D16.116.919+   D18.918.882

From the + signs we know that there will be subdivisions at the first three numbers, but not at the fourth. In the categorized list we find that D is Chemicals and Drugs, D3 is Chemicals, Organic – Heterocyclic compounds; D16 is Autonomic drugs; and D18 is Cardiovascular agents. The four hierarchies are as follows:

HETEROCYCLIC COMPOUNDS	**D3**
ALKALOIDS	**D3.132**
XANTHINE ALKALOIDS	**D3.132.956**
THEOPHYLLINE	**D3.132.956.826**
AMINOPHYLLINE	**D3.132.956.826.75**
XANTHINOL NIACINATE	**D3.132.956.826.950**

HETEROCYCLIC COMPOUNDS, 2-RING	
(NON MeSH)	**D3.438**
PURINES	**D3.438.759**
PURINONES	**D3.438.759.758**
XANTHENES	**D3.438.759.758.824**
THEOPHYLLINE	**D3.438.759.758.824.751**
AMINOPHYLLINE	**D3.438.759.758.824.751.75**
DYPHYLLINE	**D3.438.759.758.824.751.250**
XANTHINOL NIACINATE	**D3.438.759.758.824.751.950**

AUTONOMIC DRUGS	**D16**
BRONCHODILATOR AGENTS	**D16.116**
THEOPHYLLINE	**D16.116.919**
AMINOPHYLLINE	**D16.116.919.53**
DYPHYLLINE	**D16.116.919.299**

CARDIOVASCULAR AGENTS	**D18**
VASODILATOR AGENTS	**D18.918**
THEOPHYLLINE	**D18.918.882**

The heading HETEROCYCLIC COMPOUNDS, 2-RING is obviously an important step of division, but is not used for indexing; it is possible to explode on it, thus finding everything indexed by its many subdivisions.

The volume begins with a list of new or changed notation; for each term involved, the old (where appropriate) and the new notation are given, e.g.:

Occupational dermatitis	C17.174.697	C17.800.174.255.700
	C21.447.697	C17.800.815.255.700
		C21.447.270

(Replaced for 1993 by: Dermatitis, Occupational)

For each subclass notes are given; these indicate which subheadings may be used, and any particular points which need to be noted in using the headings in the subclass. For each class, a bibliographic reference is given, with a reminder of the full bibliographies to be found in the *Annotated list*. At each heading in the list, the notation is given for other places where the concept may be found; thus for each of the four locations shown above for Theophylline, the notation is also given for the other three locations.

The three parts of MeSH together form a powerful tool. There is a great deal of help for the indexer, and the list is under constant review to keep it up to date; for example in 1993 a new subdivision was introduced under N: Health care – N5 Quality, Access, Evaluation, in addition to the many other changes mentioned earlier. The *Online services reference manual* can be obtained from NTIS to give further help. While it is perhaps too closely geared to the field of medicine to act as a direct model, there are many features which other thesauri might well learn from, and a great deal of effort has obviously been expended to make sure that there will be as much consistency as possible between indexers and searchers.

The INSPEC Thesaurus

The INSPEC *Thesaurus* was first published in 1973, and is revised every two years. It is significant as the tool used to index the INSPEC database, which consists of the major abstracting services produced by the Institution of Electrical Engineers, covering physics, electronics, communications, electrical engineering, information technology, computers and computer applications: in print form, *Physics abstracts*, *Electrical and electronic engineering abstracts*, and *Computers and control abstracts*. The database now contains some four million references. In January 1995, INSPEC merged with the PHYS database of FIZ Karlsruhe, and the thesaurus was thoroughly revised.

The thesaurus is in two parts: the first and major part is the alphabetical list of terms, while the second is the list of term trees. The list contains about 15,700 terms, of which some 7,700 are preferred terms and 8,000 non-preferred entry terms (1995 edition).

All terms are in lower case, except proper nouns. Preferred terms are in bold, with non-preferred terms in normal type, e.g.:

thermal insulation
    UF   heat insulation
             insulation, thermal
heat insulation
    USE   thermal insulation

In cases where a term is used instead of the inverted form, e.g. insulation, thermal in the above example, a NT reference from the term qualified replaces the USE reference:

insulation
   NT   thermal insulation

A preferred term may be used for more than one non-preferred term, as in this example. Some terms have scope notes; these are not designated SN, but appear in italics immediately after the term. All preferred terms have the date of input (DI) given; the base date is January 1969, and new terms are added at six-monthly intervals. For terms introduced or changed since that date, the terms previously used are listed as Prior Terms (PT). Class numbers from the INSPEC classification are given (CC); one term may have more than one class number, depending on context.

aberrations   [broad term used for several specific terms]
   aberrations in optics and particle optics only
   UF   astigmatism (optical)
             barrel distortion
             chromatic aberration
             coma
             curvature of field
             optical aberrations
             pincushion distortion
             Seidel theory   [proper noun]
             spherical aberration
   RT   aspherical optics
             lenses
             optical images
             optics
             particle optics
   CC   A4180; A4230F; A4278
   DI   January 1969
integrated circuits
   UF   IC [full name preferred to abbreviation]
             microcircuits
             microelectronics
   NT   digital integrated circuits
             hybrid integrated circuits
                . . .
             superconducting integrated circuits
             thick film circuits
             thin film circuits
   BT   networks (circuits)
   TT   networks (circuits)
   RT   cryogenic electronics
             integrated circuit manufacture
             integrated circuit technology
             integrated circuit testing
                . . .

semiconductor devices
substrates
thick films
CC   B2220; B2570
DI   January 1969

Cryogenic electronics is one of the new terms introduced in this revision:

cryogenic electronics
used for low temperature operation of conventional electronics. For superconducting electronics, use 'superconducting devices' or NTs as appropriate
UF   low temperature electronics
BT   cryogenics
TT   cryogenics
RT   integrated circuits
low-temperature techniques
semiconductor devices
CC   B1200; B1300; B2500
DI   January 1995
PT   cryogenics
low-temperature techniques

Some minor oddities arise from the nature of semiconductor nomenclature. Types of semiconductor are designated by Roman numerals; these are filed as I, II, III and IV, i.e. as letters. Chemicals are normally denoted by their full names, with USE references from chemical formulae.

I-II-VI$_2$ semiconductors
USE   ternary semiconductors
II-IV-V$_2$
USE   ternary semiconductors
II-VI semiconductors
UF   2–6 semiconductors
pseudobinary semiconductors
...
pseudobinary conductors
USE   II-VI semiconductors
III-V semiconductors
III-VI semiconductors
IV-VI semiconductors
semiconductor materials
. . .
I
USE   iodine
GaAs
USE   gallium arsenide

H_3O^+ [chemical formula for hydroxonium ion]

> USE   hydrogen compounds
> positive ions

In filing, the subscript is ignored, and this files immediately after Ho USE holmium

hydroxonium ion
> *heading was preferred term between July 1975 and January 1993. Prior to 1975 'hydrogen compounds' was used*
> USE   hydrogen compounds
> positive ions

Ge
> USE   germanium

Ge–Si alloys   [exception to norm]
> UF   germanium-silicon alloys
> Si-Ge alloys
> silicon-germanium alloys
> BT   germanium alloys
> silicon alloys
> TT   alloys
> DI   July 1977
> PT   Germanium alloys
> Silicon alloys

. . .

cable television
> UF   CATV
> BT   television
> TT   telecommunication
> RT   coaxial cables
> interactive television
> communication networks
> television equipment
> CC   B6430D; D4010
> DI   January 1977
> PT   television systems

As illustrated above with integrated circuits, abbreviations are usually spelled out, but occasionally one which is widely used becomes a preferred term, e.g.:

PWM
> USE   pulse width modulation

HMO calculations
> UF   Huckel molecular orbital calculations

Where a term has changed more than once, a scope note explains what terms should be used at different times, e.g.

magnetic surface phenomena
> *heading was preferred term between January 1977 and January 1995. Prior to 1977, 'magnetic properties of substances' and 'surface phenomena' were used*
> USE surface magnetism

Occasionally this leaves the user in some doubt as to what is current practice:

holographic instruments
> *heading was preferred term between January 1973 and January 1993. Prior to 1973 'holography' was used*

This leaves us guessing as to the usage since January 1993. Is 'holography' again the preferred term? Or 'holographic optical elements'? The list does not tell us the current preferred term as it does with the previous example.

A few terms have parenthetical qualifiers to avoid confusion with homographs. In some cases this seems unnecessary, because the nature of the list makes the alternative unlikely, e.g. the improbable

bus conductors (electric)
> USE busbars

and the rather less unlikely

cables (electric)

where material on other kinds of cable might conceivably be found. Some examples are clearly necessary, e.g.

memory (physiological)
> USE brain
>   brain models
>   neural nets
>   neurophysiology
memory addresses
> USE storage allocation
monitors (computer software)
> USE supervisory programs
monitors (displays)
> USE computer displays

There are *see also* references for specific elements:

zinc
> *see also nuclei with* . . . . . .

We find a series of entries at the word "nuclei":

nuclei with mass number 1 to 5
nuclei with mass number 6 to 19
nuclei *etc* up to mass number 220 or higher

These link up with the classification, where we find

A2700   **Properties of specific nuclei listed by mass ranges**

Hierarchical display

As well as the usual BT, NT and RT links, the thesaurus gives TT for Top term in the hierarchy. In the examples above, networks (circuits) is both BT and TT to integrated circuits; alloys is the TT to Ge-Si alloys, with germanium alloys and silicon alloys as intermediate terms in the hierarchy. The hierarchies are shown in the second part of the list in alphabetical order of top terms; since there may be more than one hierarchy linking terms, a given term may appear more than once in the display, either in more than one hierarchy or more than once within the same top term. Some examples are:

Alloys
. Germanium alloys
. . Ge-Si alloys
. Silicon alloys
. . Elinvar
. . Ge-Si alloys
. Transition metal alloys
. . chromium alloys
. . . Elinvar
. . iron alloys
. . . Elinvar

receivers
. transceivers
telecommunication
. radiocommunication
. . radio equipment
. . . transceivers
transmitters
. Transceivers

. . .
semiconductor devices
. Semiconductor diodes
. . avalanche diodes
. . . IMPATT diodes
. Transit time devices
. . IMPATT diodes

English terminology is used, with reference from American spelling:

Aluminum
        USE   Aluminium

Alphabetical arrangement is word by word.

INSPEC classification

The classification referred to in the above discussion is used to arrange the abstracts in the various sections of *Science abstracts* and the accompanying *Current papers*. A brief introduction explains that this version of the scheme is for the INSPEC 2 database. The text of headings can be understood without reference to the hierarchical structure, to make use easier with the electronic version. New topics covered in the various sections, Physics, Electrical engineering and electronics, and Computers and control, are briefly listed.

A section on 'How to use the classification scheme' explains the notation. The first digit is a letter representing the section of the database:

A   Physics
B   Electrical engineering & Electronics
C   Computers & Control
D   Information technology

(These codes are not used in the actual publications, as they would be redundant.) The rest of the notation consists of four figures, plus one letter as needed. The first digit represents the first level of division; the second represents the second level; the third and fourth represent the third level; and the letter represents the fourth level, which is not always required. In the printed indexes, a point is inserted after the second digit to make the notation easier to follow.

A brief explanation shows the three ways of finding topics in the classification. The first is through the Outline of the classification; the second through cross-references in the scheme, so that if users follow up the wrong section from the outline they may still be led to the correct class number; and the third is through the alphabetical index.

Another brief section explains how the class numbers (codes) may be used in searching the database. Most of the records in the INSPEC 1 database have been reclassified in the revised scheme without difficulty, but there are some instances where problems may arise. Where the new scheme does not match the old hierarchies, records may be reclassified at a broader heading, or in a 'miscellaneous . . .' group. There is also the possibility that, with changes in the classification in areas overlapping the four main sections, an additional class number in another section may not lead to any abstracts in the database. In such a case it will be necessary to follow up the class number in the original section.

The next section is an outline of the classification to the second level. Class A is by far the most detailed, with D still in what might be described as an embryonic state. The outline gives the main headings; for example:

A00   General
A10   The physics of elementary particles and fields
A20   Nuclear physics
A30   Atomic and molecular physics
. . .
A90   Geophysics, Astronomy and Astrophysics

A91   Solid Earth physics
A96   Solar system
A97   Stars
A98   Stellar systems; Galactic and extragalactic objects and systems; Universe

which shows a reasonable progression from the very small to the very large.

D10   General & Management aspects
D20   Applications
D30   General systems and equipment
D40   Office automation – communications
D50   Office automation – computers

is the whole outline for Information Technology. There would seem to be the possibility of cross-classification with C70:

C70   Computer applications
C71   Business and administration
C72   Information science and documentation
C73   Natural sciences computing
C74   Engineering computing
C75   Other computer applications

Abstracts might perhaps be classified at more than one place; where this possibility arises, cross-references are made in the schedules to help determine the correct number. These are of three kinds: *for* . . . refer the user to the correct numbers for related subjects (USE); *see also* . . . refer to related subjects (RT); and *inc.* . . . shows topics for which there are as yet no specific place. Some cross-references are not specific; this indicates that a subject may be found at more than one place within the hierarchy referred to. If a class number has been added or changed since the start of the database, this is also noted. The hierarchy is shown by type size and weight. Some examples:

A1000   The physics of elementary particles and fields
         for cosmic rays, see A 9440 . . .
A1100   General theory of fields and particles
         (*see also A0365 . . . Quantum mechanics, A0370 Theory of quantized fields, A0380 General theory of scattering*)
A1110   Quantum field theory
A1110G   Renormalization in quantum field theories
         1973–. Before, use A1110
A1110Q   Relativistic wave equations   [gap left for hospitality]
A1117   Theories of strings and other extended objects
         (*inc. superstrings and membranes*)
         1988–. 1973–1987, use A 1240H; before, use A 1240

Cross-references may be to other sections:

A7240   **Photoconduction and photovoltaic effects; photodielectric effects**
(*see also B4210 Photoconducting materials and properties*)

The complete schedule for D1000 is as follows:

D1000   **General and management aspects**
(*inc. Contracts, planning*)
1983–
(*see also C03*)

D1010   **Consultancy services**
1983–
(*see also C0310B*)

D1030   **Training requirements**
1985–. 1983–84 use D1000
(*see also C0220*)

D1040   **Human aspects**
(*inc ergonomics, health hazards, home working*)
1983–.
(*See also D3020*)

D1050   **Legal requirements**
(*inc. Liability, regulation, taxation*)
1983–.

D1060   **Security**
(*inc. Computer crime*)
1983–.

This contrasts with the 14½ pages devoted to A9000, covering the well established fields of geophysics, astronomy and astrophysics.

The index is not a relative index, and may lead to more than one place without any qualification. As in the cross–references in the schedules, the entry may lead to a broad heading, e.g.:

Aerosols   A8270 . . .; A92 . . .

If we turn to the schedules at A92 . . ., by searching through we will find

A9260M   Particles and aerosols in the lower atmosphere
A9265V   Clouds, fog, haze, aerosols; effects of pollution.

Sometimes it is difficult to see why a second entry is made. We find:

Superconducting memory circuits B1265D; B3240C; C5320Z

If we turn to the first of these we find:

B1265   **Digital electronics**
B1265D   Memory circuits
(*inc. Semiconductor and superconducting memory circuits*)
B1265F   Microprocessors and microcomputers
(*inc. Superconducting processor chips*)

However, if we turn to the second entry, we find:

B3240	**Superconducting devices**
B3240C	Superconducting junction devices

(*inc. Josephson devices and superconducting integrated circuits*)
*for superconducting logic, memory and processor circuits see B1265B,
B1265D and B1265F, respectively*

which seems to lead back to the first number without any ambiguity. The third entry takes us to

C5320	**Digital storage**
C5320Z	Other digital storage

which must surely be regarded as a long shot.

The omission of qualifying terms does keep the size of the index down, but at a price. To check every one of the eight places listed for, e.g., stimulated emissions or strain gauges would surely become tedious.

It is not too difficult to find points of criticism in any thesaurus or classification scheme, but this should not hide the fact that the INSPEC thesaurus and classification together provide a powerful tool for information retrieval. The headings in the classification are used to arrange the printed versions, but can also be used in searching the database; terms from the thesaurus can also be used in Boolean combinations, or in combination with class numbers, to give the very specific subject searches necessary in a database of this size. Both the thesaurus and classification are updated regularly to provide users with the most effective tools possible.

At one time, the editorial panel of INSPEC decided that natural language had a number of advantages over controlled vocabularies. It is interesting to note that the database, one of the most significant in science and technology, uses both a thesaurus and a separate classification scheme to support natural language searching!

Summary

The thesauri discussed here, though important, are only a small selection from the many thesauri now in use. They do however give a good representation of the features which are to be found in most modern thesauri: an alphabetical sequence complemented by a hierarchical display, specific relationships BT, NT, RT, control over synonyms and homographs, and various kinds of scope notes. There are other more exotic forms of display, but the majority of thesauri now in use conform to the kind of pattern established here. There are a number of works which go into more detail than is possible in this text,[6] but a good way to get the feel of thesaurus construction is to carry out the kind of exercise in subject analysis described in Chapter 5.

References

1   Lancaster, F. W., 'Some observations on the performance of EJC role indicators in a mechanised retrieval system', *Special libraries*, **55** (10), 1964, 696–701.

2   *Thesaurus of scientific, technical and engineering terms*, Cambridge, Mass,

Science Information Resource Center; Hemisphere Publishing Corporation, 1988.

3 Aitchison, J., 'The Thesaurofacet: a multipurpose retrieval language tool', *Journal of documentation,* **26** (3), 1970, 187–203.

4 *BSI ROOT thesaurus,* 3rd edition, Milton Keynes, British Standards Institution, 1988. 2v.

5 One of the reasons for the high quality of MeSH was the detailed evaluation study carried out by Lancaster, which established the guidelines for future development.
Lancaster, F. W., *Evaluation of the MEDLARS demand search service,* Bethesda, MD, National Library of Medicine, 1968.
Lancaster, F. W., 'Aftermath of an evaluation', *Journal of documentation,* **27** (1), 1971, 1–10.

6 Aitchison, J. and Gilchrist, A., *Thesaurus construction: a practical manual,* 2nd edn, London, Aslib, 1987.
Foskett, D. J., 'Thesaurus', *Encyclopedia of library and information science,* NY, Dekker, v30, 1980, 416–63.
Lancaster, F. W., *Vocabulary control for information retrieval,* 2nd edn, Arlington, VA., Information Resources Press, 1986.
Townley, H. M. and Gee, R. D., Thesaurus-making : grow your own word-stock, London; Boulder, Colo., Deutsch, distributed by Westview Press, 1980.

7 *Classification: a classification scheme for the INSPEC database,* London, Institution of Electrical Engineers, 1995.

Chapter 26
Social sciences and humanities

Thesauri in the social sciences and humanities have tended to be rather more specialized than those in science and technology, and there has been no combined effort comparable with Project Lex (see p. 361). The largest single effort supported by the US government has been in the field of education.

ERIC

The Educational Resources Information Center Clearinghouses network was set up in 1966 to disseminate information in the field of educational research. The scope is the whole of education, and includes the related fields of Information Resources, Languages and linguistics, and Exceptional children. A key publication, the monthly abstract journal *Resources in education*, was begun, and the Office of Education Panel on Educational Terminology decided to sponsor a thesaurus for the indexing of this bibliography. The first, preliminary, edition was published in 1967; this contained just over 3000 descriptors, and was issued in revised form as the *Thesaurus of ERIC descriptors* (first edition). This proved to be inadequate, and a second edition, with over 6000 descriptors, was published in 1969. In addition to a greatly increased number of terms, it included a Descriptor Group display.

The sixth edition, 1975, was very well produced by comparison with the earlier editions, but the content remained very similar. In 1977, the Vocabulary Improvement Project VIP was begun, to achieve a thorough review of the quality and usefulness of the terms used. In Phase I, some 60,000 assessments of terms were made by vocabulary coordinators, users and others. Phase II involved the collation of all these assessments, revision of terminology, provision of scope notes, and a careful review of the cross-reference network. At intervals, revised versions were distributed to the Clearinghouses for discussion, and eventually the final version was published as the eighth edition by the Oryx Press with the title *Thesaurus of ERIC descriptors: completely revised*.

Figures given for the revised thesaurus showed the extent of the revision. Of the 5–6000 descriptors in the previous edition, 1000 were deleted, with 500 new descriptors added; 1400 scope notes were added or modified. All told, some 6700 changes were made, to give a 'new' thesaurus containing an entry vocabulary of over 8000 terms, of which about 5000 were preferred terms.

Further editions have been published at regular intervals, the latest available being the 12th, 1990[1] and 13th, 1995.[2] No major changes have been made, but each edition continues the process of regular updating. The 13th edition contains 10,363 entries, of which 5,759 are preferred terms; 207 of the descriptors are new, and there are 199 new USE references; in addition, there have been several hundred modifications to scope notes or cross-references.

The Preface contains a very brief introduction, and lists the names of the various members of the Vocabulary Review Group (VRG); significant is the presence of representatives of *Australian education index, British education index*, and *Canadian education index*, indicating the intention of the group to produce an internationally acceptable tool. This is followed by a list of the new descriptors added since July 1990 and thus not in the previous edition.

The next three lists are of 'Transferred descriptors', 'Invalid ("dead") descriptors' and 'Deleted descriptors'. Transferred descriptors are the 76 which have been downgraded to USE references for various reasons, e.g. Data Bases has now been replaced by Databases. Sheet metal workers, [Persons], in use from 1967–1981, has been replaced by Sheet metal work [Activity], and similarly Welders by Welding. These descriptors still appear in the entry vocabulary, and must be used when searching either the printed indexes, or the computer file back to 1980, when the ERIC file was last reloaded. The 840 descriptors transferred before the reload need not be used in computer searching, but will be found in the printed indexes produced prior to their transfer.

Invalid descriptors are those which have proved in use to be ambiguous or have been used inconsistently. They appear in the list with scope notes explaining which terms are to be used in their stead. For example, the descriptor English Education was found in the VIP project to have been used for three separate concepts; the scope note now states:

Invalid descriptor – see the more precise terms 'english teacher education,' 'english instruction,' and 'english curriculum'.

They need to be used when searching either the printed or computer file prior to September 1980, since they were then used for indexing. Because they are not direct equivalents of the replacement terms, it was not possible to substitute the new terms in the computer file.

Deleted terms no longer appear in the thesaurus, even as non-preferred terms. In the 12th and 13th editions there are no terms in this category; as a result of the VIP, 13 were deleted completely, while five were transferred to the identifier file, so the grand total is not great. Here too the terms will appear in the printed indexes prior to 1980 – but are likely to be hard to find!

Following the three lists comes an important section entitled 'ERIC's indexing and retrieval: 1995 update'. This has a brief summary of the structure of the ERIC system and of the Vocabulary Improvement Project. Since 1993 an Internet listserv has been used for all updating, which has greatly facilitated the exchange of comments and suggestions. (The inside back cover contains a flowchart of the revision process, and a diagram of the complete ERIC system, including Clearinghouses, System support services, and suppliers and users of the system.) The database held bibliographic details and abstracts of over 700,000 documents by 1990. Once the details are entered, the computer database is used to produce *Resources in education (RIE)*, covering documents other than journal articles 1966–, and *Current index to journals in education (CIJE)*, 1969–. These are available in printed form, both published monthly, with semiannual cumulations for CIJE and annual cumulations for RIE. RIE is also available on microfiche, with a main file covering 1966–1980 and monthly updates. The printed and microfiche versions have various indexes: subject, author, institution and publication type for RIE, and subject, author, and journal contents [i.e. contents pages] for CIJE. For many people, computer searching is both more convenient and more effective; the entries in the computer file can be searched on bibliographic utilities such as DIALOG and OCLC FirstSearch, but are also available on CD-ROM, with regular updates. It is stressed that ERIC is a *bibliographic* database; searches lead to bibliographic details and an abstract for each item found, but *not* the full text; for this the user must turn to the journals for CIJE, or the ERIC documents (ED. . .) for those in RIE. There are complete RIE microfiche collections at several hundred centres throughout the world to make access easier.

Since 1989, some 1200 short 'ERIC Digests' prepared by the Clearinghouses are available in full on CD-ROM, e.g. 'Equal mathematics education for female students'. About 150 new digests are prepared each year. The Clearinghouse on Information and Technology at Syracuse University is working on a pilot project to make the full text of ERIC Documents (the RIE file) available through the Internet.

A section on 'ERIC's indexing' outlines the principles used in indexing documents for the database. Two major rules are to index only what is explicit in the document, and to index at the level of specificity of the document. Full indexing rules can be seen in the *ERIC processing manual* (ED 348055, 1992) and the *ERIC indexing handbook* (ED 348069, 1992). One surprising instruction is that precoordinated descriptors are to be used wherever possible. Precoordination was shown in the second Cranfield Project to be a major cause of poor retrieval performance, and there are also many examples in the thesaurus where the precept is not followed. As a note at the bottom of each page tells us, non-preferred terms marked # are to be represented by two or more terms; for example, documents about muscular exercise are to be indexed by both Exercise and Muscular system. In a database which is searched by computer increasingly frequently, precoordination may become irrelevant.

Each document is indexed by up to six major descriptors, which are used in the printed subject indexes, in the CIJE main entry or the RIE resumé; minor descriptors may also be used, to denote educational level, methodology and other less significant aspects of the content. Major descriptors are tagged with an asterisk, e.g. *Cultural awareness, but both kinds may be searched in the computer database. Indexing by educational level is mandatory, as the database covers the whole range of levels, and the set of descriptors is given in a chart, as well as in the main sequence of descriptors. An important point is that in carrying out a broad search, it is necessary to search not only on the heading at the top of a particular hierarchy, e.g. Postsecondary education, but also on its NT subdivisions, in this case Higher education and Two year colleges. A similar set of descriptors is Age level, beginning with Neonates and concluding with Old old adults. (Adults is defined in the scope note as 'approximately 18+ years of age'; Older adults as 'approximately 65+ years of age'; and Old old adults as 'approximately 75+ years of age'.) A note warns of one possible source of ambiguity, with the use of descriptors such as Adopted children for the whole range 0 to 17 years of age; documents dealing specifically with, say, adopted adolescents, would be indexed by the terms Adopted children *and* Adolescents. This avoids the establishment of sets of parallel precoordinated descriptors for a range of subject headings which are in practice ill-defined.

In addition to descriptors, documents may be indexed by Identifiers. These are proper names, e.g. persons or organizations, or subject terms which have not been accepted as descriptors, and are listed in the *ERIC identifier authority list*. New identifiers are considered at regular intervals for addition to the list of descriptors; those which are accepted as new descriptors are listed in the monthly issues of RIE and CIJE, and removed from the *Authority list*. For those adopted before the 1980 reload, the change has been made in the computer file, but those changed since that time may be used in either way, depending on the date when the document was indexed. Identifiers are used in the subject indexes to both RIE and CIJE, and are designated major or minor in the same way as descriptors. In the printed versions they are listed separately from the descriptors, while in the computer file they are held in a separate field; thus a search for a descriptor added since 1980 may necessitate searching the identifier field as well as the descriptor field.

Documents are given one or more codes indicating their *publication type*, e.g. 110 Statistical data, 041 Doctoral dissertations. These are included in the printed version of RIE, which also has a publication type index arranged by code, but not of CIJE; however, the computer database has them for both. Publication type may also be shown by a descriptor where this is thought to be useful. This would normally be as a minor descriptor, but if the document is actually about a particular publication type, this may be used as a major descriptor; thus a set of slides about maps could have the publication type 100 Audiovisual/nonprint materials and the major descriptor Maps. There is a list of 22 forms, e.g. serials, directories, which are *not* used in the descriptor field unless they are the subject of the document, when they would be used as major descriptors. There is a table enabling indexers or searchers to find the code for a publication type, showing the publication type and pubtype code most applicable; terms not found as descriptors are shown in brackets, while the 22 which are not to be used as descriptors unless they are the subject (i.e. major descriptor) are marked with an asterisk. In many cases more than one pubtype code is suggested, while in others, several terms may lead to the same code. Some examples will clarify this:

Annotated bibliographies	131
[Archival documents]	060
Cartoons	100 (030)
[Children's books]	010 and 030
Kinescope recordings	100
Magnetic tapes	100

Resource materials   050 or 051 or 052
131 is the code for Bibliographies/annotated bibliographies
060 is the code for Historical materials; Archival materials is not a descriptor
100 is the code for Audiovisual/Nonprint materials; 030 for Creative works –
   (Literature, Drama, Fine arts); both might be appropriate
010 is the code for Books; Collected works; use both codes
050 is the code for Guides – General (use more specific code if possible);
051 is the code for Guides – Classroom use – Instructional materials (for
Learner)
052 is the code for Guides – Classroom use – Teaching guides (for Teacher)
To index a particular item use whichever of the three is most appropriate

The usual search approach is through subject, using descriptors and identifiers or, in computer searching, free text, but there are some additional access points which may be helpful. These are document language, geographical origin (as opposed to place as subject), and target audience for bias phase. Eleven specific audiences are listed, e.g. Policymakers, Practitioners, and Students. Practitioners has the five subheadings Administrators, Teachers, Counselors, Media staff, and Support staff. A document indexed by one of these five is automatically also indexed by the term Practitioners, making a generic search much easier than it is for age or educational level. Target audience has been a standard element of the full entry for both RIE and CIJE since 1984, and practitioners and/or students have been retrospectively added to some documents in RIE going back to 1975. It does not appear in the printed issues, and the method of computer searching varies depending on which utility is used. It has been found that about 25% of documents have a specific intended audience.

The next six-page section is Thesaurus construction and format. The *Thesaurus* consists of four parts, each of which is described in turn. The following notes are based on the *Thesaurus* itself, which in many ways follows what is now standard practice. The first and major section is the alphabetical list of descriptors. Preferred terms are in upper case bold; each has a note of the date of first (and last) use, the number of postings in RIE and CIJE, and the Group Code, showing which category it belongs to. Scope notes are frequent and may be either definitions or as notes for indexers or both. Possible homographs are qualified in parentheses, though it is not always clear what confusion might arise. UF shows non-preferred synonyms or quasi-synonyms, and BT, NT and RT are listed as usual, e.g.:

CURRICULUM DESIGN   *Jul. 1966*
        CIJE: 3588   RIE: 3392   GC: 320
SN   Arrangement of the component parts of
         a curriculum (note: prior to mar80, the
         use of this term was not restricted by a
         scope note)
BT   Design
RT   Course Selection (Students)

Curriculum
Curriculum Development

. . .

CURRICULUM GUIDES   *Jul.1966*
    CIJE: 678   RIE: 9030   GC: 730

SN   (Note: prior to Mar80, the thesaurus
       carried the instructions, "'course
       outlines' or 'syllabus,' use
       'curriculum guides'")
UF   Fles guides (1967 1980) #
NT   State Curriculum Guides
BT   Guides
RT   Course content
       Course descriptions
       Curriculum
       Curriculum Development

. . .

FATIGUE (BIOLOGY)
ENGLISH
ENGLISH (SECOND LANGUAGE)
ACCELERATION (EDUCATION)
ACCELERATION (PHYSICS)

The number of postings shown is a valuable guide in planning search strategy; it is clear that 'Curriculum guides' on its own will not be a useful search term, with over 9000 postings; on the other hand, we might well decide to look through the 168 postings for 'Aerobics'.

Non-preferred terms are shown in lower case bold; those which have never been preferred terms are unqualified, but those which have been transferred at some time have the dates of their use as preferred terms shown. As mentioned earlier, those to be used in conjunction with a second descriptor are marked # in the UF reference; this is reflected by the use of two (or occasionally more) terms separated by a semi-colon, e.g.:

Firemen
USE   FIRE FIGHTERS
FLES
UF   Fles Guides (1967 1980) #
       Foreign Languages in the Elementary School
Fles Guides (1967 1980)
USE   CURRICULUM GUIDES; FLES
Illegal Immigrants (1976–1984)
USE   UNDOCUMENTED IMMIGRANTS

(a nice example of political correctness!)

We may question whether the hierarchical structures are as sound as they might be, despite the VIP. Under 'Curriculum', we find as RT 'Curriculum Design', 'Curriculum Development', 'Curriculum Enrichment', 'Curriculum Evaluation', 'Curriculum Guides', 'Curriculum Problems' and 'Curriculum Research'. Since each of these is one particular aspect of Curriculum as a whole, according to the principles outlined in this book they are NT, not RT. 'Health' has some 50 RT, including some which are clearly at a different hierarchical level, e.g. 'Terminal Illness'. Even as specialized a term as 'Problem Solving' has 39 RT, some of which, e.g. 'Monte Carlo Methods', appear to be NT, while 'Problems' is surely a BT?

The Rotated Descriptor Display is a rotated index to each word used in the headings, though having found the right name, the editors then describe it as a 'permuted' index. In a thesaurus with a large number of precoordinated terms, such an index is essential, and it is made more useful by including non-preferred terms together with their Use references, and parenthetical qualifiers. A brief note at the beginning explains the filing order; at any one filing word, entries are arranged first by the words to the right, then by those to the left, e.g.:

DAY	CLASSES Use DAY PROGRAMS
DESEGREGATED	CLASSES Use CLASSROOM DESEGREGATION
EVENING	CLASSES (1967 1980) Use EVENING PROGRAMS
	CLASSES (GROUPS OF STUDENTS)
HONORS	CLASSES (1966 1980) Use HONORS CURRICULUM
INTEGRATED	CLASSES Use CLASSROOM DESEGREGATION
FORM	CLASSES (LANGUAGES)

The filing order, which is not immediately obvious, is day, desegregated, evening, groups, honors, integrated, languages. However, the list is easily scanned, and is one of the most complete of its kind. The 10,363 words in the thesaurus, preferred and non-preferred, give rise to about 21,000 entries in the rotated index, indicating that the average descriptor has about two words.

The 'Two-way Hierarchical Term Display' is so named because it shows both NT and BT relationships. Each descriptor is listed, preceded by broader terms and followed by narrower terms. (Orphans, 'Hierarchical isolates', are easily spotted!) More than one hierarchy can be shown. Each step of division is shown, by colons for BT and full stops for NT, e.g.:

```
:::::LIBERAL ARTS
::::SCIENCES
:::NATURAL SCIENCES
::PHYSICAL SCIENCES
:PHYSICS
:::::LIBERAL ARTS
:::SCIENCES
::NATURAL SCIENCES
:BIOLOGICAL sciences
BIOPHYSICS
.BIOMECHANICS
```

.BIONICS
..ROBOTICS

In the main listing we find:

BIOPHYSICS

NT   Biomechanics
           Bionics
BT   Biological sciences
           Physics

and could follow up the further steps of the hierarchy as necessary.

The final section of the thesaurus is the Descriptor groups. There are nine broad groups, e.g. Groups related to LEARNING AND DEVELOPMENT, Groups related to HUMAN SOCIETY; these are divided into a total of 41 smaller groups, each with a scope note to illustrate its coverage. The terms in the individual groups are then listed in alphabetical order. The lists include invalid descriptors with their dates of birth and death. The groups are those established by the VIP; though the size of the list has grown by over 20% since the eighth edition in 1980, the number of groups has not increased, and each group is now becoming quite large; Business, Commerce and Industry contains 62 terms, but many of the groups include over 200. The Group Code given in each entry in the main list leads to the appropriate Group, where the user can scan the list to find ideas for indexing or search formulation. This link was omitted in the eighth edition, but has obviously been found to be a useful part of the structure and restored.

The *Thesaurus* is obviously a good working tool which is kept under careful review. One cannot help feeling, however, that some opportunities were missed in the VIP to provide a firmer classificatory structure. LCSH now relies on hierarchical relationships for its BT-NT-RT links, but it is clear that this is not always the case with the ERIC *Thesaurus*. In a subject of manageable size like education, the effort would have been worth the cost.

PAIS subject headings

Public Affairs Information Service, Inc was established in 1914 to publish an index to the literature of the social sciences in general, and public policy and social policy in particular. In 1954 it was incorporated as a non-profit educational institution, and bases its work largely on the collections of the New York Public Library, where it is housed. In 1986 the name of the index changed from *Bulletin of the Public Affairs Information Service* to *PAIS Bulletin*, and again in 1991, when it became *PAIS International*. In 1972 the database was computerized, and in 1987 became available on CD-ROM; it is also available online through various services. The printed annual volumes were each self-contained in terms of the headings and cross-references used, but in 1984 a complete list was published separately. The introduction of CD-ROM prompted a close review of the headings and their structure, and the second edition was published in 1990.[3] The online database was reviewed, and now conforms to the headings in the second edition. However, if a term has not been used since 1974, it is not included as a main heading, though it may appear as a non-preferred term in the list, and may also be found in the printed volumes prior to 1974. Since the index is mainly intended as a guide to current literature (the aim is to index English-language material within two months of publication), and each printed volume was self-contained, this is not likely to be a problem.

A major reason for publishing a revised list was the number of end users searching the online and CD-ROM files. To help such users – and of course others – the number of cross-references and scope notes was increased. The introduction of CD-ROM had also indicated that the syndetic structure should be carefully reviewed. The list is thus the authority file for headings used in the print and computer-based versions; however, as new subjects arise, new headings are generated, and will be included in a subsequent edition. In searching the index since 1990, it is important to note that there may be additional headings; these will normally be self-evident, or have adequate cross-referencing to enable them to be found without difficulty.

The list consists of three parts: the main list of headings; a list of authorized subheadings (Appendix A); and a rotated index (correctly so named) giving access to words that would otherwise be lost in multi-word terms (Appendix B). In the main list, preferred terms are in bold type, with non-preferred terms in normal weight. In cross-references, bold type is not used. Although most headings are in natural language order, many are in inverted form, sometimes causing inconsistencies in format. Cross-references are in the form of *SEE* and *SEE ALSO*, with complementary *SF* (see from = USE) and *SAF* (See also from, with no precise equivalent in usual thesaurus codes). Subheadings are included in the main list in italic with a reference to Appendix A, but may also have notes indicating their use. This is a notable improvement over the first edition, where subheadings were only listed in a separate sequence. Certain main headings may also be used as subheadings, in which case notes are given referring the user to Appendix A. A few subheadings may be used as part of a multiword heading. Some headings may be subdivided geographically. The following examples will illustrate these points.

Ethiopian-Italian war, 1935–36

	SEE	Italo-Ethiopian war, 1935–36
War		
	SEE ALSO	Aerial warfare
		. . .
		Italo-Ethiopian war, 1935–36
Firefighters		
	SEE ALSO	Women firefighters
Firefighters, Volunteer		
	SF	Volunteer firefighters
Women firefighters		
	SAF	Firefighters
Protection		
	NOTE:	Use only as a subheading. See Appendix A

	SEE	United States – President – Protection

Investment

	NOTE:	Use only as a subheading. See Appendix A.

Investment advisers

. . .

Investment banking

. . .

Investments

	NOTE:	May also be used as a subheading. See Appendix A.

Investments, Foreign

	NOTE:	Subdivide geographically by country receiving the capital

Finance, Public

	NOTE:	Use for general and theoretical material on public finance not relating to a particular political jurisdiction. For the public finance or general financial conditions and institutions of a specific political jurisdiction use the subheading Finance under the appropriate geographic heading, e.g. United States – Finance

Some headings are deliberately omitted from the list. These are proper names of one kind or another for which PAIS has established a standard form. No reference is made to AACR2 or other cataloguing code, and no examples are given in the list for people, for whom users are advised to search the database for the family name. Geographic headings are based on *Webster's new geographical dictionary*; United States is used as a model heading. Ethnic groups have standardized formats: examples given in the introduction are French Canadians; Armenians; Turks in West Germany; Mexican Americans. Names of institutions are used in the form preferred by the institution, though foreign institutions have their name translated into English. For government departments, United States federal bodies are to be used as the model, while for international organizations the United Nations serves this purpose. For corporate bodies two points are worth noting: organizations with names based on personal names have the name inverted to bring the family name to the front, e.g. DU PONT DE NEMOURS (E.I.) AND COMPANY; cross-references are made from acronyms.

Appendix A lists the subheadings, each with notes showing when it may be used and under what headings, e.g.:

Assassination

Main heading which may also be used as a
subheading under names or titles of persons
assassinated, e.g. Kennedy, John Fitzgerald,
1917–63 – Assassination

Capitol

May be used under headings for individual
countries, states, etc., e.g. New Jersey –
Capitol

    SAF   Capitols

Benefits

May be used under headings for specific
population groups, e.g. Children,
Handicapped – Benefits

    SF   Benefits

May also be used under specific occupational
categories, e.g. Government employees – Benefits

    SF   Benefits

    SAF   Employees' benefit plans
                Wages and salaries – (heading for
                occupational category)

This example illustrates the advantage of listing subheadings in the main sequence.
In the first edition, the entry for Benefits in the list of subheadings is as above, but
in the main sequence we find:

Benefits

    SEE   Employees' benefit plans
                        Maternity benefits
                        Old age – Benefits
                        Sickness benefit plans
                        Survivors' benefits
                        Trade unions – Benefit funds
                        Veterans – Benefits

where only the fact that two examples are given gives a clue that it may also be used
as a subheading.

At times the notes are not as clear as one might wish:

Deinstitutionalization

    NOTE: Use for material on reductions in the
                    number of people admitted to and
                    retained in institutions. When
                    appropriate, repeat under headings
                    for specific types of institutions (e.g.,
                    Hospitals) or under headings for
                    categories of people with the

> subheading Commitment and
> detention, e.g. Mentally ill –
> Commitment and detention. See
> Appendix A.

If we turn to Appendix A, we do not find Deinstitutionalization, but we do find:

Commitment and detention
May be used under the following headings:
Drug addicts
Mentally ill
Mentally ill children
Criminals, Insane
    SF   Commitment and detention

From this we may assume that Deinstitutionalization may be used as a heading, with additional entries if necessary under the headings mentioned, but clearer instructions would have been more helpful. In the 1993 volume of *PAIS international in print* we find Deinstitutionalization with *see also* references to Community-based corrections, Group homes and House arrest, which are the three links given in the PAIS list. Deinstitutionalization did not appear at all in the first edition, reflecting a significant change in social policies during the 1980s. Another example is Default, at which heading we find in the main stream:

Default
    SF   Use only as a subheading. See
                Appendix A.
    SEE   Bankruptcy
                Loans, Bank – Default
                Loans, Foreign – Default
                Municipal bonds – Default
                Repossession
                Student loans – Default
Default judgments
    SEE   Judgments by default

If we turn to Appendix A, we find:

Default
May be used under the following headings:
Bonds
Loans, Bank
Loans, Foreign
Municipal bonds
Student loans
    SF   Default

We may ask why Bonds are not mentioned in the main sequence under Default, when the other four examples are? (Bankruptcy and Repossession do not require the subheading.) And why are compound terms involving Loans in inverted forms, whereas Bonds are not?

Appendix B is the Rotated authorized main headings list, a KWIC index to the headings in the main sequence. Subheadings are not included, so the only entry for Default is the one for Judgment by default. Deinstitutionalization is included as a main heading, but Commitment and detention is not, being only a subheading. The index was introduced in the second edition, and is a very useful addition to the list, which has many multiword headings; in the first edition, some of these words other than the first could not have been located.

The network of SF and SAF cross-references is very thorough in both editions, but some do slip through the net, e.g.

Publishing industry
[no access from Industry]

In the rotated index this can easily be located under Industry, along with over 400 other headings containing the word.

The list is a valuable tool, and reflects the experience gained in compiling the *Bulletin* over some 80 years, together with a positive attitude towards those users who wish to search the database themselves. It also shows the advantages to be gained from computer-based production, which made possible the rotated index; though the typography of this leaves something to be desired, it is a significant improvement in the second edition. Further editions will surely appear in the future.

The ASSIA thesaurus

The ASSIA *thesaurus* is used in indexing *Applied social science index and abstracts*. A database was set up in 1989 to produce the bi-monthly issues and annual cumulation, and the thesaurus was produced from this database in 1991, and reprinted in 1993.[4] It contains 8,250 terms covering the whole of the social sciences, with an emphasis on those concerned with the caring function within society. It covers core materials in Sociology and Psychology, and basic materials in Anthropology, Economics, Politics, Law and Medicine. ASSIA is intended for the *applied* social scientist, which influences the terms that are used, and also some of the relationships which are displayed.

Because of the limitations of the software used, the thesaurus contains no scope notes, and to keep the cost down, only BT-NT, USE and UF relationships are shown. It is hoped that these limitations, which are quite severe, will be avoided in a future edition. All entry terms are in bold, whether preferred or non-preferred, which means that it is not as easy as one might wish to notice the non-preferred ones. The list is in one alphabetical sequence, with no accompanying hierarchical display or rotated index, though it is fair to point out that multi-word terms, of which there are many, usually have additional entries under hidden terms. Some terms have parenthetical qualifiers, and some have comma or colon qualifiers; the difference is explained in the Introduction to the 1991 annual volume:

:   by, for, with *etc*
,   type, e.g. Accommodation, Sheltered
–   and relationship, e.g. Mother – Baby = Mother and Baby
( )   to distinguish homographs
( )   to group material on a country together, e.g. Acts of Parliament (Australia)

Entry is usually direct, but the use of the comma means that some terms are in inverted order, again with the result of revealing what would otherwise be a hidden word. Until 1993, the main sequence in ASSIA was arranged by subject headings constructed from terms in the thesaurus, and included cross-references to related headings. The accompanying author index included the journal reference, and the first two terms of the subject heading to get users to the abstract. In 1993 some important changes were made; the new arrangement is explained in the Introduction to the annual volume, but without any specific indication that it is different from previous practice. The main sequence consists of the abstracts arranged by subject headings as before, but each abstract is now numbered. There is a separate subject index giving the abstract numbers; this is constructed on chain indexing principles, and contains cross-references to related headings, using *see* and *see also* rather than the thesaurus conventions. The author index gives the abstract number but does not include the journal reference. There is also a source index, in which each issue of a periodical covered by the service is listed, leading direct to the abstract numbers for articles in that issue.

Some examples will illustrate both the thesaurus and the way it is used to construct the pre-coordinated headings used in the abstracts. There are also a few minor changes between the thesaurus, based on 1989 practice, and later use. Some of the terms do reflect the bias of the coverage as set out in the Introduction to the annual volumes and in the *Thesaurus*.

Accommodation
    NT   Boarding houses
            Caravans
            Halls of residence
            Hostels
            Housing
            Longhouses
            Residential homes
Accommodation (Psychological)
    BT   Psychological processes
Accommodation, Sheltered
    NT   Retirement communities

(Accommodation, Sheltered was changed to Sheltered accommodation in 1993.)

Adjustment, Psychological
>   *BT*   Psychological processes

Burden of proof
>   *USE*   Onus of proof

Businesses
>   *UF*   Firms

Arts
>   *BT*   Culture
>   *NT*   Art
>   Drama
>   Literature
>   Music
>   Performing arts

Performing arts
>   *BT*   Arts

Literature
>   *BT*   Arts
>   *NT*   Academic literature
>   African literature
>   Australian literature
>   Biographies
>   Fairy tales
>   Plays
>   Utopian literature
>   Western literature

Drama
>   *BT*   Arts
>   *NT*   Theatre

The facet analysis here seems to have been less precise than one might have wished; literature by form (Fiction, Biographies) is mingled with literature by country (Australian literature), literature by theme (Utopian literature), and literature by origin (Academic literature). Because of the lack of RT links, we cannot see whether there is any link between Drama, Plays, Theatre and Performing arts, which would appear to be related.

Some of the hierarchies are not worked out in as much detail as one would expect. For example, under Food we find as NT Dairy products, but also Milk, which is surely a NT to Dairy products? We have Vegetables, but also Potatoes and Sweet potatoes; Grain, but also Maize and Wheat; Meals and School meals. It can be argued that it is not essential to work these out in full detail until the list becomes larger, but surely it would save work in the long run to pursue the analysis further to begin with?

It is sometimes difficult to see how the relationships have been worked out, taking into account that there a high proportion of precoordinated terms in the thesaurus. For example, we find:

Adolescent boys [daughters, fathers, girls, mothers, parents, sons]
BT	Boys
NT	Autistic adolescent boys
	Black adolescent boys *etc*

Adolescents
NT	Black adolescents *etc*

Boys
BT	Children
NT	Adolescent boys

but there does not seem to be any way of linking Adolescents and Adolescent boys and all the other headings beginning with the adjective rather than the plural noun. The fact that no RT are listed (except one stray: Adolescents RT Young people) makes it more difficult to follow the underlying structure. It is only fair to point out that in ASSIA we *do* find Adolescents *see also* Young people and vice versa.

Countries are listed, with the normal practice being to move down to the next level of government as NT. However, under Unites States we find the States listed, including Pennsylvania, but also Philadelphia; if every substantial city in the United States is to be given as a narrower term, the list is going to be very long one! To list the states would give fifty NT, but under each state the number of cities would be limited. New York also seems to present an anomaly:

New York City
NT	Long Island

New York State
BT	United States

In this instance the alphabetical juxtaposition makes the link apparent, but this is not true of all US cities.

The thesaurus is used to construct quite complex headings for the abstracts. For example, in the main sequence in 1993 we find the heading for abstract 15704:

Terminally ill elderly people – Life-sustaining treatment – Decisions – Adult children

In the subject index, we find:

Adult children
    Decisions – Life-sustaining treatment – Terminally ill elderly people 15704
Life-sustaining treatment
    Terminally ill elderly people   15704
Terminally ill elderly people   15703–5

There is no entry for Decisions, which does not appear in the thesaurus, but we do find

Decision making
    Life-sustaining treatment   9272

which seems to muddy the waters a little.

Some of the minor changes are sensible, but others are less helpful. For example, in the thesaurus we find:

Minerals : deficiency

but in 1993 this becomes

Mineral deficiency

In the thesaurus, we find the abbreviated forms:

AIDS
>   *UF*   Acquired immunodeficiency syndrome

AIDS : virus
>   *UF*   HIV
>   Human immunodeficiency virus

but in the abstracts we find the reverse:

AIDS
>   *see*   Acquired immunodeficiency syndrome

It is not obvious why this change should have been made, from the term that is now normally used and is incorporated into the name of a number of organizations.

Compared with PAIS subject headings, the ASSIA thesaurus tends to reflect its much shorter existence as well as a different approach to the contruction of headings. The headings in PAISSH are used as they stand, whereas the ASSIA thesaurus terms are used to construct complex headings which represent as specifically as possible the subject of the document abstracted. The specificity of these headings is likely to be very helpful in arranging the abstracts – up to 20,000 each year – in order, without in any way impeding online retrieval. It will be helpful to see a new edition of the thesaurus complete with scope notes and RT links.

References

1   *Thesaurus of ERIC descriptors,* 12th edn, Phoenix, AZ, Oryx Press, 1990.
2   *Thesaurus of ERIC descriptors,* 13th edn, Phoenix, AZ, Oryx Press, May 1995.
3   *PAIS subject headings,* 2nd edn, Public Affairs Information Service, 1990.
4   ASSIA *Thesaurus,* London, Bowker-Saur. 1991, reprinted 1993.

Chapter 27
Visual art and graphics

Pictorial collections have always presented special problems in information retrieval by subject. It is usually possible to identify an 'author' – Picasso, Rodin, Dürer – or a title – *The last supper, David, Alice in Wonderland*, but subjects have proved much more intractable. If we can describe the subject in words, this may solve the problem, but very often users are interested not in the subject as a whole, but in some specific feature of a work of art. Such media as films and slides have always required special treatment to enable users to find material by subject or theme. For example, the British Film Institute has built up a detailed index to films in its collections, but this has been a very time-consuming exercise. Now of course there is also massive amounts of television material available on videotape. The situation has also changed radically since graphics became a practical feature for the desktop computer.

One of the major benefits of computer access is the availability of multimedia. However, there is little point in having access to large amounts of pictorial material if we cannot find what we want. Most of the attention paid to graphics in the computer literature has been concerned with the associated computing problems – compression, transmission, decompression, display – and very little has been said about the problems of access. In a review of the literature, Cawkell points out that not a great deal has been written about subject access to graphics.[1] The papers given at the 'Electronic imaging and the visual arts' conferences in 1993[2] and 1994[3] contain only one paper on subject access,[4] which points out that textual information is often essential to retrieve a visual image. More information can be found in a special issue of *Knowledge* organization,[5] including an article[6] on Iconclass.

Iconclass

This scheme,[7] conceived by the art historian Henri van de Waal, was intended as a classification for Western art, but it could no doubt be extended to take in images outside this particular tradition. It is a hierarchical classification, with some elements of synthesis and a great deal of detail. Van de Waal died in 1972, but the work was continued by colleagues, and publication was completed in 1985. Each section of the classification is paralleled by a bibliography, which demonstrates the scheme in use.

There are five general divisions and four special divisions. The main divisions cover:

1   Supernatural, God and Religion
2   Nature

3   Human being, Man in general
4   Society, Civilization, Culture
5   Abstract ideas or concepts.

The four special divisions cover special subjects, which may be covered in general in the five general divisions.

6   History
7   The Bible
8   Sagas, legends and tales
9   Classical mythology and Antiquities.

For example, we find:

1   Religion and magic
11   Christianity
11 D   Christ
11 D 2   Christ as child or youth
. . .

However, the Last Supper would be classified in special division 7. There is obviously scope for cross-classification here, but there is an elaborate system of cross-references in the alphabetical index, as well as notes in the schedules. The notation is simple; primary divisions are shown by up to two figures:

1   Religion and magic
11   Christianity
12   Non-Christian religions
13   Magic and occultism

Secondary divisions are shown by a single capital letter (J is not used) preceded and followed by a space; occasionally the letter is doubled to signify 'opposition':

11 A   Deity, God
11 B   Holy Trinity
25 G   Plants
25 GG   Fabulous plants

Further subdivision is by numbers in blocks of two with a space between them; in general, only 1 to 9 are used, but 0 may be used to indicate certain allegorical or symbolic representations, e.g.:

31 B   Mind, Spirit
31 B 61   Morphology of expression in general
31 B 62   Morphology of facial expression
31 B 62 1   Morphology of facial expression – eyes
31 B 62 11   looking upwards
31 B 62 14   weeping
31 B 62 31 3   smiling
. . .

31 A 41 11   blindness
31 A 41 11 0   allegorical representation of blindness

Names are used quite frequently as a useful form of subdivision; as with UDC, this can be within a class number.

11 H   Saints. Male Saints   with NAME
11 H 36   penitence
11 HH   Female Saints
11 HH (Mary Magdalene)
11 HH (Mary Magdalene) 36

Auxiliaries allow the specification of particular facets within a division, and are listed at the end of each volume under the heading Key. The notation is used in parentheses and a + is used as a facet indicator. For instance, 25 F is the main notation for animals; the key for 25 F and subdivisions lists, for example, an anatomy facet:

+3   Anatomy
+31   skeleton
+32   trunk
+33   head
+33 1   skull
+33 2   antlers, horns
. . .

We may also find cross references here:

+6   disease and death of animals
+65   caring for sick animals
                    Veterinarian 34 C 5

The citation order is normally that auxiliaries follow the main subdivisions, but this may be varied if the user prefers, e.g.:

25 F 23   Predatory animals
25 F 23 (+33) head of predatory animal
25 F 23 BEAR
25 F 23 BEAR (+33)
25 F 23 FOX
25 F 23 FOX (+33)

or:

25 F 23 BEAR
25 F 23 FOX
25 F 23 BEAR (+33)
25 F 23 FOX (+33)

which would bring all depictions of heads of predatory animals together. The classifier would need to make careful records of decisions taken in this way in an authority file.

More than one class number can be given to represent a single picture; for example, one which contained the figures of several saints could have a class mark for each; this is of course associated with a classified arrangement, as in the accompanying bibliographies. A complex subject can also be represented by more than one class number linked by colons. One example given is as follows:

73 C 52   raising of Lazarus
42 E 3   grave, tomb
73 C 52 : 42 E 3   raising of Lazarus with tomb shown

In this situation, entries would also be made under each part of such a class mark.

The index, in three volumes, is very detailed. The entry under Reading includes the following entries among a total of 22 (not alphabetically arranged!):

Reading
see also reading aloud
see also studying
reading 49 N
the penitent St Mary Magdalene (often before a cave): her long hair
covers her (naked) body, she reads, meditates or raises her tear-filled
eyes towards Heaven   11 HH (MARY MAGDALENE) 36

A collection of Dutch printers' devices classified by Iconclass is now available on CD-ROM,[8] and the scheme may well prove to be at least a partial solution to the problems of subject access to electronic images, despite having been originally intended for conventional works of art. There appears to be no reason, except perhaps cost, why it should not be expanded to take in new concepts.

Art and architecture thesaurus

Another important tool in the indexing of graphic images is the *Art and architecture thesaurus*[9] published by Oxford University Press on behalf of the Getty Art History Information Program. This detailed thesaurus took 14 years to prepare; the first edition in 1990 was not comprehensive, but was published as a valuable tool even if incomplete. Out of the then planned 40 hierarchies, 23 were worked out; these were carefully studied for overlaps and omissions, and the resulting 33 hierarchies were published in the second edition in 1994. The following description is based on the 1990 edition, with notes to indicate changes in the 1994 edition.

MeSH was taken as the model, with its alphabetical display backed up by a detailed hierarchical tree structure, and the scheme began with a selection of some 30,000 terms from LCSH. These were sorted into hierarchies, which soon revealed many gaps, so that it became necessary to gather terms from other sources. The objective was to compile a list of terms which would cover the history and the making of the visual arts and, like Iconclass, provide a link between the objects themselves and the literature about them. It was to be geographically and historically comprehensive, but would exclude terminology specifically related to iconographic themes. Although LCSH proved inadequate, it is still used as a 'home base', in that LCSH headings are used whenever they are acceptable within the framework of the thesaurus.

From 1980 to 1982 the preliminary work was funded by a grant from the National Endowment for the Humanities, (NEH), but when this stage was complete, funding was taken over by the Getty Art History Information Program, which has continued to support the work since 1983. The development had then reached a stage when rules for procedure could be laid down. The first point was to define the core and peripheral areas, so that the scope of the thesaurus could be clearly seen. The second was to recognize the necessity for a detailed authority record for each term, showing its provenance and use; scope notes would be provided for most terms to make their use clear. Subdivision lists were to be provided for common facets such as styles and periods, place, date, document types and common subjects. The hierarchies would be complete, including unsought links (called here *guide terms*) necessary to show the structure; these would be marked off by being placed in angle brackets in italic, e.g. *<processes and techniques>*. Three kinds would be sought in most hierarchies: *<by form>*, *<by function>* and *<by location or context>* but others would be used as they arose in specific subjects. There are 2752 such entries in the 1994 edition, showing the care with which the hierarchies have been worked out.

The ANSI and ISO standards on thesaurus construction were used as the main guides, with some minor modifications. Preferred terms are called *descriptors* and appear in bold type in the alphabetical list; non-preferred terms are in normal weight, and do not appear in the tree structures, which show descriptors and unsought links only. Descriptors are normally nouns, but many may also appear as adjectives, e.g. historic, circular, in 'modified descriptors', discussed later. No verbs are used, but verbal nouns (gerunds) may appear, e.g. 'repairing', with a USE reference from repair. The usual rules for singular and plural are followed; this means that some terms, e.g. building, buildings, may appear in both forms, as Activity or Objects. Natural word order is used, with USE references from inverted forms. Relationships are shown by the usual conventions: USE, UF, BT-NT, SN. However, a descriptor only has one BT; quasi-generic relationships are not shown. BT-NT relationships are generic, not partitive, except in a few places, e.g. Furniture, which has the subdivision Furniture components. In the first edition, RT was not used, as these relationships were taken to be shown by the hierarchical display. In the second edition, 3462 RT are used to link terms from different hierarchies, which in the first edition are not linked either by the display or by RT.

Terms are firmly based on literary warrant: they must appear in a document. and. most descriptors are linked to their source by abbreviated codes:

A   Avery index authority reference file
B   RIBA *Architectural periodicals index* Architectural keywords
H   BHA *Bibliography of the history of art*   (added in second edition)
L   LCSH
N   *Revised nomenclature for museum cataloging*
R   International registry of the literature of art (RILA) subject heading list

Definitions forming part of the scope notes are linked to a list of some 2000 works consulted in the selection of terms, included in the introduction. Compound terms are analysed into their component parts except where this would cause them to lose their meaning. It is good to see these rules and procedures clearly set out and followed!

By 1983 some 13,000 terms had been gathered, including about 2600 in Styles and Periods, and the first of many expert reviews took place. In these, panels of art experts have reviewed sections of the thesaurus, suggesting additional terms, possible omissions and the suitability of scope notes. There have also been reviews by thesaurus construction experts, who have commented on the hierarchies and the overall structure. These reviews have helped to ensure that the thesaurus has stayed in line with the people who will be using it in the future, from both structure and content points of view. For example, the section originally headed Fine Arts was soon broadened to Visual and verbal communication.

The scope of the thesaurus as a whole has been defined to cover three major areas. The first of these is 'Built environment: built works and the human elaboration of the natural environment', which was the first area to be considered. The second and third, which were still incomplete in the 1990 edition, are 'Furnishings and equipment: artifacts with a primarily utilitarian purpose, often embellished'; and 'Visual and verbal communication: communicative artifacts created according to aesthetic, conceptual or symbolic principles'. The terms cover objects, materials, construction techniques, physical attributes (e.g. shape, colour), persons, and concepts related to theory, history and purpose. Iconographical themes such as religious or mythical subjects are generally excluded.

In 1985 the scope was narrowed to Western art and architecture, and the scheme as it then stood was tried out in the Architectural Slide Library of the Rensselaer Polytechnic Institute. In 1989 the possibility of developing a multi-lingual thesaurus was explored with some success, and codes were added to show the hierarchies. For the second edition, it was decided to add terms used in the UK where these differed from US practice. The 1812 terms added are signalled in the alphabetical list by the code UK.

One important point was that it was soon apparent that the most common use of the scheme would be in computer-based systems, and in addition to the printed volumes, the 1990 edition was made available as a simple ASCII file. An improved version was made available in 1992; named the *Art and architecture thesaurus Authority Reference Tool* (ART), the disks included suitable retrieval software. It is available as a TSR (Terminate and Stay Resident) program for IBM-type microcomputers, so that users can get on with indexing with the thesaurus available for consultation when needed.

The scheme has been fitted into the USMARC Authorities format. The MARC tags used are:

650   subject added entry – topical term; may be used for any descriptor
654   subject added entry – faceted topical term; may be used for any descriptor
655   index term – genre/form

656	index term – occupation
657	index term – function
755	added entry – physical characteristics

There are seven facets, set out here with some examples, and MARC codes other than 650 and 654 which may be used:

1	Associated concepts	
	(beauty, privacy, connoisseurship, romanticism)	
2	Physical attributes	
	Attributes and properties (round)	755
	*Conditions and effects	755
	Design elements (exterior)	755
	Color (light green)	755
3	Styles and Periods	
	(peoples and cultures, geographical, rulers, schools)	
4	Agents (one hierarchy in 1990, split into two in 1994)	
	People (printmakers)	656
	Organizations (corporations)	656
5	Activities	
	Disciplines (archeology, engineering)	657
	Functions (analysis)	657
	Events (Contests, death)	
	*Activities	
	Processes and techniques (conservation, drawing, weaving)	657, 755
6	Materials (iron, clay, adhesives, emulsifiers, artificial ivory)	
7	Objects	
	*Object groupings and systems	
	Object genres	655
	*Components	
	Built environment	
	Settlements, [systems] and landscapes	
	Built complexes and districts (arches, rivers)	
	Single built works [and open spaces]	
	*Open spaces and site elements	
	[Building divisions and site elements (tools)]	
	[Built works components]	
	Furnishings and equipment	
	Tools and equipment	
	†Measuring devices	
	[Hardware and joints]	
	*Containers	
	†Furnishings [revised from 1990 Furniture]	
	‡Personal artifacts	
	‡Culinary artifacts	

*Costume
†Weapons and ammunition [1990 Armaments]
*Sound devices
‡Musical instruments
†Recreational artifacts
†Transportation vehicles
‡Communication artifacts
Visual and verbal communication
*Visual works   655
[1990 Drawings]
[1990 Photographs]
[1990 Paintings]
[1990 Prints]
[1990 Sculpture]
[1990 Multimedia art forms]
Information forms [1990 Document types]   655
†Exchange media
‡Communication design
‡Book arts

* indicates new in 1994
† indicates foreshadowed in 1990, present in 1994
‡ indicates foreshadowed in 1990, not specifically present in 1994
[. . .] indicates 1990 hierarchies subsumed elsewhere in 1994.

Volume 1 contains a lengthy introduction explaining the development of the thesaurus, the list of sources, guidance on using the thesaurus and rules for constructing subject headings for precoordinate indexes. There are also forms for anyone wishing to submit further terms for consideration. The second edition contains lists of terms, guide terms and UF terms which have been added, changed or deleted since the first edition. The introduction is a useful source on thesaurus construction in general.

The rules for pre-coordinate headings distinguish three kinds of heading which may result. The first is the straightforward *descriptor*, which may be used as it stands. As mentioned, LCSH headings are used where they do not conflict with the rules, so some of the descriptors will coincide with LCSH, and others will be sufficiently similar to be recognizable as a 'standard' subject heading. *Modified descriptors* are combinations of two or more AAT descriptors to form adjectival phrases. The *focus* of the phrase is the term from the latest facet, and it is modified by terms from the previous facets in schedule order as listed earlier (1 to 7). So, showing the facets in [ ] for illustration only, we could have:

Victorian [3] painted [5] wood [6] children's bedroom [7] furniture [focus]
Renaissance [3] oil [6] paintings [focus]
Oil paintings [Oil = *instrument*]

The method for constructing modified descriptors is very similar to the focus and difference procedure found in PRECIS, and gives phrases in natural language order.

The third kind of heading we can have is the *string*. This is a syntactic combination of descriptors or modified descriptors involving more than one focus, and usually represented by a prepositional phrase in natural language. The phrase is put into the passive voice and the foci written down in reverse facet order, with dashes to join the terms. This is similar to the procedures used by Coates. For example:

Paper—restoration—archivists [restoration *of* paper *by* archivists]
Wood tables—evaluation—antique dealers. [Evaluation *of* etc]

The thesaurus can thus be used either as a post-coordinate or a pre-coordinate indexing language.

Hierarchical displays

The rest of Volume 1 is devoted to the hierarchical displays, which in the second edition have expanded to occupy a second volume. Each hierarchy is carefully worked out, with subordination being shown by indentation; alternate levels of indentation are shown by vertical shaded columns, so that the structure can be followed. Within a hierarchy, terms at the same level are arranged alphabetically unless some other arrangement, e.g. chronological or size, is logically appropriate. Each hierarchy has a brief introduction, listing the scope and organization of the hierarchy, its relation to other hierarchies, descriptor form and use, and the number of descriptors. There is a synopsis, which is a summary of the hierarchy. Each line is computer-numbered as a locating device; this is *not* a notation, and differs from edition to edition as descriptors are added or deleted. It should be noted that the final line number does not coincide with the number of descriptors, as unsought links are line numbered but not counted as descriptors. As an example, we may look at the synopsis for KM Events:

KM1	Events	1994 changed to
KM2	campaigns	KM9
KM5	celebrations	KM12
KM11	ceremonies	KM19
KM12	<academic ceremonies>	KM20
. . .		
KM41	contests [*etc*]	KM50

All told there are 15 main subheadings alphabetically arranged. If we turn to the full hierarchy at KM11 we find:

KM11	ceremonies	KM19
KM12	<academic ceremonies>	KM20
KM13	commencements	KM21
KM14	convocations	KM22

For each hierarchy, examples are given at the foot of the page of ways in which the terms may be combined in precoordinate headings; for example, in Materials MT we have the footnote 'may be used in conjunction with other descriptors (e.g., marble + floors; granite + faux finishing)'. A detailed hierarchy such as that for processes and techniques can use several steps of division:

KT   *<processes and techniques>*
            <processes and techniques by specific type>
                <image-making processes and techniques>
                    <print-making and print-making techniques>
                    print-making techniques
                        <print-making techniques by transfer method>
                        relief printing
                            block printing
                                woodblock printing

The vertical bands on the display pages show the level of indentation for each line, and make it possible to follow the hierarchy through.

Alphabetical display

The remaining two volumes in the first edition hold the alphabetical listing of about 17,000 descriptors and 31,000 non-preferred terms; Volume 2 holds 1 to knotted, Volume 3 knotting to zutugil. In the second edition, the number of terms has increased to 24,496, with 63,003 non-preferred terms, in Volumes 3, 4 and 5. Descriptors are in bold, non-preferred terms in light weight type. Each descriptor has a facet and line number to locate it in the hierarchical display, and may have an indicator to show its source. Many have alternative forms marked ALT; these are often the combining form for modified descriptors, but may represent variations in practice between bibliographies and museums, e.g.:

impressionist   adjective
   ALT impressionism   noun
Buddhism   noun
   ALT Buddhist   adjective
painting   gerund
   ALT painted   adjective
museums   plural
   ALT museum   singular

Scope notes are frequent, and may be instructional or definitional. Instructional SN usually have key words which indicate when the descriptor is to be used, while definitions are often linked to the sources from which they are taken, as mentioned earlier. In the second edition, HN (History notes) are given for terms which have changed from the first edition, UK is used for British terms and UKA for alternative British terms. Each descriptor also has a class number consisting of the one-letter facet designator, two-letter heading class mark, then as many blocks of three letters as necessary to reflect its place in the hierarchy, all elements being separated by full stops. The classification is intended for computer use and is not clearly explained at any point. A few homographs occur and are indicated by parenthetical qualifiers. Some examples will illustrate these points:

bulkheads
    RT.588   (A, N)
    ALT bulkhead
    SN   walls used to resist pressure caused by rocks or water, such as to separate land and water areas (BROOKS)
    CN   V.RT.AFU.AFU.AFU.BIQ.BUE.AFU.ALO.AXC.AFU

presentation drawings
    VD.166
    SN   Use for architectural drawings presented to a client to illustrate how the building will look and function

presentation drawings (gifts)
    VD.107
    SN   finished drawings presented by the artist to a friend or patron; usually used with regard to the Renaissance-Baroque period

moorings
    RK.1323
    ALT mooring
    SN   use for semipermanent anchorages consisting of a heavy anchor, chain, moving buoy, and pennant (CFCHAP)

strong greenish blue
    DL.235
    UF   ... [41 differently named but similar colours!]

woodblock printing
    CN   K.KT.AFU.ALO.DUC.DUC.ALO.BCW.ARI.ALO.AXC

This latter class number shows the facet Activities K, heading processes and techniques KT, and the nine steps of division from Activities to Woodblock printing. Fortunately it is used only in computer manipulation and is thus completely transparent to the user, for whom it would hardly be encouraging!

The thesaurus is a major contribution to the difficult problem of indexing and searching art works and illustrations. At present it is still somewhat biased towards architecture, reflecting its origins, but the second edition, with all the outstanding hierarchies completed, is an even more valuable tool. It is already used by such works as the *Avery index to architectural periodicals*, but more widespread use of both this and Iconclass would help to solve some of the problems of subject retrieval of illustrated matter.

References

1   Cawkell, A. E., 'Imaging systems and picture collection management: a review', *Information services and use,* **12** (4), 1992, 301–25.

2   'Electronic imaging and the visual arts, London, July 1993', *Information services and use,* **13** (4), 1993, 295–419.

3   Electronic imaging and the visual arts, 1994', *Information services and use,* **14** (3), 1994, 123–251.

4   Turner, J., 'Indexing films and video images for storage and retrieval', *Information services and use,* **14** (3), 1994, 225–36.

5   'Knowledge organization in the visual arts', *Knowledge organization,* **20** (1), 1993, 2–54.

6   Grund, A., Iconclass: on subject representation of iconographic representation of art', *Knowledge organization,* **20** (1), 1993, 20–9.

7   Waal, H. Van de, *Iconclass: an iconographic classification system*; completed and edited by L. D. Couprie with R. H. Fuchs, E Tholen, Amsterdam, North-Holland Publishing Co., 1973–1985. 17v.

8   Pountain, D., 'Browsing art the Windows way', *Byte,* **17** (4), 1992, 821S 13–14, 16, 18, 20, 22, 24.

9   *Art & architecture thesaurus,* Toni Petersen, Director, New York, Oxford University Press, 1990, on behalf of the Getty Art History Information Program. 3v. A supplementary volume was issued in 1992.
    Art & architecture thesaurus, Toni Petersen, Director, 2nd ed., New York, Oxford University Press, 1994, on behalf of the Getty Art History Information Program. 5v.
    Petersen, T. and Barnett, P. J., *Guide to indexing and cataloging with the Art & architecture thesaurus,* New York, Oxford University Press, 1994, on behalf of the Getty Art History Information Program. (v6 of the complete set)
    Molholt, P. A. and Petersen, T., 'The role of the 'Art and architecture thesaurus' in communicating about visual art', *Knowledge organization,* **20** (1), 1993, 30–4.

Part V
The future

Chapter 28
Digital libraries

We have seen that increasing amounts of information are becoming available in digital form, and that this is likely to have significant consequences for information retrieval. We have had access to abstracts and indexes online for about 30 years, and for some areas, notably law, full text has also been available for much of this time, but the current ease of access to computer-held information, together with the possibility of including sound and video, means that for many other reference tools digital format has notable advantages over print. A full-scale printed encyclopedia contains far more information than any currently available on CD-ROM, but the latter will certainly be the preferred form in the future. Nearly all books are produced by computer-controlled type setting, and can thus potentially be made available online very simply. The Internet is linking computers together at an increasingly rapid rate; it has been estimated that the number of people using the World Wide Web is doubling every ten weeks. Will libraries as we know them today disappear, to be replaced by a terminal on every desktop? There will certainly be changes, but these are not likely to take place overnight, nor are we likely to discard the heritage of the past. There is still a place for the book, as the heavy use of libraries and bookshops shows. We must consider some of the factors that will influence the growth of the digital library, and some of the problems to be solved in the mixed print/digital libraries of the near future. The term digital library is used here; some writers refer to the virtual library, the online library, the desktop library or the electronic library, but 'digital library' seems to be the most straightforward.

Intellectual property

'Sir!' proclaimed Dr Johnson, 'no man but a blockhead ever wrote, except for money.' While this may be regarded as something of an exaggeration, there is no doubt that money is an essential part of publishing, whether this be commercial, academic or casual. In Chapter 4 we saw that the kind of publishing that has taken place in the past on the Internet has been non-commercial; indeed, the Internet was originally closed to commercial traffic, and it is only recently that access has become available through commercial vendors. Academic publishing is normally not undertaken primarily with immediate profit in mind; financial advantage comes indirectly rather than directly. However, this does not mean that such non-commercial publishing does not recognize the authors' rights in their intellectual property. It is now generally accepted that it is as wrong to steal someone's intellectual output without due acknowledgment as it is to steal any other goods. Information made freely available through the Internet is still the intellectual property of the originator, and should not be used without appropriate recognition.

While this recognition may not be financial for some materials, for the majority of publications money is an essential part of the transaction. Societies would not be able to continue to produce learned journals if they did not receive income from subscriptions, while for commercial publishers income from sales is their primary objective. The digital library will need to make provision for payment for the use of publications even if these do not remain permanently in its possession. This situation is of course already familiar through the use of online databases, for which libraries expect to pay on a usage basis; in the future, we shall see the same kind of provision for the use of the original materials. In an issue of its *Communications* devoted largely to the digital library,[1] the ACM also sets out its own publishing plans for the future.[2] The American Chemical Society plans to make five years of 20 primary journals published by the ACS available in SGML format in a digital library experiment;[3] as the library will occupy some 80GB of disk space, most users will be better pleased to access it online than to have to store it! The commercial publisher Elsevier is beginning to make its journals available online, and plans to have over 1000 available in this format. To keep control of use, and ensure income for the future, such publication is likely to take place through utilities such as OCLC, with its established facilities for charging.[4] The Xanadu project begun by Nelson, who coined the word hypertext, is intended to be franchised through storage vendors using the Xanadu multimedia server.[5] ADONIS, which makes available the scanned text of some 2400 biomedical journals, charges a subscription fee plus a royalty for printouts.

An unexpected cost may arise in the use of graphics in the future. One of the widely used standards for graphics on the Internet is the Graphics Interchange Format (GIF). The compression software used for this is covered by a patent held by UNISYS, who are now asking for royalties. In consequence, CompuServe may start charging for files containing GIF images.[6]

The problem is a very real one, and it is not merely coincidence that most work on digital libraries so far has taken place in university libraries or national libraries, which receive government funds to subsidize their operations, and have a responsibility to make their collections available for use as widely as possible. A notable example is the 'American memory' project of the Library of Congress, which aims to make a significant part of its Americana collections available online by the end of the century, at an estimated cost of some $60,000,000.[7] Material from the LC collections is being made available on a combination of laser disk and CD-ROM, and has been successfully tested in school and university libraries. Another is Project Gutenberg at the University of Illinois, which aims to have 10,000 books online by the end of the century.[8] Again, most of the books now available in digital form from this and other sources are 'classics' which are in the public domain. The British Library's Initiatives for Access programme aims to make important parts of the Library's collections available in digital form. This has had at least one unexpected bonus: the text of the mediaeval manuscript *Beowulf* is now available in a more readable form than for many centuries. Developments in digital photography techniques have enabled the restoration of parts of the manuscript which could not previously be deciphered.[9]

We should not only be concerned with financial recognition of an author's work. Another vital question is that of integrity. Information held in a computer can be edited and then redistributed as if it were the original. In this way, authors could find themselves apparently voicing opinions directly contrary to those they actually hold, or differing in subtle ways hard to detect. In the digital library it will be important to maintain the integrity of text as well as to ensure that authors get due recognition.

Media of presentation

As we saw in Chapter 4, there are various ways in which digital information can be distributed. Online through the Internet is likely to continue to be the most important, giving access to the latest information, but this is not always a primary factor. The American Memory project, for example, covers historical material, including large numbers of graphics, e.g. Civil War photographs. These are best distributed on laser disk or CD-ROM; graphics files are large, and downloading them online takes time and is thus expensive. For example, the Louvre has a large number of pictures from its collections in a digital library; to avoid excessive loads on the international communications network, 'mirror' collections are available, e.g. in Australia, so that the collection can be accessed locally. The National Gallery in London has made its collection of 2200 classical paintings available on CD-ROM.

On the other hand, CD-ROM can be less useful for situations when the very latest information is needed. BNB on CD-ROM was originally updated quarterly, but is now updated monthly.[10] Even monthly may not be prompt enough for some databases; to keep current, ADONIS circulates a new disk every week or so. Of course, abstracting and indexing databases must lag behind the production of the original materials, but here too online access can reduce the waiting time to a minimum. Even so, there may still be delays between original publication and access through an abstracting or indexing service, though the delays of months or even years which were regretfully tolerated in the 1950s would certainly not meet with so little complaint now!

The Internet is not well organized for those looking for information on particular subjects. One report illustrates the problems to be overcome: seven business librarians had to spend a considerable amount of time and effort locating business sources on the Internet and making them available to their clients as a manageable and focussed single source.[11] It would be short-sighted to regard this as an isolated example. A recent review of Web-searching software in Byte pointed out that users should not expect to find the Net neatly catalogued and classified like a library![12] Even those who have been using the Net for some time find problems in locating all the information likely to be use to them, and library and information professionals can certainly contribute to the marshalling of the resources now available.[13]

Implications for education

Education is one area which has been particularly affected by IT developments. This has been recognized at national levels, with the passing of the National High-Performance Computing Technology Act in 1991 in the US and the consequent setting up of the National Research and Education Network, NREN, to begin operation in 1996;[14] in the UK, in the Follett Report[15] and the upgrading of JANET; and in Australia, with the establishment of the Australian Education Network (EdNA) in 1995.[16] Recent years have seen significant developments in education, particularly at the tertiary level. There are greater numbers of students, as tertiary education is increasingly seen as the path to a good career, and many of these are now 'mature age' students, who do not undertake tertiary studies immediately upon leaving school. Many are studying externally, making use of digital materials on their home computers. Tertiary education is ceasing to be essentially associated with physical attendance at a specific location, and personal interaction with fellow-students and staff; instead, a degree will be the recognition that students have completed the requisite number of units of study at a variety of approved institutions to the satisfaction of staff who may never have actually seen them or each other. (We must hope that the resulting omelette justifies the breaking of so many valuable eggs.) In this situation, the librarian can play a valuable role by making information available, but also by teaching information skills; the librarian could become an integral part of the teaching programme.[17]

One typical project which is currently being developed is ELINOR, the digital library provided by De Montfort University for students on its Milton Keynes campus. This was started in 1992, with support from IBM and the BLR&DD. Pages from texts to be included have been scanned as images. One A4 page gives a 1MB file, but this can be compressed to about 100kB; the text of most items is in consequence rather large to be copied on to floppy disk, and the image cannot be word processed. Thus the material is freely available to students, and can be printed out, but the authors' rights are protected against plagiarism and integrity is maintained.[18] The Decomate project, involving the universities at Tilburg (Netherlands) and Barcelona and the British Library of Political and Economic Science, began in March 1995 and will run for two years; this will investigate problems of copyright in the dissemination of information in digital form.[19]

Users and the digital library

To a large extent end-users underestimate the complexity of the information world. A serious problem is the fact that users often find partial and inadequate information, but do not realize that there are better answers to be had. The librarian can help by providing training at the stage where users become aware that searching for information is not as easy as they thought! We can recognize five stages in the development of information literacy;[20] the librarian can help from stage three onwards. The user must:

1   recognize a need for information.

2   be motivated to satisfy that need.
3   develop a strategy to find the information needed.
4   carry through that strategy.
5   organize, evaluate and use the information.

The use of computer media such as CD-ROM has tended to lead to increased demands on reference librarians for explanations of how to use the materials, and to follow up references found. These demands often reveal deficiencies in library holdings, especially of journals. Users begin to have higher expectations of the library service, while librarians begin to realize that more time could have been spent in the past explaining how to use printed reference materials.[21] It has been assumed that users could make use of tools such as encyclopedias themselves, though education for librarianship should have shown that a skilled librarian can find more information more quickly than an unskilled user, even in something so apparently simple as an encyclopedia.

Problems with finding material

Even with the more user-friendly software now available, many users prefer to have their searching done by an intermediary, as we have noted in Chapter 5. One unexpected problem is that the software used for different databases is not always completely compatible, as is illustrated by an example from the bibliographic utility BRS. BRS has both some 300 bibliographic databases, and full-text databases occupying 320GB. Two parallel services are MEDLINE, containing over six million references, and the Comprehensive Core Medical Library (CCML) containing about 200,000 full-text articles from journals and textbooks. Since these are indexed by MEDLINE, it should be possible to make hypertext links between the two, but this has proved more difficult than was originally thought. As an example of the kind of problem that arises, reference 1 to this chapter contains two references to 'special issues' of journals, dealing with digital libraries. Each special issue has editors and a title, but consists of articles by several other authors as well. A citation for the whole issue may well ignore the individual authors; on the other hand, a citation for one of the articles does not usually put it in the context of the whole issue. The 'special issue' may well not occupy the whole of that issue of the journal, so that there will be other citations to the issue which have no connection with the theme of the 'special issue'. In this kind of situation it is very difficult to make suitable hypertext links consistently.

Even when we have two parallel services such as MEDLINE and CCML, BRS found that linking them may present problems. For example, let us consider an article which has the pagination 156–165. In CCML, this can be found by searching for 156 or 165, but not by searching for 156–165. By contrast, in MEDLINE it can only be found by searching for 156–165; it cannot be found by searching for 156 or 165. In neither can it be located by searching for any of the other pages.[22] Such problems may seem trivial, but they can make the difference between success and failure in a search. Only considerable experience can give the skills needed to overcome this kind of obstacle. No doubt new standards will be drawn up in due course which may gradually eliminate many of these problems. However, there are already standards for bibliographical references, e.g. BS 1629:1989,[23] but even a brief scan of professional literature will show that significant differences exist in practice between what should be standard citations.

There is also the continuing problem of subject access. Much of the material now becoming available has no better subject access than in the past. Computer searching still relies on word matching, and material available through the Internet/WWW does not usually have the DDC class numbers or LCSH headings which are at least of some assistance in searching OPACs. As the amount of material available increases, so will the difficulty of finding what we need, unless some positive steps are taken to remedy the situation. One example of a field where some positive steps towards better control are being taken is medicine.

Medical information

Medicine is a field where information has always been seen as important. Under one name or another, *Index Medicus* has been available since the 19th century; MEDLARS was one of the first computerized indexing services, and also among the first to go online, and MeSH is a model indexing language. IM is not the only service to cover medicine; we also have the European *Excerpta medica* among others. It is therefore not surprising that there has been considerable activity in recent years to take advantage of new digital technologies to provide improved access to information for medical staff and research workers.

One major initiative has been the Integrated Academic Information Management System (IAIMS). The purpose of IAIMS is to integrate all the information needed for education and research in a medical school with that needed for management and patient care in a teaching hospital. Using a fibre optic cable network throughout the buildings, it is intended to make all the information necessary to treat a patient available at the patient's bedside, as well as to research staff and students, (Patient confidentiality will of course be maintained.) The doctor treating the patient will not only have the patient's records available, but will also have access to outside sources of information, including expert systems. The goal of the system is to encourage academic medical centres to plan and implement an integrated institutional approach to information management for clinical practice, medical education and biomedical research.[24]

An important part of IAIMS is the development of a Unified Medical Language System (UMLS). This is in part a metathesaurus, so that users do not have to concern themselves with knowing the correct indexing language for whichever database they happen to be using; UMLS will serve as a glossary to map terms to a wide range of thesauri and similar tools used in medical databases: to act as a switching language. It is however intended to do much more than this. It should guide the user by providing a display of potential online information sources – databases, expert systems, full-text sources – which may be relevant. By interacting with the user UMLS can further build up the resources available to future users. The final product should feature a query interpreter and search formulator, using the metathesaurus; the output will be displayed in graphical form; and the system will have a tutorial for novice users. Grateful Med, the microcomputer-based search interface made available by the NLM in 1988, incorporated some of the features to be found in UMLS.[25]

MEDLARS is one of the world's most heavily used services, with over five million searches carried out each year. Yet a study some years ago showed that 45% of queries to MEDLINE at one medical school retrieved no documents, mainly because of the inadequacies of Boolean searching.[26] The new systems being developed should help to raise this success rate to one that is more acceptable, and could well be emulated in other subject fields.

Has technology failed us?

In a thought-provoking article,[27] Lancaster, who can hardly be accused of Luddite tendencies, suggests that as a profession librarians have become obsessed with computer-based solutions – which frequently do not work as well as expected – at the expense of user-oriented solutions. He cites the results of a research project under his direction to illustrate his point. Fifty-one searches on specific topics were carried out in the catalogue of a large academic library (4.5M items), and the results were compared with reading lists on the same topics prepared by experts. Considering only the monographic items (journal articles would not have been included in the catalogue), the results were poor; even using skilled staff to carry out lengthy and complicated searches which retrieved large numbers of items, the recall figure achieved was about 59%. The precision figure would have also become steadily lower as greater numbers of references were retrieved.

Lancaster makes the important point that the catalogue entries being searched contained inadequate subject information. As we have already seen, the average number of LCSH headings given for a book is about 1.5 (the exact figure varies from source to source, but 1.5 seems about right); there is normally an LC class number, perhaps a DDC class number, and the words in the title to add to the subject headings. When we compare this with the level of indexing of periodical articles found in databases such as MEDLINE or INSPEC, it is clear that access to books by subject is quite inadequate, a point which we have noted previously in our discussion of OPACs. However, Lancaster is pessimistic about the costs of enhanced subject access. He suggests that including contents page or book index information might have increased recall in the project to about 90%, but would have been expensive to carry out, and – more seriously – would have decreased the relevance ratio to an unacceptably low level by retrieving large numbers of documents – in which case, as we have seen in Chapter 2, the Futility Point factor would certainly have come into play. It is certainly true that the effectiveness of LCSH headings has been shown to be low in OPAC searching, but if there were, say, ten headings per document, which could be combined in Boolean searching, would this necessarily be ineffective? It appears to work for abstracting and indexing databases – but the headings used are certainly better geared to post-coordinate searching than is LCSH. Perhaps one way forward would be to continue the improvement which has been evident in LCSH over the past few years, but to direct it quite specifically to post-coordination. The vast majority of catalogues are now online, but even those which are not need not necessarily be inconvenienced unduly; as was discussed in Chapter 8, LCSH has been used in multiple entry mode for many years, long before there was any possibility of post-coordination. The problem of large library catalogues, compounded by the increase in the number of union catalogues, also seems not to be insoluble. If we consider only the two databases mentioned, MEDLINE and INSPEC, the combined number of references they hold is greater than all but the very largest library catalogue, yet it is quite possible to carry out searches on DIALOG on more than one database at a time.

There are of course problems in including contents lists and book indexes in MARC records, which have been discussed in a MARBI Committee paper.[28] The appropriate tag is 505, but when contents notes are included they are given according to AACR; this means that names are transcribed as on the source, not in the form according to an authority file. This would cause problems with, for example, conference proceedings. Analytical entries would solve the problem, by giving the full information in the form of records and subrecords, but in either case the MARC record would certainly be longer than is usual. At one time this would have caused problems of computer storage, but this is ceasing to be a significant factor with the faster computers and larger storage devices now available.

A similar problem to that identified by Lancaster was found in a study carried out for the BLR&DD.[29] The project was intended to locate as much information as possible on the costs of different methods of information storage and retrieval. Sources searched included bibliographies, card indexes maintained by specialist services, published indexes, online databases and personal contacts. Online searching – the most expensive method – located just over a quarter of the six thousand references traced; by contrast, the Russian *Referativnyi Zhurnal Informatika* provided 50% more references than all the online services together. About a fifth of the references were found in bibliographies. A significant point is that the majority of the references were found in only one of the sources checked, emphasizing the need to carry out searches in more than one reference source if high recall is needed. Computer databases are clearly not adequate as the only reference source in this situation.

Literature reviews

Are there other ways in which the information problem could be controlled? One of the recommendations of the Royal Society's Scientific Information Conference in 1948 was that more emphasis should be placed on systematic reviews of the literature. Many such reviews do now exist, and most information workers will be familiar with the *Annual review of information science and technology* and *Advances in librarianship*, as well as issues of *Library trends* and the reviews which appear in the *Journal of documentation*, to quote only four sources. In the project referred to earlier, Lancaster took as his criterion a series of bibliographies compiled by experts, but there seems to be no reason why such bibliographies should not be compiled by librarians in conjunction with subject specialists. One example of the potential significance of such reviews is again found in the field of medicine.

The Cochrane Collaboration

During the 1970s, A. L. (Archie) Cochrane became convinced of the need for systematic reviews of the results of randomized controlled trials in medicine. There are large numbers of such trials of medical procedures and pharmaceutical treatments each year, but the results are often not easily available to the doctors who are actually treating patients. Publication may be in a technical report, or a learned journal not primarily intended for the practising physician, and the patient may be totally unaware of the existence of such information. There is also the point that some trials question the effects of certain medication or treatments, and thus may conflict with vested interests. Chalmers[30] quotes Cochrane on the need for independent reviews:

> It is surely a great criticism of our profession that we have not organised a critical summary, by specialty and subspecialty, adapted periodically, of all randomised controlled trials.

Two factors are important in the production of such reviews. It takes time to gather the information and subject it to the necessary peer review, and it takes skill to write a sound and useful review. Despite the problems in meeting these requirements, an international network of Cochrane Collaboration centres, and the Cochrane database of systematic reviews have been established. A review group specializes in one subject area, e.g. pregnancy and childbirth (the first to be published), and gather information about appropriate trials to produce a systematic review. The electronic interchange of information is an important factor in making this practical on an international basis, and electronic publication means that the information can be updated relatively easily and cheaply. The pregnancy and childbirth database, for example, has an international review panel of some 30 experts and an editorial panel of four, who keep the reviews of several hundred topics, for example calcium supplementation in pregnancy, up to date. The database is published on floppy disk, with two updates each year. The complete Cochrane database is available on CD-ROM.

There are now Cochrane Collaboration centres in the UK, USA, Canada, Scandinavia, Italy and Australia. The electronic exchange of information is an essential part of keeping the database current as the results of new trials are published, or new comments are made on existing reviews. A newsletter has been started, and will also be made available through the Internet. Within a few years of its formal beginning in 1992, the Cochrane Collaboration has become a model of what can be done to keep a profession and its clients informed, using electronic media as an integral part of its functioning.

Health is of course an area where large amounts of money are involved. The widespread adoption of a successful treatment can save substantial sums, as well as improve patient care and save lives. There are however many other subject fields where the timely and accurate provision of information can be of significant value to the community, by avoiding the needless repetition of research, or by contributing to the well-informed community which is essential if democracy is to succeed.

The role of the librarian

If librarianship has a purpose, it is surely to make information available to those who need it, when it is needed, in the form in which it is needed. The subject approach is the key to this: finding known items is, as Blair[31] points out, similar to finding data; finding information by subject involves informed judgement. It also involves a knowledge of sources and the ability to organize information. Yet we seem reluctant to use our skills, or to claim them as worthwhile. Lancaster[27] refers to the lack of use made by librarians of the invaluable management information available from computerized circulation control systems. Tenopir and Neufang[21] make the point that the need to explain to readers how to use electronic media has alerted librarians to the lack of help that they have given in the past. All too often librarians have been *re*active rather than *pro*active; only in special libraries has the active intervention of the librarian been seen as something to be taken as a matter of course. Yet one study[31] showed that librarians using traditional skills searching printed bibliographies were able to achieve far better results than online searching. Printed bibliographies yielded some four times as many references as the best online search. Another important point revealed by the study was that some two-thirds of all the references were found in one source only, stressing the necessity to carry out a search in a number of sources if high recall is required. An obvious corollary is that users who restrict their searching to one catalogue or database may well find something, but nothing like a full range of answers to their queries.

In this book we have looked at various ways in which information has been organized, and the problems which have arisen, and still arise, in both manual and computer-based systems, in finding the right information at the right time. In the digital library age, either we may seize the opportunities offered to use our professional skills and judgement, or we may resign ourselves to being relegated to the role of guardians of 'intellectual supermarkets for the middle classes'. Virtually every survey done of information use has shown that the librarian is not regarded highly as a source of help and information. Yet the IAIMS project has shown that librarians, in collaboration with other professionals, can make real progress in harnessing the power of the computer to make information available when and where it is needed. The Cochrane collaboration has shown that the critical evaluation of information can serve a significant purpose; should we not be taking to the initiative to offer our skills to those working in this and similar fields? As Marx might have put it: Librarians of the world unite! You have nothing to use but your brains!

References

1   'Digital libraries', edited by E. A. Fox, R. M. Akscyn, R. K. Furuta and J. J. Leggett, *Communications of the ACM*, **38** (4), April 1995, 23–96. *Includes* Samuelson, P., 'Copyright in digital libraries', 15–21, 110.

Rao, R. *et al,* 'Rich interaction in the digital library, 29–39.

Marchionini, G. and Maurer, H., 'The roles of digital libraries in teaching and learning, 67–75.

Levy, D. M. and Marshall, C. C., 'Going digital: a look at assumptions underlying digital libraries, 77–84.

Wiederhold, G., 'Digital libraries, value, and productivity', 85–96.

and several short articles on specific examples, e.g. Stanford, Illinois, UC Berkeley and Santa Barbara, LC, BL.

See also Lunin, L. F. and Fox, E. A., editors, 'Perspectives on digital libraries', *Journal of the American Society for Information Science,* **44** (8), 1993, 440–91.

2   Denning, P. J. and Rous, B., 'The ACM electronic publishing plan', *Communications of the ACM,* **38** (4), April 1995, 97–103.

'ACM interim copyright policies', 104–9.

3   Entlich, R. *et al.* 'Making a digital library: the chemistry online retrieval experiment', *Communications of the ACM,* **38** (4), April 1995, 54. [CORE]

4   Olvey, L. D., 'Library networks and electronic publishing', *Information services and use,* **15** (1), 1995, 39–47. OCLC plans in relation to future electronic publishing.

5   Basch, R., 'Xanadu: through caverns measureless', *Online,* **15** (4), 1991, 18–19.

Nelson, T. H., 'Xanadu: document interconnection enabling re-use with automatic author credit royalty accounting', *Information services and use,* **14** (4), 1994, 255–66.

6   News item, *Byte,* **20** (4), 1995, 26.

7   The latest information on this project is available through the LC gopher marvel.loc.gov, under LC publications.

See also Polley, J. A. and Lyon, E., 'Out of the archives and into the street: American memory in American libraries', *Online,* **16** (5), 1992, 51–4, 56–7.

8   'Books online: visions, plans and perspectives for electronic text', *Online,* **15** (4), 1991, 13–23.

9   For information on the Initiatives for Access programme, gopher portico.bl.uk and follow the menu.

See also Ede, S., 'Strategic planning for the millennium: a national library perspective', *Information services and use,* **13** (1), 1993, 25–34.

10   Bevan, N., 'Transient technology? The future of CD-ROMs in libraries', *Program,* **28** (1), 1994, 1–14.

11   'The virtual library', *Special libraries,* **85** (4), 1994, 249–291, *including* Westerman, M., 'Business sources on the Net: a virtual library product', 264–9.

12   Nichols, S. J. Vaughan, 'The Web means business', *Byte,* **129** (11), 1994, 26–7.

13   Tseng, G., Poulter, A. and Hiom, D., *The library and information professional's guide to the Internet,* London, Library Association Publishing, 1995.

14   Boucher, R., 'The vision of the National High-Performance Computing Technology Act of 1991', *Information technology and libraries,* **11** (1), 1992, 56–8.

McClure, C. R. *et al.*, 'Toward a virtual library: Internet and the National Research and Education Network', *Bowker annual: library and book trade almanac, 1993*, New York, NY, Bowker, 1993, 25–45.

Reinhardt, A., 'New ways to learn', *Byte,* **20** (3), 1995, 50–2, 54–6, 58, 62, 66–7, 70, 72.

15   Joint Funding Councils' Libraries Review Group, *Report*, Bristol, Higher Education Funding Council for England, 1993. (The Follett report).
British journal of academic librarianship, 9 (1/2) 1994. Special issue.
Ford, G., '[Review of the Follett report]', *Journal of documentation,* **50** (4), 1994, 351–7.
UK Office for Library Networking. 'Networks, libraries and information: priorities for the UK', *The electronic library,* **11** (2), 1993, 109–13.

16   Crean, S., *Learning on the superhighway*, Canberra, ACT, April 1995. (Media release)
See also Schauder, D., 'Development of the E-library concept, with special reference to Australian libraries', *Australian library review,* **11** (1), 1994, 5–30. (Special issue devoted to the online electronic library, 2–89).

17   Heseltine, R., 'The challenge of learning in cyberspace', *Library Association record,* **97** (8), 1995, 432–3.

18   Arnold, K., Collier, M. W. and Ramsden, A., 'ELINOR: the electronic library project at De Montfort University Milton Keynes', *Aslib proceedings,* **45** (1), 1993, 3–6.
Ramsden, A., Wu, Z. and Zhao, D., 'Selection criteria for a document image processing system', *Program,* **27** (4), 1993, 371–87.

19   'Joint study of electronic copyright' [News item], *Library Association record,* **97** (8), 1995, 408.
For further information, http://www.blpes.lse.ac.uk/decomate

20   Fisher, J. and Bjorner, S., 'Enabling online end-user searching: an expanding role for librarians', *Special libraries,* **85** (4), 1994, 281–91.
Smith, N. R., 'The "Golden triangle" – users, librarians and suppliers in the electronic information era', *Information services and use,* **13** (1), 1993, 17–24.
Gilbert, J. D., 'Are we ready for the virtual library? Technology push, market pull and organizational response', *Information services and use,* **13** (1), 1993, 3–15.

21   Tenopir, C. and Neufang, R., 'The impact of electronic reference on reference librarians', *Online,* **16** (3), 1992, 54–6, 58, 60.

22   Stein, M. and Sheridan, C. R., 'Hypertext and the identity link', *Online review,* **14** (3), 1990, 188–96.

23   British Standards Institution. *British standard recommendations for references to published materials*, rev. ed., Milton Keynes, British Standards Institution, 1989. BS 1629:1989.

24   Broering, N. C., *Strategic planning: an integrated Academic Information Management System (IAIMS) at Georgetown University Medical Center*, Washington, DC, Georgetown University Medical Center, 1986.
Lorenzi, N. M., ed., 'A decade of IAIMS', *Bulletin of the Medical Library*

Association, **80** (3), 1993, 240–93.

25　Humphrey, B. L., 'Unified Medical Language System progress report', *International classification,* **15** (2), 1988, 85–6.

Squires, S. J., 'Access to biomedical information: the Unified Medical Language System', *Library trends,* **42**, 1993, 127–51.

Tilson, Y. and East, H., 'Academic scientists' reaction to end-user services: observations on a trial service giving access to MEDLINE using the Grateful Med software', *Online & CD-ROM review,* **18** (2), 1994, 71–7.

26　Miller, N., Kirby, M. and Templeton, E., 'End-user searching in a medical school library', *Medical references services quarterly,* **7** (1), 1988, 1–13.

27　Lancaster, F. W., 'Has technology failed us?' *in Information technology and library management,* 13th International Essen Symposium, 1990, Essen, Universitätsbibliothek Essen, 1991, 1–13.

28　'Enhancing USMARC records with table of contents', MARBI discussion paper no. 46, *Advances in online public access catalogs,* v1, New York, Meckler, 1992, 105–13.

29　Chalmers, I., 'The Cochrane Collaboration: preparing, maintaining and disseminating systematic reviews of the effects of health care', *Annals of the New York Academy of Science,* **703**, 1993, 156–65.

30　Blair, D. C. *Language and representation in information retrieval,* New York, NY, Elsevier Science Publishers, 1990. (Discussed in Chapter 5.)

31　Davison, P. and Moss, A., *International bibliographic review on costs and modelling in information retrieval,* London, British Library Research & Development Department, 1991. (Quoted in *Information market* (54).)

Indexes

This index is divided into two sections, Authors and Subjects. The author index leads to items in the chapter bibliographical references; when the same book is cited more than once, this is shown by parentheses, e.g.

Vickery, B. C.   10 (170, 199), 31 (229), 75 (95), 294

indicates that works by this author are listed on the pages shown, but the work cited on page 229 has already been cited on page 31.

The subject index is intended to demonstrate the principles set out in the text and discussed on pages 223–5, in addition to the purpose of enabling readers to find specific items quickly. *def* means that a term is defined; *irt* means in relation to.

Filing is word-by-word; abbreviations are treated as single words; the hyphen files before letters, so that CD-ROM files before CDMARC. Order within headings is alphabetical, ignoring *def* and *irt*. Figures and Tables are not indexed, nor are spelled-out forms of abbreviations, which are listed in the introductory pages.

Author index

Subject index